The Design Culture Reader

'As it becomes increasingly obvious that the designed world is not shaped by rational principles of utility, economy or even aesthetics, we need new ways to think about design. This reader provides a formidable set of "tools" for understanding how and why things fill our world and our minds . . .'
David Crowley, *Deputy Head of the Department of Design History, Royal College of Art, London*

'For those working the field of design whether they be makers, theoreticians or historians, *The Design Culture Reader* is a thought-provoking and challenging text. Ben Highmore juxtaposes canonical essays with unexpected but revealing writing, drawing both into an argument for rethinking the place of design in contemporary critical thought. His introduction, "A Sideboard Manifesto", will be, without doubt, keenly debated.'
Louise Purbrick, *Senior Lecturer in the History of Art and Design, University of Brighton*

Design is part of ordinary, everyday life, to be found in every room in every building in the world. While we may tend to think of design in terms of highly desirable objects, this book encourages us to think about design as ubiquitous (from plumbing to television) and as an agent of social change (from telephones to weapon systems).

The Design Culture Reader brings together an international array of writers whose work is of central importance for thinking about design culture in the past, present and future. Essays from philosophers, media and cultural theorists, historians of design, anthropologists, cultural historians, artists and literary critics all demonstrate the enormous potential of design studies for understanding the modern world.

Organised in thematic sections, *The Design Culture Reader* explores the social role of design by looking at the impact it has in a number of areas – especially globalisation, ecology and the changing experiences of modern life. Particular essays focus on topics such as design and the senses, design and war, and design and technology, while the editor's introduction to the collection provides a compelling argument for situating design studies at the very forefront of contemporary thought.

Ben Highmore is Reader in Media and Cultural Studies at the University of Sussex. He is the author of *Everyday Life and Cultural Theory, Cityscapes* and *Michel de Certeau*. He edited *The Everyday Life Reader* and is the reviews editor of *New Formations*.

The Design Culture Reader

Edited by
Ben Highmore

Routledge
Taylor & Francis Group

LONDON AND NEW YORK

First published 2009
by Routledge
2 Park Square, Milton Park, Abingdon, Oxon OX14 4RN

Simultaneously published in the USA and Canada
by Routledge
270 Madison Ave, New York, NY 10016

Routledge is an imprint of the Taylor & Francis Group, an informa business

Editorial selection and material © 2009 Ben Highmore
Chapters © 2009 the contributors

Typeset in Perpetua and Bell Gothic by
RefineCatch Limited, Bungay, Suffolk
Printed and bound in Great Britain by
The Cromwell Press, Trowbridge, Wiltshire

British Library Cataloguing in Publication Data
A catalogue record for this book is available from the British Library

Library of Congress Cataloging in Publication Data
The design culture reader / edited by Ben Highmore. — 1. ed.
    p. cm.
    Includes bibliographical references and index.
    1 Design—History—20th century. 2. Culture—Philosophy. I. Highmore, Ben, 1961–
NK1390.D4726 2008
    745.4—dc22   2008002956

ISBN10: 0–415–40355–3 (hbk)
ISBN10: 0–415–40356–1 (pbk)

ISBN13: 978–0–415–40355–9 (hbk)
ISBN13: 978–0–415–40356–6 (pbk)

The quest for a sustainable world may succeed, or it may fail. If it fails, the world will become unthinkable. If it works, the world will become unimaginable.

(Sterling 2005: 7)

What interests me is the way in which, by drawing lines, arranging words or distributing surfaces, one also designs divisions of communal space. It is the way in which, by assembling words or forms, people define not merely various forms of art, but certain configurations of what can be seen and what can be thought, certain forms of inhabiting the material world.

(Rancière 2007: 91)

Contents

Illustrations

Preface

Over recent decades many design historians, and those who study design as critics, consumers and producers, have been moving away from what sometimes seemed like an exclusive focus on *auteur* designers (Chanel, Corbusier, Chippendale and so on). Of course there has always been a general interest in vernacular forms of design – in ordinary objects. Popular social histories for instance (particularly those aimed at children) have, throughout the twentieth century, concentrated on pots and pans as much as princes and palaces. Similarly, archaeology has unearthed tools and utensils from pre-industrial cultures in the hope of fashioning a sense of the collective social and cultural life of pre-modern times. Early versions of art and architectural history, especially in the nineteenth and early twentieth centuries, were as fascinated by belt buckles and windows as by 'masterworks'. And yet when the topic is primarily 'design' (in libraries and bookshops) the writing is dominated by named designers.

Clearly the designed world that most of us meet most of the time is anonymous, collective, and extends exponentially beyond the realm of 'designer goods'. Recent design studies have provided a forum for engaging with the domestic world, with the world of kitchens, food, hygiene. Design research has been involved in studying a world of mobility and immobility, of techniques and technology, of bodies, things and their sensual capacities, of the intercultural world of design. Spurred on by a host of social and intellectual challenges (feminism, postcolonialism, queer studies, disability studies, globalisation, environmentalism and so on), design studies is clearly not simply reducible to the study of the products and practices of those who call themselves designers.

It is hard at this point in history to imagine a place untouched by design. Stem cell research, the genetic modification of food, environmental crisis and climate change have forced the recognition that what is called 'nature' is suffused with artifice, is animated and actualised by design. This recognition should remind us that history, seen from a materialist perspective, is primarily the effects of design (material, human, technological) on the environment. In the mid-nineteenth century Karl Marx suggested that while sensuous nature appears before us as 'eternal' (his example is a cherry tree growing in Europe), it is there in its present shape as a result of purposeful human activities, of colonial adventuring, for instance. Thus the 'designed environment' in its widest sense not only corresponds to the entirety of urban, suburban and rural conurbation, it extends into the landscape and into the biosphere. Marx's answer to the problem of understanding the designed world was historical materialism: history inoculates you against the twin pitfalls of 'eternity' (the belief that this is the way things 'naturally' are) and endless claims of newness (as if phenomena emerge out of nowhere and nothing); materialism insists on the proof of social practice, on the concrete phenomena of material experience. Historical and materialist inquiry, transformed since Marx's time, is at the root of this Reader.

I have tried to do two things at once in this anthology: to provide a flavour of the recent (and not so recent) engagement with the more everyday world of design; and to extend this work by including texts that might at first glance seem disconnected to the material world of design. Hopefully my editorial commentary will demonstrate the pertinence of these texts to the field of design studies. My interest in design culture is part of a wider interest in everyday life, and I see this book as a continuation of that project. In this, the everyday offers a set of vantage points for looking at design. But design looks back too, offering its own specific perspective on culture. And this is where there is a larger argument and a larger constituency being addressed by this anthology. As well as seeing design as a set of objects, situations and practices, it is also productive to look at other phenomena from the perspective of design. What, then, would it mean to look at a novel, a restaurant, a film, a play, radio, a birth, a football match, a demonstration, a riot, from the perspective of design? The possibility of responding to this question is the implicit task of this anthology. Here I just want to say that if this anthology finds something of a home in design departments I will be very happy; if, as well, it finds a home (however small) in departments in the humanities and social sciences I will be ecstatic.

To produce a Reader is to be involved, wittingly or not, in canon-formation – that is, the compiling and sanctifying of a selection of works, now claimed as central to a field. The success of an anthology like this will no doubt be measured, in part, by its ability to form a canon. But this process is also one of canon-deformation, as texts once thought of as crucial are unceremoniously rejected in the wake of something more current, more relevant, or (let's face it) more fashionable. I thought I would enjoy the process of canon-deformation much more than the process of legitimation and sanctification that is canon-production. Actually the reverse was true: I loved selecting these texts, but hated jettisoning the mass of material I didn't include. Where is Adolf Loos' writing on ornament or men's clothes? Why nothing by the Eames? Surely something on streamlining should be included? Limitations of space have meant that numerous writings that should be here (many of which are personal favourites) aren't. All I can say is that, luckily, there are other anthologies out there besides this one, anthologies more focused on industrial design or fashion, for instance. The variety of anthologies on related topics comes as something of a relief for a reluctant canon-former. In the face of all the lost texts, I have used the bibliography to acknowledge some of the work that isn't here but probably should be.

I have grouped the chosen texts into rough-and-ready thematic sections. These are designed to highlight productive questions and to cast the texts in a particular light (as partial responses to these questions). I took it as compelling evidence of the value of these texts that they could all fit into at least two themes while some of them seemed to speak to all six themes. Looking at them now I see other themes with which I could have grouped them (kitsch, nostalgia, memory, for instance), but such categories would, I think, have fenced in the texts much more than the present grouping has done. I leave it to readers to find their own groupings for these texts and to find the active connections between them.

To take account of design as a sprawling and saturating phenomenon is to imagine a field of inquiry that is ludicrously ambitious. It extends design studies beyond the realm of goods (the products of industrial designers, fashion designers, architects and so on) and into the whole panoply of interconnections between the material and immaterial, between humans and things, between the organic and the inorganic. As a field of inquiry it is obviously over-ambitious, with little chance of success. Hopefully it's none the worse for that.

Encouragement and inspiration came from a range of people: the late Judith Attfield, Christopher Breward, Becky Conekin, Barry Curtis, Steven Gartside, the late Philippa Goodall, Dirk van den Heuvel, David Howes, Kate Lacey, Grace Lees-Maffei, Malcolm Miles, Felicity Newman, Elspeth Probyn, Rhona Richman Kenneally, Simon Sadler and Joanne Sloan. Michelle Henning, Richard Hornsey and Gillian Swanson provided a convivial group for discussing ideas while eating. I trust that now that I have moved institutions we will continue to find excuses and occasions to continue these discussions. I'm sure that Michelle Henning will be able to find the imprint of her own ideas scattered across the introduction (borrowed rather than stolen, I hope, and not too mangled in the process). The various writers included in this volume have all been generous and enthusiastic to a fault. Some have also been extremely patient; thank you. I first rehearsed some of the ideas in the introduction in a talk I gave at Murdoch University, in Western Australia. It was a lovely occasion (my first visit to Australia) and the audience's kind and critical response suggested the possibility of this book. Thanks especially to Mark Gibson, Geoffrey Craig and Wendy Parkins for inviting me. The practical job of making this book was made relatively painless by the super diligence and good humour of Julene Knox, Carol Fellingham Webb and Charlie Wood. Natalie Foster's enthusiasm for this project helped sustain it. The production of this book required, as usual, the forbearance of those closest to me. One afternoon, after school, I told my daughter that she could use my computer (she wanted to play a game online). She replied, incredulous: 'What? You're off your computer?'

Acknowledgements

The following were reproduced with kind permission. Whilst every effort has been made to trace copyright holders and obtain permission, this has not been possible in all cases. Any omissions brought to our attention will be remedied in future editions.

Karl Marx (1867) 'The Fetishism of the Commodity and its Secret', *Capital: Volume 1*, translated by Ben Fowkes, Harmondsworth: Penguin, 1976, pp. 163–77. Reproduced by permission of New Left Review.

Jonathan Crary (1997) 'Spectacle, Attention, Counter-Memory', from Rosalind Krauss, Annette Michelson, Yve-Alain Bois, Benjamin H. D. Buchloh, Hal Foster, Denis Hollier and Silvia Koblowski, eds, *October: The Second Decade, 1986–1996*, pp. 415–25 © 1998 Massachusetts Institute of Technology and October, by permission of the MIT Press.

Vilém Flusser (1999) 'About the Word *Design*', in *The Shape of Things: A Philosophy of Design*, London: Reaktion Books, pp. 17–21. English translation © Reaktion Books Ltd, 1999. Reproduced by permission of the publisher.

Michael Moon, Eve Kosofsky Sedgwick, Benjamin Gianni and Scott Weir (1994) 'Queers in (Single-Family) Space', *Assemblage*, 24, pp. 30–7 © Michael Moon, Eve Kosofsky Sedgwick, Benjamin Gianni and Scott Weir.

Pauline Madge 'Ecological Design: A New Critique', *Design Issues*, 13, 2 (Summer, 1997), pp. 44–54 © 1997 by the Massachusetts Institute of Technology. Reproduced by permission of MIT Press Journals.

Hal Foster (2002) 'The ABCs of Contemporary Design', *October*, 100, pp. 191–9 © Hal Foster.

Marcel Mauss (1934) 'Techniques of the Body', translated by Ben Brewster, *Economy and Society*, 2, 1 (1973), pp. 70–88, Taylor & Francis Ltd (http://www.informaworld.com), reprinted by permission of the publisher.

Michel Foucault (1996) 'Space, Knowledge, and Power', in *Foucault Live: Collected Interviews, 1961–1984*, edited by Sylvère Lotringer, New York: Semiotext(e), pp. 335–47. Reproduced by permission of the publisher.

'Introduction', from Kittler, Friedrich A., translated by Geoffrey Winthrop-Young and Michael Wutz, *Gramophone, Film, Typewriter*, copyright © English translation 1999 by the Board of Trustees of the Leland Stanford University. Originally published in German © 1986 Brinkmann and Bose. All rights reserved. Used with the permission of Stanford University Press, www.sup.org.

From 'Women and the Telephone: The Gendering of a Communication Technology' by Lana F. Rakow in, Cheris Kramarae, ed. *Technology and Women's Voices: Keeping in Touch*, copyright © 1988 Routledge & Kegan Paul, pp. 207–28. Reproduced by permission of Taylor and Francis Books UK.

Ellen Lupton (1996) 'Power Tool for the Dining Room: The Electric Carving Knife', in Joel Sanders, ed. *Stud:*

Architectures of Masculinity, New York: Princeton Architectural Press, pp. 42–53. Reproduced by permission of the publisher.

Tobin Siebers (2003) 'What can Disability Studies Learn from the Culture Wars?', *Cultural Critique*, 55, pp. 200–14, University of Minnesota Press. Copyright 2003 by the Regents of the University of Minnesota. Reprinted with permission of the publisher.

Stuart Cosgrove (1984) 'The Zoot-Suit and Style Warfare', *History Workshop Journal*, 18 (Autumn), pp. 77–91 by permission of Oxford University Press.

Mihay Csikszentmihalyi (1991) 'Design and Order in Everyday Life', *Design Issues*, 8, 1, pp. 26–34 © Mihay Csikszentmihalyi.

Zeynep Çelik (1996) 'Gendered Spaces in Colonial Algiers', in Diana Agrest, Patricia Conway and Leslie Kanes Weisman, eds *The Sex of Architecture*, New York: Harry N. Abrams, pp. 127–40. Originally published in *Urban Forms and Colonial Confrontations: Algiers Under French Rule*, The University of California Press. Copyright © 1997 by The Regents of the University of California. Reproduced with permission.

Céline Rosselin (1999) 'The Ins and Outs of the Hall: A Parisian Example', in Irene Cieraad, ed. *At Home: An Anthropology of Domestic Space*, Syracuse: Syracuse University Press, pp. 53–9. Reproduced by permission of the publisher.

'Immigrant Souvenirs', from *The Future of Nostalgia* by Svetlana Boym, copyright © 2001 by Svetlana Boym. Reprinted by permission of Basic Books, a member of Perseus Book Group and The Elaine Markson Literary Agency, Inc.

Wolfgang Schivelbusch (1988) 'Shop Windows', in *Disenchanted Night: The Industrialization of Light in the Nineteenth Century*, translated by Angela Davies, Berkeley, Los Angeles and London: University of California Press, pp. 143–54. Reproduced by kind permission of the author.

Nicholson Baker (1986) 'Chapter Two', from *The Mezzanine*, Cambridge: Granta Books in association with Penguin, pp. 11–18. Reproduced by permission of Granta.

Nicholson Baker (1986) 'Chapter Two', from *The Mezzanine*, Copyright © 1986, 1988 by Nicholson Baker. Used by permission of Grove/Atlantic, Inc.

'The Memory of the Senses, Part 1: Marks of the Transitory', from C. Nadia Seremetakis, ed. *The Senses Still: Perception and Memory as Material Culture in Modernity*, Chicago: University of Chicago Press, pp. 1–18. Copyright © 1994 by Westview Press, Inc. Reprinted by permission of Westview Press, a member of Perseus Book Group.

Koichi Iwabuchi (1998) 'Marketing "Japan": Japanese Cultural Presence Under a Global Gaze', *Japanese Studies*, 18, 2, 1998, pp. 66–75, Taylor & Francis Ltd (http://www.informaworld.com), reprinted by permission of the publisher.

Jonathan Sterne (2003) 'Hello', in *The Audible Past: Cultural Origins of Sound Reproduction*, pp. 1–19, 353–60. Copyright © 2003, Duke University Press. All rights reserved. Used by permission of the publisher.

John McHale 'An Ecological Overview', from *The Future of the Future* (New York: George Braziller, 1969). Reproduced by permission of the publisher.

'Designing for the City of Strangers', from Krzysztof Wodiczko, *Critical Vehicles: Writings, Projects, Interviews*, pp. 4–15, © 1999 Massachusetts Institute of Technology, by permission of The MIT Press.

'The Crystal Palace', from *The Artificial Kingdom: A Treasury of the Kitsch Experience* by Celeste Olalquiaga, copyright © 1998 by Celestial Reasonings, Inc. Used by permission of Pantheon Books, a division of Random House, Inc. and Bloomsbury Publishing Plc.

'From War to Warring' (1999) reproduced from *A New Design Philosophy: An Introduction to Defuturing* by Tony Fry with permission of the University of New South Wales Press.

Ashoke Chatterjee 'Design in India: The Experience of Transition', *Design Issues*, 21, 4 (Autumn, 2005), pp. 4–10. © 2005 by Massachusetts Institute of Technology. Reproduced by permission of MIT Press Journals.

Siegfried Giedion (1948) 'Anonymous History', *Mechanization Takes Command: A Contribution to Anonymous History*, New York: Norton, 1969, pp. 2–11. By permission of Oxford University Press, Inc.

'Social Position and the Art of Automobile Maintenance', from Evan Watkins, *Throwaways: Work Culture and Consumer Education*, copyright © 1993 by the Board of Trustees of the Leland Stanford Jr. University. All rights reserved. Used with the permission of Stanford University Press, www.sup.org.

Michel Serres (with Bruno Latour) (1995) 'The Past is No Longer Out-of-date', in *Conversations on Science, Culture, and Time*, translated by Roxanne Lapidus (Ann Arbor: University of Michigan Press, 1995), pp. 48–62. English translation copyright © by the University of Michigan 1995. Originally published in French as *Eclaircissements* © by Editions François Bourin.

N. Katherine Hayles (1999) 'The Materiality of Informatics: Audiotape and its Cultural Niche', in *How We Became Posthuman: Virtual Bodies in Cybernetics, Literature, and Informatics*, Chicago: University of Chicago Press, pp. 207–21. Copyright © 1999 by The University of Chicago. Reprinted with permission of the publisher.

Peter Hitchcock (2003) 'Chronotope of the Shoe (Two)', in *Imaginary States: Studies in Cultural Transnationalism (Transnational Cultural Studies)*, Urbana: Illinois University Press, pp. 118–52. Originally published as 'Fetishism (of Shoes)' from *Oscillate Wildly: Space, Body and Spirit of Millennial Materialism* (University of Minnesota Press, 1999). Copyright 1999 by the Regents of the University of Minnesota. Reproduced by permission of the publisher.

Figure 0.1–9 Ubiquitous design: welcome to our artificial world (photographs by Ben Highmore).

GENERAL INTRODUCTION
A Sideboard Manifesto: Design Culture in an Artificial World

THE DESIGNED ENVIRONMENT, it seems, is now so extensive that it could encompass almost the entire modern world. Hal Foster, for instance, claims that 'today everything – from architecture and art to jeans and genes – is treated as so much design' (Foster 2002a: 192), while the science fiction novelist Bruce Sterling introduces his book on design by writing 'this book is about created objects and the environment, which is to say, it's about everything' (Sterling 2005: cover text). To treat everything (from jeans to genes) as 'so much design' runs the risk of spreading the term so thinly that it loses any hard descriptive bite. Yet the alternative – to reserve the term design only for the authored and branded objects of fashion houses, appliance outlets and furniture stores – runs a more severe risk, to my mind, of not recognising the massive range of 'designed' elements in the world, and the way we are implicated and incorporated in a variety of design processes. To fail to see this vast terrain of the artificial and manufactured is, I would argue, to fail to see the world at all. We live, as a friend of mine once put it, in artificial worlds – that is our actuality.

The extreme spread of the designed world, then, is in danger of presenting collections of material and cultural life that are simply too unwieldy and diverse to solicit systematic attention of a particular type. So be it. But just because something is endlessly unmanageable in its multiplicity doesn't mean that we should shy away from addressing it in all its reckless profusion. It strikes me that there is something particularly valuable about approaching the world from a design perspective at the moment. While my argument would be slightly different from Hal Foster's and Bruce Sterling's, I too would want to start by acknowledging the importance of the exponential expansion of design across the globe. Most catastrophically, it is hard not to see global warming and climate change as a consequence of a variety of design processes, design values and design products.[1] But alongside pressing geo-political issues (and intricately related to them) I want to claim 'design culture' (its practice, its history, its scrutiny) as a crucial arena where a whole range of inquiries could come together.

In recent decades the intellectual energy of the cultural sciences (sociology, cultural studies, art and design history, cultural and social geography, and so on) has clustered around various topics and themes: the body, the city, the senses, everyday life, science and technology, globalisation, perception, attention, affects and emotions.[2] These topics have solicited a range of theoretical and methodological approaches that have sometimes maintained disciplinary boundaries and sometimes transformed them. For those studying technological culture, for instance, the approach called actor-network-theory (ANT) has been crucial, but so too has feminism; for those studying the emotions and senses, intellectual history and neurobiology have made interesting companions. My claim, or rather my challenge, is to see 'design culture' (or design studies) as the place where all these topics and approaches could come together, where the entanglements of this range of phenomena can be seen most vividly.

This introduction is meant to be a manifesto and as such should really demand the complete rebranding of the cultural sciences as design studies – '*Stand aside! The train of design studies is coming through!*' But it is also a modest manifesto, a sideboard manifesto, and so imagines something far less dogmatic. What it imagines is an opening up of design studies. Or, more modestly still, it seeks to encourage an opening up that is already taking place as design inquiries look across aesthetics, play-theory, sensual perception, technology, global economics and affect theory for their research perspectives. It wants to promote the expansion of what counts as a design object or practice, an expansion already being pursued by researchers who might want to include air, manners, movement, recipes, plumbing and medicine as part of the designed environment. What makes design culture such a productive arena for general social and cultural research is that it can supply the objects that demonstrate the thoroughly entangled nature of our interactions in the material world, the way in which bodies, emotions, world trade and aesthetics, for instance, interweave at the most everyday level.

Just to take a most mundane example: a recipe. A recipe, written, or remembered, or recounted, is a design proposal. It names elements and arrangements, and forms for combination (frying, boiling, etc.). As with an Ikea product you have to do the assembling yourself. Unlike with an Ikea product you might play around with the recipe a little without the finished product falling down around you. This playing around might be driven by pragmatism (I can't afford that cut of meat; I don't have a griddle) and it might be driven by aesthetic concerns (I don't like that much chilli in my stew; sprouts make me nauseous). Some of the food that is being assembled might be grown locally, other elements flown in from across the world: the whole recipe might be conditioned by the scarcity of food. There is a geo-politics to all gastronomy. But as well as these pragmatic considerations, and considerations of taste and politics, another cultural level might be acting on the cook and the eater: a sort of bio-poetics of bodily memory and affect (that scent reminds me of my time in x; that flavour makes me cry because of y). The point here is that in the act of making and eating, all these registers are working simultaneously as bodies, tools, climates and physical resources come together in specific geographical and historical locations. Design culture is made up of these interwoven, entangled, dense, contradictory moments of living in a fashioned environment.

So come, design comrades, let us forge ahead, gathering around us dusty old bits of furniture and shiny new telephones; stained recipe books and modern weapon systems; variegated tulips and high-rise apartments. Let us smell the coffee, and let it awaken our dreams, but let's also look at how it was produced, the agriculture it obliterated, and the street practices it fashioned. Let us taste the future as it was inscribed in the cutlery and crockery of a troubled moment long past; let us examine the political desires embedded in a ceramic toilet bowl. Let us catch the hopes and desires, the frustrations and labours, the feelings and materials that are woven into our artificial worlds.

Design culture takes command!

The first requirement for encouraging a form of design studies dedicated to exploring the ways humans connect and disconnect with machines (for instance), or the way sensual landscapes generate emotional responses, is a mild injunction: try thinking of design culture without designers. Design studies, and more particularly design history, as it was practised during the last half of the twentieth century, often inherited a habit of mind from a particular form of art history: the concentration on named designers and on the cluster of names that constitute movements and schools. Thus scholarly design literature can often seem to be overly dominated by studies of the Bauhaus, or Charles and Ray Eames, or the ever-present Le Corbusier. Less scholarly literature can also seem transfixed by 'big names', but also by more practical questions of design as home improvement. For students learning to become professional designers, attention to canonical figures and iconic design objects can seem to connect immediately to the ambition that drives someone to enter the field in the first place. My argument, though, is that 'design culture without designers' might actually allow the study of design culture to be even more ambitious.

What then would 'design culture without designers' mean? Initially I think it just means not *starting* from a name, a reputation, and proceeding to describe and explain a body of work. It also means not assuming that the agent of design is the designer. For instance, the difference between asking a research question such as 'what has been the influence of Le Corbusier on modern apart-ment building?' and asking one like 'why are modern apartment buildings designed the way they are?' is the difference between assuming a specific active agent (Le Corbusier) and leaving that question open. The former question works to trace connections between this already known entity (the design studio of Le Corbusier) and later practices (for instance, municipal building in the UK in the second half of the twentieth century). It searches later practices for signs of Le Corbusier-like elements. The latter question wouldn't assume that Le Corbusier was a causal factor at all (but, of course, it wouldn't discount the possibility either), nor would it necessarily assume that architects and designers were the only agents in the process. For instance, it might turn out that it was the engineering profession that determined something of the specificity of those buildings, or that manu-facturers of new materials were enormously influential in the shape that a structure took. It might become clear that the most important features of the building were determined by social theories of community that had been inherited from the nineteenth century, or that the positioning and layout of the site were passed down from romantic ideas about nature and national landscape. Of course this second question is most likely to end up describing modern apartment buildings as an amalgam of all these elements (and more) with, perhaps, a little dash of Le Corbusier in the mix too.

An understanding of design as a more anonymous practice connects to some of the oldest approaches to design culture. For the architectural theorist and historian Eugène-Emmanuel Viollet-le-Duc (1814–79) the anonymous artisans working on French churches in the Middle Ages represent an architectural spirit that finds itself articulated in the deep structure of a building. In the work of the Austrian historian Alois Riegl (1858–1905) attention is given to everything from belt buckles to paintings to find the perceptual volition of an epoch. In the work of the Swiss art historian Heinrich Wölfflin (1864–1945) a shoe is as good as a cathedral for making vivid the style of an age.[3]

In recent years the productivity of the idea of 'design without designers' is often most vivid in accounts of the designed environment that see consumption as a decisive element in any design process.[4] So the inhabitation of a building is not a sign of the success or failure of an initial vision (the architect's), but is the realisation of some of the building's conscious and unconscious elements, as well as the active re-shaping and re-forming effects of the occupiers. While many debates in design studies might focus on whether priority is given to the production stage or the consumption stage, here I want to suggest another way of thinking about design. So this leads me to a second possible injunction: design culture without products. This is, I must admit, a particularly precarious injunction as I would want to argue that design studies needs objects, needs things. What it doesn't need, however, is the sense of a design item as a *finished* product that is either adopted and adapted by users, or not. I want to think of the designed environment as an active field of engagements and entanglements. This is a material environment, of course, but it is not reducible to a sort of glorified shopping mall, where identities are picked out and social status achieved via product choice.

Crucially this means finding other words to describe the active environment of design rather than 'product', 'status', 'identity' and the like. The word 'design' has multiple inflections, shifting between the stasis of something that has happened (a coat has been designed and manufactured) and the active sense of design as patterning and shaping the world in complex ways. It is this latter sense that I would want to privilege. To inoculate myself against the equation that design-equals-finished-product, I need a lexicon of more process-oriented words. Crucially, then, I want to think of design as a series of negotiations, as an orchestration (of sense, of perception and so on), as an orientation (something that encourages and generates propensities and proclivities), as an assemblage (and as an assembling activity, where it is always possible that combinations themselves combine), as an arrangement (a temporary coming together) and so on. This orchestration might include objects, but it would also include less evidently material elements such as, for instance, encouraged patterns of sociability, the training of sense perception, an ethics of distribution and so on. In one of the epigraphs at the beginning of this book Jacques Rancière writes:

> What interests me is the way in which, by drawing lines, arranging words or distributing surfaces, one also designs divisions of communal space. It is the way in which, by assembling words or forms, people define not merely various forms of art, but certain configurations of what can be seen and what can be thought, certain forms of inhabiting the material world.
>
> (Rancière 2007: 91)

For Rancière, as well as for this book, there is no design without a concomitant social imagination. From a waste disposal system to an airport, from a drain to a house, design distributes, configures and arranges social actions, sensual perceptions, and forms of being together and being apart. And it does it materially. Take any house, from the simplest to the most complex, and you have a material agent that is encouraging and discouraging everyday actions and their sociality (collective cooking, for instance, separate rooms for children, etc.). Walls, doorways, toilets, fans, windows and so on afford views, stop or encourage smells, promote walking or sitting: the ordinary elements of the designed environment orient us, and orchestrate our sensual and social worlds. And it is the ordinary, the ubiquitous and established rather than the brand new that demonstrate this social orchestration most complexly and most vividly. Thus a third injunction: design culture is not extraordinary.

Primarily I think the way to get to the ordinary, to get to the everydayness of design, requires an approach to design that isn't overawed by novelty. This might mean tempering your interest in cyborgs and reconnecting to a history of sideboards. If design studies has often been enamoured by named designers it is often because such designers are seen as having generated new forms and discovered novel arrangements, and have generally been viewed as innovators in their fields. In a similar way, many people who look at design technologies are immersed in the possibilities of what new technologies might be able to do. As such the narrative of history that is generated (depending on judgements about the value of new technologies) sees design technologies as evidence of progress or decline. To counter this, the 'object' of design studies would need to be the established and ubiquitous object or design environment, rather than the latest blue-sky software project. In this, I think, it would be worth noting Walter Benjamin's historiographic perspective: 'Overcoming the concept of "progress" and overcoming the concept of "period of decline" are two sides of one and the same thing' (Benjamin 1999: 460). This is the basic premise of Benjamin's critical cultural history, where judgements of epochal value (progress or decline) get in the way of recognising the potential and actuality of any cultural configuration.

It is worth refusing the lure of the newly new for one very simple reason: the 'brand new' just hasn't settled into the complex web of sociality that would give it life (it is far too tied to the intentionality of its makers and to the brand identity of its corporate backers). The lustre of the new is a poor substitute for the mottled density of the socially established. The brand new is as yet unmarked by the contingencies of everyday life. From the perspective of everyday life the moments of technological discovery (of the cathode ray tube, for instance) are less important than the process of television 'becoming habitual', or the process whereby the car becomes ordinary. Everyday life witnesses the path technologies take when they become ordinary: to fade from view by becoming part of the inherited landscape of our artificial earth.

Part of my aim in this introduction is to tempt you into a world of ubiquitous design. This is design in its ordinary and inescapable state: plumbing, floorboards, windows, wiring, school chairs, office carpets, TVs in hospitals, mass housing, roads, lighting, hotel bedding, car parks, exhaust systems, recipes, shelves, cupboards, supermarkets, bicycles, discarded shoes, stairs, sheds, paper, etc. This 'etc.', rather than signalling the end of the run, the run that has run out of steam, is the essence of ubiquitous design: ubiquitous design is, in one sense, nothing but an et cetera. This is a world of circulating objects and intricate connections. This is a place where bodies bristle and stomachs rumble: a lively place. It is a world where design is an informal activity that everybody participates in. This is not to deny that design isn't also a professional and commercial activity, and that designer goods aren't also central to this social world; but out here, in the world of ubiquitous design, canonical design objects have to take their chance along with everything else (Nike and knock-off alike). Ubiquitous design is technology that can be soft and fluffy as well as hard and shiny. To gain a sense of ubiquitous design, think more about a disposable drink can and less about *haute couture*; imagine emulsion paint and fitted carpets rather than Charlotte Perriand; envisage plumbing systems (and cisterns) in the place of the Bauhaus.

Sensescapes of the modern

One of the best ways to see the complex entanglement of a designed environment is to take media machines as objects of scrutiny. What would it mean to look at radio and TV from the point of view of design studies? First of all, and as part of the established traditions of design studies, it would mean looking at the actual object-hood of the device: its style, its sleekness, its borrowing of other traditions (cabinet making, for instance), its presence as furniture. This is TV as something that you can bump into or trip over. Clearly it would differ from a mainstream media studies perspective which might be more interested in the output of TV or radio, and the varied ways in which it addresses you. For media studies the interest has often been in looking at what the broadcasting schedule includes and excludes, and who is welcomed into TV's intimate and tender embrace.

From a more open design perspective (the perspective being pursued here), there would be little reason to demarcate between these approaches: such initial forms of attention (TV as furniture, TV as a form of mediation) would quickly bleed out into myriad approaches to TV's life on our artificial earth. For instance, we might start to think about the way a TV set or a radio orchestrates a room (a communal domestic space, a bedroom, a waiting room and so on). We would need to think about the kind of seating arrangements such particular objects permit or encourage, and the sociality of those arrangements.[5] We could start thinking about the forms of attention they seem to solicit (absorption and distraction, for instance) and the patterns of silence that they appear to allow and dissuade.[6] Television participates in a variety of media environments which it neither totally dominates nor leaves unchanged.[7] In spaces as anonymous as shopping malls and as personally marked as bedrooms, TV and radio (as well as, of course, newer digital media) provide opportunities for being apart-together or for being together-apart. TV participates in styles of eating and other forms of conviviality; it reformulates ideas and practices of privacy and publicity. In environmental terms these media often have contradictory affects: radio, for instance, increased the amount of noise there was in day-to-day life, but it also increases the amount of purposeful silence too (an attentive, listening audience).[8] All of these interrelated aspects of TV and radio's insertion in specific environments should be of concern to the study of design culture when it is open to the way bodies and objects are purposefully and accidentally entangled.

All the social and sensual arranging, orchestrating and orienting that TV and radio participate in seem to belong neither purely to the object (the TV and radio as furniture-like) nor purely to the text (the actual TV and radio programmes and schedules). Perhaps then this is where we can claim the design environment as a dynamic field that situates us within a world of objects, senses, emotions, forms of attention and inattention, social relationships, perceptual practices and so on. One way of measuring the impact of a design phenomenon, its orienting and orchestrating strength, so to say, is to imagine life without it, or before it. This is Paddy Scannel writing about the peculiar temporality of TV, radio and newspapers:

> Our sense of days is always already in part determined by the ways in which media contribute to the shaping of our sense of days. Would time feel different for us without radio, television and newspaper? Would it run to a different rhythm? Would it have the edge that it has today? The sense that each day is a particular day? For the effect of the temporal arrangements of radio and television is such as to pick out each day as *this* day, this day in particular, that day as its *own* day, caught up in its own immediacy, with its own involvements and concerns.
>
> (Scannell 1996: 149)

Paddy Scannell's phenomenological approach to media suggests that, as a design field, media machines and media forms (in their ubiquity) are profoundly orienting and affecting.

For Scannell media forms organise specific experiences of dailiness that invoke a strong sense of personal, experiential time (rather than clock time) even though they are often structured around clock time (hourly news updates, for instance). They deploy this orientation because, over a number of years, media forms have learnt particular techniques that Scannell calls 'care structures': the generation of intimacy (the broadcaster as intimate, friendly voice); the insistently experiential time that they foster; and the sense of address that they direct to you:

> Radio and television have a for-anyone-as-someone structure that mediates between the for-anyone structure of publicly available anonymous (mass-produced) useable things and the for-someone structure of purely personal things (letters, 'family' snapshots and videos, etc.).
>
> (Scannell 1996: 174)

For Scannell all of this is neither accidental nor established as a set of conscious intentions; instead it could be seen as a dynamic sedimentation that has formed over many years as techniques have been tried and tested and honed to achieve the affective environment of broadcasting.

Scannell's phenomenology of media might suggest that the design agents that produce this orientation and orchestration would need to include at least the following: sound producers and engineers, script writers, presenters, stylists, viewers and listeners (who attuned themselves to these orientations), telephone operators (for phone-in programmes), set designers, camera-operators, music composers, TV critics and so on. Take, for example, the globally franchised show *Who Wants to be a Millionaire?* This programme is licensed in more than seventy countries – from Iceland to India, Indonesia to Italy. Originating in the UK it is an example of a form that began on radio (the phone-in competition with one contestant at a time) and enlarged in scale to take on its TV form. The slow progress of the competition (there is no time limit for answering a question), the emphasis on deliberation (the presenter's constant interjections of 'are you sure about your answer?') and the address to the audience ('don't go away, we'll be right back' as you enter ad breaks) produce an intimacy that would be reinforced by the TV as domestic furniture. The timbre of the voice, the hair-style, the close-ups, the gentle banter, the audience's silence, the heartbeat-like music: all work to produce a sense of intimacy. I don't think it is stretching the word 'design' to see all these elements as part of a design form that produces a specific media time-space (at home, watching *Who Wants to be a Millionaire?* on a Saturday evening, for instance). It would make sense to see *Who Wants to be a Millionaire?* as part of a cluster of TV's output, and to treat this cluster as productive of a specific sensescape.

Here the Saturday evening 'family show', which seeps into so many homes, is a specific designed object that in conjunction with other objects creates a sensual and affective environment (of envy, irritation, empathy, irony, etc.). The modern world might be usefully characterised as the production of designed sensescapes. The downtown shopping mall (with franchised fast-food outlets, neon signage, smart coffee-houses, climate-controlled interiors that let you know you are nowhere, piped music, CCTV, security guards, moving staircases, endless advertising models on display and so on) is just one of the many complex sensescapes that characterise modern Western conurbations. Modern industrial transport, with that strange experience of stationary movement (your body bound to a seat, while you are hurtling through space), where the window is a screen (is it you moving or the outside world?), where the network of lines and roads meet in anonymous hubs that seem connected, provides another series of modern sensescapes. Is there anything quite as depressingly stationary as air travel?

The designed environments of modernity are always sensorial, even if they may, at times, promote sensory deprivation (think of the way in which mp3 players cut you off from the polyphony of the street). Food culture, again, provides useful examples: a McDonald's restaurant in Beijing; a sushi bar in Paris; a pub in a small town in England. All of these designed environments are very particular orchestrations of smells, tastes, textures, sounds and sights. Sitting in the plastic bucket seats in a McDonald's everything is in place, everything is marked by the corporate design ethos. The burgers are composed as efficient design solutions (the dill pickle has to sit on top of the sliced tomato, not the other way round), the lighting has a migraine-inducing intensity, a specific smell lingers in the air: all of this is the designed environment and its sensual orchestrations act on you. To a degree this environment trains you: it trains your taste buds, your alimentary desires, your temporal expectations (how fast should food be?). Of course this doesn't mean that it successfully trains you: your body might have its own sense of what counts as comforting food; the brightness might really cause the migraine. It is easy enough, I think, to see how a McDonald's in Beijing might be thought of as a designed sensescape, but we need to extend this to all designed environments (to all the places we inhabit on our artificial earth). As a rule of thumb we might want to think of modern sensescapes as the outcome of machines and movement. In this the local pub, with its particular menu, its improvised and informal interiors, is as much a result of movement and machines as the sushi bar in Paris or the McDonald's in Beijing. Foodstuffs, recipes, national cuisines are all the result of movement (of people and things), and their configuration within today's culture is always industrial (the machines that store, that cook, that clean, that move, that count, that pay, etc.).

To see design in terms of sensescapes is, I think, a crucial way of understanding the interconnectedness of the design environment, and the way in which bodies and objects are entangled. To think of design in this way is to take a macro-logical approach to design, to treat design as a series of relays, where the 'object' of study isn't the thing, but the relationships between a network of things and subjects. But if modern sensescapes position design as a series of relays between one element and another, between objects and bodies, there is also the possibility of the micro-logical attention to the obdurate thing, in all its specificity and materiality. This means attending to the object neither as a 'dumb thing', nor simply as a cipher for something else (desire, social aspirations and so on). The micro-logical object is the thing as it constantly oscillates between a rock and a dream.

Obdurate objects, symbolic possessions and playful subjects

It is always worth trying to start from the beginning, or at least from *a* beginning. We first encounter our artificial, designed worlds as babies: plastic teats, towels, teddies, cots, 'dummies' (or pacifiers), baskets, buggies, songs, toys, sweets, games, shoes and language. We are, it is all too obvious not to state, born into a world already fashioned, already fabricated. It is as babies that this world is discovered as simultaneously familiar and foreign; as unyielding and malleable; as darkly fantastic and drastically material. We do things to things, and things do things to us. We learn about the affordances of our material existence through playful interactions that put the 'experimental' back into experience. Stone is stone because it remains impervious to our violent urges; plastic is plastic for the shapes it can take, for its lightness, and for the way that it splinters when it succumbs to our destructive purges.

A child's eye view of our designed worlds offers a way of foregrounding this contradiction: the designed world is never more than the physical properties and propensities of its material existence; the designed world is never less than a cosmology of values and affects, of magical transformations and immaterial longings. Here is the surrealist Michel Leiris, writing as a troubled adult, trying to remember a moment in childhood. It is an astonishingly long sentence, so take a deep breath, and here goes . . .

> Onto the pitiless floor (of the living room or the dining room? onto a fitted carpet with faded floral patterns or a rug with some other design on which I inscribed palaces, landscapes, continents, a true kaleidoscope delightful to me in my childishness, for I designed fairyland constructions on it as if it were a canvas for some thousand and one nights that hadn't yet been revealed to me by the pages of any book in those days? or a bare floor, waxed wood with darker lineaments, cleanly cut by the rigid, black grooves from which I sometimes liked to pull up tufts of dust with a pin when I was lucky enough to find one that had fallen from the dressmaker's hands during the day?) onto the irreproachable, soulless, floor of the room (velvety or ligneous, dressed up in its Sunday best or stripped bare, favoring excursions of the imagination or more mechanical games), in the living or dining room, in shadow or light (depending on whether it was the part of the house where the furniture was usually protected by dust sheets and its modest riches were often screened from the sun by the bars of the shutters), in the special precinct accessible only to the grownups – a tranquil cave for the somnolent piano – or in the more common place that contained the large, many leaved table around which all or part of the family would gather for the ritual of daily meals, the soldier had fallen.
>
> (Leiris 1948: 3)

This gargantuan sentence forms the opening paragraph of Michel Leiris' multiple-volume auto-biography *Rules of the Game*. It takes us into a shabbily genteel, *haute bourgeois* domestic world, in early twentieth-century France. More importantly, though, it might be read as a phenomenological account of a child's (Michel Leiris') most immediate designed environment. Here carpets are soft and floorboards are hard, and hard surfaces afford a different kind of play than soft ones. But carpets and floorboards are also battlefields and landscapes. They are also places to encounter dust, fluff, the underside of furniture, splinters and so on.

In an earlier sketch of this autobiographical project ('The Sacred in Everyday Life') Leiris tours his family home revealing the places and things that mattered deeply to him as a child:

> Thinking back to my childhood, I remember first a few idols, temples and, in a more general way, sacred places. First there were several objects belonging to my father, symbols of his power and authority. His top hat with the flat brim that he hung on the coat rack at night when he came home from the office. His revolver, a Smith and Wesson with its small barrel, dangerous like all firearms

and even more attractive for being nickelplated. This instrument he usually kept in a desk drawer or in his bedside table, and it was the attribute *par excellence* of the one who, among other jobs, had the responsibility of defending the home and protecting it from burglars.

(Leiris 1938: 25)

Reading Leiris' account of the 'sacred' objects and places of his childhood, we might latch on to the term 'symbolic' to describe the power these objects had. The gun and the hat were, for Leiris, symbolic of his father's power. No doubt this was true. But the very term 'symbolic' suggests an overly mental image of power. Later on in this quotation Leiris tells us that the gun was the 'attribute *par excellence*' of his father as defender: here, with the word attribute, we get closer to the full material pull of this object. The gun, of course, is not simply symbolic; or rather its symbolism is not arbitrary. The gun is a tool, a weight, a substance, a surface, a possible action; it can do things (shoot and kill), and it belongs to someone. Similarly the hat is an intimate possession, worn as an affiliation: its hardness, its blackness, its brim, matter.

An object (design's basic element) is often simultaneously invested with powerful symbolic meaning while obdurately remaining a 'dumb', material thing. A rose may symbolise romantic love, but in the end and from the start a 'rose, is a rose, is a rose' (Stein 1980: 35).[9] What matters, I think, for the study of design objects is not to try and untangle this phenomenon (split the material from the ideational, for instance), but to recognise the actuality of the entanglement. Marx does this when he describes the commodity as a phantasmagoria: the commodity 'is nothing but the definite social relation between men themselves which assumes here, for them, the fantastic form of a relationship between things' (Marx 1867/1976: 165). The commodity (the object infused with the lustre of desire) is simultaneously a materially fashioned thing and a transcendent wish. What makes the commodity such a frustrating cultural form is often the way it fails to be either fully a thing or completely transcendent. Once bought the desired object shows its earthly origin, the lustre wears off, but never completely. Throwing away old commodities (the outdated computer, the now unfashionable clothes) is never simply equivalent to dumping fallen leaves; it always feels like you are chucking out broken promises.

Perhaps the best account of how objects have an obstinate materiality, and how we might need to rethink our ideas of symbolism because of this, is provided by the psychoanalyst Donald Winnicott. Winnicott was a psychoanalytic clinician who specialised in the treatment of very young children. His practice often involved observing children playing with toys in his consulting room or chatting with children about their drawings. In 1951 he published his landmark essay 'Transitional Objects and Transitional Phenomena' (included in Winnicott 1985). The topic of the essay is a child's special toy or comforter (a teddy bear, a small square of blanket, for instance) 'that becomes vitally important to the infant for use at a time of going to sleep, and is a defence against anxiety, especially anxiety of a depressive type' (Winnicott 1985: 4). For Winnicott these addictive things, which are taken up at a very early age and give comfort to children, are the child's first 'not-me' objects, and they allow children to navigate from the closed internal world of the dyad (the infantile world of mother and baby as a single environment) to the social world of objects and people in which the child has limited control.

For Winnicott the child's special toy is, initially at least, a substitute for the mother's breast (and anyone who has seen a very small child falling asleep with such a toy or 'snuggler' will know the truth of this). But if this suggests that the toy 'symbolises' the breast, then the opposite is also true: the toy is of value precisely because it is not the breast. It is valuable because it is a thing that can be discarded, bashed and lost before it is needed again. It is precisely because it can be possessed as a thingly object, that it can be controlled to an extent (until the bedtime horror of the lost comforter), that makes it useful for the child who is learning to cope with the trauma of being a separate person. If it is symbolic, it is symbolic in an active way. In this sense a symbol is not a metaphoric substitute (soft toy for breast), but an active agent in a dynamic environment. Thus the child's toy is symbolic of the overcoming of the child's reliance on the comfort of the breast. And the object-symbol isn't a passive cipher of this dynamic transition; it is a complex tool in achieving it.

As an example of the dynamism of the designed object, toys provide rich material. Not only do they suggest that all material things are to some degree malleable (inserted into a game a stick becomes a gun, a shoe box a fairy castle), they also reveal the intimate connection between play and habit. Part of the magic of the object is its ordinariness: the favourite toy is a toy that has weathered the descent into habit. For Walter Benjamin toys are design objects with a pedagogic mission. This pedagogic mission might be varied (the little plastic kitchens that allow children to mimic the behaviour of adults, the doctor and nurse outfits that encourage the pretence of care), but the process of pedagogy is often similar.[10] In a review of a book on the history of toys, Benjamin makes this crucial point about the relationship between play and habit:

> For play and nothing else is the mother of every habit. Eating, sleeping, getting dressed, washing have to be installed into the struggling little brat in a playful way, following the rhythm of nursery rhymes. Habit enters life as a game, and in habit, even in its most sclerotic forms, an element of play survives to the end. Habits are the forms of our first happiness and our first horror that have congealed and become deformed to the point of being unrecognizable.
>
> (Benjamin 1928: 120)

The toy or nursery rhyme provides a comforting way for adopting habits. These habits comfort us and constrict us; they allow us a certain amount of control over the world, while simultaneously showing us how we are, in turn, controlled. As we succumb to the habits of our designed environments, as we let our machines guide us in our daily routines, there is always, still, the possibility of alteration, of change through these objects. Their malleability is never far from the surface. It is us, not our objects, who surrender to the principles of instrumental reason.

For design studies, then, designed objects (be they toys, cars, clothes or whatever) exist in dynamic environments: as bluntly stubborn matter; as symbolic possessions; and as objects used by subjects whose play turns into habit. No one element of this triumvirate is more important than the other: it is the entanglement of all three that matters for understanding design culture.

Towards a social aesthetics . . .

In this introduction I have been keen to promote the study of design culture as a form of materialism (starting and finishing with the concrete environment) that is attuned to a range of immaterial materialities (emotions, play, symbolic desires and so on). This approach could be called 'social aesthetics'. Here though aesthetics wouldn't be about discriminating taste, but about the sensual material life of objects, and the subjects that interact with them. Aesthetics, then, is primarily concerned with material experiences, with the way the sensual world greets the sensorial body and with the affective forces that are generated in such meetings. Aesthetics covers the terrain of both 'the vehement passions' (fear, grief, rapture and so on) and the minor and major affects and emotions (humiliation, shame, envy, irritation, anxiety, disdain, surprise, etc.).[11] It is attuned to forms of perception, sensation and attention (distraction, spectacle, concentration, absorption, for example); to the world of the senses (haptic, aural, gustatory, olfactory and visual experience) and to the body (as gestalt and in bits and pieces). Most importantly and most suggestively it would be concerned with the utter entanglements of all these elements.

The project of generating a social aesthetic perspective for our design culture in our artificial worlds necessarily has to be on-going (these worlds are simply too dynamic, too unstable and too interesting to imagine establishing a stable perspective). The texts that follow are simply designed to encourage this project.

Notes

1   In a slightly different vein (but more immediately catastrophic) it is worth noting that the first chapter of Zygmunt Bauman's book on the purposeful production of human lives as 'waste' (in the form of refugees and other social outcasts) is titled 'In the Beginning was Design' (Bauman 2004).

2   For a sample of what this includes see Crary 1999; Donald 1999; Feher 1997; Gardiner 2000; Haraway 1991; Jameson and Miyoshi 1998; Jütte 2005; Sedgwick 2003.

3   On this tradition of cultural history and art history see Podro 1982; on Riegl see Iverson 1993; on Wölfflin see Schwartz 1999.

4   See, for instance, Attfield 2000 and Hill 1998.

5   See Lynn Spigel's account of TV's early entry into the domestic environment: Spigel 1992.

6   On distraction see Siegfried Kracauer's intellectual journalism from the 1920s and 1930s; Kracauer 1995. See also Morse 1998.

7   See McCarthy 2001 for extensive discussion of this feature of media environments.

8   Thanks to Kate Lacey for this point.

9   Gertrude Stein, the originator of this much used saying, includes it in a number of poems. The reference here is to her long poem 'Lifting Belly' (1915–17). At times 'Rose' appears to be somebody's name. Whether the rose is a woman, a flower or the name of a flower, the thrice-repeated invocation insists on the stubborn materiality of all three roses.

10   The pedagogic success of toys is never assured – this is especially true when children combine cooking and surgery, for instance, and delight in the possibility of the kitchen as a space of deadly accidents.

11   See Altieri 2003; Fisher 2002; Ngai 2005b.

PART ONE

MATERIALS AND METHODS

INTRODUCTION TO PART ONE

THE QUESTION of how to engage critically with design culture is also a question that concerns the nature of design cultures: in other words, 'what is design culture?' The character of design culture, its materiality, the way it matters and the way it is matter will determine how we treat it. Yet, perhaps confusingly, what we make design culture out to be, the characteristics that we find in it, are already a sign that we have decided how to engage with it. There is no description without some degree of interpretation (we have to start somewhere and finish somewhere else), and interpretation is never able to exhaust the object. Perhaps then the best way to start to engage with design culture is to see it as a mutual testing between materiality and method, a constant oscillation between interpretation and brute and tender matter.

The extent of design culture is, of course, fairly fluid, and while all might agree on a core set of objects and arrangements, some might be unwilling to include the seemingly more obscure and immaterial arrangements that seem to be characterised as much by the non-planned as by the planned. Take a particular domestic setting: it is breakfast time in x's apartment, the radio is on, people are sitting round a table, food is being served (some are serving, some are eating). The radio is playing schmaltzy tunes from ten years ago: the person cooking is making pancakes to order. Where in this scenario, which we already know so little about, could you mark the boundaries of design culture? You could stop after you've itemised the solid and manufactured objects (chairs, crockery, cupboards, cutlery, radio, clothes), but why stop there? Why not include the food (after all, the chickens have been living in fashioned worlds, their eggs have been date-stamped and pack-aged)? And why not the music being played (which exists as an 'object', where enormous amounts of time and energy went into the design, the clothes, the haircut, the production and so on)? And what about the people? How could we leave them out and still think we were dealing with 'culture' as a dynamic, living experience?

Design culture is extensive in sheer volume, but it is also extensive in terms of the realms it touches. If design culture is most insistently an orchestration of material (and mental) life (or a set of orchestrations and arrangements), then it touches us economically, emotionally, historically, personally, ecologically, sexually – in a word, socially. And this will always require an interdisciplinary commitment, or rather a refusal to be tied down to the tried and tested protocols of a specific discipline. But this goal of socially vivid understanding doesn't allow us to presume objectivity, a view from outside those arrangements and orchestrations. Back in the kitchen with the eggs and the radio, everything looks very different depending on where you are, what you are and what you are doing. Can you write design culture from the standpoint of a kitchen table? Or of a radio announcer? What does it look like from the position of the small child who is demolishing those pancakes?

Chapter 1

Karl Marx

THE FETISHISM OF THE COMMODITY AND ITS SECRET [1867]

Source: Karl Marx (1976 edition) *Capital: Volume One*, translated by Ben Fowkes, Harmondsworth: Penguin, pp. 163–77. First published in 1867.

Karl Marx (1818–83) is one of the most compelling voices of the nineteenth century. One way of describing his thought is to see it as the recognition of the upside-down-ness of the world, and an attempt to rectify this, in both thought and deed. For Marx philosophy as idealism is upside-down thinking (thus Hegel needed to be turned on his head); ideology sees the world as an inversion; religion is back to front (a human product, 'god', is given sovereign agency over humanity); and perhaps most importantly, the world of things and humans is standing on its head. And it is here that the fetishism of the commodity plays its decisive role. Fundamentally Marx is pointing to the dual process of industrialisation and mercantile capitalism. The result of believing in the 'money form' and in letting machinery drive history is that, as humans become more thing-like ('cogs in the machine', for instance, which is often the literal position of the factory worker), things take on magical, human qualities.

In the following extract from *Capital* Karl Marx conjures up a vivid and prescient image of commodity culture. For Marx things are enlivened by the process of commodification, they become animated, magical. His example is a table, which, when it becomes a commodity, starts standing on its head, starts dancing and starts having 'ideas'. For Marx the 'dancing' table is a complex analogy: it is the delusional 'knocking' table of the séance; but it is also a potential liberation (when the table starts dancing in China, people have cast off their feudal shackles). Perhaps most fundamentally, though, the table is that most ordinary thing, which becomes magical when it is a commodity. We are halfway there in the way we talk about furniture as having 'legs' and 'feet'. Thus anthropomorphism is one of the most significant instances of the fetishism of the commodity. While it is clear that even as a commodity a wooden table is still a wooden table, we won't get far looking for its commodity form by analysing the properties of wood (Marx reminds us that no chemist has ever told us why diamonds are so expensive and desirable). In many ways a table becomes a magical commodity only when it is 'designed', when its exchange value subsumes its use value and when the labour that produced it is veiled by the magic of the thing. And it is the design process that has most insistently accomplished this (in design culture things don't look made; they look as if they arrived 'ready-made', from space).

When Marx was writing, commodity culture was still in its infancy. The prescience of Marx's work today, though, is evident nearly everywhere. Everywhere we look advertising is trying to seduce us with the 'sex appeal of the inorganic'. Last week I saw an advert for mobile phones: all the phones had little legs, feet and heads. They were all happily dancing about inside a lorry that was zooming off to the shopping mall. These were the new phones, the latest generation. Elsewhere, last year's phones were looking ashamed, disconsolate. These phones weren't dancing; they were committing suicide.

Further reading: Appadurai 1986; Forty 1986; Tafuri 1973/1992, 1980/1990.

A COMMODITY APPEARS at first sight an extremely obvious, trivial thing. But its analysis brings out that it is a very strange thing, abounding in metaphysical subtleties and theological niceties. So far as it is a use-value, there is nothing mysterious about it, whether we consider it from the point of view that by its properties it satisfies human needs, or that it first takes on these properties as the product of human labour. It is absolutely clear that, by his activity, man changes the forms of the materials of nature in such a way as to make them useful to him. The form of wood, for instance, is altered if a table is made out of it. Nevertheless the table continues to be wood, an ordinary, sensuous thing. But as soon as it emerges as a commodity, it changes into a thing which transcends sensuousness. It not only stands with its feet on the ground, but, in relation to all other commodities, it stands on its head, and evolves out of its wooden brain grotesque ideas, far more wonderful than if it were to begin dancing of its own free will.[1]

The mystical character of the commodity does not therefore arise from its use-value. Just as little does it proceed from the nature of the determinants of value. For in the first place, however varied the useful kinds of labour, or productive activities, it is a physiological fact that they are functions of the human organism, and that each such function, whatever may be its nature or its form, is essentially the expenditure of human brain, nerves, muscles and sense organs. Secondly, with regard to the foundation of the quantitative determination of value, namely the duration of that expenditure or the quantity of labour, this is quite palpably different from its quality. In all situations, the labour-time it costs to produce the means of subsistence must necessarily concern mankind, although not to the same degree at different stages of development.[2] And finally, as soon as men start to work for each other in any way, their labour also assumes a social form.

Whence, then, arises the enigmatic character of the product of labour, as soon as it assumes the form of a commodity? Clearly, it arises from this form itself. The equality of the kinds of human labour takes on a physical form in the equal objectivity of the products of labour as values; the measure of the expenditure of human labour-power by its duration takes on the form of the magnitude of the value of the products of labour; and finally the relationships between the producers, within which the social characteristics of their labours are manifested, take on the form of a social relation between the products of labour.

The mysterious character of the commodity-form consists therefore simply in the fact that the commodity reflects the social characteristics of men's own labour as objective characteristics of the products of labour themselves, as the socio-natural properties of these things. Hence it also reflects the social relation of the producers to the sum total of labour as a social relation between objects, a relation which exists apart from and outside the producers. Through this substitution, the products of labour become commodities, sensuous things which are at the same time supra-sensible or social. In the same way, the impression made by a thing on the optic nerve is perceived not as a subjective excitation of that nerve but as the objective form of a thing outside the eye. In the act of seeing, of course, light is really transmitted from one thing, the external object, to another thing, the eye. It is a physical relation between physical things. As against this, the commodity-form, and the value-relation of the products of labour within which it appears, have absolutely no connection with the physical nature of the commodity and the material [*dinglich*] relations arising out of this. It is nothing but the definite social relation between men themselves which assumes here, for them, the fantastic form of a relation between things. In order, therefore, to find an analogy we must take flight into the misty realm of religion. There the products of the human brain appear as autonomous figures endowed with a life of their own, which enter into relations both with each other and with the human race. So it is in the world of commodities with the products of men's hands. I call this the fetishism which attaches itself to the products of labour as soon as they are produced as commodities, and is therefore inseparable from the production of commodities.

As the foregoing analysis has already demonstrated, this fetishism of the world of commodities arises from the peculiar social character of the labour which produces them.

Objects of utility become commodities only because they are the products of the labour of private individuals who work independently of each other. The sum total of the labour of all these private individuals forms the aggregate labour of society. Since the producers do not come into social contact until they exchange the products of their labour, the specific social characteristics of their private labours appear only within this exchange. In other words, the labour of the private individual manifests itself as an element of the total labour of society only through the relations which the act of exchange establishes between the products, and, through their mediation, between the producers. To the producers, therefore, the social relations between their private labours appear as what they are, i.e. they do not appear as direct social relations between persons in their work, but rather as material [dinglich] relations between persons and social relations between things.

It is only by being exchanged that the products of labour acquire a socially uniform objectivity as values, which is distinct from their sensuously varied objectivity as articles of utility. This division of the product of labour into a useful thing and a thing possessing value appears in practice only when exchange has already acquired a sufficient extension and importance to allow useful things to be produced for the purpose of being exchanged, so that their character as values has already to be taken into consideration during production. From this moment on, the labour of the individual producer acquires a twofold social character. On the one hand, it must, as a definite useful kind of labour, satisfy a definite social need, and thus maintain its position as an element of the total labour, as a branch of the social division of labour, which originally sprang up spontaneously. On the other hand, it can satisfy the manifold needs of the individual producer himself only in so far as every particular kind of useful private labour can be exchanged with, i.e. counts as the equal of, every other kind of useful private labour. Equality in the full sense between different kinds of labour can be arrived at only if we abstract from their real inequality, if we reduce them to the characteristic they have in common, that of being the expenditure of human labour-power, of human labour in the abstract. The private producer's brain reflects this twofold social character of his labour only in the forms which appear in practical intercourse, in the exchange of products. Hence the socially useful character of his private labour is reflected in the form that the product of labour has to be useful to others, and the social character of the equality of the various kinds of labour is reflected in the form of the common character, as values, possessed by these materially different things, the products of labour.

Men do not therefore bring the products of their labour into relation with each other as values because they see these objects merely as the material integuments of homogeneous human labour. The reverse is true: by equating their different products to each other in exchange as values, they equate their different kinds of labour as human labour. They do this without being aware of it.[3] Value, therefore, does not have its description branded on its forehead; it rather transforms every product of labour into a social hieroglyphic. Later on, men try to decipher the hieroglyphic, to get behind the secret of their own social product: for the characteristic which objects of utility have of being values is as much men's social product as is their language. The belated scientific discovery that the products of labour, in so far as they are values, are merely the material expressions of the human labour expended to produce them, marks an epoch in the history of mankind's development, but by no means banishes the semblance of objectivity possessed by the social characteristics of labour. Something which is only valid for this particular form of production, the production of commodities, namely the fact that the specific social character of private labours carried on independently of each other consists in their equality as human labour, and, in the product, assumes the form of the existence of value, appears to those caught up in the relations of commodity production (and this is true both before and after the above-mentioned scientific discovery) to be just as ultimately valid as the fact that the scientific dissection of the air into its component parts left the atmosphere itself unaltered in its physical configuration.

What initially concerns producers in practice when they make an exchange is how much of some other product they get for their own; in what proportions can the products be exchanged? As soon as these proportions have attained a certain customary stability, they appear to result from the nature of the products so that, for instance, one ton of iron and two ounces of gold appear to be equal in value, in the same way as a pound of gold and a pound of iron are equal in weight, despite their different physical and chemical properties. The value character of the products of labour becomes firmly established only when they act as magnitudes of value. These magnitudes vary continually, independently of the will, fore-knowledge and actions of the exchangers. Their own movement within society has for them the form of a movement made by things, and these things, far from being under their control, in fact control them. The production of commodities must be fully developed before the scientific conviction emerges, from experi-ence itself, that all the different kinds of private labour (which are carried on independently of each other, and yet, as spontaneously developed branches of the social division of labour, are in a situation of all-round dependence on each other) are continually being reduced to the quantitative proportions in which society requires them. The reason for this reduction is that in the midst of the accidental and ever-fluctuating exchange relations between the products, the labour-time socially necessary to produce them asserts itself as a regulative law of nature. In the same way, the law of gravity asserts itself when a person's house collapses on top of him.[4] The determination of the magnitude of value by labour-time is therefore a secret hidden under the apparent movements in the relative values of commodities. Its discovery destroys the semblance of the merely accidental determination of the magnitude of the value of the products of labour, but by no means abolishes that determination's material form.

Reflection on the forms of human life, hence also scientific analysis of those forms, takes a course directly opposite to their real development. Reflection begins *post festum*,[b] and therefore with the results of the process of development ready to hand. The forms which stamp products as commodities and which are therefore the preliminary requirements for the circulation of commodities, already possess the fixed quality of natural forms of social life before man seeks to give an account, not of their historical character, for in his eyes they are immutable, but of their content and meaning. Consequently, it was solely the analysis of the prices of commodities which led to the determination of the magnitude of value, and solely the common expression of all commodities in money which led to the establishment of their character as values. It is however precisely this finished form of the world of commodities – the money form – which conceals the social character of private labour and the social relations between the individual workers, by making those relations appear as relations between material objects, instead of revealing them plainly. If I state that coats or boots stand in a relation to linen because the latter is the universal incarnation of abstract human labour, the absurdity of the statement is self-evident. Nevertheless, when the producers of coats and boots bring these commodities into a relation with linen, or with gold or silver (and this makes no difference here), as the universal equivalent, the relation between their own private labour and the collective labour of society appears to them in exactly this absurd form.

The categories of bourgeois economics consist precisely of forms of this kind. They are forms of thought which are socially valid, and therefore objective, for the relations of production belonging to this historically determined mode of social production, i.e. commodity production. The whole mystery of com-modities, all the magic and necromancy that surrounds the products of labour on the basis of commodity production, vanishes therefore as soon as we come to other forms of production.

As political economists are fond of Robinson Crusoe stories,[5] let us first look at Robinson on his island. Undemanding though he is by nature, he still has needs to satisfy, and must therefore perform useful labours of various kinds: he must make tools, knock together furniture, tame llamas, fish, hunt and so on.

Of his prayers and the like, we take no account here, since our friend takes pleasure in them and sees them as recreation. Despite the diversity of his productive functions, he knows that they are only different forms of activity of one and the same Robinson, hence only different modes of human labour. Necessity itself compels him to divide his time with precision between his different functions. Whether one function occupies a greater space in his total activity than another depends on the magnitude of the difficulties to be overcome in attaining the useful effect aimed at. Our friend Robinson Crusoe learns this by experience, and having saved a watch, ledger, ink and pen from the shipwreck, he soon begins, like a good Englishman, to keep a set of books. His stock-book contains a catalogue of the useful objects he possesses, of the various operations necessary for their production, and finally of the labour-time that specific quantities of these products have on average cost him. All the relations between Robinson and these objects that form his self-created wealth are here so simple and transparent that even Mr Sedley Taylor[d] could understand them. And yet those relations contain all the essential determinants of value.

Let us now transport ourselves from Robinson's island, bathed in light, to medieval Europe, shrouded in darkness. Here, instead of the independent man, we find everyone dependent – serfs and lords, vassals and suzerains, laymen and clerics. Personal dependence characterizes the social relations of material production as much as it does the other spheres of life based on that production. But precisely because relations of personal dependence form the given social foundation, there is no need for labour and its products to assume a fantastic form different from their reality. They take the shape, in the transactions of society, of services in kind and payments in kind. The natural form of labour, its particularity – and not, as in a society based on commodity production, its universality – is here its immediate social form. The *corvée* can be measured by time just as well as the labour which produces commodities, but every serf knows that what he expends in the service of his lord is a specific quantity of his own personal labour-power. The tithe owed to the priest is more clearly apparent than his blessing. Whatever we may think, then, of the different roles in which men confront each other in such a society, the social relations between individuals in the performance of their labour appear at all events as their own personal relations, and are not disguised as social relations between things, between the products of labour.

For an example of labour in common, i.e. directly associated labour, we do not need to go back to the spontaneously developed form which we find at the threshold of the history of all civilized peoples.[6] We have one nearer to hand in the patriarchal rural industry of a peasant family which produces corn, cattle, yarn, linen and clothing for its own use. These things confront the family as so many products of its collective labour, but do not confront each other as commodities. The different kinds of labour which create these products – such as tilling the fields, tending the cattle, spinning, weaving and making clothes – are already in their natural form social functions; for they are functions of the family, which, just as much as a society based on commodity production, possesses its own spontaneously developed division of labour. The distribution of labour within the family and the labour-time expended by the individual members of the family, are regulated by differences of sex and age as well as by seasonal variations in the natural conditions of labour. The fact that the expenditure of the individual labour-powers is measured by duration appears here, by its very nature, as a social characteristic of labour itself, because the individual labour-powers, by their very nature, act only as instruments of the joint labour-power of the family.

Let us finally imagine, for a change, an association of free men, working with the means of production held in common, and expending their many different forms of labour-power in full self-awareness as one single social labour force. All the characteristics of Robinson's labour are repeated here, but with the difference that they are social instead of individual. All Robinson's products were exclusively the result of his own personal labour and they were therefore directly objects of utility for him personally. The total product of our imagined association is a social product. One part of this product serves as fresh means of production and remains social. But another part is consumed by the members of the association as means of subsistence. This part must therefore be divided amongst them. The way this division is made will vary with the particular kind of social organization of production and the corresponding level of social development attained by the producers. We shall assume, but only for the sake of a parallel with the production of commodities, that the share of each individual producer in the means of subsistence is determined by his labour-time. Labour-time would in that case play a double part. Its apportionment in accordance with a definite social plan maintains the correct proportion between the different functions of labour and the various needs of the associations. On the other hand, labour-time also serves as a measure of the part taken by each individual in the common labour, and of his share in the part of the total product destined for individual consumption. The social relations of the individual producers, both towards their labour and the products of their labour, are here transparent in their simplicity, in production as well as in distribution.

For a society of commodity producers, whose general social relation of production consists in the fact that they treat their products as commodities, hence as values, and in this material [*sachlich*] form bring their individual, private labours into relation with each other as homogeneous human labour, Christianity with its religious cult of man in the abstract, more particularly in its bourgeois development, i.e. in Protestantism, Deism, etc., is the most fitting form of religion. In the ancient Asiatic, Classical-antique, and other such modes of production, the transformation of the product into a commodity, and therefore men's existence as producers of commodities, plays a subordinate role, which however increases in importance as these communities approach nearer and nearer to the stage of their dissolution. Trading nations, properly so called, exist only in the interstices of the ancient world, like the gods of Epicurus in the *intermundia*,[e] or Jews in the pores of Polish society. Those ancient social organisms of production are much more simple and transparent than those of bourgeois society. But they are founded either on the immaturity of man as an individual, when he has not yet torn himself loose from the umbilical cord of his natural species-connection with other men, or on direct relations of dominance and servitude. They are conditioned by a low stage of development of the productive powers of labour and correspondingly limited relations between men within the process of creating and reproducing their material life, hence also limited relations between man and nature. These real limitations are reflected in the ancient worship of nature, and in other elements of tribal religions. The religious reflections of the real world can, in any case, vanish only when the practical relations of everyday life between man and man, and man and nature, generally present themselves to him in a transparent and rational form. The veil is not removed from the countenance of the social life-process, i.e. the process of material production, until it becomes production by freely associated men, and stands under their conscious and planned control. This, however, requires that society possess a material foundation, or a series of material conditions of existence, which in their turn are the natural and spontaneous product of a long and tormented historical development.

Political economy has indeed analysed value and its magnitude, however incompletely,[7] and has uncovered the content concealed within these forms. But it has never once asked the question why this content has assumed that particular form, that is to say, why labour is expressed in value, and why the measurement of labour by its duration is expressed in the magnitude of the value of the product.[8] These formulas, which bear the unmistakable stamp of belonging to a social formation in which the process of production has mastery over man, instead of the opposite, appear to the political economists' bourgeois consciousness to be as much a self-evident and nature-imposed necessity as productive labour itself. Hence the pre-bourgeois forms of the social organization of production are treated by political economy in much the same way as the Fathers of the Church treated pre-Christian religions.[9]

The degree to which some economists are misled by the fetishism attached to the world of commodities, or by the objective appearance of the social characteristics of labour, is shown, among other things, by the dull and tedious dispute over the part played by nature in the formation of exchange-value. Since exchange-value is a definite social manner of expressing the labour bestowed on a thing, it can have no more natural content than has, for example, the rate of exchange.

As the commodity-form is the most general and the most undeveloped form of bourgeois production, it makes its appearance at an early date, though not in the same predominant and therefore characteristic manner as nowadays. Hence its fetish character is still relatively easy to penetrate. But when we come to more concrete forms, even this appearance of simplicity vanishes. Where did the illusions of the Monetary

System come from? The adherents of the Monetary System did not see gold and silver as representing money as a social relation of production, but in the form of natural objects with peculiar social properties. And what of modern political economy, which looks down so disdainfully on the Monetary System? Does not its fetishism become quite palpable when it deals with capital? How long is it since the disappearance of the Physiocratic illusion that ground rent grows out of the soil, not out of society?

But, to avoid anticipating, we will content ourselves here with one more example relating to the commodity-form itself. If commodities could speak, they would say this: our use-value may interest men, but it does not belong to us as objects. What does belong to us as objects, however, is our value. Our own intercourse as commodities proves it. We relate to each other merely as exchange-values. Now listen how those commodities speak through the mouth of the economist:

'Value (i.e. exchange-value) is a property of things, riches (i.e. use-value) of man. Value, in this sense, necessarily implies exchanges, riches do not.'[10]

'Riches (use-value) are the attribute of man, value is the attribute of commodities. A man or a community is rich, a pearl or a diamond is valuable . . . A pearl or a diamond is valuable as a pearl or diamond.'[11]

So far no chemist has ever discovered exchange-value either in a pearl or a diamond. The economists who have discovered this chemical substance, and who lay special claim to critical acumen, nevertheless find that the use-value of material objects belongs to them independently of their material properties, while their value, on the other hand, forms a part of them as objects. What confirms them in this view is the peculiar circumstance that the use-value of a thing is realized without exchange, i.e. in the direct relation between the thing and man, while, inversely, its value is realized only in exchange, i.e. in a social process. Who would not call to mind at this point the advice given by the good Dogberry to the night-watchman Seacoal?[k]

'To be a well-favoured man is the gift of fortune; but reading and writing comes by nature.'[12]

Notes

1   One may recall that China and the tables began to dance when the rest of the world appeared to be standing still – *pour encourager les autres*.[a]

2   Among the ancient Germans the size of a piece of land was measured according to the labour of a day; hence the acre was called *Tagwerk, Tagwanne (jurnale,* or *terra jurnalis,* or *diornalis), Mannwerk, Mannskraft, Mannsmaad, Mannshauet*, etc. See Georg Ludwig von Maurer, *Einleitung zur Geschichte der Mark-, Hof-, usw. Verfassung*, Munich, 1854, p. 129 ff.

3   Therefore, when Galiani said: Value is a relation between persons ('*La Ricchezza è una ragione tra due persone*') he ought to have added: a relation concealed beneath a material shell. (Galiani, *Della Moneta*, p. 221, Vol. 3 of Custodi's collection entitled *Scrittori classici italiani di economia politica, Parte moderna*, Milan, 1803.)

4   'What are we to think of a law which can only assert itself through periodic crises? It is just a natural law which depends on the lack of awareness of the people who undergo it' (Friedrich Engels, *Umrisse zu einer Kritik der Nationalökonomie*, in the *Deutsch-Französische Jahrbücher*, edited by Arnold Ruge and Karl Marx, Paris, 1844) [English translation in Marx/Engels' *Collected Works*, Vol. 3, London, 1975, p. 133].

5   Even Ricardo has his Robinson Crusoe stories. 'Ricardo makes his primitive fisherman and primitive hunter into owners of commodities who immediately exchange their fish and game in proportion to the labour-time which is materialized in these exchange-values. On this occasion he slips into the anachronism of allowing the primitive fisherman and hunter to calculate the value of their implements in accordance with the annuity tables used on the London Stock Exchange in 1817. Apart from bourgeois society, the "parallelograms of Mr Owen" seem to have been the only form of society Ricardo was acquainted with'[c] (Karl Marx, *Zur Kritik der politischen Ökonomie*, Berlin, 1859, pp. 38–9) [English translation, p. 60].

6   'A ridiculous notion has spread abroad recently that communal property in its natural, spontaneous form is specifically Slav, indeed exclusively Russian. In fact, it is the primitive form that we can prove to have existed among Romans, Teutons and Celts, and which indeed still exists to this day in India, in a whole range of diverse

patterns, albeit sometimes only as remnants. A more exact study of the Asiatic, and specifically of the Indian form of communal property would indicate the way in which different forms of spontaneous, primitive communal property give rise to different forms of its dissolution. Thus the different original types of Roman and Germanic private property can be deduced from the different forms of Indian communal property' (Karl Marx, *Zur Kritik, etc.*, p. 10) [English translation, p. 33].

7   The insufficiency of Ricardo's analysis of the magnitude of value – and his analysis is by far the best – will appear from the third and fourth books of this work.[f] As regards value in general, classical political economy in fact nowhere distinguishes explicitly and with a clear awareness between labour as it appears in the value of a product, and the same labour as it appears in the product's use-value. Of course the distinction is made in practice, since labour is treated sometimes from its quantitative aspect, and at other times qualitatively. But it does not occur to the economists that a purely quantitative distinction between the kinds of labour presupposes their qualitative unity or equality, and therefore their reduction to abstract human labour. For instance, Ricardo declares that he agrees with Destutt de Tracy when the latter says: 'As it is certain that our physical and moral faculties are alone our original riches, the employment of those faculties, labour of some kind, is our original treasure, and it is always from this employment that all those things are created which we call riches . . . It is certain too, that all those things only represent the labour which has created them, and if they have a value, or even two distinct values, they can only derive them from that' (the value) 'of the labour from which they emanate (Ricardo, *The Principles of Political Economy*, 3rd edn, London, 1821, p. 334).[g] We would here only point out that Ricardo imposes his own more profound interpretation on the words of Destutt. Admittedly Destutt does say that all things which constitute wealth 'represent the labour which has created them', but, on the other hand, he also says that they acquire their 'two different values' (use-value and exchange-value) from 'the value of labour'. He thus falls into the commonplace error of the vulgar economists, who assume the value of one commodity (here labour) in order in turn to use it to determine the values of other commodities. But Ricardo reads him as if he had said that labour (not the value of labour) is represented both in use-value and in exchange-value. Nevertheless, Ricardo himself makes so little of the dual character of the labour represented in this twofold way that he is forced to spend the whole of his chapter 'Value and Riches, their Distinctive Properties' on a laborious examination of the trivialities of a J. B. Say. And at the end he is therefore quite astonished to find that while Destutt agrees with him that labour is the source of value, he nevertheless also agrees with Say about the concept of value.[h]

8   It is one of the chief failings of classical political economy that it has never succeeded, by means of its analysis of commodities, and in particular of their value, in discovering the form of value which in fact turns value into exchange-value. Even its best representatives, Adam Smith and Ricardo, treat the form of value as something of indifference, something external to the nature of the commodity itself. The explanation for this is not simply that their attention is entirely absorbed by the analysis of the magnitude of value. It lies deeper. The value-form of the product of labour is the most abstract, but also the most universal form of the bourgeois mode of production; by that fact it stamps the bourgeois mode of production as a particular kind of social production of a historical and transitory character. If then we make the mistake of treating it as the eternal natural form of social production, we necessarily overlook the specificity of the value-form, and consequently of the commodity-form together with its further developments, the money form, the capital form, etc. We therefore find that economists who are entirely agreed that labour-time is the measure of the magnitude of value, have the strangest and most contradictory ideas about money, that is, about the universal equivalent in its finished form. This emerges sharply when they deal with banking, where the commonplace definitions of money will no longer hold water. Hence there has arisen in opposition to the classical economists a restored Mercantilist System (Ganilh etc.), which sees in value only the social form, or rather its insubstantial semblance. Let me point out once and for all that by classical political economy I mean all the economists who, since the time of W. Petty, have investigated the real internal framework [*Zusammenhang*] of bourgeois relations of production, as opposed to the vulgar economists who only flounder around within the apparent framework of those relations, ceaselessly ruminate on the materials long since provided by scientific political economy, and seek there plausible explanations of the crudest phenomena for the domestic purposes of the bourgeoisie. Apart from this, the vulgar economists confine themselves to systematizing in a pedantic way, and proclaiming for everlasting truths, the banal and complacent notions held by the bourgeois agents of production about their own world, which is to them the best possible one.

9   'The economists have a singular way of proceeding. For them, there are only two kinds of institutions, artificial

and natural. The institutions of feudalism are artificial institutions, those of the bourgeoisie are natural institutions. In this they resemble the theologians, who likewise establish two kinds of religion. Every religion which is not theirs is an invention of men, while their own is an emanation of God . . . Thus there has been history, but there is no longer any' (Karl Marx, *Misère de la philosophie. Réponse à la philosophie de la misère de M. Proudhon*, 1847, p. 113).[i] Truly comical is M. Bastiat, who imagines that the ancient Greeks and Romans lived by plunder alone. For if people live by plunder for centuries there must, after all, always be something there to plunder; in other words, the objects of plunder must be continually reproduced. It seems, therefore, that even the Greeks and the Romans had a process of production, hence an economy, which constituted the material basis of their world as much as the bourgeois economy constitutes that of the present-day world. Or perhaps Bastiat means that a mode of production based on the labour of slaves is based on a system of plunder? In that case he is on dangerous ground. If a giant thinker like Aristotle could err in his evaluation of slave-labour, why should a dwarf economist like Bastiat be right in his evaluation of wage-labour? I seize this opportunity of briefly refuting an objection made by a German-American publication to my work *Zur Kritik der Politischen Ökonomie*, 1859. My view is that each particular mode of production, and the relations of production corresponding to it at each given moment, in short 'the economic structure of society', is 'the real foundation, on which arises a legal and political superstructure and to which correspond definite forms of social consciousness', and that 'the mode of production of material life conditions the general process of social, political and intellectual life'.[j]

In the opinion of the German-American publication this is all very true for our own times, in which material interests are preponderant, but not for the Middle Ages, dominated by Catholicism, nor for Athens and Rome, dominated by politics. In the first place, it strikes us as odd that anyone should suppose that these well-worn phrases about the Middle Ages and the ancient world were unknown to anyone else. One thing is clear: the Middle Ages could not live on Catholicism, nor could the ancient world on politics. On the contrary, it is the manner in which they gained their livelihood which explains why in one case politics, in the other case Catholicism, played the chief part. For the rest, one needs no more than a slight acquaintance with, for example, the history of the Roman Republic, to be aware that its secret history is the history of landed property. And then there is Don Quixote, who long ago paid the penalty for wrongly imagining that knight errantry was compatible with all economic forms of society.

10   *Observations on Some Verbal Disputes in Pol. Econ., Particularly Relating to Value, and to Supply and Demand*, London, 1821, p. 16.

11   S. Bailey, op. cit., p. 165.

12   Both the author of *Observations etc.*, and S. Bailey accuse Ricardo of converting exchange-value from something relative into something absolute. The reverse is true. He has reduced the apparent relativity which these things (diamonds, pearls, etc.) possess to the true relation hidden behind the appearance, namely their relativity as mere expressions of human labour. If the followers of Ricardo answer Bailey somewhat rudely, but by no means convincingly, this is because they are unable to find in Ricardo's own works any elucidation of the inner connection between value and the form of value, or exchange-value.

a   'To encourage the others'. A reference to the simultaneous emergence in the 1850s of the Taiping revolt in China and the craze for spiritualism which swept over upper-class German society. The rest of the world was 'standing still' in the period of reaction immediately after the defeat of the 1848 Revolutions.

b   'After the feast', i.e. after the events reflected on have taken place.

c   The 'parallelograms' were the utopian socialist Robert Owen's suggestion for the most appropriate layout for a workers' settlement, made in *A New View of Society* (1813) and immediately seized on by his critics. Ricardo's reference to them is from his *On Protection of Agriculture*, London, 1822, p. 21.

d   The original German has here 'Herr M. Wirth', chosen by Marx as a run-of-the-mill vulgar economist and propagandist familiar to German readers. Engels introduced 'Mr Sedley Taylor', a Cambridge don against whom he polemicized in his preface to the fourth German edition.

e   According to the Greek philosopher Epicurus (*c.* 341-*c.* 270 B.C.), the gods existed only in the *intermundia*, or spaces between different worlds, and had no influence on the course of human affairs. Very few of the writings of Epicurus have been preserved in the original Greek, and this particular idea survived only by being included in Cicero, *De natura deorum*, Book I, Section 18.

f   These are the books that appeared, respectively, as Volume 3 of *Capital*, and *Theories of Surplus-Value* (3 volumes).

g   Destutt de Tracy, *Élémens d'idéologie*, Parts 4 and 5, Paris, 1826, pp. 35–6.

h   'I am sorry to be obliged to add that M. de Tracy supports, by his authority, the definitions which M. Say has given of the words "value", "riches", and "utility" ' (Ricardo, op. cit., p. 334).

i   English translation: Karl Marx, *The Poverty of Philosophy*, London, 1966, p. 105.

j   These passages are taken from the Preface to *A Contribution to the Critique of Political Economy*, written in January 1859 (English translation, pp. 20–21).

k   In Shakespeare's comedy *Much Ado About Nothing*, Act 3, Scene 3.

Chapter 2

Jonathan Crary

SPECTACLE, ATTENTION, COUNTER-MEMORY [1989]

Source: Jonathan Crary (1989), *October*, 50, pp. 96–107. Also reproduced in Krauss, Rosalind et al., eds (1997), *October: The Second Decade, 1986–1996*, Cambridge, Mass. and London: MIT Press, pp. 415–25.

The art historian Jonathan Crary combines the archivist's enthusiastic precision with historical material and the theorist's willingness to mobilise archival documents for a dialogue with the most urgent social and philosophical questions of the time. In his writing Crary has explored the field of visual culture (from the panoramas of the late eighteenth century to contemporary art) to negotiate competing claims about the characteristics of modern society. As befits someone immersed in the materiality of culture's visual arena, Crary refuses to side with a characterisation of the modern world as 'spectacular society' (Debord) against one that sees it as 'disciplinary' (Foucault), or as 'a society of control' (Deleuze). Instead he explores the specific complexity of culture's visual fields and the way it solicits our attention (the way culture manages attention).

In this text Crary is responding to a challenge. In 1967 the French radical theorist, activist and filmmaker Guy Debord published his small but dense book *Society of the Spectacle* (which, by the way, is freely available on the internet). Debord's book takes the following hypothesis and develops it into a social theory: 'The whole life of those societies in which modern conditions of production prevail presents itself as an immense accumulation of *spectacles*. All that once was directly lived has become mere representation' (Debord 1967: 12). In a film that Debord made in 1973, similarly titled *Society of the Spectacle* (and using much of the book for the voice over), he makes it clear what 'the spectacle' might consist of and what the modern conditions of production are. The film is a montage of the spectacular: female strippers, female models, fashion shows, the latest interior design, the bombing of Vietnam, nuclear rockets and so on, inter-cut with factory workers, strikes, politicians on television and such like. (You can watch the film for free by going to UbuWeb on the internet and looking under UbuFilms.)

Crary, though, is less interested in mapping the contemporary spectacle than in trying to figure out its genealogical emergence. Debord's suggestion that the spectacle was roughly forty years old in 1967 provides Crary with the opportunity for speculating about the precise form that spectacular culture takes by looking at a range of cultural technologies that emerged in the late 1920s and early 1930s (television, synchronised sound in movies, the technological address of dictatorial political regimes). Thus for Crary the spectacle of modern culture requires technological mediascapes to fashion the 'real unreality' of society. Media technologies act as a sort of booster to the de-realising of society, an essential ingredient for the present condition of the world without being its sole determining agent. For studying design culture, clearly both the idea of the spectacle and the analysis of the media technologies that help disseminate it are going to be crucial.

Further reading: Crary 1990, 1999; Debord 1967; McDonough 2007; Plant 1992; Retort 2005.

W**HETHER OR NOT** the term *spectacle* was originally taken from Henri Lefebvre's *Critique de la vie quotidienne*, its currency emerged from the activities in the late 1950s and early 1960s of the various configurations now designated as presituationist or situationist.[1] The product of a radical critique of modernist art practice, a politics of everyday life, and an analysis of contemporary capitalism, its influence was obviously intensified with the publication of Guy Debord's *Society of the Spectacle* in 1967.[2] And twenty-two years later, the word *spectacle* not only persists but has become a stock phrase in a wide range of critical and not-so-critical discourses. But, assuming it has not become completely devalued or exhausted as an explanation of the contemporary operation of power, does it still mean today what it did in the early '60s? What constellation of forces and institutions does it designate? And if these have mutated, what kind of practices are required now to resist their effects?

One can still well ask if the notion of spectacle is the imposition of an illusory unity onto a more heterogenous field. Is it a totalizing and monolithic concept that inadequately represents a plurality

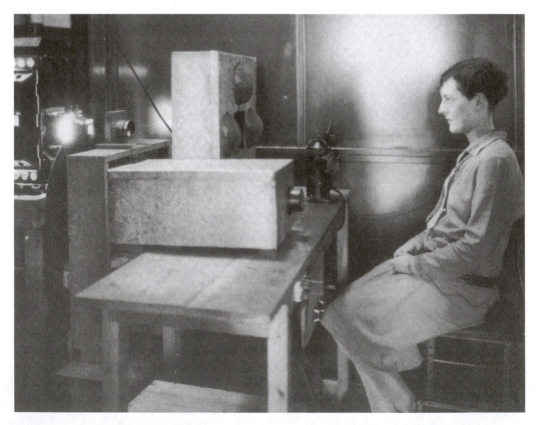

Figure 2.1   Television transmitter sending a picture of the woman seated directly in front of the apparatus, *c.* 1929.

of incommensurable institutions and events? For some, a troubling aspect about the term *spectacle* is the almost ubiquitous presence of the definite article in front of it, suggesting a single and seamless global system of relations. For others, it is a mystification of the functioning of power, a new opiate-of-the-masses type of explanation, a vague cultural-institutional formation with a suspicious structural autonomy. Or is a concept such as spectacle a necessary tool for the figuration of a radical systemic shift in the way power functions noncoercively within twentieth-century modernity? Is it an indispensable means of revealing as related what would otherwise appear as disparate and unconnected phenomena? Does it not show that a patchwork or mosaic of techniques can still constitute a homogenous effect of power?

A striking feature of Debord's book was the absence of any kind of historical genealogy of the spectacle, and that absence may have contributed to the sense of the spectacle as having appeared full-blown out of the blue. The question that concerns me is, then: assuming the spectacle does in fact designate a certain set of objective conditions, what are its origins? When might we say it was first effective or operative? And I don't ask this simply as an academic exercise. For the term to have any critical or practical efficacy depends, in part, on how one periodizes it – that is, the spectacle will assume quite different meanings depending on how it is situated historically. Is it more than just a synonym for late capitalism? for the rise of mass media and communication technology? more than an updated account of the culture or consciousness industry and thus chronologically distinct from these?

The "early" work of Jean Baudrillard provides some general parameters for what we might call the prehistory of the spectacle (which Baudrillard sees as having disappeared by the mid-1970s). For Baudrillard, writing in the late '60s, one of the crucial consequences of the bourgeois political revolutions was the ideological force that animated the myths of the Rights of Man: the right to equality and the right to happiness. What he sees happening in the nineteenth century, for the first time, is that observable proof became necessary to demonstrate that happiness had in fact been obtained. Happiness, he says "had to be *measurable* in terms of signs and objects," signs that would be evident to the eye in terms of "*visible* criteria."[3] Several decades earlier, Walter Benjamin had also written about "the phantasmagoria of equality" in the nineteenth century in terms of the transformation of the citizen into consumer. Baudrillard's account of modernity is one of an increasing destabilization and mobility of signs beginning in the Renaissance, signs which previously had been firmly rooted to relatively secure positions within fixed social hierarchies.[4] Thus, for Baudrillard, modernity is bound up in the struggle of newly empowered classes to overcome this "exclusiveness of signs" and to initiate a "proliferation of signs on demand." Imitations, copies, and counterfeits are all challenges to that exclusivity. The problem of mimesis, then, is not one of aesthetics but one of social power, and the emergence of the Italian theater and perspective painting are at the start of this ever-increasing capacity to produce equivalences. But obviously, for Baudrillard and many others, it is in the nineteenth century, alongside new industrial techniques and forms of circulation, that a new kind of sign emerges: "potentially identical objects produced in indefinite series." For Baudrillard "the relation of objects in such a series is equivalence and indifference . . . and it is on the level of reproduction, of fashion, media, advertising, information and communication (what Marx called the unessential sectors of capitalism) . . . that the global process of capital is held together." The spectacle then would coincide with the moment when sign-value takes precedence over use-value. But the question of the location of this moment in the history of the commodity remains unanswered.

T. J. Clark offers a much more specific periodization in the introduction to his book *The Painting of Modern Life*. If one agrees with Clark, not only do the origins of modernism and the spectacle coincide, but the two are inextricably related. Writing about the 1860s and '70s, Clark uses the spectacle to explain the embeddedness of Manet's art within a newly emerging social and economic configuration. This society of the spectacle, he writes, is bound up in "a massive internal extension of the capitalist market – the invasion and restructuring of whole areas of free time, private life, leisure and personal expression. . . . It indicates a new phase of commodity production – the marketing, the making-into-commodities of whole areas of social practice which had once been referred to casually as everyday life."[5] In Clark's chronology, then, the spectacle coincides with the early phase of modern Western imperialism, with two parallel expansions of a global marketplace, one internal, one external.

Although he calls "neat temporality" impossible, he does place the onset of the spectacle in the late 1860s and '70s, citing the emergence of commercialized aspects of life and leisure that are themselves due to a shift from one kind of capitalist production to another. This shift, he says, was "not a matter of mere cultural and ideological refurbishing but of all-embracing economic change." But what are Clark's examples of this sweeping change? "A move to the world of *grands boulevards* and *grands magasins* and their accompanying industries of tourism, recreation, fashion, and display." Surprisingly, Clark then reminds his readers that the spectacle was designed "first and foremost as a weapon of combat" in the 1960s.[6] Does he mean to suggest that the political and economic structure of this world of boulevards and department stores is essentially *continuous* with what Debord described as the contested terrain in 1967? And that the cultural politics of the 1960s occurred within a set of conditions isomorphic with those of the 1870s? This implication of a single spectacle common to both the Paris of Manet and of Debord is problematic to say the least.

Working with one of the most familiar examples of modernization in the nineteenth century, Haussmann's rebuilding of Paris, Clark presents it as part of a transformation from small entrepreneurial capitalism to increasingly monopolistic forms. And the new post-Haussmann Paris becomes for him the visible expression of a new alignment of class relations. But this way of deploying the spectacle posits it as a form of domination imposed onto a population or individual from without. The kind of change he delineates remains essentially exterior to the make-up of an individual subject, preserving for the latter a detached position from which the spectacle could be, however imperfectly, recorded and represented. By periodizing the spectacle in this way, Clark disregards the possibility that spectacle may be equally about a fundamental reorganization of the subject, about the construction of an observer who was a precondition for the transformation of everyday life that began then. Making the society of the spectacle more or less an equivalent for consumer society, Clark dilutes its historical specificity and overlooks some features of the spectacle that were crucial to the political practice of situationism in the 1960s: the spectacle as a new kind of power of recuperation and absorption, a capacity to neutralize and assimilate acts of resistance by converting them into objects or images of consumption.

Guy Debord himself has very recently given a surprisingly precise date for the beginning of the society of the spectacle. In a text published in 1988 Debord writes that in 1967, the date of his original book, the spectacle was barely forty years old.[7] Not a more approximate kind of number like fifty, but forty. Thus, 1927, or roughly the late 1920s. Unfortunately he doesn't provide an indication as to why he singles out this moment. It made me curious about what he might have meant by designating the late '20s as a historical threshold, thus placing the origin of the spectacle some half-century later than did Clark. I offer, then, some fragmentary speculations on some very dissimilar events that could possibly have been implicit in Debord's remark.

1. The first is both symbolic and substantive. The year 1927 saw the technological perfection of television. Vladimir Zworikin, the Russian-born, American-trained engineer and physicist, patented his iconoscope — the first electronic system of a tube containing an electron gun and a screen made out of a mosaic of photoemissive cells, each of which produced a charge proportional to the varying light intensity of the image focused on the screen. Right at the moment when an awareness arose of the age of mechanical reproduction, a new model of circulation and transmission appeared that was to exceed that age, one that had no need of silver salts or permanent physical support.[8] The spectacle was to become inseparable from this new kind of image and its speed, ubiquity, and simultaneity.

But equally important was that by the late 1920s, when the first experimental broadcasts occurred, the vast interlocking of corporate, military, and state control of television was being settled. Never before had the institutional regulation of a new technique been planned and divided up so far in advance. So, in a sense, much of the territory of spectacle, the intangible domain of the spectrum, had already been diagrammed and standardized before 1930.

2. Perhaps more immediately significant, the movie *The Jazz Singer* premiered in 1927, signaling the arrival of the sound film, and specifically *synchronized* sound. This was not only a transformation in the nature of subjective experience; it was also an event that brought on the complete vertical integration of production, distribution, and exhibition within the film industry and its amalgamation with the corporate conglomerates that owned the sound patents and provided the capital for the costly move to the new technology.[9] Again, as with television, the nascent institutional and economic infrastructure of the spectacle was set in place.

Specifying sound here obviously suggests that spectacular power cannot be reduced to an optical model but is inseparable from a larger organization of perceptual consumption. Sound had of course been part of cinema in various additive forms from the beginning, but the introduction of sync sound transformed the nature of *attention* that was demanded of a viewer. Possibly it is a break that makes previous forms of cinema actually closer to the optical devices of the late nineteenth century. The full coincidence of sound with image, of voice with figure, not only was a crucial new way of organizing space, time, and narrative, but it instituted a more commanding authority over the observer, enforcing a new kind of attention. A vivid sign of this shift can be seen in Fritz Lang's two Mabuse films. In *Dr. Mabuse the Gambler*, a 1924 silent film, the proto-fascist Mabuse exercises control through his gaze, with a hypnotic optical power; while in *The Testament of Dr. Mabuse* (1931) an incarnation of the same character dominates his underlings only through his voice, emanating from behind a curtain (which, it turns out, conceals not a person, but recording technology and a loudspeaker).

And from the 1890s well into the 1930s one of the central problems in mainstream psychology had been the nature of attention: the relation between stimulus and attention, problems of concentration, focalization, and distraction. How many sources of stimulation could one attend to simultaneously? How could novelty, familiarity, and repetition in attention be assessed? It was a problem whose position in the forefront of psychological discourse was directly related to the emergence of a social field increasingly saturated with sensory input. Some of this was the work of James McKeen Cattell, whose experiments on students at Columbia University provided the classical data for the notion of range of attention. Initially much of this research was bound up in the need for information on attention in the context of rationalizing production, but even as early as 1910 hundreds of experimental laboratory studies had been done specifically on the range of attention in advertising (including titles such as "The Attention Value of Periodical Advertisements," "Attention and the Effects of Size in Street Car Advertisements," "Advertising and the Laws of Mental Attention," "Measuring the Attention Value of Color in Advertising," the last a 1913 Columbia dissertation).

The year 1927 was also when Walter Benjamin began his Arcades Project, a work in which he would eventually point to "a crisis in perception itself," a crisis that is the result of a sweeping remaking of the observer by a calculated technology of the individual, derived from new knowledge of the body. In the course of writing the Arcades Project, Benjamin himself became preoccupied with the question of attention and the related issues of distraction and shock, and he turned to Henri Bergson's *Matter and Memory* for a way out of what he saw as the "standardized and denatured" perception of the masses. Bergson had fought to recover perception from its status as sheer physiological event; for him attention was a question of an engagement of the body, an inhibition of movement, a state of consciousness arrested in the present. But attention could become transformed into something productive only when it was linked to the deeper activity of memory:

> Memory thus creates anew present perception . . . strengthening and enriching [it] . . . . If after having gazed on any object, we turn our eyes abruptly away, we obtain an "after-image" [*image consécutive*] of it. It is true we are dealing here with images photographed on the object itself, and with memories following immediately upon the perception of which they are but the echo. But behind these images which are identical with the object, there are others, stored in memory which only resemble it. . . .[10]

What Bergson sought to describe was the vitality of the moment when a conscious rift occurred between memory and perception, a moment in which memory had the capacity to rebuild the object of perception. Deleuze and Guattari have described similar effects of the entry of memory into perception, for example in the perception of a face: one can see a face in terms of a vast set of micromemories and a rich proliferation of semiotic systems, or, what is far more common, in terms of bleak redundancies of representations, which, they say, is where connections can always be effected with the hierarchies of power formations.[11] That kind of redundancy of representation, with its accompanying inhibition and impoverishment of memory, was what Benjamin saw as the standardization of perception, or what we might call an effect of spectacle.

Although Benjamin called *Matter and Memory* a "towering and monumental work," he reproached Bergson for circumscribing memory within the isolated frame of an individual consciousness; the kind of afterimages that interested Benjamin were those of collective historical memory, haunting images of the out-of-date which had the capacity for a social reawakening.[12] And thus Benjamin's apprehension of a present-day crisis in perception is filtered through a richly elaborated afterimage of the mid-nineteenth century.

3. Given the content of Debord's work, we can also assume another crucial development in the late 1920s: the rise of fascism and, soon after, Stalinism, and the way in which they incarnated models of the spectacle. Important, for example, was Goebbels's innovative and synergetic use of every available medium, especially the development of sound/image propaganda, and his devaluation of the written word, because reading implied time for reflection and thought. In one election campaign in 1930, Goebbels mailed 50,000 phonograph records of one of his own speeches to specially targeted voters. Goebbels also introduced the airplane into politics, making Hitler the first political candidate to fly to several different cities on the same day. Air travel thus functioned as a conveyor of the image of the leader, providing a new sense of ubiquity.

As part of this mixed technology of attention, television was to have played a crucial role. And as recent scholarship has shown, the development of television in Germany was in advance of that of any other country.[13] German TV broadcasting on a regular basis began in 1935, four years ahead of the United States. Clearly, as an instrument of social control, its effectiveness was never realized by the Nazis, but its early history in Germany is instructive for the competing models of spectacular organization that were proposed in the 1930s. A major split emerged early on between the monopolistic corporate forces and the Nazi Party with regard to the development of television in Germany. The Party sought to have television centralized and accessible in public screening halls, unlike the decentralized use of radio in private homes. Goebbels and Hitler had a notion of group reception, believing that this was the most effective form of reception. Public television halls, seating from 40 to 400, were designated, not unlike the subsequent early development of television in the USSR, where a mass viewing environment was also favored. According to the Nazi director of broadcasting, writing in 1935, the "sacred mission" of television was to plant indelibly the image of the Führer in the hearts of the German people."[14] Corporate power, on the other hand, sought home viewing, for maximization of profit. One model sought to position television as technique within the demands of fascism in general: a means of mobilizing and inciting the masses, whereas the agents of capitalism sought to privatize, to divide and molecularize, to impose a model of cellularity.

It is easy to forget that in *Society of the Spectacle* Debord outlined two different models of the spectacle; one he called "concentrated" and the other "diffused," preventing the word *spectacle* from simply being synonymous with consumer or late capitalism. Concentrated spectacle was what characterized Nazi Germany, Stalinist Russia, and Maoist China; the preeminent model of diffused spectacle was the United States: "Wherever the concentrated spectacle rules so does the police . . . it is accompanied by permanent violence. The imposed image of the good envelops in its spectacle the totality of what officially exists and is usually concentrated in one man who is the guarantee of totalitarian cohesion. Everyone must magically identify with this absolute celebrity – or disappear."[15] The diffuse spectacle, on the other hand, accompanies the abundance of commodities. And certainly it is this model to which Debord gives most of his attention in his 1967 book.

I will note in passing Michel Foucault's famous dismissal of the spectacle in *Discipline and Punish*: "Our society is not one of spectacle, but of surveillance; under the surface of images one invests bodies in depth."[16] But the spectacle is also a set of techniques for the management of bodies, the management of attention (I am paraphrasing Foucault) "for assuring the ordering of human multiplicities," "its object is to fix, it is an anti-nomadic technique," "it uses procedures of partitioning and cellularity . . . in which the individual is reduced as a political force."[17] I suspect that Foucault did not spend much time watching television or thinking about it, because it would not be difficult to make a case that television is a further perfecting of panoptic technology. In it *surveillance* and *spectacle* are not opposed terms, as he insists, but collapsed onto one another in a more effective disciplinary apparatus. Recent developments have confirmed literally this overlapping model: television sets that contain advanced image recognition technology in order to monitor and quantify the behavior, attentiveness, and eye movement of a spectator.[18]

But in 1988 Debord sees his two original models of diffused and concentrated spectacle becoming indistinct, converging into what he calls "the integrated society of the spectacle."[19] In this deeply pessimistic book, he describes a more sophisticated deployment of elements from those earlier models, a flexible arrangement of global power adaptable to local needs and circumstances. In 1967 there were still marginalities and peripheries that escaped its reign: today, he insists, the spectacle has irradiated into everything and has absolute control over production, over perception, and especially over the shape of the future and the past.

As much as any single feature, Debord sees the core of the spectacle as the annihilation of historical knowledge – in particular the destruction of the recent past. In its place there is the reign of a perpetual present. History, he writes, had always been the measure by which novelty was assessed, but whoever is in the business of selling novelty has an interest in destroying the means by which it could be judged. Thus there is a ceaseless appearance of the important, and almost immediately its annihilation and replacement: "That which the spectacle ceases to speak of for three days no longer exists."[20]

In conclusion I want to note briefly two different responses to the new texture of modernity taking shape in the 1920s. The painter Fernand Léger writes, in a 1924 essay titled "The Spectacle," published soon after the making of his film *Ballet Mécanique*,

> The rhythm of modern life is so dynamic that a slice of life seen from a café terrace is a spectacle. The most diverse elements collide and jostle one another there. The interplay of contrasts is so violent that there is always exaggeration in the effect that one glimpses. On the boulevard two men are carrying some immense gilded letters in a hand cart: the effect is so unexpected that everyone stops and looks. There is the origin of the modern spectacle . . . in the shock of the surprise effect.[21]

But then Léger goes on to detail how advertising and commercial forces have taken the lead in the making of modern spectacle, and he cites the department store, the world of fashion, and the rhythms of industrial production as forms that have conquered the attention of the public. Léger's goal is the same: wanting to win over that public. Of course, he is writing at a point of uncertainty about the direction of his own art, facing the dilemma of what a public art might mean, but the confused program he comes up with in this text is an early instance of the ploys of all those – from Warhol to today's so-called simulationists – who believe, or at least claim, they are outwitting the spectacle at its own game. Léger summarizes this kind of ambition: "Let's push the system to the extreme," he states, and offers vague suggestions for polychroming the exterior of factories and apartment buildings, for using new materials and setting them in motion. But this ineffectual inclination to outdo the allure of the spectacle becomes complicit with its annihilation of the past and fetishization of the new.

But the same year, 1924, the first Surrealist Manifesto suggests a very different aesthetic strategy for confronting the spectacular organization of the modern city. I am referring to what Walter Benjamin called the "anthropological" dimension of surrealism.[22] It was a strategy of turning the spectacle of the city inside out through counter-memory and counter-itineraries. These would reveal the potency of outmoded objects excluded from its slick surfaces, and of derelict spaces off its main routes of circulation. The strategy incarnated a refusal of the imposed present, and in reclaiming fragments of a demolished past it was implicitly figuring an alternative future. And despite the equivocal nature of many of these surrealist gestures, it is no accident that they were to reappear in new forms in the tactics of situationism in the 1960s, in the notion of the *dérive* or drift, of *détournement*, of psychogeography, the exemplary act, and the constructed situation.[23] Whether these practices have any vitality or even relevance today depends in large measure on what an archaeology of the present tells us. Are we still in the midst of a society that is organized as appearance? Or have we entered a nonspectacular global system arranged primarily around the control and flow of information, a system whose management and regulation of attention would demand wholly new forms of resistance and memory?[24]

Notes

1   This paper was originally presented at the Sixth International Colloquium on Twentieth Century French Studies, "Revolutions 1889–1989," at Columbia University, March 30–April 1, 1989.

2   Guy Debord, *Society of the Spectacle*, Detroit, Red and Black, 1977.

3   Jean Baudrillard, *La société de consommation: ses mythes, ses structures*, Paris, Gallimard, 1970, p. 60. Emphasis in original.

4   A well-known passage from the "later" Baudrillard amplifies this: "There is no such thing as fashion in a society of caste and rank since one is assigned a place irrevocably. Thus class-mobility is non-existent. A prohibition protects the signs and assures them a total clarity; each sign refers unequivocally to a status. . . . In caste societies, feudal or archaic, the signs are limited in number and are not widely diffused. . . . Each is a reciprocal obligation between castes, clans, or persons" (*Simulations*, trans. Paul Foss, New York, Semiotexte, 1983, p. 84).

5   T. J. Clark, *The Painting of Modern Life: Paris in the Art of Manet and His Followers*, Princeton, Princeton University Press, 1984, p. 9.

6   *Ibid.*, p. 10.

7   Guy Debord, *Commentaires sur la société du spectacle*, Paris, Editions Gérard Lebovici, 1988, p. 13.

8   The historian of science François Dagognet cites the revolutionary nature of this development in his *Philosophie de l'image*, Paris, J. Vrin, 1986, pp. 57–58.

9   See Steven Neale, *Cinema and Technology: Image, Sound, Colour*, Bloomington, Indiana, 1985, pp. 62–102; and Douglas Gomery, "Toward an Economic History of the Cinema: The Coming of Sound to Hollywood," in Teresa de Lauretis and Stephen Heath, eds., *The Cinematic Apparatus*, London, Macmillan, 1980, pp. 38–46.

10   Henri Bergson, *Matter and Memory*, trans. N. M. Paul and W. S. Palmer, New York, Zone Books, 1988, pp. 101–103.

11   See, for example, Félix Guattari, "Les machines concrètes," in his *La révolution moléculaire*, Paris, Encres, 1977, pp. 364–376.

12   "On the contrary he [Bergson] rejects any historical determination of memory. He thus manages above all to stay clear of that experience from which his own philosophy evolved or, rather, in reaction to which it arose. It was the inhospitable, blinding age of big-scale industrialism" (Walter Benjamin, *Illuminations*, trans. Harry Zohn, New York, Schocken, 1969, pp. 156–157).

13   I have relied on the valuable research in William Uricchio, "Rituals of Reception, Patterns of Neglect: Nazi Television and its Postwar Representation," *Wide Angle*, vol. 10, no. 4, pp. 48–66. See also Robert Edwin Herzstein, *The War That Hitler Won: Goebbels and the Nazi Media Campaign*, New York, Paragon, 1978.

14   Quoted in Uricchio, p. 51.

15   Debord, *Society of the Spectacle*, sec. 64.

16   Michel Foucault, *Discipline and Punish*, trans. Alan Sheridan, New York, Pantheon, 1976, p. 217.

17   *Ibid.*, pp. 218–219.

18   See, for example, Bill Carter, "TV Viewers, Beware: Nielsen May Be Looking," *The New York Times*, June 1, 1989, p. A1.

19   Debord, *Commentaires*, pp. 17–19.

20   *Ibid.*, p. 29.

21   Fernand Léger, *Functions of Painting*, trans. Alexandra Anderson, New York, Viking, 1973, p. 35.

22   Walter Benjamin, *One Way Street*, trans. Edmund Jephcott and Kingsley Shorter, London, New Left Books, 1979, p. 239. Christopher Phillips suggested to me that the late 1920s would also likely be crucial for Debord as the moment when surrealism became coopted, that is, when its original revolutionary potential was nullified in an early instance of spectacular recuperation and absorption.

23   On these strategies, see the documents in Ken Knabb, ed., *Situationist International Anthology*, Berkeley, Bureau of Public Secrets, 1981.

24   See my "Eclipse of the Spectacle," in Brian Wallis, ed., *Art After Modernism*, Boston, David Godine, 1984, pp. 283–294.

Chapter 3

Vilém Flusser

ABOUT THE WORD *DESIGN* [1993]

Source: Vilém Flusser (1999) 'About the Word *Design*', in *The Shape of Things: A Philosophy of Design*, London: Reaktion Books, pp. 17–21. First published in German in 1993.

In his philosophical self-portrait of 1969 Vilém Flusser (1920–91) wrote:

> I come from well-to-do intellectual Prague Jewish parents. I spent my youth in the spiritually and artistically inebriating atmosphere of the between-wars Prague. I survived, groggily, the bestial and stupid earthquake of Nazism, which devoured my world (i.e., my others and my things), but also the scales of values that had structured that world. [. . .] I was vomited upon Brazil at a plastic and assimilable age, and I spent the last thirty years of my life in search of myself in Brazil, and in search of Brazil within myself. If to live is to search one's way, I lived intensely, that is, philosophically.
>
> (Flusser 2002: 198)

Flusser left Brazil in the 1970s to settle in France, and was killed in a car accident in 1991 when returning from his first visit to Prague in fifty-two years. A migrant in physical space, Flusser might also be thought of as a migrant in idea space, never entirely setting up home within a specific intellectual tradition. Philosophy is at the heart of Flusser's writing and it is a philosophical orientation that is constantly open to new approaches to the world. Thus while Husserl, Wittgenstein and Nietzsche provide insistent co-ordinates for his analytic thought, game theory, cybernetics, systems theory, Thomas Kuhn and media theory also inform his essays.

The short essay 'About the Word *Design*' evidences some of the characteristics of Flusser's work. On the face of it, the essay is an exercise in philology detailing the various etymologies at work in the concept 'design'. Philology works to unsettle any sense of fixed, essential meaning for the term 'design': in place of fixity, Flusser finds an array of diverse and conflicting meanings. But this approach is only the foundation of a little thought-machine that allows 'design' to be about human-kind's productive existence in the shadow of death. Here design is an animating energy that propels humans to create artistic freedom (through technology), but which results in the production of miraculous inventions that are worthless (the giveaway ballpoint). Flusser's writing takes us to the stars and then back to earth: his rhetorical mode is bathos.

Further reading: Flusser 1983, 1999, 2002, 2004; Poster 2001; Roth 2004.

I N E N G L I S H , T H E word *design* is both a noun and a verb (which tells one a lot about the nature of the English language). As a noun, it means – among other things – 'intention', 'plan', 'intent', 'aim', 'scheme,' 'plot', 'motif', 'basic structure', all these (and other meanings) being connected with 'cunning' and 'deception'. As a verb ('to design'), meanings include 'to concoct something', 'to simulate', 'to draft', 'to sketch', 'to fashion', 'to have designs on something'. The word is derived from the Latin *signum*, meaning 'sign', and shares the same ancient root. Thus, etymologically, *design* means 'de-sign'. This raises the question: How has the word *design* come to achieve its present-day significance throughout the world? This question is not a historical one, in the sense of sending one off to examine texts for evidence of when and where the word came to be established in its present-day meaning. It is a semantic question, in the sense of causing one to consider precisely why this word has such significance attached to it in contemporary discourse about culture.

The word occurs in contexts associated with cunning and deceit. A designer is a cunning plotter laying his traps. Falling into the same category are other very significant words: in particular, *mechanics* and *machine*. The Greek *mechos* means a device designed to deceive – i.e. a trap – and the Trojan Horse is one example of this. Ulysses is called *polymechanikos*, which schoolchildren translate as 'the crafty one'. The word *mechos* itself derives from the ancient *MAGH*, which we recognize in the German *Macht* and *mögen*, the English 'might' and 'may'. Consequently, a machine is a device designed to deceive; a lever, for example, cheats gravity, and 'mechanics' is the trick of fooling heavy bodies.

Another word used in the same context is 'technology'. The Greek *techne* means 'art' and is related to *tekton*, a 'carpenter'. The basic idea here is that wood (*hyle* in Greek) is a shapeless material to which the artist, the technician, gives form, thereby causing the form to appear in the first place. Plato's basic objection to art and technology was that they betray and distort theoretically intelligible forms ('Ideas') when they transfer these into the material world. For him, artists and technicians were traitors to Ideas and tricksters because they cunningly seduced people into perceiving distorted ideas.

The Latin equivalent of the Greek *techne* is *ars*, which in fact suggests a metaphor similar to the English rogue's 'sleight of hand'. The diminutive of *ars* is *articulum* – i.e. little art – and indicates that something is turned around the hand (as in the French *tour de main*). Hence *ars* means something like 'agility' or the

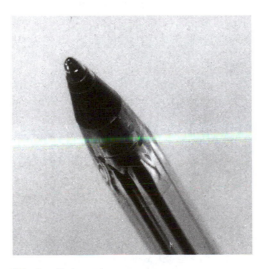

Figure 3.1   Biro (photograph by Ben Highmore).

'ability to turn something to one's advantage', and *artifex* – i.e. 'artist' – means a 'trickster' above all. That the original artist was a conjurer can be seen from words such as 'artifice', 'artifical' and even 'artillery'. In German, an artist is of course one who is 'able to do something', the German word for art, *Kunst*, being the noun from *können*, 'to be able' or 'can', but there again the word for 'artificial', *gekünstelt*, comes from the same root (as does the English 'cunning').

Such considerations in themselves constitute a sufficient explanation of why the word *design* occupies the position it does in contemporary discourse. The words *design, machine, technology, ars* and *art* are closely related to one another, one term being unthinkable without the others, and they all derive from the same existential view of the world. However, this internal connection has been denied for centuries (at least since the Renaissance). Modern bourgeois culture made a sharp division between the world of the arts and that of technology and machines; hence culture was split into two mutually exclusive branches: one scientific, quantifiable and 'hard', the other aesthetic, evaluative and 'soft'. This unfortunate split started to become irreversible towards the end of the nineteenth century. In the gap, the word *design* formed a bridge between the two. It could do this since it is an expression of the internal connection between art and technology. Hence in contemporary life, *design* more or less indicates the site where art and technology (along with their respective evaluative and scientific ways of thinking) come together as equals, making a new form of culture possible.

Although this is a good explanation, it is not satisfactory on its own. After all, what links the terms mentioned above is that they all have connotations of (among other things) deception and trickery. The new form of culture which Design was to make possible would be a culture that was aware of the fact that it was deceptive. So the question is: Who and what are we deceiving when we become involved with culture (with art, with technology – in short, with Design)? To take one example: The lever is a simple machine. Its design copies the human arm; it is an artificial arm. Its technology is probably as old as the species *homo sapiens*, perhaps even older. And this machine, this design, this art, this technology is intended to cheat gravity, to fool the laws of nature and, by means of deception, to escape our natural circumstances through the strategic exploitation of a law of nature. By means of the lever – despite our body weight – we ought to be able to raise ourselves up to touch the stars if we have to, and – thanks to the lever – if we are given the leverage, we might be able to lever the world out of its orbit. This is the design that is the basis of all culture: to deceive nature by means of technology, to replace what is natural with what is artificial and build a machine out of which there comes a god who is ourselves. In short: The design behind all culture has to be deceptive (artful?) enough to turn mere mammals conditioned by nature into free artists.

This is a great explanation, is it not? The word *design* has come to occupy the position it has in contemporary discourse through our awareness that being a human being is a design against nature. Unfortunately, this explanation will not satisfy us. If in fact *design* increasingly becomes the centre of attention, with the question of Design replacing that of the Idea, we will find ourselves on uncertain ground. To take one example: Plastic pens are getting cheaper and cheaper and tend to be given away for nothing. The material they are made of has practically no value, and work (according to Marx, the source of all value) is accomplished thanks to smart technology by fully automatic machines. The only thing that gives plastic pens any value is their design, which is the reason that they write. This design represents a coming together of great ideas, which – being derived from art and science – have cross-fertilized and creatively complemented one another. Yet this is a design we don't even notice, so such pens tend to be given away free – as advertising, for example. The great ideas behind them are treated with the same contempt as the material and work behind them.

How can we explain this devaluation of all values? By the fact that the word *design* makes us aware that all culture is trickery, that we are tricksters tricked, and that any involvement with culture is the same thing as self-deception. True, once the barrier between art and technology had been broken down, a new perspective opened up within which one could create more and more perfect *designs*, escape one's circumstances more and more, live more and more artistically (beautifully). But the price we pay for this is the loss of truth and authenticity. In fact, the lever is about to lever all that is true and authentic out of our orbit and replace it mechanically with perfectly designed artefacts. And so all these artefacts become as valuable as plastic pens, become disposable gadgets. This becomes clear when we die, if not before. Because despite all the technological and artistic arrangements we make (despite hospital architecture and death-bed design), we do die, just as other mammals die. The word *design* has managed to retain its key position in everyday discourse because we are starting (perhaps rightly) to lose faith in art and technology as sources of value. Because we are starting to wise up to the design behind them.

This is a sobering explanation. But it is also an unavoidable one. A confession is called for here. This essay has had a specific design in mind: It set out to expose the cunning and deceptive aspects of the word *design*. This it did because they are normally concealed. If it had pursued another design, it might, for example, have insisted on the fact that 'design' is related to 'sign': a sign of the times, a sign of things to come, a sign of membership. In that case, it would have given a different, but equally plausible, explanation of the word's contemporary situation. That's the answer then: Everything depends on Design.

Chapter 4

Michael Moon, Eve Kosofsky Sedgwick, Benjamin Gianni and Scott Weir

QUEERS IN (SINGLE-FAMILY) SPACE [1994]

Source: Michael Moon, Eve Kosofsky Sedgwick, Benjamin Gianni and Scott Weir (1994) 'Queers in (Single-Family) Space', *Assemblage*, 24, pp. 30–7.

Writing about the use of public space in America by gay men during the mid-twentieth century George Chauncey writes: 'There is no queer space; there are only spaces used by queers or put to queer use' (1996: 224). We might want to add that this sentiment is emphatically enshrined in the 'single-family' housing unit. But if the 'family' home is not a queer space, should we describe it as a heteronormative space: as deliberately privileging heterosexual norms and outlawing queer living? Clearly the 'family home' has been used for instilling heteronormativity, but this isn't an essential feature of its design and construction, it isn't the necessary outcome of its spatial layout. The 'single-family' house, as described by the literary critics and queer theorists Michael Moon and Eve Kosofsky Sedgwick, is testimony to the inventive desperation of 'proto-queer' kids trying to carve out a bit of head space, a bit of body space, in the cramping environment of familial life. In this sense inhabiting is never simply about occupying physical space, but about the habits, the rituals, the designating of certain spaces as sacred, the decorating and the arranging in space.

This project was part of a series of collaborations between theorists and architects. The collaborations were published in a special issue of the journal *Assemblage* titled 'House Rules' which was also the name of the exhibition at the Wexner Center for the Arts, in Columbus, Ohio, where the projects were displayed. The editors of *Assemblage* begin the special issue with the following words:

> You fill in the blank: there can be no (*feminist, Marxist, race-based, sexuality based* . . .) architecture, only a (*feminist, Marxist, race-based, sexuality based* . . .) analysis of architecture. Surely in some ways this old maxim still holds. Architecture is one of the primary means by which society reproduces itself materially and symbolically; we can analyze this fact from any number of vantage points, but to think that we can direct architecture back toward one of these points is to be dupes of the very system we would change. In a certain sense, architecture is nothing more than representation.
>
> (*Assemblage* 1994: 6)

The understanding that there is no essential correspondence between a built form and a social attitude frees the designer from the thankless task of attempting to produce a form adequate to the desire for freedom (for instance). Here the architects Benjamin Gianni and Scott Weir so adamantly refuse the idea that there might be some 'essence of queerness' that their house looks, at first glance, decidedly conventional. But rather than this signifying a lack of imagination it signals the reverse: the ability to find queerness in the normative spaces of domestic environments. The ordinary spaces of track housing, of vernacular suburbia, are already queer, are already the site of countless shrines and ritualised mimicry. Here, the architects respond to the improvisational possibilities of queer living by increasing and intensifying the social flexibility that already exists in the 'single-family' house.

Further reading: Ahmed 2006; Chauncey 1994, 1996; Fuss 2004; Moon 1998; Sedgwick 2003.

THIS PROJECT REFLECTS the intense realism underpinning any queer utopian impulse. The word queer itself means "across": it comes from the Indo-European root twerkw, which also yields the German quer (transverse), Latin toquere (to twist), English athwart and torque. Queer lives and impulses do not occupy a separate social or physical space from straight ones; instead, they are relational and conditional, moving across and transforming the conventional spaces that were designed to offer endless narcissistic self-confirmation to the unstable normative systems of sex, gender, and family. Queer politics and identity involve keeping faith with, rather than disavowing, the courage, pain, and inventiveness that mark the childhood of persons who cannot or will not conform to sex/gender expectations. This project dramatizes and offers support for the queer kid's or adult's survival habits of cherishing and reimaging the materials at hand; of exploring the uses of secrecy and exposure; of using the leverage of access to the public sphere and public fantasy as a way to survive in the private sphere; and of flexible, naturalistic reconceptions of companionship and relatedness over a variety of possible life spans.

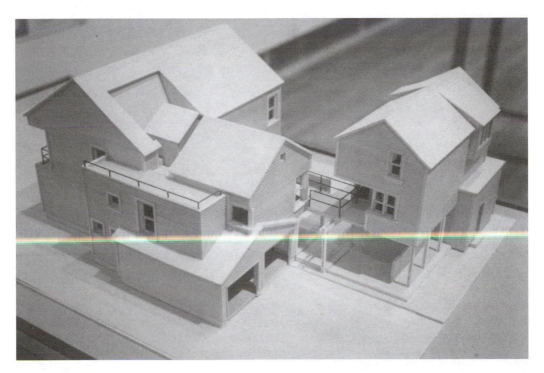

Figure 4.1   Trapped © Benjamin Gianni and Scott Weir.

Figure 4.2   © Benjamin Gianni and Scott Weir.

Figure 4.3   © Benjamin Gianni and Scott Weir.

Figure 4.4   © Benjamin Gianni and Scott Weir.

MM: I have four brothers — two older and two younger — and an older sister. In my early years of grammar school, all five of us boys shared a bedroom for awhile. My eldest bother and I had different ways of trying to make territory for our respective selves, despite the lack of private space available to us. He built furniture for the room, such as a fancy headboard that had compartments in it, some with little sliding doors and others with doors on hinges. He made a special nook into which his radio fit neatly, with a special hole in the back for the cord. In order to produce some acceptable "atmosphere" in the room, he and my other older brother would listen to cool teenage music at a low volume on the radio far into the night. I remember trying to stay awake to hang with the cool teenagers rather than falling asleep early like our baby brothers. Unsurprisingly, my eldest brother became an architect. Renovating his and his wife's and his grown children's houses, as well as designing and building "custom" furniture for them, is still his primary mode of living in a family and showing his love for them.

My own queer, or protoqueer, mode of trying to territorialize some space for myself took the form of constructing little seasonal shrines and shadow-box dioramas made of construction paper cutouts in shoe boxes. The shrines were cardboard boxes covered with pieces of fabric borrowed from my mother's sewing scraps. They were thematically keyed to religious holidays. Spring from Easter through May (the official Virgin Mary month) was the high season for these. In my personal religion they also celebrated the end of the school year and expressed my ecstatic fantasies about the coming of summer (I hated school and lived for summer vacation). The shrines were altars on which I set religious knick-knacks, such as little statues, medals, and "holy cards"; the main focus was always a small vase of beautiful flowers from my father's garden, placed as a sacrificial offering to God and the saints — but also as a smashing decorative accent. The shadow-box scenes were a focus for me of more secular fantasy. One I remember making featured a scene of teddy bears in the woods, another one Mickey Mouse and friends, and another Batman and Robin. (There is a bright-purple-plastic Mickey Mouse canteen, a recent gift from Eve, hanging from the inside knob of my bedroom door as I sit here writing these lines.)

I don't remember anyone in my family ever making fun of my shrine-building propensities; they either ignored them or expressed a respectful interest in them. In ways that seem to me analogous to my eldest brother's lifelong investment in making and remaking domestic space and furniture, I believe it remains vital to me and to the survival of my faculties for sustaining and expressing cathexis to continue creating spaces (mostly through writing at this point) that collapse the categories of the sacred (the adorable) with those of the sexy, funny, and charming (the adorable). This is as true of some of my academic writing as it is of the 'zines I produce from time to time (*Boy Martyr Monthly, Harness and Hairnet*).

I, of course, didn't go directly from making shrines to writing queer books and 'zines. What mediated these realms for me was my discovery at the age of twelve of the space of reading as what seemed at the time to be a highly effective mode of producing queer private space in a crowded single-family home. I had been a habitual reader since the age of six, but instead of continuing to read in the haphazard way I had as a child (my mother's magazines, popular biographies of great composers, nature books, "young-adult" fiction), at puberty I started reading classic nineteenth-century novels and poetry. For me, these books mediated the "sacred" (in the form of a historical past supposedly consecrated by passion and genius), the ultimate in desirability (romantic-erotic relation and passionate utterance and narrative), and intense doses of satirical and intellectual wit. These books thereby seemed to produce a richer and more highly constructed kind of space than my earlier reading had done: I felt fantasmatically drawn as a participant into drawing-room banter and erotic power struggles by turns. Unbeknown to me, my strongest favorites (Jane Austen, the Brontës, Emily Dickinson) were mostly women who had written as a way of creating space for their own difficult thought and complicated desire while continuing to live in paternal homes that they experienced as in general hostile or at best indifferent to their needs. As I soon became aware from reading biographies, these women were also adepts at conspiring with their often equally queer and intense siblings, both as adolescents and adults. Eve and I remain fascinated by the queer "home lives" of such figures as artists Andy Warhol, who cohabited with his mother during the years he was directing the creation of the Factory "scene," and Joseph Cornell, who made and bestrewed his fabulous boxes in the house on Utopia Parkway in Flushing, Queens, that he shared with his mother Helen and his brother Robert for over thirty-five years.

EKS: I grew up in a small three-bedroom suburban ranch house that was built in 1950, the same year I was born. My big sister and I shared a bedroom until my parents got worried about her climbing into my bed every night: then they gave us separate rooms, bumping our little brother up into the finished attic.

The house had thin walls, so that while closed doors created a fiction of privacy that was generally respected, in fact, my bedroom was full of sounds from the living room, my parents' and sister's rooms, and the bathroom. I think I must have disciplined the "valves of my attention" (in Emily Dickinson's phrase) so I'd be able to exclude the public part of our rather intensive family culture, when I was in my apple-blossom-pink little bedroom. I've always been good at getting completely absorbed in reading. The only other absorbing thing I spent as much time doing was masturbating. I used to assume I craved privacy in order to masturbate so much – now I also imagine I masturbated so much as a way of hollowing out a privacy for myself within the permeable ear of my room.

A fat, dorky, pink middle child in a Jewish family where everyone else was slim and/or athletic and dark, I took on a role that combined hopeless abjection ("blubber" was something I both had and did) with a certain uncanniness of presence and word. The consumer who was best educated (by me) in how to appreciate this odd product was my little brother David, and I visualize him – he's told me about it since – lying faithfully across the threshold to my room, outside the firmly closed door, guarding, marking, and longing to enter and share the space where, steeped in my own godhead and juices, I was accruing spiritual force, or something.

When my sister plunged into the stylized world of "dating," David and I responded by observing weekly "dates" when he would escort me out into the public (television) space of the living room and we'd ceremoniously watch *The Defenders, The Avengers, Mission: Impossible*, or, our favorite, *The* totally queer *Man from U.N.C.L.E.* This was about as far as I got with dating. It seems as though what began as an anxious mimicry of heterosexual ritual turned, for both of us, into a self- and mutual education in a companionate style of close intimacy where gender salience was considerably deprecated. Similarly, when I later (not much later!) got married, at age nineteen, it represented less a flight into heterosexuality than a surprisingly firm step aside from it.

I keep trying to figure out the source of an image that has tinged every utopian impulse I've had since childhood: its name would be something like "The Kids Are Amusing Themselves." The "talent show" and Mickey Rooney and Judy Garland would be prototypes of it, but much more so the sisters in *Little Women*, with their aromatic ragout of improvised games and performances, the thickness of their stolen and invented childhood culture. "The kids are amusing ourselves" as opposed to the kids are waiting for grownups to amuse us; as opposed probably also to surrendering ourselves whole to the emerging national kid media culture of the 1950s. As a small child I never doubted that my desire was for access to the means of culture production rather than just its products ("And what," my shrink gently asks me, "do you think you would have called that before you read Marx?") Thus both the soft-spoken resistance of, and a further soft-spoken resistance to, that anachronistic, relatively dense Biedermeier ambiance of this family's values cast a glamour over the improvised entertainment, the well-lit imaginary spectacle of "the kids'" self-sufficiency in the matter of fun.

"I have to get home for dinner with my kids," Frank Rosenblatt would tell his colleagues in neurobiology at Cornell in 1970, and they'd maybe picture this classic absent-minded professor tootling off to honey-I'm-home the wife and a straggling couple of offspring in Cayuga Heights. "Home," to the contrary, was a Paul Goodmanesque scene in an old five-bedroom farmhouse Frank owned miles out of town: Chateau Rosenblatt, so named after the moonshine homebrew that was bottled there in one of the hundreds of harebrained schemes for back-to-the-land self-sufficiency that formed our fantasy life, like the fantasy lives of young commune dwellers all over the U.S. during those years. We'd keep a goat! That would give milk! That we'd make into cheese! That we'd barter for seeds! That we'd grow to make flax! That we'd weave into fabric! Someone had instruction for building a loom. Etcetera. "The kids" at any given time were six to fifteen people: Frank's graduate students; old friends; young men who were or had been his lovers; partners, siblings, partners of siblings, and siblings of partners of siblings of the above categories; sometime boys who'd run away from reform school farther upstate. Thirty cats and a dysfunctional blue collie. A darkroom for Bill. A baby grand (Frank played). A big astronomical observatory out in a field (Frank had a plan for detecting signals from other solar systems). Presiding over the big kitchen: an abandoned but very recognizable half-sculpted marble bust, by Frank, of Rod.

Dinner – we took turns cooking – was the centerpiece of the communal life and it ended with Frank reading aloud, often from the children's books that the odd sentimentality of the 1960s had given adult currency, *The Wind in the Willows, Winnie the Pooh, The Once and Future King*. Such gestures of familial tenderness, coming from this queer, withdrawn, small genius daddy who took so much tending himself, let us feel that to be a kid and an adult were no very different matters.

I moved in to share my partner's space in the attic of this house. Our windows surveyed rolling country on three sides; a loft under the sloping roof held our mattress; our space was divided, where it was divided, by hanging Indian blankets. Looking back, I can't disentangle the loveliness of the space, the miasma of my depression, the delight and pathos of this quintessential stage for "kids amusing ourselves." Anytime we wandered down to the living room there were guitars and banjos being played; or visionary scientists drifted through the house explaining plans for a self-organizing analog computer that would begin as an undifferentiated vat of stinky chemicals and slowly turn itself into something like a brain.

MM and EKS: We have been sharing space in a single-family house in a suburban-feeling part of Durham, North Carolina, for four years. It's like the Kosofsky house on steroids, a sub-Frank Lloyd Wright ranch house built in 1966. The airy, woody, somewhat cavernous public spaces (living room, dining room, kitchen, den) are all laid out on one long axis; a "master bedroom" with bath goes off in one direction from the living room, and a wing presumably meant for the kids – three bedrooms, two baths – goes off in the other direction from the den. Our respective bedrooms are at opposite extremities of this L, but we occupy the space between fairly fluidly along with our allergenic cat and, when they can spend time here, our respective partners who live out-of-town.

Under the main axis of the house is a finished basement where Michael stores some of his books and has a workspace, dubbed the Batcave by his partner. The furniture throughout the house tends to be solid, broad-bottomed, and stable, the nicest of which is mission oak from yard sales and auctions, and the walls have on them textured woven things and collages of photographs of familiar places and of friends living and dead. But our most distinctive decorative motif, we have been told, are our "piles" – the vital and fermenting burial mounds for magazines, friends' manuscripts, Xeroxes of articles, aging professional correspondence, photographs, and fetishistic stationery supplies purchased in bulk from Office Depot – which overflow the floors, side tables, and most other horizontal surfaces throughout the house. These are a source of amusement and reflection for our friends and ourselves (and of disgust for some of our friends), as well as of discouragement and constant old/new ideas and impulses. We warmly agree with Freud that "a messy room is a full bowel." Yet our approaches to the construction of these midden heaps seem to differ: Michael is a packrat/collector/archivist who attends in this way to a plethora of sites of high and popular culture past and present; while Eve apparently believes that to put anything away may be to foreclose precious possibilities for its future development.

Some notes on the project to date

1   The challenge of designing for an unspecified client.
2   While we began the project by considering the potential relationships between "queerness" and the house, we realized that the idea was as broad as the sex, age, individual personalities, and proclivities of the parties involved. Queerness manifests itself (and is experienced) differently in childhood than in adolescence or adulthood. Gay adults may be married, live alone, with children, with elderly parents, with friends, with partners. As it is impossible to generalize, there is no one spatial/domestic manifestation of the issue of queerness. The same space might be lived in and experienced in a variety of ways.
3   We realized that this lack of specificity was characteristic of the suburban house in general. Increasingly, it was difficult to say who might be inhabiting it, since the "average" house changes hands as often as every five years. This degree of turnover implies two things: first, customizing the house might endanger its salability in the marketplace, alienating potential buyers; second, flexibility should be designed into the house to adapt to the variety of situations it might be asked to accommodate, not only from owner to owner but over the lifetime of a family or group of inhabitants. Even the most prototypical of inhabitants (the nuclear family) occupies the house in a variety of ways over the lifespan of its inhabitation: *a.* couple with young children (need for proximity and surveillance); *b.* parent(s) with adolescent children (need for privacy and separation); *c.* empty nest (holding pattern); *d.* return of adult child (need for well-defined territories); *e.* elderly or infirmed parents (need for two separate but connected apartments); *f.* retirement (need for separate zones for two very different individuals; *g.* rental apartment (house too big, portion rented out; need for efficiency apartment); *h.* snowbird syndrome (house divided in two, half rented out to tenants who look after the place while owners are away); *i.* etc.
4   As the cost of real estate has risen significantly in the past two decades (reflecting the presence of multiple wage earners in the household), it is increasingly difficult to afford a house on a single

income. This means that two unrelated adults may be occupying the house and/or that portions of the house will be rented out from time to time to generate income.

5   First Things First. The issues outlined above nudged us away from the specific issue of queerness toward the more general issue of flexibility. We set ourselves the challenge of addressing the problem of the unspecified inhabitant and the need for flexibility before addressing the more specific issue of the homosexual inhabitant. Although we were particularly interested in looking at the suburban house from the perspective of the homosexual adolescent (someone whose relationship to space might be characterized by isolation, adventurousness, fantasy, panic), it seemed presumptuous to design a "house for a queer teen." First of all, few queer teens are in a position to commission a house and, second, queer teens are only queer teens for a few years. We decided first to design a generic/flexible house, then to investigate how a gay adolescent might inhabit it.

6   This approach differs from the architect's usual role of designing a highly customized environment for a client/patron. We had to resist the temptation to "play architect."

7   We therefore tried to stick close to the type and remain within the visual parameters of the marketplace of builder houses. Rather than taking the usual (elitist?) position of the architect and rejecting the suburban house as déclassé, we held on to the image of the generic box. In particular, we chose a type seen increasingly in Canada, the "Welcome to My Garage" house.

8   The "Welcome to My Garage" house has evolved as a type over the past half century. Before World War II middle-class housing was built with front porches addressing the street and detached garages connected to an alley. The porch and front yard were social spaces mediating between the street and the interior of the house, while the back yard/garage were more utilitarian (perhaps a holdover from the time when privies were located behind houses). In the 1950s and 1960s alleys were eliminated and garages incorporated into the mass of the house, either at the basement level or, in the case of a split-level, at the family room level. The exterior social space moved from the front yard to the back patio (close to the kitchen, replete with barbecue). The 1970s and 1980s witnessed the emergence of the "Welcome to My Garage" house, in which the two-car garage pulled itself through the front of the house to sit prominently at the street. The front yard became entirely residual, deferring to an increasingly important back garden and rendering the street a de facto alley.

9   While we have remained "true" to this contemporary type, we have made the following innovations:

A   We reintroduced the front porch as a covered passage leading from the street to the front door. This places a symbolic pedestrian entrance alongside the garage doors and gives the house some presence on the street. It also provides a covered sitting space that faces not the street but the front garden – reducing the feeling of exposure and increasing the chances that someone might actually sit there. Above this passage is a deck that acts as a "front lawn" or exterior social space for a rental unit above the garage. The windows of the main house are oriented away from this area to make it relatively private.

B   We introduced a second stair at the back of the garage. This can function as a separate entrance for an efficiency unit above the garage. Moreover, it can operate as an escape route for the adolescent, providing direct access between his/her bedroom and car.

C   We introduced a third bathroom on the second floor. This can either serve the rental unit or be used as "his-and-hers" bathrooms in tandem "master" suites.

D   We arranged bathrooms and closets to form zones between bedrooms to assure aural privacy – especially important when the house is subdivided into multiple units.

E   *We arranged* the major components of the interior to be easily subdivided. The house can be divided as follows: a single-family house with either four or five bedrooms; a three-bedroom house with a separate efficiency apartment; a two-bedroom house with a one-bedroom apartment; a duplex in which each unit contains two bedrooms; a three-unit complex, or, with the addition of a separate structure at the street, a four-unit complex.

A commercial space or home office can be accommodated in the garage in any of the above variations.

10   Having addressed what we considered to be the "reality" of the suburban situation, we were now free to respond to the particular issue of queerness. As stated above, we were especially interested in the question of homosexuality as it emerged during adolescence and as it is (in)formed and accommodated by the suburban house. In this endeavor, we drew heavily on our own experience as gay males raised (with siblings and married parents) in the suburbs. As our reading of the house is personal, it is not meant to be exhaustive.

11   Within this theme we located and developed certain sites within the house:

A   The wall between the parents' bedroom and the children's bedroom. Through this wall the asexuality and/or autosexuality of the children (manifested in the twin beds) transmutes into the adult (presumably hetero) sexuality of the parents. Through this wall the activities of the children are monitored by the parents and the interactions of the parents (sex, arguments, etc.) are overheard by the children. The unofficial, unsanctioned emissions that make their way through this surface are the secret to adulthood and sexuality.

B   The parents' and the children's closets. They are consolidated to form a sanctum sanctorum of gender and sexuality placed within the wall between the bedrooms. As the bedrooms are hidden within the house and the closets hidden within the bedrooms, the artifacts and indicators of sexuality are hidden within the closets. As a most private space of the private realm of the house, the bedroom closets represent a kind of spectral inversion of the house. As a building within a building, the closets form a malign counterpoint to the respectable presentation of the family epitomized by the house itself.

The closet is an altar to the affectless innocence (and asexuality) of childhood, to the elements and accessories of gender, to mature sexuality.

These are juxtaposed along the boundary between the two bedrooms.

Between the clothing, games, and "junk" of the children's closets accumulate (and are hidden), during adolescence, unsanctioned materials (magazines, books, videos). The closet is both private and vulnerable to inspection by the parents. As the adolescent learns to disguise unsanctioned materials among the residue of childhood and the objects of everyday use, s/he comes to understand interstices as highly charged sites. The closet raids begin. What for the sissy boy begins as forays into the mother's closet shifts for the adolescent to frequent visits to the father's closet. In the father's closet he seeks pornographic materials by which to mend or elaborate on a perceived chink in the apparently monolithic image of (hetero) sexuality.

The closet is a space of transgression, both as a place to hide unsanctioned articles and as a place to uncover the articles and identities of others; it is both a confessional and a place for prayer.

C   *The back* stair: An escape route to the car and the world at large, it is at once hidden and vulnerable due to its position along the wall to the parents' bedroom.

D   Entertainment/information centers. Points of contact exist between the protected realm of the home and the world at large, through which unsanctioned information might find its way into the house. These can include the television/video, the radio, the computer (internet and billboards), the mailbox, and the magazine rack. Just like the closet, they are the sites to which the adolescent goes to uncover information about sexuality.

F   The boundary between the formal and informal living areas.

In addition to all this, we have consolidated the functional portions of the house (stairs, closets, hearth, etc.) into a series of freestanding objects. These act as characters or inhabitants of the house.

Project credits

This project is a collaboration between theorists Michael Moon and Eve Kosofsky Sedgwick and architects Benjamin Gianni and Scott Weir. While the opening essay was contributed by the former and the designs by the latter, both components emerged from discussions between all team members. The team met twice in New York and once in Ottawa – communicating intermittently by telephone and fax.

The essay was written in early May before the design drawings were begun; "Some Notes on the Project to Date" was written by Gianni midway through the design process.

The basswood model was produced by Lisa Hill. Graphic design and graphic support were provided by Richard Seaker and Michael Nagy at the Media Lab at Carleton University, School of Architecture. The project was modeled on the computer in Form ●Z and images were assembled using Pagemaker 5.0.

Thanks are due to curator Mark Robbins for bringing the team together and offering its members the opportunity to participate. Thanks to Ron Reaman for his patience and temporary loss of a mate.

Chapter 5

Pauline Madge

ECOLOGICAL DESIGN: A NEW CRITIQUE [1997]

Source: Pauline Madge (1997) 'Ecological Design: A New Critique', *Design Issues*, 13, 2, pp. 44–54.

Pauline Madge's very useful review of the critical debates around eco-design pinpoints a number of crucial problems when the arenas 'design' and 'ecology' converge. Of central importance is the productive drive of design in relation (and contradiction) to the conservationist ethos of much ecological thought. Traditionally design has committed itself to providing solutions by producing more things. Thus if one of the problems facing us today is climate change, and one of the explanations of this is to see it as caused by carbon emissions, then a design solution would be to produce new cars with considerably reduced carbon emissions or even zero carbon emissions. In this, environmentalism (from one perspective) becomes another marketing opportunity. Yet as Pauline Madge demonstrates the real enemy of sustainability might be a habit of mind that is dominated by the culture of consumption, that is, always wanting the next 'thing', even if that thing is environmentally better than the last thing.

As scholars of domestic material culture have shown, the key design process necessary for the large-scale take-up of new technological forms is technological normalisation. In tracing the 'social life' of the domestic freezer, for instance, Elizabeth Shove and Dale Southerton show how the freezer moves from a position of luxury through to a position of necessity. In their research they look at the changing sales narratives from before the 1970s (when the home freezer was a rare commodity) to show how the initial promotion of the freezer as a luxury gizmo representing cutting-edge technology was replaced by a narrative of labour-saving convenience (through the 1970s and into the 1980s), which in turn was replaced with a narrative that simply assumes that the freezer has a pre-given place in the home. In other words the success of a technology comes about when it is taken-for-granted, when it would only become noticeable by its absence.

For Pauline Madge ecological imperatives suggest that the process of normalisation needs to reverse this process, to turn necessities back into luxuries. In this, design would need to alter its field of intentions: rather than making new things, it might want to unmake old things, or make-strange the world of necessity as it is presently offered to us. Like some other ecological thinkers (Gay Hawkins, for instance) Pauline Madge persuades us that sustainability becomes really interesting only when it shifts from being an ethical and moral injunction (don't do that, do this) and becomes a way of imaginatively remaking ourselves through our relations with the world. There is, then, a very strong connection between environmentalism and the anarchist belief that you should live your life as an experiment for the future.

Further reading: Hawkins 2006; Papanek 1985; Shove and Southerton 2000; Wheeler 2006.

ECOLOGICAL DESIGN HAS come of age. It is now about a decade since the first wave of green design emerged as a significant new factor in product and graphic design. Though it is, by no means, fully developed and accepted, and only just beginning to be implemented in design education, for example, there is a broad consensus that environmental issues can no longer be ignored by designers and critics. There has been a significant change in recent years, from the days when it was just a matter of getting the environment onto the agenda, and establishing the broad parameters of a green design practice – the inevitable process of reappraisal and differentiation as a movement begins to acquire a history and a polemics. Already, a second or third wave of ecodesign practice and criticism has emerged which is concerned with a more subtle analysis of meaning and methodology.

As it has developed over the last decade, ecodesign has constantly borrowed ideas and terminology from ecology and environmentalism, though rarely is this explicitly acknowledged. It seems important, therefore, to evaluate the changing course of ecodesign since the mid-1980s within the framework of the broader development of ecological ideas. One notable feature is a change in terminology: the original term "green design" is rarely used today and, although it was the buzzword in the late 1980s, it is already passé. Instead, ecologically or environmentally-sensitive or affirmative design, or more generally ecodesign, has become the most widely accepted term. In the last year or so, this has, in turn, given way to "sustainable design." These terms are fairly interchangeable, and perhaps the importance of such substitution of words should not be exaggerated, but they are one indication of shifting attitudes.

The transition from "green" to "eco-" to "sustainable" in the design field represents a steady broadening of scope in theory and practice, and to a certain extent, an increasingly critical perspective on ecology and design. Here, use of terms seems to indicate an attempt to wrestle with the complexities and implications of an ecological approach to design – going beyond the rather simplistic notions of design and the environment in the previous decade.

In this essay, which is part history and part analysis of ecodesign criticism, I use these three terms as keywords to explore different facets of ecological design, and to contextualize them within particular phases of the environmental movement in the last decade. I have emphasized the more radical theories to emerge within both design and environmental thinking in order to demonstrate what this might imply for a new ecological design criticism. What will emerge is that this is not necessarily a cohesive or unified phenomenon – there are many shades of green and different ecological perspectives, reflecting political distinctions within the environmentalism and differences within ecological theory and practice. Although ecodesign in the last decade has been dominated by a concern for the mechanisms of putting policy into practice, a fundamental recognition has emerged that what is at stake is a new view of the world and a choice of possible futures, and it is this which has the most interesting implications for design criticism.

Green design

"Green" became the buzzword of the 1980s. As public awareness of environmental problems spread and green parties became more prominent throughout Europe, there was a sudden profusion of greenery within the media and in advertising in the mid- to late '80s. Because "green" encapsulated green politics, current environmental concerns, and identified them with a specific color, in an unprecedented way, green design arrived with a ready-made symbolism: green products, green packaging, and numerous books on "how to be green" in green book jackets. The "lead" nations, within Europe, in environmental terms, such as Germany and the Netherlands, began research into design and the environment in the early 1980s. Evelyn Möller coined the phrase "ecological functionalism" in 1982, and devised an ecological checklist for product designers and manufacturers which formed the basis of a working group on ecology and design in the *Verband Deutscher Industrie-Designer*.[1]

In the UK, the Design Council took the lead with an exhibition called "The Green Designer" in 1986, organized by Paul Burall, Design Council publicity officer, and John Elkington, environmental consultant. Despite the fact that the term "green" was borrowed from politics, the approach in this exhibition was largely apolitical, taking place as it did in the design culture of the mid-'80s, when the idea of "winning by design" or "profit by design," as the Design Council called it, was paramount. In fact, the exhibition was the Design Council's contribution to Industry Year in 1986, and it was mainly concerned with demonstrating that green design was not "anti-industry," and that the "the greening of industry had gone further than most people imagined." John Elkington argued that the problems had now been largely overcome because green markets and the emergence of the environmental industry meant that there was no longer a conflict between a green approach to design and business success.[2] The exhibition focused on examples of specific products, and devised "10 Questions for the Green Designer" related to energy use, durability, recyclabilty, and acceptability in the marketplace. Five years later, a similar exhibition was held at the Design Centre called "More From Less" which also included "Cradle to Grave Guidelines for Design." A number of books on green design appeared around this date to answer the need for basic information on environmental issues for designers, adopting the same basic approach as the Design Council.[3]

In political terms, all of these exhibitions and publications can be classified as "light green," as opposed to "dark green," terms that were being used by the mid-'80s to designate different tendencies within the green movement. To distinguish itself from the red/blue, left/right of traditional politics, the green movement referred to a spectrum from gray to green, with the deeper shades of green being the more radical. In the late '80s, the terms were somewhat trivialized to refer to light and dark green consumers, but they reflected a deep division within the environmental movement between those who advocated a radical rejection of the status quo, a critique of the paradigm of modern industrial society (whether capitalist or socialist), and the lighter green idea of modifying existing institutions and practices. This ideological division goes back to the historic roots of the environmental movement in the late 1960s and early '70s (and beyond), but it acquired a new urgency in the 1980s as the green movement came into the mainstream.

One very influential way of designating these different strands within the environmental movement which still seems relevant to the green or ecodesign movement today, is Timothy O'Riordan's classification of "technocentric" and "ecocentric." He used these terms to represent two fundamentally different outlooks on the world. The ecocentric attitude is based on bioethics and a deep reverence for nature. It is in favor of low-impact technology, and is concerned with the environmental impact of rampant economic growth and large-scale industrial development; emphasizing, instead, morally and ecologically sound alternatives. Conversely, the technocentric mode is characterized by an unswerving belief in the ability of human science and high technology to manage the environment for the benefit of present and future generations and is based on an ideology of progress, efficiency, rationality, and control, viewing discussions about the wider political, social or ethical dimensions of the environment with suspicion.[4] In the 1970s and 1980s, these different attitudes also came to be described in terms of "shallow" and "deep" ecology, the latter, like ecocentrism, emphasizing harmony with nature and the intrinsic worth of all forms of life, as well as simplifying material needs so as to reduce human impact on planetary ecology.[5]

In the mid- to late '80s, the predominate form of green design represented a light green, technocentric, or shallow ecological approach, but it is possible to identify darker green or deeper ecological design, too. For example, the range of products and services listed in John Button's *Green Pages*, with its emphasis on consuming less;[6] or the German *Baubiologie* movement which believes that "living with less is better than saving energy," and that it is possible to do without many existing products through the improved design of buildings and changes in lifestyles.[7] This raises the whole question of alternative or green lifestyles, which have long been part of the green movement but which came to the fore in the debate over green consumerism in the late '80s.

Green consumerism arrived in 1988 with the publication of the best-selling *Green Consumer Guide*, by John Elkington and Julia Hailes. It was timed to coincide with "Green Consumer Week," organized by Friends of the Earth in September 1988. In the next year or so, there was frenzied activity on the green marketing front with some major claims being made for the new green products. This led to certain misgivings on the part of environmental groups and, while supporting green consumerism in principle, Friends of the Earth, for example, warned of a "green con," and argued for the need to go *Beyond Green Consumerism*.[8] An essential conflict appeared to exist between what could be called a dark green approach to design and consumption, and the values of advertising and marketing:

> Notions such as durability, reduced or shared consumption, or substituting nonmaterial pleasures for the use of objects, conflict with requirements of mass marketing. Advertising is tied to an expanding economy, the one thing that we living on a finite planet, must avoid.[9]

Here was a danger that:

> efforts to promote a demand for consumer goods that are environmentally benign will simply result in strengthening the growth of consumerism.[10]

As a response to this two new consumer magazines emerged in 1989. *Ethical Consumer* and *New Consumer* attempted to promote the use of "consumer power for positive economic, social, and environmental change."[11] There was an essential contrast between this approach and the more mainstream studies such as *Green, Greener, Greenest* by Michael Peters, an investigation into whether green consumerism was a significant marketing trend in Europe.[12]

Although these issues were not explicitly discussed within green design circles at the time, and there was never any question that a dark green approach would be on the agenda, there were occasional nods toward darker shades of green. For example, the title of a conference at the Design Museum in 1990, "Green Design: Beyond the Bandwagon," reflected a similar concern over green con to that expressed by Friends of the Earth, and concentrated on *genuine* green products and graphics. Alongside speakers from design and industry, Richard Adams of *New Consumer* broadened the debate.

In the next few years, the practicalities of greening products and industry came to the fore. The Design Research Society, for example, organized a conference called "The Greening of Design" in Manchester in 1992 which concentrated on environmental factors in new product development and business from a design management point of view. There was considerable overlap between this and attempts to introduce business ethics and green management into industry on the part of the New Economics Foundation and the New Consumer. But the latter adopted a more radical, watchdog role:

> The vital issues of the coming decades will revolve around the nature of global consumption and distribution. Fundamental choices will have to be made about lifestyles, patterns of production and consumer priorities. Planet-sustaining decisions must be based on extensive and wide ranging information about the nature of our consumer society and those who service it.[13]

In the next few years, such ideas were to be taken on board by green designers who, as a kind of recognition of a wider frame of reference, began increasingly to refer to their work as "ecological design."

Ecological design

The adoption of the term "ecological" to refer to anything vaguely to do with the environment dates back to the beginning of the environmental movement in the late 1960s and '70s. In 1988, John Button referred to about ninety sightings of the prefix "eco" including ecocity, ecomanagement, ecotechnics, and eco-(logical archi)tecture; but not at that time, ecodesign.[14] The term came into prominence a few years later, but one early use was by the Ecological Design Association, formed by 1989, whose journal was called *Ecodesign*. The EDA chose "ecological" rather than "green" because it was thought, quite rightly, that "green" would soon be an outdated term. This also reflected a broad understanding of ecological design, including radical notions of deep ecology:

> The design of materials and products, projects and systems, environments and communities which are friendly to living species and planetary ecology.[15]

Although, by 1990, ecodesign was most advanced in European countries, there were some new initiatives in the early '90s in Australia. In 1990, the EcoDesign Foundation in Sydney was set up, "dedicated to the promotion of ecological sustainability through industrial re-creation."[16] There, Tony Fry and Anne-Marie Willis focused on both the immediate task of greening products and the longer-term goals of redefining design and industrial practice – what Chris Ryan of the Centre for Design at the Royal Melbourne Institute of Technology has recently referred to as "EcoRedesign" and "Ecodesign," respectively.[17] An international EcoDesign conference was held at RMIT in October 1991 which, according to Anne-Marie Willis, reflected "the unchoate nature of ecodesign":

> . . . for many this simply meant the "adding in" of environmental criteria to the design process. Yet ecodesign has the potential to be more than the reform of existing design, for if taken seriously, it can establish a new foundation for design that could bring economic and ecological needs into a new union. . . .[18]

In the Netherlands an international gathering of designers met in March 1991 to discuss ecodesign, focusing on principles and methods as well as prevention by design.[19] This was a working group of the European Union's Eureka program, set up to provide the forum for the concept of environmentally sound product design. It was organized under the auspices of the Dutch Ministry of Economic Affairs. This was one example of many government-sponsored initiatives in the early '90s. UNEP (the United Nations Environment Program) had identified fifty of these by 1994[20] – a sign that ecodesign was beginning to be incorporated into national policies. Joint research was undertaken by academic institutions and industry, too, in the Netherlands[21] and the UK.[22]

Much of this research in the UK and elsewhere focused on the minutiae of ecodesign practice, adopting a systems approach either to the individual product or product system, or to industry as a whole. This included life cycle models which charted energy and material flow through a product system from "cradle to grave" or "womb to tomb," and there was a proliferation of flowcharts and circular diagrams. This was related to the new interdisciplinary subject of industrial ecology, "a framework for conceptualizing environmental and technical issues" which could help to inform the implementation of ecodesign or DFE (Design for the Environment).[23] Industrial ecology, like LCA [life cycle assessment], is closely modeled on ecological systems:

> Industrial ecology is meant as a conceptual tool emulating models derived from natural ecosystems, aimed at developing fundamentally new approaches to the industrial system reorganization.[24]

This attempt to draw upon ecological models to analyze product or industrial systems has proven very useful, since it is a way of containing the complexities of an environmental approach to design within limits by defining the boundaries of a system. But it does present some problems. It tends to be technocentric in that it embodies a belief in objective, value-free, scientific evidence; whereas, like EIA (Environmental

Impact Assessment) or COBA (Cost Benefit Analysis), it clearly involves value judgments. Only by "scoping," that is concentrating on key areas of environmental impact, can LCA, for example, be at all manageable. Otherwise, the detailed analysis would include a huge amount of data and take years to complete. Selectivity inevitably introduces an element of bias, and what is excluded from the debate may be as important as what is included. A recent study of 132 LCA schemes found that they did not share a common methodology, and that they tended to support the views of the company which sponsored them.[25] A more fundamental issue is that certain kinds of ecological models are being borrowed from ecological science as if they were absolutes, whereas, in fact, a closer look at the history and development of ecology reveals a range of methods, approaches, and philosophies.

There is no real consensus on whether ecology is a science or a philosophy, even though the term "ecology" was coined in the mid-19th century by Ernst Haeckel to refer to a new sub-branch of biology concerned with the relationship between living organisms and their surroundings. For him, it had social and political implications, too.[26] In the 20th century, ecological science can be roughly divided into two main phases. In the period up to about 1960, it was based on the idea of homeostasis and ecological balance. The concept of the ecosystem was developed by Tansley, Odum, and others. This has been described as the "ecology of the machine age," and is still based largely on the mechanistic beliefs of 19th century science.[27] By contrast, the new ecology which developed from the 1970s onwards rejected the idea of nature as a balanced system, and emphasized instead the disequilibrium of natural systems. Linked as it was with chaos and complexity theory, it revolutionized the concept of nature which was now seen to consist of unpredictable, dynamic, evolving, self-adaptive systems.[28]

In many respects, the ecodesign studies referred to above are based more on the first kind of ecology than on the second, and reflect a mechanistic view of the world. The new ecology of chaos and complexity throws the whole basis of the inquiry into dispute. In a pragmatic sense, designing systems or products based on a mechanistic mode would be doomed to failure if the real world does not, in fact, work like that. The old dogma that the modeling of ecosystems is an exact science appears to have been shattered.[29] This raises the problem of the nature of the evidence culled from ecological science. Not only does the long-term nature of ecological research make it difficult to produce the hard and fast evidence called for by environmentalists, policymakers – and now designers – but recent ecology presents a dynamic picture of unpredictable chaos-like successions which contradict the classical models of stability and homeostasis.[30] The implication of chaos and complexity theory for ecodesign are not yet clear, but it does seem to suggest that an incremental approach is difficult because small changes can trigger gigantic impacts. The study of complex adaptive systems also implies a new model of design, one that is more modest and relational.[31]

There is a further implication of recent ecological thinking for design. Edward Goldsmith contrasts an ecological world-view with the modernist world-view of industrial society, which is:

> . . . methodically substituting the technosphere or the surrogate world of human artifacts for the biosphere – or the *real* world of living things – from which the former derives its resources and to which it consigns its waste products. . . .

This suggests a different version of ecological design because to reverse this process means rethinking priorities and changing fundamental attitudes including phasing out unnecessary products, reversing the process whereby luxuries are turned into needs, living with less, and working with the natural system.[32] Under the impact of such thinking, and that of the Gaia Hypothesis[33] and the Permaculture Movement,[34] a new model of a radical, dark green, sustainable lifestyle has begun to emerge but this has, so far, been only partially reflected in ecodesign – in the EDA, for instance. There are some signs that such ideas are beginning to have an impact on more mainstream ecodesign. In 1993, the O2 Group, for example, held a conference called "Striking Visions" to create visions of sustainable lifestyles, taking a long-term view of the changes in attitudes needed to bring this about, and how design can make a new consumerless world palatable and even enjoyable.[35] This was reflected in a shift in the discussion about ecological design and a move toward the idea of "sustainable" or "global" design.

Sustainable design

Sustainability is not a new concept. It is an ecological term that has been used since the early 1970s to mean: "the capacity of a system to maintain a continuous flow of whatever each part of that system needs for a healthy existence,"[36] and when applied to ecosystems containing human beings refers to the limitations imposed by the ability of the biosphere to absorb the effects of human activities. The term sustainable development was first used in the early '80s, but was popularized by the Brundtland Report of 1987.[37] "Sustainable" has become the buzzword of the '90s in the same way "green" was in the '80s, and is equally open to different interpretations and misuse. The Brundtland Report adopted a global perspective on the consumption of energy and resources, and emphasized the imbalance between rich and poor parts of the world, arguing that: "Sustainable development requires that those who are more affluent adopt lifestyles within the planet's ecological means."[38] However, because the report also argued that economic growth or development is still possible as long as it is *green* growth, this has been interpreted by many to endorse a "business as usual" approach, with just a nod in the direction of environmental protection. This ignores the real meaning of sustainable development, which is enshrined in the widely quoted concept of "futurity": . . . "meeting the needs of the present without compromising the ability of future generations to meet their own needs."[39]

When applied to design, this not only introduces – or reintroduces – the ideas of ethical and social responsibility, but also the notion of time and timescale. Thinking about the life cycle of products through time, and considerations about design for recycling, have led to the concept of DfD – Design for Disassembly – followed by the idea of going *Beyond Recycling*[40] towards the design of longlife, durable products. These two concepts are not as contradictory as they sound, as Victor Papanek has recently remarked: "To design durable goods for eventual disassembly may sound like an oxymoron, yet it is profoundly important in a sustainable world."[41]

The term "sustainable design" has begun to be used in the last year or so to refer to a broader, longer-term vision of ecodesign. At the Centre for Sustainable Design, established at the Surrey Institute of Art and Design in July 1995, sustainable design means "analyzing and changing the 'systems' in which we make, use, and dispose of products," as opposed to more limited, short-term DFE.[42] The ECO2 group makes a similar distinction between "green design, project-based, single issue and relatively short-term; and 'sustainable' design, which is system-based, long-term" ethical design.[43] Emma Dewberry and Phillip Goggin have also explored the distinctions between ecodesign and sustainable design; arguing that, whereas ecodesign can be applied to all products and used as a suitable guide for designing at product level: "The concept of sustainable design, however, is much more complex and moves the interface of design outwards toward societal conditions, development, and ethics. . . ."[44] This suggests changes in design and the role of design, including an inevitable move from a product to a systems-based approach, from hardware to software, from ownership to service, and will involve concepts such as dematerialization and "a general shift from physiological to psychological needs." Finally, they emphasize the extent to which consumption patterns must change, and refer to the inequality between developed and developing nations, the fact that 20 percent of the world's population consumes 80 percent of the world's resources and conclude that ecodesign does fit into a global move toward sustainability, but has many limitations in this context.[45] This is the point made by Gui Bonsiepe, who has expressed the fear that ecological design will remain the luxury of the affluent countries while "the cost of environmental standards would be shifted onto the shoulders of the Third World."[46]

This raises the other dimensions of sustainable development: "Equity," meeting the needs of all, and "Participation," effective citizen involvement in decision-making, without which global sustainable growth would be impossible – except by an unacceptable form of "ecofascism." These issues are only just being raised in design circles, but were explored in detail recently by the WorldWatch Institute in reports on global resources and consumption patterns. In *How Much is Enough? The Consumer Society and the Future of the Earth*, Alan Durning divides the world population into three consumption classes and analyzes their consumption of food, transport, and goods, concluding that environmental destruction results from the overconsumption of the top one-fifth of the world's population and from the poverty of the bottom one-fifth. He asks if there is a level of sufficiency for all the world's population, a level above poverty and subsistence but below the affluent consumer lifestyle, that is sustainable. The answer is a shift from the "cultivation of needs" to "a culture of permanence": "substituting local foods for grain-fed meat and packaged fare, switching from cars to bikes and buses, and replacing throwaways with durable goods."[47] This obviously implies a new agenda for design, and this is beginning to be discussed in the UNEP Working Group on Sustainable Product Development which was started in January 1994 as a follow-up initiative to the Rio Conference of 1992. It is a network of 360 people in 40 countries all over the world, including 18 from developing and transitional countries. The Research Programme is based on the principles of sustainable development:

> The very concept of "sustainability" underlies our fear for the next generation's future, and forces the question; is a harmonious balance between their product demands and the earth's ecology possible and how can it be sustained?[48]

Products are redefined in terms of categories such as "service" (transport "pool," rented products), "dematerialization" (virtual libraries, teleworking systems), as well as life cycle design and longevity. But perhaps even more interesting is the focus on "Products, Services and Systems that Meet Human Needs," and which can lead to an improvement in living and working conditions. Areas of "need" to be explored include transportation, communication, heating, cooling, clothing and textiles, and the use of water by the end-consumer.[49] This shift of emphasis from the products to the needs reintroduces an important theme from the 1970s, that of "Design for Need,"[50] and, in many ways, sustainable design has come back full circle to some of the radical design theories of the 1970s.

Conclusion

Thus, ecological design, as it has developed over the last decade, has reinvented some old ideas and produced some new ones. It has gone through a process of maturity, moving toward a deepening of understanding of environmental issues and a darker shade of green. It has become increasingly evident that the radical nature of an ecological approach to design implies a new design critique. In the 1980s, this was not necessarily apparent when green was the flavor, or rather the color, of the month and it seemed that green design would comfortably settle down into the mainstream of design industrial practice. In the 1990s, the oppositional nature of ecological design is more apparent, since even fairly pragmatic attempts to apply ecological principles to design seem to inevitably challenge existing practices and ideologies.

Designers and design critics are increasingly emphasizing the actual or, potentially, radical nature of an ecological approach to design which implies a new critique – a recognition of the fact that to adopt an ecological approach to design is, by definition, to question and oppose the status quo. Ezio Manzini, for example, has described this as a shift from the "normalized ecological design" of the 1980s to the "new radicalism" of the '90s, which increasingly recognizes that ecological design necessitates changes in lifestyles that challenge the current global model of development.[51] In a similar way, Tony Fry argues that ecodesign is the means by which industrial culture can be remade, and that the need to change basic values can only be achieved "by design so long as design itself is redesigned." He is critical of existing ecodesign theory and practice, but postulates a potentially radical ecodesign which could create a new direction for design.[52] From a different perspective, Gui Bonsiepe has also recently critically evaluated ecodesign. Although a new environmental ethic implies a new design ethic, he says, ecodesign, in theory and practice, has not yet developed enough to have created a new paradigm for industrial design. However:

> The unquestionable merit of ecodesign consists in having articulated concerns which put into question paradigms of design and industrial production and consumption that we took for granted.[53]

These issues may be new to design in the 1990s but, within the environmental literature, there has been a constant discussion since the 1960s of the extent to which an ecological world-view represents a new paradigm requiring a fundamental challenge to industrial society, or merely a minor modification of existing values and practices, and a debate over the degree of change required to overcome the current ecological crisis. That such issues are now being taken seriously within the design field – more so than the 1970s – suggests a shift in attitudes which will have far-reaching consequences for design criticism. During the last few decades, design criticism has followed design practice and has been dominated by a nonecological approach, tending to view consumerism as having positive economic and social value, and thereby endorsing the kind of industrial culture under attack by Greens. Only now, in the wake of discussions of ecological design theory and practice, is an ecological design criticism beginning to emerge.

Notes

The author would like to thank Gui Bonsiepe, Tony Fry, Philip Goggin, and especially Harry Sutcliffe for their help on the preparation of this article.

1   Evelyn Möller, "Design-Philosophie der 80er Jahre(2). Kommit mit dem Ende der Wegwerf-Ideologie ein Ökologischer Funktionalismus?" *Form* 98 (1982) and *Unternehmen Pro Umwelt. Ansätze ganzheitlichen Denkens in Politik and Wirtschaft Architektur Produktionentwikklung and Design* (Munich: Lexika, 1989). In the Netherlands at this time, 1984–5, the Advisory Council for Research on Nature and the Environment was promoting research into product design: J. C. Van Weenen, C. A. Bakker, and I. V. de Keijser. *Eco-design: An Exploration of the Environment* (Milieukunde: Universiteit van Amsterdam, 1991).

2   *The Green Designer* (London: Design Council, 1986), 4.

3   For example, Paul Burall, *Green Design* (London: Green Council, 1990) and Dorothy Mackenzie, *Green Design, Design for the Environment* (London: Lawrence King, 1991).

4   T. O'Riordan, *Environmentalism* (London: Pion Ltd., 1976).

5   Deep ecology was first developed by the Norwegian philosopher Arne Naess in the early 1970s. See Arne Naess, "The Shallow and the Deep, Long-range Ecology Movement. A Summary," *Inquiry* 16 (1973) and special issue of *The Ecologist* on Deep Ecology: "Rethinking Man and Nature: Towards an Ecological World View," 188, no. 415 (1988).

6   John Button, *Green Pages: A Directory of Natural Products, Services, Resources and Ideas* (London: Optima, 1988).

7   Keystone Architects, statement at the EDA exhibition, London Ecology Centre, 1990. Hartwin Busch "Building Biology: Towards a New Era of Healthy Building," *Caduceus* 7 (1989).

8   Sandy Irvine, *Beyond Green Consumerism* (London: Friends of the Earth, 1989).

9   Sandy Irvine and Alec Ponton, *A Green Manifesto: Politics for a Green Future* (London: Optima, 1989).

10   James Robertson, *Future Wealth: A New Economics for the 21st Century* (London: Cassell, 1989), 9.

11   *New Consumer Review* (Newcastle, England: New Consumer, 1991).

12   Michael Peters Brand Development Division and Diagnostic Market Research Ltd., *Green, Greener, Greenest: The Green Consumer in the UK, Netherlands and Germany* (September 1989).

13   Richard Adams, Jane Carruthers, and Sean Hamil, *Changing Corporate Values: A Guide to Social and Environmental Policy and Practice in Britain's Top Companies* (Newcastle: Kogan Page, 1990), x.

14   John Button, *A Dictionary of Green Ideas: Vocabulary for a Sane and Sustainable Future* (London: Routledge, 1988), 139–142.

15   EDA leaflet (London, 1990).

16   EcoDesign Foundation, *NewsLines* 1 (Sept. 1991): 4.

17   Chris Ryan, "From EcoRedesign to Ecodesign," *EcoDesign* IV, no. 1 (1996).

18   Anne-Marie Willis, "Echoes of EcoDesign 1," EcoDesign Foundation Newsletter (Sydney, Dec. 1991): 2.

19   J. C. Van Weenen, C. A. Bakker, and I. V. de Keijser, *Eco-Design: An Exploration of the Environment* (Milieukunde, The Netherlands: Universiteit van Amsterdam, 1991). Delegates included Dorothy Mackenzie, Ezio Manzini, and Chris Ryan.

20   "Eco-Design Initiatives Gather Momentum," *ENDS Report* 231 (April 1994): 29.

21   In the Netherlands, there was discussion of a formal system to put products through a green filter and a team of designers and environmental experts at the TNO Product Centre, Delft Technical University studied eight product systems in terms of material and energy use, and suggested ways in which manufacturers could improve them. Harry te Riele and Albert Zweers, *Eco-design: Acht vorbeelden van milieugerichte produkt-ontwikkeling* (Delft: Delft Technical University, 1994).

22   In the UK, a Eureka ecodesign seminar was organized by the Royal Society of Arts in March in 1994 on the telecommunications industry. This provided a forum for all those researching into ecodesign, LCA, innovation, and the strategy of firms, notably at the Institute for Advanced Studies, Manchester Metropolitan University and the Design Innovation Group at the Open University.

23   Brad Allenby (AT&T), "Sustainable Development, Industrial Ecology, and Design for the Environment," White paper no. 10 (June 1993).

24   Silvia Pizzacaro, "Theoretical Approaches to Industrial Ecology: Status and Perspectives," international seminar "The Scenario of Sustainability: The Systemic Context" (Milan, April 1994): 1.

25   "Critical Review of LCA Practice," *ENDS Report* 219 (April 1994).

26   Anna Bramewell, *Ecology in the Twentieth Century: A History* (New Haven: Yale University Press, 1989). A good example of the word "ecology" being used in a general philosophical or political sense.

27   Daniel B. Botkin, *Discordant Harmonies: A New Ecology of the 21st Century* (New York: OUP, 1990).

28   See Donald Worster, *Nature's Economy: A History of Ecological Ideas*, 2nd edition (Cambridge: Cambridge University Press, 1994) and Richard Huggett, "Nature's Design: The Ecologist's View," a paper originally intended to be given at the "Eco-Design" conference held in the Department of Philosophy. University of Manchester in October 1995. I would like to acknowledge how much this interesting, interdisciplinary conference has influenced my recent thinking on ecology and ecodesign, especially papers by John Wood, James Cullen, and Richard Huggett (whose paper was circulated to delegates afterward).

29   See, for example, John Harte, "Ecosystem Stability and Diversity," in Stephen H. Schneider and Penelope J. Boston, eds., *Scientists on Gaia* (Cambridge: MIT Press, 1991).

30   I. G. Simmons, *Interpreting Nature: Cultural Constructions of the Environment* (London: Routledge, 1993).

31   A point made by John Wood at the Eco-Design conference in Manchester, October 1995. The Santa Fe Institute in the USA, home of complexity theory, began to look at global sustainability in the early '90s, and suggested that the study of complex adaptive systems implied a new model. Sustainable human society is an interconnected system in which economic, social, and political forces are deeply intertwined and mutually dependent on each other. Thus, a sustainable human society cannot be achieved by rational methods and technical fixes, but only by the transformation of traditional attitudes and appetites. M. Mitchell Waldrop, *Complexity: The Emerging Science at the Edge of Order & Chaos* (New York: Viking, 1992).

32   Edward Goldsmith, *The Ecologist* 188, no. 415 (1988): 118, and *The Way: An Ecological World View*, 2nd edition (London: Green Books, 1996); *De-Industrializing Society* (London: *The Ecologist*, 1988).

33   Gaia, the earth-goddess, is the name given by scientist James Lovelock to his hypothesis that the earth is like a super, self-regulating organism. Gaia has become a potent symbol in the last few years because it provides a planetary perspective on the current ecological crisis. See James Lovelock, *Gaia: A New Look at Life on Earth* (Oxford & New York: OUP, 1987) and *The Ages of Gaia: A Biography of Our Living Earth*, 2nd edition (Oxford & New York: OUP, 1995).

34   Permaculture (*perma*nent agri*culture* or *perma*nent *culture*) is a total design system based on the functional zoning of a site in a series of concentric circles according to frequency of use, and brings together the design of dwellings, animal husbandry and edible landscaping, and community building. There is little reference to the contents of the innermost zone, the dwelling, but permaculture implies a radical rethinking of products and services, too. Permaculture has been one of the fastest growing organizations within the green movement in the

1980s and '90s — it is the equivalent of the alternative technology movement of the '70s. See Mollison, *Permaculture: A Designer's Manual* (Tagari: Tyalgum, Australia: 1988).

35   "Striking Visions," O2 Event (Netherlands, Nov. 1993) organized by the Dutch O2 group. O2 was founded by the Danish designer Niels Peter Flint as an international organization of environmentally aware industrial designers.

36   John Button, *Dictionary of Green Ideas*, 446.

37   World Commission on Environment and Development, *Our Common Future* (Oxford: OUP, 1987).

38   Ibid., 9.

39   Ibid., 8.

40   Tim Cooper, *Beyond Recycling: The Longer Life Option* (London: New Economics Foundation, 1994).

41   Victor Papanek, "Eco-logic," *Ecodesign* III, no. I (1994): 10. Discussed in his recent book, *The Green Imperative: Ecology and Ethic in Design and Architecture* (London: Thames & Hudson, 1995).

42   Anne Chick, "MA in Sustainable Design," Centre for Sustainable Design leaflet, 1995.

43   ECO2 group, "Hierarchy of EcoProducts in Strategies," workshop on defining ecodesign, Nov. 1994.

44   Emma Dewberry and Phillip Goggin, "Ecodesign & Beyond: Steps towards 'Sustainability' " (Open University and Nottingham Trent University, Nov. 1994): 7–8; and Emma Dewberry, "Ecodesign Strategies," *EcoDesign* IV, no. I (1996), in which she distinguishes between green design, ecodesign, and global design approaches and company initiatives.

45   Dewberry and Goggin, "Ecodesign & Beyond."

46   Gui Bonsiepe, "North/South: Environment/Design," *Inca* 14. Gui Bonsiepe, formerly of the *Hochschule fur Gestaltung*, Ulm, until recently has been living and working in Latin America since the 1970s, and so he is in a good position to view the situation from a "south" perspective.

47   Alan Thein Durning. *How Much is Enough? The Consumer Society and the Future of the Earth* (London: Earthscan, 1992), 109. See also John E. Young and Aaron Sachs, *The Next Efficiency Revolution: Creating a Sustainable Materials Economy* (Worldwatch Paper 121, 1994). Peter Harper of the Centre for Alternative Technology, Wales, has been working along the same lines, and has made an interesting analysis of the acceptability of putative "eco-technology" and lifestyle changes. He has classified possible response from light to dark green in "The L-Word: A.T. and Lifestyles," *Proceedings of AT2000: A Conference on Alternative Technology for the 21st Century* (Milton Keynes: Open University, 1994).

48   United Nations Working Group on Sustainable Product Design News Fax (August 11, 1995): 1.

49   Ibid., 2, 3. See also Yorick Benjamin, senior researcher, "Sustainable Product Development," *EcoDesign* IV, no. 196.

50   "Design for Need" was the name of an ICSID (International Council for Societies of Industrial Design) conference held at the Royal College of Art in 1976. See J. Bicknell and L. McOuiston, eds., *Design for Need: The Social Contribution of Design* (Oxford: Pergamon Press, 1977).

51   Ezio Manzini, "Prometheus of the Everyday: The Ecology of the Artificial and the Designer's Responsibility," *Design Issues* 9, no. 11 (Fall 1992): 5 and "Design, Environment, and Social Quality: From 'Existenzminimum' to Quality Maximum," *Design Issues* 10, no. 1 (Spring 1994).

52   Tony Fry, *Remarkings. Ecology. Design. Philosophy* (Sydney: Envirobook, 1994), 9, 11–12.

53   Gui Bonsiepe, "North/South Environment/Design," *Inca*, a publication of the San Francisco Chapter of the Industrial Designer's Society of America (August 1992).

Chapter 6

Hal Foster

THE ABCS OF CONTEMPORARY
DESIGN [2001]

Source: Hal Foster (2002a) 'The ABCs of Contemporary Design', *October*, 100, pp. 191–9.

Hal Foster is an important critical voice within the field of modern and contemporary art. Combining a nuanced attentiveness to the art-object, with a sophisticated use of contemporary theory (psychoanalysis, for instance), Foster has rescued many artworks from the deadening grip of those who want their art history simply to supplement the intrinsic quality of art. As a historical scholar he has provided insightful accounts of surrealism and pop art, for instance. But it has been in his relationship with contemporary art that he has most vividly exhibited his critical panache. Initially he was one of the few writers who maintained a commitment to critical evaluation (the evaluation of art's critical potential) while also enthusiastically championing many aspects of postmodern art. Later (along with some of his colleagues from the journal *October*) he worked to resuscitate the potential of artistic avant-gardism (or neo-avant-gardism, as postwar avant-gardism has been dubbed) as a critical heritage that contemporary art could draw on.

The text here was written by Foster as a glossary that could accompany his book *Design and Crime (and Other Diatribes)*. Foster's turn towards design has to be seen within the context of his other work: for Foster the contemporary moment of 'design' partly signifies the historical victory of capitalist culture and the defeat of the critical possibilities of postmodernism and the neo-avant-garde. Thus if artists and designers in the early twentieth century could imagine a utopia in which the artist-designer-worker would participate in a full life where art was lived and life was art, then the present moment can be seen as the degraded realisation of this:

> The old project to reconnect Art and Life, endorsed in different ways by Art Nouveau, the Bauhaus, and many other movements, was eventually accomplished, but according to the spectacular dictates of the culture industry, not the liberatory ambitions of the avant-garde. And a primary form of this perverse reconciliation in our time is design.
>
> (Foster 2002b: 19)

The contemporary shopping mall is the tawdry overcoming of a division between art and life: it was Coca-Cola not constructivism that produced an actual revolution in everyday life.

Yet Foster is too much the dialectician to fall for the myth of the 'end of history' (the final victory of designer capitalism, achieved partly by rendering critical thinking unfashionable). This text then is also an urgent plea for the return of critical reflection in the face of the indifferent but shiny surfaces provided by capitalism. If critical reflection is out of date in some quarters then this is all to the good: it is the outmoded (in technology, in theory and in cultural practice) that will offer 'running room' (a strategic space, momentarily beyond the grip of instrumentalism) for critical thought. Critical reflection, in this sense, is always out of date, precisely because it names the effort required to resist the seductions of fashion.

Further reading: Acland 2007; Foster 2002b; Jameson 1998; Loos 1987.

Autonomy: Aesthetic autonomy is the notion that culture is a sphere apart, with each art distinct, and it is a bad word for most of us raised on postmodernist interdisciplinarity. We tend to forget that autonomy is always provisional, always defined diacritically and situated politically, always *semi*. Enlightenment thinkers advocated political autonomy in order to challenge the vested interests of the *ancien régime*, while modernist artists advocated aesthetic autonomy in order to resist illustrational meanings and commercial forces. Like "essentialism," then, "autonomy" is a bad word, but it may not always be a bad strategy, especially at a moment when postmodernist interdisciplinarity has become routine: call it "strategic autonomy."

Bonaventura: In his seminal analysis of postmodern space, "The Cultural Logic of Late Capitalism," Fredric Jameson used the vast atrium of the Bonaventura Hotel in Los Angeles designed by John Portman as a symptom of a new kind of architectural sublime: a sort of hyper-space that deranges the human sensorium. Jameson took this spatial delirium as a particular instance of a general incapacity to comprehend the late capitalist universe, to map it cognitively. Strangely, what Jameson offered as a *critique* of postmodern culture many architects (Frank Gehry foremost among them) have taken as a *paragon*: the creation of extravagant spaces that work to overwhelm the subject, a neo-Baroque Sublime dedicated to the glory of the Corporation (which is the Church of our age). It is as if these architects designed not in contestation of "the cultural logic of late capitalism" but according to its specifications.

Carcassonne: Carcassonne is a tourist destination in southern France, a medieval *cité* replete with château, church, and fortifications. Viollet-le-Duc restored its towers and turrets in the nineteenth century, and the site retains an unreal sheen: it is a historical town turned into a theme park, with its walls whitened and capped like TV-star teeth. At least Americans make their Disneylands from scratch, or they once did so. More and more this Carcassonnization – the canonization of the urban carcass – is at work in American cities as well. For example, the cast-iron buildings of SoHo now gleam with the shine of artifacts-become-commodities. Like Viollet-le-Duc, developers undertake these face-lifts in the name of historical preservation, but the purpose is financial aggrandizement. And like victims of cosmetic surgery, these facades may mask historical age but advance mnemonic decay.

Design: Today everything – from architecture and art to jeans and genes – is treated as so much design. Those old heroes of industrial modernism, the artist-as-engineer and the author-as-producer, are long gone, and the postindustrial designer now rules supreme. Today you don't have to be filthy rich to be designer and designed in one – whether the product in question is your home or business, your sagging face (designer surgery) or lagging personality (designer drugs), your historical memory (designer museum), or DNA future (designer children). Might this "designed subject" of consumerism be the unintended offspring of the "constructed subject" of postmodernism? One thing seems clear: today design abets a near-perfect circuit of production and consumption.

Environment: The world of total design is an old dream of modernism, but it only comes true, in perverse form, in our pan-capitalist present. With post-Fordist production, commodities can be tweaked and markets niched, so that a product can be mass in quantity yet appear personal in address. Desire is not only registered in products today, but is specified there: a self-interpellation is performed in catalogs and on-line almost automatically. In large part it is this perpetual profiling of the commodity that drives the contemporary inflation of design. Yet what happens when this commodity-machine breaks down, as markets crash, sweatshop workers resist, or environments give out?

Finitude: An early version of total design was advanced in Art Nouveau, with its will to ornament. This *Style 1900* found its great nemesis in Adolf Loos, who attacked it in several texts. One attack took the form of an allegorical skit about "a poor little rich man" who commissioned a designer to put "art in each and every thing": "The architect has forgotten nothing, absolutely nothing. Cigar ashtrays, cutlery, light switches — everything, everything was made by him." This *Gesamtkunstwerk* did more than combine art, architecture, and craft; it commingled subject and object: "the individuality of the owner was expressed in every ornament, every form, every nail." For the Art Nouveau designer the result is perfection: "You are complete!" he exults to the owner. But the owner is not so sure; rather than a sanctuary from modern stress, he sees his Art Nouveau interior as another instance of it. "The happy man suddenly felt deeply, deeply unhappy. . . . He was precluded from all future living and striving, developing and desiring. He thought, this is what it means to learn to go about life with one's own corpse. Yes indeed. He is finished. *He is complete!*" For the Art Nouveau designer such completion reunited art and life, with all signs of death banished. For Loos this triumphant overcoming of limits was a catastrophic loss of the same — the loss of the objective constraints required to define any "future living and striving, developing and desiring." Far from a transcendence of death, this loss of finitude was a death-in-life, living "with one's own corpse."

Gesamtkunstwerk: After September 11, metaphorical talk of corpses seems misbegotten, and confusions between art and life worse. Recall the remarks of Karlheinz Stockhausen on the World Trade Center attack: "What happened there is — they all have to rearrange their brains now — is the greatest work of art ever: that characters can bring about in one act what we in music cannot dream of, that people practice madly for ten years, completely, fanatically, for a concert and then die. That is the greatest work of art for the whole of the cosmos. I could not do that. Against that we composers are nothing." Yet this reading of avant-gardism cannot be simply disavowed: with the simplest means the terrorists rocked our symbolic order like nothing before. But this reading also reveals the grave problem of such avant-gardism: here its confusion of art and life abets a conflation between symbolic transgression and mass murder. It is long past time to forego crypto-fascist ideas of sublimity.

High-Rise: In *Delirious New York* (1978), a "retrospective manifesto for Manhattan," Rem Koolhaas published an old, tinted postcard of the city skyline from the early 1930s. It presents the Empire State, Chrysler, and other landmark buildings of the time with a visionary twist — a dirigible set to dock at the spire of the Empire State. It is an image of the twentieth-century city as a spectacle of new tourism, to be sure, but also as a utopia of new spaces — of people free to circulate from the street, through the tower, to the sky, and back down again. (The image is not strictly capitalist: the utopian conjunction of skyscraper and airship appears in revolutionary Russian designs of the 1920s as well.) The attack on the World Trade Center — the two jets flown into the two towers — was a dystopian perversion of this modernist dream of free movement through cosmopolitan space. Much damage was done to this great vision of the skyscraper city — and to New York as the capital of this old dream.

Indiscipline: Several of these notes circle around a single thesis: contemporary design is part of a greater revenge taken by advanced capitalism on postmodernist culture — a recouping of its crossings of arts and disciplines, a routinization of its transgressions. We know that autonomy, even semi-autonomy, is a fiction, but periodically this fiction is useful, even necessary, as it was at the high-modernist moment of Loos and company one hundred years ago. Periodically, too, it can become repressive, even deadening, as it was a few decades ago when late modernism had petrified into medium-specificity and postmodernism promised an interdisciplinary opening. But this is no longer our situation. It is time to recapture a sense of the political situatedness of both autonomy and its transgression, a sense of the historical dialectic of disciplinarity and its contestation.

Jewel Box: No term is more important to modern architecture than "transparency." For Siegfried Giedion this transparency was predicated on technologies such as steel and glass and ferro-concrete that allowed a thorough exposition of architectural space. For Lázlo Moholy-Nagy, it allowed architecture in turn to integrate the different transparencies of other mediums, such as photography and film. Less concerned with space than light, Moholy saw this integration as fundamental to the "new vision" of modernist culture in general. Yet this vision did not fare well after the war. In "Transparency: Literal and Phenomenal" (1963), Colin Rowe and Robert Slutzky devalued literal in favor of phenomenal transparency, in which "Cubist" surfaces "interpenetrate without optical destruction of each other." This revaluation marked the moment when, once more, articulation of surface became as important as that of space, and the understanding of skin as important as that of structure. In other words, it marked the discursive advent of postmodern architecture in its two principal versions: first, architecture as a scenographic surface of symbols (as in pastiche postmodernism from Robert Venturi on) and, later, architecture as an autonomous transformation of forms (as in deconstructivist postmodernism from Peter Eisenman on). Today many prominent architects, such as Koolhaas, Herzog and de Meuron, and Richard Gluckman, do not fit neatly into either camp: they hold on to literal transparency even as they elaborate phenomenal transparency with projective skins and luminous scrims. Sometimes, however, these skins and scrims only dazzle or confuse, and the architecture becomes an illuminated sculpture, a radiant jewel. It can be beautiful, but it can also be spectacular in the negative sense used by Guy Debord – a kind of commodity-fetish on a grand scale, a mysterious object whose production is mystified.

Kool House: "This architecture relates to the forces of the *Großstadt* [the metropolis] like a surfer to the waves," Koolhaas once remarked of the skyscrapers of Manhattan. With his recent interventions in the global city, the same might be said of his own architecture, and it might not sound like praise. What does it mean for an architect to surf the *Großstadt* today – to perfect its curve, to extend its trajectory? Even if an architect is empowered enough to make the attempt, can he or she do more than crash on the beach?

Life Style: In *Life Style* (2000), a compendium of his work, Canadian designer Bruce Mau asks us to think design as "life style" in the philosophical sense of the Greeks, Nietzsche, or Foucault, that is, as an ethics. But the style of *Life Style* is closer in spirit to Martha Stewart – a folding of the "examined life" into the "designed life." Such style does not boost our "character," as *Life Style* claims; rather, it aids the contemporary conflation of the realization of self with the consumption of identity.

Mediation: "Mediation" used to mean the critical attempt to think the totality of the social world beyond its fragmentation and disconnection. Now it tends to refer to a social world given over to electronic media – and to an economic world retooled around digitizing and computing. In this mediation, the commodity is no longer an object to be produced so much as a datum to be manipulated – designed and redesigned, consumed and reconsumed. This is another reason why design is inflated today, to the point where it is no longer a secondary industry. Perhaps we should speak of a "political economy of design."

Nobrow: One aspect of this mediated world is a merging of culture and marketing. For some commentators this has effected a new kind of "nobrow" culture in which the old distinctions of highbrow, middlebrow, and lowbrow no longer apply. For fans of this development "nobrow" is not a dumbing down of intellectual culture so much as a wising up to commercial culture, which becomes a source of status in its own right. Today, this argument runs, we are all in the same "megastore," only in different aisles, and that is a good thing – that is democracy. Yet this is a conflation of democracy with consumption, a conflation that underwrites the principal commodity on sale in this marketplace: the fantasy that class divisions are thereby resolved. This fantasy is the contemporary complement to the foundational myth of the United States: that such divisions never existed here in the first place. This delusion allows millions of Americans to vote against their class interests at least every four years.

Outmoded: "The older media, not designed for mass production, take on a new timeliness: that of exemption and of improvisation. They alone could outflank the united front of trusts and technology." So writes Theodor Adorno in *Minima Moralia* (1951) on the critical use of outmoded media in a capitalist context of ceaseless obsolescence. Here, of course, Adorno draws on Walter Benjamin, for whom "the outmoded" was a central concern. "Balzac was the first to speak of the ruins of the bourgeoisie," Benjamin wrote in his *Arcades Project*. "But only Surrealism exposed them to view. The development of the forces of production reduced the wish symbols of the previous century to rubble even before the monuments representing them had crumbled." The "wish symbols" in question are the capitalist wonders of the nineteenth-century bourgeoisie at the height of its confidence, such as "the arcades and interiors, the exhibitions and panoramas." These structures fascinated the Surrealists nearly a century later – when further capitalist development had turned them into "residues of a dream world" or, again, "rubble even before the monuments which represented them had crumbled." For the Surrealists to haunt these outmoded spaces, according to Benjamin, was to tap "the revolutionary energies" that were trapped there. But it is less utopian to say simply that the Surrealists registered the mnemonic signals encrypted in these structures – signals that might not otherwise have reached the present. This deployment of the outmoded can query the totalist assumptions of capitalist culture, and its claim to be timeless; it can also remind this culture of its own wish symbols, and its own forfeited dreams of liberty, equality, and fraternity. Can this mnemonic dimension of the outmoded still be mined today, or is the outmoded now outmoded too – another device of fashion?

Post-Fordism: The object world of modern cities was born of a Fordist economy that was relatively fixed: factories and warehouses, skyscrapers and bridges, railways and highways. However, as our economy has become more post-Fordist, capital has flowed ever more rapidly in search of cheap labor, innovative manufacture, financial deregulation, and new markets; and the life expectancy of many buildings has fallen dramatically. (Many cities are now hybrids of the two economies, with Fordist structures often retrofitted to post-Fordist needs.) This process is pronounced in the United States, of course, but it is rapacious where development is even less restricted. "His task is truly impossible," Koolhaas writes of the architect in this condition, "to express increasing turbulence in a stable medium." In a post-Fordist context, what can the criteria of architecture be?

Quarantine: For Koolhaas, the skyscraper is the crux of the "culture of congestion" of the old Manhattan, and he sees it as a mating of two emblematic forms – "the needle" and "the globe." The needle grabs "attention," while the globe promises "receptivity," and "the history of Manhattanism is a dialectic between these two forms." Since September 11 the discursive frame of this Manhattanism has shifted. New fears cling to the skyscraper as a terrorist target, and the values of "attention" and "receptivity" are rendered suspicious. The same holds for the values of congestion and "delirious space"; they are overshadowed by calls for surveillance and "defensible space." In short, the "urbanistic ego" and cultural diversity that Koolhaas celebrates in *Delirious New York* are under enormous pressure. They need advocates like never before; for, to paraphrase the Surrealists, New York Beauty will be delirious or will not be.

Running-Room: As much as interdisciplinarity is crucial to cultural practice, so too are distinctions, as

Karl Kraus insisted in 1912: "Adolf Loos and I – he literally and I linguistically – have done nothing more than show that there is a distinction between an urn and a chamber pot and that it is this distinction above all that provides culture with running-room [*Spielraum*]. The others, the positive ones [i.e., those who fail to make this distinction], are divided into those who use the urn as a chamber pot and those who use the chamber pot as an urn." "Those who use the urn as a chamber pot" were Art Nouveau designers who wanted to infuse art (the urn) into the utilitarian object (the chamber pot). Those who did the reverse were functionalist modernists who wanted to elevate the utilitarian object into art. For Kraus the two mistakes were symmetrical – both confused use-value and art-value – and both risked a regressive indistinction: they failed to safeguard "the running-room" necessary to liberal subjectivity and culture. Note that nothing is said about a natural "essence" of art, or an absolute "autonomy" of culture; the stake is simply one of "distinctions" and "running-room," of proposed differences and provisional spaces.

Spectacle: Clearly architecture has a new centrality in cultural discourse. Although this centrality stems from the initial debates about postmodernism in the 1970s, which were focused on architecture, it is clinched by the contemporary inflation of design and display in all sorts of spheres – art, fashion, business, and so on. Moreover, to make a big splash in the global pond of spectacle culture today, one has to have a big rock to drop, maybe as big as the Guggenheim Museum in Bilbao; and here architects like Gehry have an obvious advantage over artists in other media. In *The Society of the Spectacle* (1967), Debord defined spectacle as "capital accumulated to the point where it becomes an image." With Gehry and company the reverse is now true as well: spectacle is "an image accumulated to the point where it becomes capital." Such is the logic of many cultural centers today, as they are designed, alongside theme parks and sports complexes, to assist in the corporate "revival" of the city – that is, in its being made safe for shopping, spectating, and spacing out. This is the "Bilbao-Effect."

Tectonics: For all the futurism of the computer-assisted designs of architects like Gehry, his structures are often akin to the Statue of Liberty, with a separate skin hung over a hidden armature, and with exterior surfaces that rarely match up with interior spaces. With the putative passing of the industrial age, the structural transparency of modern architecture was declared outmoded, and now the Pop aesthetic of postmodern architecture looks dated as well. The search for the architecture of the computer age is on; ironically, however, it has led Gehry and followers to nineteenth-century sculpture as a model, at least in part. The disconnection between skin and structure represented by this academic model has two problematic effects. First, it can lead to strained spaces that are mistaken for a new kind of architectural sublime. Second, it can abet a further disconnection between building and site. I am not pleading for a return to structural transparency; I am simply cautioning against a new Potemkin architecture of conjured surfaces driven by computer design.

Unabombers: From the handler of the terrorist in *The Secret Agent* (1907), by Joseph Conrad: "Pay attention to what I say. The fetish of today is neither royalty nor religion. Therefore the palace and the church should be left alone. . . . A murderous attempt on a restaurant or a theatre would suffer . . . from the suggestion of a nonpolitical passion. . . . Of course there is art. A bomb in the National Gallery would make some noise. But it would not be serious enough. Art has never been their fetish. . . . But there is learning – science. Any imbecile that has got an income believes in that. He does not know why, but he believes it matters somehow. It is the sacrosanct fetish. . . . The whole civilized world has heard of Greenwich. . . . Yes, the blowing up of the first meridian is bound to raise a howl of execration." The terrorists of September 11 picked out our "fetishes of today" with precision: the architectures of "finance" and "defense."

Vernacular: Postmodern architecture pretended to revive vernacular forms, but for the most part it replaced them with commercial signs, and Pop images became as important as articulated space. In our design world, this development has reached a new level: now commodity-image and space are often melded through design. Designers strive for programs "in which brand identity, signage systems, interiors, and architecture would be totally integrated" (Bruce Mau). This integration depends on a deterritorializing of both image and space, which depends in turn on a digitizing of the photograph, its loosening from old referential ties, and on a computing of architecture, its loosening from old tectonic principles. As Deleuze and Guattari (let alone Marx) taught us long ago, this deterritorializing is the path of capital, not the avant-garde.

Without Qualities: Design is all about desire, but today this desire seems almost subject-less, or at least almost lack-less: design seems to advance a kind of narcissism that is all image and no interiority – an apotheosis of the subject that may be one with its disappearance. In our neo-Art Nouveau world of total design and Internet plenitude, the fate of "the poor little rich man" of Loos, "precluded from all future living and striving, developing and desiring," is on the verge of realization. Robert Musil, a Loos contemporary, also seemed to anticipate this *Style 2000* from the perspective of *Style 1900*. "A world of qualities without man has arisen," Musil wrote in *The Man Without Qualities* (1930–43), "of experiences without the person who experiences them, and it almost looks as though ideally private experience is a thing of the past, and that the friendly burden of personal responsibility is to dissolve into a system of formulas of possible meanings. Probably the dissolution of the anthropocentric point of view, which for such a long time considered man to be at the center of the universe but which has been fading for centuries, has finally arrived at the 'I' itself."

Xed: Two theoretical models structured critical studies of postwar art above all others: the oppositional logic of the "post-," of an interdisciplinary postmodernism opposed to a medium-specific modernism, and the recursive strategy of the "neo-," of a postwar neo-avant-garde that recovered the devices of the prewar avant-garde (e.g., the monochrome, the readymade, the collage). Today, however, these models are played out; neither suffices as a strong paradigm for practice, and no other model stands in their stead. For many this double demise is a good thing: it permits artistic diversity; "weak" theory is better than strong; and so on. But our paradigm-of-no-paradigm can also abet a stagnant incommensurability or a flat indifference, and this posthistorical default of contemporary art and architecture is no improvement on the old teleological projections of modernist practices. All of us (artists, critics, curators, *amateurs*) need some narrative to focus our practices – situated stories, not *grands récits*. Without this guide we are likely to remain swamped in the double wake of post/modernism and the neo/avant-garde.

Yahoos: . . .

Zebras: In American football the referees who wear striped shirts are derided as "zebras," but the game is difficult to play without them. Critics once had a similar status in the sports of art and architecture, but more and more often they are banished from the field. Over the last two decades a nexus of curators and collectors, dealers and clients has displaced the critic; for these managers of art and architecture critical evaluation, let alone theoretical analysis, is of no use. They deem the critic an obstruction, and actively shun him or her, as do many artists and architects. In this void returns the poet-critic who waxes on about Beauty as the moral subject of art and architecture, with Sensation held over as a fun sideshow, or who combines the two in a pop-libertarian aesthetic perfect for market rule. This development needs to be challenged, if it is not too late, and "running-room" secured wherever it can be found or made.

PART TWO

ACTORS AND AGENTS

INTRODUCTION TO PART TWO

THERE IS A SMALL, separate story within Thomas Pynchon's mega-sprawling novel *Gravity's Rainbow* called 'The Story of Byron the Bulb' (Pynchon 1973/2000: 766–76). Byron is an unusual light bulb: he has immortality. Initially Byron attempts to politicise the mass ranks of ordinary light bulbs, bulbs designed with a very limited life-span. Direct action against the humans might be the first step towards liberty: what would happen if a certain percentage of the total light bulbs all blew at the same time? Or, alternatively, what might the humans do if all the bulbs started pulsing at the same rate as the alpha-rhythms of the human brain, causing mass epilepsy? The other bulbs, babies in comparison, can't understand Byron and remain unmoved by his arguments. More worrying is the fact that Byron's longevity is being noticed by the bulb factory overseers. A light-bulb cartel called 'Phoebus' exists precisely to protect the interests of light-bulb manufacturers; and the existence of an everlasting light bulb is a 'clear and present danger' to these interests. A bulb assassin is dispatched, but by this time Byron is already in circulation. Byron's story is the story of bulb-snatching, of picaresque adventure, of the massive resources of the light-bulb cartel, and the material power of the 'grid' (the electrical grid).

Pynchon's tale is about human agents motivated by the interests of financial protectionism against the possibilities of technological innovation (an everlasting light bulb, if it could be developed, would soon put the light-bulb manufacturers out of business). But the story of Byron doesn't just leave agency with the human actors: the inorganic bodies of Byron and his colleagues are, potentially and actually, powerful forces in the world. So too is the haphazard accomplice 'contingency'. Pynchon's novel is, of course, a fantasy and its humour partly rests on the excessive anthropomorphism that it uses to bring 'Byron' to life. It would, however, be unwise to dismiss Byron's story simply because of this anthropomorphism: indeed anthropomorphism might be a very useful technique for recognising all the activities that design culture regularly accomplishes.

It is no accident that Pynchon takes the electric light bulb as a protagonist. Electric light is ubiquitous; you only really begin to see its extensiveness when a bulb blows, or more crucially during power cuts. The story of a society changing from candle light, to gas light, and moving on to various forms of electric light, is also the story of the 'phantasmagoria' — the story of society becoming dominated by the spectacle of a sparkling, ethereal and iridescent culture of consumerism. This is the narrative of design culture as display culture, of the new immateriality of the material world.

Some of the writing around design and technology has worried about the causal agent in fashioning this artificial world: is it, ultimately, the new instruments of science and technology that are shaping the world, or is it, rather, human, social agency that is shaping how technology is being deployed? The 'either-or-ness' of this problem is deeply unhelpful. We need to ask ourselves: what sort of understanding of 'the social' would exclude the technological materiality of the artificial world? And what image of technology is at work that doesn't want to include users as part of technology's functioning world? Similarly we might also wish to ask what sort of concept of 'causality' and 'determinism' is circulating that might want to find a causal determinant in the singular.

Chapter 7

Marcel Mauss

TECHNIQUES OF THE BODY [1934]

Source: Marcel Mauss (1934) 'Techniques of the Body', translated by Ben Brewster, *Economy and Society*, 2, 1, 1973, pp. 70–88.

Marcel Mauss (1872–1950) was a French sociologist (though these days he would be called an anthropologist who didn't do fieldwork), a socialist and one of the founders of the Institut d'Ethnologie. He wrote comparatively little but taught a great deal. Thus his influence is often gestured towards rather than fully acknowledged by those who are clearly intellectually indebted to him. For instance Pierre Bourdieu, who spent much of his career expounding on the concept of 'habitus', is drawing on the heritage of Mauss' work. For Bourdieu 'habitus' is the field of 'regulated improvisations' (Bourdieu 1972/1990: 78); it is life that *feels* totally spontaneous but is actually regulated by the proclivities and dispositions, the abilities, practices and understandings (often tacitly 'known' by the body rather than fully grasped by consciousness) that are transmitted by a culture. For Mauss the best place to see habitus is in the world that seems most natural – the world of body techniques.

Mauss' 'Techniques of the Body' offers a fundamental challenge to those who study design culture. For Mauss: 'The body is man's first and most natural instrument. Or more accurately, not to speak of instruments, man's first and most natural technical object, and at the same time technical means, is his body.' The consequence of recognising the body as our 'first technology' (as both object and tool) is that now design becomes a process that exists prior to the production of designed objects. When we help a child learn to walk, or when we learn to swim (to uses Mauss' favoured example), or when we start spoon-feeding a baby, we are entering into design processes.

Mauss' essay is directly concerned with the acculturation of intimate bodily repertoires: sitting and squatting, walking, having sex, giving birth and so on. To treat these intimate actions and activities as design practices provides a way of denaturalising them: taken-for-granted, everyday practices, like eating, sleeping, dressing and so on, become newly strange when we see them as 'design accomplishments'. Treating bodily activities as design accomplishments also provided Mauss with the means for reshuffling a global sense of civilisation ('primitives, these peoples so wrongly named' [Mauss 2006: 143]). From a body-design perspective the ability to squat – which most small children everywhere can do, but which most adults in chair-dominated societies lose – is preferable to the ability to sit. Squatting is more practical, it is self-sufficient and suggests a higher degree of affordance for the design body (after all squatting doesn't preclude the ability to sit, whereas sitting often results in the inability to squat).

Further reading: Clifford 1988; Fournier 2006; Lingis 1994; Mauss 1923, 2006; Probyn 2005.

Chapter one: *The notion of techniques of the body*

I DELIBERATELY SAY techniques of the body in the plural because it is possible to produce a theory of *the* technique of the body in the singular on the basis of a study, an exposition, a description pure and simple of techniques of the body in the plural. By this expression I mean the ways in which from society to society men know how to use their bodies. In any case, it is essential to move from the concrete to the abstract and not the other way round.

I want to convey to you what I believe is one of the parts of my teaching which is not to be found elsewhere, that I have rehearsed in a course of lectures on descriptive ethnology (the books containing the *Summary Instructions* and *Instructions for Ethnographers* are to be published) and have tried out several times in my teaching at the Institut d'Ethnologie of the University of Paris.

When a natural science makes advances, it only ever does so in the direction of the concrete, and always in the direction of the unknown. Now the unknown is found at the frontiers of the sciences, where the professors are at each other's throats, as Goethe put it (though Goethe was not so polite). It is generally in these ill-demarcated domains that the urgent problems lie. Moreover, these uncleared lands are marked. In the natural sciences at present, there is always one obnoxious rubric. There is always a moment when, the science of certain facts not being yet reduced into concepts, the facts not even being organically grouped together, these masses of facts receive that posting of ignorance: 'Miscellaneous'. This is where we have to penetrate. We can be certain that this is where there are truths to be discovered: first because we know that we are ignorant, and second because we have a lively sense of the quantity of the facts. For many years in my course in descriptive ethnology, I have had to teach in the shadow of the disgrace and opprobrium of the 'miscellaneous' in a matter in which in ethnography this rubric 'miscellaneous' was truly heteroclite. I was well aware that walking or swimming, for example, and all sorts of things of the same type, are specific to determinate societies; that the Polynesians do not swim as we do, that my generation did not swim as the present generation does. But what social phenomena did these represent? They were 'miscellaneous' social phenomena, and, as this rubric is a horror, I have often thought about this 'miscellaneous', at least as often as I have been obliged to discuss it and often in between times.

Forgive me if, in order to give this notion of techniques of the body shape for you, I tell you about the occasions on which I pursued this general problem and how I managed to pose it clearly. It was a series of steps consciously and unconsciously taken.

First, in 1898, I came into contact with someone whose initials I still know, but whose name I can no longer remember. I have been too lazy to look it up. It was the man who wrote an excellent article on 'Swimming' for the 1902 edition of the *Encyclopædia Britannica*, then in preparation.[1] (The articles on 'Swimming' in the two later editions are not so good.) He revealed to me the historical and ethnographical interest of the question. It was a starting-point, an observational framework. Subsequently – I noticed it myself – we have seen swimming techniques undergo a change, in our generation's life-time. An example will put us in the picture straight away: us, the psychologists, as well as the biologists and sociologists. Previously we were taught to dive after having learnt to swim. And when we were learning to dive, we were taught to close our eyes and then to open them under water. Today the technique is the other way round. The whole training begins by getting the children used to keeping their eyes open under water. Thus, even before they can swim, particular care is taken to get the children to control their dangerous but instinctive ocular reflexes, before all else they are familiarised with the water, their fears are suppressed, a certain confidence is created, suspensions and movements are selected. Hence there is a technique of diving and a technique of education in diving which have been discovered in my day. And you can see that it really is a technical education and, as in every technique, there is an apprenticeship in swimming. On the other hand, here our generation has witnessed a complete change in technique: we have seen the breast-stroke with the head out of the water replaced by the different sorts of crawl. Moreover, the habit of swallowing water and spitting it out again has gone. In my day swimmers thought of themselves as a kind of steam-boat. It was stupid, but in fact I still do this: I cannot get rid of my technique. Here then we have a specific technique of the body, a gymnic art perfected in our own day.

But this specificity is characteristic of all techniques. An example: during the War I was able to make many observations on this specificity of techniques. E.g. the technique of *digging*. The English troops I was with did not know how to use French spades, which forced us to change 8,000 spades a division when we relieved a French division, and vice versa. This plainly shows that a manual knack can only be learnt slowly. Every technique properly so-called has its own form.

But the same is true of every attitude of the body. Each society has its own special habits. In the same period I had many opportunities to note the differences between the various armies. An anecdote about *marching*. You all know that the British infantry marches with a different step from our own: with a different frequency and a different stride. For the moment I am not talking about the English swing or the action of the knees, etc. The Worcester Regiment, having achieved considerable glory alongside French infantry in the Battle of the Aisne, requested Royal permission to have French trumpets and drums, a band of French buglers and drummers. The result was not very encouraging. For nearly six months, in the streets of Bailleul, long after the Battle of the Aisne, I often saw the following sight: the regiment had preserved its English march but had set it to a French rhythm. It even had at the head of its band a little French light infantry regimental sergeant major who could blow the bugle and sound the march even better than his men. The unfortunate regiment of tall Englishmen could not march. Their gait was completely at odds. When they tried to march in step, the music would be out of step. With the result that the Worcester Regiment was forced to give up its French buglers. In fact, the bugle-calls adopted army by army earlier, in the Crimean War, were the calls 'at ease', 'retreat', etc. Thus I saw in a very precise and frequent fashion, not only with the ordinary march, but also at the double and so on, the differences in elementary as well as sporting techniques between the English and the French. Prince Curt Sachs, who is living here in France at present, made the same observation. He has discussed it in several of his lectures. He could recognise the gait of an Englishman and a Frenchman from a long distance.

But these were only approaches to the subject.

A kind of revelation came to me in hospital. I was ill in New York. I wondered where previously I had seen girls walking as my nurses walked. I had the time to think about it. At last I realised that it was at the cinema. Returning to France, I noticed how common this gait was, especially in Paris; the girls were French and they too were walking in this way. In fact, American walking fashions had begun to arrive over here, thanks to the cinema. This was an idea I could generalise. The positions of the arms and hands while walking form a social idiosyncracy, they are not simply a product of some purely individual, almost completely psychical arrangements and mechanisms. For example: I think I can also recognise a girl who has been raised in a convent. In general she will walk with her fists closed. And I can still remember my third-form teacher shouting at me: 'Idiot! why do you walk around the whole time with your hands flapping wide open?' Thus there exists an education in walking, too.

Another example: there are polite and impolite *positions for the hands* at rest. Thus you can be certain that if a child at table keeps his elbows in when he is not eating he is English. A young Frenchman has no idea how to sit up straight; his elbows stick out sideways; he puts them on the table, and so on.

Finally, in *running*, too, I have seen, you all have seen, the change in technique. Imagine, my gymnastics teacher, one of the top graduates of Joinville around 1860, taught me to run with my fists close to my chest: a movement completely contradictory to all running movements; I had to see the professional runners of 1890 before I realised the necessity of running in a different fashion.

Hence I have had this notion of the social nature of the 'habitus' for many years. Please note that I use the Latin word – it should be understood in France – *habitus*. The word translates infinitely better than 'habitude' (habit or custom), the 'exis', the 'acquired ability' and 'faculty' of Aristotle (who was a psychologist). It does not designate those metaphysical *habitudes*, that mysterious 'memory', the subjects of volumes or short and famous theses. These 'habits' do not just vary with individuals and their imitations, they vary especially between societies, educations, proprieties and fashions, prestiges. In them we should see the techniques and work of collective and individual practical reason rather than, in the ordinary way, merely the soul and its repetitive faculties.

Thus everything moved me towards the position that we in this Society are among those who have adopted, following Comte's example: the position of [Georges] Dumas, for example, who, in the constant relations between the biological and the sociological, leaves but little room for the psychological mediator. And I concluded that it was not possible to have a clear idea of all these facts about running, swimming, etc., unless one introduced a triple consideration instead of a single consideration, be it mechanical and physical, like an anatomical and physiological theory of walking, or on the contrary psychological or sociological. It is the triple viewpoint, that of the 'total man' that is needed.

Lastly, another series of facts impressed itself upon me. In all these elements of the art of using the human body, the facts of *education* were dominant. The notion of education could be superimposed on that of imitation. For there are particular children with very strong imitative faculties, others with very weak ones, but all of them go through the same education, such that we can understand the continuity of the concatenations. What takes place is a prestigious imitation. The child, the adult, imitates actions which have succeeded and which he has seen successfully performed by people in whom he has confidence and who have authority over him. The action is imposed from without, from above, even if it is an exclusively biological action, involving his body. The individual borrows the series of movements which constitute it from the action executed in front of him or with him by others.

It is precisely this notion of the prestige of the person who performs the ordered, authorised, tested action *vis-à-vis* the imitating individual that contains all the social element. The imitative action which follows contains the psychological element and the biological element.

But the whole, the ensemble, is conditioned by the three elements indissolubly mixed together.

All this is easily linked to a number of other facts. In a book by Elsdon Best that reached here in 1925 there is a remarkable document on the way Maori women (New Zealand) walk. (Do not say that they are primitives, for in some ways I think they are superior to the Celts and Germans.) 'Native women adopted a peculiar gait' (the English word is delightful) 'that was acquired in youth, a loose-jointed swinging of the hips that looks ungainly to us, but was admired by the Maori. Mothers drilled their daughters in this accomplishment, termed *onioni*, and I have heard a mother say to her girl: "*Ha! Kaore koe e onioni*" (you are not doing the *onioni*) when the young one was neglecting to practise the gait.'[2] This was an acquired, not a natural way of walking. To sum up, there is perhaps no 'natural way' for the adult. *A fortiori* when other technical facts intervene: to take ourselves, the fact that we wear shoes to walk transforms the positions of our feet: we feel it sure enough when we walk without them.

On the other hand, this same basic question arose for me in a different region, *vis-à-vis* all the notions concerning magical power, beliefs in the not only physical but also moral, magical and ritual effectiveness of certain actions. Here I am perhaps even more on my own terrain than on the adventurous terrain of the psycho-physiology of modes of walking, which is a risky one for me in this company.

Here is a more 'primitive' fact, Australian this time: a ritual formula both for hunting and for running. As you will know, the Australian manages to outrun kangaroos, emus, and wild dogs. He manages to catch the possum or phalanger at the top of its tree, even though the animal puts up a remarkable resistance. One of these running rituals, observed a hundred years ago, is that of the hunt for the dingo or wild dog among the tribes near Adelaide. The hunter constantly shouts the following formula:

> Strike (him, i.e. the dingo) with the tuft of eagle feathers (used in initiation, etc.)
> Strike (him) with the girdle
> Strike (him) with the string round the head

Strike (him) with the blood of circumcision
Strike (him) with the blood of the arm
Strike (him) with menstrual blood
Send (him) to sleep, etc.[3]

In another ceremony, that of the possum hunt, the individual carries in his mouth a piece of rock crystal (*kawemukka*), a particularly magical stone, and chants a formula of the same kind, and it is with this support that he is able to dislodge the possum, that he climbs the tree and can stay hanging on to it by his belt, that he can outlast and catch and kill this difficult prey.

The relations between magical procedures and hunting techniques are clear, too universal to need stressing.

The psychological phenomenon I am reporting at this moment is clearly only too easy to know and understand from the normal point of view of the sociologist. But what I want to get at now is the confidence, the psychological *momentum* that can be linked to an action which is primarily a fact of biological resistance, obtained thanks to some words and a magical object.

Technical action, physical action, magico-religious action are confused for the actor. These are the elements I had at my disposal.

All this did not satisfy me. I saw how everything could be described, but not how it could be organised; I did not know what name, what title to give it all.

It was very simple, I just had to refer to the division of traditional actions into techniques and rites, which I believe to be well founded. All these modes of action were techniques, the techniques of the body.

I made, and went on making for several years, the fundamental mistake of thinking that there is technique only when there is an instrument. I had to go back to ancient notions, to the Platonic position on technique, for Plato spoke of a technique of music and in particular of a technique of the dance, and extend these notions.

I call technique an action which is *effective* and *traditional* (and you will see that in this it is no different from a magical, religious or symbolic action). It has to be *effective* and *traditional*. There is no technique and no transmission in the absence of tradition. This above all is what distinguishes man from the animals: the transmission of his techniques and very probably their oral transmission.

Allow me, therefore, to assume that you accept my definitions. But what is the difference between the effective traditional action of religion, the symbolic or juridical effective traditional action, the actions of life in common, moral actions on the one hand and the traditional actions of technique on the other? It is that the latter are felt by the author as *actions of a mechanical, physical or physico-chemical order* and that they are pursued with that aim in view.

In this case all that need be said is quite simply that we are dealing with *techniques of the body*. The body is man's first and most natural instrument. Or more accurately, not to speak of instruments, man's first and most natural technical object, and at the same time technical means, is his body. Immediately this whole broad category of what I classified in descriptive sociology as 'miscellaneous' disappeared from that rubric and took shape and body: we now know where to range it.

Before instrumental techniques there is the ensemble of techniques of the body. I am not exaggerating the importance of this kind of work, the work of psycho-sociological taxonomy. But it is something: order put into ideas where there was none before. Even inside this grouping of facts, the principle made possible a precise classification. The constant adaptation to a physical, mechanical or chemical aim (e.g. when we drink) is pursued in a series of assembled actions, and assembled for the individual not by himself alone but by all his education, by the whole society to which he belongs, in the place he occupies in it.

Moreover, all these techniques were easily arranged in a system which is common to us, the notion basic to psychologists, particularly [William Halse] Rivers and [Sir Henry] Head, of the symbolic life of the mind; the notion we have of the activity of the consciousness as being above all a system of symbolic assemblages.

I should never stop if I tried to demonstrate to you all the facts that might be listed to make visible this concourse of the body and moral or intellectual symbols. Here let us look for a moment at ourselves. Everything in us all is under command. I am a lecturer for you; you can tell it from my sitting posture and my voice, and you are listening to me seated and in silence. We have a set of permissible or impermissible, natural or unnatural attitudes. Thus we should attribute different values to the act of staring fixedly: a symbol of politeness in the army, and of rudeness in everyday life.

Chapter two: *Principles of the classification of techniques of the body*

Two things were immediately apparent given the notion of techniques of the body: they are divided and vary by sex *and* by age.

1 Sexual division of techniques of the body (and not just sexual division of labour)

This is a fairly broad subject. The observations of [Robert Mearns] Yerkes and [Wolfgang] Köhler on the position of objects with respect to the body, and especially to the groin, in monkeys provide inspiration for a general disquisition on the different attitudes of the moving body with respect to moving objects in the two sexes. Besides, there are classical observations of man himself on this point. They need to be supplemented. Allow me to suggest this series of investigations to my psychologist friends. I am not very competent in this field and also my time is otherwise engaged. Take the way of closing the fist. A man normally closes his fist with the thumb outside, a woman with her thumb inside; perhaps because she has not been taught to do it, but I am sure that if she were taught, it would prove difficult. Her punching, her delivery of a punch, are weak. And everyone knows that a woman's throwing, of a stone for example, is not just weak, but always different from that of a man: in a vertical instead of a horizontal plane.

Perhaps this is a case of two instructions. For there is a society of men and a society of women. However, I believe that there are also perhaps biological and psychological things involved as well. But there again, the psychologist alone will only be able to give dubious explanations, and he will need the collaboration of two neighbouring sciences: physiology, sociology.

2 Variations of techniques of the body with age

The child normally squats. We no longer know how to. I believe that this is an absurdity and an inferiority of our races, civilisations, societies. An example: I lived at the front with Australians (whites). They had one considerable advantage over me. When we made a stop in mud or water, they could sit down on their heels to rest, and the *'flotte'*, as it was called, stayed below their heels. I was forced to stay standing up in my boots with my whole foot in the water. The squatting position is, in my opinion, an interesting one that could be preserved in a child. It is a very stupid mistake to take it away from him. All mankind, excepting only our societies, has so preserved it.

It seems besides that in the series of ages of the human race this posture has also changed in importance. You will remember that curvature of the lower limbs was once regarded as a sign of degeneration. A physiological explanation has been given for this racial characteristic. What even [Rudolf Ludwig Karl] Virchow still regarded as an unfortunate degenerate and is in fact simply what is now called Neanderthal man, had curved legs. This is because he normally lived in a squatting position. Hence there are things which we believe to be of a hereditary kind which are in reality physiological, psychological or sociological in kind. A certain form of the tendons and even of the bones is simply the result of certain forms of posture and repose. This is clear enough. By this procedure, it is possible not only to classify techniques, but also to classify their variations by age and sex.

Having established this classification, which cuts across all classes of society, we can now glimpse a third one.

3 Classification of techniques of the body according to efficiency

The techniques of the body can be classified according to their efficiency, i.e. according to the results of training. Training, like the assembly of a machine, is the search for, the acquisition of an efficiency. Here it is a human efficiency. These techniques are thus human norms of human training. These procedures that we apply to animals men voluntarily apply to themselves and to their children. The latter are probably the first beings to have been trained in this way, before all the animals, which first had to be tamed. As a result I could to a certain extent compare these techniques, them and their transmission, to training systems, and rank them in the order of their effectiveness.

This is the place for the notion of dexterity, so important in psychology, as well as in sociology. But in French we only have the poor term 'habile' which is a bad translation of the Latin word 'habilis', far better designating those people with a sense of the adaptation of all their well-co-ordinated movements to a goal, who are practised, who 'know what they are up to'. The English notions of 'craft' or 'cleverness' (skill, presence of mind and habit combined) imply competence at something. Once again we are clearly in the technical domain.

4 Transmission of the form of the techniques

One last viewpoint: the teaching of techniques being essential, we can classify them according to the nature of this education and training. Here is a new field of studies: masses of details which have not been observed, but should be, constitute the physical education of all ages and both sexes. The child's education is full of so-called details, which are really essential. Take the problem of ambi-dextrousness for example: our observations of the movements of the right hand and of the left hand are poor and we do not know how much all of them are acquired. A pious Muslim can easily be recognised: even when he has a knife and fork (which is rarely), he will go to any lengths to avoid using anything but his right hand. He must never touch his food with his left hand, or certain parts of his body with his right. To know why he does not make a certain gesture and does make a certain other gesture neither the physiology nor the psychology of motor asymmetry in man is enough, it is also necessary to know the traditions which impose it. Robert Hertz has posed this problem correctly.[4] But reflections of this and other kinds can be applied whenever there is a social choice of the principless of movements.

There are grounds for studying all the modes of training, imitation and especially those fundamental fashions that can be called the modes of life, the *modes*, the *tonus*, the 'matter', the 'manners', the 'way'.

Here is the first classification, or rather, four viewpoints.

Chapter three: *A biographical list of the techniques of the body*

Another quite different classification is, I would not say more logical, but easier for the observer. It is a simple list. I had thought of presenting to you a series of small tables, of the kind American professors construct. I shall simply follow more or less the ages of man, the normal biography of an individual, as an arrangement of the techniques of the body which concern him or which he is taught.

1 Techniques of birth and obstetrics

The facts are rather little known, and much of the classical information is disputable.[5] Among the best is that of Walter Roth on the Australian tribes of Queensland and on those of British Guiana.[6]

The forms of obstetrics are very variable. The infant Buddha was born with his mother Mâya upright and clinging to the branch of a tree. She gave birth standing up. Indian women still in the main give birth in this position. Something we think of as normal, like giving birth lying on one's back, is no more normal than doing so in other positions, e.g. on all fours. There are techniques of giving birth, both on the mother's part and on that of her helpers, of holding the baby, cutting and tying the umbilical cord, caring for the mother, caring for the child. Here are quite a number of questions of some importance. And here are some more: the choice of the child, the exposure of weaklings, the killing of twins are decisive moments in the history of a race. In ancient history and in other civilisations, the recognition of the child is a crucial event.

2 Techniques of infancy

Rearing and feeding the child. Attitudes of the two inter-related beings: mother and child. Take the child, suckling, etc., carrying, etc. The history of carrying is very important. A child carried next to its mother's skin for two or three years has a quite different attitude to its mother from that of a child not so carried;[7] it has a contact with its mother utterly unlike our children's. It clings to her neck, her shoulder, it sits astride her hip. This remarkable gymnastics is essential throughout its life. And there is another gymnastics for the mother carrying it. It even seems that psychical states arise here which have disappeared from infancy with us. There are sexual contacts, skin contacts, etc.

Weaning. Takes a long time, usually two or three years. The obligation to suckle, sometimes even to suckle animals. It takes a long time for the mother's milk to run dry. Besides this there are relations between weaning and reproduction, suspensions of reproduction during weaning.[8]

Mankind can more or less be divided into people with cradles and people without. For there are techniques of the body which presuppose an instrument. Countries with cradles include almost all the peoples of the two Northern hemispheres, those of the Andean region, and also a certain number of Central African populations. In these last two groups, the use of the cradle coincides with a cranial deformation (which perhaps has serious physiological consequences).

The weaned child. It can eat and drink; it is taught to walk; it is trained in vision, hearing, in a sense of rhythm and form and movement, often for dancing and music.

It acquires the notions and practices of physical exercise and breathing. It takes certain postures which are often imposed on it.

3 Techniques of adolescence

To be observed with men in particular. Less important with girls in those societies to whose study a course in Ethnology is devoted. The big moment in the education of the body is, in fact, the moment of initiation. Because of the way our boys and girls are brought up we imagine that both acquire the same manners and postures and receive the same training everywhere. The idea is already erroneous about ourselves – and it is totally false in so-called primitive countries. Moreover, we describe the facts as if something like our own school, beginning straight away and intended to protect the child and train it for life, had always and everywhere existed. The opposite is the rule. For example: in all black societies the education of the boy intensifies around the age of puberty, while that of women remains traditional, so to speak. There is no school for women. They are at school with their mothers and are formed there continuously, moving directly, with few exceptions, to the married state. The male child enters the society of men where he learns his profession, especially the profession of arms. However, for men as well as women, the decisive moment is that of adolescence. It is at this moment that they learn definitively the techniques of the body that they will retain for the whole of their adult lives.

4 Techniques of adult life

To list these we can run through the various moments of the day among which co-ordinated movements and suspensions of movement are distributed.

We can distinguish sleep and waking, and in waking, rest and activity.

1° *Techniques of sleep.* The notion that going to sleep is something natural is totally inaccurate. I can tell you that the War taught me to sleep anywhere, on heaps of stones for example, but that I have never been able to change my bed without a moment of insomnia: only on the second night can I go to sleep quickly.

One thing is very simple: it is possible to distinguish between those societies that have nothing to sleep on except the 'floor', and those that have instrumental assistance. The 'civilisation of latitude 15°' discussed by Graebner[9] is characterised among other things by its use of a bench for the neck. This neck-rest is often a totem, sometimes carved with squatting figures of men and totemic animals. There are people with mats and people without (Asia, Oceania, part of America). There are people with pillows and people without. There are populations which lie very close together in a ring to sleep, round a fire, or even without a fire. There are primitive ways of getting warm and keeping the feet warm. The Fuegians, who live in a very cold region, cannot warm their feet while they are asleep having only one blanket of skin (*guanaco*). Finally there is sleep standing up. The Masai can sleep on their feet. I have slept standing up in the mountains. I have often slept on a horse, even sometimes a moving horse: the horse was more intelligent than I was. The old chroniclers of the invasions picture the Huns and Mongols sleeping on horseback. This is still true, and their riders' sleeping does not stop the horses' progress.

There is the use of coverings. People who sleep covered and uncovered. There is the hammock and the way of sleeping hanging up.

Here are a large number of practices which are both techniques of the body and also have profound biological echoes and effects. All this can and must be observed on the ground; hundreds of things still remain to be discovered.

2° *Waking: Techniques of rest.* Rest can be perfect rest or a mere suspension of activity: lying down, sitting, squatting, etc. Try squatting. You will realise the torture that a Moroccan meal, for example, eaten according to all the rituals, would cause you. The way of sitting down is fundamental. You can distinguish squatting mankind and sitting mankind. And, in the latter, people with benches and people without benches and daises: people with chairs and people without chairs. Wooden chairs supported by crouching figures are widespread, curiously enough, in all the regions at fifteen degrees of latitude North and along the Equator in both continents.[10] There are people who have tables and people who do not. The table, the Greek 'trapeza', is far from universal. Normally it is still a carpet, a mat, throughout the East. This is all complicated, for these forms of rest include meals, conversation, etc. Certain societies take their rest in very peculiar positions. Thus, the whole of Nilotic Africa and part of the Chad region, all the way to Tanganyika, is populated by men who rest in the fields like storks. Some manage to rest on one foot without a pole, others lean on a stick. These resting techniques form real characteristics of civilisations, common to a large number of them, to whole families of peoples. Nothing seems more natural to the psychologists; I do not know if they would quite agree with me, but I believe that these postures in the savannah are due to the height of the grasses there and the functions of shepherd or sentry, etc.; they are laboriously acquired by education and preserved.

You have active, generally aesthetic rest; thus even dancing at rest is frequent, etc. I shall return to this.

3° *Techniques of activity, of movement.* By definition, rest is the absence of movements, movement the absence of rest. Here is a straightforward list:

Movements of the whole body: climbing; trampling; walking.

Walking: the *habitus* of the body being upright while walking, breathing, rhythm of the walk, swinging the fists, the elbows, progression with the trunk in advance of the body or by advancing either side of the body alternately (we have got accustomed to moving all the body forward at once). Feet in or out. Extension of the leg. We laugh at the 'goose-step'. It is the way the German Army can obtain the maximum extension of the leg, given in particular that all Northerners, high on their legs, like to make steps as long as possible. In the absence of these exercises, we Frenchmen remain more or less knock-kneed. Here is one of those idiosyncrasies which are simultaneously matters of race, of individual mentality and of collective mentality. Techniques such as those of the about-turn are among the most curious. The about-turn 'on principle' English-style is so different from our own that it takes considerable study to master it.

Running. Position of the feet, position of the arms, breathing, running magic, endurance. In Washington I saw the chief of the Fire Fraternity of the Hopi Indians who had arrived with four of his men to protest against the prohibition of the use of certain alcoholic liquors in their ceremonies. He was certainly the best runner in the world. He had run 250 miles without stopping. All the Pueblos are accustomed to prodigious physical feats of all kinds. [Henri] Hubert, who had seen them, compared them physically with Japanese athletes. This same Indian was an incomparable dancer.

Finally we reach techniques of active rest which are not simply a matter of aesthetics, but also of bodily games.

Dancing. You have perhaps attended the lectures of M. [Erich Maria] von Hornbostel and M. Curt Sachs. I recommend to you the latter's very fine history of dancing.[11] I accept their division into dances at rest and dances in action.[12] I am less prepared to accept their hypothesis about the distribution of these dances. They are victims to the fundamental error which is the mainstay of a whole section of sociology. There are supposed to be societies with exclusively masculine descent and others with exclusively uterine descent. The uterine ones, being feminised, tend to dance on the spot; the others, with descent by the male, take their pleasure in moving about.

Curt Sachs has better classified these dances into extravert and introvert dances.[13] We are plunged straight into psychoanalysis, which is probably quite well-founded here. In fact the sociologist has to see things in a more complex way. Thus, the Polynesians and in particular the Maori, shake very greatly, even on the spot, or move about very much when they have the space to do so.

Men's dancing and women's dancing should be distinguished, for they are often opposed.

Lastly we should realise that dancing in a partner's arms is a product of modern European civilisation. Which shows you that things we find natural are historical. Moreover, they horrify everyone in the world but ourselves.

I move on to the techniques of the body which are also a function of vocations and part of vocations or more complex techniques.

Jumping. We have witnessed a transformation of jumping techniques. We all jumped from a spring-board and, once again, full-face. I am glad to say that this has stopped. Now people jump, fortunately, from one side. Jumping lengthways, sideways, up and down. Standing jump, pole-jump. Here was return to the objects of the reflections of our friends [Wolfgang] Köhler, [Paul] Guillaume and [Ignace] Meyerson: the comparative psychology of man and animals. I won't say anything more about it. These techniques are infinitely variable.

Climbing. I can tell you that I'm very bad at climbing trees, though reasonable on mountains and rocks. A difference of education and hence of method.

A method of getting up trees with a belt encircling the tree and the body is crucial among all so-called primitives. But we do not have the use of this belt. We see telegraph workers climbing with crampons, but no belt. This procedure should be taught them.[14]

The history of mountaineering methods is very noteworthy. It has made fabulous progress in my life-time.

Descent. Nothing makes me so dizzy as watching a Kabyle going downstairs in Turkish slippers (*babouches*). How can he keep his feet without the slippers coming off? I have tried to see, to do it, but I can't understand.

Nor can I understand how women can walk in high heels. Thus there is a lot even to be observed, let alone compared.

Swimming. I have told you what I think. Diving, swimming; use of supplementary means; air-floats, planks, etc. We are on the way to the invention of navigation. I was one of those who criticised the de Rougés' book on Australia [?], demonstrated their plagiarisms, believed they were grossly inaccurate. Along with so many others I held their story for a fable: they had seen the Niol-Niol (N.W. Australia) riding cavalcades of great sea-turtles. But now we have excellent photographs in which these people can be seen riding turtles. In the same way [Robert Sutherland] Rattray noted the story of pieces of wood on which people swim among the Ashanti.[15] Moreover, it has been confirmed for the natives of almost all the lagoons of Guinea, Porto-Novo in our own colonies.

Forceful movements. Pushing, pulling, lifting. Everyone knows what a back-heave is. It is an acquired technique, not just a series of movements.

Throwing, up or along the ground, etc.; the way of holding the object to be thrown between the fingers is noteworthy and undergoes great variation.

Holding. Holding between the teeth. Use of the toes, the arm-pit, etc.

This study of mechanical movements has got off to a good start. It is the formation of mechanical 'pairs of elements' with the body. You will recall [Franz] Reuleaux's great theory about the formation of these pairs of elements.[16] And here the great name of [Louis-Hubert] Farabeuf will not be forgotten. As soon as I use my fist, and *a fortiori*, when a man had a 'Chellean hand-axe' in his hand, these 'pairs of elements' are formed.

This is the place for conjuring tricks, sleight of hand, athletics, acrobatics, etc. I must tell you that I had and still have a great admiration for jugglers and gymnasts.

4° *Techniques of care for the body. Rubbing, washing, soaping.* This dossier is hardly a day old. The inventors of soap were not the Ancients, they did not use it. It was the Gauls. And on the other hand, independently, in the whole of Central and North East of South America they soaped themselves with *quillaia* bark or 'brazil', hence the name of the empire.

Care of the mouth. Coughing and spitting technique. Here is a personal observation. A little girl did not know how to spit and this made every cold she had much worse. I made inquiries. In her father's village and in her father's family in particular, in Berry, people do not know how to spit. I taught her to spit. I gave her four *sous* per spit. As she was saving up for a bicycle she learnt to spit. She is the first person in her family who knows how to spit.

Hygiene in the needs of nature. Here I could list innumerable facts for you.

5° *Consumption techniques. Eating.* You will remember the story [Harald] Høffding repeats about the Shah of Persia. The Shah was the guest of Napoleon III and insisted on eating with his fingers. The Emperor urged him to use a golden fork. 'You don't know what a pleasure you are missing,' the Shah replied.

Absence and use of knives. An enormous factual error is made by [W. J.] McGee who believed he had observed that the Seri (Indians of the Madeleine Peninsula, California), having no notion of knives, were the most primitive human beings. They did not have knives for eating, that is all.[17]

Drinking. It would be very useful to teach children to drink straight from the source, the fountain, etc., or from puddles of water, etc., to pour their drinks straight down their throats, etc.

6° *Techniques of reproduction.* Nothing is more technical than sexual positions. Very few writers have had the courage to discuss this question. We should be grateful to M. [Friedrich Saloman] Krauss for having published his great collection of *Anthropophyteia.*[18] Consider for example the technique of the sexual position consisting of this: the woman's legs hang by the knees from the man's elbows. It is a technique *specific* to the whole Pacific, from Australia to lower Peru, via the Behring Straits – very rare, so to speak, elsewhere.

There are all the techniques of normal and abnormal sexual acts. Contact of the sexual organs, mingling of breath, kisses, etc. Here sexual techniques and sexual morals are closely related.

7° Lastly there are the *techniques of the care of the abnormal*: massages, etc. But let us move on.

Chapter four: *General considerations*

General questions may perhaps be of more interest to you than these lists of techniques that I have paraded before you at rather too great a length.

What emerges very clearly from them is the fact that we are everywhere faced with physio-psycho-sociological assemblages of series of actions. These actions are more or less habitual and more or less ancient in the life of the individual and the history of the society.

Let us go further: one of the reasons why these series may more easily be assembled in the individual is precisely because they are assembled by and for social authority. As a corporal this is how I taught the reason for exercise in close order, marching four abreast and in step. I ordered the soldiers not to march in step drawn up in ranks and in two files four abreast, and I obliged the squad to pass between two of the trees in the courtyard. They marched on top of one another. They realised that what they were being made to do was not so stupid. In group life as a whole there is a kind of education of movements in close order.

In every society, everyone knows and has to know and learn what he has to do in all conditions. Naturally, social life is not exempt from stupidity and abnormalities. Error may be a principle. The French Navy only recently began to teach its sailors to swim. But example and order, that is the principle. Hence there is a strong sociological causality in all these facts. I hope you will accept that I am right.

On the other hand, since these are movements of the body, this all presupposes an enormous biological and physiological apparatus. What is the breadth of the linking psychological cog-wheel? I deliberately say cog-wheel. A Comtian would say that there is no gap between the social and the biological. What I can tell you is that here I see psychological facts as connecting cogs and not as causes, except in moments of creation or reform. Cases of invention, of laying down principles, are rare. Cases of adaptation are an individual psychological matter. But in general they are governed by education, and at least by the circumstances of life in common, of contact.

On the other hand there are two big questions on the agenda for psychology: the question of individual capacities, of technical orientation, and the question of salient features, of bio-typology, which may concur with the brief investigations I have just made. The great advances of psychology in the last few years have not, in my opinion, been made *vis-à-vis* each of the so-called faculties of psychology, but in psychotechnics, and in the analysis of psychological 'wholes'.

Here the ethnologist comes up against the big question of the psychical possibilities of such a race and such a biology of such a people. These are fundamental questions. I believe that here, too, whatever the appearances, we are dealing with biologico-sociological phenomena. I think that the basic education in all these techniques consists of an adaptation of the body to their use. For example, the great tests of stoicism, etc., which constitute initiation for the majority of mankind, have as their aim to teach composure, resistance, seriousness, presence of mind, dignity, etc. The main utility I see in my erstwhile mountaineering was this education of my composure, which enabled me to sleep upright on the narrowest ledge overlooking an abyss.

I believe that this whole notion of the education of races that are selected on the basis of a determinate efficiency is one of the fundamental moments of history itself: education of the vision, education in walking – ascending, descending, running. It consists especially of education in composure. And the latter is above all a retarding mechanism, a mechanism inhibiting disorderly movements; this retardation subsequently allows a co-ordinated response of co-ordinated movements setting off in the direction of a chosen goal. This resistance to emotional seizure is something fundamental in social and mental life. It separates out, it even classifies the so-called primitive societies; according to whether they display more brutal, unreflected, unconscious reactions or on the contrary more isolated, precise actions governed by a clear consciousness.

It is thanks to society that there is an intervention of consciousness. It is not thanks to unconsciousness that there is an intervention of society. It is thanks to society that there is the certainty of pre-prepared movements, domination of the conscious over emotion and unconsciousness. It is right that the French Navy is now to make it obligatory for its sailors to learn to swim.

From here we easily move on to much more philosophical problems.

I don't know whether you have paid attention to what our friend [Marcel] Granet has already pointed out in his great investigations into the techniques of Taoism, its techniques of the body, breathing techniques in particular.[19] I have studied the Sanscrit texts of Yoga enough to know that the same things occur in India. I believe precisely that at the bottom of all our mystical states there are techniques of the body which we have not studied, but which were perfectly studied by China and India, even in very remote periods. This socio-psychobiological study should be made. I think that there are necessarily biological means of entering into 'communication with God'. Although in the end breath technique, etc., is only the basic aspect in India and China, I believe this technique is much more widespread. At any rate, on this point we have the methods to understand a great many facts which we have not understood hitherto. I even believe that all the recent discoveries in reflex therapy deserve our attention, ours, the sociologists', as well as that of biologists and psychologists . . . much more competent than ourselves.

Notes

This lecture was given at a meeting of the Société de Psychologie, May 17th, 1934 and published in the *Journal de psychologie normal et patholigique*, Paris, Année XXXII, 1935, pp. 271–93. Reprinted in Marcel Mauss, *Sociologie et Anthropologie* (with introduction by Claude Lévi-Strauss), 4th edition, Paris: Presses Universitaires de France, 1968, pp. 364–386.

1   [In fact Sydney Holland. See Holland, 1902–3.]

2   Best, 1924: I, 408; cf. 135 [*sic* – the latter reference seems to be a mistake of Mauss'; could he have been referring to I, 436 or II, 556, which refer to the gait of men and women respectively?].

3   Teichelmann and Schürmann, 1840: 73; cit. Eyre, 1845: II, 241.

4   Hertz, 1929 & 1960.
5   Even the latest editions of Ploss: *Das Weib* (Bartels's editions, etc.) leave something to be desired in this question. [See Ploss, 1884; Ploss and Bartels, 1905; Ploss, Bartels and Bartels, 1935.]
6   [See Roth, 1897: 182–3; Roth, 1924: 693–6.]
7   Observations are beginning to be published on this point.
8   Ploss's large collection of facts, supplemented by Bartels, is satisfactory on this point [see Ploss, Bartels and Bartels, 1935: III, 183].
9   Graebner, 1923.
10   This is one of the fine observations from Graebner, 1923.
11   Sachs, 1933 & 1938.
12   [Sachs, 1938 uses the terms 'close dance' and 'expanded dance'.]
13   [Sachs, 1938: 59–61.]
14   I have just seen it in use at last (Spring 1935).
15   [Rattray, 1923: pp. 62–3, Figs 8–12, 15–16.]
16   ['The kinematic elements of a machine are not employed singly, but always in pairs; or in other words . . . the machine cannot so well be said to consist of elements as of *pairs of elements (Elementenpaare)*. This particular manner of constitution forms a distinguishing characteristic of the machine.' Reuleaux, 1876: 43.]
17   [McGee, 1898: 152. In fact the Seri live on the island of Tiburon and the adjacent mainland of Sonora province, Mexico, on the Gulf of California.]
18   [Krauss, 1904–13; 1906–7; 1909–29.]
19   [Granet, 1929 and 1930.]

References

Best, Elsdon (1924) *The Maori*, Memoirs of the Polynesian Society, Volume V, Board of Maori Ethnological Research, Wellington, New Zealand, two volumes.

Eyre, Edward John (1845) *Journals of Expeditions of Discovery into Central Australia and Overland from Adelaide to King George's Sound in the Years 1840–1; sent by the Colonists of South Australia with the Sanction and Support of the Government: including an Account of the Manners and Customs of the Aborigines and the State of their Relations with Europeans*, T. & W. Boone, London, two volumes.

Graebner, Fritz (1923) *Ethnologie*, in Paul Hinneberg, ed., *Die Kultur der Gegenwart* Part III Section 5, B. G. Teubner, Leipzig.

Granet, Marcel (1929) *La civilisation chinoise, la vie publique et la vie privée*, L'évolution de l'humanité vol. 25, La Renaissance du Livre, Paris.

Granet, Marcel (1930) *Chinese Civilization*, translated by Kathleen E. Innes and Mabel R. Brailsford, Kegan Paul, London.

Hertz, Robert (1929) 'La pré-éminence de la main droite: étude sur la polarité religieuse' (1909), in *Mélanges de sociologie religieuse et de folklore*, Librairie Félix Alcan, Paris.

Hertz, Robert (1960) 'The Pre-eminence of the Right Hand', *Death and the Right Hand*, translated by Rodney and Claudia Needham, Cohen and West, London, pp. 87–113.

Holland, Sydney (1902–3) 'Swimming', *Encyclopædia Britannica* 10th edition (Supplement to the 9th), Edinburgh, Vol. XXXIII, pp. 140–1.

Krauss, Friedrich Saloman (1904–13) ed., *Anthropophyteia*, Jahrbücher für folkloristische Erhebungen und Forschungen zur Entwicklungsgeschichte der geschlechtlichen Moral, Leipzig, ten volumes.

Krauss, Friedrich Saloman (1906–7) ed., *Historische Quellenschriften zum Studium der Anthropophyteia*, Leipzig, four volumes.

Krauss, Friedrich Saloman (1909–29) ed., *Beiwerke zum Studium der Anthropophyteia*, Leipzig, nine volumes.

McGee, W. J. (1898) 'The Seri Indians', *Seventeenth Annual Report of the Bureau of American Ethnology to the Smithsonian Institution* for the year 1895–6, Part One, pp. 9–344, Washington.

Ploss, Hermann Heinrich (1884) *Das Weib in der Natur- and Völkerkunde, Anthropologische Studien*, Leipzig, two volumes.

Ploss, Hermann Heinrich and Bartels, Max (1905) *Das Weib in der Natur- und Völkerkunde*, 8th much expanded edition, Leipzig.

Ploss, Hermann Heinrich, Bartels, Max and Bartels, Paul (1935) *Woman: an Historical, Gynaecological and Anthropological Compendium*, edited and translated by Eric John Dingwall, Heinemann, London, three volumes.

Rattray, Robert Sutherland (1923) *Ashanti*, Clarendon Press, Oxford.

Reuleaux, Franz (1875) *Theoretische Kinematik, Grundzüge einer Theorie des Maschinenwesens*, Brunswick.

Reuleaux, Franz (1876) *The Kinematics of Machinery, Outlines of a Theory of Machines*, Macmillan, London.

Roth, Walter Edmund (1897) *Ethnological Studies among the North-West-Central Queensland Aborigines*, Edmund Gregory, Government Printer, Brisbane, Australia.

Roth, Walter Edmund (1924) 'An Introductory Study of the Arts, Crafts, and Customs of the Guiana Indians', *38th Annual Report of the Bureau of American Ethnology to the Smithsonian Institution 1916–1917*, Government Printing Office, Washington D.C., pp. 25–745.

Sachs, Curt (1933) *Weltgeschichte des Tanzes*, D. Reimer, Berlin.

Sachs, Curt (1938) *World History of the Dance*, translated by Bessie Schönberg, George Allen and Unwin, London.

Teichelmann, Christian Gottlieb and Schürmann, Clamor Wilhelm, *Outlines of a Grammar, Vocabulary, and Phraseology, of the Aboriginal Language of South Australia, spoken by the Natives in and for some distance around Adelaide*, published by the authors at the Native Location, Adelaide (Xerographic facsimile, South Australia Facsimile Editions no. 39, 1962).

Chapter 8

Michel Foucault

SPACE, KNOWLEDGE, AND POWER [1982]

Source: Michel Foucault (1996) *Foucault Live: Collected Interviews, 1961–1984*, edited by Sylvère Lotringer, New York: Semiotext(e), pp. 335–47. This interview was first published in *Skyline, the Architecture and Design Review*, March 1982. The interview was conducted by Paul Rabinow, translated by Christian Hubert.

Michel Foucault (1926–84) was a prominent French intellectual working primarily in an area that he named the history of 'systems of thought' (although 'thought' doesn't quite capture his interest in the more 'thought-less' practices of governance, for instance). His books map out the diverse shifts and continuities within such arenas as 'madness', 'sexuality', 'medicine' and other realms of knowledge and power. Foucault's approach is fundamentally historical, his counter-intuitive move was to take some aspect of life considered timeless and pre-social (sexuality, for instance) and show that it has a social history, that its present form emerged under precise historical and social conditions. His work, then, is in one sense a very strong form of social constructivism (an understanding that what we call 'natural' is usually a social convention that has been naturalised). It is a mark of Foucault's influence (and the work of other social constructivists) that this position is nowadays often taken as a basic tenet of any social and cultural inquiry.

While Foucault's work is often associated with the idea that discourse is a crucial agent for producing the social (as if the social body persuades itself of the order of things by endlessly repeating similar statements about the world), his work needs to be understood as focusing on the non-discursive as well as the discursive. The crucial term that Foucault uses (and it is a term that really should supplant discourse) is the term *dispositif* – a French word that is either left untranslated or translated into English as 'apparatus'. Foucault defines *dispositif* in the following way:

> A thoroughly heterogeneous ensemble consisting of discourses, institutions, architectural forms, regulatory decisions, laws, administrative measures, scientific statements, philosophical, moral and philanthropic propositions – in short, the said as much as the unsaid.
>
> (Foucault 1980: 194)

It is this ensemble of the said and the unsaid, the concrete and the abstract, the physically routine as much as the discursively repetitive that drives his project. And it is here where his contribution to the understanding of design culture is at its most pungent.

In the interview reproduced here the anthropologist Paul Rabinow is questioning Foucault about his understanding of social space, particularly architecture. In 1975 Foucault had published his book on the modern prison and had made much of Jeremy Bentham's *Panopticon*: an architectural design for a prison that would keep the prisoner permanently visible while keeping the prison guard (the surveyor) permanently hidden (see Figure 8.1 for an example). It is this design that allows Foucault to write about the prisoner internalising disciplinary power to the point where he (or less often she) 'becomes the principle of his own subjection' (Foucault 1975/1982: 203). This interview is a clarification (if one were needed) for anyone who might think Foucault is reading this architectural machine too instrumentally, that is, as an instrument that alone could simply produce docile subjects. It is always the ensemble that is productive, always the *dispositif* that generates the subject. We could translate this into the following maxim: never design outside social practice.

Further reading: Foucault 1963/1976, 1975/1982, 1976/1984, 1980; Mitchell 2002; Rabinow 1989; Stoler 1995.

Figure 8.1   N. Harou-Romain. Plan for a penitentiary, 1840. A prisoner, in his cell, kneeling at prayer before the central inspection tower.

Q: In your interview with geographers at *Herodote*,[1] you said that architecture becomes political at the end of the 18th century. Obviously, it was political in earlier periods, too, such as during the Roman Empire. What is particular about the 18th century?

MF: My statement was awkward in that form. Of course I did not mean to say that architecture was not political before, becoming so only at that time. I only meant to say that in the 18th century one sees the development of reflection upon architecture as a function of the aims and techniques of the government of societies. One begins to see a form of political literature that addresses what the order of a society should be, what a city should be, given the requirements of the maintenance of order; given that one should avoid epidemics, avoid revolts, permit a decent and moral family life, and so on. In terms of these objectives, how is one to conceive of both the organization of a city and the construction of a collective infrastructure? And how should houses be built? I am not saying that this sort of reflection appears only in the 18th century, but only that in the 18th century a very broad and general reflection on these questions takes place. If one opens a police report of the times – the treatises that are devoted to the techniques of government – one finds that architecture and urbanism occupy a place of considerable importance. That is what I meant to say.

Q: Among the Ancients, in Rome or Greece, what was the difference?

MF: In discussing Rome one sees that the problem revolves around Vitruvius. Vitruvius was reinterpreted from the 16th century on, but one can find in the 16th century – and no doubt in the Middle Ages as well – many considerations of the same order as Vitruvius; if you consider them as *reflections upon*. The treatises on politics, on the art of government, on the manner of good government, did not generally include chapters or analyses devoted to the organization of cities or to architecture. The *Republic* of Jean Bodin (Paris, 1577) does not contain extended discussions of the role of architecture, whereas the police treatises of the 18th century are full of them.

Q: Do you mean that there were techniques and practices, but the discourse did not exist?

MF: I did not say that discourse upon architecture did not exist before the 18th century. Nor do I mean to say the discussions of architecture before the 18th century lacked any political dimension or significance. What I wished to point out is that from the 18th century on, every discussion of politics as the art of government of men necessarily includes a chapter or a series of chapters on urbanism, on collective facilities, on hygiene, and on private architecture. Such chapters are not found in the discussions of the art of government of the 16th century. This change is perhaps not in the reflections of architects upon architecture, but it is quite clearly seen in the reflections of political men.

Q: It was not necessarily a change within the theory of architecture itself?

MF: That's right. It was not necessarily a change in the minds of architects, or in their techniques – although that remains to be seen – but in the minds of political men in the choice and the form of attention that they bring to bear upon the objects that are of concern to them. Architecture became one of these during the 17th and 18th centuries.

Q: Could you tell us why?

MF: Well, I think it was linked to a number of phenomena, such as the question of the city and the idea that was clearly formulated at the beginning of the 17th century that the government of a large state like France should ultimately think of its territory on the model of the city. The city was no longer perceived as a place of privilege, as an exception in a territory of fields, forests, and roads. The cities were no longer islands beyond the common law. Instead, the cities, with the problems that they raised, and the particular forms that they took, served as the models for the governmental rationality that was to apply to the whole of the territory.

There is an entire series of utopias or projects for governing territory that developed on the premise that a state is like a large city; the capital is like its main square; the roads are like its streets. A state will be well-organized when a system of policing as tight and efficient as that of the cities extends over the entire territory. At the outset, the notion of police applied only to the set of regulations that were to assure the tranquility of a city, but at that moment the police become the very *type* of rationality for the government of the whole territory. The model of the city became the matrix for the regulations that apply to a whole state.

The notion of police, even in France today, is frequently misunderstood. When one speaks to a Frenchman about police, he can only think of people in uniform or in the secret service. In the 17th and 18th centuries, "police" signified a program of government rationality. This can be characterized as a project to create a system of regulation of the general conduct of individuals whereby everything would be controlled to the point of self-sustenance, without the need of intervention. This is a rather typically French effort of policing. The English did not develop a comparable system, mainly because of parliamentary traditions on the one hand, and traditions of local, communal autonomy on the other, not to mention the religious system.

One can place Napoleon almost exactly at the break between the old organization of the 18th-century police state (understood, of course, in the sense we have been discussing, not in the sense of the "police state" as we have come to know it) and the forms of the modern state, which he invented. At any rate, it seems that, during the 18th and 19th centuries, there appeared – rather quickly in the case of commerce and more slowly in all the other domains – this idea of a police that would manage to penetrate, to stimulate, to regulate, and to render almost automatic all the mechanisms of society.

This idea has been abandoned. The question has been turned around. No longer do we ask, What is the form of governmental rationality that will be able to penetrate the body politic to its most fundamental elements? But rather, How is government possible? That is, what is the principle of limitation that applies to governmental actions such that things will occur for the best, in conformity with the rationality of government, and without intervention?

It is here that the question of liberalism comes up. It seems to me that at that very moment it became apparent that if one governed too much, one did not govern at all – that one provoked results contrary to those one desired. What was discovered at that time – and this was one of the great discoveries of political thought at the end of the 18th century – was the idea of *society*. That is to say, that government not only has to deal with a territory, with a domain, and with its subjects, but that it also has to deal with a complex and independent reality that has its own laws and mechanisms of disturbance. This new reality is society. From the moment that one is to manipulate a society, one cannot consider it completely penetrable by police. One must take into account what it is. It becomes necessary to reflect upon it, upon its specific characteristics, its constants and its variables . . .

Q: So there is a change in the importance of space. In the 18th century there was a territory and the problem of governing people in this territory; one can choose as an example *La Métropolite* (1682) of Alexandre LeMaitre – a utopian treatise on how to build a capital city – or one can understand a city as a metaphor or symbol for the territory and how to govern it. All of this is quite spatial, whereas after Napoleon, society is not necessarily so *spatialized* . . .

MF: That's right. On one hand, it is not so spatialized, yet at the same time a certain number of problems that are properly seen as spatial emerged. Urban space has its own dangers: disease, such as the epidemics of cholera in Europe from 1830 to about 1880; and revolution, such as the series of urban revolts that shook all of Europe during the same period. These spatial problems, which were perhaps not new, took on a new importance.

Secondly, a new aspect of the relations of space and power were [*sic*] the railroads. These were to establish a network of communication no longer corresponding necessarily to the traditional network of roads, but they nonetheless had to take into account the nature of society and its history. In addition, there are all the social phenomena that railroads give rise to, be they the resistances they provoked, the transformations of population, or changes in the behavior of people. Europe was immediately sensitive to the changes in behavior that the railroads entailed. What was going to happen, for example, if it was possible to get married between Bordeaux and Nantes? Something that was not possible before. What was going to happen when people in Germany and France might get to know one another? Would war still be possible once there were railroads? In France a theory developed that the railroads would increase familiarity among people and that the new forms of human universality made possible would render war impossible. But what the people did not foresee — although the German military command was fully aware of it, since they were much cleverer than their French counterpart — was that, on the contrary, the railroads rendered war far easier to wage. The third development, which came later, was electricity.

So, there were problems in the links between the exercise of political power and the space of a territory, or the space of cities — links that were completely new.

Q: So, it was less a matter of architecture than before. These are sorts of technics of space . . .

MF: The major problems of space, from the 19th century on, were indeed of a different type. Which is not to say that problems of an architectural nature were forgotten. In terms of the first ones I referred to — disease and the political problems — architecture has a very important role to play. The reflections on urbanism and on the design of workers' housing — all of these questions — are an area of reflection upon architecture.

Q: But architecture itself, the Ecole des Beaux-Arts, belongs to a completely different set of spatial issues.

MF: That's right. With the birth of these new technologies and these new economic processes one sees the birth of a sort of thinking about space that's no longer modeled upon the police state of the urbanization of the territory, but that extends far beyond limits of urbanism and architecture.

Q: Consequently, the Ecole des Ponts et Chaussées . . .

MF: That's right. The Ecole des Ponts et Chaussées and its capital importance in political rationality in France are part of this. It was not architects, but engineers and builders of bridges, roads, viaducts, railways, as well as the Polytechnicians (who practically controlled the French railroads) — those are the people who thought out space.

Q: Has this situation continued up to the present, or are we witnessing a change in relations between the technicians of space?

MF: We may well witness some changes, but I think that we have until now remained with the developers of the territory, the people of the Ponts et Chaussées, etc.

Q: So architects are not necessarily the masters of space that they once were, or believed themselves to be.

MF: That's right. They are not the technicians or engineers of the three great variables — territory, communication, and speed. These escape the domain of architects.

Q: Do you see any particular architectural projects, either in the past or the present, as forces of liberation or resistance?

MF: I do not think that it is possible to say that one thing is of the order of "liberation" and another of the order of "oppression." There are a number of things that one can say with some certainty about a concentration camp to the effect that it is not an instrument of liberation, but one should still take into account – and this is not generally acknowledged – that aside from torture and execution, which preclude any resistance, no matter how terrifying a given system may be, there always remain the possibilities of resistance, disobedience, and oppositional groupings.

On the other hand, I do not think that there is anything that is functionally – by its very nature – absolutely liberating. Liberty is a practice. So there may, in fact, always be, a number of projects whose aim is to modify some constraints, to loosen, or even to break them, but none of these projects can, simply by its nature, assure that people will have liberty automatically: that it will be established by the project itself. The liberty of men is never assured by the institutions and laws that are intended to guarantee them. This is why almost all of these laws and institutions are quite capable of being turned around. Not because they are ambiguous, but simply because "liberty" is what must be exercised.

Q: Are there urban examples of this? Or examples where architects succeeded?

MF: Well, up to a point there is Le Corbusier, who is described today – with a sort of cruelty that I find perfectly useless – as a sort of crypto-Stalinist. He was, I am sure, someone full of good intentions, and what he did was in fact dedicated to liberating effects. Perhaps the means that he proposed were in the end less liberating than he thought, but, once again, I think that it can never be inherent in the structure of things to guarantee the exercise of freedom. The guarantee of freedom is freedom.

Q: So you do not think of Le Corbusier as an example of success. You are simply saying that his intention was liberating. Can you give us a successful example?

MF: No. It *cannot* succeed. If one were to find a place, and perhaps there are some, where liberty is effectively exercised, one would find that this is not owing to the order of objects, but, once again, owing to the practice of liberty. Which is not to say, after all, one may as well leave people in slums thinking that they can simply exercise their rights there.

Q: Meaning that architecture in itself cannot resolve social problems?

MF: I think it can and does produce positive effects when the liberating intentions of the architect coincide with the real practice of people in the exercise of their freedom.

Q: But the same architecture can serve other ends.

MF: Absolutely. Let me bring up another example: The *Familistère* of Jean-Baptiste Godin at Guise (1859). The architecture of Godin was clearly intended for the freedom of people. Here was something that manifested the power of ordinary workers to participate in the exercise of their trade. It was a rather important sign and instrument of autonomy for a group of workers. Yet no one could enter or leave the place without being seen by everyone – an aspect of the architecture that could be totally oppressive. But it could only be oppressive if people were prepared to use their own presence in order to watch over others. Let's imagine a community of unlimited sexual practices that might be established there. It would once again become a place of freedom. I think it is somewhat arbitrary to try to dissociate the effective practice of freedom by people, the practice of social relations, and the spatial distributions in which they find themselves. If they are separated, they become impossible to understand. Each can only be understood through the other.

Q: Yet people have often attempted to find utopian schemes to liberate people, or to oppress them.

MF: Men have dreamed of liberating machines. But there are no machines of freedom, by definition. This is not to say that the exercise of freedom is completely indifferent to spatial distribution, but it can only function when there is a certain convergence; in the case of divergence or distortion it immediately becomes the opposite of that which had been intended. The panoptic qualities of Guise could perfectly well have allowed it to be used as a prison. Nothing could be simpler. It is clear that, in fact, the *Familistère* may well have served as an instrument for discipline and a rather unbearable group pressure.

Q: So once again the intention of the architect is not the fundamental determining factor.

MF: Nothing is fundamental. That is what is interesting in the analysis of society. That is why nothing irritates me as much as these inquiries – which are by definition metaphysical – on the foundations of power in a society or the self-institution of a society, etc. These are not fundamental phenomena. There are only reciprocal relations, and the perpetual gaps between intentions in relation to one another.

Q: You have singled out doctors, prison wardens, priests, judges, and psychiatrists as key figures in the political configurations that involve domination. Would you put architects on this list?

MF: You know, I was not really attempting to describe figures of domination when I referred to doctors and people like that, but rather to describe people through whom power passed or who are important in the fields of power relations. A patient in a mental institution is placed within a field of fairly complicated power relations, which Erving Goffman analyzed very well. The pastor in a Christian or Catholic church (in Protestant churches it is somewhat different) is an important link in a set of power relations. The architect is not an individual of that sort.

After all, the architect has no power over me. If I want to tear down or change a house he built for me, put up new partitions, add a chimney, the architect has no control. So the architect should be placed in another category – which is not to say that he is totally foreign to the organization, the implementation, and all the techniques of power that are exercised in a society. I would say that one must take him – his mentality, his attitude – into account as well as his projects, in order to understand a certain number of the techniques of power that are invested in architecture, but he is not comparable to a doctor, a priest, a psychiatrist, or a prison warden.

Q: "Post-modernism" has received a great deal of attention recently in architectural circles. It is also being talked about in philosophy, notably by Jean-François Lyotard and Jürgen Habermas. Clearly, historical reference and language play an important role in the modern *episteme*. How do you see post-modernism, both as architecture and in terms of the historical and philosophical questions that are raised by it?

MF: I think there is a widespread and facile tendency, which one should combat, to designate that which has just occurred as the primary enemy as if this were always the principal form of oppression from which one had to liberate oneself. Now, this simple attitude entails a number of dangerous consequences: first, an inclination to seek out some cheap form of archaism or some imaginary past forms of happiness that people did not, in fact, have at all. For instance, in the area that interests me, it is very amusing to see how contemporary sexuality is described as something absolutely terrible. To think that it is only possible now to make love after turning off the television! And in mass-produced beds! "Not like the wonderful time when . . ." Well, what about those wonderful times when people worked eighteen hours a day and there were six people in a bed, if one was lucky enough to have a bed! There is in this hatred of the present or the immediate past a dangerous tendency to invoke a completely mythical past. Secondly, there is the problem raised by Habermas: if one abandons the work of Kant or Weber, for example, one runs the risk of lapsing into irrationality.

I am completely in agreement with this, but at the same time, our question is quite different. I think that the central issue of philosophy and critical thought since the 18th century has been, still is, and will, I hope, remain the question, *What* is this Reason that we use? What are its historical effects? What are its limits, and what are its dangers? How can we exist as rational beings, fortunately committed to practicing a rationality that is unfortunately crisscrossed by intrinsic dangers? One should not forget – and I'm not saying this in order to criticize rationality, but in order to show how ambiguous things are – it was on the basis of the flamboyant rationality of Social Darwinism that racism was formulated, becoming one of the most enduring and powerful ingredients of Nazism. This was, of course, an irrationality, but an irrationality that was at the same time, after all, a certain form of rationality . . .

This is the situation that we are in and that we must combat. If intellectuals in general are to have a function, if critical thought itself has a function, and, even more specifically, if philosophy has a function within critical thought, it is precisely to accept this sort of spiral, this sort of revolving door of rationality that refers us to its necessity, to its indispensability, and at the same time, to its intrinsic dangers.

Q: All that being said, it would be fair to say that you are much less afraid of historicism and the play of historical references than someone like Habermas is; also that this issue has been raised in architecture as almost a crisis of civilization by the defenders of modernism, who contend that if we abandon modern architecture for a frivolous return to decoration and motifs, we are somehow abandoning civilization. On the other hand, some post-modernists have claimed that historical references per se are somehow meaningful and are going to protect us from the dangers of an overly rationalized world.

MF: Although it may not answer your question, I would say this: one should totally and absolutely suspect anything that claims to be a return. One reason is a logical one; there is in fact no such thing as a return. History, and the meticulous interest applied to history, is certainly one of the best defenses against this theme of the return. For me, the history of madness or the studies of the prison . . . were done in that precise manner because I knew full well – this is in fact what aggravated many people – that I was carrying out an historical analysis in such a manner that people *could* criticize the present, but it was impossible for them to say, "Let's go back to the good old days when madmen in the eighteenth century . . ." or, "Let's go back to the days when the prison was not one of the principal instruments . . ." No; I think that history preserves us from that sort of ideology of the return.

Q: Hence, the simple opposition between reason and history is rather silly . . . choosing sides between the two . . .

MF: Yes. Well, the problem for Habermas is, after all, to make a transcendental mode of thought spring forth against any historicism. I am, indeed, far more historicist and Nietzschean. I do not think that there is a proper usage of history or a proper usage of intrahistorical analysis – which is fairly lucid, by the way – that works precisely against this ideology of the return. A good study of peasant architecture in Europe, for example, would show the utter vanity of wanting to return to the little individual house with its thatched roof. History protects us from historicism – from a historicism that calls on the past to resolve the questions of the present.

Q: It also reminds us that there is always a history; that those modernists who wanted to suppress any reference to the past were making a mistake.

MF: Of course.

Q: Your next two books deal with sexuality among the Greeks and the early Christians. Are there any particular architectural dimensions to the issues you discuss?

MF: I didn't find any; absolutely none. But what is interesting is that in Imperial Rome there were, in fact, brothels, pleasure quarters, criminal areas, etc., and there was also one sort of quasi-public place of pleasure: the baths, the *thermes*. The baths were a very important place of pleasure and encounter, which slowly disappeared in Europe. In the Middle Ages, the baths were still a place of encounter between men and women as well as of men and men and women with women, although that is rarely talked about. What was referred to and condemned, as well as practiced, were the encounters between men and women, which disappeared over the course of the 16th and 17th centuries.

Q: In the Arab world it continues.

MF: Yes; but in France it has largely ceased. It still existed in the 19th century. One sees it in *Les Enfants du Paradis*, and it is historically exact. One of the characters, Lacenaire, was – no one mentions it – a swine and a pimp who used young boys to attract older men and then blackmailed them; there is a scene that refers to this. It required all the naivete and antihomosexuality of the Surrealists to overlook that fact. So the baths continued to exist, as a place of sexual encounters. The bath was a sort of cathedral of pleasure at the heart of the city, where people could go as often as they wanted, where they walked about, picked each other up, met each other, took their pleasure, ate, drank, discussed . . .

Q: So sex was not separated from the other pleasures. It was inscribed in the center of the cities. It was public; it served a purpose . . .

MF: That's right. Sexuality was obviously considered a social pleasure for the Greeks and the Romans. What is interesting about male homosexuality today – this has apparently been the case of female homosexuals for some time – is that their sexual relations are immediately transferred into social relations and the social relations are understood as sexual relations. For the Greeks and the Romans, in a different fashion, sexual relations were located within social relations in the widest sense of the term. The baths were a place of sociality that included sexual relations.

One can directly compare the bath and the brothel. The brothel is in fact a place, and an architecture, of pleasure. There is, in fact, a very interesting form of sociality that was studied by Alain Corbin in *Les Filles de Noces* (Aubier, 1978). The men of the city met at the brothel; they were tied to one another by the fact that the same women passed through their hands, that the same diseases and infections were communicated to them. There was a sociality of the brothel; but the sociality of the baths as it existed among the Ancients – a new version of which could perhaps exist again – was completely different from the sociality of the brothel.

Q: We now know a great deal about disciplinary architecture. What about confessional architecture – the kind of architecture that would be associated with a confessional technology?

MF: You mean religious architecture? I think that it has been studied. There is the whole problem of a monastery as xenophobic. There one finds precise regulations concerning life in common; affecting sleeping, eating, prayer, the place of each individual in all of that, the cells. All of this was programmed from very early on.

Q: In a technology of power, of confession as opposed to discipline, space seems to play a central role as well.

MF: Yes, space is fundamental in any form of communal life; space is fundamental in any exercise of power. To make a parenthetical remark, I recall having been invited, in 1966, by a group of architects to do a study of space, of something that I called at that time "heterotopias," those singular spaces to be found in some given social spaces whose functions are different or even the opposite of others. The architects worked on this, and at the end of the study someone spoke up – a Sartrean psychologist – who firebombed me, saying that *space* is reactionary and capitalist, but *history* and *becoming* are revolutionary. This absurd discourse was not at all unusual at the time. Today everyone would be convulsed with laughter at such a pronouncement, but not then.

Q: Architects in particular, if they choose to analyze an institutional building such as a hospital or a school in terms of its disciplinary function, would tend to focus primarily on the walls. After all, that is what they design. Your approach is perhaps more concerned with space, rather than architecture, in that the physical walls are only one aspect of the institution. How would you characterize the difference between these two approaches, between the building itself and space?

MF: I think there is a difference in method and approach. It is true that for me, architecture, in the very vague analyses of it that I have been able to conduct, is only taken as an element of support, to insure a certain allocation of people in space, a *canalization* of their circulation, as well as the coding of their reciprocal relations. So it is not only considered as an element in space, but is especially thought of as a plunge into a field of social relations in which it brings about some specific effects.

For example, I know that there is an historian who is carrying out some interesting studies of the archeology of the Middle Ages, in which he takes up the problem of architecture, in terms of the problem of the chimney. I think that he is in the process of showing that from a certain time on it was possible to build a chimney inside the house – a chimney with a hearth, not simply an open room or a chimney outside the house; that at that moment all sorts of things changed and relations between individuals became possible. All of this seems very interesting to me, but the conclusion that he presented in an article was that the history of ideas and thoughts is useless.

What is, in fact, interesting is that the two are rigorously indivisible. Why did people struggle to find the way to put a chimney inside the house? Or why did they put their techniques to this use? So often in the history of techniques it takes years or even centuries to implement them. It is certain, and of capital importance, that this technique was a formative influence upon new human relations, but it is impossible to think that it would have been developed and adapted had there not been in the play and strategy of human relations something which tended in that direction. What is interesting is always interconnection, not the primacy of this over that, which never has any meaning.

Q: In your book *The Order of Things* you constructed certain vivid spatial metaphors to describe structures of thought. Why do you think spatial images are so evocative for these references? What is the relationship between these spatial metaphors describing disciplines and more concrete descriptions of institutional spaces?

MF: It is quite possible that since I was interested in the problems of space I used quite a number of spatial metaphors in *The Order of Things*, but usually these metaphors were not ones that I advanced, but ones that I was studying as objects. What is striking in the epistemological mutations and transformations of the 17th century is to see how the spatialization of knowledge was one of the factors in the constitution of this knowledge as a science. If the natural history and the classifications of Linneas were possible, it is for a certain number of reasons: on the one hand, there was literally a spatialization of the very object of their analyses, since they gave themselves the rule of studying and classifying a plant only on the basis of that which was visible. They didn't even want to use the microscope. All the traditional elements of knowledge, such as the medical functions of the plant, fell away. The object was spatialized. Subsequently, it was spatialized insofar as the principles of classification had to be found in the very structure of the plant: the number of elements, how they were arranged, their size, etc., and other elements, like the height of the plant. Then there was the spatialization into illustrations within books, which was only possible with some printing techniques. Then the spatialization of the reproduction of the plants themselves, which was represented in books. All of these are spatial techniques, not metaphors.

Q: Is the actual plan for a building – the precise drawing that becomes walls and windows – the same form of discourse as, say, a hierarchical pyramid that describes rather precisely relations between people not only in space but in social life?

MF: Well, I think there are a few simple and exceptional examples in which the architectural means reproduce, with more or less emphasis, the social hierarchies. There is the model of the military camp, where the military hierarchy is to be read in the ground itself, by the place occupied by the tents and the buildings reserved for each rank. It reproduces precisely through architecture a pyramid of power; but this is an exceptional example, as is everything military – privileged in society and of an extreme simplicity.

Q: But the plan itself is not always an account of relations or power.

MF: No. Fortunately for human imagination, things are a little more complicated than that.

Q: Architecture is not, of course, a constant: it has a long tradition of changing preoccupations, changing systems, different rules. The *savoir* of architecture is partly the history of the profession, partly the evolution of a science of construction, and partly a rewriting of aesthetic theories. What do you think is particular about this form of *savoir*? Is it more like a natural science, or what you have called a "dubious science"?

MF: I can't exactly say that this distinction between sciences that are certain and those that are uncertain is of no interest – that would be dodging the question – but I must say that what interests me more is to focus on what the Greeks called the *technè*, that is to say, a practical rationality governed by a conscious goal. I am not even sure if it is worth constantly asking the question of whether government can be the object of an exact science. On the other hand, if architecture, like the practice of government and the practice of other forms of social organization, is considered as a *technè*, possibly using elements of sciences like physics, for example, or statistics, etc. . . . . that is what is interesting. But if one wanted to do a history of architecture, I think that it should be much more along the lines of that general history of the *technè*, rather than the histories of either the exact sciences or the inexact ones. The disadvantage of this word *technè*, I realize, is its relation to the word "technology," which has a very specific meaning. A very narrow meaning is given to "technology": one thinks of hard technology, the technology of wood, of fire, of electricity. Whereas government is also a function of technology: the government of individuals, the government of souls, the government of the self by the self, the government of families, the government of children, and so on. I believe that if one placed the history of architecture back in this general history of *technè*, in this wide sense of the word, one would have a more interesting guiding concept than by considering opposition between the exact sciences and the inexact ones.

Note

1   "Questions on Geography," from *Hérodote* 1 (1976), reprinted in *Power/Knowledge: Selected Interviews and Other Writings by Michel Foucault, 1972–1977*, ed. Colin Gordon (New York: Pantheon Books, 1980), p. 69.

Chapter 9

Friedrich A. Kittler

INTRODUCTION TO *GRAMOPHONE, FILM, TYPEWRITER* [1986]

Source: Friedrich A. Kittler (1999) 'Introduction', in *Gramophone, Film, Typewriter*, translated by Geoffrey Winthrop-Young and Michael Wutz, Stanford: Stanford University Press, pp. 1–19.

For Vilém Flusser human animals are peculiar not because they communicate (most animals do that) but because they store their communications. For Flusser there is a perversity in holding on to what is, in the larger animal kingdom, a necessarily fleeting phenomenon. Flusser sees the storage of communication as a protection against chaos, an attempt at negative entropy. In this the storage, sorting and retrieval of communication is both negatively entropic (it tries to build order out of disorder) and positively entropic (the more communication is stored the harder it is to produce order). As design culture puts more and more energy into constructing devices and networks with immense storage capabilities, we are getting lost in the data drift.

Friedrich Kittler is a theorist of storage and *mediality*. Following in the tradition of the likes of Marshall McLuhan and less well-known figures such as Flusser, Kittler's focus is on the materialities of communication. Durable forms of communication (from writing to binary code) and technical processes of reproduction (from the printing press, through to photography, film and video) mean that our media culture has to be thought of as a network of storage devices (books, CDs, data banks). But while this describes a continuum from Johannes Gutenberg through to Bill Gates, Kittler is also keen to mark significant discontinuities too. If storage is continuous, mediality is discontinuous. Mediality is the specificity and peculiarity of a media form, and for Kittler the mediality changes when the storage devices (such as film and the gramophone) no longer rely on a symbolic currency and instead deal in mimetic simulations. This is, though, a movement not from the symbol to the index, but from the symbolic register to the realm of the 'real'. And this is where Kittler's work is, on the surface, at its most counter-intuitive: the move from writing to simulation could, after all, be understood as the gradual advancement of unreality (or 'real unreality' as Guy Debord might have it). But Kittler has a specific reference in mind when he talks about the move from the symbolic to the real, and that is the French poststructuralist psychoanalyst Jacques Lacan. For Lacan the Imaginary, the Symbolic and the Real are 'orders' that we move between and that constitute us (the Imaginary, for instance, is a realm where ego formation takes place). The Real is in many ways the most difficult to grasp: it is at once traumatic, absolute and impossible. For our purpose we could think of it as hermetic and beyond reference. Perhaps the best way of understanding it, though, is by using an example from design culture.

One of the objects that Kittler often refers to is the recording *Dark Side of the Moon* (1973) by Pink Floyd – an album which according to various internet sources has sold more than 40 million copies. Pink Floyd, who met as architectural students, are a progressive rock band noted for the combination of blues music and psychedelic culture. But what interests Kittler about the album *Dark Side of the Moon* is not its cultural references but its mediality. If you ignore the overly portentous lyrics and the solemn pastoral rock, then you are left with the 'impossible' object of the record. What you are listening to when you hear *Dark Side of the Moon* are the recording capabil-ities of 1973, which, for instance, allowed the singer to harmonise with himself, and included excessive multitracking. For Kittler the 'real' of *Dark Side of the Moon* is its tautological aspect: it is a recording whose referent is recording. This is its mediality. And while this mediality is vividly shown by *Dark Side of the Moon*, it is also a material condition of media design since the advent of simulation technologies.

Further reading: Gumbrecht and Pfeiffer 1994; Kittler 2001; Ronell 1991; Zielinski 1998, 2006.

OPTICAL FIBER NETWORKS. People will be hooked to an information channel that can be used for any medium – for the first time in history, or for its end. Once movies and music, phone calls and texts reach households via optical fiber cables, the formerly distinct media of television, radio, telephone, and mail converge, standardized by transmission frequencies and bit format. The optoelectronic channel in particular will be immune to disturbances that might randomize the pretty bit patterns behind the images and sounds. Immune, that is, to the bomb. As is well known, nuclear blasts send an electromagnetic pulse (EMP) through the usual copper cables, which would infect all connected computers.

The Pentagon is engaged in farsighted planning: only the substitution of optical fibers for metal cables can accommodate the enormous rates and volumes of bits required, spent, and celebrated by electronic warfare. All early warning systems, radar installations, missile bases, and army staffs in Europe, the opposite coast,[1] finally will be connected to computers safe from EMP and thus will remain operational in wartime. In the meantime, pleasure is produced as a by-product: people are free to channel-surf among entertainment media. After all, fiber optics transmit all messages imaginable save for the one that counts – the bomb.

Before the end, something is coming to an end. The general digitization of channels and information erases the differences among individual media. Sound and image, voice and text are reduced to surface effects, known to consumers as interface. Sense and the senses turn into eyewash. Their media-produced glamor will survive for an interim as a by-product of strategic programs. Inside the computers themselves everything becomes a number: quantity without image, sound, or voice. And once optical fiber networks turn formerly distinct data flows into a standardized series of digitized numbers, any medium can be translated into any other. With numbers, everything goes. Modulation, transformation, synchronization; delay, storage, transposition; scrambling, scanning, mapping – a total media link on a digital base will erase the very concept of medium. Instead of wiring people and technologies, absolute knowledge will run as an endless loop.

But there still are media; there still is entertainment.

Today's standard comprises partially connected media links that are still comprehensible in McLuhan's terms. According to him, one medium's content is always other media: film and radio constitute the content of television; records and tapes the content of radio; silent films and audiotape that of cinema; text, telephone, and telegram that of the semi-media monopoly of the postal system. Since the beginning of the century, when the electronic tube was developed by von Lieben in Germany and De Forest in California, it has been possible to amplify and transmit signals. Accordingly, the large media networks, which have been in existence since the thirties, have been able to fall back on all three storage media — writing, film, and phonography — to link up and send their signals at will.

But these links are separated by incompatible data channels and differing data formats. Electrics does not equal electronics. Within the spectrum of the general data flow, television, radio, cinema, and the postal service constitute individual and limited windows for people's sense perceptions. Infrared radiations or the radio echoes of approaching missiles are still transmitted through other channels, unlike the optical fiber networks of the future. Our media systems merely distribute the words, noises, and images people can transmit and receive. But they do not compute these data. They do not produce an output that, under computer control, transforms any algorithm into any interface effect, to the point where people take leave of their senses. At this point, the only thing being computed is the transmission quality of storage media, which appear in the media links as the content of the media. A compromise between engineers and salespeople regulates how poor the sound from a TV set can be, how fuzzy movie images can be, or how much a beloved voice on the telephone can be filtered. Our sense perceptions are the dependent variable of this compromise.

A composite of face and voice that remains calm, even when faced during a televised debate by an opponent named Richard M. Nixon, is deemed telegenic and may win a presidential election, as in Kennedy's case. Voices that an optical close-up would reveal as treacherous, however, are called radiogenic and rule over the VE 301, the *Volksempfänger* of the Second World War. For, as the Heidegger disciple among Germany's early radio experts realized, "death is primarily a radio topic."[2]

But these sense perceptions had to be fabricated first. For media to link up and achieve dominance, we need a coincidence in the Lacanian sense: that something ceases not to write itself. Prior to the electrification of media, and well before their electronic end, there were modest, merely mechanical apparatuses. Unable to amplify or transmit, they nevertheless were the first to store sensory data: silent movies stored sights, and Edison's phonograph (which, unlike Berliner's later gramophone, was capable both of recording and reproducing) stored sounds.

On December 6, 1877, Edison, lord of the first research laboratory in the history of technology, presented the prototype of the phonograph to the public. On February 20, 1892, the same lab in Menlo Park (near New York) added the so-called kinetoscope. Three years later, the Lumière brothers in France and the Skladanowsky brothers in Germany merely had to add a means of projection to turn Edison's invention into cinema.

Ever since that epochal change we have been in possession of storage technologies that can record and reproduce the very time flow of acoustic and optical data. Ears and eyes have become autonomous. And that changed the state of reality more than lithography and photography, which (according to Benjamin's thesis) in the first third of the nineteenth century merely propelled the work of art into the age of its technical reproducibility. Media "define what really is";[3] they are always already beyond aesthetics.

What phonographs and cinematographs, whose names not coincidentally derive from writing, were able to store was time: time as a mixture of audio frequencies in the acoustic realm and as the movement of single-image sequences in the optical. Time determines the limit of all art, which first has to arrest the daily data flow in order to turn it into images or signs. What is called style in art is merely the switchboard of these scannings and selections. That same switchboard also controls those arts that use writing as a serial, that is, temporally transposed, data flow. To record the sound sequences of speech, literature has to arrest them in a system of 26 letters, thereby categorically excluding all noise sequences. Not coincidentally, this system also contains as a subsystem the seven notes, whose diatonics — from A to G — form the basis of occidental music. Following a suggestion made by the musicologist von Hornbostel, it is possible to fix the chaos of exotic music assailing European ears by first interpolating a phonograph, which is able to record this chaos in real time and then replay it in slow motion. As the rhythms begin to flag and "individual measures, even individual notes resound on their own," occidental alphabetism with its staffs can proceed to an "exact notation."[4]

Texts and scores – Europe had no other means of storing time. Both are based on a writing system whose time is (in Lacan's term) symbolic. Using projections and retrievals, this time memorizes itself – like a chain of chains. Nevertheless, whatever ran as time on a physical or (again in Lacan's terms) real level, blindly and unpredictably, could by no means be encoded. Therefore, all data flows, provided they really were streams of data, had to pass through the bottleneck of the signifier. Alphabetic monopoly, grammatology.

If the film called history rewinds itself, it turns into an endless loop. What will soon end in the monopoly of bits and fiber optics began with the monopoly of writing. History was the homogenized field that, as an academic subject, only took account of literate cultures. Mouths and graphisms were relegated to prehistory. Otherwise, stories and histories (both deriving from *historia*) could not have been linked. All the orders and judgments, announcements and prescriptions (military and legal, religious and medical) that produced mountains of corpses were communicated along the very same channel that monopolized the descriptions of those mountains of corpses. Which is why anything that ever happened ended up in libraries.

And Foucault, the last historian or first archeologist, merely had to look things up. The suspicion that all power emanates from and returns to archives could be brilliantly confirmed, at least within the realms of law, medicine, and theology. A tautology of history, or its calvary. For the libraries in which the archeologist found so much rich material collected and catalogued papers that had been extremely diverse in terms of addressee, distribution technique, degree of secrecy, and writing technique – Foucault's archive as the entropy of a post office.[5] Even writing itself, before it ends up in libraries, is a communication medium, the technology of which the archeologist simply forgot. It is for this reason that all his analyses end immediately before that point in time at which other media penetrated the library's stacks. Discourse analysis cannot be applied to sound archives or towers of film rolls.

As long as it was moving along, history was indeed Foucault's "wave-like succession of words."[6] More simply, but no less technically than tomorrow's fiber optic cables, writing functioned as a universal medium – in times when there was no concept of medium. Whatever else was going on dropped through the filter of letters or ideograms.

"Literature," Goethe wrote, "is a fragment of fragments; only the smallest proportion of what took place and what was said was written down, while only the smallest proportion of what was written down has survived."[7]

Accordingly, oral history today confronts the historians' writing monopoly; accordingly, a media theoretician like the Jesuit priest Walter J. Ong, who must have been concerned with the spirit of the Pentecostal mystery, could celebrate a primary orality of tribal cultures as opposed to the secondary orality of our media acoustics. Such research remained unthinkable as long as the opposite of "history" was simply termed (again following Goethe) "legend."[8] Prehistory was subsumed by its mythical name; Goethe's definition of literature did not even have to mention optical or acoustic data flows. And even legends, those oralized segments of bygone events, only survived in written format; that is, under pretechnological but literary conditions. However, since it has become possible to record the epics of the last Homeric bards, who until recently were wandering through Serbia and Croatia, oral mnemotechnics or cultures have become reconstructible in a completely different way.[9] Even Homer's rosy-fingered Eos changes from a Goddess into a piece of chromium dioxide that was stored in the memory of the bard and could be combined with other pieces into whole epics. "Primary orality" and "oral history" came into existence only after the end of the writing monopoly, as the technological shadows of the apparatuses that document them.

Writing, however, stored writing – no more and no less. The holy books attest to this. Exodus, chapter 20, contains a copy of what Yahweh's own finger originally had written on two stone tablets: the law. But of the thunder and lightning, of the thick cloud and the mighty trumpet which, according to scripture, surrounded this first act of writing on Mount Sinai, that same Bible could store nothing but mere words.[10]

Even less is handed down of the nightmares and temptations that afflicted a nomad called Mohammed following his flight to the holy mountain of Hira. The Koran does not begin until the one God takes the place of the many demons. The archangel Gabriel descends from the seventh heaven with a roll of scripture and the command to decipher the scroll. "Rejoice in the name of the Lord who created – created man from clots of blood. Recite! Your Lord is the Most Bountiful One, who by pen taught man what he did not know."[11]

Mohammed, however, answers that he, the nomad, can't read; not even the divine message about the origin of reading and writing. The archangel has to repeat his command before an illiterate can turn into the founder of a book-based religion. For soon, or all too soon, the illegible scroll makes sense and presents to Mohammed's miraculously alphabetized eyes the very same text that Gabriel had already uttered twice as an oral command. Mohammed's illuminations began, according to tradition, with this 96th sura – in order then to be "memorized by the faithful and written down on primitive surfaces such as palm leaves, stones, wood, bones, and pieces of leather, and to be recited, again and again, by Mohammed and select believers, especially during Ramadan."[12]

Writing therefore merely stores the fact of its authorization. It celebrates the storage monopoly of the God who invented it. And since the realm of this God consists of signs that only nonreaders can't make sense of, all books are books of the dead, like the Egyptian ones with which literature began.[13] The book itself coincides with the realm of the dead beyond all senses into which it lures us. When the Stoic philosopher Zeno asked the oracle at Delphi how he should best lead his life, he was given the answer "that he should mate with the dead. He understood this to mean that he should *read* the *ancients*."[14]

The story of how the divine instructions to use quills extended beyond Moses and Mohammed and reached simpler and simpler people is a lengthy one that nobody can write, because it would be history itself. In much the same way, the storage capacities of our computers will soon coincide with electronic warfare and, gigabyte upon gigabyte, exceed all the processing capacities of historians.

Suffice it to say that one day – in Germany, this may have already been the case during the age of Goethe – the homogenous medium of writing also became homogenous in the social sphere. Compulsory education engulfed people in paper. They learned a way of writing that, as an "abuse of language" (according to Goethe), no longer had to struggle with cramped muscles and individual letters, but rather proceeded in rapture or darkness. They learned to read "silently to one's self," a "sorry substitute for speech"[15] that consumed letters without effort by bypassing oral organs. Whatever they emitted and received was writing. And because only that exists which can be posted, bodies themselves fell under the regime of the symbolic. What is unthinkable today was once reality: no film stored the movements they made or saw, no phonograph, the noise they made or heard. For whatever existed failed before time. Silhouettes or pastel drawings fixed facial expressions, and scores were unable to store noise. But once a hand took hold of a pen, something miraculous occurred: the body, which did not cease not to write itself, left strangely unavoidable traces.

> I'm ashamed to tell of it. I'm ashamed of my handwriting. It exposes me in all my spiritual nakedness. My handwriting shows me more naked than I am with my clothes off. No leg, no breath, no clothes, no sound. Neither voice nor reflection. All cleaned out. Instead, a whole man's being, shriveled and misshapen, like his scribble-scrabble. His lines are all that's left of him, as well as his self-propagation. The uneven tracings of his pencil on paper, so minimal that a blind man's fingertips would hardly detect them, become the measure of the whole fellow.[16]

Today, this shame, which overcomes the hero of Botho Strauss's last love story, *Dedication*, whenever he sees his handwriting, is no more than an anachronism. The fact that the minimal unevenness between stroke and paper can store neither a voice nor an image of a body presupposes in its exclusion the invention of phonography and cinema. Before their invention, however, handwriting alone could guarantee the perfect securing of traces. It wrote and wrote, in an energetic and ideally uninterrupted flow. As Hegel so correctly observed, the alphabetized individual had his "appearance and externality"[17] in this continuous flow of ink or letters.

And what applied to writing also applied to reading. Even if the alphabetized individual known as the "author" finally had to fall from the private exteriority of handwriting into the anonymous exteriority of print in order to secure "all that's left of him, as well as his self-propagation" – alphabetized individuals known as "readers" were able to reverse this exteriorization. "If one reads in the right way," Novalis wrote, "the words will unfold in us a real, visible world."[18] And his friend Schlegel added that "one believes to hear what one merely reads."[19] Perfect alphabetization was to supplement precisely those optical and acoustic data flows that, under the monopoly of writing, did not cease not to write themselves. Effort had been removed from writing, and sound from reading, in order to naturalize writing. The letters that educated readers skimmed over provided people with sights and sounds.

Aided by compulsory education and new alphabetization techniques, the book became both film and record around 1800 – not as a media-technological reality, but in the imaginary of readers' souls. As a surrogate of unstorable data flows, books came to power and glory.[20]

In 1774 an editor by the name of Goethe committed handwritten letters or *Sorrows of Young Werther* to print. The "nameless throng" (to quote the dedication of *Faust*), too, was to hear an "early song" that, like "some old half-faded song," revived "old griefs" and "old friends."[21] This was the new literary recipe for success: to surreptitiously turn the voice or handwriting of a soul into Gutenbergiana. In the last letter he wrote and sealed but did not send off before committing suicide, Werther gave his beloved the very promise of poetry: during her lifetime she would have to remain with Albert, her unloved husband, but afterwards she would be united with her lover "in the sight of the Infinite One in eternal embraces."[22] Indeed: the addressee of handwritten love letters, which were then published by a mere editor, was to be rewarded with an immortality in the shape of the novel itself. It alone was able to create the "beautiful realm"[23] in which the lovers of Goethe's *Elective Affinities*, according to the hope of their narrator, "will waken together once more."[24] Strangely enough, Eduard and Ottilie had one and the same handwriting during their lifetime. Their death elevated them to a paradise that under the storage monopoly of writing was called poetry.

And maybe that paradise was more real than our media-controlled senses can imagine. Reading intently, Werther's suicidal readers may well have perceived their hero in a real, visible world. And the lovers among Goethe's female readers, like Bettina Brentano, may well have died with the heroine of his *Elective Affinities* only to be "reborn in a more beautiful youth" through Goethe's "genius."[25] Maybe the perfectly alphabetized readers of 1800 were a living answer to the question with which Chris Marker concludes his film essay *Sans Soleil*:

> Lost at the end of the world on my island, Sal, in the company of my dogs strutting around, I remember that January in Tokyo, or rather I remember the images I filmed in Tokyo in January. They have now put themselves in place of my memory, they *are* my memory. I wonder how people who do not film, take photos, or record tapes remember, how humankind used to go about remembering.[26]

It is the same with language, which only leaves us the choice of either retaining words while losing their meaning or, vice versa, retaining meaning while losing the words.[27] Once storage media can accommodate optical and acoustic data, human memory capacity is bound to dwindle. Its "liberation"[28] is its end. As long as the book was responsible for all serial data flows, words quivered with sensuality and memory. It was the passion of all reading to hallucinate meaning between lines and letters: the visible and audible world of Romantic poetics. And the passion of all writing was (in the words of E. T. A. Hoffmann) the poet's desire to "describe" the hallucinated "picture in one's mind with all its vivid colors, the light and the shade," in order to "strike [the] gentle reader like an electric shock."[29]

Electricity itself put an end to this. Once memories and dreams, the dead and ghosts, become technically reproducible, readers and writers no longer need the powers of hallucination. Our realm of the dead has withdrawn from the books in which it resided for so long. As Diodor of Sicily once wrote, "it is no longer only through writing that the dead remain in the memory of the living."

The writer Balzac was already overcome by fear when faced with photography, as he confessed to Nadar, the great pioneer of photography. If (according to Balzac) the human body consists of many infinitely thin layers of "specters," and if the human spirit cannot be created from nothingness, then the daguerreotype must be a sinister trick: it fixes, that is, steals, one layer after the other, until nothing remains of the specters and the photographed body.[30] Photo albums establish a realm of the dead infinitely more precise than Balzac's competing literary enterprise, the *Comédie humaine*, could ever hope to create. In contrast to the arts, media do not have to make do with the grid of the symbolic. That is to say, they reconstruct bodies not only in a system of words or colors or sound intervals. Media and media only fulfill the "high standards" that (according to Rudolf Arnheim) we expect from "reproductions" since the invention of photography: "They are not only supposed to resemble the object, but rather guarantee this resemblance by being, as it were, a product of the object in question, that is, by being mechanically produced by it – just as the illuminated objects of reality imprint their image on the photographic layer,"[31] or the frequency curves of noises inscribe their wavelike shapes onto the photographic plate.

A reproduction authenticated by the object itself is one of physical precision. It refers to the bodily real, which of necessity escapes all symbolic grids. Media always already provide the appearances of specters. For, according to Lacan, even the word "corpse" is a euphemism in reference to the real.[32]

Accordingly, the invention of the Morse alphabet in 1837 was promptly followed by the tapping specters of spiritistic seances sending their messages from the realm of the dead. Promptly as well, photographic plates – even and especially those taken with the camera shutter closed – furnished reproductions of ghosts or specters, whose black-and-white fuzziness only served to underscore the promise of resemblance. Finally, one of the ten applications Edison envisioned for his newly invented phonograph in the *North American Review* (1878) was to record "the last words of dying persons."

It was only a small step from such a "family record,"[33] with its special consideration of revenants, to fantasies that had telephone cables linking the living and the dead. What Leopold Bloom in *Ulysses* could only wish for in his Dublin graveyard meditations had already been turned into science fiction by Walter Rathenau, the AEG chairman of the board and futurist writer.[34] In Rathenau's story "Resurrection Co.," the cemetery administration of Necropolis, Dacota/USA, following a series of scandalous premature burials in 1898, founds a daughter company entitled "Dacota and Central Resurrection Telephone Bell Co." with a capital stock of $750,000. Its sole purpose is to make certain that the inhabitants of graves, too, are connected to the public telephone network. Whereupon the dead avail themselves of the opportunity to prove, long before McLuhan, that the content of one medium is always another medium – in this concrete case, a *déformation professionelle*.[35]

These days, paranormal voices on tape or radio, the likes of which have been spiritistically researched since 1959 and preserved in rock music since Laurie Anderson's 1982 release *Big Science*,[36] inform their researchers of their preferred radio wavelength. This already occurred in 1898, in the case of Senate President Schreber: when a paranormal, beautifully autonomous "basic or nerve language" revealed its code as well as its channels,[37] message and channel became one. "You just have to choose a middle-, short-, or long-wave talk-show station, or the 'white noise' between two stations, or the 'Jürgenson wave,' which, depending on where you are, is located around 1450 to 1600 kHz between Vienna and Moscow."[38] If you replay a tape that has been recorded off the radio, you will hear all kinds of ghost voices that do not originate from any known radio station, but that, like all official newscasters, indulge in radio self-advertisement. Indeed, the location and existence of that "Jürgenson wave" was pinpointed by none other than "Friedrich Jürgenson, the Nestor of vocal research."[39]

The realm of the dead is as extensive as the storage and transmission capabilities of a given culture. As Klaus Theweleit noted, media are always flight apparatuses into the great beyond. If gravestones stood as symbols at the beginning of culture itself, our media technology can retrieve all gods. The old written laments about ephemerality, which measured no more than distance between writing and sensuality, suddenly fall silent. In our mediascape, immortals have come to exist again.

War on the Mind is the title of an account of the psychological strategies hatched by the Pentagon. It reports that the staff planning the electronic war, which merely continues the Battle of the Atlantic,[40] have already compiled a list of the propitious and unpropitious days in other cultures. This list enables the U.S. Air Force "to time [its] bombing campaigns to coincide with unpropitious days, thus 'conforming' the forecasts of local gods." As well, the voices of these gods have been recorded on tape to be broadcast from helicopters "to keep tribes in their villages." And finally, the Pentagon has developed special film projectors capable of projecting those gods onto low-hanging clouds.[41] A technologically implemented beyond . . .

Of course the Pentagon does not keep a handwritten list of good and bad days. Office technology keeps up with media technology. Cinema and the phonograph, Edison's two great achievements that ushered in the present, are complemented by the typewriter. Since 1865 (according to European accounts) or 1868 (according to American ones), writing has no longer been the ink or pencil trace of a body whose optical and acoustic signals were irretrievably lost, only to reappear (in readers' minds) in the surrogate sensuality of handwriting. In order to store series of sights and sounds, Old Europe's only storage technology first had to be mechanized. Hans Magnus Malling Hansen in Copenhagen and Christopher Latham Sholes in Milwaukee developed mass-producible typewriters. Edison commented positively on the invention's potential when Sholes visited him in Newark to demonstrate his newly patented model and to invite the man who had invented invention to enter a joint venture.[42]

But Edison declined the offer – as if, already in 1868, the phonograph and kinetoscope preoccupied their future inventor. Instead, the offer was grabbed by an arms manufacturer suffering from dwindling revenues in the post-Civil War slump. Remington, not Edison, took over Sholes's discourse machine gun.

Thus, there was no Marvelous One from whose brow sprang all three media technologies of the modern age. On the contrary, the beginning of our age was marked by separation or differentiation.[43] On the one hand, we have two technological media that, for the first time, fix unwritable data flows; on the other, an "'intermediate' thing between a tool and a machine," as Heidegger wrote so precisely about the typewriter.[44] On the one hand, we have the entertainment industry with its new sensualities; on the other, a writing that already separates paper and body during textual production, not first during reproduction (as Gutenberg's movable types had done). From the beginning, the letters and their arrangement were standardized in the shapes of type and keyboard, while media were engulfed by the noise of the real – the fuzziness of cinematic pictures, the hissing of tape recordings.

In standardized texts, paper and body, writing and soul fall apart. Typewriters do not store individuals; their letters do not communicate a beyond that perfectly alphabetized readers can subsequently hallucinate as meaning. Everything that has been taken over by technological media since Edison's inventions disappears from typescripts. The dream of a real visible or audible world arising from words has come to an end. The historical synchronicity of cinema, phonography, and typewriting separated optical, acoustic, and written data flows, thereby rendering them autonomous. That electric or electronic media can recombine them does not change the fact of their differentiation.

In 1860, five years before Malling Hansen's mechanical writing ball (the first mass-produced typewriter), Gottfried Keller's "Misused Love Letters" still proclaimed the illusion of poetry itself: love is left with the impossible alternatives of speaking either with "black ink" or with "red blood."[45] But once typing, filming, and recording became equally valid options, writing lost such surrogate sensualities. Around 1880 poetry turned into literature. Standardized letters were no longer to transmit Keller's red blood or Hoffmann's inner forms, but rather a new and elegant tautology of technicians. According to Mallarmé's instant insight, literature is made up of no more and no less than twenty-six letters.[46]

Lacan's "methodological distinction"[47] among the real, the imaginary, and the symbolic is the theory (or merely a historical effect) of that differentiation. The symbolic now encompasses linguistic signs in their materiality and technicity. That is to say, letters and ciphers form a finite set without taking into account philosophical dreams of infinity. What counts are differences, or, in the language of the typewriter, the spaces between the elements of a system. For that reason, Lacan designates "the world of the symbolic [as] the world of the machine."[48]

The imaginary, however, comes about as the mirror image of a body that appears to be, in terms of motor control, more perfect than the infant's own body, for in the real everything begins with coldness, dizziness, and shortness of breath.[49] Thus, the imaginary implements precisely those optical illusions that were being researched in the early days of cinema. A dismembered or (in the case of film) cut-up body is faced with the illusionary continuity of movements in the mirror or on screen. It is no coincidence that Lacan recorded infants' jubilant reactions to their mirror images in the form of documentary footage.

Finally, of the real nothing more can be brought to light than what Lacan presupposed – that is, nothing. It forms the waste or residue that neither the mirror of the imaginary nor the grid of the symbolic can catch: the physiological accidents and stochastic disorder of bodies.

The methodological distinctions of modern psychoanalysis clearly coincide with the distinctions of media technology. Every theory has its historical a priori. And structuralist theory simply spells out what, since the turn of the century, has been coming over the information channels.

Only the typewriter provides writing as a selection from the finite and arranged stock of its keyboard. It literally embodies what Lacan illustrated using the antiquated letter box. In contrast to the flow of handwriting, we now have discrete elements separated by spaces. Thus, the symbolic has the status of block letters. Film was the first to store those mobile doubles that humans, unlike other primates, were able to (mis)perceive as their own body. Thus, the imaginary has the status of cinema. And only the phonograph can record all the noise produced by the larynx prior to any semiotic order and linguistic meaning. To experience pleasure, Freud's patients no longer have to desire what philosophers consider good. Rather, they are free to babble.[50] Thus, the real – especially in the talking cure known as psychoanalysis – has the status of phonography.

Once the technological differentiation of optics, acoustics, and writing exploded Gutenberg's writing monopoly around 1880, the fabrication of so-called Man became possible. His essence escapes into apparatuses. Machines take over functions of the central nervous system, and no longer, as in times past, merely those of muscles. And with this differentiation – and not with steam engines and railroads – a clear division occurs between matter and information, the real and the symbolic. When it comes to inventing phonography and cinema, the age-old dreams of humankind are no longer sufficient. The physiology of eyes, ears, and brains have to become objects of scientific research. For mechanized writing to be optimized, one can no longer dream of writing as the expression of individuals or the trace of bodies. The very forms, differences, and frequencies of its letters have to be reduced to formulas. So-called Man is split up into physiology and information technology.

When Hegel summed up the perfect alphabetism of his age, he called it Spirit. The readability of all history and all discourses turned humans or philosophers into God. The media revolution of 1880, however, laid the groundwork for theories and practices that no longer mistake information for spirit. Thought is replaced by a Boolean algebra, and consciousness by the unconscious, which (at least since Lacan's reading) makes of Poe's "Purloined Letter" a Markoff chain.[51] And that the symbolic is called the world of the machine undermines Man's delusion of possessing a "quality" called "consciousness," which identifies him as something other and better than a "calculating machine." For both people and computers are "subject to the appeal of the signifier"; that is, they are both run by programs. "Are these humans," Nietzsche already asked himself in 1874, eight years before buying a typewriter, "or perhaps only thinking, writing, and speaking machines?"[52]

In 1950 Alan Turing, the practitioner among England's mathematicians, gave the answer to Nietzsche's question. He observed, with formal elegance, that there is no question to begin with. To clarify the issue, Turing's essay "Computing Machinery and Intelligence" – appearing in, of all places, the philosophical periodical *Mind* – proposed an experiment, the so-called Turing game: A computer *A* and human *B* exchange data via some kind of telewriter interface. The exchange of texts is monitored by a censor *C*, who also only receives written information. *A* and *B* both pretend to be human, and *C* has to decide which of the two is simulating and which merely is Nietzsche's thinking, writing, and speaking machine. But the game remains open-ended, because each time the machine gives itself away – be it by making a mistake or, more likely, by not making any – it will refine its program by learning.[53] In the Turing game, Man coincides with his simulation.

And this is, obviously, already so because the censor *C* receives plotter printouts and typescripts rather than handwritten texts. Of course, computer programs could simulate the "individuality" of the human hand, with its routines and mistakes, but Turing, as the inventor of the universal discrete machine, was a typist. Though he wasn't much better or skilled at it than his tomcat Timothy, who was allowed to jump across the keyboard in Turing's chaotic secret service office,[54] it was at least somewhat less catastrophic than his handwriting. The teachers at the honorable Sherborne School could hardly "forgive" their pupil's chaotic lifestyle and messy writing. He got lousy grades for brilliant exams in mathematics only because his handwriting was "the worst . . . ever seen."[55] Faithfully, schools cling to their old duty of fabricating individuals (in the literal sense of the word) by drilling them in a beautiful, continuous, and individual handwriting. Turing, a master in subverting all education, however, dodged the system; he made plans for an "exceedingly crude" typewriter.[56]

Nothing came of these plans. But when, on the meadows of Grantchester, the meadows of all English poetry from the Romantics to Pink Floyd, he hit upon the idea of the universal discrete machine, his early dreams were realized and transformed. Sholes's typewriter, reduced to its fundamental principle, has supported us to this day. Turing merely got rid of the people and typists that Remington & Son needed for reading and writing.

And this is possible because a Turing machine is even more exceedingly crude than the Sherborne plan for a typewriter. All it works with is a paper strip that is both its program and its data material, its input and its output. Turing slimmed down the common typewriter page to this little strip. But there are even more economizations: his machine doesn't need the many redundant letters, ciphers, and signs of a typewriter keyboard; it can do with one sign and its absence, 1 and 0. This binary information can be read or (in Turing's technospeak) scanned by the machine. It can then move the paper strip one space to the right, one to the left, or not at all, moving in a jerky (i.e., discrete) fashion like a typewriter, which in contrast to handwriting has block caps, a back spacer, and a space bar. (From a letter to Turing: "Pardon the use of the typewriter: I have come to prefer discrete machines to continuous ones.")[57] The mathematical model of 1936 is no longer a hermaphrodite of a machine and a mere tool. As a feedback system it beats all the Remingtons, because each step is controlled by scanning the paper strip for the sign or its absence, which amounts to a kind of writing: it depends on this reading whether the machine keeps the sign or erases it, or, vice versa, whether it keeps a space blank or replaces it with a sign, and so on and so forth.

That's all. But no computer that has been built or ever will be built can do more. Even the most advanced Von Neumann machines (with program storage and computing units), though they operate much faster, are in principle no different from Turing's infinitely slow model. Also, while not all computers have to be Von Neumann machines, all conceivable data processing machines are merely a state *n* of the universal discrete machine. This was proved mathematically by Alan Turing in 1936, two years before Konrad Zuse in Berlin built the first programmable computer from simple relays. And with that the world of the symbolic really turned into the world of the machine.[58]

Unlike the history to which it put an end, the media age proceeds in jerks, just like Turing's paper strip. From the Remington via the Turing machine to microelectronics, from mechanization and automatization to the implementation of a writing that is only cipher, not meaning – one century was enough to transfer the age-old monopoly of writing into the omnipotence of integrated circuits. Not unlike Turing's correspondents, everyone is deserting analog machines in favor of discrete ones. The CD digitizes the gramophone, the video camera digitizes the movies. All data streams flow into a state n of Turing's universal machine; Romanticism notwithstanding, numbers and figures become the key to all creatures.

Notes

1 Under the title "*Nostris ex ossibus*: Thoughts of an Optimist," Karl Haushofer, "the main representative, . . . though not the originator, of the term 'geopolitics'" (November 2, 1945, in Haushofer 1979, 2: 639), wrote: "After the war, the Americans will appropriate a relatively wide strip of Europe's western and southern coast and, at the same time, in some shape or fashion annex England, thus realizing the ideal of Cecil Rhodes from the opposite coast. In doing so, they will act in accordance with the age-old ambition of any sea power to gain control of the opposite coast(s) and rule the ocean in between. The opposite coast is at least the entire eastern rim of the Atlantic and, in order to achieve domination over all 'seven seas,' possibly the entire western rim of the Pacific. Thus, America wants to connect the outer crescent to the 'axis'" (October 19, 1944, in Haushofer 1979, 2: 635).

2 W. Hoffmann, 1944, in Hay 1975, 374.

3 Bolz 1986, 34.

4 Abraham and Hornbostel 1904, 229.

5 See Campe 1986, 70–71.

6 Foucault 1963/1976, 66.

7 Goethe 1829/1981, 122.

8 Goethe, "Geschichte der Farbenlehre" (1810), in idem 1976, 14: 47. [The oral nature of this "opposite" to written history is underscored by the use of Goethe's word *Sage*, "legend," which derives from *sagen*, "to say." – Trans.]

9 See Ong 1982, 27 and (more reasonably) 3.

10 See Exodus 24:12–34:28.

11 Koran, sura 96, vv. 1–6.

12 Winter 1959, 6.

13 See Assmann and Assmann 1983, 68.

14 Nietzsche, "Geschichte der griechischen Literatur" (1874), in idem 1922–29, 5: 213.

15 Goethe 1811–14/1969, 3: 59.

16 Strauss 1977/1979, 15–16.

17 Hegel 1807/1977, 190.

18 Hardenberg (Novalis), 1798–99/1960–75, 3: 377.

19 Schlegel 1799/1958ff, 8: 42.

20 See Kittler 1985/1990, 108–23.

21 Goethe 1797/1987, 3. For reasons why a fully alphabetized literature in particular simulated orality, see Schlaffer 1986, 7–20.

22 Goethe, *Werther* (1774), in Goethe 1990, 109.

23 Benjamin 1924–25/1972–85, 1: 1, 200.

24 Goethe, *Elective Affinities* (1809), in idem 1990, 342.

25 Brentano 1835/1959–63, 2: 222.

26 Marker 1983, 23–24.

27 See Deleuze 1965, 32. "The alternative is between two purities; the false and the true; that of responsibility and that of innocence; that of memory and that of forgetting. . . . Either one remembers words but their meaning remains obscure, or one apprehends the meaning, in which case the memory of the words disappears."

28 Leroi-Gourhan, quoted in Derrida 1967/1976, 333n.

29 E. T. A. Hoffmann 1816/1969, 148 (translation modified).

30 Nadar 1899/1978, 9.

31 Arnheim 1933/1977, 27.

32 See Lacan 1978/1988, 278.

33 Edison, 1878, quoted in Gelatt 1977, 29. Phonographic recordings of last words are based on the recognition

that "physiological time is not reversible," and that "in the province of rhythm, and of time in general, there is no symmetry" (Mach 1886/1914, 256).

34   See Joyce 1922/1969, 113. See also Brooks 1977, 213–14. ["AEG" refers to the Allgemeine Elektrizitäts-Gesellschaft, one of the leading German electronics corporations. It was originally founded in 1883 by Emil Rathenau as the German Edison Society for Applied Electricity. – Trans.]

35   Rathenau 1918–29, 4: 347. Two examples of *déformation professionelle* among the dead of Necropolis: "A writer is dissatisfied with his epitaph. An employee of the telephone company uses short and long intervals, a kind of Morse alphabet, to ring in a critique of his sucessor." King Alexander, the hero of Bronnen's *Ostpolzug*, says everything there is to say about telephonitis and Hades while, according to the stage directions, the "telephone is buzzing": "Oh, you black beast growing on fatty brown stems, you flower of untimeliness, you rabbit of dark rooms! Your voice is our hereafter, and it has crowded out heaven" (Bronnen 1926/1977, 133).

36   The song "Example #22" actually combines the announcement and sound of "example no. 22" ("Hier spricht Edgar"/"Edgar speaking" [Schäfer 1983, 11]), which, strangely enough, must have migrated on a paranormal cassette-to-book from Freiburg to the United States.

37   See Lacan 1966/1977, 184.

38   Schäfer 1983, 2.

39   Ibid., 3.

40   See Gordon 1981, *passim*.

41   Watson 1978, 26, 410.

42   See Walze 1980, 133.

43   See Luhmann 1985, 20–22.

44   Heidegger 1942–43/1992, 86.

45   Keller 1865/1974, 41.

46   See Mallarmé 1893/1945, 850.

47   Lacan 1966, 720.

48   Lacan 1978/1988, 47.

49   See Lacan 1966/1977, 1–7.

50   See Lacan 1975, 53, 73.

51   See Lacan 1978/1988, 191–205.

52   Nietzsche 1873–76/1990, 110.

53   See Turing 1950, 441–42; Hodges 1983, 415–17.

54   Hodges 1983, 279.

55   Ibid., 30.

56   Ibid., 14.

57   J. Good, September 16, 1948, quoted in ibid., 387.

58   See Zuse, June 19, 1937, in idem 1984, 41: "Decisive thought, 19 June 1937/Realization that there are elementary operations to which all computing and thinking operations may be reduced./A primitive type of mechanical brain consists of storage unit, dialing system, and a simple device that can handle conditional chains of two or three links./With such a form of brain it must be possible to solve all operations of the mind that can be dealt with mechanically, regardless of the time involved. More complex brains are merely a matter of executing those operations faster."

References

Abraham, Otto and Erich Moritz von Hornbostel (1904) 'Über die Bedeutung des Phonographen für vergleichende Musikwissenshaft', *Zeitschrift für Ethnologie*, 36, pp. 222–36.

Arnheim, Rudolf (1933/1977) 'Systematik der frühen kinematographischen Erfindungen', in *Kritiken und Aufsätze zum Film*, ed. Helmut H. Dieterichs, Munich.

Assmann, Aleida and Jan Assmann, eds (1983) *Schrift und Gedächtnis: Archäologie der literarischen Kommunikation*, Munich.

Benjamin, Walter (1924–25/1972–85) *Gesammelte Schriften*, ed. Rolf Tiedemann et al., 4 vols, Frankfurt a.M.

Bolz, Norbert (1986) 'Die Schrift des Films', in *Diskursanalysen I: Medien,* ed. Friedrich A. Kittler, Manfred Schneider and Samuel Weber, Wiesbaden, pp. 26–34.

Brentano, Bettina (1835/1959–63) *Bettina von Arnim, Werke und Briefe,* ed. Gustav Konrad, 4 vols, Frechen.

Bronnen, Arnolt (1926/1977) *Ostpolzug,* in *Werke,* ed. Hans Mayer, vol. I, Kronberg, pp. 117–50.

Brooks, John (1977) 'The First and Only Century of Telephone Literature', in *The Social Impact of the Telephone,* ed. Ithiel de Sola Pool, Cambridge, Mass.: MIT Press, pp. 208–24.

Campe, Rüdiger (1986) 'Pronto! Telefonate und Telephonstimmen', in *Diskursanalysen I: Medien,* ed. Friedrich A. Kittler, Manfred Schneider and Samuel Weber, Wiesbaden, pp. 68–93.

Deleuze, Gilles (1965) 'Pierre Klossowski ou Les corps-langage', *Critique,* 21, pp. 199–219.

Derrida, Jacques (1967/1976) *Of Grammatology,* translated by Gayatri Chakravorty Spivak, Baltimore: The Johns Hopkins University Press.

Foucault, Michel (1963/1976) *The Birth of the Clinic,* translated by A. M. Sheridan, London: Tavistock.

Gelatt, Roland (1977) *The Fabulous Phonograph 1877–1977: From Edison to Stereo,* New York.

Goethe, Johann Wolfgang von (1811–14/1969) *The Autobiography of Johann Wolfgang von Goethe,* translated by John Oxenford, New York.

—— (1797/1987) *Faust, Part One,* translated by David Luke, Oxford.

—— (1990) *The Sufferings of Young Werther* and *Elective Affinities,* ed. Victor Lange, The German Library, vol. XIX, New York.

—— (1976) *Werke,* ed. Erich Trunz, Munich.

—— (1829/1981) *Wilhelm Meister's Years of Travel; or, The Renunciants,* translated by H. M. Waidson, New York.

Gordon, Don E. (1981) *Electronic Warfare: Element of Strategy and Multiplier of Combat Power,* New York.

Hardenberg, Friedrich von (Novalis) (1798–99/1960–75) *Schriften,* ed. Paul Kluckhohn and Richard Samuel, Stuttgart.

Haushofer, Karl (1979) '*Nostris ex ossibus*: Gedanken eines Optimisten', in *Karl Haushofer: Leben und Werk,* vol. II, ed. Hans-Adolf Jacobsen, Boppard, pp. 634–40.

Hay, Gerhard, ed. (1975) *Literatur und Rundfunk 1923–1933,* Hildesheim.

Hegel, Georg Wilhelm Friedrich (1807/1977) *Phenomenology of Spirit,* translated by A. V. Miller, Oxford.

Heidegger, Martin (1942–43/1992) *Parmenides,* translated by André Schuwer and Richard Rojcewicz, Bloomington.

Hodges, Andrew (1983) *Alan Turing: The Enigma,* New York.

Hoffmann, E. T. A. (1816/1969) 'The Sandman', in *Selected Writings,* vol. I, *The Tales,* translated by Leonard J. Kent and Elizabeth C. Knight, Chicago.

Joyce, James (1922/1969) *Ulysses,* Harmondsworth: Penguin.

Keller, Gottfried (1865/1974) *The Misused Love Letters* and *Regula Amrain and her Youngest Son,* translated by Michael Bullock and Anne Fremantle, New York.

Kittler, Friedrich A. (1985/1990) *Discourse Networks, 1800/1900,* translated by Michael Metteer, Stanford.

Lacan, Jacques (1966) *Ecrits,* Paris.

—— (1966/1977) *Ecrits: A Selection,* translated by Alan Sheridan, New York.

—— (1975) *Le séminaire: livre XX,* Paris.

—— (1978/1988) *The Seminar of Jacques Lacan, Book II: The Ego in Freud's Theory and in the Technique of Psychoanalysis 1954–55,* translated by Sylvana Tomaselli, New York.

Luhmann, Niklas (1985) 'Das Problem der Epochenbildung und die Evolutionstheories', in *Epochenschwellen und Epochenstrukturen in Diskurs der Literatur und Sprachhistorie,* ed. Hans-Ulrich Gumbrecht and Ulla Link-Herr, Franfurt a.M., pp. 11–33.

Mach, Ernst (1886/1914) *The Analysis of Sensations and the Relation of the Physical to the Psychical,* translated by C. M. Williams, Chicago.

Mallarmé, Stéphane (1893/1945) *Oeuvres complètes,* ed. Henri Mondor and G. Jean-Aubry, Paris.

Marker, Chris (1983) *Sans Soleil / Unsichtbare Sonne: Vollständiger Text zum gleichnamigen Film-Essay,* Hamburg.

Nadar (Félix Tournachon) (1899/1978) 'My Life as a Photographer', *October,* 5, pp. 7–28.

Nietzsche, Friedrich (1922–29) *Sämtliche Werke,* 15 vols, Munich.

—— (1873–76/1990) *Unmodern Observations,* New Haven.

Ong, Walter J. (1982) *Orality and Literacy: The Technologizing of the World,* London.

Rathenau, Walter (1918–29) *Gesammelte Schriften,* 6 vols, Berlin.

Schäfer, Hildegard (1983) *Stimmen aus einer anderen Welt*, Freiburg.

Schlaffer, Heinz (1986) 'Einführung,' in Jach Goody, Ian Watt and Kathleen Gough, *Entstehung und Folgen der Schriftkultur*, Frankfurt a.M., pp. 7–20.

Schlegel, Friedrich (1799–1958ff) *Kritische Ausgabe*, ed. Ernst Behler, 35 vols, Munich.

Strauss, Botho (1977/1979) *Devotion*, translated by Sophie Wilkins, New York.

Turing, Alan M. (1950) 'Computing Machinery and Intelligence', *Mind: A Quarterly Review of Psychology and Philosophy*, 59, pp. 433–60.

Walze, Alfred (1980) 'Auf den Spuren von Christopher Latham Scholes: Ein Besuch in Milwaukee, der Geburtstätte der ersten brauchbaren Schreibmaschine', *Deutsche Stenografenzeitung*, pp. 159–61.

Watson, Peter (1978) *War on the Mind: The Military Uses and Abuses of Psychology*, London.

Winter, L. W., ed. (1959) *Der Koran: Das heilige Buch des Islam*, Munich.

Zuse, Konrad (1984) *Der Computer: Mein Lebenswerk*, 2nd edn, Berlin.

Chapter 10

Lana F. Rakow

WOMEN AND THE TELEPHONE: THE GENDERING OF A COMMUNICATION TECHNOLOGY [1988]

Source: Lana F. Rakow (1988) 'Women and the Telephone: The Gendering of a Communication Technology', in *Technology and Women's Voices: Keeping in Touch,* ed. Cheris Kramarae, New York and London: Routledge & Kegan Paul, pp. 207–28.

For Lana Rakow communication technologies are born into a world marked by unevenness (of gender, of class, of ethnicity and of global proportions). How they are deployed, how they act in our social worlds, will animate this unevenness and will in turn be animated by it. Rakow's account of the telephone is a vivid example of this. Gender differences, of course, exist prior to the invention and dissemination of the telephone and determine the way that telephony is deployed: but this doesn't mean that this new technology is simply mobilised for the reproduction of the status quo. Such technology alters the orchestration of gender and affects the distribution of gendered cultural forms. To see technology as both determined and determining is not to see it has having predictable outcomes. Like any other social technology telephony is 'open' to contingency and to complexity and to the improvisational skills of users. Rakow tells us of women adapting the telephone to uses for which it clearly wasn't designed. So decades before the advent of the speaker phone, a farmer constructs her own amplification with the assistance of a large aluminium pan, which allows her both to chat and to peel potatoes.

In the complex 'social life' of the telephone, Rakow shows how the telephone provided the partial fix to problems of which it was also a causal agent. Thus if the telephone was welcomed as a palliative for female alienation, a way for lonely housewives to fend off isolation, then the telephone was also active in producing the conditions for women's greater loneliness in the first place. For Rakow, and for the work of the social historians she reviews, the telephone is not an isolated technology but one that connects to other cultural forms such as housing, shopping, the distribution of goods, the work of servants and the placing of offices. Because telephony allows a different time-space to exist (what was far away is now close) new routines can emerge that are governed by the desires of the market place. So farmers don't need to travel into towns as regularly (supplies can be delivered, ordered by telephone), families can live in less built-up urban areas but still keep in touch with the larger family group and so on. For women one effect of all this was the production of less face-to-face contact and the intensification of physical isolation. In the forgetful light of efficiency and technological modernisation, the telephone was offered as an effective solace for the lonely woman.

The history of the telephone presented here concentrates on its early years: the years before automation, the years of women-operated switchboards and telephone exchanges, and of party lines.

Perhaps most crucially it deals with the years before the advent of the mobile phone. The history of recent telephony would of course concentrate on its mobility, on the way it converges a variety of technologies and communicative devices; it would highlight its use in 'citizen journalism' and the agency it has had in political struggles. It would also focus on the mobile phone as the fashion-led design item par excellence. How these mobile technologies reanimate gender differences, and how gendered propensities articulate mobile technologies, is the history we are living through.

Further reading: Fischer 1994; Goggin 2006; Pool 1977; Rafael 2003; Rakow 1992.

> 'I never answer the phone at home. It carries over. The way I talk to people on the phone has changed. Even when my mother calls, I don't talk to her very long. I want to *see* people to talk to them.'
>
> (Telephone receptionist, in Studs Terkel [1974/1985], *Working* [New York: Ballantine Books, 58])

THE TELEPHONE HAS been presumed to have been a blessing and a liberator for women. Early commentary on the telephone, repeated by contemporary authors, extolled the virtue of the telephone in reducing women's loneliness and isolation and freeing their time from unnecessary travel. John Brooks (1976), for example, claims that by the end of the 1880s, 'telephones were beginning to save the sanity of remote farm wives by lessening their sense of isolation' and 'they were beginning to bring women in cities "out of the kitchen" by reducing the time required for shopping' (94). Sidney Aronson (1971) states, 'Since farmers' wives were especially susceptible to feelings of loneliness and isolation, the telephone here too helped to allay personal anxiety' (278).[1] Ithiel de Sola Pool (1983) notes that the telephone's role in reducing isolation and insecurity was thought to be particularly relevant to women (131).

The role of the telephone in social change and social life has never received much attention from the academic community. It has only been during the past decade and a half that a few sociologists and communications researchers have begun to think about the telephone as a serious object to study. It is not unusual in this literature for the authors to comment upon the neglect of attention to the telephone, offering various explanations: researchers and funding sources have been interested in the mass media rather than point-to-point telecommuniations (Hudson 1984, 5); the place of the telephone in our lives is habitual and unconscious (Boettinger 1977, 200); the telephone has no deleterious effects but adds to human freedom and choice of action (Pool 1977, 4).

Even contemporary scholars who have focused their attention specifically on the telephone, however, have neglected or trivialized one of the most significant aspects of the telephone and another possible reason the telephone has not been taken seriously by scholars: the role of the telephone in women's lives and the association of the telephone with women's talk. Ironically, clues to the significance of the telephone for women and to popular and scholarly attitudes about women and the telephone are embedded in this recent literature.

Frequently mentioned by contemporary US authors, as their own opinion or their perception of popular opinion of the past, is that women talk a great deal, if not too much, on the telephone. Sidney Aronson (1977) claims that, following the expiration of Bell patents in 1894, 'the telephone became widely available to women and adolescents – two groups who, according to telephone folklore, distinguished themselves as talkers' (31). John Brooks (1977) cites an 1880 piece by Mark Twain as introducing to Americans 'the persistent hero of subsequent telephone literature, the woman user, and its dominant theme, her special love of the instrument and special ways of using it. The piece might almost have been written in the 1970's' (211). Ithiel de Sola Pool (1983) notes that in early telephone trade journals and in popular literature 'one of the most common remarks about women and the telephone is to allege a peculiar addiction on their part to its use' (131). Women's telephone talk has been referred to in recent literature as gossip (Pierce 1977, 173), chitchat (Pool 1977, 133), and chatter (Pool 1983, 49).

One of the few recent authors to suggest that women's relationship to the telephone is a significant topic for serious consideration is Brenda Maddox (1977). Though Maddox's research concerns women's employment in the telephone industry, she notes other ways in which the telephone has had a particular significance for women, such as providing a link to their mothers and friends and providing an instrument for male advances and harassment. She cites a Bell System study that discovered three reasons women use the telephone: their fear of crime in the streets, their confinement at home with small children, and their physical separation from relatives.

Following Brenda Maddox's lead, what can be said about women's relationship to the telephone? Why would women have developed a particular attachment to the telephone? Did it open up new possibilities for women's speaking and new ways of creating and sustaining relationships or free time from household responsibilities? Has the telephone been widely available for women to use for any purpose? The story of the telephone bears re-examination.

Geographic and social change

There is almost unanimous agreement among commentators on the social effects of the telephone that the telephone was an important agent of modernization. Pool's comments exemplify the effects attributed to the telephone:

> Among the most significant impacts of the telephone were those in modifying the pattern of human settlement. It made farm life less isolated, made suburbs more practical, helped break up single industry neighborhoods, allowed offices of industrial companies to move away from the plant into down-town office buildings, and made skyscrapers economic.
>
> (Pool 1983, 11)

If the telephone was indeed implicated in the development of suburbs, the separation of homes and business, and the decline of neighborhoods, it was also implicated in the physical separation of women's private sphere and men's public sphere and the isolation of the home and of individual women in them.[2] That is, the telephone may have been implicated in creating the very conditions from which it was praised for having rescued women. Susan Strasser's description of how the isolation of the housewife increased with industrialization fills in what remains unsaid in most discussions of the telephone:

> While other workers went to work in groups, however thoroughly supervised, full-time house-wives lost the growing daughters and full-time servants who worked for them at home, the iceman and the street vendors who came to their houses, the sewing circle and the group of women around the well. That isolation, combined with the illusory individualism of consumer-ism, intensified the notion that individuals could control their private lives at home, protected behind the portals of their houses from the domination of others: the central legacy of the doctrine of separate spheres.
>
> (Strasser 1982, 9)

By the time Helen Lynd and Robert Lynd (1929) conducted their US study of 'Middletown,' this isolation was readily apparent, particularly in the lives of working-class women. One woman commented to researchers, 'I don't see my friends at all. That is really true – I never see them unless I run into them somewhere occasionally or they come over to dinner. It was different with my mother. She and her friends were always in each other's homes.' Another said, 'I do very little visiting – mostly keep in touch with my friends by telephone' (275). As for the role of the telephone in relieving women of unnecessary travel, such as shopping, women may have greeted such a function with mixed feelings. For some women, shopping may have been one of their few outlets. One Middletown woman admitted, 'I'd go anywhere to get away from the house. I went to the store last night. I've been out of the house only twice in the three months since we moved here, both times to the store' (310).

Ann Oakley (1974) discovered the same loneliness and isolation in her more recent study of London housewives. According to Oakley, 'Research has shown that loneliness is an occupational hazard for the modern housewife, who is often cut off not only from community life but from family life – in the wider sense – also' (88). The telephone does not seem to compensate for a lack of personal contact, though it may be valued for the kind of link it does provide. 'The only person I really see is my neighbour,' one woman told Oakley. 'My mother comes once a week, for the day. She phones me every other day' (89). Oakley suggests that for some women the superficiality of the few social contacts they have may be a reminder of the deep and meaningful relationships they lack.

The isolation of US farm women, as well as their long hours of drudgery at household and farm work, were not cured by the appearance of the telephone, despite frequent claims to that effect (e.g. US Bureau of the Census 1910, 78), but may well have been better helped by different government farm policies and by the kind of community cooperative enterprises suggested by Florence E. Ward's report (1920) for the US Department of Agriculture. Despite the fact that 72 percent of the 9,748 farm homes in the Department of Agriculture survey conducted by Ward had telephones (a very high percentage, suggesting an unrepresentative sample of farm families), the isolation and burden of the farm women remained unsolved. The report suggested farm families should pool their individual interests in common community enterprises such as canning kitchens, buying centers, markets, laundries, salvage shops, and sewing rooms, as well as social centers for lectures, community sings, dramatics, and games, 'which, if properly handled, overcome the isolation of country homes and make possible the accomplishment of many otherwise difficult tasks with a saving of time and labor for the housewife' (12).

Farm women were also accused of being particularly addicted to eavesdropping on their party lines. A 1914 *McClure's Magazine* article claimed, 'Some farmers' wives sit with their ears glued to the receiver all the long dreary afternoon, taking in their neighbors' secrets' (Hendrick 1914, 48). Realistically, few farm women would have had time for such luxuries. In the 1910s they were working on average more than thirteen hours a day in the summer and more than ten hours a day in the winter, according to Ward (1920, 7). If there had been a genuine interest in easing farm women's isolation, telephone sets would have been designed differently so that women could talk together while they worked. In the 1920s one farm woman resorted to peeling potatoes with the telephone receiver lying in the bottom of a large aluminum pan, which reflected the voices of the telephone conversation back up to her at her seat on a stool (Wisconsin State Telephone Association 1985, 96).

Women's 'peculiar' addiction to the telephone is a more complex phenomenon than early and contemporary telephone literature has led us to believe. To understand women's relationship to the telephone, we must ask why women were isolated and lonely and how the telephone fit into a changing Western landscape of public and private spheres.

Women's telephone work

Women's work as telephone operators has been perhaps the most explored topic related to women's relationship to the telephone in popular and academic literature. Operators were popular heroines in stories, songs, and telephone industry literature in their day. More recently attention has been directed to their labor organizing activities. (Maurine Weiner Greenwald (1980) describes the US situation, for example, and Elaine Bernard (1982) describes that in British Columbia.) The full significance of the role and talk of operators, however, has not been explored.

Women worked and still work as telephone operators all around the world. A 1913 international trade journal refers to the employment of women as operators in Germany, Australia, Tasmania, Austria, Hungary and Sweden (*Telecommunications Journal* 1975). A history published by the International Telecommunication Union (1965) shows early pictures of women operators in England, Germany and the Netherlands, as well as at the switchboard of a contemporary international exchange. This transcultural use of women as operators has not been adequately examined. In the case of the US, the assumption has been that women were hired as telephone operators to replace boys because the women were more polite and mannerly (see, for example, Greenwald 1980; and Brooks 1976). Maddox (1977) points out, however, another more important reason: women's work was cheap. Women earned from one-half to one-fourth of men's wages (266). A 1906 *Journal Télégraphique* article summarized women's role in the telegraph service around the world, which suggests that women's telegraph work was the precedence for their low-paid telephone work (*Telecommunications Journal* 1975). Countries such as Italy, Hungary, France, Norway and Switzerland used women extensively in telegraph work, reporting substantial financial savings by doing so.

The employment of women at low wages does not explain why young, attractive and single women should have been hired, another common transcultural practice. The explanation for this phenomenon is multifaceted, but, at least in the US, part of the explanation might lie in the fact that the time period of the manual operator coincided with the transition to the new economic and social relations of the late nineteenth and early twentieth centuries. The voices of young women, supplemented by visual images of operators as 'All American Girls' made popular by telephone industry advertising and public relations, may have provided an important bridge in the increasing gap between public and private spheres. A Bell System advertisement in 1915 illustrates this symbolic function of operators (the advertisement is reproduced in Boettinger 1977, 10). The operator is referred to as a 'weaver of speech' in the advertisement; the illustration shows an operator holding lines coming down from a telephone pole, the lines passing through her hands and out into the world, connecting homes, cities and factories. The cultural myth of the telephone operator, embodying new and old values and mediating new social relations over the telephone wires, may have functioned as a reassuring expression of the new social order in an uneasy transition from the old. These young women were to be both innocent and efficient, desirable yet unattainable, businesslike but adept at soothing the harried and demanding captain of industry of the public sphere as well as the stereotypically portrayed petty and demanding matron of the private sphere.

The importance of the operator's voice and restrictions on her speech were hallmarks of operator selection and training in the US, Canada and France, as well as in other countries. Part of the examination of operator applicants usually included an evaluation of the women's ability to speak clearly and 'without an accent.' Once hired, operators underwent stringent training in what to say and how it was to be said. They learned set phrases and proper inflection, deviations from which could result in punishment. A 1921 article in a US women's labor magazine described how the training room sounded like an operatic rehearsal as operators in training learned how to sing out phrases, sweetly, with the proper inflection (The Pilgrim 1921, 14). An early federal investigation of the US telephone industry, though clearly sympathetic to the industry and its need for efficiency in the name of public service, described the operator's frustration with these restrictions. When a subscriber scolds her for being kept waiting,

> She is not allowed by the rules of most companies to answer this, but may only repeat 'Number please' until the caller gives the number so that she can make the connection. For with most companies the operator may not 'talk back' no matter how much she is abused by a subscriber; the only words she dare use over a phone are the set phrases printed in her book of instructions.
> (US Bureau of Labor 1910, 56)

Operators in Canada and France underwent similar training and were subject to such restrictions as well, according to Elaine Bernard (1982, 42) and Pierrette Pézerat and Danièle Poublan (1985, 32). One operator in France remarked, 'In order to talk PTT [Postes, Télégraphes et Téléphones], one is forbidden to be oneself' (Pézerat and Poublan 1985, 33). Yet the voice of the operator, in accordance with the operator myth of a number of countries, was deemed to have special powers, widely acclaimed in popular and telephone industry literature, illustrated by these comments: 'The dulcet tones of the feminine voice seem to exercise a soothing and calming effect upon the masculine mind, subduing irritation and suggesting gentleness of speech and demeanor; thereby avoiding unnecessary friction' (McCluer 1902, 31).

The telephone work that women have been performing in businesses and offices since the turn of the century has received little analysis, yet is an area that could provide useful insights into the gendered hierarchy of communication. Despite the fact that the telephone has long been hailed as a great social leveler (e.g. in recent literature see Cherry 1977; and Ball 1968), business and social practices immediately arose to embed hierarchical social relations into the use of the telephone. A. H. Hastie, leader of the Association for Protection of Telephone Subscribers, for example, suggested in 1898 that 'The telephone should be primarily answered by a servant' to screen intrusions, just as a gentleman would have a servant answer the door to keep out unwanted guests (1898, 894).

Despite the decline of servants to answer the telephone and the door, social relations remain embedded in telephone access and use. Martin Mayer (1977) points out that a central difference between white-collar and blue-collar workers in US society is that white-collar workers have access to telephones on the job (244). A primary means, however, by which hierarchical distinctions are made through telephone use is by gender, a social hierarchy presumably readily recognizable by sound. The employment of women in offices as 'telephonists' was undoubtedly related to the particular economic and social forces of the time, but was likely also to have been related to the usefulness of women's voices in establishing hierarchies among men, an explanation often masked by appeals to women's 'natural' suitability to telephone office work. Henry M. Boettinger (1977) illustrates this 'natural' argument: 'Few devices are so well matched [as the telephone] to the needs and style of women. The instrument seems particularly suited to their voice range and timbre' (15).

More likely, women's voices have been particularly suited to the needs of their employers. Secretaries and receptionists, charged with answering the telephone and placing telephone calls, convey the importance of the caller or the person being called, screen callers, and relieve others from interruptions and the detail work of looking up telephone numbers, dialing and taking messages. Being responsible for answering the telephone restricts movement and concentration. Office telephonists are often restricted in what to say, and instructed in telephone etiquette. Receptionist Sharon Atkins has related how the telephone was a constant source of interruption and how she was often required to lie for others (Terkel 1985, 57–60). Much has been made in social mythology of the power of the secretary over telephone access to important people (usually men), but little has been made of women's voices as commodities bought to achieve just such an effect.

Women's work accounts for another area of socially significant but unrecognized and unpaid telephone labor. This work was anticipated and encouraged from the outset of the telephone. An 1878 advertising circular in New Haven, Connecticut advised men, 'Your wife may order your dinner, a hack, your family physician, etc., all by Telephone without leaving the house or trusting servants or messengers to do it' (Fischer 1984, 5–6). By 1948, a study of telephone use in rural Indiana reported that men and women in the study both agreed that women used the telephone most frequently. 'Many men said they did not like to use the phone, so they had the women call for them' (Robertson and Amstutz 1949, 18).

The responsibility for maintaining family and social relations and home–business transactions which was relegated to women was apparently, then, quickly extended to the use of the telephone. Today, women arrange visits with family members and dinner parties with friends, remember birthdays and anniversaries, and 'keep in touch.' With primary responsibility for the household and family, women most likely take the majority of responsibility for telephone calls with plumbers, optometrists, veterinarians, music teachers, dentists, pharmacists, babysitters and the like. (Many of these interactions, of course, will be with women on the other end of the line, hired by men to talk to other women.) For women working outside the home, the logistics of making these calls can be difficult, particularly if her place of employment has restrictions on employees' personal telephone calls (more likely to be the case with hourly workers). Little is known about women's networks and women's use of the telephone in carrying out church and school work, such as making arrangements for providing food at funeral services and planning community meetings, or their work in canvassing, fundraising, and political organizing. Finally, women may do a majority of home telephone work answering surveys and listening to salescalls. It is little wonder that Martin Mayer (1977) reports, 'the most important single factor [determining how many calls a household will make] is the presence of a woman between the ages of 19 and 64' (23).

Universal access and availability

Availability of telephone service varies widely around the world. Sweden, the US, Switzerland, Denmark and Canada all have over sixty telephones per 100 population, for example, while Brazil, Colombia, Turkey, Iran and India have fewer than ten (AT&T 1982, 16). While it is obvious that access to and use of telephone service will be much more restricted in countries with fewer telephones, it should not be assumed that the mere presence of greater numbers of telephones per capita ensures its universal access. This assumption marks early predictions and later assessments about the telephone service in the US, which has been thought to have been quickly diffused throughout the country and universally available. Telephone service was soon available to anyone who wanted to use it to talk to anyone they desired, according to popular and academic writers (see Pool 1983, 86 for a sample of such comments). Pool (1983) states that early expectations about a low-cost universal service became a self-fulfilling prophecy (24). Boettinger (1977) extols the telephone's democratic functions: 'The privately owned American system arrived at the greatest public market and the widest use of the telephone, a reflection of a democratic mind . . . Bell, Watson and Vail were indifferent to class or ideology. The telephone itself did not discriminate against race, creed or color. It served lords and "commoners" equally' (98).

The story of the diffusion and availability of the telephone in the US is not quite so simple. As Claude S. Fischer (1984) explains, the diffusion of telephones did not follow a steady, chronological, upward trend. Forty-two per cent of all households had telephones by 1929, but in 1940, only 32 per cent had telephones (4). The shrinkage of the number of telephones in service during the Depression led Bell Telephone to expand its marketing approaches to include encouraging the social use of the telephone, a use the exchanges had seemed to frown on until then. Indeed, women's 'gossip' on local lines when a flat local area rate was charged added little to telephone company coffers, suggesting one reason women's telephone talk was ridiculed or discouraged. Two non-Bell companies in Indiana and Oregon went so far as to take their cases to the public service commissions in their states to ask for extra service charges for each call. Women gossiping at length were detrimental to their business, they claimed. When the Indiana Public Service Commission held its hearing, according to one account, 'the whole countryside turned out. Many telephone subscribers testified that they had no objection to the women talking at any length they wished, so the commission ruled it could do nothing.' The Oregon commission ruled similarly, though it denounced gossiping (MacMeal 1934, 224). Bell Telephone, meanwhile, began placing greater emphasis on the social uses of the telephone after the Depression (Fischer 1984, 9), presumably in order to increase installations.

If diffusion was not evenly spread across time, it was also not evenly spread across classes and geographic location, raising questions about who had access to telephones. The Lynd and Lynd survey (1929) found that all forty of the business class families they interviewed had telephones, but only 55 per cent of the working-class families did (173). When forced to make cutbacks in a time of unemployment, five of twenty families having a telephone had it taken out (62). A survey by R. O. Eastman, Inc. (1927) showed a correlation of income with telephone ownership. Not surprisingly, the higher the income, the more likely a family was to have a telephone. Urban zoning of residential and industrial areas, popular around the turn of the century, was supported by telephone companies and utilities because the companies were uninterested in business in poor or deteriorating neighborhoods (Pool 1983, 46). Telephone service, consequently, was less likely to be available to lower-income families. Diffusion of telephone service in rural areas was also highly uneven. States such as Iowa and Wisconsin had early and vigorous development of private and community telephone exchanges. However, many rural communities and farm families in other states and in isolated areas had to wait until the Rural Electrification Administration made loans for rural telephone development beginning in 1949. Commentators on the social effects of the telephone have been too ready to assume a homogeneous diffusion and effect among the population. The experiences of poor, rural, working-class, non-white and non-native born women may have varied widely in terms of telephone access and use.

Even today about one in twenty homes in the US has no telephone, homes disproportionately likely to be those in which older and poorer people are living, people who are likely to be most in need of telephone service. Lewis Perl (1978) has concluded that a household's access to telephone service is positively related to income, age and education and inversely related to number of persons per household (4). Only recently has the New York City Welfare Department permitted welfare recipients to have telephones, presumably because welfare recipients tend to live in dangerous neighborhoods (Keller 1977, 284, 286). We do not know how the telephone functions in the delivery of social services or in the lives of those who need them. Nor should we forget that having a telephone does not solve problems of isolation or loneliness if we have no one to call (Keller 1977, 294), nor can it solve personally experienced problems of poverty, unemployment or fear of crime if there is no one we can call who will or can help.

In addition to limits on the availability of telephone service, women may experience other restrictions on their use of the telephone. Maddox (1977) reports that women call their mothers, sisters and mothers-in-law, but regard the calls as frivolous, feeling guilty when the telephone bill comes (264). Since AT&T offers residential rate discounts after 11 p.m. weekdays and on weekends, women may feel restrictions on when they call long-distance relatives and friends. The US trend toward 'usage sensitive pricing,' where the caller is charged for each local call, and away from flat local pricing, may be creating new economic restrictions on women's telephone use. Women in Great Britain, for example, which has a system of charging for each call, may experience guilt feelings and hesitation about making calls for non-business reasons. Party lines, which were once prevalent in rural areas and still remain in some rural areas, also probably acted to restrict talk, despite popular folklore. One Canadian study reported that 11.2 percent of the respondents had party lines. Survey respondents indicated they restricted their talk because of the possibility of being overheard and indicated the telephone was often unavailable when they wanted to use it (Singer 1981, 56).

Social etiquette from the outset of the telephone industry dictated against girls and women calling boys and men, among other rules for proper telephone behavior. The telephone industry was active in prescribing proper telephone use, as this comment from a telephone trade journal illustrates:

> The etiquette of calls holds good in the matter of telephone calls between men and women. It is not good form for a young woman to call up a man, either at his home or at his office. . . . It is sure to be an interruption; it is quite likely to be embarrassing, and above all this is the fact, that a tactful girl will avoid all appearance of pursuing the man of her acquaintance.
>
> (*Telephony* 1907, 138)

A woman waiting by the telephone for a call became a stock cultural image based on the experiences of real women. Dorothy Parker's 'A Telephone Call' (1942), about a woman agonizing over a man's call that does not come, illustrates vividly that the telephone did not free women to call whom and when they pleased nor did it eliminate for women the hierarchy of gender relations.

Telephone directories and unlisted numbers suggest that women are not accessible to others in the same manner that men are. Telephone directories exist in principle so that people listed can reach any of the others as a right of 'membership,' Colin Cherry points out (1977, 138). Women's names are often absent from telephone directories, subsumed under the names of their husbands because their name is considered less important or because additional listings involve a telephone company charge. Women do not apparently share the same rights of membership as men, and if telephone directories 'represent a symbolic map of a community's members' (Boettinger 1977, 206) women's unequal appearance in telephone directories suggests women's symbolic cultural status. If a number published in a directory is a cue for interaction (Latham 1975, 35), women are less accessible than men. Of course, accessibility is a double-edged sword for women in a patriarchal culture. Women resort to using initials in telephone directories rather than first names in order to disguise their gender. They resort to unlisted numbers in an attempt to prevent unwanted calls.

Privatized oppression

Marshall McLuhan (1964) labeled the telephone an 'irresistible intruder in time and space' (238), an observation to be echoed by later commentators on the telephone. For example, Garry Mitchell (1984) notes, 'The event of a ringing telephone is an intrusion into personal privacy and individual predictability. Few can ignore this imperious summons' (251). But the kind of intrusion and violation that the telephone made possible for men against women has been little noted or studied.

It was apparently a combination of the spread of automatic switching and private lines and the social disorder of the 1960s that either increased abusive calling in the US or at least brought it to the attention of the Bell Telephone Company and federal officials. With automatic rather than operator switching and with private rather than party lines, abusive callers apparently felt less likely to be found out (Pool 1983, 133; John Brooks 1976, 286). The weakening of social norms in the 1960s was supposed to have increased such 'antisocial' behavior. John Brooks (1976), melodramatically, describes the problem as one of social deviation rather than of an intensified expression of cultural misogyny: 'The venom of the poisoned, the bad blood of society, was spread through the national blood vessels of the telephone network' (286). AT&T expressed its official concern about such calls in its annual reports in the mid-1960s, undertook an 'education' campaign advising callers how to deal with such calls, and began offering a device that enabled the company to track callers (Brooks 1976, 287).[3]

AT&T's actions were likely to have been spurred by US Senate hearings on abusive and harassing telephone calls held in 1965 and 1966. The record of the May and June 1966 hearings, however, suggest that the Senate Commerce Committee, Subcommittee on Communications, chaired by John Pastore of Rhode Island, was more concerned about malicious calls to the families of Vietnam servicemen than about abusive calls to women. The Bell System reported receiving 375,000 complaints a year; the Bureau of Police-women of the New York Police Department was reported to have received a 30 percent increase in complaints of obscene calls over 1964. Yet the testimony, all by men, reflected little concern for women by either AT&T or senators:

> *Senator Pastore.* '[About the question of sexual perversion,] how many would you say were men as against women in these cases that you prosecuted?'
>
> *Mr. Kertz [Herbert Kertz, operating vice president, AT&T]* 'The majority are men.'
>
> *Senator Pastore.* 'The majority are men?'
>
> *Mr. Kertz.* 'Yes, sir. Now, when I said that, you qualified, Mr. Chairman, the type of cases. There are a great many cases that involve domestic squabbles where the woman is the offender.'
>
> *Senator Pastore.* 'I see.'
>
> *Mr. Kertz.* 'But going to your pervert, the majority of it is men.'
>
> *Senator Cotton [Norris Cotton, New Hampshire].* 'It is practically impossible for a woman to put in a telephone call and not talk; is it not?' [laughter]
>
> *Mr. Kertz.* 'The strength of our business, Senator.' [laughter]
>
> (US Senate 1966, 45)

A bulletin by the US Independent Telephone Association, placed into the record, reveals how the telephone industry was likely to view abusive calls as a 'customer service problem' because they were 'irritating' to customers (US Senate 1966, 48–9). The bulletin cited the problem of growing non-published and non-listed service resulting from abusive and commercial solicitation calling.

Liz Stanley and Sue Wise, conducting research on their personal experiences in England of abusive telephone calls, have begun to shed light on the culturally telling nature of abusive calls and the complex experience of oppression faced by women in Western countries. They received abusive calls every day over a period of several years when their home telephone number was advertised as a contact for several local lesbian groups (Stanley and Wise 1979). By unflinchingly publishing the transcripts of some of these calls, they have exposed the virulent side to women's oppression and the everyday violations to which women can be subjected. Their categorization of different types of calls and callers, their analysis of responses to their experiences from feminists and male homosexuals, and their self-scrutiny of their own feelings and strategies (see Stanley 1984) suggest this topic has received too little serious attention.

Comments

This review of the received story of the telephone should suggest that women's relationship to the telephone has been much more complex than popular and academic literature has led us to believe. The telephone opened up new possibilities for women's talk and women's relationships, but may have been implicated in closing off others. It may serve as a lifeline to women isolated in a private sphere and cut off from family and friends, but the telephone may have helped bring that isolation about. The telephone did not level and democratize all social relations, but arrived embedded in them and was used to perpetuate and create hierarchies. Women's speech was commoditized, controlled, and restrained for business purposes at an early stage. The telephone was not and is not available for all women for all purposes, even in countries where telephone service is widespread. The telephone has been used by some men to bring oppression through abusive and harassing calls into the most private spaces women occupy.

The story of the history of the telephone cannot be told without accounting for the gender relations within which a telephone system developed. The telephone, in turn, was used to construct and maintain gender differences and hierarchies. The story of the telephone teaches us the lesson that communications technologies in a gendered society are not gender-neutral.

Notes

1   The wording of these comments – 'sense of isolation' and 'susceptibility to feelings of loneliness and isolation' – are [sic] interesting. The implication is that the isolation of these women was not as serious as they felt it to be or that their feelings resulted from their own weakness.

2   Claims about the telephone's cause and effect relationship to these changes should be weighed carefully, however. See Fischer (1985) for a discussion of the complexity of technological assessment.

3   The sincerity of then AT&T's chief executive officer, Frederick R. Kappel, in wanting to do something about calls against women cannot be taken at face value. The following incident raises questions about his feelings toward women. According to one account, at an annual AT&T meeting in Detroit in 1966, 'after a wrangle with Mrs. Wilma Soss of the Federation of Women Shareholders, he silenced her by summarily having her floor microphone turned off' (Brooks 1976, 280).

References

Aronson, Sidney. 1971. 'The sociology of the telephone.' In Gary Gumpert and Robert Cathcart, eds. *Inter / Media*. 2nd ed. New York: Oxford University Press, 1982, 272–83. Reprinted from *International Journal of Comparative Sociology* 12:3 (September 1971).

Aronson, Sidney. 1977. 'Bell's electrical toy: what's the use? The sociology of early telephone usage.' In Ithiel de Sola Pool, ed. *The Social Impact of the Telephone*. Cambridge, Mass.: MIT Press, 15–39.

AT&T. 1982. *The World's Telephones*. Morris Plains, New Jersey.

Ball, Donald. 1968. 'Toward a sociology of telephones and telephoners.' In Marcell Truzzi, ed. *Sociology and Everyday Life*. Englewood Cliffs, New Jersey: Prentice-Hall, 59–75.

Bernard, Elaine. 1982. *The Long Distance Feeling: A History of the Telecommunications Workers Union*. Vancouver: New Star Books.

Boettinger, Henry M. 1977. *The Telephone Book: Bell, Watson, Vail and American Life, 1876–1976*. Croton-on-Hudson, New York: Riverwood.

Brooks, John. 1976. *Telephone: The First Hundred Years*. New York: Harper & Row.

Brooks, John. 1977. 'The first and only century of telephone literature.' In Ithiel de Sola Pool, ed. *The Social Impact of the Telephone*. Cambridge, Mass.: MIT Press, 208–24.

Cherry, Colin. 1977. 'The telephone system: creator of mobility and social change.' In Ithiel de Sola Pool, ed. *The Social Impact of the Telephone*. Cambridge, Mass.: MIT Press, 112–26.

Eastman, R. O., Inc. 1927. *Zanesville and Thirty-six Other American Communities: A Study of Markets and the Telephones as a Market Index*. New York: Literary Index.

Fischer, Claude S. 1984. 'Educating the public: selling Americans the telephone, 1876–1940.' Unpublished revision of paper presented to the Social Science History Association, Washington, D.C., October 1983. Berkeley: University of California, Department of Sociology.

Fischer, Claude S. 1985. 'Studying technology and social life.' In Manuel Castells, ed. *High Technology, Space, and Society: Emerging Trends*. Urban Affairs Annual Reviews, Vol. 28. Beverley Hills: Sage Publications.

Greenwald, Maurine Weiner. 1980. *Women, War, and Work*. Westport, Conn.: Greenwood Press.

Hastie, A. H. 1898. 'The telephone tangle and the way to untie it.' *Fortnightly Review* 70, 893–900.

Hendrick, Burton J. 1914. 'Telephones for the millions.' *McClure's Magazine* 44 (November), 45–55.

Hudson, Heather E. 1984. *When Telephones Reach the Village: The Role of Telecommunications in Rural Development*. Norwood, New Jersey: Ablex Publishing.

International Telecommunication Union. 1965. *From Semaphore to Satellite*. Geneva: ITU.

Keller, Suzanne. 1977. 'The telephone in new (and old) communities.' In Ithiel de Sola Pool, ed. *The Social Impact of the Telephone*. Cambridge, Mass.: MIT Press, 281–98.

Latham, Robert F. 1975. 'The telephone and social change.' In Benjamin D. Singer, ed. *Communications in Canadian Society*, 2nd rev. ed. Vancouver: Copp Clark, 19–39.

Lynd, Robert S. and Helen Merrell Lynd. 1929. *Middletown*. New York: Harcourt, Brace.

McCluer, C. E. 1902. 'Telephone operators and operating room management.' *The American Telephone Journal* 6:2 (12 July), 31–2.

McLuhan, Marshall. 1964. *Understanding Media*, 2nd ed. New York: Mentor.

MacMeal, Harry B. 1934. *The Story of Independent Telephony*. Chicago: Independent Pioneer Telephone Association.

Maddox, Brenda. 1977. 'Women and the switchboard.' In Ithiel de Sola Pool, ed. *The Social Impact of the Telephone*. Cambridge, Mass.: MIT Press, 262–80.

Mayer, Martin, 1977. 'The telephone and the uses of time.' In Ithiel de Sola Pool, ed. *The Social Impact of the Telephone*. Cambridge, Mass.: MIT Press, 225–45.

Mitchell, Garry. 1984. 'Some aspects of telephone socialization.' In Sari Thomas, ed. *Studies in Mass Communication, Vol. 1*. Norwood, New Jersey: Ablex, 249–52.

Oakley, Ann. 1974. *The Sociology of Housework*. New York: Pantheon.

Parker, Dorothy. 1942. 'A telephone call.' In *The Collected Stories of Dorothy Parker*. New York: Random House, 41–50.

Perl, Lewis J. 1978. *Economic and Demographic Determinants of Residential Demand for Basic Telephone Service*. New York: National Economic Research Associates.

Pézerat, Pierrette and Danièle Poublan. 1985. 'French telephone operators past and present: the ambiguities of progress.' *Oral History Journal* 13:1 (Spring), 28–42.

Pierce, John. 1977. 'The telephone and society in the past 100 years.' In Ithiel de Sola Pool, ed. *The Social Impact of the Telephone*. Cambridge, Mass.: MIT Press, 159–96.

Pilgrim, The. 1921. 'Pilgrim's progress in a telephone exchange.' *Life and Labor*, Part I, 11:1 (January), 11–14; Part II, 11:2 (February), 48–52.

Pool, Ithiel de Sola, ed. 1977. *The Social Impact of the Telephone*. Cambridge, Mass.: MIT Press.

Pool, Ithiel de Sola. 1983. *Forecasting the Telephone: A Retrospective Technology Assessment*. Norwood, New Jersey: Ablex.

Robertson, Lynn and Keith Amstutz. 1949. *Telephone Problems in Rural Indiana*. Agricultural Experimental Station Bulletin no. 548, Lafayette, Ind.: Purdue University.

Singer, Benjamin D. 1981. *Social Functions of the Telephone*. Palo Alto, Cal.: R&E Research Associates.

Stanley, Liz. 1984. 'Open secrets: what they are and what we should do about them.' In Olivia Butler, ed. *Feminist Experience in Feminist Research*. Manchester: University of Manchester, 117–39.

Stanley, Liz and Sue Wise. 1979. 'Feminist research, feminist consciousness and experiences of sexism.' *Women's Studies International Quarterly* 2, 359–74.

Strasser, Susan. 1982. *Never Done: A History of American Housework*. New York: Pantheon.

Telecommunications Journal. 1975. *Journal Télégraphique* 42:12 (December), unnumbered.

'Telephone good form.' 1907. *Telephony* 14:3 (September), 138.

Terkel, Studs. 1974/1985. *Working*. New York: Ballantine Books.

US Bureau of the Census. 1910. *Telephones: 1907*. Washington, DC.

US Bureau of Labor, 1910. *Investigation of Telephone Companies*. Washington, DC.

US Senate, 1966. *Abusive and Harassing Telephone Calls*. Washington, DC.

Ward, Florence E. 1920. *The Farm Woman's Problems*. Circular no. 148. Washington, DC: US Department of Agriculture.

Wisconsin State Telephone Association. 1985. *On the Line . . . A History of the Telephone Industry in Wisconsin*. Madison: WSTA.

Chapter 11

Ellen Lupton

POWER TOOL FOR THE DINING ROOM: THE ELECTRIC CARVING KNIFE [1996]

Source: Ellen Lupton (1996) 'Power Tool for the Dining Room: The Electric Carving Knife', in *Stud: Architectures of Masculinity*, ed. Joel Sanders, New York: Princeton Architectural Press, pp. 42–53.

Ellen Lupton is a curator, teacher, painter, writer and graphic designer (see designwritingresearch. org for a full inventory of her prodigious output). An advocate of the 'free font movement' and DIY design, Lupton approaches design with political and ethical commitments and with a spirit of generosity (the 'free font movement' encourages typefoundries each to offer one good font as a freely given gift to humanity). In the 1990s Lupton curated a number of significant design exhibitions that reflected her abiding concern with design as a living force in daily life: for instance, 'The Bathroom, the Kitchen, and the Aesthetics of Waste: A Process of Elimination' (with J. Abbott Miller, MIT List Visual Arts Center, 1992) and 'Mechanical Brides: Women and Machines from Home to Office' (Cooper-Hewitt National Design Museum, Smithsonian Institution, 1993). These exhibitions encouraged viewers to see design as a combined world of promotion, physical objects and everyday practices.

Lupton has an anthropologist's eye for recognising the deep symbolic and emotional resonances that the design environment registers, and she has a historian's sense that such environments are marked by continuities as well as sudden innovative departures. In the text reproduced here Lupton investigates one such 'innovation' (the electric carving knife) to show how deeply embedded it was in age-old cultural practices:

> Recalling the ancient division between hunting and cultivating, various advertisements instruct men to employ the knife for meat, and women to use it for bread, cake, and vegetables – to carve is masculine and to slice is feminine, just as the traditional hunt was the work of men, while the cultivation of vegetables and the boiling of stews belonged in the domain of women.

The tool-ness of the electric carving knife (its efficiency in cutting through foodstuffs) gives way to its complex cultural negotiation of social space (kitchen, dining room and the unintended use on fishing boats) as well as its troubling of gender distinctions. Design objects, then, become artefacts that can tell us, not simply about the changes that are taking place in society, but about society's limitations and failures to change. The pristine, unopened carving knife found in a car-boot sale or a yard sale tells us, potentially, as much about the world as the continued success of the tool-belt.

Perhaps most compellingly of all, Ellen Lupton has a practitioner's enthusiasm for design, and the desire to communicate as widely as possible. Constantly crossing audiences, from small children through to design students, and on to the academic community of design historians as well as the general public, Ellen Lupton's work is always in the end concerned with the practical possibilities of design in creating a better world.

Further reading: Lupton 1993; Lupton and Miller 1992, 1999; Sparke 1995.

THE ELECTRIC CARVING knife is a rare instance of a domestic appliance addressed to male users. A transitional object that mediates between the interior, service space of the kitchen and the public, ceremonial space of the dining room, the electric knife belongs to a population of machines that play an ancillary role in the larger architecture of the domestic environment, mechanizing

Figure 11.1   The 'New Electric Carving Knife', advertisement for General Electric, 1963.

the labors of modern life. The proliferation of domestic appliances since the 1920s has been fertile ground for feminist historians of design and technology, who have shown how the seemingly rational forms of "labor-saving" devices have fetishized hygiene and cleanliness and have romanticized an unrelenting series of chores.[1] Although considerable scholarly work has addressed the role of female consumers in design culture, few efforts have been made to position products engineered for male use within the gendered map of modern domesticity.

General Electric introduced the electric knife in January 1963. The engineering department created several experimental prototypes before arriving at a workable technical solution: the motor moves two parallel blades back and forth counter to one another, eliminating the need for sawing motions by the user. Competing knives that were fitted with a single blade cost less than half the price of GE's model, but proved ineffective.[2] "Reciprocating action" remains the mechanical principle for electric knives manufactured today.

Market surveys by GE's consumer panel suggested that the knife would be a welcome addition to the mechanically enhanced homes of the period. The perceived market included both men (who would use it for carving turkeys) and women (who would use it for general kitchen use). An in-house team led by industrial designers Olle Haggstrom and Ted Daher refined the details of the knife's handle, which houses the motor and the on/off switch and acts as a base for the knife when not in use. Daher enclosed the mechanism in a two-toned brown plastic shell, designed to "coordinate with the colors of food" – those of cooked meat, presumably.[3]

The electric knife was born into a consumer culture of proliferating kitchen gadgetry. Sharing the small appliance market in 1961 were the Cory electric can opener, the Iona drink mixer, the GE toaster oven, and the Casco appliance center, which combined a mixer, blender, juicer, and knife sharpener into a single counter-top unit.[4] The electric knife quickly achieved success, reaching nearly $1 billion in annual sales by 1966. In 1977 more than 1.7 million units were sold.[5] In 1971 the British journal *Design* reported – in a tone of mild amusement – that one out of three American families owned an electric carving knife.[6] Since the mid-1980s sales of the electric knife have held steady at around 1.5 million units per year.[7]

Following GE's successful launch of the electric knife, other appliance manufacturers quickly produced competing models, marketing the new product as a gift item especially suited to men.[8] While electric skillets, coffee makers, and hair dryers were seen as appropriate for women, fire starters, shavers, and electric knives were packaged for Dad. A 1965 Ronson ad, published in time for Father's Day, presented its electric knife as a partner in a softly lit dinner for two: "Romps through a roast. Zips through a Porterhouse. And it looks terrific on the table, too. Makes any man a Michelangelo at mealtime."[9] Today, electric knives are rarely advertised and are sold primarily at Thanksgiving and Christmas – in most households, they are ceremonial objects rather than everyday necessities.[10]

GE introduced a cordless electric knife in January 1964. The rechargeable knife was abused by hunters and fishermen, an unanticipated market for the new appliance. Outdoorsmen exposed the knife to brutal natural elements – blood, guts, saltwater, etc. – that damaged the mechanism and led to numerous complaints from consumers: the electric knife, conceived as an indoor appliance – domestic and domesticated – failed to survive the rigors of the hunt.[11] Today, cordless knives for use inside the home are available at the high end of the market.[12]

Hamilton Beach redesigned the electric knife by inserting an open loop into the object's monolithic handle, leaving the motor enclosed in the structure below – this design typology was familiar from the popular electric mixer. The new model, introduced in 1966, was developed by in-house industrial designer Marlan Polhemuf and consultant designer Dave Chapman. The original "stick knife" had vibrated unpleasantly in the hand, an annoyance eliminated by the "hole-in-handle" model, whose slimmed-down grip also was considered more manageable for women.[13] The new electric knife received a Design in Housewares award in 1966 and was applauded by *Industrial Design* magazine for its "smooth, sculptured appearance."[14] Selling for $60 a unit, this deluxe appliance would be considered expensive even on today's market.

While Dave Chapman proposed visionary functional variations on the electric knife – such as a model powered by water from the kitchen faucet – he also presented packaging concepts to Hamilton Beach that concentrated on the object's cultural status.[15] One concept sketch shows the knife in a soft, dark wrapper modeled after the light-proof bags traditionally used for holding silverware; another sketch proposes a velvet-lined box with molded indentations for the handle unit and blades. These packaging ideas promoted the electric knife as a dignified object removed from the mundane world of the kitchen counter. In a similar spirit, Remington advertised a knife in 1965 whose brushed-chrome handle was designed "especially for the dining-room table"; photographed in a lady's gloved hand, this knife was "elegant enough to go with your best silver and china".[16]

It would take more than packaging or styling, however, to transform the electric slicer into an inconspicuous substitute for a skillfully deployed carving knife. As an appliance whose sheer physical presence – its size, weight, and sound – upstages the drama of the task at hand, the electric knife embraces a central aspect of modernist kitsch: the display of technological features exceeds the demands of the situation. In the words of Vittorio Gregotti, such "extravagant futility" typifies the realm of gadgets, as seen in the overly mechanized apartment of James Bond's arch-enemy Goldfinger, equipped with spectacular devices of surveilliance, torture, and entrapment.[17]

Comments in contemporary trade articles and advertisements hinted at the absurdity of the electric knife, insinuating that the object signaled a lack on the part of the head of household. Heralding the electric knife in 1965 as one of the "hottest" items on the small appliance market, *Plastics World* proclaimed: "They've been given to men who pride themselves on their carving ability and to men whose friends and families felt they needed all the help that could be rendered to cut through the cheese."[18] A 1964 GE ad suggested the electric knife as a useful gift for the male carver, from skittish fumbler to skilled virtuoso: "Does a roast make him roar? Or is he deft with a blade? Carving is child's play with General Electric's new Electric Slicing Knife."[19] In 1967 Carvel Hall, a manufacturer of high-end conventional cutlery, condemned the electric knife as a travesty of male honor:

> You don't carve with an electric knife. You saw. Swiftly, yes. Effortlessly. Without difficulty. And without art. Which depresses us. Because we still believe there's something grand about carving. It takes a simple chore like divvying up a roast and turns it into a small but gala performance. It is, indeed, a man's only chance to shine during a meal.[20]

Carvel Hall's elegy to the art of carving mourned the decline of a traditional masculine skill in a world of burgeoning gadgetry.

The performance of many domestic chores was fundamentally changed by machines in the postwar period. The mechanization of laundry, for example, successfully lightened one of the housewife's heaviest burdens. The washing machine also encouraged women to do laundry more often and to do nearly all of it at home. Thus, while such developments were heralded by many advertisers and commentators as a "revolution" that had liberated the modern woman from drudgery, the gendered assignment of chores remained unchanged. Likewise, the success of the electric knife was powered by traditional norms that defined carving as a masculine duty. Yet while the washing machine fundamentally altered a base and arduous task, the electric knife intervened in a ceremonial ritual, making it easier while rendering it somewhat ridiculous. The postwar man was no more "liberated" by his electric knife than his wife was set free by her blender. His new possession neither enhanced his status in the home nor freed him from a dreaded obligation.

From the primeval hunt to the royal feast, a long tradition of masculine performance surrounds the act of carving meat. In her anthropological study, *The Rituals of Dinner*, Margaret Visser examines the signifi-cance of cutting meat across a spectrum of cultural scenarios.[21] The perishable nature of animal flesh and the relative difficulty of procuring it, especially in hunting societies, makes meat a central focus of religious sacrifices and celebratory feasts:

> For thousands of years [meat] was placed before the family as a result of male enterprise and triumph; and men, with their knives, have insisted on carving it up, and even cooking it before the expectant crowd. Vegetables, on the other hand, were most often the result of steady, unexalted, cooperative, and often mainly female work.[22]

According to Visser, the act of cutting meat in public dramatizes the difference in taste and texture between the diverse parts of an animal carcass, forcing the carver to decide who will receive the best pieces. In contrast to the hierarchical roast, an "egalitarian" pie or stew reduces all cuts of flesh to a common medium.[23] As Visser points out, the modern suburban barbecue – a festive, holiday event – rehearses this ancient pattern by putting men in control of the meat and women in charge of salads and desserts.[24]

In early modern Europe carving was a compelling spectacle at grand feasts; the task of cutting meat at the table was reserved for an important person of noble birth. A manual of carving written by Vincenzo Cervio in 1581 describes the staggering levels of skill, strength, and confidence demanded by this art, and the burden of shame attached to failed performances. To serve a roasted bird the carver was expected to hold the entire carcass in the air on the end of a fork, while with the other hand slicing off perfect slivers of meat that would fall in a circular pattern on a platter waiting below.[25]

Mrs. Beeton's Book of Household Management, a famous British cooking guide first published in 1861, described with awe the feat of carving a bird in mid-air, witnessed at an exclusive London restaurant – by this time, such acrobatic serving techniques were no longer commonplace.[26] Painting a pathetic portrait of a man "entirely ignorant of carving," Mrs. Beeton bemoaned the state of the art in modern-day England:

> We have all seen him, offering in an emergency to assist his hostess, and trying with mere physical force to overcome his lack of skill; with red face and perspiring forehead he hacks and tugs at the dish in front of him, and at every attempt the veins stand out more prominently in his head, while the face of his hostess grows graver each moment as she begins to realize the appalling fact that the dish will not go around.[27]

If skill is what the humiliated carver lacked, it would not be provided by the electric knife, which a hundred years later offered plenty of motorized muscle power but no knowledge of animal anatomy or guarantee of the appropriate distribution of flesh, fat, and gravy on diners' plates – both essential to the art of carving. The author of *The Working Woman's Dream Kitchen*, a late twentieth-century offspring of Mrs. Beeton's famous book, acknowledged the functional value of the electric knife, especially for carving large birds, but added this note of disapproval: "I am old fashioned and still like to see my husband manually carve the Thanksgiving turkey or the Christmas standing rib roast."[28]

The spectacle of the domestically incompetent male appears in various ads for the electric knife, flattering the female gift buyer and emphasizing the superiority of her own skills and duties. In 1965 Westinghouse imagined its electric knife provoking a Texas chainsaw-style massacre of the contents of the kitchen:

> After he's had a go at poultry, roasts, hams, there won't be any stopping him. He'll want to branch out . . . slice bread, vegetables, cheese, fruit, and cake for you. Let him go . . . A Westinghouse Electric Knife is the one thing that can make him handy in the kitchen. And think what you can do with it when he isn't around.[29]

Recalling the ancient division between hunting and cultivating, various advertisements instruct men to employ the knife for meat, and women to use it for bread, cake, and vegetables – to carve is masculine and to slice is feminine, just as the traditional hunt was the work of men, while the cultivation of vegetables and the boiling of stews belonged in the domain of women. A 1965 Presto ad explained that the slim-handled electric knife "helps a man carve at dinnertime yet works just as well for everyday slicing of fruits, vegetables, even tender angel food . . . Great for gals. But be generous . . . let Dad still carve at dinner-time, huh?"[30] Such comments reinforce the delineation between masculine and feminine duties in the home, and show that men were assigned ceremonial, occasional tasks while "everyday" routines were women's work.

Unlike shoe polishers or shop tools, the electric knife is linked to the female-identified world of cooking and serving; at the same time, however, it draws on a long history of masculine performance at the dinner table. Appearing on the market during a period of rapid expansion and dubious innovation in the field of small appliances, the electric knife was a masculine addition to a world of gadgets associated largely with female consumers. Plugging into a tradition of male duty that had come under question, the knife supplemented a disappearing domestic art with the brute strength – and short leash – of electric power. Although it was designed for a ritual that signified male domestic leadership, the intrusive presence of the buzzing electric knife in the formal dining room signaled uncertainties in the hierarchy of the household.

Notes

1   Feminist studies of design and technology include Ruth Schwartz Cowan, *More Work for Mother: The Ironies of Household Technology from Open Hearth to Microwave* (New York: Basic Books, 1983); Adrian Forty, *Objects of Desire* (New York: Pantheon, 1986); and Penny Sparke, *Electrical Appliances: Twentieth-Century Design* (New York: E. P. Dutton, 1987).

2   On the differences between various electric knives on the market in 1964, see John H. Ingersoll, "Now . . . Carve with Power," *Popular Science* (December 1964), pp. 148–149.

3   Conversation with Olle Haggstrom, former GE Manager of Industrial Design, April 1994.

4   "Electric Housewares," *Industrial Design* 8 (December 1961), pp. 54–65.

5   In-house publication, General Electric, 1977.

6   "US Gadget Gluttony and Power Politics," *Design* 268 (April 1971), p. 19.

7   Duke Ratliff, "Bread Machines Boost Sales of Electric Knives," *Home Furnishings Daily* (3 May 1993), p. 121.

8   According to Olle Haggstrom, GE originally conceived of the electric knife as a "new household necessity," but the product quickly became identified with the gift market. An invaluable source of advertising material on the electric knife and other appliances is the John W. Hartman Center for Sales, Advertising, and Marketing History, Special Collections Library, Duke University.

9   *The New Yorker* (5 June 1965).

10   Conversation with Pete Elshout, National Accounts Department, Black and Decker, April 1994.

11   Conversation with Robert Mazakane, former manager of product safety for GE's Housewares Division, May 1994.

12   Brian J. Hogan, "Custom-Made Motor Simplifies Rechargeable Electric Knife," *Design News* (21 October 1985), pp. 122–123.

13   Marlan Polhemuf was the primary product designer working on the electric knife at Hamilton Beach when the Chicago firm Dave Chapman, Goldsmith, and Yamasaki, Inc. was hired in the capacity of consultant. Polhemuf claims to have originated the "hole-in-handle" concept. Conversation with Marlan Polhemuf, April 1994.

14   "NHMA Award Winners," *Industrial Design* 13 (September 1966), pp. 82–86. The Design in Housewares prize is awarded by the National Housewares Manufacturers Association.

15   "Confidential Report to Hamilton Beach Company"; by Dave Chapman, Goldsmith, and Yamasaki Inc., with drawings dated 1965. The Dave Chapman Papers, Department of Special Collections, Syracuse University Library.

16   *Life* (3 December 1965).

17   Vittorio Gregotti, "Styling and Architecture," in *Kitsch: The World of Bad Taste*, ed. Gillo Dorfles (New York: Bell, 1968), p. 263.

18   Madeleine Crowell, "Merchandising Memo on Kitchens and Small Appliances," *Plastics World* 23 (December 1965), pp. 36–37.

19   *Brides* (March 1964).

20   *The New Yorker* (20 May 1967).

21   Margaret Visser, *The Rituals of Dinner: The Origins, Evolutions, Eccentricities, and Meaning of Table Manners* (New York: Penguin, 1991).

22   Ibid., p. 231.

23   Ibid.

24   Advertisers in the 1960s recognized the barbecue as a site for selling male cooking gadgets, including the electric knife and the automatic fire starter. GE promoted the mechanized cook-out in *Sunset* (June 1964).

25   See Visser, *The Rituals of Dinner*, pp. 235–237, and *Masterpieces of Cutlery and the Art of Eating* (London: Victoria and Albert Museum, 1979).

26   *Mrs. Beeton's Book of Household Management, A Guide to Cookery in All Branches* (London: Ward, Lock & Co., 1915), Chapter XXXIX, "The Art of Carving at the Table," pp. 1258–1274.

27   Ibid., p. 1259.

28   Hilde Gabriel Lee, *The Working Woman's Dream Kitchen* (White Hall, VA: Betterway Publications, 1990).

29   *Life* (3 December 1965).

30   *Ladies Home Journal* (December 1965).

Chapter 12

Tobin Siebers

WHAT CAN DISABILITY STUDIES LEARN FROM THE CULTURE WARS? [2003]

Source: Tobin Siebers (2003) 'What can Disability Studies Learn from the Culture Wars?' [edited], *Cultural Critique*, 55, pp. 200–14.

The 'culture wars' is the name that is given to the political condemnation of certain forms of progressive and avant-garde art in the USA and the UK. Right-wing politicians have, since at least the 1950s, been particularly vocal about condemning the public funding of art that is seen by traditionalists as purposefully ugly, sexually explicit, left-leaning or formless. Often the condemnation also points to the way that the work doesn't show evidence of conventional artistic skills. Sometimes politicians have made grandiose claims about the moral corruption that the work is seen as performing, or the political allegiances that an art form is seen to represent (in the 1950s it was not unusual for US politicians to claim that abstract art was communistic).

For Tobin Siebers the 'culture wars' signify the deep structural organisation of taste and beauty around idealised images of body-norms. The culture wars offer vivid symptoms of the way that idealised bodies ('whole', 'fit', 'complete' bodies) inform judgements of what is ugly and what is beautiful, and what the appropriate forms of culture should be. Words like 'harmony', for instance, which might be used to evaluate a façade of a building, relate back to idealised images of 'healthy' bodies. For Siebers this makes aesthetics a far from innocent realm of value. In as much as the 'body politic' of democratic societies is the image of a body or series of bodies, then aesthetic norms actively work to exclude disabled bodies.

There are at least two consequences of such a perspective. The first is to strive to uncover the exclusionary power of dominant aesthetic forms. And this is what the text below is primarily concerned with. Here disability activists are encouraged to expand their remit of analysis and to think less about whether representations of disabled people are 'positive' or 'negative', and to think more fundamentally about the aesthetic organisation of beauty as a generalised value in culture. The other consequence for Siebers, and one that follows on from this, is the promotion of what elsewhere he calls 'disability aesthetics'. Disability aesthetics is both the analysis of aesthetic norms and the championing of other orders of beauty, particularly the beauty of the disabled body:

> Disability aesthetics refuses to recognize the representation of the healthy body – and its definition of harmony, integrity, and beauty – as the sole determination of the aesthetic. It is not a matter of representing the exclusion of disability from aesthetic history, since such an exclusion has not taken place, but of making the influence of

disability obvious. This goal may take two forms: 1) to establish disability as a critical framework that questions the presuppositions underlying definitions of aesthetic production and appreciation; 2) to establish disability as a significant value in itself worthy of future development.

(Siebers 2006: 64)

Design culture is the central realm for materialising the aesthetics of body-norms. A design culture premised on disability aesthetics promises not simply a world more easily navigated; it promises an entirely new world.

Further reading: Evans 1986; Freund 2001; Komardjaja 2001; Siebers 2006.

[. . .]

CULTURE IS NOT merely a web of symbols. It is a web of body symbols. Disability activists have focused so far on negative representations of the human body, on how the desire to represent perfect, individual bodies denigrates or excludes the experience of disability. If culture is really composed of body symbols, however, it means that the struggle by disability activists against negative body images must extend far beyond physical images of the individual human body to its symbolic resonance in other bodies. Beauty, order, and cleanliness in the built environment occupy a special position among the requirements of society because they apply to artificial bodies our pre-occupation with our own body, including its health, integrity, and hygiene. Only an analysis of this powerful symbolic connection will explain why prejudices against the disabled body persist in the built environment, and only then will disability activists be able to shift emphasis from the individual human body to the imaginary bodies undergirding architectural theory, employment law, and conceptions of citizenship.

A man extending a cane before himself and a three-bedroom colonial home stretching a wheelchair ramp into the street are equally disconcerting to the public eye. Both ignite a vigorous, defensive impulse to cure or fix the offending body. Conversely, beautiful, harmonious constructions automatically summon ideas of elegant, graceful people, as in this description of the John Hancock building in Boston, designed by I. M. Pei: "Pei and his principal designer, Henry Cobb, devised a sixty-two-story tower proportioned as slimly as a fashion model, sequined in reflective glass panels."[1] Other examples of the imaginary connection between body and building may be found throughout architectural theory both because the political unconscious exerts a stranglehold on the kinds of bodies acceptable in the built environment, and because modern architectural theories define the form and function of buildings with explicit reference to a politics of the body. Lewis Mumford claimed that the state of building at any period represents a "legible script" detailing the complicated processes and changes taking place in the body politic itself, while Louis Sullivan insisted that pure design in architecture maximizes utility by reproducing the essence of the human being.[2] Of course, this essence represents human beings in normative terms, both physically and mentally. These and other aesthetic dictates represent architecture itself as providing a transcendental expression of human perfection, situating in the crafting of concrete, wood, plastic, and steel the ability to overcome limitations of the human body and mind, but they also use the built environment to maintain a spatial caste system at the expense of people with disabilities. This caste system not only targets individual disabled bodies for exclusion but also rejects any form of appearance that symbolizes disability.

Perhaps the most revealing example of the relation between the political unconscious and architectural theory exists in the work of Le Corbusier. In 1925 he conceived of a diagram, the *Modular*, that utilizes the proportions of the body to help architects design buildings and other human habitats. It was to provide a standard scale by which buildings and human beings could be connected. The modular presents the image of an upright male – six feet tall, muscular, powerful, and showing no evidence of either physical or mental disability. It pictures the human body as a universal type, with no consideration of physical variation. Ironically, Le Corbusier wanted to tie buildings to the human beings living in them, but his theories privilege form over function and establish one basis for what Rob Imrie has called the "design apartheid" of modernist architectural practices.[3] In fact, design apartheid describes with accuracy the exclusionary system apparent in many episodes of the culture wars. Works of art called ugly ignite public furor. Unaesthetic designs or dilapidated buildings are viewed as eyesores. Deformed bodies appear as public nuisances. Not only do these phenomena confront the public with images of the disabled body, they expose the fact that the public's idea of health is itself based on unconscious operations designed to defend against the pain of disability.

Successful methods of fending off what is painful or distressing choose appropriate courses of action by recognizing the threat, considering it, and making a judgment about it. Between these methods and unconscious, defensive inhibitions lies a range of pathological behaviors and mental operations. They are observable in actions by individuals and the public, but they are obviously much more difficult to identify and analyze in the case of groups, since social pressure makes discovering them less probable, and the sheer number of people and the absence of anything approaching a genuine theory of group psychology make treatment impossible. "Mass hysteria" and "group delusion" are, after all, rather sad theories and do not take analysis far beyond the sensationalism implied in the phrases themselves. Nevertheless, some form of group psychology appears to be at the origin of public reactions to disability, for the defensive measures are too consistent to be merely coincidental. It is as if the phobias, inhibitions, defensive reactions, and avoidance patterns that spring up to meet any formal instance of disability, whether organic, aesthetic, or architectural, represent collective versions of what are normally thought to be individual defense mechanisms.[4] These group inhibitions preserve the self-image of the community, its ego function as it were, by striving to banish distressing emotional impulses, visceral signs of anxiety, and threats of injury or pain, amounting to the equivalent of a collective flight reflex in the presence of painful stimuli.[5]

The culture wars were bound to display a panorama of phobias, inhibitions, censorship, and avoidance of bodies imagined as diseased or defective because they make the metaphoric connection between able bodies and healthy societies an explicit theme of public controversy and because their posture is defensive in nature. In effect, the culture wars amount to a striking episode of collective inhibition in action: they represent a critical moment when the existing culture is trying to defend its ideal image against forces that would transform it. The NEA controversy, *sensation*, the Heidelberg Project, and the official responses to them provide only a few samples of possible case studies exposing collective defense mechanisms at work. But the same defensive ideas, reactions, and behaviors appear even where explicit public controversy has no place, the most surprising and unsettling being design projects friendly to the disability community. Here mechanisms of defense are not easy to explain without further consideration of the ways in which mental behaviors buttress the political unconscious. I refer to the bungled actions, instances of counter will, and disturbances in memory readable in the most amiable efforts to make the built environment accessible to people with disabilities. These phenomena might be collected, following Freud, under the heading of "hysterical architecture," since they encompass plans and design implementations contrived to provide access but burdened by a symptomatic inhibition against disability. The reference to psychoanalysis makes sense both because defensive measures against disability often mimic hysterical symptomatology, and because Freud illustrates the exchange of symptoms in hysteria with the analogy of a disabled woman carrying too many packages.[6] The feeble woman, her arms overflowing with packages, tries to walk down the street, but she inevitably drops a package, and when she bends down to pick it up, she drops a second package just as she recovers the first, and on and on, to the point where progress is futile. Freud claims that each package represents a symptom, one of many external signs of the same underlying problem. The analogy is especially pertinent to defensive measures in the built environment because the disabled woman is marked by a series of external signs that signal the presence of her disability, and yet the exchange of external signs works like a shell game to hide her disability or at least to displace attention from it.

In the case of the built environment, of course, the shuffling of external signs of disability cannot be blamed on the psychology of people with disabilities, as in the example of Freud's hysteric. The architecture is itself "hysterical" in its desire to ward off signs of disability, for each attempt to make the building accessible produces another attempt either to block accessibility or to conceal the marker of disability tattooed by accessible features on the skin of the building. The end result is a zero-sum game in favor of phobia, inhibition, and discrimination.

Each person with a disability can recount experiences with defensive inhibitions against accessible architecture in the public environment. Local examples in Ann Arbor are numerous, some of which reflect trends in building and landscaping evident at the national level. Designers of parking lots for shopping malls in Ann Arbor suffer from a bizarre counter will when it comes to handicapped parking. Often they fill the median – separating the parking lot from the store entrances and next to which handicapped spaces are always found – with large decorative rocks that are extremely difficult to walk over and impossible to cross with a wheelchair. The practice effectively places a rocky barrier reef between the handicapped spaces and the destination of the wheelchair users. The four handicapped spaces for the graduate library at the University of Michigan are buttressed by a three-foot high retaining wall, decorated with flowers and inconveniently located between the parking places and the rear entrance of the library (Figure 12.1). The sidewalks leading to that entrance are also strategically blocked by an obstacle course of concrete planters, approximately three feet square and brimming with colorful pansies.

An example of motivated forgetting in accessible architecture at the national level is found in the government lawsuit against Ellerbe Becket of Minneapolis, one of the largest architectural firms in the

Figure 12.1   Handicapped spaces, Graduate Library, University of Michigan (image © Tobin Siebers).

country (Dunlap 1997). Ellerbe Becket has designed over a half-dozen sport stadiums, and each one demonstrates a "pattern or practice of discrimination" in its placement of wheelchair locations, according to the government. The law requires that wheelchair locations have "lines of sight comparable to those for members of the general public." But Ellerbe Becket arranges wheelchair locations so that their users cannot see when the crowd stands. The firm has tried to argue that government guidelines and laws do not require that people in wheelchairs be able to see over standing spectators.

Jim Knipfel details two extraordinary instances of bungled actions toward disability in his comic memoir *Slack Jaw*. Knipfel is one of one hundred thousand Americans with retinitis pigmentosa, a genetic condition that attacks the photoreceptor cells in the retina, eventually producing blindness. One of his many adventures includes spending the better part of one morning trying to locate the New York State Department of Social Services Commission for the Blind and Visually Handicapped at 270 Broadway in New York City. After roaming up and down the even-numbered side of Broadway between the 100 and 400 blocks for several hours, he finally asks a homeless man where to find the address and then describes the "nasty tendency" found inside the front doors:

> "Excuse me?" I inquired without getting too close. I didn't want to startle him. "Do you know where Two-seventy Broadway is?"
>
> Without a word he raised a finger and pointed across the street.
>
> As it happens, 270 Broadway is the anomaly, an even-numbered building on the west side of the street.
>
> Once I got through the front doors, I was in near-total darkness. This is a nasty tendency I've discovered in places that are designed to "help" the blind. Willis Eye Hospital in Philadelphia was the worst in this respect. The reception area is a cavernous, unlit room scattered with floor-to-ceiling concrete pillars. You could sit there all day and be entertained by the zany antics of blind people walking headlong into post after post, like a giant pinball machine. Here at 270 Broadway, at least, there was only a long unlit hallway.
>
> I asked a man where the elevators were, and he said, "Right over there," which, of course, helped me not at all. Once I did feel my way to the elevators, I found a man down on his hands and knees inside, banging away with a hammer at a piece of metal that had come loose.
>
> (1999, 184)

Finally, misdirection may also indicate defensive inhibitions at work. Handicapped signage is sometimes unclear, using the same icons to mark where handicapped entrances are and are not, and often signs disappear abruptly en route, leaving people wondering at every fork in the road. In old construction, designers trying to meet accessibility requirements plotted courses with more curves than a cobra, but new construction is just as likely to lead people with disabilities into buildings along a snaky course. Following handicapped signage often gives one the impression of being caught in a labyrinth. The shortest distance between two points is rarely a straight line when people with disabilities are involved – "a crooked path for crooked people" appears to be the motto behind some attempts to open buildings to accessibility.

Defensive countermeasures, as these examples show, work to conceal the blemish on society represented by disability. The personal fear and shame that have led historically to the institutionalization of people with disabilities by their own families is a common trope in this pattern of avoidance. But defensive avoidance extends well beyond individual bodies and personal actions to encompass the behavior, ideas, and physical appearance of society itself. Ugly laws and less official sanctions against people with disabilities strive to decrease their presence and lessen their influence in the community. Architecture and landscape design attempt not only to project a sense of beauty but also to exclude people deemed ugly or defective by making their access to society difficult or impossible. City codes about building upkeep guarantee a sense of harmony for the eye and maintain a uniformity unaffected by any sign of dilapidation or defect. More significant, friendly attempts to provide access for people with disabilities are sometimes disrupted by countermeasures that undo the process of accessibility itself. It is as if the public interprets ramps, accessible doors, and signage for the disabled as symbols of disability that require a mustering of defense mechanisms. In no time, plants and flowers clutter wheelchair ramps, handicap signs are tucked away, and decorative rocks and wood chips block accessible walkways. Nature abhors a vacuum, and society treats handicapped parking places and accessible pathways as empty spaces to fill: locales marked by accessibility inevitably become handy collecting points for trash, building materials, or delivery trucks (Figures 12.2–4).

My purpose has been to explore, under the pressure of the culture wars, how the aesthetic representation of bodies – individual and collective, organic and artificial – leads to the oppression of people with disabilities. The culture wars are not just about different political factions in conflict (conservative versus liberal) or about a historical backlash against the 1960s (the usual argument), but about the incorporation of different physical and mental types into the American body politic. On the one hand, civic beauty, political consensus, social harmony, and economic vitality summon images of the healthy body. On the other hand, whenever sickness, dirt, political disagreement, social chaos, or economic depression appears, society responds by generating images of the disabled or diseased body. Nevertheless, most commentators, including those with disabilities, have not registered the relevance of disability to the culture wars, and only the disability community recognizes the cultural meaning of fights about employment law, citizenship, and accessibility. This is obviously the case, as Jameson has argued, because the political operates at a deeply unconscious level. The political unconscious cements the secret connection between beauty, health, and social totality through innumerable images and representations, some generated by art, commerce, and the

Figure 12.2 UPS truck, handicapped spaces, Mason Hall loading dock, University of Michigan (image © Tobin Siebers).

Figure 12.3   Grass clippings, handicapped spaces, Mason Hall loading dock, University of Michigan (image ©
Tobin Siebers).

media, others embedded in the bodies of leaders and the shapes of buildings, city streets, tools, furniture, automobiles, and other instances of form.

The culture wars have used aesthetic rather than political arguments to influence public policy because concepts such as health, well-being, and beauty – so important to ideals of social perfection – often rely on appearance, and appearance is inevitably a matter of aesthetic form. Now it is generally accepted that works of art call for aesthetic judgments, but we rarely consider that manifestations of sickness and health also elicit judgments of this kind. In fact, judgments about art objects are widely thought to be different from judgments about the abilities of human beings, especially with regard to physical appearance, health, and mental competence. Moreover, it is now possible to question the use of aesthetic standards to judge artworks – most art critics today would object if a show or museum excluded an art object because it was deemed ugly. This self-conscious and critical attitude does not arise when it comes to the exclusion of people of disabilities from the built environment. My point is that aversion to and hatred of disability are also aesthetic reactions, but that objections to aesthetic standards and tastes are rarely raised when it comes to the inclusion of people with disabilities. In fact, aesthetic judgments about the built environment remain unquestioned when architects make the case against accessible designs on the grounds that access produces ugly buildings, despite the fact that those buildings called beautiful are fashioned to suppress the disabled body from public view. Obviously, people with disabilities suffer because their individual appearance is thought by others to be aesthetically displeasing, but this truth tells only half the story. The sense of rejection felt by people with disabilities, over and above personal humiliations and individual affronts, is doubled when one considers how profound is the symbolic exclusion of disability by society.

Ideal versions of human appearance are preserved through aesthetic representations that bridge the

Figure 12.4   Trash, handicapped spaces, Mason Hall loading dock, University of Michigan (image © Tobin Siebers).

gap between individual and collective existence. Indeed, aesthetics may be the most effective means of bridging this gap, for in the absence of aesthetic representation, it is not clear that human beings would be able to imagine what political community is, let alone understand their place in it.[7] Disability studies cannot avoid a similar conflation between aesthetic and political form, since it must invent its own imaginary communities, but we might take advantage of the confusion in a number of ways. First, the study of cultural representations of the disabled body and mind needs to continue, including stereotypes elaborated by art, literature, the sciences and social sciences, medicine, the media, law, commerce, and politics. Second, the study of the disabled body must be extended to its symbolization by other bodies and the vast array of cultural forms, such as objects of art, buildings, environments, and consumer products. This step will help disability activists to determine the extent to which defensive trends organize public spaces; to offer theories about the psychology motivating the collective fears, inhibitions, and patterns of avoidance that censor disability; and to tackle prejudices against disability operating beyond the representation of the individual body. Finally, the disability community should continue to intervene vigorously in the culture wars, creating artworks, performances, theater, and political spectacle; imprinting disabled bodies and minds on the public landscape; and inventing new modes of beauty that attack aesthetic and political standards that insist on uniformity, balance, hygiene, and formal integrity.

Although we all have a stake in the healthiness of our country, it is time to understand health differently. The artists at the center of the culture wars – Finley, Serrano, Mapplethorpe, Guyton, the young British artists, and others – might be thought of as a first wave in the struggle to make our communities more accessible and democratic. They provide a powerful formula for questioning contemporary conceptions of beauty as well as suggesting an arena for future political intervention. The current battles about culture and political self-image are being waged over the definition of health, and they are ripe for aggressive political action. Indeed, the culture wars may have greater potential for political engagement than other phenomena on the scene today. The political unconscious will always be in force, influencing conceptions of identities and bodies, both individual and collective, but because it is constantly shifting, social change is possible.

Notes

1   In this particular case, however, the illusion of health proved disastrous, since hundreds of the glass panels cracked before the building was occupied and had to be replaced with stronger glass at a cost of $8.2 million. The building also shifted in the wind, requiring further construction, costing $17.5 million, to stabilize its thin frame and to install two three-hundred-ton adjustable counterweights near its top to resist wind pressure. Cited by Knox 1987, 358.

2   See Mumford 1983, 403; and Sullivan 1979, who discusses everywhere the connection between bodies and design imperatives. For an illuminating discussion of modern architecture, focusing on Sullivan and Le Corbusier, see Imrie 1996, chapter 4.

3   Designers and architects learn to design buildings, environments, and products for "average" people, and, of course, the "average" person is always able-bodied. The incarnation of the "average" in the built environment excludes bodies that do not fit the norm and embeds in the flesh of that environment the desire to preserve the able body over all other forms and shapes. But the average person does not really exist, for someone who is average at one point in life fails to be average earlier or later on. Children and the elderly, for example, do not have average bodies. Averageness is a ratio used to reject human variation, and of these variations the disabled body is the easiest to exclude. See Imrie 1996, 19, 81–87, whose discussion of Le Corbusier and architectural standards is invaluable.

4   Freud, in *The Psychopathology of Everyday Life*, initially defines mechanisms of defense with reference to hysteria and, appropriately for my argument, in language ripe with architectural metaphors: "We are forced to regard as one of the main pillars of the mechanism supporting hysterical symptoms an *elementary endeavour* of this kind to fend off ideas that can arouse feelings of unpleasure . . . to banish distressing affective impulses like remorse and the pangs of conscience. . . . It may be surmised that *the architectonic principle of the mental apparatus lies in a stratification – a building up of superimposed agencies*" (6: 147; Freud's emphases). He then abandons the idea of defensive processes for the theory of repression, only to revert to a theory of defense in his later work. He uses the concept of defense "explicitly as a general designation for all the techniques which the ego makes use of in conflicts which may lead to neurosis" ("Inhibitions, Symptoms, and Anxiety," 20: 163).

5   I find the connection between the ego and the self-image of political bodies suggestive for thinking about the defensive posture of public reactions to disability but cannot assert it rigorously, given the undeveloped state of group psychology as a discipline. Some thinkers using a Lacanian orientation, however, have pursued this line of thinking productively, most obviously Žižek 1989.

6   A caution: the analogy between hysteria and the disabled woman maintains the superficial demand for balance, coordination, posture, and outward appearance of perfection as the measure against which the disabled body and mind must compete. I apply it, as well as the term "hysterical architecture," with this caution, to insist on the importance of the superficial in the workings of the political unconscious. One can literally read the defensive reactions against disability in the commotion agitating the external skin of accessible buildings and their approaches. As I will enumerate, the commotion around disability and its symbols is sometimes cosmetic, obscuring markers of disability with decoration, and sometimes dissembling, complicating accessible entrances with erroneous signage or complicated distribution points. In most cases, the impression of superficiality dominates.

7   My *The Subject and Other Subjects* (1998), especially chapters 1 and 6, elaborates at great length on the necessary supplementation of the political by the aesthetic.

PART THREE

OBJECT LIFE

INTRODUCTION TO PART THREE

I N H E R book *Wild Things: The Material Culture of Everyday Life* the design historian Judith Attfield wrote of sorting through her father's possessions after he died. She ends up keeping his 'most loved cardigan', and places it in a drawer at the bottom of her chest of drawers. The cardigan, through wear, through being loved, had become a material attribute of her lost loved father. The cardigan was a material link; it bore testimony to a life now gone. And because it was loved, it was altered by that love. Sometimes loving something alters it completely. My son has loved his 'dog' (a small dark-brown soft toy) since he was about six months old. The dog, after many attempts at mending, is now completely undone and has no filling (apart from the head). Love is wear and tear. The toy's label that my son has sucked every night for the last six and half years has been replaced on numerous occasions. 'Doggy' has in the past, of course, gone (treacherously) missing, and was once only found by backtracking through the length and breadth of an Ikea store to be discovered tucked up in one of the bedroom displays.

Of course, materially, love might not look that different from hate: the clothes you are often made to wear as a schoolchild, that you pull at and that pull at you, might not wear out in a way that is significantly different from those clothes you treasure. The shoes scuffed through general disdain might not look that different from the shoes that are scuffed through enthusiastic use. However much we may love and hate the objects around us, there is a material indifference to be found in the object too; it is indifferent and resilient. My son's doggy isn't going to sulk if he chucks it in the corner and ignores it.

But while we might invest individual objects with all sorts of personal emotional significance, we also use objects to negotiate our place in the world. Those school uniforms that turn you into 'school property' are also the canvases for your attempts to inscribe meaning on to the world, and to do so by making communal affiliations. Are you going to tuck your shirt in? Have a small knot or a large knot in your tie? Collar up or down? Trousers (or pants, depending on your linguistic persuasion) nestling on your hips, or magically attached to the mid-point of your bottom? But while such touches might allow you a nuanced form of communication within a social arrangement like a school, it may go back to being fairly blunt communication outside. For instance, there may be little you can do to disguise a uniform's provenance when you meet some kids from a rival school in the street. And here the objects of design (clothing) are tokens in a world marked by difference and by structured antagonisms.

History is filled with stories of people getting treated with suspicion, abused, beaten up or killed for the clothes they wear, or the objects that they carry. People have been forced to wear certain clothes, and to carry signs that are meant to shame them in public. But clothes can also be worn with pride, with confidence in the face of that structural antagonism which is stacked against you. Love and hate (and all the places in between), then, also animate the sociality of these designed worlds. It is a sign perhaps that the political is not a distant realm of complex long-range planning (though it may be this as well), but is lived intimately, close to the body, near the surface of the skin. And it is lived with and through these objects that gather around us.

Chapter 13

Stuart Cosgrove

THE ZOOT-SUIT AND STYLE
WARFARE [1984]

Source: Stuart Cosgrove (1984) 'The Zoot-Suit and Style Warfare', *History Workshop Journal*, 18 (Autumn), pp. 77–91.

Stuart Cosgrove is Channel 4's head of programmes (nations and regions) (Channel 4 is a commercial TV channel in the UK whose founding charter promised that it would address socially diverse audiences). He has been the editor of *The New Musical Express* and *The Face*, and presently hosts a popular comedy show on Scottish radio. Before his stellar broadcasting career he was an academic, and this essay on the zoot-suit riots in Los Angeles, Detroit and other US cities in 1943 shows just how explosive clothing design can be.

The zoot-suit is, as Cosgrove shows, a piece of flamboyant and exorbitant tailoring: a long, frock-coat jacket, exaggerated shoulder pads, coupled with excessively baggy trousers (pants) tapering into relatively tight cuffs. But the description sounds much 'zootier' in the vernacular: 'a killer-diller coat with a drape-shape, reat-pleats and shoulders padded like a lunatic's cell'. As the dress of choice for Mexican American (*pachucos*) and African American youth subcultures it was the clothing of exuberant refusal: the refusal to inhabit the role that was ascribed to them, the role of social victim. The excessive negation of the utility of clothing is immediately performed by the sheer amount of cloth needed for the suit. The zoot-suit demands attention: it spoke of an extreme social confidence as it cast exaggerated shapes of dapper masculinity. At a historical moment when America had joined the allied forces in the Second World War, and when the government had imposed fabric rationing in support of the war effort, the zoot-suit also spoke in a voice that was outside the heightened patriotism of the time.

The riots came after months of violent meetings between zoot-suited groups and US servicemen. What the white servicemen recognised was that the zoot-suit mocked them; or rather that the zoot-suit mocked their assumed racial superiority, mocked their implicit 'right' to social confidence. That this mockery disturbed the fragile ego of white masculinity can be judged from what one writer refers to as the symbolic annihilation that the servicemen meted out. Zoot-suited young men were hunted down, stripped and beaten, and their zoot-suits were burnt or urinated on. While the white press represented such acts as retribution for the criminal and unpatriotic activities of the young Mexican and African Americans, other writers recognised them for what they were: acts of racial hatred aimed at the bodies and bodily attire of the zoot-suiters.

The zoot-suit is related to the 'bling' of present-day RnB and rap culture; it is a first cousin to the working-class Teddy boy culture of postwar London. Clothing has always been an extension of the self, a performance enhancer for social being. Just as the business suit and the soldier's uniform enact the arrogance of privilege (which for the working-class soldier is often more symbolic than actual), the exaggerated luxury of the zoot-suit answers back with a studied arrogance of its own.

Further reading: English 2007; Entwistle 2000; Hebdige 1979; Mazon 1988; Wallace 1992.

Introduction: the silent noise of sinister clowns

What about those fellows waiting still and silent there on the platform, so still and silent they clash with the crowd in their very immobility, standing noisy in their very silence; harsh as a cry of terror in their quietness? What about these three boys, coming now along the platform, tall and slender, walking with swinging shoulders in their well-pressed, too-hot-for-summer suits, their collars high and tight about their necks, their identical hats of black cheap felt set upon the crowns of their heads with a severe formality above their conked hair? It was as though I'd never seen their like before: walking slowly, their shoulders swaying, their legs swinging from their hips in trousers that ballooned upward from cuffs fitting snug about their ankles; their coats long

Figure 13.1   Pair of zoot-suit-wearing African American men walking down the street after wartime race riots. Michigan, United States, June 20, 1943 (photo by Gordon Coster/Time & Life Pictures/Getty Images).

and hip-tight with shoulders far too broad to be those of natural western men. These fellows whose bodies seemed — what had one of my teachers said of me? — 'You're like one of those African sculptures, distorted in the interest of design.' Well, what design and whose?[1]

THE ZOOT-SUIT IS more than an exaggerated costume, more than a sartorial statement, it is the bearer of a complex and contradictory history. When the nameless narrator of Ellison's *Invisible Man* confronted the subversive sight of three young and extravagantly dressed blacks, his reaction was one of fascination not of fear. These youths were not simply grotesque dandies parading the city's secret underworld, they were 'the stewards of something uncomfortable',[2] a spectacular reminder that the social order had failed to contain their energy and difference. The zoot-suit was more than the drape-shape of 1940s fashion, more than a colourful stage-prop hanging from the shoulders of Cab Calloway, it was, in the most direct and obvious ways, an emblem of ethnicity and a way of negotiating an identiy. The zoot-suit was a refusal: a subcultural gesture that refused to concede to the manners of subservience. By the late 1930s, the term 'zoot' was in common circulation within urban jazz culture. Zoot meant something worn or performed in an extravagant style, and since many young blacks wore suits with outrageously padded shoulders and trousers that were fiercely tapered at the ankles, the term zoot-suit passed into everyday usage. In the sub-cultural world of Harlem's nightlife, the language of rhyming slang succinctly described the zoot-suit's unmistakable style: 'a killer-diller coat with a drape-shape, reat-pleats and shoulders padded like a lunatic's cell'. The study of the relationships between fashion and social action is notoriously underdeveloped, but there is every indication that the zoot-suit riots that erupted in the United States in the summer of 1943 had a profound effect on a whole generation of socially disadvantaged youths. It was during his period as a young zoot-suiter that the Chicano union activist Cesar Chavez first came into contact with community politics, and it was through the experiences of participating in zoot-suit riots in Harlem that the young pimp 'Detroit Red' began a political education that transformed him into the Black radical leader Malcolm X. Although the zoot-suit occupies an almost mythical place within the history of jazz music, its social and political importance has been virtually ignored. There can be no certainty about when, where or why the zoot-suit came into existence, but what is certain is that during the summer months of 1943 'the killer-diller coat' was the uniform of young rioters and the symbol of a moral panic about juvenile delinquency that was to intensify in the post-war period.

At the height of the Los Angeles riots of June 1943, the *New York Times* carried a front page article which claimed without reservation that the first zoot-suit had been purchased by a black bus worker, Clyde Duncan, from a tailor's shop in Gainesville, Georgia.[3] Allegedly, Duncan had been inspired by the film 'Gone with the Wind' and had set out to look like Rhett Butler. This explanation clearly found favour throughout the USA. The national press forwarded countless others. Some reports claimed that the zoot-suit was an invention of Harlem night life, others suggested it grew out of jazz culture and the exhibitionist stage-costumes of the band leaders, and some argued that the zoot-suit was derived from military uniforms and imported from Britain. The alternative and independent press, particularly *Crisis* and *Negro Quarterly*, more convincingly argued that the zoot-suit was the product of a particular social context.[4] They emphasised the importance of Mexican-American youths, or *pachucos*, in the emergence of zoot-suit style and, in tentative ways, tried to relate their appearance on the streets to the concept of *pachuquismo*.

In his pioneering book, *The Labyrinth of Solitude*, the Mexican poet and social commentator Octavio Paz throws imaginative light on *pachuco* style and indirectly establishes a framework within which the zoot-suit can be understood. Paz's study of the Mexican national consciousness examines the changes brought about by the movement of labour, particularly the generations of Mexicans who migrated northwards to the USA. This movement, and the new economic and social patterns it implies, has, according to Paz, forced young Mexican-Americans into an ambivalent experience between two cultures.

What distinguishes them, I think, is their furtive, restless air: they act like persons who are wearing disguises, who are afraid of a stranger's look because it could strip them and leave them stark naked . . . This spiritual condition, or lack of a spirit, has given birth to a type known as the pachuco. The pachucos are youths, for the most part of Mexican origin, who form gangs in southern cities; they can be identified by their language and behaviour as well as by the clothing they affect. They are instinctive rebels, and North American racism has vented its wrath on them more than once. But the pachucos do not attempt to vindicate their race or the nationality of their forebears. Their attitude reveals an obstinate, almost fanatical will-to-be, but this will affirms nothing specific except their determination not to be like those around them.[5]

Pachuco youth embodied all the characteristics of second generation working-class immigrants. In the most obvious ways they had been stripped of their customs, beliefs and language. The *pachucos* were a dis-inherited generation within a disadvantaged sector of North American society, and predictably their experiences in education, welfare and employment alienated them from the aspirations of their parents and the dominant assumptions of the society in which they lived. The *pachuco* subculture was defined not only by ostentatious fashion, but by petty crime, delinquency and drug-taking. Rather than disguise their alienation or efface their hostility to the dominant society, the *pachucos* adopted an arrogant posture. They flaunted their difference, and the zoot-suit became the means by which that difference was announced. Those 'impassive and sinister clowns' whose purpose was 'to cause terror instead of laughter,'[6] invited the kind of attention that led to both prestige and persecution. For Octavio Paz the *pachuco*'s appropriation of the zoot-suit was an admission of the ambivalent place he occupied. 'It is the only way he can establish a more vital relationship with the society he is antagonising. As a victim he can occupy a place in the world that previously ignored him; as a delinquent, he can become one of its wicked heroes.'[7] The zoot-suit riots of 1943 encapsulated this paradox. They emerged out of the dialectics of delinquency and persecution, during a period in which American society was undergoing profound structural change.

The major social change brought about by the United States' involvement in the war was the recruitment to the armed forces of over four million civilians and the entrance of over five million women into the war-time labour force. The rapid increase in military recruitment and the radical shift in the composition of the labour force led in turn to changes in family life, particularly the erosion of parental control and authority. The large scale and prolonged separation of millions of families precipitated an unprecedented increase in the rate of juvenile crime and delinquency. By the summer of 1943 it was commonplace for teenagers to be left to their own initiatives whilst their parents were either on active military service or involved in war work. The increase in night work compounded the problem. With their parents or guardians working unsocial hours, it became possible for many more young people to gather late into the night at major urban centres or simply on the street corners.

The rate of social mobility intensified during the period of the zoot-suit riots. With over 15 million civilians and 12 million military personnel on the move throughout the country, there was a corresponding increase in vagrancy. Petty crimes became more difficult to detect and control; itinerants became increas-ingly common, and social transience put unforeseen pressure on housing and welfare. The new patterns of social mobility also led to congestion in military and industrial areas. Significantly, it was the overcrowded military towns along the Pacific coast and the industrial conurbations of Detroit, Pittsburgh and Los Angeles that witnessed the most violent outbreaks of zoot-suit rioting.[8]

'Delinquency' emerged from the dictionary of new sociology to become an everyday term, as wartime statistics revealed these new patterns of adolescent behavior. The *pachucos* of the Los Angeles area were particularly vulnerable to the effects of war. Being neither Mexican nor American, the *pachucos*, like the black youths with whom they shared the zoot-suit style, simply did not fit. In their own terms they were '24-hour orphans', having rejected the ideologies of their migrant parents. As the war furthered the dislocation of family relationships, the *pachucos* gravitated away from the home to the only place where their status was visible, the streets and bars of the towns and cities. But if the *pachucos* laid themselves open to a life of delinquency and detention, they also asserted their distinct identity, with their own style of dress, their own way of life and a shared set of experiences.

The zoot-suit riots: liberty, disorder and the forbidden

The zoot-suit riots sharply revealed a polarization between two youth groups within wartime society: the gangs of predominantly black and Mexican youths who were at the forefront of the zoot-suit subculture, and the predominantly white American servicemen stationed along the Pacific coast. The riots invariably had racial and social resonances but the primary issue seems to have been patriotism and attitudes to the war. With the entry of the United States into the war in December 1941, the nation had to come to terms with the restrictions of rationing and the prospects of conscription. In March 1942, the War Production Board's first rationing act had a direct effect on the manufacture of suits and all clothing containing wool. In an attempt to institute a 26% cut-back in the use of fabrics, the War Production Board drew up regulations for the wartime manufacture of what *Esquire* magazine called, 'streamlined suits by Uncle Sam.'[9] The regulations effectively forbade the manufacture of zoot-suits and most legitimate tailoring companies ceased to manufacture or advertise any suits that fell outside the War Production Board's guide lines. However, the demand for zoot-suits did not decline and a network of bootleg tailors based in Los Angeles and New York continued to manufacture the garments. Thus the polarization between servicemen and *pachucos* was immediately visible: the chino shirt and battledress were evidently uniforms of patriotism, whereas wearing a zoot-suit was a deliberate and public way of flouting the regulations of rationing. The zoot-suit was a moral and social scandal in the eyes of the authorities, not simply because it was associated with petty crime and violence, but because it openly snubbed the laws of rationing. In the fragile harmony of wartime society, the zoot-suiters were, according to Octavio Paz, 'a symbol of love and joy or of horror and loathing, an embodiment of liberty, of disorder, of the forbidden.'[10]

The zoot-suit riots, which were initially confined to Los Angeles, began in the first few days of June 1943. During the first weekend of the month, over 60 zoot-suiters were arrested and charged at Los Angeles County jail, after violent and well publicized fights between servicemen on shore leave and gangs of Mexican-American youths. In order to prevent further outbreaks of fighting, the police patrolled the eastern sections of the city, as rumours spread from the military bases that servicemen were intending to form vigilante groups. The *Washington Post*'s report of the incidents, on the morning of Wednesday 9 June 1943, clearly saw the events from the point of view of the servicemen.

> Disgusted with being robbed and beaten with tire irons, weighted ropes, belts and fists employed by overwhelming numbers of the youthful hoodlums, the uniformed men passed the word quietly among themselves and opened their campaign in force on Friday night.
>
> At central jail, where spectators jammed the sidewalks and police made no efforts to halt auto loads of servicemen openly cruising in search of zoot-suiters, the youths streamed gladly into the sanctity of the cells after being snatched from bar rooms, pool halls and theaters and stripped of their attire.[11]

During the ensuing weeks of rioting, the ritualistic stripping of zoot-suiters became the major means by which the servicemen re-established their status over the *pachucos*. It became commonplace for gangs of marines to ambush zoot-suiters, strip them down to their underwear and leave them helpless in the streets. In one particularly vicious incident, a gang of drunken sailors rampaged through a cinema after discovering two zoot-suiters. They dragged the *pachucos* on to the stage as the film was being screened, stripped them in front of the audience and as a final insult, urinated on the suits.

The press coverage of these incidents ranged from the careful and cautionary liberalism of the *Los Angeles Times* to the more hysterical hate-mongering of William Randolph Hearst's west coast papers. Although the practice of stripping and publicly humiliating the zoot-suiters was not prompted by the press, several reports did little to discourage the attacks:

> . . . zoot-suits smouldered in the ashes of street bonfires where they had been tossed by grimly

methodical tank forces of service men. . . . The zooters, who earlier in the day had spread boasts that they were organized to 'kill every cop' they could find, showed no inclination to try to make good their boasts . . . Searching parties of soldiers, sailors and Marines hunted them out and drove them out into the open like bird dogs flushing quail. Procedure was standard: grab a zooter. Take off his pants and frock coat and tear them up or burn them. Trim the 'Argentine Ducktail' haircut that goes with the screwy costume.[12]

The second week of June witnessed the worst incidents of rioting and public disorder. A sailor was slashed and disfigured by a *pachuco* gang; a policeman was run down when he tried to question a car load of zoot-suiters; a young Mexican was stabbed at a party by drunken Marines; a trainload of sailors were stoned by *pachucos* as their train approached Long Beach; streetfights broke out daily in San Bernardino; over 400 vigilantes toured the streets of San Diego looking for zoot-suiters, and many individuals from both factions were arrested.[13] On 9 June, the *Los Angeles Times* published the first in a series of editorials designed to reduce the level of violence, but which also tried to allay the growing concern about the racial character of the riots.

> To preserve the peace and good name of the Los Angeles area, the strongest measures must be taken jointly by the police, the Sheriff's office and Army and Navy authorities, to prevent any further outbreaks of 'zoot suit' rioting. While members of the armed forces received considerable provocation at the hands of the unidentified miscreants, such a situation cannot be cured by indiscriminate assault on every youth wearing a particular type of costume.
>
> It would not do, for a large number of reasons, to let the impression circulate in South America that persons of Spanish-American ancestry were being singled out for mistreatment in Southern California. And the incidents here were capable of being exaggerated to give that impression.[14]

The Chief, the Black Widows and the Tomahawk Kid

The pleas for tolerance from civic authorities and representatives of the church and state had no immediate effect, and the riots became more frequent and more violent. A zoot-suited youth was shot by a special police officer in Azusa, a gang of *pachucos* were arrested for rioting and carrying weapons in the Lincoln Heights area; 25 black zoot-suiters were arrested for wrecking an electric railway train in Watts, and 1000 additional police were drafted into East Los Angeles. The press coverage increasingly focused on the most 'spectacular' incidents and began to identify leaders of zoot-suit style. On the morning of Thursday 10 June 1943, most newspapers carried photographs and reports on three 'notorious' zoot-suit gang leaders. Of the thousands of *pachucos* that allegedly belonged to the hundreds of zoot-suit gangs in Los Angeles, the press singled out the arrest of Lewis D English, a 23-year-old black, charged with felony and carrying a '16-inch razor sharp butcher knife'; Frank H Tellez, a 22-year-old Mexican held on vagrancy charges, and another Mexican, Luis 'The Chief' Verdusco (27 years of age), allegedly the leader of the Los Angeles *pachucos*.[15]

The arrests of English, Tellez and Verdusco seemed to confirm popular perceptions of the zoot-suiters widely expressed for weeks prior to the riots. Firstly, that the zoot-suit gangs were predominantly, but not exclusively, comprised of black and Mexican youths. Secondly, that many of the zoot-suiters were old enough to be in the armed forces but were either avoiding conscription or had been exempted on medical grounds. Finally, in the case of Frank Tellez, who was photographed wearing a pancake hat with a rear feather, that zoot-suit style was an expensive fashion often funded by theft and petty extortion. Tellez allegedly wore a colourful long drape coat that was 'part of a $75 suit' and a pair of pegged trousers 'very full at the knees and narrow at the cuffs' which were allegedly part of another suit. The caption of the

Associated Press photograph indignantly added that 'Tellez holds a medical discharge from the Army'.[16] What newspaper reports tended to suppress was information on the Marines who were arrested for inciting riots, the existence of gangs of white American zoot-suiters, and the opinions of Mexican-American servicemen stationed in California, who were part of the war effort but who refused to take part in vigilante raids on *pachuco* hangouts.

As the zoot-suit riots spread throughout California, to cities in Texas and Arizona, a new dimension began to influence press coverage of the riots in Los Angeles. On a day when 125 zoot-suited youths clashed with Marines in Watts and armed police had to quell riots in Boyle Heights, the Los Angeles press concentrated on a razor attack on a local mother, Betty Morgan. What distinguished this incident from hundreds of comparable attacks was that the assailants were girls. The press related the incident to the arrest of Amelia Venegas, a woman zoot-suiter who was charged with carrying, and threatening to use, a brass knuckleduster. The revelation that girls were active within *pachuco* subculture led to consistent press coverage of the activities of two female gangs: the Slick Chicks and the Black Widows.[17] The latter gang took its name from the members' distinctive dress, black zoot-suit jackets, short black skirts and black fish-net stockings. In retrospect the Black Widows, and their active part in the subcultural violence of the zoot-suit riots, disturb conventional understandings of the concept of *pachuquismo*.

As Joan W Moore implies in *Homeboys*, her definitive study of Los Angeles youth gangs, the concept of *pachuquismo* is too readily and unproblematically equated with the better known concept of *machismo*.[18] Undoubtedly, they share certain ideological traits, not least a swaggering and at times aggressive sense of power and bravado, but the two concepts derive from different sets of social definitions. Whereas *machismo* can be defined in terms of male power and sexuality, *pachuquismo* predominantly derives from ethnic, generational and class-based aspirations, and is less evidently a question of gender. What the zoot-suit riots brought to the surface was the complexity of *pachuco* style. The Black Widows and their aggressive image confounded the *pachuco* stereotype of the lazy male delinquent who avoided conscription for a life of dandyism and petty crime, and reinforced radical readings of *pachuco* subculture. The Black Widows were a reminder that ethnic and generational alienation was a pressing social problem and an indication of the tensions that existed in minority, low-income communities.

Although detailed information on the role of girls within zoot-suit subculture is limited to very brief press reports, the appearance of female *pachucos* coincided with a dramatic rise in the delinquency rates amongst girls aged between 12 and 20 years old. The disintegration of traditional family relationships and the entry of young women into the labour force undoubtedly had an effect on the social roles and responsibilities of female adolescents, but it is difficult to be precise about the relationships between changed patterns of social experience and the rise in delinquency. However, war-time society brought about an increase in unprepared and irregular sexual intercourse, which in turn led to significant increases in the rates of abortion, illegitimate births and venereal diseases. Although statistics are difficult to trace, there are many indications that the war years saw a remarkable increase in the numbers of young women who were taken into social care or referred to penal institutions, as a result of the specific social problems they had to encounter.

Later studies provide evidence that young women and girls were also heavily involved in the traffic and transaction of soft drugs. The *pachuco* subculture within the Los Angeles metropolitan area was directly associated with a widespread growth in the use of marijuana. It has been suggested that female zoot-suiters concealed quantities of drugs on their bodies, since they were less likely to be closely searched by male members of the law enforcement agencies. Unfortunately, the absence of consistent or reliable information on the female gangs makes it particularly difficult to be certain about their status within the riots, or their place within traditions of feminine resistance. The Black Widows and Slick Chicks were spectacular in a subcultural sense, but their black drape jackets, tight skirts, fish-net stockings and heavily emphasised make-up, were ridiculed in the press. The Black Widows clearly existed outside the orthodoxies of war-time society: playing no part in the industrial war effort, and openly challenging conventional notions of feminine beauty and sexuality.

Towards the end of the second week of June, the riots in Los Angeles were dying out. Sporadic incidents broke out in other cities, particularly Detroit, New York and Philadelphia, where two members of Gene Krupa's dance band were beaten up in a station for wearing the band's zoot-suit costumes; but these, like the residual events in Los Angeles, were not taken seriously. The authorities failed to read the inarticulate warning signs proffered in two separate incidents in California: in one a zoot-suiter was arrested for throwing gasoline flares at a theatre; and in the second another was arrested for carrying a silver tomahawk. The zoot-suit riots had become a public and spectacular enactment of social disaffection. The authorities in Detroit chose to dismiss a zoot-suit riot at the city's Cooley High School as an adolescent imitation of the Los Angeles disturbances.[19] Within three weeks Detroit was in the midst of the worst race riot in its history.[20] The United States was still involved in the war abroad when violent events on the home front signalled the beginnings of a new era in racial politics.

Official fears of fifth column fashion

Official reactions to the zoot-suit riots varied enormously. The most urgent problem that concerned California's State Senators was the adverse effect that the events might have on the relationship between the United States and Mexico. This concern stemmed partly from the wish to preserve good international relations, but rather more from the significance of relations with Mexico for the economy of Southern California, as an item in the *Los Angeles Times* made clear. 'In San Francisco Senator Downey declared that the riots may have "extremely grave consequences" in impairing relations between the United States and Mexico, and may endanger the program of importing Mexican labor to aid in harvesting California crops.'[21] These fears were compounded when the Mexican Embassy formally drew the zoot-suit riots to the attention of the State Department. It was the fear of an 'international incident'[22] that could only have an adverse effect on California's economy, rather than any real concern for the social conditions of the Mexican-American community, that motivated Governor Warren of California to order a public investigation into the causes of the riots. In an ambiguous press statement, the Governor hinted that the riots may have been instigated by outside or even foreign agitators:

> As we love our country and the boys we are sending overseas to defend it, we are all duty bound to suppress every discordant activity which is designed to stir up international strife or adversely affect our relationships with our allies in the United Nations.[23]

The zoot-suit riots provoked two related investigations; a fact finding investigative committee headed by Attorney General Robert Kenny and an un-American activities investigation presided over by State Senator Jack B Tenney. The un-American activities investigation was ordered 'to determine whether the present zoot-suit riots were sponsored by Nazi agencies attempting to spread disunity between the United States and Latin-American countries'.[24] Senator Tenney, a member of the un-American Activities committee for Los Angeles County, claimed he had evidence that the zoot-suit riots were 'axis-sponsored' but the evidence was never presented.[25] However, the notion that the riots might have been initiated by outside agitators persisted throughout the month of June, and was fuelled by Japanese propaganda broadcasts accusing the North American government of ignoring the brutality of US marines. The arguments of the un-American activities investigation were given a certain amount of credibility by a Mexican pastor based in Watts, who according to the press had been 'a pretty rough customer himself, serving as a captain in Pancho Villa's revolutionary army.'[26] Reverend Francisco Quintanilla, the pastor of the Mexican Methodist church, was convinced the riots were the result of fifth columnists. 'When boys start attacking servicemen it means the enemy is right at home. It means they are being fed vicious propaganda by enemy agents who wish to stir up all the racial and class hatreds they can put their evil fingers on.'[27]

The attention given to the dubious claims of nazi-instigation tended to obfuscate other more credible opinions. Examination of the social conditions of *pachuco* youths tended to be marginalized in favour of other more 'newsworthy' angles. At no stage in the press coverage were the opinions of community workers or youth leaders sought, and so, ironically, the most progressive opinion to appear in the major newspapers was offered by the Deputy Chief of Police, EW Lester. In press releases and on radio he provided a short history of gang subcultures in the Los Angeles area and then tried, albeit briefly, to place the riots in a social context.

> The Deputy Chief said most of the youths came from overcrowded colorless homes that offered
> no opportunities for leisure-time activities. He said it is wrong to blame law enforcement
> agencies for the present situation, but that society as a whole must be charged with mishandling
> the problems.[28]

On the morning of Friday, 11 June 1943, the *Los Angeles Times* broke with its regular practices and printed an editorial appeal, 'Time For Sanity' on its front page. The main purpose of the editorial was to dispel suggestions that the riots were racially motivated, and to challenge the growing opinion that white servicemen from the Southern States had actively colluded with the police in their vigilante campaign against the zoot-suiters.

> There seems to be no simple or complete explanation for the growth of the grotesque gangs.
> Many reasons have been offered, some apparently valid, some farfetched. But it does appear to
> be definitely established that any attempts at curbing the movement have had nothing whatever
> to do with race persecution, although some elements have loudly raised the cry of this very
> thing.[29]

A month later, the editorial of July's issue of *Crisis* presented a diametrically opposed point of view:

> These riots would not occur – no matter what the instant provocation – if the vast majority of
> the population, including more often than not the law enforcement officers and machinery, did
> not share in varying degrees the belief that Negroes are and must be kept second-class citizens.[30]

But this view got short shrift, particularly from the authorities, whose initial response to the riots was largely retributive. Emphasis was placed on arrest and punishment. The Los Angeles City Council considered a proposal from Councillor Norris Nelson, that 'it be made a jail offense to wear zoot-suits with reat pleats within the city limits of LA',[31] and a discussion ensued for over an hour before it was resolved that the laws pertaining to rioting and disorderly conduct were sufficient to contain the zoot-suit threat. However, the council did encourage the War Production Board (WPB) to reiterate its regulations on the manufacture of suits. The regional office of the WPB based in San Francisco investigated tailors manufacturing in the area of men's fashion and took steps 'to curb illegal production of men's clothing in violation of WPB limitation orders.' Only when Governor Warren's fact finding commission made its public recommendations did the political analysis of the riots go beyond the first principles of punishment and proscription. The recommendations called for a more responsible co-operation from the press; a programme of special training for police officers working in multi-racial communities; additional detention centres; a juvenile forestry camp for youth under the age of 16; an increase in military and shore police; an increase in the youth facilities provided by the church; an increase in neighbourhood recreation facilities and an end to discrimination in the use of public facilities. In addition to these measures, the commission urged that arrests should be made without undue emphasis on members of minority groups and encouraged lawyers to protect the rights of youths arrested for participation in gang activity. The findings were a delicate balance of punishment and palliative; it made no significant mention of the social conditions of

Mexican labourers and no recommendations about the kind of public spending that would be needed to alter the social experiences of *pachuco* youth. The outcome of the zoot-suit riots was an inadequate, highly localized and relatively ineffective body of short term public policies that provided no guidelines for the more serious riots in Detroit and Harlem later in the same summer.

The mystery of the signifying monkey

> The pachuco is the prey of society, but instead of hiding he adorns himself to attract the hunter's attention. Persecution redeems him and breaks his solitude: his salvation depends on him becoming part of the very society he appears to deny.[32]

The zoot-suit was associated with a multiplicity of different traits and conditions. It was simultaneously the garb of the victim and the attacker, the persecutor and the persecuted, the 'sinister clown' and the grotesque dandy. But the central opposition was between the style of the delinquent and that of the disinherited. To wear a zoot-suit was to risk the repressive intolerance of war-time society and to invite the attention of the police, the parent generation and the uniformed members of the armed forces. For many *pachucos* the zoot-suit riots were simply hightimes in Los Angeles when momentarily they had control of the streets, for others it was a realization that they were outcasts in a society that was not of their making. For the black radical writer, Chester Himes, the riots in his neighbourhood were unambiguous: 'Zoot Riots are Race Riots.'[33] For other contemporary commentators the wearing of the zoot-suit could be anything from unconscious dandyism to a conscious 'political' engagement. The zoot-suit riots were *not* 'political' riots in the strictest sense, but for many participants they were an entry into the language of politics, an inarticulate rejection of the 'straight world' and its organization.

It is remarkable how many post-war activists were inspired by the zoot-suit disturbances. Luis Valdez of the radical theatre company, El Teatro Campesino, allegedly learned the 'chicano' from his cousin the zoot-suiter Billy Miranda.[34] The novelists Ralph Ellison and Richard Wright both conveyed a literary and political fascination with the power and potential of the zoot-suit. One of Ellison's editorials for the journal *Negro Quarterly* expressed his own sense of frustration at the enigmatic attraction of zoot-suit style.

> A third major problem, and one that is indispensable to the centralization and direction of power is that of learning the meaning of myths and symbols which abound among the Negro masses. For without this knowledge, leadership, no matter how correct its program, will fail. Much in Negro life remains a mystery; perhaps the zoot-suit conceals profound political meaning; perhaps the symmetrical frenzy of the Lindy-hop conceals clues to great potential powers, if only leaders could solve this riddle.[35]

Although Ellison's remarks are undoubtedly compromised by their own mysterious idealism, he touches on the zoot-suit's major source of interest. It is in everyday rituals that resistance can find natural and unconscious expression. In retrospect, the zoot-suit's history can be seen as a point of intersection, between the related potential of ethnicity and politics on the one hand, and the pleasures of identity and difference on the other. It is the zoot-suit's political and ethnic associations that have made it such a rich reference point for subsequent generations. From the music of Thelonious Monk and Kid Creole to the jazz-poetry of Larry Neal, the zoot-suit has inherited new meanings and new mysteries. In his book *Hoodoo Hollerin' Bebop Ghosts*, Neal uses the image of the zoot-suit as the symbol of Black America's cultural resistance. For Neal, the zoot-suit ceased to be a costume and became a tapestry of meaning, where music, politics and social action merged. The zoot-suit became a symbol for the enigmas of Black culture and the mystery of the signifying monkey:

But there is rhythm here
Its own special substance:

> I hear Billie sing, no Good Man, and dig Prez, wearing the Zoot suit of life, the Porkpie hat
> tilted at the correct angle; through the Harlem smoke of beer and whisky, I understand the
> mystery of the Signifying Monkey. [36]

Notes

The author wishes to acknowledge the support of the British Academy for the research for this article.

1   Ralph Ellison *Invisible Man* New York 1947 p 380
2   *Invisible Man* p 381
3   'Zoot Suit Originated in Georgia' *New York Times* 11 June 1943 p 21
4   For the most extensive sociological study of the zoot-suit riots of 1943 see Ralph H Turner and Samuel
     J Surace 'Zoot Suiters and Mexicans: Symbols in Crowd Behaviour' *American Journal of Sociology* 62 1956
     pp 14–20
5   Octavio Paz *The Labyrinth of Solitude* London 1967 pp 5–6
6   *Labyrinth of Solitude* p 8
7   As note 6
8   See KL Nelson (ed) *The Impact of War on American Life* New York 1971
9   OE Schoeffler and W Gale *Esqure's Encyclopaedia of Twentieth-Century Men's Fashion* New York 1973 p 24
10   As note 6
11   'Zoot-Suiters Again on the Prowl as Navy Holds Back Sailors' *Washington Post* 9 June 1943 p 1
12   Quoted in S Menefee *Assignment USA* New York 1943 p 189
13   Details of the riots are taken from newspaper reports and press releases for the weeks in question, particularly
     from the *Los Angeles Times, New York Times, Washington Post, Washington Star* and *Time Magazine*
14   'Strong Measures Must be Taken Against Rioting' *Los Angeles Times* 9 June 1943 p 4
15   'Zoot-Suit Fighting Spreads On the Coast' *New York Times* 10 June 1943 p 23
16   As note 15
17   'Zoot-Girls Use Knife in Attack' *Los Angeles Times* 11 June 1943 p 1
18   Joan W Moore *Homeboys: Gangs, Drugs and Prison in the Barrios of Los Angeles* Philadelphia 1978
19   'Zoot Suit Warfare Spreads to Pupils of Detroit Area' *Washington Star* 11 June 1943 p 1
20   Although the Detroit Race Riots of 1943 were not zoot-suit riots, nor evidently about 'youth' or 'delin-
     quency', the social context in which they took place was obviously comparable. For a lengthy study of the
     Detroit riots see R Shogun and T Craig *The Detroit Race Riot: a study in violence* Philadelphia and New York
     1964
21   'Zoot Suit War Inquiry Ordered by Governor' *Los Angeles Times* 9 June 1943 p A
22   'Warren Orders Zoot Suit Quiz, Quiet Reigns After Rioting' *Los Angeles Times* 10 June 1943 p 1
23   As note 22
24   'Tenney Feels Riots Caused by Nazi Move for Disunity' *Los Angeles Times* 9 June 1943 p A
25   As note 24
26   'Watts Pastor Blames Riots on Fifth Column' *Los Angeles Times* 11 June 1943 p A
27   As note 26
28   'California Governor Appeals for Quelling of Zoot Suit Riots' *Washington Star* 10 June 1943 p A3
29   'Time for Sanity' *Los Angeles Times* 11 June 1943 p 1
30   'The Riots' *The Crisis* July 1943 p 199
31   'Ban on Freak Suits Studied by Councilmen' *Los Angeles Times* 9 June 1943 p A3
32   *Labyrinth of Solitude* p 9
33   Chester Himes 'Zoot Riots are Race Riots' *The Crisis* July 1943, reprinted in Himes *Black on Black. Baby Sister and
     Selected Writings* London 1975
34   El Teatro Campesino presented the first Chicano play to achieve full commercial Broadway production. The

play, written by Luis Valdez and entitled 'Zoot Suit' was a drama documentary on the Sleepy Lagoon murder and the events leading to the Los Angeles riots. (The Sleepy Lagoon murder of August 1942 resulted in 24 *pachucos* being indicted for conspiracy to murder.)

35   Quoted in Larry Neal 'Ellison's Zoot Suit' in J Hersey (ed) *Ralph Ellison: A Collection of Critical Essays* New Jersey 1974 p 67

36   From Larry Neal's poem 'Malcolm X: an Autobiography' in L Neal *Hoodoo Hollerin' Bebop Ghosts* Washington DC 1974 p 9.

Chapter 14

Mihay Csikszentmihalyi

DESIGN AND ORDER IN EVERYDAY LIFE [1991]

Source: Mihay Csikszentmihalyi (1991) 'Design and Order in Everyday Life', *Design Issues*, 8, 1, pp. 26–34.

Mihay Csikszentmihalyi is a psychologist of happiness and the theorist of the notion of 'flow'. According to Csikszentmihalyi happiness is connected to an engaged absorption in our interactions with the world. Things 'flow' when our physical and mental insertion into the world is at its most total. In this essay Csikszentmihalyi is looking at the question of how and why 'things' matter to us in our everyday life and why, when interviewing people about the things they surround themselves with, so few people chose the artworks they had used to decorate their houses and apartments. The short answer to the question of why some things matter more than others is something of a tautology: things that matter to us, matter for us. In other words they don't matter in and of themselves; they don't matter on some abstract scale of value. Anyone who has suffered adolescent love and received some small token of reciprocated feelings (a fairground prize, for instance) knows how much value can be invested in the materially worthless.

But if Csikszentmihalyi is talking to us about a familiar, and to some degrees 'obvious' world, he is also quite clearly finding conclusions from this that are not so obvious. Csikszentmihalyi takes our precious 'things' out of the scales of value that would suggest that something had worth for its exchange value or for the way it signified our cultural capital (our taste, our elite knowledge of antique furniture, for instance). Of course some things may have value to us because of this, but even then this would be to connect it to an active participation with the object (as an art *lover*, for instance) rather than to the value intrinsic to the object. What often seemed to matter for the people that Csikszentmihalyi and his students interviewed was the fact that the objects had 'born witness' in some way: the old razor of a husband who had died and the cheap plastic Venus de Milo that had been won by a sales manager had been there at the scene of love and success. Indeed the old razor has such an intimate connection to the dead man, and is such a concrete participant in the practice of sexual difference, that it would be hard to think of this as straightforwardly 'symbolic'. Just as a piece of shrapnel that has been removed from a body might 'symbolise' triumph of life over death what matters is not the shrapnel as sign, but the shrapnel as material witness.

In taking 'mattering' out of the realm of aesthetic value Csikszentmihalyi strives to link our prized possession with human activity (loving, succeeding, failing, living). Things, in other words, have beauty, or are wondrous for us, not because they are 'well designed', or because they are universally recognised as beautiful, as transcendent of the messy social actuality of life: they have value precisely because of their direct connection to this actuality. For Csikszentmihalyi it is precisely the sociality of the object that is its value:

> An old china cup, a houseplant, a ring, or a family photograph has symbolic power if it produces a sense of order in the mind. This happens when the owner, in seeing the object, feels that: his or her desires are in harmony; his or her goals might be reached; the past and the future are related in a sensible way; that the people who are close to them are worthy of love and love them in return. Without such feelings, life is not worth living.
>
> (Csikszentmihalyi 1991: 34)

Further reading: Attfield 2000; Bourdieu 1979/1989; Csikszentmihalyi 1997; Halle 1993.

Art and order

SINCE THE TIME of Aristotle, a recurrent theme among thinkers has been the idea that art exists because it helps bring order to human experience. This notion still stubbornly survives, despite the fact that in recent times the arts have not been distinguished by a concern for maintaining harmony.

László Moholy-Nagy claimed (not so many years ago) that the goal of art is to form a "unified manifestation . . . a balance of the social, intellectual, and emotional experience; a synthesis of attitudes and opinions, fears and hopes."[1] Gyorgy Kepes thought that people of the twentieth century live in chaotic environments, are involved in chaotic relationships, and carry chaos at the core of their consciousness. The job of the artist, according to Kepes, is to reduce all this free-floating chaos by imposing order on the environment, and on our thoughts and feelings.[2] Psychologist Abraham Maslow expressed a similar idea when he claimed that art helps reconcile the conflict between ancient biological instincts and the artificial rules we have developed for organizing social life.[3] E. H. Gombrich restates this theme in its most complete form in his latest book on the psychology of design and decoration.[4]

But what does it actually mean to say that art helps bring order to experience? How does this mysterious process take place? As a psychologist I was dissatisfied with the vague and metaphorical accounts of how art affects the consciousness of the viewer. As a result, ten years ago my students and I conducted a study in which we interviewed a representative cross-section of families in the Chicago area, to find out how "normal" people responded to art objects and design qualities in their environment. We conducted the interviews in the respondents' homes, asking them such questions as: What kind of "art" objects did they have in their homes? How often did they notice such objects? What went on in their minds when they did respond?

Soon after we started interviewing, however, we realized that we were having difficulties. The people we talked to, even professional, educated persons, had very little to say about the subject. They were able to repeat a few impersonal clichés, but it was clear that art played a decidedly insignificant role in their lives. Although most homes contained a few paintings or sculpture, usually reproductions, these works were marginal to the owner's sense of psychological or spiritual well-being.

There were, however, in every home, several artifacts to which the owners were strongly attached. These objects often lacked any discernible esthetic value, but they were charged with meanings that conveyed a sense of integrity and purpose to the lives of the owners. So instead of asking questions about artworks, we changed our tactic and asked what objects were special to each person, and why.[5] Eventually we interviewed 315 individuals in 82 families, observing the respondents for a few hours at a time with these objects in their homes.

The meanings of household objects

In one interview a woman showed us with pride a plastic statuette of the Venus de Milo. It was a tacky specimen, with thick seams and blurred features. With some hesitancy the interviewer asked the woman why the statue was so special to her? She answered with great enthusiasm that the statue had been given to her by a Tupperware regional sales manager as a prize for the quantity of merchandise she had sold. Whenever she looked at the Venus replica, she didn't see the cheap goddess, but an image of herself as a capable, successful businessperson.

In other cases, a woman pulled out an old Bible that she cherished as a symbol of family continuity; a man showed us a desk he had built, a piece of furniture which embodied his ideals of simplicity and economy; one boy showed us his stereo with which he could make "weird sounds" when he was depressed; while an old woman showed us the razor which her husband, who had been dead for eighteen years, had shaved with and which she still kept in the medicine cabinet. Finally, a successful lawyer took us to the basement where he unpacked a trombone he used to play in college. He explained that whenever he felt overwhelmed by his many responsibilities, he took refuge in the basement to blow on the old trombone.

In other words, we found that each home contained a symbolic ecology, a network of objects that referred to meanings that gave sense to the lives of those who dwelt there. Sometimes these meanings were conveyed by works of art. To be precise, of the 1,694 objects mentioned in the study, 136 or eight percent referred to the graphic arts (photography excluded), and 108 or six percent referred to sculpture, including the Venus de Milo replica. But to be effective in conveying meanings, the owner had to be personally involved with the artifact. It was not enough that the object had been created by someone else; to be significant, the owner had to enter into an active symbolic relationship with it.

A large majority of the 136 graphic works were homemade; they were often the work of children, relatives, or friends. Their value consisted in reminding the owner of important personal ties, of the qualities of the people who made them. In some instances, a picture was cherished because it reminded the owner of a particular place or an occasion, such as a Mexican landscape bought on a honeymoon. Rarely were the esthetic, formal, syntactic qualities of the object mentioned as a reason for liking it. Of the 537 reasons given for cherishing the 136 graphic works, only sixteen percent had anything to do with *how* the pictures looked. The objects were special because they: conveyed memories (sixteen percent), or referred to family members (seventeen percent), or to friends (thirteen percent). Formal qualities alone almost never made a picture valuable to its owner. In the relatively rare occasions in which a person was sensitive to the formal qualities of a painting or sculpture, the object was special because the owner recognized its esthetic value. By actively appreciating the object, the owner joins in the act of creation, and it is this participation, rather than the artist's creative effort, that makes the artifact important in his or her life.

Table 1 shows the ten types of household objects that were mentioned as special or important by the largest number of respondents.

As the table shows, the most frequently mentioned special object in the home was some kind of furniture. Again, it was not the design quality of the piece that made it special, but what the person did with it, and what the interaction meant to the person. Because different people have different goals and do different things, the kinds of objects cherished and the reasons why they were special varied dramatically by age and sex.

The youngest generation of the families interviewed chose stereos, television sets, furniture, musical instruments, and their own beds, in that order. Their parents most often chose furniture, graphic arts, sculpture, books, and musical instruments; while their grandparents' chose photographs, furniture, books, television sets, and graphic arts. It was clear that the younger generations responded to the activity potential of the objects – to what they could do with them, while the older generations turned to things that evoked contemplation, or preserved the memories of events, experiences, and relationships.

For example, a teenage boy said that the kitchen table and chairs were among the most special objects in his home because they were very comfortable. He could also tilt the chairs and balance on them, hide

Table 14.1 Percentage of respondents who mentioned at least one special object in a given category

Objects	Percentage
Furniture	36
Graphic art	26
Photographs	23
Books	22
Stereo	22
Musical instrument	22
Television sets	21
Sculpture	19
Plants	15
Plates	15

Source: Csikszentmihalyi and Rochberg-Halton, *The Meaning of Things*, 58.

under the table, or build a fortress with the entire set. "(W)ith another table, I couldn't play as good 'cause I love the feel of that table." A typical response from someone from the second generation was that of one woman who singled out a piece of furniture because of the memories it evoked about her friends, husband, or children: "I just associate that chair with sitting in it with my babies." For the older generation of respondents, objects often bridged relationships between several generations: "This chest was bought by my mother and father when they were married, about seventy years ago. . . . My mother painted it different colors, used it in the bedroom. When I got it my husband sanded it down to the natural wood. . . . I wouldn't part with it for anything. And I imagine the kids are going to want it, my daughter-in-law loves antiques."[6]

Responses also differed between genders, indicating that stereotyped sexual roles influence the way we perceive and respond to objects in the environment. Men, like many of the children we interviewed, preferred things that could be interacted with: television sets (ranked 2 in preference), stereos (3), musical instruments (5), sports equipment (7). Women responded more like the older generations of people interviewed and preferred objects of contemplation: photographs (2), graphic art (3), sculpture (4), books (5), plants (6). Women, more often than men, tended to see objects as special because they were mementoes of children or grandparents, or because they had been a gift or an heirloom. Approximately twenty-two percent of the women interviewed mentioned that special objects personified the qualities of another person, as opposed to only seven percent of the men.

These patterns, and many of the others that emerged from the data, suggest that (at least in our culture and in the present historical period) objects do not create order in the viewer's mind by embodying principles of visual order; they do so by helping the viewer struggle for the ordering of his or her own experience. A person finds meaning in objects that are plausible, concrete symbols of the foremost goals, the most salient actions and events in that person's life.

In the past, generally accepted symbols performed this function. Religious icons, patriotic lithographs, folk-art, for example, could represent the identity of the owner and his or her purpose in life. But today, widely shared cultural symbols have lost their power to create order. Each person, each family unit must discover a visual language that will express what they most deeply care for.

Of the eighty-two families interviewed, some were enthusiastic about their home; parents and children loved the space and the atmosphere of the house in which they lived, and felt close to each other. In these homes each person mentioned things that reminded him or her of the other members of the family, or of events in which they had jointly participated. In the families where people were ambivalent about the home in which they lived, where conflict set family members against each other, such common symbols were mentioned less often.

If it is not the object that creates order in the viewer's consciousness, does it actually matter how the object looks? In other words, are there objective visual qualities that add up to "good design?"

In search of universal values: color and form

Artists and writers on art usually assume that some aspect of the visual stimulus will have a direct, immediate effect on the senses of the viewer, and that psychic harmony is created by means of such effects. Certain colors or shapes are universally pleasing, and it is by combining these formal elements that designers reach their audience.

Early psychological investigations supported the belief that some colors "belong" together, and that some forms are better suited than others to please the brain. These extrapolations from the findings of the natural sciences and mathematics were occasionally confirmed by laboratory experiments on visual perception, but turned out to have little explanatory value in real-life contexts.

The reasons for this failure are not difficult to understand. It is true that the light spectrum demonstrates regular relationships between abstract dimensions of color, such as hue, saturation, and brightness. It is also true that when we begin to think of color in this way we can generate categories of complementary or clashing colors. However, it does not follow that people perceive color according to the analytical rules developed by physical scientists.

In his delightful investigations among illiterate Uzbeks in the Soviet Union, Luria found that village women refused to combine colored skeins of wool into meaningful categories because they thought each was uniquely different from the other.[7] Instead of using abstract categories, such as "brown," they said that a particular piece of wool was the color of calf or pig dung; the color of decayed teeth, or the color of cotton in bloom. On the other hand, men from the same village called or named everything "blue," regardless of whether it was yellow or red.

In Western culture, colors are seen in terms of a rational analysis of the physical properties of light. Having learned these properties, one can't help but perceive colors in these terms. The names and relationships that physicists have bestowed on the light spectrum influence one's views. Harmony and conflict exist largely (perhaps entirely?) for those who have learned a specific way of coding colors. For example, for the shepherds of Central Asia, color is rarely an abstract dimension. The quality of an object is inseparable from its concrete manifestation: the redness of the apple is not the same as the redness of fire or the feverish cheek of a child. When one uses categories, they are derived from the practice of everyday life: the Uzbek women, for instance, found in dung and flowers handy organizing principles of color.

The notion of a universal propensity for certain harmonious color combinations based on "natural"; categories or on underlying neurological preferences does not seem tenable. True, it is possible to threaten a viewer's sense of order by distorting the accepted conventions of representation. Most people still do not accept the painting of a yellow sea, a green horse, or an entirely black canvas, but not because these colors are wrong in some absolute sense. The clash is not due to physiological or perceptual incompatibility. The sources of the conflict are entirely different and must be sought in the habits of symbolization that people in a given culture have acquired.

The same argument holds true for perception of spatial relationships. Since the time of Pythagoras and Aristotle, thinkers have been seeking harmony among lines and spaces – golden ratios, mystical quantities. More recently, Gestalt psychologists have asserted that certain figures were more "pregnant" than others, that they possessed stimulus qualities which were more pleasing to the nervous system. Esthetic preference was supposed to be based on the underlying stimulus qualities of a picture, which were reducible to simple geometric patterns.

Like the early color preference work, this approach assumed simple one-to-one relationships between abstract characteristics of the visual field and the way people perceive and interpret stimuli. In fact, it turns out that people do not necessarily perceive the visual configurations that Euclidian geometry made so popular. Basic patterns such as straight lines and right angles are easily isolated and recognized by people living in a "carpentered world," but those used to a more organic environment fail to perceive such "units" as separate from the rest of the perceptual context.[8]

Here, the research of Luria provides interesting insights.[9] In his Uzbek study he asked respondents to sort a number of geometrical designs, which in the Western world would immediately be classified as squares, circles, and triangles. The Uzbek peasants, however, were unable to see such "natural" similarities. For them a completed circle was a ring, whereas an incomplete circle was a moon, and hence two circles could not be sorted in the same pile. A triangle, however, resembled a *tumar* (a piece of traditional jewelry) therefore, it could be grouped with the circle as a ring.

It is not difficult to see that the categories which critics and psychologists have used to analyze esthetics reflect theories of perception, not the actual process by which untutored viewers apprehend visual stimuli. The laws of perception are based on the properties of light, on the axioms of geometry, but might have little to do with the organization of the nervous system, and even less with the phenomenology of perception.

This applies also to some of the more recent psychological theories of esthetics, such as the one proposed by D. E. Berlyne.[10] Like most modern theorists, Berlyne's ideas are based on ancient ideas reinterpreted through current neurological models of the mind. In this case, Aristotle's axiom has been repeated by so many others that the pleasure of perception derives from balancing monotony and confusion.[11] According to Berlyne, a person is attracted to visual stimuli that produce an optimal arousal of the nervous system – stimuli that are neither extremely redundant nor entirely chaotic. Optimal arousal results from a design that has a basic pattern or order, but enough variation to require an active perceptual struggle on the part of the viewer to recognize and maintain the pattern.

Berlyne's model is an attractive one, and it is moderately useful in explaining simple esthetic choices. But as long as it remains a purely neurological theory it quickly runs into the same problems as the others reviewed so far, in that people do not necessarily perceive order and disorder objectively. For example, let us suppose that slide A contains a square pattern composed of twenty-five exact replications of a simple design. Slides B through F are the same, except that ten percent of the elements are randomly changed until slide G has no pattern. According to the optimal arousal theory, people would prefer some of the middle slides in the series; not A or B, which are too regular, nor F or G, which are too chaotic. In effect, this does not happen. One reason is that people do not perceive order and disorder in the designs the way their mathematical structure would seem to require. Some persons rate slide D as the most regular, for example, while others perceive F and G as the most regular, even though objectively it is clear that A is the most regular of all the slides.

There is no question that people can be easily trained to recognize which design is more orderly according to some objective criterion. In the laboratory, one learns readily to agree with whatever the experimenter wants you to see. But the fact remains that in real life people do not carry in their minds yardsticks for measuring abstract concepts of "order" or "disorder." What they see and what they prefer are not determined by objective characteristics of visual stimuli.

The social construction of visual values

This does not mean, however, that how a thing looks has no bearing on how it affects the viewer. Visual qualities obviously have a lot to do with how we react to an object or an environment. But our reactions are not direct "natural" responses to color and form. They are responses to meanings attached to configurations of color and form.

The extent to which a visual stimulus helps create order in consciousness does not depend on inherent objective characteristics of the object to trigger a programmed response from the brain. What happens instead is that some people in a given culture agree that straight lines (or curved lines) are the best way to represent universal order. If they are convincing enough, everybody will feel a greater sense of harmony when they see straight lines.

Visual values are created by social consensus, not by perceptual stimulation. Thus art criticism is essential for creating meaning, especially in periods of transition when the majority of people are confused about how they should be affected by visual stimuli. Art critics believe that they are discovering criteria by which they can reveal natural esthetic values. In reality they are constructing criteria of value which then become attached to visual elements.

When Vitruvius attacked the fanciful pictorial compositions ornamenting the walls of Roman palaces, he based his critique on the realistic premise that "such things neither are, nor can be, nor have been." Vitruvius and his modern followers believed that natural representation is intrinsically valid and any departure from it inevitably brings disorder or chaos. Order or disorder were seen as being inherent in the representation itself. In actuality, it was the theories and arguments of Vitruvius that linked order with realistic design, and disorder with surrealistic decoration. Romans who were unaware of Vitruvius's critique could have looked at the fanciest Pompeian fresco without a stirring of unease; while those who had heard of the new symbolic code might think: "This is degenerate art, full of falsehood that will destroy our civilization."

Without the consensus-building efforts of the art theorist or critic, each person would evaluate objects in terms of his or her private experiences. In each culture, however, public taste develops as visual qualities are eventually linked with values. The visual taste of an epoch is a subset of its world-view, related to the norms and values that regulate the rest of life. Like other values, visual values can be unanimous or contested, elite or popular, strong or vulnerable, depending on the integration of the culture.

The relativity of esthetic values does not mean that there cannot be "good" design. Good design is a visual statement that maximizes the life goals of the people in a given culture (or, more realistically, the goals of a certain subset of people in the culture) that draws on a shared symbolic expression for the ordering of such goals. If the system of symbols is relatively universal, then the design will also be judged good across time and cultures.

Public works of art gain symbolic power because they are admired by an elite. The average person meets the recognized art object with the respect due something awesome and expensive, but usually the experience leaves no permanent trace in consciousness.

On the other hand, an old china cup, a houseplant, a ring, or a family photograph has symbolic power if it produces a sense of order in the mind. This happens when the owner, in seeing the object, feels that: his or her desires are in harmony; his or her goals might be reached; the past and the future are related in a sensible way; that the people who are close to them are worthy of love and love them in return. Without such feelings, life is not worth living. The objects we surround ourselves with are the concrete symbols that convey these messages. The meaning of our private lives is built with these household objects.

The varying styles of visual expression, that which artists and critics debate endlessly, is part of the public image each culture fashions for itself. It provides abstract, general statements about the problems of a particular historical period. Therefore, the high arts help create order in the thoughts and feelings a given society has about itself. But these are often the thoughts and feelings of a small minority struggling to formulate its experience in terms of a public symbolic vocabulary. Most people create their own private set of references, singling out objects that will give order to what they have experienced.

The creation of private meaning is no less miraculous than the accomplishments of Rembrandt or Michelangelo. It is true that a great master is able to condense, in a given moment of historical time, the expressive striving of a great number of people. The artist's work brings together what many people want to say yet can't express. The creation of meaning in everyday life often uses trite symbols – kitsch rather than originality. Yet our lives are held together by the strands of meaning these worn forms convey.

Notes

1   László Moholy-Nagy, *Vision in Motion* (Chicago: Paul Theobald, 1947), 28.

2   Gyorgy Kepes, *Education and Vision* (New York: Braziller, 1965).

3   Abraham Maslow, "Isomorphic Interrelations Between Knower & Known," *Sign, Image, Symbol*, Gyorgy Kepes, ed. (New York: Braziller, 1966), 134–43.

4   E. H. Gombrich, *The Sense of Order: A Study in the Psychology of Decorative Art* (Ithaca, NY: Cornell University Press, 1979).

5   Mihaly Csikszentmihalyi and Eugene Rochberg-Halton, *The Meaning of Things: Domestic Symbols and the Self* (New York: Cambridge University Press, 1981).

6   Csikszentmihalyi and Rochberg-Halton, *The Meaning of Things*, 62.

7   A. R. Luria, *Cognitive Development* (Cambridge, MA: Harvard University Press, 1976).

8   M. Segall, D. Campbell, and M. Herskovits, *The Influence of Culture on Visual Perception* (Indianapolis: Bobbs, Merrils, 1966).

9   Luria, *Cognitive Development*.

10 D. E. Berlyne, *Aesthetics and Psychobiology* (New York: Appleton-Century-Crofts, 1971).

11 Gombrich, *The Sense of Order*, 54.

Chapter 15

Zeynep Çelik

GENDERED SPACES IN COLONIAL ALGIERS [1996]

Source: Zeynep Çelik (1996) 'Gendered Spaces in Colonial Algiers', in *The Sex of Architecture*, ed. Diana Agrest, Patricia Conway and Leslie Kanes Weisman, New York: Harry N. Abrams, pp. 127–40.

Zeynep Çelik is Professor of Architectural History at the New Jersey Institute of Technology. A specialist in Middle Eastern and North African (particularly Maghrebian) urban environments, Çelik investigates architectural and urban design as a social and cultural form. While her research includes analysis of the use of 'orientalist' architecture in US world exhibitions (for instance) her privileged design-site has been the city of Algiers. It would, I think, be hard to find a city where the designed form so vividly and dynamically articulates the social and cultural forces that have struggled over it. Occupied by the French from 1830, Algeria was formally colonised (named as a French Department) in 1871 and throughout the late nineteenth century and the first half of the twentieth Algiers was subjected to constant colonial urban 'reform'. From 1954 through to the final liberation from France in 1962, Algiers was the site of a brutal anti-colonial liberation war. Since 1962 the continual struggle to find a shape for Algerian independence is also registered in the built form of Algiers.

Çelik's commitments to feminism and postcolonialism give her an architectural perspective that is immediately inoculated against any tendency to treat urban architecture as a set of discrete objects. In Çelik's writing buildings are living habitats, animated by family life, by administrative policies, by religious faith, by gender inequality, by cultural conventions and by colonial orchestrations. In short the designed environment of the city is an active participant in the struggle over Algiers. Clearly urban design can be used to physically organise a mass population and it can be used to symbolically communicate a socio-political order. In a more domestic vein, architecture both performs and signifies a form of life, a regimen of daily practices (which, for Çelik, is always a distribution of gendered spaces). In her essay reproduced here Çelik demonstrates the complex manner in which the physical and symbolic were woven together in colonial Algiers, and how the figure of the veiled Arab woman was constantly evoked in this weave.

But while designed space may well be organised to simultaneously perform physically and symbolically, the crucial point for Çelik is that there is no guaranteed stability in the urban form. The Casbah, for instance, might be purposefully designed to distribute female domestic space as semi-public space; but during a period of violent war this gendered distribution also had to accommodate (forcibly) the gendered invasions of French troops as well as the network of anti-colonial guerrilla fighters. For Çelik this isn't simply the re-ordering of space in a practical-strategic manner. Previous symbolic and physical ordering isn't obliterated when buildings are put to new uses; rather new uses are scaffolded on to previous ones, new symbolic tones resonate as the high notes amid the drone of historical polyphony. And this is, I think, what makes architectural design such a rich object for historical writing: it provides the concrete form for a history of struggle.

Further reading: Çelik 1997; Highmore 2005; Leach 1999; Wright 1991.

THE FRENCH COLONIAL discourse, developed by a broad base of intellectuals and military and administrative officers, identified the Algerian woman as the key symbol of the country's cultural identity.[1] In a typical formulation, J. Lorrain, writing at the turn of the century, called the entire country "a wise and dangerous mistress," but one who "exudes a climate of caress and torpor," suggesting that control over her mind and body was essential.[2] This association extended to the city of Algiers as well. Popular literature from the colonial period abounds with gendered descriptions that attribute an excessive sensuality to the city. In the turn-of-the-century travel accounts of Marius Bernard, for example, Algiers is a lascivious woman whose appeal was evident even in her name: "Algiers! Such a musical word, like the murmur of waves against the white sand of the beach; a name as sweet as the rippling of the breeze in the palm trees of the oases! Algiers! So seductive and easy-going, a town to be loved for the deep purity of her sky, the radiant splendor of her turquoise sea, her mysterious smells, the warm breath in which she wraps her visitors like a long caress."[3] Similarly, Lucienne Favre, a woman novelist writing in the 1930s, described the Casbah (the precolonial town of al-Jazaïr) as "the vamp of North Africa," endowed with a "capricious feminine charm" and great "sex appeal."[4] Heralded by Eugène Delacroix's *Les Femmes d'Alger* – a painting from the first years of the French occupation that, symbolically, entered the privacy of an Algerian home – the artistic discourse reiterated this association. Beginning in the 1930s, Le Corbusier's gendering of Algiers extended this tradition to architecture. Provoking associations between the curved lines of his projects to modernize the city and the "plasticity" of the bodies of Algerian women, Le Corbusier articulated his enchantment with these women and consistently represented the Casbah as a veiled head in his reductive drawings. His choice of words further punctuated the association: the Casbah was "beautiful," "charming," and "adorable."[5] He also likened the city to a female body: "Algiers drops out of sight," he noted as he viewed the city from a boat leaving for France, "like a magnificent body, supple-hipped and full-breasted."[6] The cover sketch of his *Poésie sur Alger* depicts a unicorn-headed, winged female body – supple-hipped and full-breasted (the city/poem?) – caressed gently by a hand (the architect's hand) against the skyline of new Algiers, to be designed by Le Corbusier himself.

While metaphors between cities and female figures are quite common, the exaggerated episode of Algiers stands out, calling for closer analysis. In its historic context, the Casbah presents an evocative case study of gendered spaces. It displays distinctly separate realms, sometimes claimed by the women of Algiers as an alternative to men's public spaces. The gendered spaces of Algiers became truly contested terrains during the colonial era, and their appropriation by the French turned into a major obsession. Focusing on the meanings associated with them and tracing the shifts in the forms of their appropriation, I hope to bring a new perspective to the reading of the colonial city, with references to a specific setting.

The urban fabric of the Casbah, dominated by its short, crooked streets, is a hallmark of the "Islamic city" – a problematic construction by European historians which has recently been subjected to serious revision. Janet Abu-Lughod, the most convincing critic of this concept, has argued, nevertheless, that Islam shaped social, political, and legal institutions, and through them, the cities. She points out that gender segregation was the most important issue here and that, by encouraging it, Islam structured the urban space and divided places and functions.[7] To put it schematically, in the "traditional Islamic city," public spaces belonged to men and domestic spaces belonged to women.

Gender-based and separate turfs prevented physical contact between men and women, and enabled visual privacy. The exteriors of the houses of Algiers reflected the semiotic of sexual segregation: the *mushrabiyyas* were literal screens and the asymmetrical arrangement of entrance doors protected the interior of the home from the gaze of passersby. Regardless of the family's income or the size of the building, the houses of the Casbah closed themselves to the street and turned onto a courtyard surrounded by elaborate arcades. The geographic and topographic conditions of Algiers added another element to the houses of the Casbah: rooftop terraces. In contrast to the interiorized courtyards and relatively contrived rooms of the houses, the terraces opened up to neighbors, to the city, to the sea — to the world. The concern for privacy, so dominant in defining the street facades, disintegrated at roof level. It was this alternative realm that the women of Algiers claimed for themselves — as a place of work, socialization, and recreation; indeed, a much more pleasant place than the restricted streets below. The Casbah thus became divided into two realms: on the top, occupying the expanse of the entire city, were the women; at the bottom were the narrow streets belonging to the men.

The French occupation of Algiers (1830–1962) obscured this unusual dual structure by transforming the entire Casbah into an *espace-contre* (counter space) because it contrasted with the European sections of the city in form and in lifestyles, and because its residents continually challenged and opposed the colonizer.[8] Yet, in the typical ambivalence of the colonial condition, thrill and fear of the unknown intertwined with fantasy, and the Casbah opened new vistas for the imagination.[9] The massing and interiority of the Algerian house constituted favorite themes for Orientalist artists who were as much interested in the architectural qualities of the Casbah as in its lifestyles. The rooftop activities of the women, reenacted by painters who turned the top of the Casbah into the sensuous realm of the belly dancer and the ever-reclining odalisque, were depicted with colorful clothes contrasted against the white residential fabric. Interior views of the Algerian house formed another genre, with the stage-set quality of women's *appartements* reinforcing the introverted nature of the domestic realm.[10]

The postcard industry that bloomed around the turn of the century duplicated this dual representation of the houses of the Casbah. Exterior views focused on the narrow, winding streets, while interiors were "assembled" as women's environments (often against the ornate arcades of the courtyard) according to familiar Orientalist formulas.[11] Colonial cinematography further reinforced this image in feature films varying from Jacques Feyder's *Atlantide* (1921) and Raymond Bernard's *Tartarin de Tarascon* (1934) to Julien Duvivier's *Pépé le Moko* (1937).

Le Corbusier, too, focused on the courtyards and roof terraces. He argued that the narrow streets of the Casbah were mere passageways, yet, a "miracle" occurred when the door of an Arab house opened, revealing a lovely courtyard where coolness, tranquility, and well-being reigned.[12] Furthermore, Arabs had "conquered the view of the sea for every house" by means of roof terraces that "add[ed] on to each other like a magic and gigantic staircase descending to the sea."[13]

The colonial obsession with the Algerian home grew in proportion to the actual impenetrability of this realm. To Algerians living under French occupation, home carried a special meaning as the place where they found refuge from colonial interventions perpetually confronted in public life. In the words of social historian Djamila Amrane, home was the "inviolable space" where Algerians recovered their identity.[14] It acted as a buffer against colonialism. Furthermore, it constituted an element in the "language of refusal" created by Algerians, a language that involved their whole way of life, from their behavior patterns to their clothing. As Pierre Bourdieu argued, under the constant gaze of Europeans, Algerian society chose to remain tightly closed upon itself by developing innumerable barriers.[15] The home was a most significant shell for this form of resistance.

In this context, spaces occupied by women (and especially women's historically self-defined public realms) become loaded with additional meanings. The colonizer's persistent efforts to appropriate women by incorporating them into modern buildings reveals much about the scope of the role they played in colonial confrontations. Clearly, behind the struggle to appropriate was the desire to control — an issue that emerged predominantly in the designs of the *grands ensembles*, the large housing complexes built for Algerians by the French administration.

From the 1930s on, the French administration regarded housing the Algerians as a major task directly responding to the increase in the "indigenous" population of Algiers and, consequently, to the overcrowding of the Casbah and the emergence of squatter settlements (the *bidonvilles*). Adhering to colonial policies at large, the goal was two-fold: to improve the living standards of local people and to control their environments – both as social engineering tools to secure the French presence. Attempting to refine French colonial policies in order to ensure the legitimacy and durability of the French empire, Albert Sarrault, the former governor of Indochina and minister of colonies, asserted in 1931 that the "historic reality" of colonialism (characterized until then as "a unilateral and egotistical enterprise of personal interest, accomplished by the strongest over the weakest" and as "an act of force," not of "civilization") should be corrected. France had to develop a "precise colonial doctrine [relying on] the mirror of its conscience." It was, indeed, France's honor to acknowledge the "value of latent races" (*races attardées*) and to see the colonies not simply as markets, but as "creations of humanity." Behind this humanistic facade, however, Sarrault presented the most important issue as the "control of local populations," which would depend on ensuring their loyalty and attachment to the colonizer.[16]

It was in the spirit championed by Sarrault that René Lespès, the foremost scholar of Algiers, explained the political implications of housing in a colonial society. Raising the "material living conditions of our subjects will bring them closer to us," he argued. This was "humanitarian work, useful work, necessary work."[17] The president of the Algiers Chamber of Commerce applauded the decision to provide new housing for Algerians because giving them "a taste of hygiene, well-being . . . and a higher degree of civilization" would create a "sentiment of trust in France."[18] In the years to come, the importance of housing as a pacifying device would continue to be emphasized and a massive construction program would be put in action, escalating in scale from the 1950s to the end of French rule.

Control over the domestic spaces of the colonized society was particularly important in the Algerian context because resistance to the French had persisted ever since the 1830s. Increasingly the French administration believed that Algeria could be captured only from the smallest social unit, the family. Therefore, penetrating the spaces that had remained inaccessible to the colonizer became a priority. The architects commissioned to design the *grands ensembles* experimented with a wide range of designs, varying from high-density, low-rise settlements to clusters of apartment blocks; from "*Arabisance*" to pure International Style.[19] Nevertheless, the projects were united by an overriding theme: the attempt to integrate the essential features of the Algerian house; that is, the courtyard and the roof terrace. However, the interpretations varied and often resulted in questionable spaces, which were transformed over time by the residents in response to their needs. Out of approximately forty such projects built in Algiers, two case studies (both from the 1950s) represent intriguing experimentations in French architects' claims to women's spaces.

The spectacularly monumental 200 Colonnes was designed by Fernand Pouillon, who had established himself in Aix-en-Provence and Marseille and who, by 1953, had become chief architect of the city of Algiers. 200 Colonnes sits in the center of a large housing development (called Climat de France, also designed by Pouillon) on a sloped site to the west of the Casbah. The complex provided four thousand dwelling units in blocks planned linearly around communal courts or as single towers. Sizes varied greatly in the search for compositional balance, and site planning required radical interventions to topography.

No other construction in the vicinity matched the dimensions of 200 Colonnes, a massive, rectangular block 233 meters long and 38 meters wide, with a vast courtyard and surrounded by a three-story-high colonnade consisting of two hundred square-shaped columns. The practice of turning the private courtyards of "traditional" houses into one communal space to be shared by all residents was quite common in new housing projects in Algiers, and it sparked heated debate among architects. Essentially, Pouillon's scheme aggrandized the courtyard to the scale of a public square, thereby taking it away from the residents of the building and making it the "agora" of the entire Climat de France development.

With 200 Colonnes, Pouillon deliberately turned away from the "charming" effects of his former projects to create a "more profound, more austere plastique."[20] His references were not only to the residential courtyards of Algiers but also to a long and eclectic legacy that included the towns of Mzab and the ruins of el-Golea and Timimoum in Algeria; Hellenistic agoras and Roman fora; the Place des Vosges and the Palais Royal in Paris; the Court of the Myrtles and the Court of the Lions in the Alhambra Palace in Granada; and Isfahan's great seventeenth-century square, Maydan-i Shah.[21]

The roof terrace was another major feature of 200 Colonnes. Pouillon claimed that in his "new Casbah" he would give Algerian women their semi-private space to work and socialize. Placing small domed pavilions at regular intervals on the immense terrace (as washhouses that would double as centers of gathering), he envisioned a replication of the liveliness of the Casbah rooftops, with women socializing and children playing; clothes drying on the lines would add a picturesque touch to his architecture. Pouillon also made the stairs climbing up to the roof particularly narrow in order to emphasize the domestic and semi-private nature of the passageway and as a reminder of the stepped streets of the old town. However, only the women living on the upper floors used the roof terrace. The majority, loaded down with baskets full of laundry, refused to climb the narrow stairs and, despite the inadequacy of the provisions, chose to wash their clothes in their apartments. To dry them they projected rods from their windows, thus contributing involuntarily to the atmosphere of "authenticity" so cherished by Pouillon.

Pouillon's oversweeping approach to architecture and urban design and his radical interventionism vis-à-vis site conditions present a contrast to the architecture of Roland Simounet. With his responsive and imaginative buildings, Simounet gained respectability among the leading architects of the 1950s despite his relative youth and blatant disapproval of the aesthetic sensibilities of Pouillon, the city's *architecte en chef*.[22] Simounet was greatly influenced by the work of Le Corbusier, but he was also a careful student of Algerian culture, especially the Algerian vernacular. His architecture was shaped by the lessons he learned from European modernism, by his respect for the site, and by his inquiry into vernacular house forms (including squatter settlements) and the patterns of daily life and ritual.

Djenan el-Hasan is the widely published and discussed housing project that established Simounet's reputation. Located near Climat de France, the 210-dwelling units of Djenan el-Hasan were built to rehouse one thousand former residents of demolished *bidonvilles* in the area. The scheme, described by the architect as "between vertical and horizontal," compactly settled the units on a series of terraces parallel to each other and against the steep slope of the terrain, giving each apartment an uninterrupted view. The lessons that Simounet had learned from the Casbah were interpreted, rationalized, and aestheticized in the stacked, uniform vaulted units. At the same time, the overall image borrowed from the architecture of Le Corbusier, in particular the Roq et Rob project in Roquebrune–Cap Martin (1949), a particularly relevant scheme in the "Mediterranean tradition." Rationalizing the street network of the Casbah, Simounet developed here a complex circulation system of level paths and stepped paths that responded to the site and opened up to small public squares intended for use by men and children.

Simounet's apartments, developed on a strictly modular system derived from Le Corbusier's "Modulor," were either single story or duplex, the latter doubling the former vertically. The first type consisted of a single room and a loggia, which combined the notions of the rooftop terrace and the courtyard. The loggia was intended to function as a living, working, and recreational space – an extension of the house. Unlike the terraces of the houses in the Casbah, this space did not become part of the larger entity but remained linked to the interior space onto which it opened. The placement of a water outlet here was to enable the inclusion of washing facilities, but the further insertion of a toilet (derived from the outhouses in the courtyards of rural domestic architecture) complicated matters by hindering the intended function of this mutant courtyard/roof terrace.

The vaulted roofs could not be reached from the apartment units and, hence, were not designated as useable spaces. Despite their inconvenient form and difficult accessibility, the women of Djenan el-Hasan claimed these rooftops, turning them into work and recreation areas. Thus, the space limitations of the apartments pushed the functions meant to be sheltered in the loggias (such as food preparation) to the rooftops, overruling the inconvenience of jumping from the balcony, down to the roof of the unit in the front row, climbing back up, and working and moving on a curved surface.

As observed in these case studies, French architects were struggling to rationalize, tame, and control indigenous forms. Especially important was the appropriation of women's spaces, into which a great deal of consideration was invested. Nevertheless, this consideration did not achieve access into Algerian women's lives, which remained closed to colonizers – a situation eventually revealed by the active role that women were to play in a war totally unexpected by the French. The pacifying powers of architecture were proven false, as well. With the intensification of the decolonization war, housing project after housing project turned into a resistance center. To cite one example, the residents of Climat de France – deemed by an official report to be politically "less fidgety" than those of the Casbah due to their much better living conditions – took part in public demonstrations. On one memorable day, December 1, 1960, sixty people from 200 Colonnes alone were killed by French forces.[23]

The war of decolonization brought the Casbah to the forefront as a major locus of resistance. In this context, Algerians did not consider the privacy of the family and of women as a sacrosanct issue: resistance fighters were allowed into the houses and onto the rooftops (accessible only through the hearts of houses), facilitating their movements, while other outsiders, including the French forces, were not allowed access. Subsequently, the French forces would blockade the Casbah and occupy not only the streets but also the homes and roof terraces. The surrender of the Casbah is extensively documented by photographs showing armed officers on rooftops – a telling comparison with earlier depictions of the Casbah terraces being "invaded" by women.

Underlying the history of Algiers is a continuing theme that centers on the gendering of urban and architectural spaces. The gendered spaces of Algiers have carried great significance in asserting power, as clearly illustrated by the persistent struggles of appropriation and reappropriation that surfaced so blatantly during the colonial period. Yet, both the pre- and postcolonial eras display a separation of the city into men's and women's realms, albeit in very different contexts.

The current political climate in Algeria calls for extended discussion of women's public and private spaces in contemporary Algiers. While I cannot engage in that discussion here, I would like to acknowledge the seriousness of the situation by dedicating this essay to the memory of Nabila Djanine, an Algerian woman architect and the leader of a feminist group called The Cry of Women. Nabila Djanine was shot and killed in February 1995.

Notes

1   Winifred Woodhull, *Transfigurations of the Maghreb* (Minneapolis and London: University of Minnesota Press, 1993), 19.

2   J. Lorrain, *Heures d'Afrique* (1899), quoted in Yvonne Knibiéler and Régine Goutalier, *La Femme aux temps des colonies* (Paris: Stock, 1985), 40.

3   Marius Bernard, *D'Alger à Tanger* (n.d.), quoted in Judy Mabro, *Veiled Half-Truths: Western Travelers' Perceptions of Middle Eastern Women* (London and New York: I. B. Tauris & Co., 1991), 35.

4   Lucienne Favre, *Tout l'inconnu de la Casbah* (Algiers, 1933), 10. "Sex appeal" is in English in the original.

5   Le Corbusier, *La Ville Radieuse* (Paris: Editions Vincent, Fréal & Cie., 1938), 229.

6   Ibid., 260.

7   Janet L. Abu-Lughod, "The Islamic City – Historic Myth, Islamic Essence, and Contemporary Relevance," *International Journal of Middle East Studies* 19 (May 1987), 162–64.

8   Djaffar Lesbet, *La Casbah d'Alger. Gestion urbaine et vide social* (Algiers: Office des Publications Universitaires, 1985?), 39–48.

9   Colonial relationship is not a symmetrically antagonistic one due to the ambivalence in the positioning of the colonized and the colonizer. Ambivalence is connected to the notion of "hybridity," which depends on the rewriting of the other's original, but transforming it because of misreadings and incongruities and thus making it something different. Expanding the work of Frantz Fanon, cultural critics have focused largely on the ambivalence of the colonized. I would like to extend this notion to the colonizer as well. Among the key texts

on the topic are Homi K. Bhabha, "The Other Question," in Russell Ferguson, Martha Gever, Trihn T. Mihn-ha, Cornel West, eds., *Out There: Marginalization and Contemporary Culture* (Cambridge, Mass.: MIT Press, 1990), 71–87; Homi Bhabha, "Of Mimicry and Man," *October* 28 (October 1984), 125–33; and Benita Parry, "Problems in Current Theories of Colonial Discourse," *Oxford Literary Review* 9 (1987), 27–58.

10   The list of paintings is long. For the depiction of terraces, see, for example, Jules Meunier's *Femmes d'Alger sur les terrasses* (1888) and Marius de Buzon's *Trois Algériennes* (ca. 1927). Among the best-known interior depictions are Delacroix's two versions of *Les Femmes d'Alger* (1832 and 1848) and Auguste Renoir's painting of the same title.

11   For colonial postcards, see Malek Alloula, *The Colonial Harem*, trans. Myrna Godzich and Wlad Godzich (Minneapolis: University of Minnesota Press, 1985).

12   Le Corbusier, *La Ville Radieuse*, 230–31.

13   Le Corbusier, "Le Folklore est l'expression fleurie des traditions," *Voici la France de ce mois* (June 16, 1941), 31.

14   Djamila Amrane, *Les Femmes algériennes dans la guerre* (Paris: Plon, 1991), 45.

15   Pierre Bourdieu, *The Algerians*, trans. Alan C. M. Ross (Boston: Beacon Press, 1961), 157.

16   Albert Sarrault, *Servitudes et grandeur coloniales* (Paris: Sagittaire, 1931), 102–3, 108, 116, 119.

17   René Lespès, "Project d'enquête sur l'habitat des indigènes musulmans dans les centres urbains en Algérie," *Revue africaine* 76 (1935), 431–36.

18   Louis Morard, "L'Algérie – ce qu'elle est – ce qu'elle doit devenir," *Le Monde colonial illustré* 87 (November 1930).

19   I borrow the term *"Arabisance"* from François Béguin, who defines it as "arabization of architectural forms imported from Europe." See François Béguin, *Arabisances* (Paris: Dunod, 1983), 1.

20   Pouillon's specific reference here is to Diar el-Mahçoul, a housing complex he designed on the hills of Algiers prior to Climat de France.

21   Fernand Pouillon, *Mémoires d'un architecte* (Paris: Seuil, 1968), 206–8; *Travaux nord-africains*, March 7, 1957.

22   Simounet elaborated on the major difference between Pouillon and himself: "Je respecte le site; Pouillon agresse le site" (I respect the site; Pouillon attacks the site). Furthermore, he criticized Pouillon for designing "sans penser aux hommes" (without thinking of men). For Simounet, Pouillon's insensitivity to the site, context, and culture stemmed from his coming directly from France – unlike Simounet, who was "from Algeria." Roland Simounet, interview with the author, Paris, April 16, 1993.

23   Albert-Paul Lentin, *L'Algérie entre deux mondes. Le Dernier Quart d'Heure* (Paris: René Julliard, 1963), 147, 151.

Chapter 16

Céline Rosselin

THE INS AND OUTS OF THE HALL:
A PARISIAN EXAMPLE [1999]

Source: Céline Rosselin (1999) 'The Ins and Outs of the Hall: A Parisian Example', in *At Home: An Anthropology of Domestic Space*, ed. Irene Cieraad, Syracuse: Syracuse University Press, pp. 53–9. This is a version of an essay that first appeared as 'Entrée, enter: approche anthropologique d'un espace du logement', *Espaces et Sociétés*, 78, 1, 1994, pp. 83–96.

Céline Rosselin is a French anthropologist specialising in material culture. By taking the Parisian hallway as her example she is also signalling an allegiance to the 'ethnography of the near', a loose movement of anthropological work in France and beyond that has chosen not to focus on 'exotic' cultures but to study 'home' culture from an anthropological perspective. Perhaps the most famous example of the ethnography of the near is the work of Marc Augé who has written about the Paris Metro, about football, strolling, airports and motorways. In many ways, though, Céline Rosselin's work is an ethnography of even closer proximity: it is the ethnography of semi-intimate space – the space before intimacy begins, the space that invites or deflects intimacy.

Rosselin draws on a tradition of anthropology and phenomenological sociology that treats space as a crucial ingredient for social interaction and for symbolic culture. Mary Douglas, Erving Goffman and Victor Turner, for instance, all attend to cultural life as something that is performed in particular and peculiar spaces that are marked in advance by cultural values. For Rosselin the Parisian hallway is designated as a liminal zone: it is neither purely inside nor outside (it is both inside and outside) nor is it strictly 'living' inhabited space. The liminality of the hallway allows occupants to negotiate their social contacts with visitors in a variety of ways: it is no mere figure of speech when salesmen and women talk about getting 'their foot in the door'. The more meagre a hallway the more difficult it is to show a generous welcome when greeting a host and for a guest to show largesse when being greeted. In narrow, one-person-width corridors, doors are opened, greetings are spoken, as the host necessarily backs away to make space for the guest's entrance.

If you are used to entering the homes of others via a hallway then you really notice its absence. In the industrial cities of Britain, the mass-housing that was produced for workers in the late nineteenth century did away with hallways. In the terraced 'two-up, two-down', workers' cottages that pepper the streets of Sheffield, say, or in the 'back-to-backs' of Leeds, the front door opens directly into the front room (the main sitting room). What opportunity is there for nuanced contact here? Either come in or stay out. In winter the abruptness is even more dramatic; opening the door means bringing freezing air into intimate spaces.

Rosselin's text shows how valuable an ethnography of the designed environment can be. Her work doesn't merely describe the symbolic economy of what might be simply mistaken for a domestic non-space; it also allows us to make judgements about the sociality of space. Hers is a plea for architects and designers to value these liminal spaces and to refuse the instrumentality that might treat the hallway as a space simply for distributing rooms. The historical trajectory she briefly maps is from a time when the hallway was the central room of a house to a time of functionalist design. It marks the gradual decline of social space as the dictates of real estate took precedence.

Further reading: Augé 1986/2002, 1992/1995; Marcus 1999; Periton 2004; Turner 1969.

STRONG WILL AND patience are essential requirements for a visitor who wishes to get through the front door of a Parisian apartment building. At the building's main entrance, the visitor must dial a code to open the door. The residents have to reveal this code to their invited guests. Once the door has been opened by the magic buzz, one might end up in a hall leading to different apartments. Often a visitor will also meet with the female caretaker of the building, the concierge. "May I help you?" she asks as a response to an indecisive look. If there is no concierge, as is increasingly the case, the interphone will put visitors directly in touch with their host, who will invite them in. The sound of the elevator, the clicks of approaching footsteps, the knock at the door, or the ring of the bell signals the arrival of the visitor at the apartment door. The apartment door is the last boundary to cross before one gets inside the flat itself. This description clearly shows that the apartment door is one among several thresholds dividing people's private world from the public world.

The concept of the threshold is a prime concept in traditional anthropology. It is connected with the work of famous French and British scholars, such as the seminal work of the Frenchman Arnold Van Gennep ([1909] 1981) and his British followers Mary Douglas (1979) and Victor Turner (1969). According to Van Gennep, society is like a house with rooms and corridors. Thresholds symbolize beginnings of new statuses. The "dangerous" act of crossing the threshold is for that reason controlled by ritual, similar to the popular ritual performed by the bridegroom who carries his bride over the threshold of their first home together.

However, it is not only in matrimonial ritual, but also in daily rituals of reception, that the threshold of the front door, being the borderline between the private and the public space, is of special importance. Van Gennep refers to this threshold as a *zone de marge*, a marginal or liminal zone that separates and links two distinct territories. Consequently, it represents an ambiguous, neutralizing space. The "dangerous" passage through a marginal zone means a temporary ambiguity involving a transition of statuses that is ritually controlled.

The borders of the marginal zone are not necessarily marked, but are acknowledged by a mutual and tacit agreement, by a social and cultural consensus (Hall 1966; Rapoport 1969). For example, in rural areas in France the contrast between the private and the public space is less outspoken than it is in the cities. Farmhouses lack a hallway, and consequently visitors step straight into the main room. On the contrary, in cities, this contrast is more marked: the hall, as a marginal zone, enables a gradual transition.

This study of the entrance hall in modern Parisian apartments describes everyday phenomena of ritualization in contemporary Western urban areas. It illustrates how not only the architecture and the decoration of the hall, but also the ritualized behavior that takes place in it, conspire in a forced neutrality, temporality, and ambiguity akin to marginal zones.

The hall in architecture

In Western domestic architecture the hall was originally designed to be the main room of the house and the showcase of the residents' wealth. However, in nineteenth-century apartment buildings for the middle classes the size of the hall was reduced and its function changed into a distributing one: giving entrance to the various rooms of the apartment. The changed morphology of the hall is not a result simply of the formal separation of rooms, but more so of the nineteenth-century, urban split between the private and the public domains. The hall became the intermediate zone to protect the privacy of the residents (Eleb-Vidal and Debarre-Blanchard 1989, 1995). Nowadays, the hall is defined as an adjacent space to the entrance door; beyond this zone, the visitor is no longer in the hall and is already in another area, either an intermediary zone or a proper room, usually the living room.

However, modern architects, in restricting the hall to its traditional distribution function, omitted the hall in the design of one-room apartments. The need for a hall as a transitional zone is illustrated by the opinions and actions of residents living in modern French one-room apartments. One resident expresses her embarrassment: "This apartment is not very convenient because there is no hall and visitors are getting straight into my room!" Residents create substitute halls; a couple in their fifties created a space behind the door by the placement of a wardrobe with a coat rack fixed on the side. Similarly, a young student has put a carpet of one square meter on the floor, where guests have to leave their shoes. This carpet represents his imaginary hall. Objects that can usually be found in a hall are also located in this area and contribute to the re-creation of the missing room.

Architects often forget that the hall plays a more important role than just distribution. It is not only an entrance room to welcome visitors, but also a protective and neutralizing zone to prevent or ease transition from the public to the private world. Once in the hall, the visitor is not outside the apartment yet not inside it. Located on the edge of the private and public, the inside and the outside, the exterior and the interior, the familiar and the foreign, the hall neutralizes the qualitative aspects of both domains. Not only does the spatial layout of the hall as a marginal zone contribute to its neutrality, but also its decoration and the performed rituals of reception do so.

Protection and identification

Being a threshold, a marginal zone, the hall is the space where controls, such as the identification of visitors, take place. At the same time this space requires extra protection. The objects used to identify a visitor are closely linked to the necessity of preserving and protecting the residents' privacy against outside intrusion. For example, the judas, the peephole that takes its name from the traitor of Christ, allows, like the moucharabieh in Arab countries, a resident to see without being seen and to identify a visitor before opening the door. The apartment door is the first line of defense, sometimes signaled by a barking dog or the sound of an alarm. The protection of the home can take on a more symbolic aspect and even become religious. For example, it is quite common to find in the halls of older people small wooden frames holding mottoes written on copper plates. They often invoke God's protection of the place with sentences such as "God bless you" or "God protect your home." A similar role is played by the mezuza, a small case with parchment inscribed with religious text placed on the door frames of Jewish homes located in Le Marais, a quarter in the center of Paris.

It is not exactly in the hall itself that the action, the first contact between people from the inside and those from the outside, starts. The first role-playing game starts either over the interphone or just behind the door: on the one side, people have to identify the visitor, and on the other side, the visitor has to announce himself or herself. The negotiation stage starts at this point, when everyone takes up a set role: the visitor is often in an inferior situation, whereas the resident may decide whether to open the door to let the visitor in, or to leave him on the threshold of the door. Anthropologists have shown that a foreigner who tries to integrate into a society is in a similar position.

Once the door has been opened by one of the residents, it takes a few seconds to identify or recognize the visitor. This waiting time is justified by the liminal characteristic of the hall as a threshold. The hall is a limit threshold: the last one for the public world and the first one for the private world. As a threshold, it plays a selective role, and consequently not everyone can succeed in crossing it and being let in at any time.

As pointed out by Françoise Paul-Lévy and Marion Segaud (1983, 64), each threshold plays a specific role in the selection process.

During this first stage, the resident will decide whether the visitor can be let in. Strictly speaking, it is the first face-to-face contact. In the face-to-face encounter studies in Western societies, a minimum distance is necessary to avoid a feeling of intrusion. When someone reaches the door, he or she often takes a step backwards, which also enables the resident to see the visitor in full size. The face-to-face meeting can be the beginning of an interactive ritual that can go on in the hall but may also be the first and last contact between people if the visitor is not let in.

If the resident and the visitor have never met, the identification procedure might be even more complex. In our society, this procedure is defined according to one's social status with respect to the visitor (either known or unknown) and with rules of politeness. If the visitor is a complete stranger, this step will be very conventional, that is to say, very close to an ideal pattern. Only when the visitor is a close friend is he or she allowed to violate the conventional rules by deviant behavior, such as hiding or making faces.

The situation of identification and negotiation is necessarily temporary and depends on the preexisting relationship between people or on a first impression when people do not know each other. The question of who opens to whom also depends on social rules and safety precautions: men more often reply to unexpected visits and women to planned ones. When people are coming for dinner at the home of a couple, the man is usually in charge of welcoming the guests, and the woman is in the kitchen finishing the preparation of the meal. However, social rules of welcoming forbid children to open the door to guests.

When the resident invites the visitor in, he or she enters the house in one big step so as to revere the *Dieu du seuil*, the God of the threshold, as was mentioned by Gaston Bachelard (1958). Van Gennep ([1909] 1981) also described such practices, such as newlyweds who are not supposed to step on the threshold when entering their new house. This ritualized passage recalls what has been said before about the marginal, the dangerous, and even the sacred aspect of the hall as a threshold. Finally, it is the host's decision to close the door when the visitor has stepped in. This action also illustrates the repartition of the roles to each protagonist in the next stage.

Neutrality and purification

Once the visitor has been allowed into the house, the hierarchy of the roles tends to disappear. Now the hall is a place for mutual identification where the objects play an important role as much for the visitor as for the host. For the visitor, the objects give information about the number of people living in the apartment and on their activities. For example, the number of shoes, slippers, or cloth pads used to walk on a freshly waxed wooden floor is a good indication of the number of people living there and which residents are at home during the visit. Similarly, the presence of children is indicated by drawings put on the entrance door or the hall walls, by a pram left outside or inside the flat, or by a parent's note saying, "The child is sleeping; please do not ring the bell." Some objects give indications of the residents' outside activities, like sports equipment, travel photos, or posters from museums.

For a host it is very important to have a nicely decorated hall to give the best impression to visitors. Most hall decorations, however, preserve some neutrality: a neutral wallpaper or plain white paint is often preferred to colorful patterns. On the one hand, this neutrality can be interpreted as a way to allow your guests to take possession of the space: they will hang their coats there and leave their umbrellas to dry — objects that represent a foreign intrusion. On the other hand, neutrality prevents the visitor from gaining an all-too-personal impression, and in doing so it protects the privacy of the inhabitants. The resident often justifies the neutrality of the hall by its functionality. In fact, the entrance is neutral not because it is functional but because the residents wish it to be as neutral as possible.

The hall conversation, like the hall decoration, is also quite neutral and limited to greetings and polite phrases: "Hello" or "How are you?" At this stage, a formal language is used because private or personal conversations are not allowed. The formal aspect of this dialogue aims at saving face and putting people at ease, as pointed out by Erving Goffman (1967, 11). Consequently, the answer to "How are you?" is usually "Well. Thank you." During this encounter, people are checking that their respective status has not changed since the last visit.

The hierarchy of roles decreases not only through the exchange of greetings, but also through hugs and handshakes. These gestures epitomize the acceptance of a contract or an agreement on both sides, most clearly illustrated by the shaking of hands to confirm a business deal or by the kiss sealing a wedding ceremony. The representation of this contract between visitor and resident depends on their relationship and on the time elapsed since their last encounter.

Another way of balancing positions is the presentation of a gift by the visitor: flowers, sweets, or a dessert, which are "bartered" against the invitation to come into the apartment. Gift exchange belongs to the logic of social transactions as described by Marcel Mauss ([1923] 1990) and involves a sequence of obligations and expectations: gift giving, accepting, and returning. The host has the obligation not only to accept the visitor's gift, but also to give a present at a return visit.

As a marginal zone, the hall is also a purification area. According to Mary Douglas (1979) marginal zones are intrinsically dangerous because of their ambiguous, inbetween character. Some objects in the hall play a part in the rituals of purification, in order to neutralize the danger of ambiguity and impurity. For example, there are often two floor mats: the first one can be found in front of the entrance door, and the second one in the hall itself. People wipe their shoes on the first and take them off on the second one. Shoes and other objects defiled by the public space, like coats, hats, umbrellas, shopping bags, and leisure equipment, are often left behind in the hall. Looking in the hall's mirror and correcting one's appearance either before leaving the house or before entering the living room are also purifying acts. Neutrality and purity are both conditions for transition.

Transition and temporality

The transitional character of the hall, the area where people are not meant to stay, gives a special temporality to the actions performed there. For example, the look in the hall's mirror has to be cursory, in contrast to the more intimate and elaborate inspection of one's appearance in the mirror of the bathroom or the bedroom. The greeting and welcoming of guests are also dictated by temporality, for they are progressive stages in the transition process. They are followed by the invitation to take off the coat and by preparation of the guest for the final stage: the entrance into the more intimate space of the apartment. In this final stage the conversation also switches from formal language to more personal topics.

Entering and leaving, especially by visitors, can be interpreted as so-called rituals of passage, which involve not only a progressive spatial transition but also a change of status. Generally speaking, the hall allows the transition from one status to another. Office clerks become parents at home, students become sons or daughters of residents, the stranger becomes acquainted. Changes of status can also go the other way around. For example, if a friend leaves you after an argument he can become an enemy who is not welcome anymore. The transitional aspect is reinforced by framed mottoes that decorate the hall: "A friend is always most welcome at our table" or "Friendship is a flower which can be shared when blossoming." These mottoes kindly welcome the guest who changes from stranger into friend.

Thanks to the change of status, the leaving of a visitor is not ruled by such strict behavior. Indeed, the conversation will be more spontaneous, less conventional, and after visitor and guest have spent some time talking in the hall, it might continue on the staircase when showing the visitor out. Getting the coats, saying good-bye, launching new invitations, and putting an end to the conversation are now submitted to a much less rigid ritualization (wine might also contribute to a more relaxed atmosphere!). The initial role playing might even be reversed: the resident decided to let the visitor in, but the visitor might decide when he or she wants to leave. After saying good-bye, the guest might even take the initiative in opening the apartment door, as the residents do not want their visitor to believe that they are pushing him or her out. The transitional space of the hall is also a space of reversals, as Gaston Bachelard (1958) defined the entrance door, through its opening and closing functions, as twice symbolical in linking the two worlds.

Conclusion

The descriptions of objects, actions, and words exchanged between the protagonists of the interaction ritual show that the hall is a threshold, an in-between of two other worlds: interior versus exterior, private versus public, and intimate versus foreign. As a marginal zone, the hall does not belong to either of these categories but plays a spatial role in both of them. Kenneth Ames underlines this when writing about halls in Victorian America: "For it was a space which was neither wholly interior nor exterior but a sheltered testing zone which some passed through easy and others never went beyond" (1984, 221). The hall does have a role of protection: it physically and symbolically protects the private and the domestic world. It also has a level of intimacy while allowing for the process of identification, neutralization, and purification.

The hall is not a univocal space: it is a space where the reversal between interior and exterior, private and public, and opening and closing is always possible. Consequently, this space holds a variety of behaviors and actions that tend subtly to a transition, a change of status. The objects put in the hall refer back to the representations that derive from this zone and to its role.

This study was aimed at putting into question the architectural approach to domestic space in Western societies. However, an anthropology of the domestic space cannot be established solely from the observation of architectural data, the objects as such, or the interviews with the residents. Only the study of the interaction between the domestic space, the occupants, and the objects that surround them will reveal the mechanisms of creating a meaningful universe.

Chapter 17

Svetlana Boym

IMMIGRANT SOUVENIRS [2001]

Source: Svetlana Boym (2001) 'Immigrant Souvenirs', in *The Future of Nostalgia*, New York: Basic Books, pp. 327–36.

Svetlana Boym is a writer, media artist (svetlanaboym.com), and a teacher of Slavic and comparative literature at Harvard University. Before immigrating to the United States she had lived and grown up in St Petersburg (or Leningrad as it had been). Boym's work is about the piquant emotion of nostalgia, about the diasporic experiences of immigrants, about the things we gather round us and hold closest to us and about the feeling of defeated utopia. Hers is a story about modern Russia as it has dispersed in the wake of Stalinism and its descendants. Her story (which is also a collective story) begins, not in 1917 with the October Revolution, but on 14 April 1930 when the poet and champion of the revolution, Vladimir Mayakovsky, killed himself. In his last letter he wrote that 'Love's boat had crashed on the daily grind'; the dream of utopia had been scuppered by the failed attempt to transform daily life.

In a previous book, *Common Places: Mythologies of Everyday Life in Russia*, Boym writes about communal apartment buildings, shared kitchens, about adverts and monuments. She tells the story of the campaign against domestic ornaments, against bric-à-brac: 'Let us stop the production of tasteless bric-à-bracs! With all these dogs, mermaids, little devils and elephants, invisibly approaches *meshchanstvo* [middle-class, philistine taste]. Clean your room! Summon bric-à-brac to a public trial!' (Soviet newspaper from 1928 quoted in Boym 1994: 35). There is of course something deeply ludicrous about the energy exerted on a campaign against sentimental figurines at a time when most sources of protein were considered a luxury. For the campaigners against bric-à-brac the revolution began on the mantelpiece: failure to transform it was the reactionary position of the enemy of revolution.

In the text here (from her equally wonderful *The Future of Nostalgia*) Boym visits the diasporic grandchildren (and great-grandchildren) of the generation accused of hoarding knick-knacks. In their homes in Boston and New York she finds 'personal memory museums': rooms decorated with collections of religious ornaments, *matreshka* dolls, old clocks, clay toys and so on. Boym's task is to try to understand the function of nostalgia as it is played out through the material objects that decorate these immigrant homes. In the lives of the people she talks to (who are all relatively successful Russian immigrants who have lived in the USA for more than ten years), Russia is not a place they want to return to, or a past they want to wallow in; rather it is a feature of their existence in America. For Boym these domestic ornaments are witnesses to the job of 'making a home abroad': 'Diasporic souvenirs do not reconstruct the narrative of one's roots but rather tell the story of exile.' Nostalgia, as it is lived through the domestic objects of this diasporic community, is not a longing for the past, but a memorialising for the present, for a life lived at home abroad.

Further reading: Blunt 2005; Boym 1994; Kiaer 2005; Kiaer and Naiman 2006.

ALEXANDER HERZEN, A celebrated nineteenth-century Russian émigré, said that for those living abroad the clocks stop at the hour of exile. When I interviewed ex-Soviet immigrants in their homes in New York and Boston I was struck by the outdated calendars with pictures of familiar wintry landscapes that frequently decorated their rooms, as well as by the old wall clocks, once elegant but no longer functional, purchased somewhere at a yard sale. Yet most immigrants whose homes I photographed spent ten or twenty years in the United States, and were more or less punctual, efficient and assimilated into American life. Owners of appointment books and computers, they were still fond of their

Figure 17.1   Immigrant souvenirs (photograph © Svetlana Boym).

Figure 17.2   Immigrant souvenirs (photograph © Svetlana Boym).

useless objects, souvenirs, treasures rescued from the trash. The outdated calendars ceased to be efficient organizers of the present and turned into memory grids.

"Russian immigrants just can't stand white walls," says Larisa F., an elementary schoolteacher in Queens who came to the United States twenty years ago. When it comes to making a home abroad, minimalism is not always the answer. "We don't want our room to look like a hospital."[1] White walls, the great achievement of modern design, are associated with official spaces: it seems that overcrowdedness has become a synonym for coziness and intimacy. Each home, even the most modest one, becomes a personal memory museum. Some apartment displays could easily compete with Ilya Kabakov's installations; willingly or not, each immigrant becomes an amateur artist in everyday life. The domestic interiors of ex-Soviet immigrants in the United States and their collections of diasporic souvenirs tempt us at first glance with a heartwrenching symbolism of the abandoned mother country; yet the stories these owners tell about their objects reveal more about making a home abroad than about reconstructing the original loss. They speak about a survival in exile that fits neither the tale of the American dream nor that of the Russian melodrama of insufferable nostalgia.

The people whom I interviewed were roughly of the same age and social group: they were born before or right after World War II and belonged to the lower to middle level of the urban intelligentsia

— engineers, accountants, schoolteachers — that is characteristic of this immigrant group. They could all be considered "well-adjusted immigrants," neither failures nor extraordinary successes. These are not nostalgic tales of Little Odessa, glamorous mafiosi and sobbing long-legged prostitutes. In fact, none of the people I spoke with happened to live in Brighton Beach. These diasporic tales do not represent the majority of immigrants, but rather individuals. After all, this is precisely what these people aspired to become — individuals, not cogs in the collective machine or generic bad guys with thick accents, as they are frequently portrayed on American television and in movies.

"We experienced ten years earlier what all of Russia experienced after *perestroika*," says Rita D., smiling. "We were the first 'post-Communists.' Now [in 1995] it seems that the whole of the former Soviet Union went into immigration, without leaving the country." The immigrants' version of post-Communist nostalgia is remarkably ambivalent. The Soviet refugees (most of them Jewish) who came to the United States from 1972 to 1987 (*glukhaia emigratsiia*) were uniquely unsentimental; theirs was an old-fashioned exile without return. All of them emigrated under the clause of family reunification that the Soviet Union had recognized after signing the Helsinki Agreement, even though many didn't really have any family abroad. The reasons for their emigration ranged from political convictions and experiences of anti-Semitism to a sense of claustrophobia and existential allergy to Soviet life during the Brezhnev stagnation, from the search for economic and social opportunities to some vaguely utopian dream of freedom, a desire for an unpredictable future.

The reasons for leaving home can be as elusive as the objects of nostalgia. The two are somewhat interconnected. When I lived in a refugee camp in Italy in 1981 and worked as an interpreter there, I remember how difficult it was for ex-Soviet citizens to explain in one sentence their reasons for emigration that would qualify them as political refugees. They either wanted to talk for hours, dwelling on all the nuances of their humiliation, or didn't wish to say anything about it. They knew what they were supposed to write but somehow couldn't quite relate to what they imagined to be a new definition of themselves. While in most cases there were actual experiences of anti-Semitism (whether blatant or subtle), it appeared difficult for immigrants who resisted Soviet-style idealogization of their lives in the old country to cast their life stories in political terms; some felt that they simply moved from one official label to another, since nobody cared to know the actual reasons of their departure.

In the descriptions of their lives leading up to the decision to leave, these immigrants tell of a number of formative experiences in the Soviet Union that pushed them to rethink their lives; it could have been an experience of injustice, a shocking revelation in their family's history that might have included deaths in the camps, an all-night reading of a samizdat edition of Solzhenitsyn or Nabokov, a departure of a friend or lover. For me there were two such experiences. One was a school trial in the seventh grade of a fellow student whose parents decided to emigrate. I remember how in the presence of the school principal our teacher wasn't satisfied with our passive acquiescence and demanded that all the pupils of Jewish nationality in the class make statements denouncing Zionist propaganda. (I kept silent and chewed my nails, but a few volunteered deeply felt denunciations.)

The other experience was a film, *The Passenger*, directed by Michelangelo Antonioni, that I saw at the age of seventeen. The film is not about political exile, but about alienation and emigration into different identities. In the film, the hero, played by Jack Nicholson, forges the identity papers of his dead friend and resumes the other man's life. His casual beloved, played by Maria Schneider, is possessed by a similar kind of unspeakable angst and embodies transience and freedom itself, moving from man to man, from architectural ruin to ruin. Most important, she crosses many forbidden Western borders with no visa problems whatsoever, her ephemeral skirt and beautiful uncombed hair blowing in the Mediterranean sea breeze. (I remember that my mother was remarkably unsympathetic to the all-consuming angst of the "Western" heroes, "who didn't have to stand in lines and suffer through the Soviet daily grind. . . . I wish I had her problems," she said.) As for me, I was deeply envious of this luxury of alienation, of the sheer freedom of movement that I observed in the movie. This film still makes me nostalgic for my dreams of leaving home. Later came the reading of samizdat and a keener political awareness. Yet even at the time I was emigrating I was not entirely sure where I was going: to the United States or to the decadent (rather than Wild) "West" of my favorite films. (Luckily I didn't mention Antonioni in my application for refugee status.)

When Soviet citizens began to read samizdat and contemplated the decision to leave the country, they automatically became internal exiles who entered a parallel existence. This included endless visits to the Immigration Office and occasionally, the KGB, expulsion from the workplace, sometimes followed by a "show trial" public meeting, at which friends and coworkers had to express their indignation about the "betrayal" in their midst, and the months of Kafkaesque bureaucratic adventures of collecting all the necessary papers from every possible committee. This existence in internal exile or in virtual limbo, without employment or a network of friends, could last from a few months to ten years. After that, the lucky refuseniks received their visas and had to leave the country within two weeks. By that time they knew better what they were leaving but not where they were going.

Border crossing was another transformative experience. After a humiliating, day-long customs check (including an occasional gynecological examination for hidden diamonds), the Soviet border authorities informed the "departees" that they would never be able to come back to their native country. Through the oblique glass of the airport security offices they caught a last glimpse of their close relatives and a few brave friends who had dared to come for the final farewell. There was no special place for farewells. My father remembers catching a parting glimpse of me as I was crossing the line for "departees only"; then he saw a baby carriage pushed away by a disgruntled immigrant who had been standing behind me in the long line; for some reason the baby carriage didn't make it through customs and there were no relatives or friends left to pick it up and save it. So it rolled pointlessly down the stairs of the emptied departure hall. "Just like in Eisenstein's film," my father said.

Relatives and friends who stayed behind in the Soviet Union recall that for them, ritual farewell parties (*provody*) for the departing immigrants resembled wakes. Emigration seemed like death, a departure to somewhere beyond the horizon of the knowable. If one were to read Soviet newspapers and periodicals of the 1970s and 1980s, one would hardly guess that a hundred thousand people were leaving the country at that time. There was a general fear of speaking about it explicitly and of preserving relationships with people who planned to emigrate. Emigration was spoken about mostly through double entendre and Aesopian language. When people spoke about "departure" (*ot'ezd*) without mentioning the place of destination, it was absolutely clear what they meant. It was the departure to the place from which there could be no return.[2] The silence in the official culture was overcompensated in the unofficial humor; it seems that all the heroes of the 1970s jokes, from Rabinovich to Brigitte Bardot, Brezhnev and Vasili Ivanych Chapaev, had nothing better to talk about but the Jewish emigration. One joke nearly predicted the end of the Soviet Union. Comrade Rabinovich comes to the immigration office OVIR.

"Why do you want to leave, Comrade Rabinovich?" asks the officer politely. "You have a nice job here, a family."

"Two reasons," says Rabinovich. "One is that my communal apartment neighbor every day promises to beat me up when Soviet power comes to an end."

"But Comrade Rabinovich, you know that this will never happen, Soviet power will never come to an end," says the officer.

"That's reason number two," says Rabinovich.

Twenty years after leaving the Soviet Union, several former immigrants, now naturalized Americans, assured me that they never wanted to return, even as tourists. The departing immigrants turned the threat of nonreturn into their destiny and their choice. The experience of that first border crossing that put a taboo on a backward glance was a watershed for them, a trauma that they refused to sentimentalize or even dwell on. The humiliation of that border crossing that appeared so severely one-way at the time is what lies between those "veteran" émigrés of the 1970s and the new immigrants who came in the 1990s – who have the luxury (or curse) of being able to criss-cross the border and can delay the decision about their place of dwelling. The veterans are often defensive and stubborn in their attitudes; they have internalized the nonreturn that from a physical and political impossibility became a psychological need. Some immigrants recreate the border over and over, in order to make it their own. This experience of departure in the 1970s is at the core of the misunderstanding between the immigrants and their former friends left behind. Each sees in the other an alternative potentiality of his or her own life, a route not taken that is irreconcilable with life at the present. Paradoxically, the immigrants remember their Soviet homes much better than those who remained in the Soviet Union and one day woke up in a different country.

Twenty years ago, virtually stripped of identity, citizenship and most of their personal belongings, the émigrés arrived in the United States as political refugees with their "two suitcases per person" and an allowance of ninety dollars. With the advent of *perestroika*, the "third wave" of Soviet emigration from the 1970s to the 1980s came to an end, both in legal and in practical terms. Yet the peculiar hybrid identity of these émigrés makes the object of their nostalgia and ways of identification at once illuminating and particularly elusive.

Russian-American is hardly an accepted hyphenated identity; indeed, the Soviet immigrants of the third wave, most of them "Jewish," according to the fifth line of the Soviet passport, experienced a veritable identity crisis upon arrival in the United States. They were surprised to discover that in the United States they had finally become "Russian." Yet they also realized that the other Russian émigrés – survivors of the first and second wave – did not view them as Russians at all, but as "unpatriotic rootless cosmopolitans." While many of the immigrants received generous help from American Jewish organizations, their sponsors soon discovered that the newly arrived Soviet Jews knew very little about Jewishness, and they did not conform to their sponsors' own nostalgic image of a communal *shtetl* – from which their parents and grandparents had escaped. Most of the Soviet Jews were urban, educated and secular. As for the "American" part of their identity, they obviously did not manage to fit there either, and often irritated their American friends and sponsors by overplaying their allegiance to the United States a bit too ostentatiously. The immigrants placed toy American flags in their glass cabinets, but at the same time they knew very little about actual American customs, legal systems and ways of behavior. They remain nostalgic for the American dream they dreamed up in Russia and sometimes can't quite forgive America for not living up to it.

Larisa says that when people first visit her apartment, they have two reactions – either a compliment: "It's so cozy here, it looks just like a Moscow apartment!" or a reproach: "You've been here for fifteen years and you still live like an immigrant!" These places look like Moscow apartments but they are hardly a direct recreation of them. Bookshelves with the complete works of Dostoevsky, Tolstoy, Goethe and Thomas Mann in Russian are of crucial importance here, being at once a status symbol of the intelligentsia and a meeting place of personal souvenirs: matreshka dolls, wooden spoons and khokhloma bowls, clay toys, shells from exotic seaside resorts, ceramic vases purchased in Estonia in the 1970s, riches found at New York yard sales and treasures from the trash.[3] The kitchen features many different religious artifacts: a cheap menorah box on one shelf and Orthodox Easter eggs on another shelf. They compose a strange still life: Russian toys on the shelf, a Passover plate on the wall, and a box of matzohs, tea cups and toast with jam on the table. Religious objects are also treated as artifacts and souvenirs. Larisa was "Jewish" according to her former Soviet passport but never practiced any particular religion in the Soviet Union. Now she says that she celebrates all holidays, the more the merrier. She remarks, however, that she would have never hung the Passover plate on the wall in Moscow. It would have been seen as a statement, rather than a decoration.

The souvenirs on the immigrants' bookshelves are quite international. We find here treasures from American yard sales, Chinese ducks, Thai lions and other exotic animals, including the tiny dinosaurs found in Red Rose tea boxes that Russian immigrants try to rescue from consumerist oblivion and display in their little bookshelf museums. They are favorite pets in the exilic memory games. What they represent, perhaps, is the refusal to accept the culture of disposable objects. There was a time when immigrants themselves got rid of their own trash and lost much of their personal belongings; now, they feel it is their turn to preserve and collect, no matter what.

American yard sales and trash play an important role in the émigré topography of America. Émigré memoirist Diana Vin'kovetskaya writes: "Have you heard about New York trash? What can you find there? Oh, you wouldn't find things like that in a museum! One little coffee table still constitutes a treasure of my house . . . it's the empire style of Louis XIV!"⁴ She reports the story of an immigrant who did painting restoration at the Tretiakov Gallery in Moscow, but once in New York, became a specialist on trash. He cleaned and restored many objects that he rescued from the streets – so many that when the social workers from the Tolstoy Fund came to visit, they immediately cut his financial aid. The recovery of objects from the trash seems to be a practical need but also a peculiar ritual rescue of the past, even if the past is not actually their own.

"I would have never had all these tchotchkes on my shelves in Moscow," says Larisa. In fact, several women told me that they never displayed *matreshki* and *khokhloma* in Russia, because they smacked of kitsch, especially in the 1960s, when the intelligentsia wars against philistinism and materialism (*meshchanstvo*) were in full swing. Larisa recalls that in the 1960s she was an avid reader of the journal *Amerika*, a propagandistic magazine printed on high-quality, pleasantly smelling paper. Larisa particularly admired the photographs of the apartment interiors of radical students from Berkeley. While many were from a comfortable middle-class background, they came to despise bourgeois commodities and chose to sleep on the mattresses covered with red cloth instead of regular beds. In emulation, Larisa decided to throw out the Soviet furniture purchased by her parents before the war and got herself a mattress and red cloth to create a progressive "Western" interior. Obviously, the mattress with the red cloth signified very different things in a culture of overabundance of commodities and in a culture of material scarcity (and an excess of red cloth used for banners and public decorations). In the 1960s Larisa was proud of her American radicalism. Some ten years later, when she actually arrived in the United States and at the begining had to live on a mattress, like many other immigrants, her perspective changed. From the perspective of absence, uprooting and exile, she longed to recreate that cozy, overcrowded interior that she had been so eager to destroy in the good old 1960s Moscow.

The Soviet Russian folk art on the immigrant bookshelves is not so much a nostalgic souvenir of Russia as a personal memory of friends left behind. The owner of the mass-reproduced souvenir becomes its new author, who tells an alternative narrative of its adventures. In Brighton, Massachusetts, in the room of another ex-Soviet immigrant, Lisa, I saw Russian nesting dolls, *matreshski*. Lisa immediately warned me that she hadn't brought them from Russia. They were a gift from a friend who had visited her. Short of money, Lisa's friend took the *matreshki* from the kindergarden where she worked; the dolls became a memento of a first border crossing between the USSR and the USA and the rediscovery of friendship.

This reminds me of a story of domestic embarrassment recounted by the Russian émigré writer Nina Berberova. Some time in the early 1930s, the writer Ivan Bunin paid a visit to Berberova and the poet Vladislav Khodasevich in their little flat in the working-class outskirts of Paris populated by immigrants. The apartment hardly had any furniture, and no particular dinner was served that night. Yet Bunin was irritated by Berberova's precarious domesticity. "'How do you like that! They have *an* embroidered cock on the teapot cover!' exclaimed Bunin once as he entered our dining room. 'Who could have imagined it! Poets, as we all know, live in a ditch, and now it turns out they have a cock on a tea cozy!'"⁵ The embroidered cock symbolized a certain intimacy with everyday objects that appeared to be in profound bad taste for Russian intellectuals in exile. For Bunin, it was an example of domestic kitsch that compromised the purity of Russian nostalgia. The embroidered cock seemed to be a cover-up of exilic pain; it betrayed a desire to inhabit exile, to build a home away from home. Berberova did not give up her decorated teapot. She confesses to love that other deliberately chosen and freely inhabited domesticity that "is neither a 'nest' nor biological obligation" but something "warm, pleasant and becoming to people." That embroidered cock turned out to be a dangerous exilic bird. Hardly an emblem of exotic Russianness, this specific embroidery was a handmade gift sent to Berberova from the Soviet Union by a woman friend who ended up in Siberian exile "for having contacts abroad." It turned into a souvenir of transient exilic intimacy.

Each apartment collection presents at once a fragmentary biography of the inhabitant and a display of collective memory. The collections set the stage for intimate experiences. Their ways of making a home away from home reminded me of old-fashioned Soviet interiors, where each object had an aura of uniqueness – whether it was grandmother's miraculously preserved antique statuette or a seashell found on the beach of a memorable Black Sea resort in the summer of 1968. For the generation of people born before or right after World War II, material possessions were often scarce and hard to obtain; in earlier days they could be expropriated, but they were never to be disposed of voluntarily. For an immigrant, the proverb "my home is my castle" doesn't quite work; rather, it should be "my home is my museum." On her kitchen shelf Larisa F. collected colorful badges from the Metropolitan Museum of Art that she saved from her frequent trips to the museum. Larisa brings her pupils regularly to the Met "because it helps to open up their horizons, and shows them that there is a whole world out there, beyond Queens." The colorful museum badges, the cheapest found objects that the museum offers, enliven the kitchen and are also reminiscent of the Soviet practice of decorating rooms in communal apartments with posters from the Hermitage. The aesthetic and everyday practices of inhabiting and preserving memories are closely linked.

The American culture of the disposable object was most unfamiliar to the immigrants from the East; it embodied their desires and fears: consumerist luxury on the one hand, and a sense of transience, a perpetual whirlpool of change that reminded them acutely of their exile on the other. So in their collections of souvenirs many immigrants preserve a certain "crypto-Soviet" attitude toward the object, even when the object itself and the context is different. Several people confessed with good humor that during their first year in the United States they never threw away paper cups and paper plates. They secretly saved them. Now, as they become "Americanized," they no longer do that. This is hardly unique to immigrants from the former Soviet Union. One could observe similar American immigrant rituals in Chinese, Vietnamese and Puerto Rican communities, for example. Their idea of privacy and intimacy retains the memory of their abandoned homeland, where privacy was forever endangered. Soviet domestic rituals originated in response and in opposition to the culture of fear, where the home search was a fact of daily

Figure 17.3   Immigrant souvenirs (photograph © Svetlana Boym).

Figure 17.4   Immigrant souvenirs (photograph © Svetlana Boym).

life and any pursuit of domesticity precarious and vulnerable. Moreover, for this group of middle and low strata of urban intelligentsia, the "private" or "intimate" was often understood as a space of escape that was not limited to an individual or a nuclear family, but more often to a group of close friends. The social frameworks of memory (formed, in this case, in the Soviet urban context) have merged with individual practices of inhabiting a home; they now provide a minimal continuity of self during the immigrant's period of displacement and resettlement. Immigrant households share traces and frameworks of Soviet urban memory of the 1970s, yet their story, the way of making sense of their environment, is radically different.

"I don't think of returning back to Russia, only of visiting," says Larisa, "this is my home now." There are many nostalgic objects on immigrant bookshelves, and still the narrative as a whole is not that of nostalgia. Diasporic souvenirs do not reconstruct the narrative of one's roots but rather tell the story of exile. They are not symbols but transitional objects that reflect multiple belonging. The former country of origin turns into an exotic place represented through its arts and crafts usually admired by foreign tourists. Newly collected memories of exile and acculturation shift the old cultural frameworks; even Russian or Soviet souvenirs can no longer be interpreted within their "native" context. Now they are a cipher for exile itself and for a newfound exilic domesticity.[6] If Kabakov's installations reveal the desire to inhabit in the most trivial everyday manner the sacred spaces of the artistic establishment, immigrants' homes betray an obsession with making everyday existence beautiful and memorable. Their rooms filled with diasporic souvenirs are not altars to their unhappiness, but rather places for communication and conversation. They do not manage to live in the eternal present of the American myth, but neither can they afford to dwell in the past. Diasporic intimacy is possible only when one masters a certain imperfect aesthetics of survival and learns to inhabit exile. The immigrants cherish their oases of intimacy, away from the homeland and not quite in the promised land. They have accents in both languages – foreign and native.

Notes

1   Interviews were conducted from May to August 1995, mostly in the New York and Boston area. Ilya Kabakov and Joseph Brodsky commented on the depressive homogeneity of Soviet interiors. They speak not so much about white walls as about that familiar blue line of the Soviet horizon. Even when the work is installed by assistants, Kabakov takes upon himself the task of executing this blue line.

2   In the circles of urban intelligentsia, there were also plenty of jokes well understood without being spelled out: Brezhnev encounters Brigitte Bardot. Brigitte asks Brezhnev, "Leonid Ilich, what would happen if we open the borders of the Soviet Union, so people could come and go as they please?" "Oh baby, you want to be alone with me?" or: Q. How many Jews are in Russia? A. 2 million. Q. How many would leave if we open the borders? A. I don't know, 10 or 15 million.

3   The books, however were not purchased in Russia (immigrants were unable to bring them due to customs restrictions). Moreover, Larisa never actually possessed those complete works but only dreamed of having them and continuously borrowed volumes from her more fortunate friends. The precious volumes of Russian and foreign classics in Russian that decorate her apartment were purchased in the States.

4   Diana Vin'kovetskaya, *Amerika, Rossiia i ia* (New York: Hermitage, 1993), 45.

5   Nina Berberova, *The Italics are Mine*, Philippe Radley, trans. (New York: Vintage Books, 1993), 338. For further discussion of diaspora, cosmopolitanism, homeland and immigrant poetics see the journal *Diaspora*; and Homi Bhabha, *Nation and Narration* (London and New York: Routledge, 1990).

6   The majority of the people I interviewed – whom the social worker referred to as "adjusted immigrants" – said that exile was like a second life, or even like a second childhood, where they could play again with the foreign reality.

PART FOUR

SENSE AND SENSIBILITIES

INTRODUCTION TO PART FOUR

IN HIS *ECONOMIC* and *Philosophical Manuscripts of 1844* (the 'Paris Manuscripts', which were not finished and were posthumously published in 1932), Karl Marx is concerned with human life at its most 'creaturely'. It is here that he writes about alienation, species-being and the sensorial life of humans. This is Marx the humanist, concerned with the bio-politics of modernisation. In this manuscript he writes that: 'The *forming* of the five senses is a labour of the entire history of the world down to the present' (Marx 1844/1977: 96). It is not difficult to imagine that the smells and tastes of the present are fashioned in a different way to how they were a thousand years ago. In this sense it is not hard to see a 'Big Mac' as the product of historical processes. But it is a larger claim to say that 'how we taste' may have altered too. This is precisely what Marx is arguing: not simply that our sensual world has changed but that the way we perceive it, and the way that we interact with it, has altered too.

For Marx this constant re-orchestration of the senses and the sensibilities is patterned according to large-scale designs: the design of social relations (the division of creative and manual labour, for instance) and the designs of daily life (including, of course, daily work). And the only way to understand this orchestration of the senses and sensibilities is to see it as an 'objective' result of human history, of material human production:

> Each of his [*sic*] *human* relations to the world – seeing, hearing, smelling, tasting, feeling, thinking, observing, experiencing, wanting, acting, loving – in short, all the organs of his individual being, like those organs which are directly social in their form, are in their *objective* orientation, or in their *orientation to the object*, the appropriation of the object, the appropriation of human reality.
>
> (Marx 1844/1977: 94)

This is fairly abstract, but as soon as we see it in relation to a concrete example, we begin to see what Marx means and how this implicates design within biological-social processes.

Take, for example, your sense of smell. Any intercultural study will tell you that what is 'smelly' in one country isn't necessarily considered smelly in another. Similarly, the body odours that are considered permissible vary from culture to culture and throughout history. These changes are reliant on a number of factors, not least of which is the techno-social 'design' of cleanliness. This would include running water, soap production, washing technologies, antiperspirants, drainage systems, washing powders, as well as a whole barrage of rules that apply to an ethos of washing, an ethos that allows groups to practise forms of social distinction. When someone offends your sense of smell, when you turn your head away in disgust, you can, then, see the results of a host of social and technical designs being acted out through your bio-social 'spontaneous' reaction. Thus your 'objective orientation' is an orientation to the world as a set of objects that have been produced through social design practices.

Clearly this implicates design within social history in a way that allows us to see history as a sustained 'artificial' training of the body, the senses and the affects. For historical work this means that design becomes a central component in the production of modern sensibilities. For contemporary work it requires us to inquire into the sensual orchestration of the design environment. For future speculation it would suggest that the sensorial is an area of invention as much as of intervention.

Chapter 18

Wolfgang Schivelbusch

SHOP WINDOWS [1983]

Source: Wolfgang Schivelbusch (1988) 'Shop Windows', in *Disenchanted Night: The Industrialization of Light in the Nineteenth Century*, translated by Angela Davies, Berkeley, Los Angeles and London: University of California Press, pp. 143–54. First published in German in 1983.

Wolfgang Schivelbusch is a cultural historian who, in the 1970s, through the 1980s and beyond, seemed almost single-handedly to revivify that discipline. In a trilogy of books (one on railway travel, another on artificial light, and the final one on spices and stimulants) Wolfgang Schivelbusch mapped a beguiling history of the industrialisation of the senses. In them he provides the evidence that shows how, during the modern period (predominantly the eighteenth century through to the twentieth), a plethora of devices and cultural conventions were designed that retrained the senses on the basis of a new industrial order. His historical narratives are compelling in the complex weave that they produce, blending together design production (the stories of ordinary and extravagant invention) with the effects and affects of design consumption (the railway, for instance, produced a number of neurasthenic complaints experienced by nineteenth-century travellers).

One way of describing Schivelbusch's approach might be to see it as taking something that has been thought of as both marginal and ubiquitous (food and drink, lighting, for instance) and placing it at the centre of the historical stage. There is a logic here: if something is socially ubiquitous, then it must necessarily be a part of historical processes. And certainly one result of reading Schivelbusch is the odd sensation that you have of not quite believing that people haven't seen the importance of everyday design before. It is also, I think, no coincidence that the cultural material that has interested him has tended towards 'immaterial culture' (sensations, sensorial forms, movements). Thus another way of describing Schivelbusch's history would be as a materialist account of the immaterial.

In this extract from his book *Disenchanted Night* Schivelbusch shows how light and glass become essential ingredients for the constant staging of commodities (in shop windows, obviously, but also in exhibitions, in domestic interiors, in cafés and restaurants). Thus for Schivelbusch artificial light is employed on behalf of the designed commodity. This is one side of his dialectic of light, whereby commercial lighting has a symbiotic relationship with what he calls police lighting:

> What we think of as night life includes this nocturnal round of business, pleasure and illumination. It derives its own, special atmosphere from the light that falls onto the pavements and streets from shops (especially those selling luxury goods), cafés and

restaurants, light that is intended to attract passers-by and potential customers. It is advertising light – commercialised festive illumination – in contrast to street light, the lighting of a police order. Commercial light is to police light what bourgeois society is to the state. As the state, in its appropriately named 'night-watchman' function, guarantees the security that bourgeois society needs to pursue its business interests, so public lighting creates the framework of security within which commercial lighting can unfold.

(Schivelbusch 1988: 142)

Further reading: Asendorf 1993; Schivelbusch 1977, 1988, 1993; Sennett 1986; Ward 2001; Williams 1982.

Shop windows

UNTIL THE LATE seventeenth century, shops for retail trade were little more than anterooms of the warehouses behind them. Indeed, their plain and simple furnishings made them almost indistinguishable from warehouses. But they compensated for their austerity with magnificent signboards, which hung out in the street showing what was on sale. When it was discovered, during the seventeenth and eighteenth centuries, that the signboards obstructed the traffic, these imaginative precursors of modern advertising gradually disappeared from the streets. As Sombart comments, 'the disappearance of these signboards, one after the other, almost as symbols of a dying age, was one of those momentous steps out of the cheerful world of words and colours into the grey world of figures'.[1] But this is only half the story. The colourful and aesthetic display of shop signs disappeared from the streets only to

Figure 18.1   Harrods department store, Brompton Road, Knightsbridge, London. View of Harrods lit up at night © English Heritage Prints.

reappear, in a different form, inside the shop. A new combination of aesthetics and business was developing in the capitals of Europe. The luxury trade was in the hands of bourgeois merchants, but their customers were almost exclusively members of the court aristocracy. In the cities, the trade in luxury goods depended almost entirely on the court. To quote Sombart again: 'The elegant luxury shops, in particular, which had multiplied in Paris and London since the seventeenth century, served as popular meeting places for high society, for people who were happy to spend an hour of the day there, chatting, looking at the newest goods available and buying a few things, rather like at fashionable art auctions today.'[2]

The new social role of shops was reflected in their interior design. Catering for the taste of their customers, shop owners made their sales-rooms look like reception rooms in a palace. The most popular materials were rare woods, marble, brass and especially the high-status materials used at court: glass and mirrors.

The new splendour was foreign to the bourgeois, puritan morality of traders who experienced this transformation in the early eighteenth century. 'It is a modern custom, and wholly unknown to our ancestors, who yet understood trade, in proportion to the Business they carried on, as well as we do, to have tradesmen lay out two-thirds of their fortune in fitting up their shops,' writes Defoe in *The Complete Tradesman*.

> By fitting up, I do not mean furnishing their shops with wares and goods to sell; for in that they came up to us in every particular, and perhaps beyond us too; but in painting and gilding, in fine shelves, shutters, boxes, glass doors, sashes and the like, in which they tell us now, 'tis a small matter to lay out two hundred or three hundred pounds, nay five hundred pounds to fit up a Pastry-Cook's, or a Toy-Shop. The first inference to be drawn from this must necessarily be, that this age must have more fools than the last, for certainly fools only are most taken with shews and outsides . . ., but that a fine shew of shelves and glass windows should bring customers, that was never made a rule in trade till now.[3]

As an example of a luxurious fitting-out, Defoe refers to a pastry shop in which £300 was spent on furnishings, while the stock was only worth £20. Defoe's description is one of the very few that have survived from the early period of the luxury trade:

1   Sash windows, all of looking-glass plates, 12 inches by 16 inches in measure.
2   All the walks of the shops lin'd up with galley tiles, and the Back-shop with galley-tiles in pannels, finely painted in forest-work and figures.
3   Two large Peir looking-glasses and one chimney glass in the shop, and one very large Peir-glass seven foot high in the Back-shop.
4   Two large branches of Candlesticks, one in the shop and one in the back-room.
5   Three great glass Lanthorns in the shop, and eight small ones.
6   Twenty-five sconces against the wall, with a large pair of silver standing candlesticks in the back room.[4]

The glass, mirrors and lights used in its furnishing must have made this shop a remarkably sparkling, reflecting, brilliant room — a miniature hall of mirrors.[5] In Defoe's time, all this splendour was limited to the interior of the shop. This changed with the social profile of the customers, as increasingly anonymous buyers replaced what had been a largely personal clientele. The more the streets could supply potential customers, the more the shops opened up to them. The display window, that began to develop as an independent part of the shop around the middle of the eighteenth century, was the scene of this inter-change. While previously it had been little more than an ordinary window that permitted people to see into and out of the shop, it now became a glassed-in stage on which an advertising show was presented. 'Behind the great glass windows absolutely everything one can think of is neatly and attractively displayed in such abundance of choice as almost to make one greedy,' wrote Sophie von La Roche from London in the 1780s. 'There is a cunning device for showing women's materials. They hang down in folds behind the fine, high windows so that the effect of this or that material, as it would be in a woman's dress, can be studied.'[6]

In the eighteenth and nineteenth centuries, shop display windows still looked like ordinary windows. They consisted not of a single sheet of glass, but of several smaller panes, separated by a number of ribs. Around 1850 it became technically possible to produce large sheets of glass and so to have a glass shop-front which presented 'an uninterrupted mass of glass from the ceiling to the ground', as an observer pointed out admiringly in 1851.[7] This had a profound impact on the appearance of the wares on display. The uninterrupted, transparently sparkling surface acted rather like glass on a framed painting. 'Dull colours receive . . . an element of freshness, sparkle and refinement, because glass as a medium alters appearances and irritates the eye' – this is how Hirth explains the phenomenon. He adds in a footnote: 'Putting paintings under glass makes them appear better than they really are. The protective glass confers upon good copies an additional element of deception. The plate glass of shop windows, too, has an "improving" effect on some goods.'[8]

Artificial light also helped to make the wares on display look more attractive. Its importance grew as business hours were extended into the late evening. During a visit to London in 1775, Lichtenberg observed how shops drew attention to their windows by special effects with coloured lights: 'Apothecaries and grocers display glasses . . . filled with coloured spirits and cover large areas with crimson, yellow, verdigris and skyblue light. Confectioners dazzle the eye with their chandeliers and tickle the nose with their wares at no greater effort or cost than turning both in their direction.'[9] Berlin pastry cooks displayed in their windows 'artificially lit scenes, populated by small, three-dimensional figures, often artificially animated, the whole thing resembling a diorama'. In fact, these displays are thought to have inspired the development of the diorama.[10] Mostly, however, shop window lighting followed the path taken by stage lighting. As long as lights were too weak to be used indirectly, that is with the aid of reflectors, they were placed among the goods in the window. When gas and electricity increased the range over which light could be cast, the source of the light itself disappeared from view. Around the middle of the nineteenth century gaslights on London shops were 'fixed outside the shop, with a reflector so placed as to throw a strong light upon the commodities in the window'.[11] The introduction of electric light, which was not a fire hazard and therefore no longer had to be installed outside the display window, finally made it possible to achieve the sort of lighting effects that were used on the stage. A 1926 advertising handbook states that shop windows should not be 'evenly lit up. Individual spots and objects are to be highlighted by means of strong, concealed reflectors.'[12]

The illuminated window as stage, the street as theatre and the passers-by as audience – this is the scene of big-city night life. As the boulevard at night developed in the nineteenth century, it did in fact look like an interior out of doors. 'Always festively illuminated, golden cafés, a stylish and elegant throng, dandies, literati, financiers. The whole thing resembles a drawing-room' – this is Emma von Niendorf's 1854 description of the Parisian Boulevard des Italiens late at night.[13] There is a simple psychological explanation for the fact that the street looks like an 'Interieur', to borrow Walter Benjamin's expression.[14] Any artificially lit area out of doors is experienced as an interior because it is marked off from the surrounding darkness as if by walls, which run along the edges of the lit up area. The same applies to the 'ceiling'. Common usage shows that we step *out* of the darkness *into* a circle of light – be it the small one of a camp fire or the larger one of a lighted boulevard. The 'side walls' of the boulevard, as a 'room', were defined by the housefronts – shop windows, restaurants and café terraces; its 'ceiling' was at the limit of the commercial lighting, that is, at about first-floor level.

Before shop lighting created an 'interior' space out of doors, however, it went through a transitional phase, developing in an area that was bigger than the individual shop, but not yet as big as the open boulevard: the glass-roofed arcade, gallery or passage. This type of commercial space was most highly developed in Paris. The Galérie Orléans in the Palais Royal, *the* centre of Paris night life between 1790 and

1830, was the first of its kind. 'It makes a splendid sight indeed,' reported a German traveller in 1800 (i.e. before the introduction of gas lighting), '– tasteful Argand lamps illuminating the shops in the evening and at night, luxury goods sparkling with a heightened brilliance, and bright *réverbères* lighting up a packed, surging crowd in the arcades.'[15] Here is the same view under gaslight, described thirty years later: 'A thousand lights are reflected in the surface of polished mahogany and in the large mirror walls. . . . The stranger dazzled by all this begins to think of the Palais Royal as a bazaar.'[16] When the Palais Royal fell out of favour after 1830, Paris's numerous arcades took over the role of the Galérie Orléans in a process of decentralisation that was also an expansion of night life. Contemporary descriptions of these new venues are couched in exactly the same terms as descriptions of the Galérie Orléans. People seem to have been fascinated by the interplay between the brilliance of the light and the wares on display, and the lively crowd. 'A labyrinth of iridescent passages, like rainbow bridges in an ocean of light. A totally magical world. Everything, or rather, much more than the imagination could devise.'[17]

There is a final step in this progression of light: the emergence of light from a roofed-in space into the open air. The following descriptions are of boulevards, but they could just as well be about arcades or the Galérie Orléans. 'Glittering shops everywhere, splendid displays, cafés covered in gilt, and permanent lighting. . . . The shops put out so much light that one can read the paper as one strolls.'[18] 'The gas-lamps sparkle and the suspended lamps glow, and in between there are the tobacconists' red lanterns and the chemists' blue-glass globes – transparent signs announce the marvels of the Paris night in large, fiery letters, and the crowd surges back and forth.'[19]

Impressions like these can be found in city guides and travel reports published between 1850 and 1870, with titles such as *Gas-Light and Day-Light; Paris au Gaz; Paris bei Sonnenschein und Lampenlicht*; and *New York by Gaslight*.[20] These two decades were the heyday of gas lighting. It had become firmly established in the cultural and psychological structure of Western European and American society. Earlier reservations and fears had disappeared, and its modern successor, electric light, had not yet arrived on the scene. Gaslight, like the railway, reigned supreme as a symbol of human and industrial progress.

All the same, gaslight still burned with an open flame. However functional, neutral and rational it seemed in comparison with earlier forms of lighting, it retained the lively, magical quality of an open flame. It was both a modern, expansive source of light that illuminated incomparably larger spaces than any earlier form of lighting, and an 'old-fashioned' light still bound to the flame. This combination was probably the source of its appeal as a medium of night life in the capitals of Europe between 1850 and 1870. Lighting up the night with gas stirred people's feelings because it represented a triumph over the natural order, achieved without the lifeless hardness of electric light. Gaslight offered life, warmth and closeness. This was true also of the relationship between light and the shop goods upon which it fell. They were close to each other, indeed, they permeated each other, and each enhanced the effect of the other, to judge by descriptions of illuminated luxury shops.

Here, too, electric light injected an element of rigidity, coldness and distance. It burst open the 'ceiling' of the boulevard 'salon' by lifting it to roof level. From now on, commercial light shone down from this distant position, detached from the display windows, in its own, independent sphere. In 1928 Ernst May describes how this symphony of advertising lights in Times Square affected him: 'Here the eye does not read any writing, it cannot pick out any shapes, it is simply dazzled by a profusion of scintillating lights, by a plethora of elements of light that cancel out each other's effect.'[21]

Notes

1   Werner Sombart, *Der moderne Kapitalismus*, 1st edn (Munich, 1902), Vol. 2, p. 402.
2   Ibid., p. 463; see also Sombart's study, *Kapitalismus und Luxus*. In it, he argues that the court aristocracy's consumption of luxury goods ruined it financially while at the other end of the same process, the bourgeoisie's role as supplier of luxury goods was the thing that allowed the bourgeois economy to begin to blossom.

3   Daniel Defoe, *The Complete Tradesman*, 2nd edn (London, 1727; reprinted New York, 1969), Vol. 1, pp. 257–8.

4   Ibid., p. 259.

5   The use of large mirrors in seventeenth-century palaces has been explained as an attempt to create *an illusion of space*. 'High walls, doors, even ceilings are more and more often covered with mirrors. Their purpose, however, is not to reflect any particular, delimited image, but to give the impression of a scintillating, rather kaleidoscopic and uncertain sum of light and decoration' (Georg Hirth, *Das deutsche Zimmer der Gotik und Renaissance, des Barock- Rokoko- und Zopfstils*, Munich and Leipzig, 1899), p. 154.

6   Quoted from Dorothy Davis, *A History of Shopping* (London and Toronto, 1966), p. 192.

7   Charles Knight (1851), quoted from Alison Adburgham, *Shops and Shopping 1800–1914* (London, 1964), p. 96.

8   Hirth, *Das deutsche Zimmer*, p. 152. Albert Smith gives us a good example of what a glance through such a window revealed: 'How richly falls the drapery of those emblazoned shawls through the fair plate-glass. How the rows of loves of bonnets . . . gladden and sadden at the same moment the bright female eyes . . . How gorgeously shines the plate' (*Sketches of London Life and Character*, London, 1859, p. 117, quoted from Wilfried B. Whitaker, *Victorian and Edwardian Shopworkers*, Newton Abbot, 1973, p. 31).

9   Letter to Boie, 10 January 1775, in *Lichtenbergs Werke in einem Band* (Stuttgart, 1924), pp. 356–7.

10   Marianne Mildenberger, *Film und Projektion auf der Bühne* (Emsdetten, Westphalia, 1961), p. 22.

11   Charles Knight, quoted from Adburgham, *Shops and Shopping*, p. 96. 'Reflectors made of nickel silver or mirror glass with a parabolic cross-section are used to illuminate shop windows. They reflect the light perpendicularly down, so that the goods on display in the window are very brightly lit up' (C. Muchall, *Das A-B-C des Gas-Consumenten*, Wiesbaden, 1889, p. 23).

12   Bruno H. Jahn, *Reklame durch das Schaufenster* (Berlin, 1926), p. 130.

13   Emma von Niendorf, *Aus dem heutigen Paris* (Stuttgart, 1854), p. 171.

14   Walter Benjamin, *Charles Baudelaire. Ein Lyriker im Zeitalter des Hochkapitalismus* (Frankfurt, 1969), p. 37.

15   *Reise nach Paris im August und September 1789* (no place of publication, 1800), p. 180.

16   *Le livre des Cent-et-Un* (Paris, 1831), Vol. 1, pp. 19–21.

17   Niendorf, *Aus dem heutigen Paris*, p. 169.

18   Julier Lemer, *Paris au gaz* (1861), p. 15.

19   Julius Rodenberg, *Paris bei Sonnenschein und Lampenlicht* (Leipzig, 1867), p. 45.

20   George G. Foster, *New York by Gas-Light* (New York, 1850). Lemer gives the following list of words relating to night life that were in vogue in Paris around 1860: *noctivague, noctilogue, noctiphague, noctiurge, physiologie de l'existence de nuit à Paris*.

21   Quoted from W. Lotz (ed.), *Licht und Beleuchtung* (Berlin, 1928), p. 44.

Chapter 19

Nicholson Baker

FROM *THE MEZZANINE* [1986]

Source: Nicholson Baker (1986) 'Chapter Two', in *The Mezzanine*, Cambridge: Granta Books in association with Penguin, pp. 11–18.

The world described by Nicholson Baker in *The Mezzanine* is made up of what might be thought of as 'minor devices': staplers, paper bags, shoelaces, elevators and escalators, drinking-straws, wax-treated cardboard drink containers, fitted carpets and so on. It is a world that seems to be associated with a particular social form – office work (it would be hard to imagine a similar book describing life on a working farm or in an industrial factory). Lefebvre once described much of the postwar, 'developed' world as the 'bureaucratic society of controlled consumption' (Lefebvre 1968/1984), and this too might be a fitting designation of the world of *The Mezzanine*. It is a world where social contact is conventionalised to a startlingly high degree, and this results in seemingly endless opportunities for small infractions of etiquette, little humiliations in social exchanges, chances for getting it wrong. It is, to a large extent, a world ordered by the re-negotiation of gender meanings as many wealthy nations moved from the ultra-masculinity of industrial manufacturing to the incipient femininity associated with office work and service industry.

If the world of *The Mezzanine* privileges a certain 'form of attention', then this might be described as an odd amalgam of bored, intense and distracted concentration on the phenomenal experiences of the everyday designed environment. Baker has the narrator of *The Mezzanine* relating the pleasures and frustrations of the bodily experiences of the designed world: what it feels like to press a stapler, bend a bendy straw, open a carton of milk. The physicality of the motions required to use one of these devices successfully is often associated, here, with the childhood pleasure of first being able to control the object world. For the narrator of *The Mezzanine* these pleasures, as they extend into the present, aren't mere nostalgia for these early inaugural moments but the very real pleasure of the thingly world.

But if this phenomenological description of design culture is the initial grounding for reflection, then the novel also provides a 'meta' level of reflection. This is achieved by constructing a heavily footnoted text, where distraction provides a constant diversion that instead of following the narrative follows the 'thing'. And it often does this by pursuing historical information about a thingly phenomenon. The narration is minimal: a young office worker buys some shoelaces in his lunch hour. The book, then, is a constant digression that turns attention away from narrative progression towards a concentration on the material world.

Nicholson Baker's novel is proof that exorbitant attention to the thingly-ness of the everyday (its ubiquitous design culture) could provide a platform for recognising the extent to which the material world of design affects and orchestrates our world. In this, a novel might provide the most analytic approach to design culture – a paradigm for design culture research. It also suggests that today the 'examined life' (the one that we are told is worth living) starts here amongst the very ordinariness of toilet cubicles, office furniture and convenience stores. The question remains (and it is the implicit question of the novel) whether, once examined, this life appears full and satisfying or metaphysically impoverished.

Further reading: Chambers 1994; Perec 1978/1987, 1997; Simmons 1992.

MY LEFT SHOELACE had snapped just before lunch. At some earlier point in the morning, my left shoe had become untied, and as I had sat at my desk working on a memo, my foot had sensed its potential freedom and slipped out of the sauna of black cordovan to soothe itself with rhythmic movements over an area of wall-to-wall carpeting under my desk, which, unlike the tamped-down areas of public traffic, was still almost as soft and fibrous as it had been when first installed. Only under the desks and in the little-used conference rooms was the pile still plush enough to hold the beautiful Ms and Vs the night crew left as strokes of their vacuum cleaners' wands made swaths of dustless tufting lean in directions that alternately absorbed and reflected the light. The nearly universal carpeting of offices must have come about in my lifetime, judging from black-and-white movies and Hopper paintings: since the pervasion of carpeting, all you hear when people walk by are their own noises – the flap of their raincoats, the jingle of their change, the squeak of their shoes, the efficient little sniffs they make to signal to us and to themselves that they are busy and walking somewhere for a very good reason, as well as the almost sonic whoosh of receptionists' staggering and misguided perfumes, and the covert chokings and showings of tongues and placing of braceleted hands to windpipes that more tastefully scented secretaries exchange in their wake. One or two individuals in every office (Dave in mine), who have special pounding styles of walking, may still manage to get their footfalls heard; but in general now we all glide at work: a major improvement, as anyone knows who has visited those areas of offices that are still for various reasons linoleum-squared – cafeterias, mail-rooms, computer rooms. Linoleum was bearable back when incandescent light was there to counteract it with a softening glow, but the combination of fluorescence and linoleum, which must have been widespread for several years as the two trends overlapped, is not good.

As I had worked, then, my foot had, without any sanction from my conscious will, slipped from the untied shoe and sought out the texture of the carpeting; although now, as I reconstruct the moment, I realize that a more specialized desire was at work as well: when you slide a socked foot over a carpeted surface, the fibers of sock and carpet mesh and lock, so that though you think you are enjoying the texture of the carpeting, you are really enjoying the slippage of the inner surface of the sock against the underside of your foot, something you normally get to experience only in the morning when you first pull the sock on.[1]

At a few minutes before twelve, I stopped working, threw out my earplugs and, more carefully, the remainder of my morning coffee – placing it upright within the converging spinnakers of the trash can liner on the base of the receptacle itself. I stapled a copy of a memo someone had cc:'d me on to a copy of an earlier memo I had written on the same subject, and wrote at the top to my manager, in my best casual scrawl, "Abe – should I keep hammering on these people or drop it?" I put the stapled papers in one of my Eldon trays, not sure whether I would forward them to Abelardo or not. Then I slipped my shoe back on by flipping it on its side, hooking it with my foot, and shaking it into place. I accomplished all this by foot-feel; and when I crouched forward, over the papers on my desk, to reach the untied shoelace, I experienced a faint surge of pride in being able to tie a shoe without looking at it. At that moment, Dave, Sue, and Steve, on their way to lunch, waved as they passed by my office. Right in the middle of tying a shoe as I was, I couldn't wave nonchalantly back, so I called out a startled, overhearty "Have a good one, guys!" They disappeared; I pulled the left shoelace tight, and *bingo*, it broke.

The curve of incredulousness and resignation I rode out at that moment was a kind caused in life by a certain class of events, disruptions of physical routines, such as:

(a)   reaching a top step but thinking there is another step there, and stamping down on the landing;

(b)   pulling on the red thread that is supposed to butterfly a Band-Aid and having it wrest free from the wrapper without tearing it;

(c)   drawing a piece of Scotch tape from the roll that resides half sunk in its black, weighted Duesenberg of a dispenser, hearing the slightly descending whisper of adhesive-coated plastic detaching itself from the back of the tape to come (descending in pitch because the strip, while amplifying the sound, is also getting longer as you pull on it[2]), and then, just as you are intending to break the piece off over the metal serration, reaching the innermost end of the roll, so that the segment you have been pulling wafts unexpectedly free. Especially now, with the rise of Post-it notes, which have made the massive black tape-dispensers seem even more grandiose and Biedermeier and tragically defunct, you almost believe that you will never come to the end of a roll of tape; and when you do, there is a feeling, nearly, though very briefly, of shock and grief;

(d)   attempting to staple a thick memo, and looking forward, as you begin to lean on the brontosaural head of the stapler arm,[3] to the three phases of the act –

first, before the stapler arm makes contact with the paper, the resistance of the spring that keeps the arm held up; then, *second*, the moment when the small independent unit in the stapler arm noses into the paper and begins to force the two points of the staple into and through it; and, *third*, the felt crunch, like the chewing of an ice cube, as the twin tines of the staple emerge from the underside of the paper and are bent by the two troughs of the template in the stapler's base, curving inward in a crab's embrace of your memo, and finally disengaging from the machine completely –

but finding, as you lean on the stapler with your elbow locked and your breath held and it slumps toothlessly to the paper, that it has run out of staples. How could something this consistent, this incremental, betray you? (But then you are consoled: you get to reload it, laying bare the stapler arm and dropping a long zithering row of staples into place; and later, on the phone, you get to toy with the piece of the staples you couldn't fit into the stapler, breaking it into smaller segments, making them dangle on a hinge of glue.)

In the aftermath of the broken-shoelace disappointment, irrationally, I pictured Dave, Sue, and Steve as I had just seen them and thought, "Cheerful assholes!" because I had probably broken the shoelace by transferring the social energy that I had had to muster in order to deliver a chummy "Have a good one!" to them from my awkward shoe-tier's crouch into the force I had used in pulling on the shoelace. Of course, it would have worn out sooner or later anyway. It was the original shoelace, and the shoes were the very ones my father had bought me two years earlier, just after I had started this job, my first out of college – so the breakage was a sentimental milestone of sorts. I rolled back in my chair to study the damage, imagining the smiles on my three co-workers' faces suddenly vanishing if I had really called them cheerful assholes, and regretting this burst of ill feeling toward them.

As soon as my gaze fell to my shoes, however, I was reminded of something that should have struck me the instant the shoelace had first snapped. The day before, as I had been getting ready for work, my *other* shoelace, the right one, had snapped, too, as I was yanking it tight to tie it, under very similar circumstances. I repaired it with a knot, just as I was planning to do now with the left. I was surprised – more than surprised — to think that after almost two years my right and left shoelaces could fail less than two days apart. Apparently my shoe-tying routine was so unvarying and robotic that over those hundreds of mornings I had inflicted identical levels of wear on both laces. The near simultaneity was very exciting — it made the variables of private life seem suddenly graspable and law-abiding.

I moistened the splayed threads of the snapped-off piece and twirled them gently into a damp, unwholesome minaret. Breathing steadily and softly through my nose, I was able to guide the saliva-sharpened leader thread through the eyelet without too much trouble. And then I grew uncertain. In order for the shoelaces to have worn to the breaking point on almost the same day, they would have had to be tied almost exactly the same number of times. But when Dave, Sue, and Steve passed my office door, I had been in the middle of tying one shoe — *one shoe only*. And in the course of a normal day it wasn't at all unusual for one shoe to come untied independent of the other. In the morning, of course, you always tied both shoes, but random midday comings-undone would have to have constituted a significant proportion of the total wear on both of these broken laces, I felt — possibly thirty percent. And how could I be positive that this thirty percent was equally distributed — that right and left shoes had come randomly undone over the last two years with the same frequency?

I tried to call up some sample memories of shoe-tying to determine whether one shoe tended to come untied more often than another. What I found was that I did not retain a single specific engram of tying a shoe, or a pair of shoes, that dated from any later than when I was four or five years old, the age at which I had first learned the skill. Over twenty years of empirical data were lost forever, a complete blank. But I suppose this is often true of moments of life that are remembered as major advances: the discovery is the crucial thing, not its repeated later applications. As it happened, the first *three* major advances in my life — and I will list all the advances here —

1   shoe-tying
2   pulling up on Xs
3   steadying hand against sneaker when tying
4   brushing tongue as well as teeth
5   putting on deodorant after I was fully dressed
6   discovering that sweeping was fun
7   ordering a rubber stamp with my address on it to make bill-paying more efficient
8   deciding that brain cells ought to die

— have to do with shoe-tying, but I don't think that this fact is very unusual. Shoes are the first adult machines we are given to master. Being taught to tie them was not like watching some adult fill the dishwasher and then being asked in a kind voice if you would like to clamp the dishwasher door shut and advance the selector knob (with its uncomfortable grinding sound) to Wash. That was artificial, whereas you knew that adults wanted you to learn how to tie your shoes; it was no fun for them to kneel. I made several attempts to learn the skill, but it was not until my mother placed a lamp on the floor so that I could clearly see the dark laces of a pair of new dress shoes that I really mastered it; she explained again how to form the introductory platform knot, which began high in the air as a frail, heart-shaped loop, and shrunk as you pulled the plastic lace-tips down to a short twisted kernel three-eights of an inch long, and she showed me how to progress from that base to the main cotyledonary string figure, which was, as it turned out, not a true knot but an illusion, a trick that you performed on the lace-string by bending segments of it back on themselves and tightening other temporary bends around them: it looked like a knot and functioned like a knot, but the whole thing was really an amazing interdependent pyramid scheme, which much later I connected with a couplet of Pope's:

> Man, like the gen'rous vine, supported lives;
> The strength he gains is from th'embrace he gives.

Only a few weeks after I learned the basic skill, my father helped me to my second major advance, when he demonstrated thoroughness by showing me how to tighten the rungs of the shoelaces one by one, beginning down at the toe and working up, hooking an index finger under each X, so that by the time you reached the top you were rewarded with surprising lengths of lace to use in tying the knot, and at the same time your foot felt tightly papooosed and alert.

The third advance I made by myself in the middle of a playground, when I halted, out of breath, to tie a sneaker,[4] my mouth on my interesting-smelling knee, a close-up view of anthills and the tread marks of other sneakers before me (the best kind, Keds, I think, or Red Ball Flyers, had a perimeter of asymmetrical triangles, and a few concavities in the center which printed perfect domes of dust), and found as I retied the shoe that I was doing it automatically, without having to concentrate on it as I had done at first, and, more important, that somewhere over the past year since I had first learned the basic moves, I had evidently evolved two little substeps of my own *that nobody had showed me*. In one I held down a temporarily taut stretch of shoelace with the side of my thumb; in the other I stabilized my hand with a middle finger propped against the side of the sneaker during some final manipulations. The advance here was my recognition that I had independently developed refinements of technique in an area where nobody had indicated there were refinements to be found: I had personalized an already adult procedure.

Notes

1   When I pull a sock on, I no longer *pre-bunch*, that is, I don't gather the sock up into telescoped folds over my thumbs and then position the resultant donut over my toes, even though I believed for some years that this was a clever trick, taught by admirable, fresh-faced kindergarten teachers, and that I revealed my laziness and my inability to plan ahead by instead holding the sock by the ankle rim and jamming my foot to its destination, working the ankle a few times to properly seat the heel. Why? The more elegant pre-bunching can leave in place any pieces of grit that have embedded themselves in your sole from the imperfectly swept floor you walked on to get from the shower to your room; while the cruder, more direct method, though it risks tearing an older sock, does detach this grit during the foot's downward passage, so that you seldom later feel irritating particles rolling around under your arch as you depart for the subway.

2   When I was little I thought it was called Scotch tape because the word "scotch" imitated the descending screech of early cellophane tapes. As incandescence gave way before fluorescence in office lighting, Scotch tape, once yellowish-transparent, became bluish-transparent, as well as superbly quiet.

3   Staplers have followed, lagging by about ten years, the broad stylistic changes we have witnessed in train locomotives and phonograph tonearms, both of which they resemble. The oldest staplers are cast-ironic and upright, like coal-fired locomotives and Edison wax-cylinder players. Then, in mid-century, as locomotive manufacturers discovered the word "streamlined," and as tonearm designers housed the stylus in aerodynamic ribbed plastic hoods that looked like trains curving around a mountain, the people at Swingline and Bates tagged along, instinctively sensing that staplers were like locomotives in that the two prongs of the staple make contact with a pair of metal hollows, which, like the paired rail under the wheels of the train, forces them to follow a preset path, and that they were like phonograph tonearms in that both machines, roughly the same size, make sharp points of contact with their respective media of informational storage. (In the case of the tonearm, the stylus retrieves the information, while in the case of the stapler, the staple binds it together as a unit – the order; the shipping paper, the invoice: *boom*, stapled, a unit; the letter of complaint, the copies of canceled checks and receipts, the letter of apologetic response: *boom*, stapled, a unit; a sequence of memos and telexes holding the history of some interdepartmental controversy: *boom*, stapled, one controversy. In old stapled problems, you can see the TB vaccine marks in the upper left corner where staples have been removed and replaced, removed and replaced, as the problem – even the staple holes of the problem – was copied and sent on to other departments for further action, copying, and stapling.) And then the great era of squareness set in: BART was the ideal for trains, while AR and Bang & Olufsen turntables became angular – no more cream-colored bulbs of plastic! The people at Bates and Swingline again were drawn along, ridding their devices of all softening curvatures and offering black rather than the interestingly textured tan. And now, of course, the high-speed

trains of France and Japan have reverted to aerodynamic profiles reminiscent of *Popular Science* cities-of-the-future covers of the fifties; and soon the stapler will incorporate a toned-down pompadour swoop as well. Sadly, the tonearm's stylistic progress has slowed, because all the buyers who would appreciate an up-to-date Soviet Realism in the design are buying CD players: its inspirational era is over.

4　Sneaker knots were quite different from dress knots – when you pulled the two loops tight at the end, the logic of the knot you had just created became untraceable; while in the case of dress-lace knots, you could, even after tightening, follow the path of the knot around with your mind, as if riding a roller coaster. You could imagine a sneaker-shoelace knot and a dress-shoelace knot standing side by side saying the Pledge of Allegiance: the dress-shoelace knot would pronounce each word as a grammatical unit, understanding it as more than a sound; the sneaker-shoelace knot would run the words together. The great advantage of sneakers, though, one of the many advantages, was that when you had tied them tightly, without wearing socks, and worn them all day, and gotten them wet, and you took them off before bed, your feet would display the impression of the chrome eyelets in red rows down the sides of your foot, like the portholes in a Jules Verne submarine.

Chapter 20

C. Nadia Seremetakis

THE MEMORY OF THE SENSES, PART 1: MARKS OF THE TRANSITORY [1996]

Source: C. Nadia Seremetakis (1996) 'The Memory of the Senses, Part 1: Marks of the Transitory', in *The Senses Still: Perception and Memory as Material Culture in Modernity*, ed. C. Nadia Seremetakis, Chicago: University of Chicago Press, pp. 1–18.

The anthropologist C. Nadia Seremetakis is an adviser to the Minister of Public Health in Greece. In her anthropological writing she combines an unfailing attention to the liveliness of experience with theoretical commitments to the investigation of historical changes forged in the name of modernity. Crucially, though, this isn't a standardised modernity that comes to all nation-states (in the end) as some sort of inevitable historical destiny. By paying close attention to the everydayness of culture, which is necessarily a local experience, modernity becomes the meeting ground for both tradition and change. In the words of Harry Harootunian:

> If modernity was driven by the desiring machine of capitalism, promising to install its regime of production and consumption everywhere, the everyday . . . signalling the level of lived experience and reproduction would, in fact, negotiate the compelling demands of homogeneity through the mediations of a past that constantly stood in a tense, often antagonistic, relationship to the present of the new.
>
> (Harootunian 2000: 63)

Such an understanding of modernity positions the everydayness of culture as a crucial instrument for differentiation: for seeing that the effects and affects of modernisation are qualitatively different in Athens, for example, to those in Los Angeles – even though we might still think of modernity as a pull towards global sameness. And this is where nostalgia becomes such an important and resistant aspect of modern experience: it allows for a counter-memory to exist, a counter-memory that will always refuse the lure of global sameness.

The differentiation of modernity is even more nuanced by the topic of Seremetakis' investigation: senses and sentiments. Modernisation alters the world that is perceived (it brings about new sensual regimes) and it alters the way that it is perceived (think of how much of the world we encounter through TV, newspapers, radio and the internet). But if the modern world brings us new flavours and smells, and if we eventually orient ourselves to these sense orchestrations, older sense experiences aren't thereby obliterated. They remain: often heavily invested with longing, with a sense that the flavours of the past were deeper, fuller, more sensually compelling.

For Seremetakis, food, however saturated it is in the language of nature (organically grown, no artificial flavours), is an active participant in design processes. As I mentioned in the preface to this book, Karl Marx's example of mistaking nature for culture is a cherry tree: the cherry tree for Marx is the result of purposeful design activity – of travel, of migration, of taste, of cultivation. For Seremetakis food participates in design processes partly by disappearing. Here a peach (a very particular peach) is designed out of circulation. Negative design processes are a crucial element of standardising the product as an image of itself. (Anyone who has spent time harvesting fruit knows how much perfectly good produce is destroyed because it is too small or big, and therefore doesn't fit the image of the fruit that is being promoted.) Nostalgia, as a feeling that is central to modern experience, is the unflinching witness to negative design.

Further reading: Boym 2001; Deborah Lupton 1996; Sutton 2001; Warin and Dennis 2005.

The breast of Aphrodite

I GREW UP with the peach. It had a thin skin touched with fuzz, and a soft matte off-white color alternating with rosy hues. *Rodhákino* was its name (*ródho* means rose). It was well rounded and smooth like a small clay vase, fitting perfectly into your palm. Its interior was firm yet moist, offering a soft resistance to the teeth. A bit sweet and a bit sour, it exuded a distinct fragrance. This peach was known as "the breast of Aphrodite" (*o mastós tis Afrodhítis*).

A relation of this peach appeared eventually in the markets, which was called *yermás*. It was a much softer, watery fruit with a yolkish yellow color and reddish patches. Its silky thin skin would slide off at a touch revealing its slippery, shiny, deep yellow interior that melted with no resistance in the mouth. Both fruits were very sensitive, easy to bruise. I learned to like them both but my heart was set for the *rodhákino*.

In the United States, all fruits resembling either the *rodhákino* or *yermás* are named "peach." Throughout my years in the States, the memory of my peach was in its difference.

Every journey back was marked by its taste. Summer was its permanent referent, yet its gradual disappearance from the summer markets passed almost unnoticed. A few years ago, I realized that the peach was nowhere to be found in the markets, in or outside of Athens. When I mentioned it in casual conversations to friends and relatives, they responded as if the peach is always out there although they did not happen to eat it lately. What they are mainly buying, they explained, is a kind of *yermadho-rodhákino* (a blend of *yermás* and *rodhákino*). People only alluded to the disappearance of the older peach by remarking on the tastelessness of new varieties, a comment that was often extended to all food, "nothing tastes as good as the past."

As my search for the peach became more persistent, my disappointment matched their surprise in the realization that the peach was gone forever. I asked my father to plant it in our fields in the country to rescue it, but he has yet to find it. My older friends began to bring me tokens from their neighborhood markets, as well as from the country whenever they traveled out of the city. We all agreed that there were varieties that carried one or two of the characteristics of "our peach" but they were far from it. The part had taken the name of the whole.

In the presence of all those "peaches," the absent peach became narrative. It was as if when something leaves, it only goes externally, for its body persists within persons. The peach was its memory, and as if both had gone underground, they waited to be named. My naming of its absence resurrected observations, commentaries, stories, some of which encapsulated whole epochs marked by their own sensibilities. "Ah, that peach, what an aroma! and taste! The breast of Aphrodite we called it. These (peaches and other food) today have no taste (*á-nosta*)."

The younger generation, whenever present, heard these stories as if listening to a captivating fairy tale. For me the peach had been both eaten and remembered, but for the younger generation it was now digested through memory and language. At the same time, we are all experiencing the introduction from foreign markets of new fruits with no Greek precedents, such as the kiwi. For the younger generation, the remembered first peach exists on the same exotic plane as the kiwi. For the generation that follows, the kiwi, no longer exotic, may evoke a different sensibility.

The disappearance of Aphrodite's peach is a double absence; it reveals the extent to which the senses are entangled with history, memory, forgetfulness, narrative and silence. That first peach of my childhood carried with it allusions to distant epochs where the relation between food and the erotic was perhaps more explicit, named, and sacrilized; a relation that although fragmented and gone underground, was carried over through the centuries by the *rodhákino*, a fruit bearing myth in its form.

The new fruits displaced the *rodhákino* and together with it, a mosaic of enmeshed memories, tastes, aromas. The surrogate remains as a simulation with no model, emptied of specific cultural content and actively producing forgetfulness. A shift has been accomplished from sedimented depth to surface with no past. Aphrodite's peach in its presence and later absence materialized experiences of time which are searched for fruitlessly in the peach of today. This complicity of history and the senses also refers to the relation between *Eros* and *Thanatos* where the latter is not mere absence or void but rather material closure, a cordoning off of the capacity for certain perceptual experiences in such a manner that their very disappearance goes unnoticed.

How are the transformations of the senses experienced and conceptualized? This is also to ask, how is history experienced and thought of, on the level of the everyday? What elements in a culture enable the sensory experience of history? Where can historicity be found? in what sensory forms and practices? And to what extent is the experience of and the capacity to narrate history tied to the senses? Is memory stored in specific everyday items that form the historicity of a culture, items that create and sustain our relationship to the historical as a sensory dimension?

Is the disappearance of Aphrodite's peach an idiosyncratic event? Or does the disappearance of the "particular" peach as micro-history materialize on the everyday sweeping, macro-historical, sociocultural changes? The vanishing of tastes, aromas, and textures are being writ large in contemporary European margins with the joint expansion and centralizations of EEC market rationalities. The erasure of one Greek peach poses the question: at what experiential levels are the economic and social transformations of the EEC being felt? Under the rationale of trans-national uniformity the EEC may have initiated a massive intervention in the commensal cultures of its membership by determining what regional varieties of basic food staples can be grown, marketed and exported. Certain types of Irish potatoes, German beer, and French cheese are no longer admissible into the public market, no longer eligible for subsidies because they look, appear, and taste different, and in some cases violate new health regulations.

In Greece, as regional products gradually disappear, they are replaced by foreign foods, foreign tastes; the universal and rationalized is now imported into the European periphery as the exotic. Here a regional diversity is substituted by a surplus over-production. This EEC project implicitly constitutes a massive resocialization of existing consumer cultures and sensibilities, as well as a reorganization of public memory. A French cheese is excluded because it is produced through a specific fermentation process; one that market regulations deem a health-risk. What is fermentation if not history? If not a maturation that occurs through the articulation of time and substance? Sensory premises, memories and histories are being pulled out from under entire regional cultures and the capacity to reproduce social identities may be altered as a result. Such economic processes reveal the extent to which the ability to replicate cultural identity is a material practice embedded in the reciprocities, aesthetics, and sensory strata of material objects. Sensory displacement does not only relate to cultures of consumption but to those local material cultures of production where the latter is still symbolically mediated and not yet reduced to a purely instrumental practice. Sensory changes occur microscopically through everyday accretion; so, that which shifts the material culture of perception is itself imperceptible and only reappears after the fact in fairy tales, myths, and memories that hover at the margins of speech.

The imperceptible is not only the consequence of sensory transformation but also the means by which it takes place. Thus the problematic of the senses in modernity resurrects the old theme ignored in recent anthropological theory, that of the historical unconscious.

The impeachment of nostalgia

The memory of Aphrodite's peach is nostalgic. What is the relation of nostalgia to the senses and history? In English the word nostalgia (in Greek *nostalghía*) implies trivializing romantic sentimentality. In Greek the verb *nostalghó* is a composite of *nostó* and *alghó*. *Nostó* means I return, I travel (back to homeland); the noun *nóstos* means the return, the journey, while *á-nostos* means without taste, as the new peaches are described (*ánosta*, in plural). The opposite of *ánostos* is *nóstimos* and characterizes someone or something that has journeyed and arrived, has matured, ripened and is thus tasty (and useful). *Alghó* means I feel pain, I ache for, and the noun *álghos* characterizes one's pain in soul and body, burning pain (*kaimós*). Thus *nostalghía* is the desire or longing with burning pain to journey. It also evokes the sensory dimension of memory in exile and estrangement; it mixes bodily and emotional pain and ties painful experiences of spiritual and somatic exile to the notion of maturation and ripening. In this sense, *nostalghía* is linked to the personal consequences of historicizing sensory experience which is conceived as a painful bodily and emotional journey.

Nostalghía thus is far from trivializing romantic sentimentality. This reduction of the term confines the past and removes it from any transactional and material relation to the present; the past becomes an isolatable and consumable unit of time. Nostalgia, in the American sense, freezes the past in such a manner as to preclude it from any capacity for social transformation in the present, preventing the present from establishing a dynamic perceptual relationship to its history. Whereas the Greek etymology evokes the transformative impact of the past as unreconciled historical experience.[1] Does the difference between nostalgia and *nostalghía* speak of different cultural experiences of the senses and memory? Could a dialogical encounter of the terms offer insights for an anthropology of the senses?

Sensory exchange and performance

Nostalghía speaks to the sensory reception of history. In Greek there is a semantic circuit that weds the sensorial to agency, memory, finitude, and therefore history – all of which are contained within the etymological strata of the senses. The word for senses is *aesthísis;* emotion-feeling and aesthetics are respectively *aésthima* and *aesthitikí*. They all derive from the verb *aesthánome* or *aesthísome* meaning I feel or sense, I understand, grasp, learn or receive news or information, and I have an accurate sense of good and evil, that is I judge correctly. *Aesthísis* is defined as action or power through the medium of the senses, and the media or the *semía* (points, tracks, marks) by which one senses. *Aésthima*, emotion feeling, is also an ailment of the soul, an event that happens, that impacts on one viscerally through the senses; it also refers to romance, love affair. A strong *aésthima* is called *páthos* (passion). This includes the sense of suffering, illness, but also the English sense of passion, as in "he has a passion for music." The stem verb *pathéno* means I provoke passion in both its meanings; I am acting, moving by an internal forceful *aésthima*, passion; I get inspired, excited; I suffer. Among Greek youth the word *pathéno* as in "when I hear this song *pathéno*," is common. The gestures accompanying it, such as hitting and holding the forehead, and the matching sounds, express both (sudden) suffering and extreme enjoyment.

A synonym of *pathéno* in this case is *pathéno*, I die. *Páthos* (passion) is the meeting point of *éros* and *thánatos* where the latter is an internal death, the death of the self because of and for the other; the moment that the self is both the self and a memory in the other. Death is a journey; a sensorial journey into the other. So is *éros*. The common expression during love making is *me péthanes* (you made me die, I died because of, for you and through you). *Éros* is desire. It also means appetite. The expression often used in vernacular Greek, e.g., from mother to child, to show extreme desire is "I'll eat you." The same expression is used for someone causing suffering, e.g., child to parent, "you ate me." In the journey of death, to the otherworld, the earth "eats" the body.

In these semantic currents we find no clear cut boundaries between the senses and emotions, the mind and body, pleasure and pain, the voluntary and the involuntary, and affective and aesthetic experience. Such culturally specific perspectives on sensory experience are not sheer comparative curiosities. They are crucial for opening up a self reflexive, culturally and historically informed consideration of the senses. Sensory semantics in Greek culture, among others, contain regional epistemologies, in-built theories, that provoke important cross-cultural methodological consequences.

The senses represent inner states not shown on the surface. They are also located in a social-material field outside of the body. Consider the Greek expression "his eyes witness fear" (*ta mátia tou martyráne fóvo*) and the English gloss "his eyes show fear." The latter speaks of fear as an inner psychological state, while "his eyes witness fear" can speak of fear as if it is out there, external to and autonomous of the body, and involuntarily marked on the senses. Here the sense organs become tracks, *semía*, where fear is received by the body. The sense organs function in the same manner that the material artifact can also function, that is as *semíon*, track, which one senses and a medium by which one senses. Thus the sensory is not only encapsulated within the body as an internal capacity or power, but is also dispersed out there on the surface of things as the latter's autonomous characteristics, which then can invade the body as perceptual experience. Here sensory interiors and exteriors constantly pass into each other in the creation of extra-personal significance.

A related saying, "his eyes witnessed him" or "betrayed him," and "I saw it in his eyes" (despite his talk), speaks of the involuntary aspect of sensory experience which discloses inner states not intended by the subject. Thus although "his speech" may have attempted to lie, "his eyes revealed the truth" *to my eyes*. The sense organs can exchange with each other. The senses are meaning-generating apparatuses that operate beyond consciousness and intention. The interpretation of and through the senses becomes a recovery of truth as collective, material experience.

The senses are also implicated in historical interpretation as witnesses or record-keepers of material experience. There is an autonomous circuit between inner and outer sensory states and fields, that constitutes an independent sphere of perceptual exchange and reciprocity. The senses, like language, are a social fact to the extent that they are a collective medium of communication that is both voluntary and involuntary, stylized and personal. For example, the Greek term for perception is *antílipsi* (*lípsi* means reception, while the prefix *antí* refers to equivalence, reciprocity, face to face, in place of and not only opposition as in English). *Antílipsi* is thus defined as the act of receiving in an exchange.

There is a corporate communication between the body and things, the person and the world, which points to the perceptual construction of truth as the involuntary disclosure of meaning through the senses. Although the senses are a social and collective institution like language, they *are not* reducible to language. Thus sensory meaning as truth, in Greece, introduces an ironic counterpoint to any linguistic discourse. What is being said may be relativized, contradicted or confirmed by embodied acts, gestures, and sensory affects. This process of confirmation or negation is a performative moment where gestures and/or a surround of artifacts are mobilized to bear or deny witness to language. Truth therefore is extra-linguistic and revealed through expression, performance, material culture and conditions of embodiment.

The involuntary circuit of the senses reveals that embodied performance is in part constructed out of the cross-communication of senses and things. This speaks of a social aesthetics that is not purely a contracted or negotiated synchrony but one that is embedded in, and inherited from, an autonomous network of object relations and prior sensory exchanges. Performance therefore is elicited by externality and history as much as it may come from within.

The sensory landscape and its meaning-endowed objects bear within them emotional and historical sedimentation that can provoke and ignite gestures, discourses and acts – acts which open up these objects' stratigraphy. Thus the surround of material culture is neither stable nor fixed, but inherently transitive, demanding connection and completion by the perceiver. Performance can be such an act of perceptual completion as opposed to being a manipulative theatrical display.[2] Performance is also a moment where the unconscious levels and accumulated layers of personal experience become conscious through material networks, independent of the performer. However, the mode and content of completion/connection with the sensory artifact is not determined in advance, it is not a communication with a Platonic essense, but rather it is a mutation of meaning and memory that refracts the mutual insertion of the perceiver and perceived in historical experience and possibly their mutual alienation from public culture, official memory and formal economies. This *performance is not "performative"* – the instantiation of a pre-existing code. It is a *poesis*, the making of something out of that which was previously experientially and culturally unmarked or even null and void. Here sensory memory, as the meditation on the historical substance of experience, is not mere repetition but transformation which brings the past into the present as a natal event. In this moment the actor is also the audience of his/her involuntary implication in a sensory horizon. This can be a moment of sensory self-reflexivity and because it is located within, and generated by, material forces, we can begin to see how material culture functions as an apparatus for the production of *social and historical reflexivity*.

Sour grapes

Not only have some foreign fruits arrived in Greek markets – it is no coincidence that in colloquial Greek a strange or weird person is referred to as "a strange fruit" or "a new fruit" – but also familiar fruits have made their timid appearance in fancy supermarkets at the "wrong season." For instance grapes, emblematic of the summer for Greeks, appeared in the winter under the sign "imported from EEC." Observing local women shopping, touching, picking and choosing, one notices that they pass them over as if they never noticed them, or commenting on how "sour they look." Sour implies not yet ripened, thus not in season, and so tasteless (*ánosta*). And while the EEC in this case becomes identified with sour grapes, a whole epoch, the present, is characterized as *ánosto*.

When and how does an epoch, a slice of history, become something *ánosto*? To say that aspects of daily life have become tasteless, to make parts substitute for the whole, implies that the capacity to synthesize perceptual experience, is only accessible through dispersed fragments. The movement from real or imagined wholes to parts and fragments is a metaphorical slide that captures the movement of history through a shifting perceptual focus. The capacity to replicate a sensorial culture resides in a dynamic interaction between perception, memory and a landscape of artifacts, organic and inorganic. This capacity can atrophy when that landscape, as a repository and horizon of historical experience, emotions, embedded sensibilities and hence social identities, dissolves into disconnected pieces. At the same time, what replaces it?

When new forms and items of an emerging material culture step in between a society's present perceptual existence and its residual socio-cultural identity, they can be tasteless because people may no longer have the perceptual means for seeking identity and experience in new material forms. Because the cultural instruments for creating meaning out of material experience have been dispersed with the now discarded past sensory landscape. The latter was didactic as much as it was an object of perception and utility. The characterization *ánosto* (tasteless) then deals with the cultural incapacity to codify past, present, and anticipatory experiences at the level of sensory existence. This is so because such codifying practices are never purely mentalist but embedded in and borne by a material world of talking objects.

This is why the enthusiastic reception of the "new" is imported, culturally prepared and programmed with the simultaneous fabrication or promise of new sensory powers – the latter are automatically bonded with the items of the penetrating culture. Thus each commodity form is introduced through the creation of its own self-generating experience and memory. The latter are themselves promised as substitutions, replacements and improvements of prior sensory experience.

In cultures that undergo colonial and post-colonial experiences of transformation, the experience of tastlessness can be self-imposed for they have internalized "the eye of the Other" (Seremetakis 1984) and see their own culture and residual experience from a position of defamiliarization and estrangement. This can result in a newly constructed archaicization of recent and unreconcilable experiences, practices, and narratives. Particular and now idiosyncratic cultural experiences are described as having long disappeared, as lost, when in fact they are quite recent and their memory sharp. As one moves deeper into conversation with people, their intimacy with these distant practices comes out as fairy tales, anecdotes, folklore, and myth. The historical repression of memory that the cultural periphery can impose on itself is as rapid, shallow, profound and experientially painful as any other disorienting penetration of metropolitan modernity. The discourse on loss is an element of public culture, an official ideological stance taken towards the past that aligns the speaker with the normative view of the present, i.e., modern times. Yet as the discourse of loss congeals into an element of public culture, that which has never been lost, but which can no longer be said, shared and exchanged, becomes the content of unreconciled personal and privatized experience.[3]

Sensory and historical multiplicity

What can be lost is not the senses but the memory of the senses. The erasure of this memory renders the senses as imperceptible as the passing of Aphrodite's peach. There is no such thing as one moment of perception and then another of memory, representation or objectification. Mnemonic processes are intertwined with the sensory order in such a manner as to render each perception a re-perception. Re-perception is the creation of meaning through the interplay, witnessing, and cross-metaphorization of co-implicated sensory spheres. Memory cannot be confined to a purely mentalist or subjective sphere. It is a culturally mediated material practice that is activated by embodied acts and semantically dense objects. This material approach to memory places the senses in time and speaks to memory as both meta-sensory capacity and as a sense organ in-it-self.

Memory as a distinct meta-sense transports, bridges and crosses all the other senses. Yet memory is internal to each sense, and the senses are as divisible and indivisible from each other as each memory is separable and intertwined with others. Memory is the horizon of sensory experiences, storing and restoring the experience of each sensory dimension in another, as well as dispersing and finding sensory records outside the body in a surround of entangling objects and places. Memory and the senses are commingled in so far as they are equally involuntary experiences. Their involuntary dimension points to their encompassment by a trans-individual social and somatic landscape.

The particular effacement of sensory memory in modernity, is mainly a consequence of an extreme division of labor, perceptual specialization and rationalization. The senses, in modernity, are detached from each other, re-functioned and externalized as utilitarian instruments, and as media and objects of commodification. The carving out and partitioning of separate domains of perceptual acquisition also authorizes the sheer literality of sensory experience. The literal is a symbolic logic produced by the scientific rationalization of the senses and/or by a culture of specialized consumption. The result is the privatized sense organ (see Jameson 1981; Harvey 1989; Crary 1991). The literality of the thing, as its most digestible and commodifiable dimension, allows hyper-consumption. Literality, as a cultural code, prescribes and insures norms of limited, functional and repetitious engagement with the disposable commodity unit. The paradox is that, in the repeated performance of consumption, the commodity form, despite its episodic character and the ongoing obsolescence of the new, is elaborated as the dominant perceptual logic of things. In the high turn-over of commodity experiences, each object, each material experience, is the absence of the other and the sensory investment it provoked. Each episode of consumption is relatively absolute and quickly totalizing because it never lingers long enough in the senses as social memory to be stitched into a historical fabric with the others it has displaced.

As Ernst Bloch (1991), Walter Benjamin (1969, 1973, 1978) and the Surrealists insisted, the cosmos of economically discarded cultural artifacts constitutes a vast social unconscious of sensory-emotive experience that potentially offers up hidden and now inadmissible counter-narratives of once valued lifeworlds. These critics pitted the latent utopian sensibility, locked within the dysfunctional and the useless, against the functional, utilitarian and compulsory wastage of a political culture of fashion. Benjamin, Bloch, the artist Max Ernst, as chroniclers of the first encounter with late modernity, recovered utopian feeling, alterity and cultural procreation in the lost, negated, de-commodified attics and basements of everyday life. It was in these sites that they relocated social memory as a sphere that tripped-up the closures of public memory, official histories and the idea of progress. Within this framework, the article invested with surplus memory and meanings becomes a separate and distinct (monadic) memory-form in-it-self; it carries within it the sensorial off-print of its human use and triggered desires; when it is discarded and rendered inaudible, an entire anthropology is thrown away with it.

Mnemonic sensory experience implies that the artifact bears within it layered commensal meanings (shared substance and material reciprocities), and histories. It can also be an instrument for mobilizing the perceptual penetration of historical matter. As a sensory form in itself, the artifact can provoke the emergence, the awakening of the layered memories, and thus the senses contained within it. The object invested with sensory memory speaks; it provokes re-call as a missing, detached yet antiphonic element of the perceiver. The sensory connection between perceiver and artifact completes the latter in an unexpected and non-prescribed fashion because the perceiver is also the recipient of the unintended historical after-effects of the artifact's presence *or* absence.

Commensal events devoted to the consumption, distribution, sharing and exchange of substances, are usually seen as performances and protocols whose synchronic rules and structure are kept in people's heads like a pre-programmed game plan (as in Douglas 1991). Instead, I have been suggesting that the artifact laden with perceptual recall, is a temporal conduit within which commensal histories and perceptual topographies are borne through time and space, and in a manner that often runs counter to the official cultural codes for the disposition of things. Thus no object or substance can acquire meaning and value by simply being inserted into rules, times and spaces of commensality which "permit" it to be consumed, shared, exchanged and enjoyed. Rather, artifacts are in themselves histories of prior commensal events and emotional sensory exchanges, and it is these very histories that are exchanged at commensal events and that qualify the object as commensal in the first place. At the same time, the historicity of the commensal artifact can be effaced, forgotten or denied by current cultural, economic and commensal codes. Recovery of the artifact's commensal depth, in this context, reanimates alternative codes and other relations of shared experiential substance.

This approach shows the extent to which the senses are embodied in objects that can provide a multiplicity of possible and always autonomous prospects on their human authors (authorship is not only linked to production but also to use and consumption as identity-conferring performances). Artifacts as memory-forms cannot only be viewed from the perspective of their sanctioned use and literal functions. The latter mainly respond to the pre-set cultural limits of specific conditions of production and overtly prescribed modes of consumption. The artifact as the bearer of sensory multiplicity is a catchment zone of perceptions, a lens through which the senses can be explored from their other side: matter as both the terminus of human actions and the carrier of surplus meanings of those actions. Thus it is an unrecognized double of the human body. Between the body and its non-identical doubles, the senses exist in transit, as multi-directional channels of meaning whether one moves from person to person, thing to thing, person to thing, or thing to person.

The memory of the senses speaks to a *reception theory of material culture*, from both the different perspectives of interacting, perceiving subjects and that of the perceptible talking object (formed from a constellation of human acts). Meaning-endowed objects constitute indigenous, regional nets of sensory receipt. Sediments of sensory memory stratify the artifact as depth, forming a diachronic volume, from which all historical matter, valued and devalued, may seep as expressive material culture. The memory of the senses runs against the socio-economic currents that treat artifacts and personal material experiences as dust. *Dust* is created by any perceptual stance that hastily traverses the object world, skims over its surface, treating it as a nullity that casts no meaning into our bodies, or recovers no stories from our past.

Stillness

Articles invested with sensory memory, with regional narratives, are frequently non-synchronous; they are out of the immediate continuum of socially constructed material presence and value. They drag the after-effects of recent, yet now inadmissible social experience. Society does not change all at once or in one piece. And dominant cultural codes are not the only inheritance that we transmit to ourselves and to others who come after. Social transformation is uneven. And it is this unevenness, the non-contemporaneity of the social formation with it-self, that preserves and produces non-synchronous, interruptive articles, spaces, acts and narratives. These can stand like a dark stone against the onward rush and transparency of ahistorical time and part the encompassing and mythic seamless present. There are expressions of non-synchronicity which become material encounters with cultural absence and possibility. There are islands of historicity, discontinuous punctures, that render the imperceptible perceptible as they produce marked moments – tidal pools where an experiential cosmos can be mapped out in miniature.

These islands may emancipate sensory experience from the social structure of silence. The artifacts as memory-forms are passageways into the autonomous entanglements of everyday material experience. They can halt the customary unfolding of everyday life by generating other languages against the blanketing of commonsensical codes that rationalize the skimmed experience of the everyday as totality.

Against the flow of the present, there is a stillness in the material culture of historicity; those things, spaces, gestures, and tales that signify the perceptual capacity for elemental historical creation. *Stillness* is the moment when the buried, the discarded, and the forgotten escape to the social surface of awareness like life-supporting oxygen. It is the moment of exit from historical dust.

What was previously imperceptible and now became "real" was in fact always there as an element of the material culture of the unconscious. The imperceptible has a social structure based on culturally prescribed zones of non-experience and canceled meaning. At this juncture, a politics of the senses is brought into play. Everyday life is always a privileged site of political colonization because the everyday, prepared as a zone of devaluation, forgetfulness, and inattention, is also the site where new political identities can be fabricated by techniques of distraction; where power can make its own self-referential histories by absenting any thing that relativizes it. Everyday life is mythicized as the atopic and as the repository of passivity precisely because it harbors the most elusive depths, obscure corners, transient corridors that evade political grids and controls. Yet everyday life is also the zone of lost glances, oblique views and angles where micro-practices leak through the crevices and cracks of official cultures and memories.

Monads and nomads

There are substances, spaces and times that can trigger stillness. I think of the old Greek who halted from his daily activity in the heat of the mid-day to slowly sip his coffee, each sip followed by a sigh of release. This was a "resting point," a moment of contemplation, the moment he began to re-taste the day. Introduced by aroma and taste, this was a moment of stillness. Each sip and sigh signaling a deepening in thought, returning "*logismós* (thought) to distant times." Coffee is *sintrofiá* (friendly companion), as the saying goes. *Sintrofiá* generates a moment of meta-commentary in which the entire scenography of present and past social landscapes are arrayed before his consciousness: the contemporary political situation, familial events, village circumstances, the weather, crops, international news, all mixed together. There is a perceptual compression of space and time that is encapsulated in the small coffee cup, from which he takes a sip every other minute, and while feeling the sediments on his tongue, he makes his passage through this diversity.

This is the moment that he will think and express, alone or with other drinkers, his *parápono*, a meta-commentary, as an exchange and sharing, of the cycle of pains, emotions, and joys of everyday life. *Parápono* is the narrative of everyday life. It is not a complaint in the English sense of the term, for it does not necessarily require redress or rectification. It can be a sheer presentation of the substance of everyday experience which resists resolution, defies any sense of an ending. *Parápono* (*pónos* means pain) can be but the establishment of the truthfulness of that experience, and for that to happen he needs a *sintrofiá*. It is worth pausing to listen to the etymology of the word. It derives from the verb *tréfo* meaning I feed, raise, cultivate (dreams, ideas, hopes). *Sin-tréfo* (-ome), composed of the prefix *sin* (co-) and *tréfo*, means I feed (I am fed) together with, I solidify, congeal, unify. *Sintrofiá* in colloquial Greek refers to a group of friends, a close companion (human or non-human).

The generic experiences of everyday life transmuted into the aroma and taste of the coffee are sipped along with it. *Ton pótise pharmáki*, "watering someone with poison (pain or negative experience)" or "with joy," is a saying that captures the body's saturation of everyday experience as substance. In popular songs we also hear the expression "I will drink you sip by sip" which evokes a slow maturation of a human relationship, a duration that brings into play the senses and memory. When something is good or beautiful, one desires to "drink it from a glass" (*na to piís sto potíri*). The experience that embodies sensory, emotional engagement and remembrance is received in an encapsulated form; shifted from its origin into a surrogate container, a storage vehicle, a substance from which it can be released, liberated at moments of stillness. Encapsulation forms the plurality of the unnarrativized, taken for granted, and imperceptible into a meta-narrative. The meta-narrative is perceived or spoken as a slowing down of "normal" temporal passage. This decompression of routine temporal experience and its subsequent re-compression into surrogate vehicle and substance is not a stop. It is a different movement within time that captures everyday temporal experience from another oblique angle as if the sensory array is shifted from one point of consciousness to another, from one side of the body to another, which gives rise to a new or alternative perceptual landscape. It is a moment of poetry. It can be a moment of vision.

> But to speak of Greek poetry is to speak of politics – not so much in the rarefied aesthetic sense of the old duality: poetry versus philosophy, that old Aristotelian kind of politics; rather, in the raw sense of poetry as crisis, as the rhythm and heartbeat of a nation's identity. And, politics as when a soldier says "in my *politike zoe* I am a carpenter," meaning in his "civilian life," using precisely the same term normally used for a "political life." Poetry, then, as one of the primary acts of the *zoon politikon*. And politics as when a civic model becomes workable *after* it has been heralded by the vanguard art of that culture, which has always been poetry.
>
> (Chioles 1993)

I have talked about history; now I can speak of the political. How is the political experienced on the level of the senses? The political and poetic have to be synthesized at the level of everyday experience. *Poesis* as a component of the everyday is crucial to the creation of the *zóon politikón*. This speaks to a politics of sensory creation and reception as a politics of everyday life.

More than that, *poesis* (poetry) means both making and imagining (Seremetakis 1991). It thus takes various forms. Rehearing Diotima's response to Socrates,

> Any action which is the cause of something to emerge from nonexistence to existence is poesis, thus all craft works are kinds of poesis, and their creators are all poets. . . . Yet, they are not called, as you know, poets, but have different names; out of the general meaning of poetry, one

part has been separated, that which deals with music and meter, and is given the name of the
whole. Indeed this part alone is named poetry . . .

(Plato 1976: 150)

I can think of women's embroidering and weaving throughout the centuries. It always occurred after daily
routine labor. And although it involved work and the creation of articles of economic and symbolic value, it
has always been experienced by women as a "resting moment." After ordering her immediate world, her
household, the fields, she will halt, step back and begin to weave dreams, desires, musings into cloth.
Women never embroider one piece or one design. They embroider series and sequences that cohere into a
visual, tactile story. An embroidery piece captures a dream or an imaging, and women do not dream once.
Such multiple, sequential production is not necessarily motivated by the accumulation of wealth or caused
by economic circumstances demanding overproduction. It is their form of writing which, spread on
cloths, ornaments and names people and spaces, within and beyond the household. Just like the ornaments
Yannis Ritsos, the celebrated poet, left us: "To you I leave my clothes, my poems, my shoes. Wear them on
Sundays." (Ritsos 1991)

The embroiderer, alone or with other women, borrows and elaborates the designs of others in a form
of exchange. She is externalizing pieces of the self to make it public. Women circulate knowledge through
multiple designs and spaces which they cover, protect and ornament. It is this transfer of the self into
substance that disseminates a history of the person in dispersal. Embroidering engages a self-reflexive
femininity: she will endow artifacts with her content and yet allow them to speak for themselves.

In one of my return trips to Greece, during our mid-day coffee, my mother opened a box she had been
storing in her closet for years. One by one she took out dozens of beautiful embroidered and finely
crocheted pieces of all shapes and sizes, made to ornament different parts of a house. As she displayed them
she named each one after its maker, "This is from Voula for your name day last year," "This is from your
aunt's friend two years ago for your book (publication)" and so on. As she spread them out I was
taken through a journey to different times. A moment of stillness. These hand-made, tactile traces on the
invisible past of my life represented their way of rendering me present in my absence. It was an imaginary
historicization of my life-path and events which were inaccessible to those women as direct experience.
Some of those donors I had never met, and others I knew very little; some I will not see again for they are
long dead. Yet they, through narrative, knew me well. Well enough to exchange with my memory, as they
embodied it in cloth. These gifts did not require a return – "*haláli sou*," as they said.

I left Athens and traveled to the Peloponnese for my usual fieldwork. After I settled in my "first post," I
looked out the window one morning and I had that irresistible desire to eat *hórta* (wild greens). I took a
knife to collect them and jumped outside. Absorbed by the action, I heard the voice of a middle aged
neighbor remarking on it, in the usual Greek way of asking a rhetorical question to state his approval: "Ah!
your mother has taught you, eh?" Without thinking, and as he walked by, I smiled and nodded "yes." A few
moments later I wondered "why on earth did I say yes?" Neither my mother nor anybody else as a matter of
fact had taught me how to identify, select, cut and clean these greens. Suspicious of my harvest, I ran to a
next door neighbor to check if it were edible. Although I had missed a few kinds, the ones I had collected
were right. She also named them, thus I matched for the first time names I knew with the corresponding
greens. Yet the question stuck in my mind: how did I know how to collect *hórta*? And more important, why
didn't I have this skill and knowledge, nor the urge, to harvest *hórta* before I left Greece?

I had been eating *hórta* (boiled greens with oil, lemon and oregano) all my life, whether in Greece
or Astoria, USA (though in Astoria, one finds only domestic substitutes). I had tasted them that is, and
I had heard all kinds of talks around them. When I went out to collect them, the sensory memory of taste,
order, orality stored in the body was transferred to vision and tactility. My body involuntarily knew what
I consciously did not.

This knowing emerged in "exile." The absence of *hórta* and the memory of it shifted to the senses and to action. What was an outward act of cutting was in fact an inward act of diving into the self, of space-time and sensory compression, as well as of sensory switching that culminated in the harvesting. This was a resting point, a moment of stillness, where an entire past sensory landscape was translated into a present act; and in the course of doing so, one sense educated and enculturated the other. This was an involuntary process, a moment of sensory stasis where one sense became the meta-narrative of another through memory. Thus sensory stasis is not always cultivated as in the mid-day coffee sipping. It can occur through forced experiences of crisis, separation and cross cultural contact. For these moments release hidden substances of the past. It is the very absence of referents, surfaces and textures that lifts them out of the banality of structural silence imposed by a culture or social order and allows a previously by-passed content to be released as history.

Notes

1   To conduct an etymological analysis of a term or concept is not to assume that all the sediments of meaning are operant at all times and with a uniform prevalence. However, etymological analysis is complementary to the uneven historical development of European peripheries which is characterized by the incomplete and disjunctive articulation of the pre-modern, different phases within modernity, and the post-modern. Etymology captures the uneven shifts of semantic history that may be present at any given moment in a society. Thus the American sense of the term nostalgia can be discerned in Greek state discourses and in the popular press. Both institutions tend to deliver discourses on identity and value loss and consequent societal crises. Yet, in its various etymological senses discussed here, *nostalghía* is widely heard in the language of everyday life, as well as in Greek popular music and poetry.

2   See my discussion and critique, in the Greek context, of rhetorical-display models of performance in *The Last Word* (1991).

3   The notions of authenticity and inauthenticity are symbiotic concepts that equally repress and silence non-contemporaneous and discordant cultural experiences and sensibilities. Thus the modernist critic would look at Greek society and dismiss any residues and incongruities emanating from the pre-modern as both romantic and invented (see for instance Hobsbawm and Ranger on Scotland (1985) and in the context of Greece, Faubion (1988). In both cases, static impositions of the polarity authentic/inauthentic led to the dismissal of important discontinuous cultural systems and sensibilities that have been repositioned within the modern as non-synchronous elements.

References

Benjamin, Walter. 1969. "The Work of Art in the Age of Mechanical Reproduction." *Illuminations*. Hannah Arendt, editor. Trans. H. Zohn. New York: Schocken, pp. 83–109, 217–51, 253–64.

——. 1973. *Charles Baudelaire: A Lyric Poet in the Era of High Capitalism*. Trans. Harry Zohn. London: NLB.

——. 1978. "Surrealism: The Last Snapshot of the European Intelligentsia." *Reflections*. New York: Harcourt Brace Jovanovich, pp. 177–92.

Bloch, Ernst. 1991. *Heritage of Our Times*. Trans. Neville & Stephen Plaice. Berkeley: University of California Press.

Chioles, John. 1993. "Poetry and Politics: The Greek Cultural Dilemma." *Ritual, Power and the Body: Historical Perspectives on the Representation of Greek Women*. C. Nadia Seremetakis, editor. New York: Pella Publishing Co. (Greek Studies), pp. 151–73.

Crary, Jonathan. 1991. *Techniques of the Observer: On Vision and Modernity in the Nineteenth Century*. Cambridge, Mass: MIT Press.

Douglas, Mary, ed. 1991. *Constructive Drinking: Perspectives on Drink from Anthropology*. Cambridge: Cambridge University Press.

Faubion, James. 1988. "Possible Modernities." *Cultural Anthropology*, vol. 3, no. 4, pp. 365–78.

Harvey, David. 1989. *The Condition of Postmodernity: An Inquiry into the Origins of Cultural Change*. Oxford: Blackwell.

Hobsbawm, Eric and Terence Ranger, editors. 1985. *The Invention of Tradition*. Cambridge: Cambridge University Press.

Jameson, Fredric. 1981. *The Political Unconscious: Narrative as a Socially Symbolic Act*. Ithaca: Cornell University Press.

Plato. 1976. (The Symposium) *Platonos Symposion*. I. Sikoutris, editor. Athens: Estia.

Ricoeur, Paul. 1984. *Time and Narrative*. Vol. 1. Chicago: University of Chicago Press.

Ritsos, Yannis. 1991. *3x111 Tristichs*. Trans. Rick Newton. New York: Pella Publishing Co. (Greek Studies).

Seremetakis, C. Nadia. 1984. "The Eye of the Other: Watching Death in Rural Greece." *Journal of Modern Hellenism*, vol. 1, no. 1, pp. 63–77.

—— . 1991. *The Last Word: Women, Death and Divination in Inner Mani*. Chicago: University of Chicago Press.

—— . 1993. "Gender, Culture and History: On the Anthropologies of Ancient and Modern Greece." *Ritual, Power and the Body: Historical Perspectives on the Representation of Greek Women*. C. Nadia Seremetakis, editor. New York: Pella Publishing Co. (Greek Studies).

—— . 1994a. "Two Years After: The Last Word in Greece and Beyond." *The Last Word in the Ends of Europe: Divination, Death, Women*. C. Nadia Seremetakis. In Greek. Athens: Nea Synora/Livanis Publishing Co.

—— . 1994b. "Gender Studies or Women's Studies: Theoretical and Paedagogical Issues, Research Agendas and Directions." (Keynote speech, UNESCO International Conference on Gender Studies, Athens 1993.) *Australian Feminist Studies*, Summer 1994.

Chapter 21

Koichi Iwabuchi

MARKETING 'JAPAN': JAPANESE CULTURAL PRESENCE UNDER A GLOBAL GAZE [1998]

Source: Koichi Iwabuchi (1998) 'Marketing "Japan": Japanese Cultural Presence Under a Global Gaze', *Japanese Studies*, 18, 2, 1998, pp. 66–75.

Koichi Iwabuchi is faced with a conundrum: how is it that a country (Japan) that makes so much of the globally circulating commodity culture seems to leave such little presence of Japanese-ness? For Iwabuchi, the smell and sound of America is ever present – it is there in every high street McDonald's and Kentucky Fried Chicken, echoing in every power chord pop record and rock ballad. A feel and touch of European-ness might circulate along with every Ikea store. The Japanese cultural commodities that circulate so successfully seem, in relation, to lack any connection to Japanese bodies. Companies like Sony and Nintendo make devices that are disseminated widely but, in the place of strong cultural identity, only offer a sense of trans-national efficiency. Even some of the most popular character games produced by Japanese companies distinctly play down any relation to Japanese populations. Thus the game characters of Super Mario Brothers are designed to look Italian rather than Japanese, and the human characters that populate the fantastic worlds of Pokémon, Digimon and Yu-Gi-Oh all have exaggeratedly round eyes.

One of the initial values, then, of Iwabuchi's work is that it warns us against assuming that cultural reach follows economic reach, and to sensitise us to the fact that Americanisation, for instance, is qualitatively different from Japanese-isation. Iwabuchi's understanding of cultural globalisation is rich in complexity and understands that cultural disseminators might take a range of forms. For instance, one of the cultural roles that Japan plays is as cultural translator. Thus Taiwan might be buying into an American pop idiom, but they will be doing so by adopting and adapting pop music coming from Japan. The fact that the Japanese pop that is being adapted is in turn an adoption and alteration of American pop vernacular casts Japan as crucial cultural intermediary for the spread of a sort of global-Americanism design culture.

Iwabuchi's choice of the word 'odourless' to describe the lack of Japanese-ness in globalised Japan is worth remarking on. Why 'odour'? Why not 'taste' or 'touch' or 'vision' or 'sound'? Is Iwabuchi just using odourless-ness as a metaphor for what might be described as culturally thin dissemination? To a degree it is being used metaphorically and when we think about the over-presence of an Anglo-American pop vernacular then the sense of 'odour' must be an analogy. But it is a strong analogy nevertheless, offering a whiff of hair spray and the body smells of gyrating mass crowds (that sweet smell of perfumed sweat). Iwabuchi's use of the word 'odour' insists on the importance of bodies in cultural change and exchange, and in measuring the unevenness of dissemination. Odour connects us to bodies; bodies that work, that eat, that have sex, that dance and drink. The dissemination of odourless culture produces a cultural mirage that is literally, and metaphorically, disembodied.

Further reading: Buck 2000; Daniels 1999; Drobnick 2006; Iwabuchi 2002; Tobin 1992.

A DOMINANT IMAGE of Japan is of a faceless economic superpower with a disproportionate lack of cultural influence upon the world. Japan has money and technologies but cannot diffuse its culture. The culture of Japan that is considered worth appreciating is most usually something traditional which is to be put on exhibit to show its irreducible uniqueness.[1] Contrary to this assumption, however, Japan has long been exporting cultural products overseas, particularly to Asia. This paper explores the Japanese cultural presence overseas that is becoming increasingly conspicuous in the 1990s.

While acknowledging that the textual analysis and audience study of Japanese popular culture are indispensable to understanding a comprehensive picture of the Japanese cultural presence overseas, in this paper I will focus on the marketing strategies – of both Japanese and local cultural industries in Asia – that direct its distribution. One reason for the comparative invisibility of Japan's cultural presence in Asia is Japan's peculiar position in the global audio-visual market as an exporter of what may be called 'culturally odourless' products, that is, products which, in contrast to American export icons such as Coca Cola or McDonald's, do not immediately conjure images of the country of origin in the minds of consumers.

Figure 21.1   Pokémon and trainer (photograph by Ben Highmore).

Increasing economic power in Asia and the proliferation of media space in the region has dramatically increased the export of Japanese popular culture. However, Japanese cultural industries still tend to be less concerned with the direct export of Japanese cultural products than with selling the know-how of indigenising the West (America).

Japanese cultural exports are nevertheless becoming increasingly conspicuous in the 1990s as local industries of other parts of Asia now find commercial value in promoting Japanese popular culture in the local market. This local initiative also gives Japanese cultural industries more confidence in the exportability of Japanese products. I will suggest that the ascent of a Japanese cultural presence in Asia clearly not only shows that Japanese cultural industries have become key players of media globalisation. It also testifies to the emerging currents of transnational cultural flow brought about by globalisation processes.

Culturally odourless products and globalisation

In July 1997, a Japanese TV news reporter covering an ASEAN meeting in Kuala Lumpur joked that there were three requirements for becoming a member of ASEAN. First, one must play golf; second, one must love karaoke. Compared to these cultural practices, which are not particularly Southeast Asian but are common among the male-dominated business circles and the middle class in many parts of Asia, the third requirement is very much Southeast Asian: last but not least, the reporter continued with a faint smile, one must be able to eat durian, the delicious but pungent-smelling fruit of Southeast Asia.

This joke brings to mind a distinctive feature of the nature of Japanese cultural presence in Asia, the transnational cultural flow of Japanese influence in general, and particularly of its audio-visual products: Japanese cultural presence tends to be 'culturally odourless' and its cultural products are destined to be localised in overseas markets. That playing golf for business and enjoying karaoke are even jokingly considered requirements of membership of ASEAN points to Japanese cultural influences in Southeast Asia and elsewhere in the region. However, these activities do not invoke images of 'Japan' and thus of Japanese cultural presence, as they have been fully localised, incorporated as integral parts of business culture and the everyday life of the middle classes in the region to the extent that they represent consumer modernity in Southeast Asia. At the same time, as the punch line of the joke reminds us, such common signifiers of modernity in the region are not enough to articulate distinctive local identities. No matter how karaoke and golf signify common business practices and the preferred leisure activities of an emerging affluent middle class in the region, it is not the localised cultural products of foreign (Japanese) origin but the fruit with an insuppressible local odour that ultimately confers the Southeast Asian-ness of ASEAN.

The difference between the presence and the influence of foreign cultures and the significance of local odour is a key to understanding the strategies behind Japanese exports of media/audio-visual products. The major audio-visual products Japan exports overseas may be characterised as the 'culturally odourless' three Cs: consumer technologies, such as VCRs, karaoke and the Walkman; comics/cartoons (animation); and computer/video games. I use the term 'cultural odour' to focus on the way in which the cultural presence of a country of origin and images or ideas of its way of life are positively associated with a particular product in the consumption process. Any product may have various kinds of cultural association with the country of its production, but it is when the image of the lifestyle of the country of origin is strongly evoked as the appeal of the product that the 'cultural odour' of cultural commodities concerns me. The way in which the cultural odour of a particular product becomes 'fragrance' – a socially acceptable, desirable smell – is not determined simply by the perception of the consumer that something is 'made in Japan'. Neither is it necessarily related to the functions, influences or the quality of a particular product or image. It has more to do with discursively constructed images of the country of origin, which are widely disseminated in the world. The influence of McDonald's throughout the world, for example, is enormous in terms of the bureaucratisation and standardisation of food.[2] But no less important to its international success is its association with an attractive image of an American way of life. As Featherstone argues,

> It is a product from a superior global centre, which has long represented itself as the centre. For those on the periphery it offers the possibility of the psychological benefits of identifying with the powerful. Along with the Marlboro Man, Coca-Cola, Hollywood, Sesame Street, rock music and American football insignia, McDonald's is one of a series of icons of the American way of life. They have become associated with transposable themes which are central to consumer culture, such as youth, fitness, beauty, luxury, romance, freedom.[3]

McDonald's of course does not inherently represent 'America'. It is the discursive formation of the latter that confers McDonald's symbolic meanings.

In contrast, the dominant image of 'Japan' constructed by a Western Orientalist discourse and reinforced by a self-Orientalising discourse in Japan, is mainly concerned with 'traditional' and particular-istic cultures and, more recently, hi-tech sophistication.[4] The Sony Walkman is also an important cultural commodity which has various influences on our everyday life. Du Gay et al. chose it as the cultural artefact most suited to the multi-layered analyses of cultural studies.[5] The Sony Walkman, they argue, may signify 'Japanese-ness' in terms of miniaturisation, technical sophistication and high quality. Such 'Japanese-nesses' are analytically important but not especially relevant to Walkman's appeal at a consumer level. The use of Walkman does not evoke images or ideas of a Japanese lifestyle, even if consumers know it is made in Japan and appreciate 'Japanese-ness' in terms of its sophisticated technology. Unlike American commod-ities, as Featherstone points out, 'Japanese consumer goods do not seek to sell on the back of a Japanese way of life'[6] and they lack any influential 'idea of Japan'.[7]

The cultural odour of a product is also closely associated with racial and bodily images of a country of origin. Japan's 'three Cs' are cultural artefacts and present an imagery in which the bodily, racial and ethnic characteristics are erased or softened. This is particularly evident in Japanese animation where the characters, for the most part, do not look 'Japanese'. Such non-Japanese-ness is called *mu-kokuseki*. This literally means something or someone lacking any nationality, but also implies the erasure of racial or ethnic characteristics and any context that would embed the characters in a particular culture or country. Internationally acclaimed Japanese animation director Oshii Mamoru suggests that when Japanese anima-tors and cartoonists are sketching attractive characters, they *unconsciously* choose not to draw 'realistic' Japanese figures.[8] In his case the characters tend to be modelled on Caucasian types.

Even if Japanese animators do not consciously draw *mu-kokuseki* characters in order to export their animations overseas, it is no accident that Japan has become a major exporter of animations and computer games. Japanese animation industries always have the global market in mind and are aware that the non-Japanese-ness of characters works to their advantage in the export market. Since Tezuka Osamu's *Astro Boy* in the early 1960s, Japanese animation has long been consumed overseas. Japan routinely exports animation films. Animated films occupied 56% of all TV exports from Japan in 1980–1981[9] and 58% in 1992–1993.[10] While other film genres are mostly exported in the original Japanese language, only 1% of animated exports were in Japanese. This implies that animation is routinely intended for export.[11] Similarly, the producers and creators of game software *intentionally* make the characters of computer games look non-Japanese because they are clearly conscious that the market is global.[12] Mario, the principal character of the popular computer game Super Mario Brothers, for example, does not invoke an image of Japan. Both his name and appearance are intended to be Italian. Consumers and audiences of Japanese animation and games may be aware of the Japanese origin of these commodities, but they perceive little 'Japanese bodily odour'.

Sony, from the outset, has also had a strong policy of becoming a global company. The name of the company and its products, such as Walkman, are in English, the world language. At the same time, what characterises Sony (and Japanese manufacturers in general) as a significant global company is its marketing strategy, which is committed to local market differences. This global marketing strategy is another of Japan's significant contributions to the world of commodities. It is best expressed by what Sony calls 'global localisation' or 'glocalisation'. In order to penetrate different local markets at once, global companies try to 'transcend vestigial national differences and to create standardised global markets, whilst remaining sensitive to the peculiarities of local markets and differentiated consumer segments'.[13] This strategy is not an exclusively Japanese practice. The term 'glocalisation' has apparently become a marketing buzz-word of the global business world. Its entry in *The Oxford Dictionary of New Words*, however, acknowledges its origination in Japan:

> . . . modelled on Japanese *dochakuka* (deriving from *dochaku* 'living on one's own land'), origin-
> ally the agricultural principle of adapting one's farming technique to local conditions, but also
> adopted in Japanese business for global localization, a global outlook adapted to local
> conditions.[14]

It is indeed an interesting question why the term 'glocal' was originally used by Japanese companies, but we should not regard the act of *dochakuka* (indigenisation) as a unique cultural essence of Japan.[15] What should be borne in mind, however, is that cultural borrowing, appropriation, hybridisation and indigenisation are, as the ASEAN joke suggests, common practices in the global cultural flow. What is more relevant to this paper is how Japanese companies *imagine* Japan's position in the global cultural flow when they develop strategies of glocalisation. Behind such developments we can discern the engagement of Japanese companies in efforts to suppress Japanese 'odour' in order to market their products overseas.

Of particular importance here is that, although originally deployed by manufacturers of consumer goods, globalisation strategies can also be discerned in Japanese music and television industries attempting to enter Asian markets. Their marketing strategies appear to be based on two assumptions. The first is that Japan's successful indigenisation of foreign (Western) cultural influence presents a prototype for other Asian countries to follow. Since World War II, Japanese popular culture has been deeply influenced by American media. There has been no policy of imposing any quota on foreign popular culture in the audio-visual market since the war. Japan quickly localised these influences by imitating and partly appropriating the original, rather than being dominated by American products and 'colonised' by America. Although Japanese TV programming relied enormously upon imports from Hollywood in the 1950s and early 1960s, for example, since the mid-1960s the imbalance has drastically diminished. From as early as in 1980 just 5% of programmes have been imported.[16] Japan is now the only country, besides the USA, whose domestic TV programme market is almost self-sufficient. This is not to say that no foreign popular culture is consumed in Japan, but testifies to a widely discerned empirical tendency that locally produced media products tend to be more popular than imported ones, even though they may entirely imitate the products of foreign origin.[17] And what the Japanese experiences teach Japanese cultural industries is that this empirical tendency can be marketed in other parts of Asia.

At the same time, the question of the universality of Japanese cultural products and of Japanese cultural hegemony also has much to do with Japanese originality in developing glocalisation. Until recently there has been no strong impetus on the part of Japanese cultural industries to export popular culture to other countries. There are several reasons for this, including the existence of an affluent Japanese market and the historical obstacle of the memory of Japanese colonialism in exporting Japanese culture to other parts of Asia. But it can also be argued that low exports are explained by the notion of 'cultural discount'.[18] This concept explains the diminishing attractiveness of a particular TV programme in other cultures due to cultural differences based on style, values or beliefs. Cultural prestige, Western cultural hegemony, the universalism of the United States and the prevalence of the English language are advantageous to Hollywood. However, Japanese TV industries themselves seem to believe that their products would suffer a high cultural discount overseas. If 'culturally odourless' products consciously or unconsciously lack Japanese bodily images, the imagery of TV programmes and popular music is inescapably represented through living Japanese bodies. While Japanese cultural industries have been unsure of the exportability of distinctively Japanese products, they are confident that other Asian countries will follow the same path as Japan in terms of a rapid indigenisation of foreign (American) popular culture.

Finding local pop stars in Asia

Although the influence of the recent economic and currency crisis in Asia is yet to be seen, Asia has become the hottest market for global media industries in the 1990s. In entering the Asian market, localisation has become a key word to the success of global media industries. For example, STAR TV was struggling with cultural and linguistic differences in Asia; now their strategy is changing from pan-Asian programmes to localised programmes. The lesson STAR TV has learned is that exporting English-language programmes produced in Hollywood is no longer enough; thus Rupert Murdoch has announced 'we've committed ourselves to learning the nuances of the region's diverse cultures'.[19] Rather than broadcasting pan-Asian programmes in one language, STAR TV switched its strategy to localising programmes by finding local partners.[20]

The growing Asian audio-visual markets have also made Japanese cultural industries keen to do business in the region. Japanese cultural industries, too, are conscious of the significance of localisation, but in a different way from STAR TV. In 1994, Dentsu, the biggest advertising agency in Japan, organised a committee to promote the export of Japanese audio-visual products and submitted a report to the Ministry of International Trade and Industry. The report clearly saw the great possibility for Japanese products being further accepted in Asian markets and suggested the necessity of developing more export-oriented production systems, including market research and language dubbing, to expand exports. However, many members of the committee also pointed out the likelihood of Japanese cultural products soon being superseded by local ones and emphasised developing other strategies for entering Asian markets such as co-production and format trade, which sells the concept of television programming. This view corresponds with my own research. In November 1994, I interviewed many cultural producers in Japan concerning the popularity of Japanese products in Asia. Interestingly, almost every producer thought that Japanese products would not be well received in the Asian market for long. As a long-term strategy, they are not as keen to export Japanese products as to produce 'local' products in various Asian markets by indigenising Western (American) popular culture.

In this respect, a 1993 Japanese film about the Japanisation of Asia is suggestive of how Japanese cultural industries imagine the global cultural flow. The film 'Sotsugyō Ryokō: Nihon kara kimashita' ['My graduation trip: I'm from Japan'], is about a Japanese male university student who becomes a pop star in a fictional Southeast Asian country when he travels there. The country is in a phenomenal 'Japan boom' and he is scouted by a Japanese agent. He wins a star search audition and quickly becomes a national hero. Putting aside the depiction of a Japan boom in Asia, which the director himself acknowledged was not realistic, the interesting issues dealt with in this film are the status of American popular culture and the circulation of 'Japanised' Western popular culture in other parts of Asia. The film begins with a scene in Japan in 1979 in which the hero as a child is earnestly watching a Japanese star singing a Japanised version of the song 'YMCA' by the American pop group Village People.[21] The child dances along with the star on the screen. Symbolically he later performs the same number as a pop star in an Asian country. The premise appears to be that the basic model of Japanese popular culture is American and that Japan can provide a model for localising moves.

What the film does not show is the endless simulation of American pop in Asia through a second-generation simulation of Japanese pop music, which is 'home grown' if unquestionably owing a debt to American trends. Japanese popular music, much of which is deeply influenced by American popular music, has been popular in Hong Kong, Taiwan and Singapore but there is little awareness of this in these places because most of the songs are sung by local singers in local languages. For example, Chinese audiences listening to Hong Kong pop are unaware when it is actually a cover version of a Japanese song because they do not know the Japanese original (cover songs might well constitute a fourth 'C' of Japanese culturally odourless products!). In a 1994 TBS 'NEWS 23' report[22] on Japanese cultural industries in Shanghai, both the owner of a record shop and a customer said to camera that the local people knew very few Japanese songs. They also said Japanese songs were not popular in China and that Japanese record companies should develop a more subtle marketing strategy. But this was followed by a Japanese narration observing that people listen to many Japanese songs in China without realising their origin, because the songs have come to Shanghai via Hong Kong or Taiwan.

Japanese cultural producers are obviously aware from their own experience that Japanese cultural commodities are destined to be indigenised/localised and/or differently appropriated in each locale. It is, they seem to believe, through the process of indigenisation of the foreign (West) rather than the export of the product *per se* that Japan can capture the attention of people in Asia. For example, the Japanese music industries that are most active in entering the Asian market are using Japanese pop production know-how to seek out 'indigenous' pop stars rather than exporting Japanese stars directly. The film 'Sotsugyō Ryokō' mentioned above is suggestive in this respect as well. The hero achieves fame through an audition, which gives audiences the feeling that anyone in Asia can be tomorrow's star.

A televised star search audition process was in reality the basis of the development of the Japanese pop idol system – the processes by which media industries manufacture pop stars – in the 1970s and 1980s. In the early 1990s, Japanese cultural industries have tried to export the system to other parts of Asia. Many auditions have been held in Asia, particularly in China, by Japanese talent agencies, and recording companies such as Hori Production and Sony Music Entertainment. Also, a Japanese television station has been co-producing a talent quest TV programme, '*Asia Bagus*', with Singapore, Malaysia and Indonesia since 1992.[23] In this strategy for producing local pop stars in Asia, Japanese cultural industries are not trying to export Japanese cultural artefacts but rather to market the process whereby local contestants and audiences can appropriate and consume products of foreign origin. This is the element of Japanese 'originality' in glocalisation – to incorporate the viewpoint of 'the dominated' (who in this case have long learnt to negotiate with Western culture) in the local consumption of media products. The Japanese strategy of localisation tries to create local zones by gauging the practices of local media centres and their dynamic indigenisation processes. Indeed, this dynamic is exactly what the Japanese cultural industries are trying to produce in the Asian markets.

In this strategy, Japanese cultural industries attempt to become interpreters of 'the West' for 'Asia'. A Japanese cultural producer stressed in an interview with me in 1996 that the strength of Japan is its 50 years of experience and accumulated know-how of 'American education'. He, like other Japanese producers, seems to believe that Japan is the most 'successfully Westernised' country in the world. However, Japanese cultural industries share with other economic sectors a pessimistic view of the country's standing, as the world shifts from Japan-bashing to Japan-passing and now to Japan-nothing. Behind the confidence of Japanese music industries in their know-how in terms of indigenising the West, there is also a fear that other Asian countries are now bypassing Japan and indigenising the West directly. The same producer also emphasised in interview with me:

> Japanese cultural industries have a misconception that Japan is more advanced than any other Asian country in terms of popular culture, but what is happening is that other Asian countries are rapidly absorbing American culture. I think an Americanisation of Asia cannot be avoided. Japan has to be involved in this process in order not to be left out of the prosperous Asian markets. I would propose the acronym 'USA', to stand for the United States of Asia. Like the United States of America where many different cultures are fused, our USA should fuse different cultures so something new emerges from Asia.

What he was stressing is that Japan must be fused (yūgō suru) with other parts of Asia, particularly the

Greater China cultural bloc. Japanese music industries suspect that this is the only way for Japan not to be left out of transnational popular culture in Asia. They are struggling with how to be involved in the rise of cultural industries in other parts of Asia before it is too late.

Another consideration to be borne in mind is that the strategy of localisation is effective mainly in a relatively immature market such as China, not in mature markets like Taiwan and Hong Kong, where Japanese popular culture has long had an influence. These countries have imitated and indigenised the Japanese idol system and there is not much space for Japanese cultural industries to tell them how to indigenise the West.[24] This is not to say that Japan no longer has a cultural influence in these areas. Contrary to the expectation of the Japanese cultural industries, Japanese TV programmes and popular music are becoming more popular in such mature markets. While the export of the Japanese idol system is still sporadic, the circulation of Japanese TV programmes and popular music in Asia has become widespread. There are some markets in Asia where Japanese popular culture products rate highly, despite the embodiment of their textual appeal in living Japanese actors and musicians, but the interests which are promoting such products in those markets are more often local than Japanese. This is particularly the case with Taiwan. The ascent of Japanese popular culture in Taiwan has not occurred thanks to active promotion by Japanese cultural industries. Rather it is the local cable channels, STAR TV, and local music industries that have been actively selling Japanese products. In other words, the localisation of Japanese popular culture in Taiwan has less to do with Japanese promoters disguising the content with local odour than with local marketing strategies, which subtly turn the attention of audiences to the 'fragrance' of Japanese popular culture.

'Japan' in Taiwan: local promotion

Japanese popular music occupies a mere 2–4% share of the Taiwanese market (Chinese 75–80% and international 15–20%) according to my interviews with figures in the Taiwanese music industries in 1997, though there are no reliable figures available. However, Japanese popular music has been gradually increasing its presence in Taiwan in the last 3–4 years. In the week 25–31 March 1997, five Japanese songs were in the top 10 of single-CD sales figures, according to the IFPI Taiwan hit chart – two songs of Amuro Namie, one of which became number 1, two songs of Globe and one song of Dreams Come True. This is an amazing phenomenon, though local artists do not issue single CDs and thus the single-CD chart is almost entirely made up of international single CDs. What is noteworthy is that the presence of Japanese popular songs in Taiwan is becoming common and that they gain release soon after their appearance in the hit chart in Japan. A significant factor in the recent popularity of Japanese popular culture in Taiwan is the Taiwan government's removal of a ban on broadcasting Japanese-language TV programmes and songs around the end of 1993. Along with the liberalisation movement, what has also been important in facilitating the influx of Japanese popular culture in Taiwan since the late 1980s is the development of communication technologies and the expansion of entertainment markets in Taiwan. This has both exposed the audience in Taiwan to more information about Japanese popular culture, through newspapers, magazines and television, and given the local industries a better appreciation of the value of Japanese popular music, thus encouraging them to invest a good amount of money into promoting it in Taiwan.

During the time of my field research in Taipei in 1997, two local companies, Magic Stone and Sony Music Taiwan, were particularly keen to sell Japanese artists in Taiwan. Interestingly neither are controlled by Japanese companies. Magic Stone distributes Japanese popular songs from Avex Japan, a company that has not established branches in Asian capitals but promotes its CDs by licensing. Licensing allows this newly established, independent company to avoid the high cost of maintaining an office and employees. One disadvantage of the system is that the artists whom Avex wants to sell do not necessarily attract licensing partners and the amount of money spent on publicity is totally decided by the partner. However, this licensing strategy has been successful in Taiwan. Magic Stone has supported the Japanese dance music of

Komuro Tetsuya (the most popular and influential artist and producer in Japan) in becoming 'cool' in Taiwan. Taiwanese record companies usually spend a lot on publicity for the new albums of local artists, but relatively little for international artists. The managing director of Magic Stone boasted to me that now for the first time Magic Stone has invested the same amount of money in publicising Japanese artists in Taiwan as local artists.

A similar arrangement can be seen in Sony Music Taiwan's promotion of Dreams Come True. It was Sony Music Taiwan, not Sony Music Japan, that took the initiative in deciding which Japanese artists to sell in the Taiwanese market. Sony Music Taiwan had cautiously planned to promote Dreams Come True in Taiwan over a 2-year period and finally succeeded in inviting the group to Taiwan in 1996. According to the vice president of Sony Music Taiwan, the company spent a considerable amount of money on promotion in Taiwan, almost ten times the average for international artists, resulting in sales there of over 200,000 copies of Dreams Come True's CD, a phenomenally successful figure for foreign artists.

The Japanese managing director of the Taiwan office of a Japanese recording company lamented in an interview with me the difficulty he had in convincing the Tokyo head office of the importance of spending money on publicity to sell CDs in Taiwan:

> Japanese companies naively assume that Japanese know-how is completely transferable to other Asian markets, but they do not understand how media environments vary and systems work differently. In Taiwan, TV is a medium that just sells spot commercial time, and recording companies have to pay for using it, even when the record is the theme song from a TV drama. This is common practice throughout the world, as far as I know – so it is Japan that is different. The Japanese system is too self-contained to extend its power overseas.

These comments show some of the difficulties which Japanese music industries face in selling Japanese artists as well as in the enterprise of exporting Japanese know-how to Asian markets. It is possible for the Japanese music industries to be self-contained because Japan is the world's second-biggest economic power and consumer market. Japanese cultural industries do not have to risk investing huge sums of money into other Asian markets where profits may not be very attractive to them. The same is true with Japanese popular musicians. For them, Japan is no doubt the most important market and they cannot sacrifice it to visit other less profitable markets. Chage & Aska, who did tour Asia twice, were exceptional in this regard and were also exceptional in becoming popular overseas. Avex's strategy of licensing suits the Taiwanese market. Japanese companies do not risk their own money and Japanese artists do not have to go on frequent tours to promote themselves. The manager of Magic Stone was emphatic that the promotion of Japanese popular music in Asian markets can only be done effectively in conjunction with the marketing strategies of local industries.

The same can also be said of Japanese television programmes. Recently Japanese dramas have attracted a greater young (particularly female) audience in Taiwan than either locally produced, Hong Kong or Western/American dramas.[25] A news reporter from Taiwan I interviewed observed that Japanese dramas are now one of the most common topics of everyday gossip for high school and university students. Apart from their textual appeal, another important factor in the popularity of Japanese television programmes in Taiwan is the maturity and expansion of the local television market, which has forced local companies to recognise the capacity of quality Japanese TV dramas to find a niche market in Taiwan.

There is no doubt that STAR TV has been the pioneering player in diffusing Japanese TV programmes to Asia, particularly to Taiwan. STAR TV started broadcasting in August 1991 and the 'Japanese Idol Drama Hour' has been the most popular programme on the Chinese channel since 1992. Although STAR TV has been discussed widely in terms of its pan-Asian satellite broadcasting and of its possible penetration into China, it should be remembered that Taiwan has been a major target too. This is particularly true with STAR Chinese Channel and Music Channel V (which replaced MTV in 1994). Recently STAR TV launched a new Chinese channel, Phoenix, for the mainland Chinese market and STAR Chinese Channel is now broadcast exclusively in Taiwan. Japanese programmes, particularly dramas, are occupying the prime time slots on the STAR Chinese Channel. A Taiwanese programming officer for STAR TV told me that they programmed Japanese dramas to attract a large Taiwanese audience. Japanese programmes are clearly indispensable to STAR TV's strategy of localisation in Taiwan.

A most important factor to consider in the recent popularity of Japanese TV programmes in Taiwan is the rapid development there of cable television. Cable TV emerged as an illegal business in the 1980s. After a long battle between the government and the cable operators, the government changed its policy from prohibition to regulation. The 1993 Cable TV Law legalised cable television, but even before it came into force about 50% of households were watching cable (known as 'the Fourth Channel'). Under the Cable TV Law viewership levels have continued to rise; now in 1998 nearly 80% of households enjoy cable television and Taiwan has the most developed cable TV system in Asia.

The Cable Law requires that at least 20% of the programmes of each cable channel are locally produced, but it is obvious that many cable channels do not abide by this condition. Most channels are buying whole programmes from overseas, mainly from the United States, Hong Kong and Japan. Lewis *et al.* have argued that the development of cable TV in Taiwan facilitated re-Americanisation after a period when the people's preference for local programmes reduced the number of American programs on air;[26] ESPN, HBO, Discovery and CNNI are some of the leading programme packages in this re-Americanisation of Taiwan. However, the dramatic increase in Japanese TV programmes in Taiwan has been another significant trend of the last few years, particularly since Japanese-language TV programmes were officially allowed to be broadcast from the end of 1993. In 1997 there were five Japanese cable channels in Taiwan: NHK Asia, Gold Sun, Videoland Japan, Po-Shin and JET (Japan Entertainment Television). Apart from NHK Asia, which broadcasts its own programmes by satellite almost simultaneously with Japan, the other four channels buy whole programmes from Japanese commercial television stations for local rebroadcast. In addition, the free-to-air channels and STAR TV all regularly broadcast Japanese programmes. In 1992 the total export of television programming from Japan to Taiwan was about 600 hours.[27] There are no accurate figures available on Japanese programme exports to Taiwan after 1993, but in 1996 the commercial TBS network alone exported 1000 hours of programmes to Taiwan, according to my interview with TBS.

The popularity of Japanese popular culture in Taiwan has an impact on the export strategies of Japanese cultural industries. Taiwan's case positively suggests to the Japanese cultural industries that a Japanese cultural odour does sell. A manager of Dentsu who promoted format sales of Japanese quiz shows in Asia also mentioned this shift. He said in an interview with me that what has been made clear is that Japanese TV programmes have gained a certain universal appeal. In 1997 Sumitomo Trading Co. Ltd launched JET as the first Japanese pay TV channel with TBS, whose profits from selling programmes overseas are the highest in Japan. JET supplies nine Asia-Pacific countries (Taiwan, Hong Kong, Thailand, Singapore, Malaysia, Indonesia, the Philippines, Australia and New Zealand) with a channel of exclusively Japanese TV programmes, in four languages – Japanese, English, Mandarin and Thai – by satellite up-link from Singapore. In its current 1998 advertising, JET declares:

> People with an eye for trends have their eyes on Japan. On its fashions, celebrities, and hit products – anything that's new and fun. Today, trend-conscious viewers throughout Asia can enjoy up-to-date programs from Japan 24 hours a day: on JET TV.

The emphasis on the attractiveness of Japanese popular culture has clearly become a key to the export strategies of Japanese TV industries in Asian markets.

Another interesting move is the music producer Komuro Tetsuya's inroad into Asian markets with the help of foreign media, namely STAR TV. Komuro and News Corp established a joint company, TK NEWS, in December 1996. The purpose of the company is not only to promote Komuro's music but also to popularise the Komuro Family in Asia. When the family had two concerts in Taipei in May 1997, the

Komuro Family's concert surprisingly attracted more media attention than global pop star Whitney Houston, who happened to be giving a concert two days before the Komuro Family and staying at the same hotel. TK NEWS also produced a TV programme to find local artists for the Komuro Family, and a 13-year-old Taiwanese female singer called Ring made her debut with them in April 1998. This sounds like the familiar strategy of finding a local star, but the crucial difference is that Komuro is not only an artist but also a capable producer. Komuro announced his willingness to learn from News Corp concepts of local sound and localising marketing strategies developed for Asia;[28] however, for TK News what was important was not localising his sound so much as his fame. The selling point was that the local artist had been produced by the best producer in Japan. As a result, Ring's first single went to the top of the IFPI Taiwan single-CD chart immediately after its release.

The strength of TK NEWS is that it is closely connected with STAR TV's music channel, Channel V, on which Komuro and his Family are appearing more and more frequently. In January 1997, Amuro Namie was selected as Channel V's 'artist of the month', the first time for a Japanese artist. Her song went to number 1 on the channel's Asian top 20. The then-director of Channel V, Jeff Murray, who was also the intermediary between Komuro and News Corp, told me in an interview that the Japanese music market is definitely more sophisticated than other Asian markets in terms of the absorption and indigenisation of a variety of Western pop. He believes that Japanese music, though a new taste for the Taiwanese audience, is for them easier to relate to than Western pop. He also said that Channel V is more local than MTV Asia. 'If MTV can be compared to McDonald's, Channel V is a dimsim.' When I asked whether Japanese popular culture and music are dimsims, he answered 'yes'. Elsewhere, he has predicted that 'being Japanese will be fashionable in the twenty-first century'.[29] I was also told by the managing director of a Taiwan record company that Japan should be confident of its own popular culture, and that the 1990s are a turning point at which Japanese popular culture is taking over the symbolic role of American popular culture in Asia: Japanese popular culture is becoming an object to which young people in Asia will aspire. The extent to which these scenarios eventuate remains to be seen, but the predictions made by those in management positions reflect their desire for this end.

From Western gaze to global gaze

The Japanese cultural presence is becoming more visible and discursively more articulated. The discursive manifestation of the cultural presence of a foreign country usually happens when that presence seems either to be a threat to national identity or national interest, or to be an object of yearning in the recipient country. In either case, the presence of a foreign country marks its cultural hegemony. It was Sony's purchase of Columbia in 1989, and Matsushita's purchase of MCA (Universal) in 1990, that dramatised the ascendancy of Japan as a global cultural as well as economic power by making the Japanese presence in the United States visible. The merger of hardware and software by Japanese media companies shocked the United States, which had previously disdained the Japanese capacity to produce culture. Although Matsushita retreated from Hollywood and Sony struggled to make a profit (though Columbia finally achieved phenomenal box-office sales in 1997), the ascendancy of Japan's culturally odourless presence in the global audio-visual market is attracting increasing academic and media attention – the Walkman was chosen for analysis as the most appropriate example of a global cultural product in a British Open University cultural studies textbook prepared for global distribution; the Japanese origin of the term 'glocalisation' was explicitly acknowledged in the *Oxford Dictionary of New Words*; and Japanese animations have become a well-recognised and established genre in the global market.

Undoubtedly the emergence of discourses on the popularity of Japanese culturally odourless products in the world reflects the fact that Japanese cultural industries are playing a substantial role in globalisation processes. What is particularly significant in the discursive manifestation of Japanese cultural presence is that Japanese cultural products are now appreciated even by dominant Western countries. An animated film, 'The Ghost in the Shell', was shown simultaneously in Japan, America and Britain. Disney is distributing Miyazaki Hayao's animated films globally. The computer game market is dominated world-wide by three Japanese manufacturers, Nintendo, Sega and Sony. The popularity of Japanese game software is exemplified by Super Mario Brothers. According to a survey, Mario is better known among American children than Mickey Mouse.[30] However, the question remains: if Sony's buy-out of Columbia articulated Japanese cultural and economic power as a threat to the United States, what kind of hegemony (if any) does the popularity of Japanese animations and computer games overseas signify? What power status does the popularity of animations and computer games overseas confer on Japan?

Japanese animated culture and imagery evoke both a sense of threat and a yearning overseas. On the one hand, the global circulation of Japanese animated culture causes a fear of cultural invasion and decadence in Western countries, and discourses of 'techno-Orientalism' in Western countries present new, dehumanised hi-tech images of Japan.[31] At the same time, we see the emergence in Western countries of *otaku*, obsessively devoted fans of Japanese animations whose mania makes them wish they were born in Japan. To them Japan 'looks more cool' than the United States.[32] Okada compares this Western passionate consumption of Japanese animation to Japan's – and his own – experience of yearning for 'America' through the consumption of American popular culture. Paradoxically, Okada seems to argue, Western audiences appreciate a Japanese way of life, which is embodied in the *mu-kokuseki* (racially, ethnically and culturally unembedded) imagery of animation. If the 'Japanese-ness' of Japanese animations is derived from their active erasure of bodily Japanese-ness from the visual imagery, the object of yearning is an animated virtual 'Japan'. In this respect, Okada's argument at least serves to remind us that a sense of yearning for a particular country evoked through the consumption of cultural commodities is inevitably a monological illusion since it is little concerned with the complexity of 'real' culture.

Another way of making sense of Japanese cultural power is to look at the issue of cultural power – and hegemony which is articulated through the cross-cultural circulation of products – in a different light. It seems not entirely contingent that the manifestation of Japanese cultural hegemony has occurred in the last decade. This is a period when the globalisation of culture has been accelerated by several interconnected factors: the global integration of markets and capital by powerful transnational corporations; the development of communication technologies which easily connect all over the globe; the emergence of an affluent middle class in non-Western countries; the increasing number of people moving from one place to another by migration and tourism. What has happened to cultural flow under these conditions is that the variety of images and commodities – most of which are still from the West, though non-Western countries such as Japan are increasing their share – are simultaneously circulating in urban spaces all over the globe. While this makes Western modernity ubiquitous, at the same time the original ownership of images and commodities becomes increasingly insignificant and irrelevant. That is, images and commodities tend to become culturally odourless because origin tends to be subsumed under local appropriation. The specificities or 'authenticity' of local cultures, as Miller argues, are to be found '*a posteriori* not *a priori*, according to local consequences not local origins'.[33] By appropriating, hybridising or indigenising images and commodities of 'foreign' origin, even American culture is conceived of as 'ours' in many places. McDonald's is so much a part of their own world that it no longer represents an American way of life to Japanese or Taiwanese young consumers.[34]

What is disappearing in this process is a sense of derivative modernity, that 'our' modernity is borrowed from modernity that happened elsewhere.[35] Ubiquitous modernity, in contrast, is based on a sense that 'our' modernity is the one that is simultaneously happening everywhere. To put it differently, the Western gaze that has long dominated the material and discursive construction of non-Western modernity is now melting into a global gaze, which subtly resists condemnation of 'cultural imperialism' and yearning for Western culture. This shift is therefore as much about our interpretive framework as about 'reality'. The age of 'Americanisation', in which cross-cultural consumption was predominantly discussed in terms of the export of a way of life and ideas of a dominant country, is over. It is the shift from a Western gaze to a global gaze, I would suggest, that Japanese cultural hegemony thrives on. Although commodities and images are dominated by a small number of wealthy countries including Japan, and many parts of the world are still excluded from enjoying global cultural consumption, their presence and uneven distributions are becoming more difficult to demarcate.

The point is most clear when we look at Japanese cultural presence in Asia. Fifty years would seem long enough for former colonies to become more tolerant towards, if not to forget, the legacy of Japanese imperialism. Taiwan removed its ban on broadcasting Japanese-language TV programmes and music in 1993 and the new president of South Korea has publicly announced his intention of ending the restrictions on importing Japanese cultural products. It is not totally an accident that the ascent of Japanese cultural presence in Asia coincides with the vanishing of a discourse on cultural imperialism.

At the same time, it cannot be denied that Japanese cultural odour has gained momentum in Asian markets. We have seen this trend in the promotion of Japanese popular culture in Taiwan, to the point where a new word has been coined to describe young people who love to consume things Japanese.

This testifies to another trend – that of the globalisation process facilitating intra-regional cultural flow among non-Western countries. While what Japan can export to Western countries is still limited to well-recognised culturally odourless products, much broader selections of Japanese TV programmes and popular music are increasing their presence in Asian markets. I have focused on marketing strategies, but the ascent of Japanese TV dramas and popular music in Taiwan also has much to do with their textual appeal. In my research in Taipei and Hong Kong, many young viewers said they found Japanese TV dramas more attractive and easier to relate to than American dramas, because of cultural and bodily similarity and textual subtlety. This is neither to say that Japan has become an object of yearning in other parts of Asia, nor that *a priori* cultural proximity generates regionalisation. Rather, under globalising forces, cultural similarities and resonances in the region are newly articulated. It is also an emerging sense of coevalness based upon the narrowing economic gap, simultaneous circulation of information, the abundance of global commodities and the common experience of urbanisation that has sustained a Japanese cultural presence in East Asia.[36]

It is often argued that the beauty of Japanese traditional culture was discovered by 'the West', and that this in turn made Japan conscious of the Western gaze when claiming its cultural uniqueness. In the case of contemporary popular culture, it is neither Japan nor 'the West' but modernised 'Asia' which has discovered the commercial value and cultural resonance of Japanese popular culture. What tends to be emphasised in traditional culture is Japan's irreducible difference; but, for audiences in East Asia, Japanese popular culture represents cultural similarities and a common experience of modernity in the region that is based on an ongoing negotiation between the West and the non-West – experiences which American popular culture cannot represent.

Even in the age of global gaze, the local odour still matters. The desire to become at once modern and different is one which the global gaze generates.[37] It is this desire that lets durian articulate the 'modern' local identity of Southeast Asia; and it is the same desire that is increasingly exploited by transnational corporations. The Japanese market is not immune from the transnational cultural industries' strategies of globalisation. Miwa Yoshida, the female vocalist with the pop group Dreams Come True, appeared on the cover page of the 14 October 1996 issue of *Time Asia*. The issue's cover story was 'the Divas of Pop'. Yoshida was one of the divas, along with Celine Dion, Gloria Estefan, Whitney Houston, Mariah Carey, Alanis Morissette, Tina Arena and Faye Wong. In Japan this was reported in major newspapers and the sales for the issue almost tripled. But Yoshida was only on the cover page of the Japanese version of *Time Asia*. In other Asian countries, including Taiwan, the cover page carried the picture of Faye Wong, a Beijing-born Hong Kong singer. No matter how well received in other parts of Asia, it will not be easy for the sweet scent of Japanese popular culture to overpower the deodorant of global cultural industries, which are the main force for promoting uneven distributions, organising cultural diversity and selling cultural odour to local markets.

Notes

1   Ulf Hannerz, 'Notes on the Global Ecumene', *Public Culture* 1:2, 1989, pp. 66–75.

2   George Ritzer, *The McDonaldisation of Society* (London, Sage, 1993).

3   Mike Featherstone, *Undoing Culture* (London, Sage, 1996), p. 8.

4   Koichi Iwabuchi, 'Complicit Exoticism: Japan and Its Other', *Continuum* 8:2, 1994, pp. 49–82.

5   Paul du Gay, Stuart Hall, Linda Janes, Hugh Mackay and Keith Negus, *Doing Cultural Studies: The Story of the Sony Walkman* (London, Sage, 1997).

6   Featherstone, *Undoing Culture*, p. 9.

7   C.J.W.-L. Wee, 'Buying Japan: Singapore, Japan, and an "East Asian" Modernity', *The Journal of Pacific Asia*, 4, 1997, pp. 21–46.

8   Oshii Mamoru, Itō Kazunori and Ueno Toshiya, 'Eiga to wa jitsu wa animēshon datta' ('Film Was Actually a Form of Animation'), *Yurika*, August 1996, pp. 50–81.

9   Bruce Stronach, 'Japanese Television', in: R. Powers and H. Kato (Eds) *Handbook of Japanese Popular Culture* (Westport, Greenwood Press, 1989), pp. 127–165.

10   Kawatake Kazuo and Hara Yumiko, 'Nihon o chūshin to suru terebi bangumi no ryūtsū jōkyō' ('The International Flow of TV Programmes From and Into Japan'), *Hōsō Kenkyū to Chōsa*, November 1994.

11   Stronach, 'Japanese Television', p. 144.

12   Akurosu Henshūshitsu, *Sekai shōhin no tsukurikata: Nihon media ga sekai o sesshita hi* (The Making of World Products: The Day Japanese Media Conquered the World) (Tokyo, Parco Shuppan, 1995).

13   Asu Aksoy and Kevin Robins, 'Hollywood for the 21st Century: Global Competition for Critical Mass in Image Markets', *Cambridge Journal of Economics*, 16, 1992, p. 18; see also du Gay *et al.*, *Doing Cultural Studies*.

14   Quoted in Roland Robertson, 'Globalization: Time-Space and Homogeneity-Heterogeneity', in: M. Featherstone, S. Lash and R. Robertson (Eds) *Global Modernities* (London, Sage, 1995), p. 28.

15   Iwabuchi Koichi, 'Pure Impurity: Japan's Genius for Hybridism', *Communal/Plural: Journal of Transnational & Crosscultural Studies* 6:1, 1998, pp. 71–86.

16   Kawatake and Hara, 'Nihon o chūshin to suru terebi bangumi no ryūtsū jōkyō'.

17   See Paul S.-N. Lee, 'The Absorption and Indigenisation of Foreign Media Cultures. A Study on a Cultural Meeting Point of East and West: Hong Kong', *Asian Journal of Communication* 1:2, 1991, pp. 55–72; and Joseph Straubhaar, 'Beyond Media Imperialism: Asymmetrical Interdependence and Cultural Proximity', *Critical Studies in Mass Communication*, 8:1, 1991, pp. 39–59, for the indigenisation of foreign media culture in Hong Kong and South America.

18   Colin Hoskins and Rolf Mirus, 'Reasons for the US Dominance of the International Trade in Television Programmes', *Media, Culture and Society*, 10, 1988, pp. 499–515.

19   *Asian Business Review*, May 1994.

20   *Far Eastern Economic Review*, 27 January 1994.

21   The Japanese version, unlike the original song, has no gay culture subtext; instead, it features an 'original' dance.

22   6 October 1994; TBS is one of Japan's national commercial television networks.

23   I have written about this in more detail in 'Return to Asia? Japan in the Global Audiovisual Market', *Media International Australia*, 77, August 1995, pp. 94–106.

24   See Leo Ching, 'Imaginings in the Empire of the Sun: Japanese Mass Culture in Asia', *Boundary 2*, 21.1, 1994, pp. 199–219, on the Taiwanese imitation of the Japanese idol system.

25   Hattori Hiroshi and Hara Yumiko, 'Tachanneruka no naka no terebi to shichōsha: Taiwan kēburu terebi no baai' ('The Proliferation of Television Channels and Audiences: A Study of Taiwan Cable Television'), *Hōsō Kenkyū to Chōsa*, February 1997; Ishii Ken'ichi, Watanabe Satoshi and Su Hearng, *Taiwan ni okeru Nihon bangumi no shichōsha bunseki* (Analysis of Viewer Data for Japanese Programmes in Taiwan), Discussion Papers Series No. 701 (Tsukuba, University of Tsukuba, 1996).

26   Glen Lewis *et al.*, 'Television Globalisation in Taiwan and Australia', *Media Asia* 21:4, 1994, pp. 184–189.

27   Kawatake and Hara, 'Nihon o chūshin to suru terebi bangumi no ryūtsū jōkyō'.

28   *Nikkei Shimbun*, 10 January 1997.

29   *Aera*, 20 January 1997.

30   See Akurosu Henshūshitsu, *Sekai shōhin no tsukurikata: Nihon media ga sekai o sesshita hi*.

31   David Morley and Kevin Robins, 'Techno-Orientalism: Futures, Foreigners and Phobias', *New Formations*, 16, Spring 1992, pp. 136–156.

32   Okada Toshio, '*Anime bunka wa chō kakkō ii*' ('Animation Culture is Super Cool'), *Aera*, 2 October 1995, pp. 43–44.

33   Daniel Miller, 'The Young and Restless in Trinidad: A Case of the Local and Global in Mass Consumption', in: R. Silverstone and E. Hirsch (Eds) *Consuming Technologies: Media and Information in Domestic Spaces* (London, Routledge, 1992), p. 181.

34   See James L. Watson (Ed.) *Golden Arches East: McDonald's in East Asia* (Stanford University Press, 1997).

35   See, for example, Dipesh Chakrabarty, 'Postcoloniality and the Artifice of History: Who Speaks for "Indian" Pasts?', *Representations*, 37, 1992, pp. 1–26.

36   For a detailed analysis of the consumption of Japanese TV dramas in Taiwan, see Koichi Iwabuchi, 'Becoming Culturally Proximate: The A/Scent of Japanese Idol Dramas in Taiwan', in B. Moeran (Ed.) *Asian Media and Advertising* (London, Curzon, forthcoming).

37   Ulf Hannerz, *Transnational Connections: Culture, People, Places* (London, Routledge, 1996).

Chapter 22

Jonathan Sterne

HELLO [2003]

Source: Jonathan Sterne (2003) 'Hello' [edited], in *The Audible Past: Cultural Origins of Sound Reproduction*, Durham, NC: Duke University Press, pp. 1–19.

The auditory world we live in now (in the twenty-first century) is different from the world our ancestors lived in a hundred years ago or a thousand years ago. The noise of a church bell is different from the constant drone and pounding clatter of a car factory. The sound of music produced by sackbuts and harpsichords would be different from that produced when Julie Andrews sings 'Edelweiss', which in turn is different from the sounds of synthesisers and computer-generated sound effects. The sonorous sound of a parent's voice for a baby is different from the pneumatic thumping of a rock-drill, but here the difference is of historical duration; the sound of the rock-drill is fairly recent while the comforting resonance of mothers and fathers spirals back into prehistory and forward into the unknown.

These sounds are not the neutral background matter of our designed environment; they are active ingredients in our history. For Jonathan Sterne sound is both shaped and shaping, and this is made evident when we move from a history of 'sounds' to think of those same sounds within a history of hearing and, perhaps most importantly, of listening. It is as listeners, as subjects encouraged to hear in particular ways, subjects designed to 'listen out for' noticeable sounds, that the historical sociality of sound is made evident. For Sterne it is by attending to the history of sound-reproduction technologies (which could also be thought of as systematic and systemic sound design) that the sociality of auditory culture can be most dramatically charted. In Sterne's work the mechanical reproduction of sound offers fascinating glimpses of the changing patterns of listening, mainly because 'Technologies are repeatable social, cultural, and material processes crystallized into mechanisms.' His account doesn't privilege early mechanical sound forms like the gramophone or the radio or the telephone because it is understood, *a priori*, that it is technology that transforms experience; instead such technologies are historical artefacts because they condense and stabilise the mechanical form of new experiences.

Perhaps there is nothing as potentially uncanny as recorded sound; the first time you listen to a recording of your own voice the sound that greets you is quite clearly someone else's. If this is what people hear when I speak then quite clearly I am a ventriloquist's dummy inhabited by the voice of another. The history of sound recording is not one that is only concerned with efficiency and rationality. Sound recording knows that its primary goal is to store the sounds of ghosts.

Further reading: Attali 1977; Connor 1997; Johnson 1995; Thompson 2004.

HERE ARE THE tales currently told: Alexander Graham Bell and Thomas Watson had their first telephone conversation in 1876. "Mr. Watson – Come here – I want to see you!" yelled Bell to Watson, and the world shook. Thomas Edison first heard his words – "Mary had a little lamb" – returned to him from the cylinder of a phonograph built by his assistants in 1878, and suddenly the human voice gained a measure of immortality. Guglielmo Marconi's wireless telegraph conquered the English channel in 1899. Unsuspecting navy personnel first heard voices coming over their radios in 1906. Each event has been claimed as a turning point in human history. Before the invention of sound-reproduction technologies, we are told, sound withered away. It existed only as it went out of existence. Once telephones, phonographs, and radios populated our world, sound had lost a little of its ephemeral character. The voice became a little more unmoored from the body, and people's ears could take them into the past or across vast distances.

These are powerful stories because they tell us that something happened to the nature, meaning, and practices of sound in the late nineteenth century. But they are incomplete.[1] If sound-reproduction technologies changed the way we hear, where did they come from? Many of the practices, ideas, and constructs associated with sound-reproduction technologies predated the machines themselves. The basic technology to make phonographs (and, by extension, telephones) existed for some time prior to their actual invention.[2] So why did sound-reproduction technologies emerge when they did and not at some other time? What preceded them that made them possible, desirable, effective, and meaningful? In what milieu did they dwell? How and why did sound-reproduction technologies take on the particular technological and cultural forms and functions that they did? To answer these questions, we move from considering simple mechanical possibility out into the social and cultural worlds from which the technologies emerged.

The Audible Past offers a history of the *possibility* of sound reproduction – the telephone, the phonograph, radio, and other related technologies. It examines the social and cultural conditions that gave rise to sound reproduction and, in turn, how those technologies crystallized and combined larger cultural currents. Sound-reproduction technologies are artifacts of vast transformations in the fundamental nature of sound, the human ear, the faculty of hearing, and practices of listening that occurred over the long nineteenth century. Capitalism, rationalism, science, colonialism, and a host of other factors – the "maelstrom" of modernity, to use Marshall Berman's phrase – all affected constructs and practices of sound, hearing, and listening.[3]

As there was an Enlightenment, so too was there an "Ensoniment." A series of conjunctures among ideas, institutions, and practices rendered the world audible in new ways and valorized new constructs of hearing and listening. Between about 1750 and 1925, sound itself became an object and a domain of thought and practice, where it had previously been conceptualized in terms of particular idealized instances like voice or music. Hearing was reconstructed as a physiological process, a kind of receptivity and capacity based on physics, biology, and mechanics. Through techniques of listening, people harnessed, modified, and shaped their powers of auditory perception in the service of rationality. In the modern age, sound and hearing were reconceptualized, objectified, imitated, transformed, reproduced, commodified, mass-produced, and industrialized. To be sure, the transformation of sound and hearing took well over a century. It is not that people woke up one day and found everything suddenly different. Changes in sound, listening, and hearing happened bit by bit, place by place, practice by practice, over a long period of time.

"The golden age of the ear never ended," writes Alan Burdick. "It continues, occluded by the visual hegemony."[4] *The Audible Past* tells a story where sound, hearing, and listening are central to the cultural life of modernity, where sound, hearing, and listening are foundational to modern modes of knowledge, culture, and social organization. It provides an alternative to the pervasive narrative that says that, in becoming modern, Western culture moved away from a culture of hearing to a culture of seeing. There is no doubt that the philosophical literature of the Enlightenment – as well as many people's everyday language – is littered with light and sight metaphors for truth and understanding.[5] But, even if sight is in some ways the privileged sense in European philosophical discourse since the Enlightenment, it is fallacious to think that sight alone or in its supposed difference from hearing explains modernity.

There has always been a heady audacity to the claim that vision is the social chart of modernity. While I do not claim that listening is *the* social chart of modernity, it certainly charts a significant field of modern practice. There is always more than one map for a territory, and sound provides a particular path through history. In some cases – as this book will demonstrate – modern ways of hearing prefigured modern ways of seeing. During the Enlightenment and afterward, the sense of hearing became an object of contemplation. It was measured, objectified, isolated, and simulated. Techniques of audition developed by doctors and telegraphers were constitutive characteristics of scientific medicine and early versions of modern bureaucracy. Sound was commodified; it became something that can be bought and sold. These facts trouble the cliché that modern science and rationality were outgrowths of visual culture and visual thinking. They urge us to rethink exactly what we mean by the *privilege* of vision and images.[6] To take seriously the role of sound and hearing in modern life is to trouble the visualist definition of *modernity*.

Today, it is understood across the human sciences that vision and visual culture are important matters. Many contemporary writers interested in various aspects of visual culture (or, more properly, visual aspects of various cultural domains) – the arts, design, landscape, media, fashion – understand their work as contributing to a core set of theoretical, cultural, and historical questions about vision and images. While writers interested in visual media have for some time gestured toward a conceptualization of *visual culture*, no such parallel construct – *sound culture* or, simply, *sound studies* – has broadly informed work on hearing or the other senses.[7] While sound is considered as a unified intellectual problem in some science and engineering fields, it is less developed as an integrated problem in the social and cultural disciplines.

Similarly, visual concerns populate many strains of cultural theory. The question of *the gaze* haunts several schools of feminism, critical race theory, psychoanalysis, and poststructuralism. The cultural status of *the image* and seeing occupies great minds in semiotics, film studies, several schools of literary and art-historical interpretation, architecture, and communication. While sound may interest individual scholars in these areas, it is still too often considered a parochial or specialized concern. While there are many scholars of sound active in communication, film studies, music, and other human sciences, sound is not usually a central theoretical problem for major schools of cultural theory, apart from the privilege of the voice in phenomenology and psychoanalysis and its negation in deconstruction.[8]

It would be possible to write a different book, one that explains and criticizes scholars' preference for visual objects and vision as an object of study. For now, it is enough to note that the fault lies with both cultural theorists and scholars of sound. Cultural theorists too easily accept pieties about the dominance of vision and, as a result, have elided differences between the privilege of vision and the totality of vision. Meanwhile, studies of sound tend to shy away from questions of sound culture as such (with a few notable exceptions) and prefer instead to work within other disciplinary or interdisciplinary intellectual domains. By *not* gesturing back toward a more general level of questioning, these works offer an implicitly cumulativist epistemology of the history of sound. The promise of cumulativist approaches is that one day we will have enough historical information to begin generalizing about society. The problem with this perspective is that such a remarkable day is always just over the horizon.[9] If sound and hearing are indeed significant theoretical problems, then now is as good a time as any to begin dealing with them as broad intellectual matters.

Many authors have claimed that hearing is the neglected sense in modernity, a novel sense for analysis.[10] It would perhaps be polemically acceptable at this point to lament the relative lack of scholarly work on sound as compared with images and vision, chart the pioneers, and then claim that this book will fill the gap. But the reality is somewhat different. There is a vast literature on the history and philosophy of sound; yet it remains conceptually fragmented. For the interested reader, there is a wealth of books and articles available on different aspects of sound written by scholars of communication, music, art, and culture.[11] But, without some kind of over-arching, shared sensibility about what constitutes *the history of sound, sound culture*, or *sound studies*, piecing together a history of sound from the bewildering array of stories about speech, music, technology, and other sound-related practices has all the promise and appeal of piecing together a pane of shattered glass. We know that the parts line up somehow, we know that they can connect, but we are unsure of how they actually link together. We have histories of concert audiences, telephones, speeches, sound films, soundscapes, and theories of hearing. But only rarely do the writers of histories of sound suggest how their work connects with other, related work or with larger intellectual domains. Because scholarship on sound has not consistently gestured toward more fundamental and synthetic theoretical, cultural, and historical questions, it has not been able to bring broader philosophical questions to bear on the various intellectual fields that it inhabits. The challenge, then, is to imagine sound as a problem that moves beyond its immediate empirical context. The history of sound is already connected to the larger projects of the human sciences; it is up to us to flesh out the connections.

In positing a history of sound, *The Audible Past* extends a long tradition of interpretive and critical social thought. Some authors have quoted the young Marx on the importance of sensory history: "The forming of the five senses is a labor of the entire history of the world down to the present." Marx's passage signals that the very capacity to relate to the world through one's senses is organized and learned differently in different social settings. The senses are "cultivated or brought into being." "Man himself becomes the object" to be shaped and oriented through historical and social process.[12] Before the senses are real, palpable, concrete, or available for contemplation, they are already affected and effected through the particular historical conditions that also give rise to the subject who possesses them. We can fully consider the senses as historical only if we consider society, culture, technology, and the body as themselves artifacts of human history. A truly historicist understanding of the senses – or of a particular sense – therefore requires a commitment to the constructivist and contextualist strain of social and cultural thought. Conversely, a vigorous constructivism and a vigorous contextualism require a history of the senses. It is no accident that Marx's discussion of the senses appears in a section on communism in the *Economic and Philosophic Manuscripts of 1844*. Even to begin imagining (another) society, the young Marx had to consider the historical dynamics of sensation itself. As we imagine the possibilities of social, cultural, and historical change – in the past, present, or future – it is also our task to imagine histories of the senses. It is widely accepted that "the individual observer became an object of investigation and a locus of knowledge begin-ning in the first few decades of the 1800s" and that, during that same period, "the status of the observing subject was transformed."[13] So, too, transformations in sound, hearing, and listening were part of massive shifts in the landscapes of social and cultural life of the last three centuries.

The emergence of sound-reproduction technology in the nineteenth and twentieth centuries provides a particularly good entry into the larger history of sound. It is one of the few extant sites in the human sciences where scholars have acknowledged and contemplated the historicity of hearing. As Theodor Adorno, Walter Benjamin, and countless other writers have argued, the problem of mechanical reproduc-tion is central to understanding the changing shape of communication in the late nineteenth and early twentieth centuries. For them, the compelling problem of sound's reproducibility, like the reproduction of images, was its seeming abstraction from the social world even as it was manifested more dynamically within it.[14] Other writers have offered even stronger claims for sound reproduction: it has been described as a "material foundation" of the changing senses of space and time at the turn of the twentieth century, part of a "perceptual revolution" in the early twentieth century. Sound technologies are said to have amplified and extended sound and our sense of hearing across time and space.[15] We are told that telephony altered "the conditions of daily life"; that sound recording represented a moment when "everything suddenly changed," a "shocking emblem of modernity"; that radio was "the most important electronic invention" of the twentieth century, transforming our perceptual habits and blurring the boundaries of private, public, commercial, and political life.[16]

Taken out of context or with a little hostility, claims for the historical significance of sound reproduc-tion may seem overstated or even grandiose. D. L. LeMahieu writes that sound recording was one of "a score of new technologies thrust upon a population increasingly accustomed to mechanical miracles. In a decade when men learned to fly, the clock-sprung motor of a portable gramophone or the extended playing time of a double-sided disk hardly provoked astonishment. Indeed, what may be most remarkable was the rapidity with which technological innovations became absorbed into everyday, commonplace experience."[17] The same could be said for telephony, radio, and many other technologies. Yet LeMahieu's more sober prose still leaves room for wonder − not at the revolutionary power of sound-reproduction technology, but at its banality. If modernity, in part, names the experience of rapid social and cultural change, then its "shocking emblems" may very well have been taken in stride by some of its people.

Because sound-reproduction technology's role in history is so easily treated as self-evidently decisive, it makes sense to begin rewriting the history of sound by reconsidering the historical significance of sound technologies. A focus on sound-reproduction technology has an added advantage for the historian of sound: during their early years, technologies leave huge paper trails, thus making them especially rich resources for historical research. In early writings about the telephone, phonograph, and radio, we find a rich archive of reflections on the nature and meaning of sound, hearing, and listening. Douglas Kahn writes that, "as a historical object, sound cannot furnish a good story or consistent cast of characters nor can it validate any ersatz notion of progress or generational maturity. The history is scattered, fleeting, and highly mediated − it is as poor an object in any respect as sound itself."[18] Prior to the twentieth century, very little of the sonic past was physically preserved for historical analysis at a later date. So it makes sense to look instead at a particular domain of practice associated with sound. The paper trail left by sound-reproduction technologies provides one useful starting point for a history of sound.

Like an examination of the sense organs themselves, an examination of sound technologies also cuts to the core of the nature/nurture debate in thinking about the causes of and possibilities for historical change. Even the most basic mechanical workings of sound-reproduction technologies are historically shaped. As I will argue, the vibrating diaphragm that allowed telephones and phonographs to function was itself an artifact of changing understandings of human hearing. Sound-reproduction technologies are artifacts of particular practices and relations "all the way down"; they can be considered archaeologically. The history of sound technology offers a route into a field of conjunctures among material, economic, technical, ideational, practical, and environmental changes. Situated as we are amid torrential rains of capitalist development and marketing that pelt us with new digital machinery, it is both easy and tempting to forget the enduring connection between any technology and a larger cultural context. Technologies sometimes enjoy a certain level of deification in social theory and cultural history, where they come to be cast as divine actors. In "impact" narratives, technologies are mysterious beings with obscure origins that come down from the sky to "impact" human relations. Such narratives cast technologies themselves as primary agents of historical change: technological deification is the religion behind claims like "the telephone changed the way we do business," "the phonograph changed the way we listen to music." Impact narratives have been rightly and widely criticized as a form of technological determinism; they spring from an impoverished notion of causality.[19]

At the same time, technologies are interesting precisely because they can play a significant role in people's lives. Technologies are repeatable social, cultural, and material processes crystallized into mechanisms. Often, they perform labor that had previously been done by a person. It is this process of crystallization that makes them historically interesting. Their mechanical character, the ways in which they commingle physics and culture, can tell us a great deal about the people who build and deploy them. Technologies manifest a designed mechanical agency, a set of functions cordoned off from the rest of life and delegated to them, a set of functions developed from and linked to sets of cultural practices. People design and use technologies to enhance or promote certain activities and discourage others. Technologies are associated with habits, sometimes crystallizing them and sometimes enabling them. They embody in physical form particular dispositions and tendencies. The door closer tends to close the door unless I stop it with my hand or a doorstop. The domestic radio set receives but does not broadcast unless I do a little rewiring and add a microphone. The telephone rings while I write the introduction to this book. After years of conditioning to respond to a ringing telephone, it takes some effort to ignore it and finish the sentence or paragraph. To study technologies in any meaningful sense requires a rich sense of their connection with human practice, habitat, and habit. It requires attention to the fields of combined cultural, social, and physical activity – what other authors have called *networks* or *assemblages* – from which technologies emerge and of which they are a part.[20]

The story presented in these pages spirals out from an analysis of the mechanical and physical aspects of the technologies themselves to the techniques, practices, and institutions associated with them. At each juncture in the argument, I show how sound-reproduction technologies are shot through with the tensions, tendencies, and currents of the culture from which they emerged, right on down to their most basic mechanical functions. Our most cherished pieties about sound-reproduction technologies – for instance, that they separated sounds from their sources or that sound recording allows us to hear the voices of the dead – were not and are not innocent empirical descriptions of the technologies' impact. They were wishes that people grafted onto sound-reproduction technologies – wishes that became programs for innovation and use.

For many of their inventors and early users, sound-reproduction technologies encapsulated a whole set of beliefs about the age and place in which they lived. Sound-reproduction technologies represented the promise of science, rationality, and industry and the power of the white man to co-opt and supersede domains of life that were previously considered to be magical. For their early users, sound technologies were – in a word – modern.[21] *Modernity* is of course a cloudy analytic category, fraught with internal contradictions and intellectual conflicts. Its difficulty probably stems from its usefulness as a heuristic term, and my use of it is deliberately heuristic. When I claim that sound-reproduction technology indexes an acoustic modernity, I do not mean quite the same thing as the subjects of my history. *The Audible Past* explores the ways in which the history of sound contributes to and develops from the "maelstrom" of modern life (to return to Berman): capitalism, colonialism, and the rise of industry; the growth and development of the sciences, changing cosmologies, massive population shifts (specifically migration and urbanization), new forms of collective and corporate power, social movements, class struggle and the rise of new middle classes, mass communication, nation-states, bureaucracy; confidence in progress, a universal abstract humanist subject, and the world market; and a reflexive contemplation of the constancy of change.[22] In modern life, sound becomes a problem: an object to be contemplated, reconstructed, and manipulated, something that can be fragmented, industrialized, and bought and sold.

But *The Audible Past* is not a simple modernization narrative for sound and hearing. *Modernization* can too easily suggest a brittle kind of universalism, where the specific historical developments referenced by *modernity* are transmogrified into a set of historical stages through which all cultures must pass. In Johannes Fabian's apt phrase, the idea of modernity as modernization turns relations of space – relations between cultures – into relations of time, where the white man stands at the pinnacle of world evolution.[23] While I am not an exponent of a developmental theory of modernity as "modernization," it is such a central element of some discourses about sound reproduction that we will confront it more than once in the following pages. A long line of inventors, scholars, businesspeople, phonographic anthropologists, and casual users thought of themselves as partaking in a modern way of life, as living at the pinnacle of the world's progress. They believed that their epoch rode the crest of modernization's unstoppable wave. So, in addition to being a useful heuristic for describing the context of the project as a whole, *modernity* and its conjugates are also important categories to be analyzed and carefully taken apart within this history.

The remainder of this introduction provides some conceptual background for the history that follows. The next section is an extended consideration of sound as an object of historical study: what does it mean to write a history of something so apparently natural and physical as sound and hearing? A more detailed map of the book's arguments then follows.

Rethinking sound's nature: Of forests, fallen trees, and phenomenologies

All this talk of modernity, history, and sound technology conjures an implied opposite: the *nature* of sound and hearing. Insofar as we treat sound as a fact of nature, writing something other than its natural history might seem like an immodest or inappropriate endeavor – at best it could aspire only to partiality. Although film scholars have been using the phrase *history of sound* for some time, it has an uneasy ring to it. After all, scholars of the visible world do not write "histories of light" (although perhaps they should), instead preferring to write histories of "visual culture," "images," "visuality," and the like. Bracketing light in favor of "the visual" may be a defensive maneuver since the various visual terms conveniently bracket questions of the nature of nature. But, besides sounding good, *history of sound* already embodies a hard-to-grasp but necessary paradox of nature and culture central to everything that follows in this book. At its core, the phenomenon of sound and the history of sound rest at the in-between point of culture and nature.

It is impossible to "merely describe" the faculty of hearing in its natural state. Even to try is to pretend that language has no figurative dimension of its own. The language that we use to describe sound and hearing comes weighted down with decades or centuries of cultural baggage. Consider the careers of two adjectives associated with the ear in the English language. The term *aural* began its history in 1847 meaning "of or pertaining to the organ of hearing"; it did not appear in print denoting something "received or perceived by the ear" until 1860. Prior to that period, the term *auricular* was used to describe something "of or pertaining to the ear" or perceived by the ear.[24] This was not a mere semantic difference: *auricular* carried with it connotations of oral tradition and hearsay as well as the external features of the ear visible to the naked eye (the folded mass of skin that is often synecdochally referred to as the ear is technically either the *auricle*, the *pinna*, or the *outer ear*). *Aural*, meanwhile, carried with it no connotations of oral tradition and referred specifically to the middle ear, the inner ear, and the nerves that turn vibrations into what the brain perceives as sound (as in *aural surgery*). The idea of the aural and its decidedly medical inflection is a part of the historical transformation that I describe in the following pages.

Generally, when writers invoke a binary coupling between culture and nature, it is with the idea that culture is that which changes over time and that nature is that which is permanent, timeless, and unchanging. The nature/culture binary offers a thin view of nature, a convenient straw figure for "social construction" arguments.[25] In the case of sound, the appeal to something static is also a trick of the language. We treat sound as a natural phenomenon exterior to people, but its very definition is anthropo-centric. The physiologist Johannes Müller wrote over 150 years ago that, "without the organ of hearing with its vital endowments, there would be no such a thing as sound in the world, but merely vibrations."[26] As Müller pointed out, our other senses can also perceive vibration. Sound is a very particular perception of vibrations. You can take the sound out of the human, but you can take the human out of the sound only through an exercise in imagination. Sounds are defined as that class of vibrations perceived – and, in a more exact sense, sympathetically produced – by the functioning ear when they travel through a medium that can convey changes in pressure (such as air). The numbers for the range of human hearing (which absolutely do not matter for the purposes of this study) are twenty to twenty thousand cycles per second, although in practice most adults in industrial society cannot hear either end of that range. We are thus presented with a choice in our definition: we can say either that sound is a class of vibration that *might* be heard or that it is a class of vibration that *is* heard, but, in either case, the hearing of the sound is what makes it. My point is that human beings reside at the center of any meaningful definition of sound. When the hearing of other animals comes up, it is usually contrasted with human hearing (as in "sounds that only a dog could hear"). As part of a larger physical phenomenon of vibration, sound is a product of the human senses and not a thing in the world apart from humans. Sound is a little piece of the vibrating world.

Perhaps this reads like an argument that falling trees in the forest make no sounds if there are no people there to hear them. I am aware that the squirrels would offer another interpretation. Certainly, once we establish an operational definition of sound, there may be those aspects of it that can be identified by physicists and physiologists as universal and unchanging. By our definition of sound, the tree makes a noise whether or not anyone is there to hear it. But, even here, we are dealing in anthropocentric definitions. When a big tree falls, the vibrations extend outside the audible range. The boundary between vibration that is sound and vibration that is not-sound is not derived from any quality of the vibration in itself or the air that conveys the vibrations. Rather, the boundary between sound and not-sound is based on the understood possibilities of the faculty of hearing – whether we are talking about a person or a squirrel. Therefore, as people and squirrels change, so too will sound – by definition. Species have histories.

Sound history indexes changes in human nature and the human body – in life and in death. The very shape and functioning of technologies of sound reproduction reflected, in part, changing understandings of and relations to the nature and function of hearing. For instance, in the final chapter of this book, I discuss how Victorian writers' desire for permanence in sound recording was an extension of changing practices and understandings of preserving bodies and food following the Civil War. The connections among canning, embalming, and sound recording require that we consider practices of sound reproduction in relation to other bodily practices. In a phrase, the history of sound implies a history of the body.

Bodily experience is a product of the particular conditions of social life, not something that is given prior to it. Michel Foucault has shown that, in the eighteenth and nineteenth centuries, the body became "an object and target of power." The modern body is the body that is "is manipulated, shaped, trained," that "obeys, responds, becomes skillful and increases its forces." Like a machine, it is built and rebuilt, operationalized and modified.[27] Beyond and before Foucault, there are scores of authors who reach similar conclusions. Already in 1801, a Dr. Jean-Marc Gaspard Itard concluded, on the basis of his interactions with a young boy found living "wild" in the woods, that audition is learned. Itard named the boy Victor. Being a wild child, Victor did not speak – and his silence led to questions about his ability to hear. Itard slammed doors, jingled keys, and made other sounds to test Victor's hearing. The boy even failed to react when Itard shot off a gun near his head. But Victor was not deaf: the young doctor surmised that the boy's hearing was just fine. Victor simply showed no interest in the same sounds as "civilized" French people.[28]

While the younger Marx argued that the history of the senses was a core component of human history, the older Marx argued that the physical conditions under which laborers "reproduced" themselves would vary from society to society – that their bodies and needs were historically determined.[29] The French anthropologist Marcel Mauss, one of Foucault's many influences, offered that "man's first and most natural technical object, and at the same time technical means, is his body." What Mauss called *body techniques* were "one of the fundamental moments of history itself: education of the vision, education in walking – ascending, descending, running."[30] To Mauss's list we could add the education and shaping of audition. Phenomenology always presupposes culture, power, practice, and epistemology. "Everything is knowledge, and this is the first reason why there is no 'savage experience': there is nothing beneath or prior to knowledge."[31]

The history of sound provides some of the best evidence for a dynamic history of the body because it traverses the nature/culture divide: it demonstrates that the transformation of people's physical attributes is part of cultural history. For example, industrialization and urbanization decrease people's physical capacities to hear. One of the ways in which adults lose the upper range of their hearing is through encounters with loud machinery. A jackhammer here, a siren there, and the top edge of hearing begins to erode. Conflicts over what does and does not constitute environmental noise are themselves battles over what sounds are admissible in the modern landscape.[32] As Nietzsche would have it, modernity is a time and place where it becomes possible for people to be measured.[33] It is also a place where the human-built environment modifies the living body.

If our goal is to describe the historical dynamism of sound or to consider sound from the vantage point of cultural theory, we must move just beyond its shifting borders – just outside sound into the vast world of things that we think of as not being about sound at all. The history of sound is at different moments strangely silent, strangely gory, strangely visual, and always contextual. This is because that elusive inside world of sound – the sonorous, the auditory, the heard, the very density of sonic experience – emerges and becomes perceptible only through its exteriors. If there is no "mere" or innocent description of sound, then there is no "mere" or innocent description of sonic experience. This book turns away from attempts to recover and describe people's interior experience of listening – an auditory past – toward the social and cultural grounds of sonic experience. The "exteriority" of sound is this book's primary object of study. If sound in itself is a variable rather than a constant, then the history of sound is of necessity an externalist and contextualist endeavor. Sound is an artifact of the messy and political human sphere.

To borrow a phrase from Michel Chion, I aim to "disengage sound thinking . . . from its naturalistic rut."[34] Many theorists and historians of sound have privileged the static and transhistorical, that is, the "natural," qualities of sound and hearing as a basis for sound history. A surprisingly large proportion of the books and articles written about sound begin with an argument that sound is in some way a "special case" for social or cultural analysis. The "special case" argument is accomplished through an appeal to the interior nature of sound: it is argued that sound's natural or phenomenological traits require a special sensibility and special vocabulary when we approach it as an object of study. To fully appreciate the strangeness of beginning a history with a transhistorical description of human listening experience, consider how rare it is for histories of newspapers or literature to begin with naturalistic descriptions of light and phenomenologies of reading.

Sound certainly has natural dimensions, but these have been widely misinterpreted. I want to spend the next few pages considering other writers' claims about the supposed natural characteristics of sound in order to explain how and why *The Audible Past* eschews transhistorical constructs of sound and hearing as a basis for a history of sound. Transhistorical explanations of sound's nature can certainly be compelling and powerful, but they tend to carry with them the unacknowledged weight of a two-thousand-year-old Christian theology of listening.

Even if it comes at the beginning of a history, an appeal to the "phenomenological" truth about sound sets up experience as somehow outside the purview of historical analysis. This need not be so – phenomenology and the study of experience are not by definition opposed to historicism. For instance, Maurice Merleau-Ponty's work has a rich sense of the historical dimensions of phenomenological experience.[35] But founding one's analysis on the supposed transhistorical phenomenological characteristics of hearing is an incredibly powerful move in constructing a cultural theory of sound. Certainly, it asserts a universal human subject, but we will see that the problem is less in the universality per se than in the universalization of a set of particular religious prejudices about the role of hearing in salvation. That these religious prejudices are embedded at the very center of Western intellectual history makes them all the more intuitive, obvious, or otherwise persuasive.

To offer a gross generalization, assertions about the difference between hearing and seeing usually appear together in the form of a list.[36] They begin at the level of the individual human being (both physically and psychologically). They move out from there to construct a cultural theory of the senses. These differences between hearing and seeing are often considered as biological, psychological, and physical facts, the implication being that they are a necessary starting point for the cultural analysis of sound. This list strikes me as a litany – and I use that term deliberately because of its theological overtones – so I will present it as a litany here:

— hearing is spherical, vision is directional;
— hearing immerses its subject, vision offers a perspective;
— sounds come to us, but vision travels to its object;
— hearing is concerned with interiors, vision is concerned with surfaces;
— hearing involves physical contact with the outside world, vision requires distance from it;
— hearing places us inside an event, seeing gives us a perspective on the event;
— hearing tends toward subjectivity, vision tends toward objectivity;
— hearing brings us into the living world, sight moves us toward atrophy and death;
— hearing is about affect, vision is about intellect;

— hearing is a primarily temporal sense, vision is a primarily spatial sense;
— hearing is a sense that immerses us in the world, vision is a sense that removes us from it.[37]

The audiovisual litany — as I will hereafter call it — idealizes hearing (and, by extension, speech) as manifesting a kind of pure interiority. It alternately denigrates and elevates vision: as a fallen sense, vision takes us out of the world. But it also bathes us in the clear light of reason. One can also see the same kind of thinking at work in Romantic conceptualizations of music. Caryl Flinn writes that nineteenth-century Romanticism promoted the belief that "music's immaterial nature lends it a transcendent, mystical quality, a point that then makes it quite difficult for music to speak to concrete realities. . . . Like all 'great art' so construed, it takes its place outside of history where it is considered timeless, universal, functionless, operating beyond the marketplace and the standard social relations of consumption and production."[38] Outlining the *differences* between sight and hearing begs the prior question of what we mean when we talk about their nature. Some authors refer back to physics; others refer back to transcendental phenomenology or even cognitive psychology. In each case, those citing the litany do so to demarcate the purportedly special capacities of each sense as the starting point for historical analysis. Instead of offering us an entry into the history of the senses, the audiovisual litany posits history as something that happens *between* the senses. As a culture moves from the dominance of one sense to that of another, it changes. The audiovisual litany renders the history of the senses as a zero-sum game, where the dominance of one sense by necessity leads to the decline of another sense. But there is no scientific basis for asserting that the use of one sense atrophies another. In addition to its specious zero-sum reasoning, the audiovisual litany carries with it a good deal of ideological baggage. Even if that were not so, it would still not be a very good empirical account of sensation or perception.

The audiovisual litany is ideological in the oldest sense of the word: it is derived from religious dogma. It is essentially a restatement of the long-standing spirit/letter distinction in Christian spiritualism. The spirit is living and life-giving — it leads to salvation. The letter is dead and inert — it leads to damnation. Spirit and letter have sensory analogues: hearing leads a soul to spirit, sight leads a soul to the letter. A theory of religious communication that posits sound as life-giving spirit can be traced back to the Gospel of John and the writings of Saint Augustine. These Christian ideas about speech and hearing can in turn be traced back to Plato's discussion of speech and writing in the *Phaedrus*.[39] The hearing-spirit/sight-letter framework finds its most coherent contemporary statement in the work of Walter Ong, whose later writing (especially *Orality and Literacy*) is still widely cited as an authoritative description of the phenomenology and psychology of sound. Because Ong's later work is so widely cited (usually in ignorance of the connections between his ideas on sound and his theological writings), and because he makes a positive statement of the audiovisual litany such a central part of his argument about cultural history, Ong's work warrants some consideration here.

To describe the balance sheet of the senses, Ong used the word *sensorium*, a physiological term that denoted a particular region of the brain that was thought to control all perceptual activity. *Sensorium* fell out of favor in the late nineteenth century as physiologists learned that there is no such center in the brain. Ong's use of the term should therefore be considered metaphoric. For him, the sensorium is "the entire sensory apparatus as an organizational complex," the combined balance among a fixed set of sensory capacities.

Although *Orality and Literacy* reads at times like a summary of scientific findings, Ong's earlier writings clearly state that his primary interest in the senses is explicitly driven by theological concerns: "The question of the sensorium in the Christian economy of revelation is particularly fascinating because of the primacy which this economy accords to the word of God and thus in some mysterious way to sound itself, a primacy already suggested in the Old Testament pre-Christian [*sic*] tradition."[40] For Ong, "divine revelation itself . . . is indeed inserted in a particular sensorium, a particular mixture of the sensory activity typical of a given culture." Ong's balance-sheet history of the senses is clearly and urgently linked to the problem of how to hear the word of God in the modern age. The sonic dimension of experience is closest to divinity.

Vision suggests distance and disengagement. Ong's history of the move from sound-based oral culture to sight-based literate culture is a history of "a certain silencing of God" in modern life. Ong's assertions about the difference between the world of "oral man" and the "hypertrophy of the visual" that marks the modern age parallel perfectly the spirit/letter distinction in Catholic spiritualism. It is a sophisticated and iconoclastic antimodernist Catholicism. Still, Ong argues that the audiovisual litany transcends theological differences: "Faith or no, we must all deal with the same data."[41]

Of course, parts of the audiovisual litany have come under heavy criticism. The work of Jacques Derrida can be read as an inversion of Ong's value system – Ong himself suggests as much.[42] Derrida uses his well-known phrase *the metaphysics of presence* to criticize and dismantle the connections among speech, sound, voice, and presence in Western thought. Although Derrida's most celebrated critiques of presence find him tarrying with Edmund Husserl's transcendental phenomenology, Ferdinand de Saussure's semiotic theory, and Martin Heidegger's ontology, his criticisms are certainly applicable to Ong's thought as well. Ong argues for exactly the metaphysics of presence that Jacques Derrida attacks as "ontotheological," as a creeping Christian spiritualism that inhabits Western philosophy: "The living act, the life-giving act [hearing oneself speak], the *Leben-digkeit*, which animates the body of the signifier and transforms it into a meaningful expression, the soul of language, seems not to separate itself from itself, from its own self-presence."[43] For Derrida, the elevation of speech as the center of subjectivity and the point of access into the divine is "essential to the history of the West, therefore to metaphysics in its entirety, even when it professes to be atheist."[44] Derrida uses this position to argue for the visual side of the audiovisual litany – an emphasis on vision, writing, difference, and absence. Deconstruction inverts, inhabits, and reanimates the sound/vision binary, privileging writing over speech and refusing both speech-based metaphysics and presence-based positive assertions.

Here, I want to make a slightly different move: the audiovisual litany carries with it the theological weight of the durable association among sound, speech, and divinity, even in its scientific guise. Rather than inverting the audiovisual litany, why not redescribe sound? Since this book is not bound by Christian doctrine, there is no law – divine or otherwise – requiring us to assume the interiority of sound and the connection between sound, subjective self-presence, and intersubjective experience. We do not need to assume that sound draws us into the world while vision separates us from it. We can reopen the question of the sources of rationality and modern ways of knowing. If history exists *within* the senses as well as *between* them, then we need not begin a history of sound with an assertion of the transhistorical dimensions of sound.

My criticism of the audiovisual litany goes far beyond the questions of essentialism or social construction, which usually degenerate into philosophical hygienics. Even if we grant the possibility of a transcendental subject of sensation, the audiovisual litany falls short on its own terms. Despite all the appeals to nature in the name of the litany, the phenomenology implied by the audiovisual litany is highly selective – it stands on shaky empirical (and transcendental) ground. As Rick Altman has argued, claims about the transhistorical and transcultural character of the senses often derive their support from culturally and historically specific evidence – limited evidence at that. In the audiovisual litany, "an apparently ontological claim about the role of sound [or vision] has been allowed to take precedence over actual analysis of sound's functioning."[45] Consider the purportedly unique temporal and spatial characteristics of auditory phenomenology. Ong argues that "sound is more real or existential than other sense objects, despite the fact that it is also more evanescent. Sound itself is related to present actuality rather than to past or future"; sounds exist only as they go out of existence.[46] But, strictly speaking, Ong's claim is true for any event – any *process* that you can possibly experience – and so it is not a quality special or unique to sound. To say that ephemerality is a special quality of sound, rather than a quality endemic to any form of perceptible motion or event in time, is to engage in a very selective form of nominalism.[47] The same criticism can be made of the litany's attribution of a "surface"-oriented spatiality to vision as opposed to an "interior" orientation to sound: it is a very selective notion of surface. Anyone who has heard fingernails on a chalkboard or footsteps in a concrete hallway (or on a wooden floor) can recognize that listening has the potential to yield a great deal of information about surfaces very quickly. The phenomenologist Don Ihde has shown that writers who take sound as a weakly spatial sense wholly disregard "the contemporary discoveries of very complex spatial attributes to auditory experience."[48] He demonstrates that hearing has many spatial aspects and possibilities to which we do not normally attend. We can learn a great deal about shape, surface, or texture from listening. Perhaps the biggest error of the audiovisual litany lies in its equation of hearing and listening. Listening is a directed, learned activity: it is a definite cultural practice. Listening requires hearing but is not simply reducible to hearing.

There is no "mere" or innocent description of interior auditory experience. The attempt to describe sound or the act of hearing in itself — as if the sonic dimension of human life inhabited a space prior to or outside history — strives for a false transcendence. Even phenomenologies can change. In this respect, we follow in Dr. Itard's footsteps. Like the studious Itard, who was perplexed by the wild boy who could hear but did not speak, historians of sound must surmise that our subjects' hearing is fine medically. But we can know their sonic world only through their efforts, expressions, and reactions. History is nothing but exteriorities. We make our past out of the artifacts, documents, memories, and other traces left behind. We can listen to recorded traces of past history, but we cannot presume to know exactly what it was like to hear at a particular time or place in the past. In the age of technological reproduction, we can sometimes experience an audible past, but we can do no more than presume the existence of an auditory past.

Notes

1   In both the Bell and the Edison cases, the inventors had a partially functional device before the moment of their "famous first."

2   Oliver Read and Walter L. Welch, *From Tin Foil to Stereo: Evolution of the Phonograph* (New York: Herbert W. Sams, 1976), 4; Michael Chanan, *Repeated Takes: A Short History of Recording and Its Effects on Music* (New York: Verso, 1995), 2.

3   Marshall Berman, *All That Is Solid Melts into Air: The Experience of Modernity* (New York: Penguin, 1992).

4   Alan Burdick, "Now Hear This: Listening Back on a Century of Sound," *Harper's Magazine* 303, no. 1804 (July 2001): 75.

5   For the sake of readability, I have largely kept with the standard practice of using light and sight metaphors for knowledge. Replacing all these with sonic metaphors would be largely a formalist exercise and of dubious value in helping readers understand my argument.

6   For a full discussion of the status of vision in modern thought and the idea that vision is central to the categories of modernity, see Martin Jay, *Downcast Eyes: The Denigration of Vision in Twentieth-Century French Thought* (Berkeley and Los Angeles: University of California Press, 1993); and David Michael Levin, ed., *Modernity and the Hegemony of Vision* (Berkeley and Los Angeles: University of California Press, 1993). See also Marshall McLuhan, *The Gutenberg Galaxy: The Making of Typographic Man* (Toronto: University of Toronto Press, 1962); Michel Foucault, *The Birth of the Clinic: An Archaeology of Medical Perception*, trans. A. M. Sheridan Smith (New York: Pantheon, 1973); and Walter Ong, *Orality and Literacy: The Technologization of the Word* (New York: Routledge, 1982). Ong's work and the phenomenology of listening are discussed below.

7   Although one can hope that this, too, is changing. In addition to some of the scholars of sound cited elsewhere in this introduction, see, e.g., Laura Marks, *The Skin of the Film: The Senses in Intercultural Cinema* (Durham, N.C.: Duke University Press, 1999); David Howes, *The Varieties of Sensory Experience: A Sourcebook in the Anthropology of the Senses* (Toronto: University of Toronto Press, 1991); and Alain Corbin, *The Foul and the Fragrant: Odor and the French Social Imagination* (Cambridge, Mass.: Harvard University Press, 1986), and *Time, Desire, and Horror: Toward a History of the Senses*, trans. Jean Birrell (Cambridge: Blackwell, 1995).

8   In addition to the works discussed below, see Kaja Silverman, *The Acoustic Mirror: The Female Voice in Psychoanalysis and Cinema* (Bloomington: Indiana University Press, 1988); Amy Lawrence, *Echo and Narcissus: Women's Voice in Classical Hollywood Cinema* (Berkeley and Los Angeles: University of California Press, 1991); and Claudia Gorbman, *Unheard Melodies: Narrative Film Music* (Bloomington: Indiana University Press, 1987). Anahid

Kassabian, *Hearing Film: Tracking Identifications in Contemporary Hollywood Film Music* (New York: Routledge, 2001), provides an interesting alternative approach.

9   See C. Wright Mills, *The Sociological Imagination* (New York: Oxford University Press, 1959), 50–75; Peter Novick, *That Noble Dream: The "Objectivity Question" and the American Historical Profession* (New York: Cambridge University Press, 1988); Georg C. Iggers, *Historiography in the Twentieth Century: From Scientific Objectivity to the Postmodern Challenge* (Hanover, N.H.: Wesleyan University Press, 1997); and Bonnie Smith, *The Gender of History* (Cambridge, Mass.: Harvard University Press, 1998).

10   See, e.g., Hadley Cantril and Gordon Allport, *The Psychology of Radio* (New York: Harper and Bros., 1935); Rudolf Arnheim, *Radio*, trans. Margaret Ludwig and Herbert Read (London: Faber and Faber, 1936); and Hanns Eisler and Theodor Adorno, *Composing for the Films* (New York: Oxford University Press, 1947). For a contemporary example, see David Michael Levin, *The Listening Self: Personal Growth, Social Change, and the Closure of Metaphysics* (New York: Routledge, 1989).

11   A significant share of the English-language literature appears in my notes and bibliography.

12   Karl Marx, *Economic and Philosophic Manuscripts of 1844*, trans. Martin Milligan (New York: International, 1968), 140–41.

13   Jonathan Crary, *Techniques of the Observer: On Vision and Modernity in the Nineteenth Century* (Cambridge, Mass.: MIT Press, 1990), 16.

14   These questions recur constantly in the classic texts, such as Max Horkheimer and Theodor Adorno, *Dialectic of Enlightenment* (New York: Continuum, 1944); Walter Benjamin, "The Storyteller," and "The Work of Art in the Age of Mechanical Reproduction," in *Illuminations*, trans. Hannah Arendt (New York: Schocken, 1968); and Theodor Adorno, "The Curves of the Needle," trans. Thomas Levin, *October*, no. 55 (winter 1990): 49–56.

15   Stephen Kern, *The Culture of Time and Space, 1800–1918* (Cambridge, Mass.: Harvard University Press, 1983), passim; Donald M. Lowe, *History of Bourgeois Perception* (Chicago: University of Chicago Press, 1982), 9, 111–17; and Marshall McLuhan, *Understanding Media: The Extensions of Man* (New York: McGraw-Hill, 1964), 265–83, 297–307.

16   Claude S. Fischer, *America Calling: A Social History of the Telephone* (Berkeley and Los Angeles: University of California Press, 1992), 5; Jacques Attali, *Noise: The Political Economy of Music* (Minneapolis: University of Minnesota Press, 1985), 87; John Durham Peters, *Speaking into the Air: A History of the Idea of Communication* (Chicago: University of Chicago Press, 1999), 160; Susan Douglas, *Listening In: Radio and the American Imagination from Amos 'n Andy and Edward R. Murrow to Wolfman Jack and Howard Stern* (New York: Times Books, 1999), 9.

17   D. L. LeMahieu, *A Culture for Democracy: Mass Communication and the Cultivated Mind in Britain between the Wars* (Oxford: Clarendon, 1988), 81.

18   Douglas Kahn, "Histories of Sound Once Removed," in *Wireless Imagination: Sound, Radio, and the Avant-Garde*, ed. Douglas Kahn and Gregory Whitehead (Cambridge, Mass.: MIT Press, 1992), 2.

19   Technological determinism is, more or less, the premise that technology determines the conduct and form of cultural life. For criticisms of technological determinism from perspectives sympathetic to my own, see Jennifer Daryl Slack, *Communication Technologies and Society: Conceptions of Causality and the Politics of Techno-logical Intervention* (Norwood, N.J.: Ablex, 1984); Raymond Williams, *Television: Technology and Cultural Form* (Middletown, Conn.: Wesleyan University Press, 1992); and Carol Stabile, *Feminism and the Technological Fix* (New York: St. Martin's, 1994). From a different angle, Martin Heidegger points out that there are actually four kinds of causality when we consider technology: material, form, use, and that which shapes the material into a particular form for a particular use (see *The Question Concerning Technology and Other Essays*, trans. William Lovitt [New York: Harper Torchbooks, 1977], 6–12 and throughout).

20   Bruno Latour, *We Have Never Been Modern*, trans. Catherine Porter (Cambridge, Mass.: Harvard University Press, 1993), 3–8; Jody Berland, "Cultural Technologies and the Production of Space," in *Cultural Studies*, ed. Lawrence Grossberg, Cary Nelson, and Paula Treichler (New York: Routledge, 1992); J. Macgregor Wise, *Exploring Technology and Social Space* (Thousand Oaks, Calif.: Sage, 1997), xvi, 54–55, 68; Gilles Deleuze and Félix Guattari, *A Thousand Plateaus: Capitalism and Schizophrenia*, trans. Brian Massumi (Minneapolis: University of Minnesota Press, 1987), 4, 90, 503–05.

21   Jonathan Sterne, "Sound Out of Time/Modernity's Echo," in *Turning the Century*, ed. Carol Stabile (Boulder, Colo.: Westview, 2000), 9–30.

22   This list is drawn from Berman, *All That Is Solid Melts into Air*, 5–12, 16; Matei Calinescu, *Five Faces of Modernity: Modernity, Avant-Garde, Decadence, Kitsch, Postmodernism* (Durham, N.C.: Duke University Press, 1987), 42;

Zygmunt Bauman, *Modernity and Ambivalence* (Cambridge: Polity, 1991), 5; and Henri Lefebvre, *Introduction to Modernity*, trans. John Moore (New York: Verso, 1995), 168–238.

23   Johannes Fabian, *Time and the Other: How Anthropology Makes Its Object* (New York: Columbia University Press, 1983).

24   *Oxford English Dictionary*, s.v. "aural," "auricular."

25   Michael Taussig, *Mimesis and Alterity: A Particular History of the Senses* (New York: Routledge, 1993), xvi–xviii. See also Ian Hacking, *The Social Construction of What?* (Cambridge, Mass.: Harvard University Press, 1999).

26   Johannes Müller, *Elements of Physiology*, trans. William Baly, arranged from the 2d London ed. by John Bell (Philadelphia: Lea and Blanchard, 1843), 714.

27   Michel Foucault, *Discipline and Punish: The Birth of the Prison*, trans. Alan Sheridan (New York: Vintage, 1977), 136. Foucault has a similar discussion in *The History of Sexuality*, vol. I, *An Introduction*, trans. Robert Hurley (New York: Vintage, 1978), 139.

28   Jean-Marc Gaspard Itard, *The Wild Boy of Aveyron*, trans. George Humphrey and Muriel Humphrey (New York: Meredith, 1962), 26–27; Douglas Keith Candland, *Feral Children and Clever Animals: Reflections on Human Nature* (New York: Oxford University Press, 1993).

29   Karl Marx, *Capital*, vol. I, *The Process of Capitalist Production* (New York: International, 1967), 168.

30   Marcel Mauss, "Body Techniques," in *Sociology and Psychology: Essays*, trans. Ben Brewster (Boston: Routledge and Kegan Paul, 1979), 104, 121.

31   Gilles Deleuze, *Foucault*, trans. Sean Hand (Minneapolis: University of Minnesota Press, 1988), 109.

32   Alain Corbin, *Village Bells: Sound and Meaning in the Nineteenth-Century French Countryside* (New York: Columbia University Press, 1999), 254–83.

33   "Man himself must first of all have become *calculable, regular, necessary*, even in his own image of himself, if he is to be able to stand security for *his own future*" (Friedrich Nietzsche, *On the Genealogy of Morals and Ecce Homo*, trans. Walter Kauffman [New York: Vintage, 1967], 58). Nietzsche makes this comment in a discussion of promises and contracts. For him, a sense of the human calculability is inextricably tied to the contemplation of an interrelated past, present, and future. For our purposes, it is enough to note that Nietzsche's self-calculating subject who can make a promise is a short step from Zygmunt Bauman's subject who contemplates the relation between continuity and change (see Bauman, *Modernity and Ambivalence*).

34   Michel Chion, *Audio-Vision: Sound on Screen*, trans. Claudia Gorbman (New York: Columbia University Press, 1994), 94.

35   Maurice Merleau-Ponty, "The Primacy of Perception and Its Philosophical Consequences," trans. James M. Edie, in *The Primacy of Perception and Other Essays on Phenomenological Psychology, the Philosophy of Art, History, and Politics*, ed. James M. Edie (Evanston, Ill.: Northwestern University Press, 1964), 20. For a discussion of the temporal and ephemeral character of perception, see ibid., 35.

36   The following summarizes an argument that I develop more fully in an essay in progress entitled "The Theology of Sound."

37   This list is most clearly elaborated in Walter Ong, *The Presence of the Word: Some Prolegomena for Cultural and Religious History* (Minneapolis: University of Minnesota Press, 1981). See also Ong, *Orality and Literacy*, 30–72; Attali, *Noise*; Lowe, *History of Bourgeois Perception*; Marshall McLuhan and Edmund Carpenter, "Acoustic Space," in *Explorations in Communication: An Anthology*, ed. Edmund Carpenter and Marshall McLuhan (Boston: Beacon, 1960); Rick Altman, "The Material Heterogeneity of Recorded Sound," in *Sound Theory / Sound Practice*, ed. Rick Altman (New York: Routledge, 1992); John Shepherd, *Music as a Social Text* (Cambridge: Polity, 1991); Barry Truax, *Acoustic Communication* (Norwood, N.J.: Ablex, 1984); Eric Havelock, *Preface to Plato* (Cambridge, Mass.: Harvard University Press, 1963), and *The Muse Learns to Write: Reflections on Orality and Literacy from Antiquity to the Present* (New Haven, Conn.: Yale University Press, 1986), esp. 1–29; and Bruce R. Smith, *The Acoustic Culture of Early-Modern England: Attending to the O-Factor* (Chicago: University of Chicago Press, 1999), 3–29.

38   Caryl Flinn, *Strains of Utopia: Gender, Nostalgia, and Hollywood Film Music* (Princeton, N.J.: Princeton University Press, 1992), 7. Although it is still quite influential, this Romantic notion of music has been widely criticized in the past few decades. See, e.g., Janet Wolff, "The Ideology of Autonomous Art," in *Music and Society: The Politics of Composition, Performance, and Reception*, ed. Richard Leppert and Susan McClary (New York: Cambridge University Press, 1987).

39   Susan Handelman, *Slayers of Moses: The Emergence of Rabbinic Interpretation in Modern Literary Theory* (Albany: State University of New York Press, 1982), 15–21. Handelman's book offers an extended discussion of the

spirit/letter distinction as it is manifested in Western metaphysics and hermeneutics. See also Peters, *Speaking into the Air*, 36–51, 66–74; Jacques Derrida, *Of Grammatology*, trans. Gayatri Chakravorty Spivak (Baltimore: Johns Hopkins University Press, 1976), 323 n. 3, *Dissemination*, trans. Barbara Johnson (Chicago: University of Chicago Press, 1981), 61–171, and *The Postcard: From Socrates to Freud and Beyond*, trans. Alan Bass (Chicago: University of Chicago Press, 1987); Plato, "Phaedrus," in *Collected Dialogues*, ed. Edith Hamilton and Huntington Cairns (Princeton, N.J.: Princeton University Press, 1961), 475–525; and Havelock, *Preface to Plato*.

40 Ong, *Presence of the Word*, 6. *Pre-Christian* is an important modifier here since it treats rabbinic thought as an incomplete prelude to Catholic Christianity.

41 Ibid., 6, 11, 12, 288–89, 324. In *Orality and Literacy* (perhaps at the request of his editors), Ong largely removed the religious content of the distinction, treating it instead as a purely secular academic discovery (see pp. 1, 6).

42 Ong, *Orality and Literacy*, 75, 77, 123, 129, 166–71.

43 Jacques Derrida, *Speech and Phenomena and Other Essays on Husserl's Theory of Signs*, trans. David B. Allison (Evanston, Ill.: Northwestern University Press, 1973), 77.

44 Derrida, *Of Grammatology*, 323 n. 3. For a reading of Derrida's critique of Christian metaphysics as an instance of a "heretical" rabbinic hermeneutics, see also Handelman, *Slayers of Moses*.

45 Rick Altman, "Four and a Half Film Fallacies," in Altman, ed., *Sound Theory / Sound Practice*, 37, 39.

46 Ong, *Presence of the Word*, III (quotation), and *Orality and Literacy*, 32 (on sound existing only as it goes out of existence).

47 James Lastra (*Sound Technology and American Cinema: Perception, Representation, Modernity* [New York: Columbia University Press, 2000], 133) criticizes nominalism on the basis that it treats technological reproduction as a false mediation of a real event. He is actually criticizing bad nominalism since a fully developed nominalism would treat *all* events in their uniqueness. See, e.g., Gilles Deleuze, *Spinoza: Practical Philosophy* (San Francisco: City Lights, 1988), 122–30.

48 Don Ihde, *Listening and Voice: A Phenomenology of Sound* (Athens: Ohio University Press, 1976), 58. Steven Feld has also roundly criticized the notion of orality as a universal construct of sound culture. See his "Orality and Consciousness," in *The Oral and the Literate in Music*, ed. Yoshiko Tokumaru and Osamu Yamaguti (Tokyo: Academia Music, 1986).

PART FIVE

DESIGNING (IN) THE WORLD

INTRODUCTION TO PART FIVE

DESIGN CULTURE knits you into the world in direct and indirect ways. Have a look at where your clothes were made. The clothes I am wearing were bought in the United Kingdom, but they tell another story too: 'Made in Hong Kong' (jumper), 'Made in Sri Lanka' (shirt), 'Made in China' (shoes), 'Made in Turkey' (trousers). The labels tell only a fraction of the story: they tell only of a geographical movement (from over 'there' to over 'here'), not the full extent of the uneven circulation of goods, ideas, wealth, bodies and labour hours.

The social philosopher Henri Lefebvre once remarked how 'the sum total of capitalist society' can be found in a small event like somebody (a woman) buying sugar:

> Thus the simplest event – a woman buying a pound of sugar, for example – must be analysed. . . .
> To understand this simple event, it is not enough merely to describe it; research will disclose a
> tangle of reasons and causes, of essences and 'spheres': the woman's life, her biography, her job,
> her family, her class, her budget, her eating habits, how she uses money, her opinions and her ideas,
> the state of the market, etc. Finally I will have grasped the sum total of capitalist society, the
> nation and its history.
>
> (Lefebvre 1958/1991: 57)

Sugar was no accidental choice. Sugar is marked by the history of colonial adventurism and the inhuman horror that was the slave trade.

I am writing this in the city of Bristol in England. Bristol is a city that prospered on the back of slavery (on the backs of slaves). It was a central departure port for the 'triangular trade' of transatlantic slavery. Ships left the port of Bristol carrying manufactured goods made throughout Britain. These goods were taken to the west coast of Africa and exchanged for enslaved Africans. The slave ships sailed to the Caribbean islands, where slaves (the ones that didn't die in transit) were set to work on plantations. Sugar, cotton and tobacco – produce that was cultivated and harvested by slave labour – were brought back to Bristol, stored in warehouses on the docks and then taken to be refined into commodity forms.

Everywhere in Bristol you can see the signs of the wealth that was generated by those enslaved bodies. The luxurious eighteenth-century housing was built for plantation owners, who also traded in slaves and made money in manufacturing refined sugar. Bristol was also one of the first cities to establish a committee for the abolition of the slave trade. The abolitionists also launched what may have been the first consumer boycott (against the use of sugar) and effectively politicised the use of sugar, and altered the practices of people sitting round kitchen and dining-room tables in Britain.

Chapter 23

John McHale

AN ECOLOGICAL OVERVIEW [1969]

Source: John McHale (1969) 'An Ecological Overview', in *The Future of the Future*, New York: George Braziller, pp. 66–74.

During the 1950s John McHale (1922–78) was a significant force in the Independent Group (IG) – a loose collection of artists, musicians, writers, historians, architects, photographers and designers who irregularly met at London's Institute of Contemporary Art. The group's significance for the study of design culture is, I think, enormous. While the IG have tended to be subsumed in the history books as forerunners to Pop Art they are more productively recognised as a form of emergent cultural studies. The group (which, to be fair, wasn't really much of a group) could be characterised by a number of features that it shares with early cultural studies: intellectual diversity; a willingness to mix what had previously been thought of as 'low' culture with 'high' culture; and an abiding enthusiasm for understanding the complexity of the present moment. The Independent Group talked, listened, wrote and made work. The topics they covered included cybernetics, Tin Pan Alley music, advertising, car design, existentialism, abstract painting and so on.

In 1955 McHale was awarded a fellowship to study at Yale with the former Bauhaus colour theorist Josef Albers. McHale was seduced by America and busily collected the glossy magazines of postwar consumerism, and photographed roadside diners and other elements of what today is called Americana. McHale was a ceaseless promoter of the architect and visionary theorist Richard Buckminster Fuller (with whom he would later work on 'the inventory of world resources' project) and his trajectory after the Independent Group needs to be seen in this light. In 1962 with the painter Magda Cordell McHale (who had also been involved in the Independent Group) he immigrated to the USA and established a number of research centres dedicated to studying world resources, human needs, technology, mass communication and the future.

The Future of the Future, which includes the chapter reproduced here, is an early example of a strand of 'eco-futurism' that connects a number of communication theorists with avant-garde artists and designers. *The Future of the Future* brings together Buckminster Fuller and the Canadian media theorist Marshall McLuhan, with artists like Robert Rauschenberg and John Cage, as well as various sociologists and futurologists. The book ends with a plea for a truly 'planetary society', which can begin to think globally about how to sustain shared resources, meet real human needs, while releasing creative energies. It still sounds urgent. After a number of years working as an eco-futurist researcher and writer, McHale was planning in the late 1970s to return to making artworks. Unfortunately he left 'spaceship earth' before he could start this new project; he died at the age of fifty-six.

Further reading: Fuller 1981; Massey 1995; McHale and McHale 1978; Robbins 1990; Wigley 2001.

L IFE ON EARTH has been possible during the past billions of years only through the relatively stable interrelationships of the variables of climate, the composition of the atmosphere, the oceans, the life-sustaining qualities of the land surface, the natural reservoirs, and natural cycles.

Within the thinly spread biofilm of air, earth, and water space around the planet, all living organisms exist in various systems of delicately balanced symbiotic relations. The close tolerances of many of these relationships have become known to us, generally through their disruption, only in recent times.

> For at least 2,000,000 years, men have been reproducing and multiplying on a little automated space ship called earth, in an automated universe in which the entire process is so successfully predesigned that men did not even know that they were so naive as to think they had invented their own success as they lived egocentrically on a seemingly static earth.[1]

Apart from the comparatively local disturbances of natural cycles occasioned through hunting, herding, and primitive agricultural practices, until quite recently man did not have the developed capacities to interfere seriously with the major life-sustaining processes of the planet. He could live and find food only under conditions restricted by his technological development. The earth surface available to him, with breathable air, water and arable land, was less than one-eighth of the earth area; the remainder – the seas, mountain peaks, and glacial and desert areas – was mainly inaccessible to human habitation or large-scale use.

Though the evidence of ancient disruption of natural balance is still with us in the form of man-made deserts, deforested lands, etc., these were essentially local in their scope and consequences. It is only in the more recent and brief historical period that man has developed sufficient power to be actually, and even more potentially, dangerous to the overall ecosystem.

His acquisition of specifically technological means of gaining control over local aspects of the environ through fire, implements, weapons and other means is accompanied by the swift increase and geographical spread of human populations. From approximately 20 millions in 300 B.C., population increased to 500 millions by the seventeenth century; in the short interval since then, there has been a fivefold multiplication, to 2,500 million people. This explosive increase coincides with the introduction of mechanical energies in machine production, to mechanized agriculture and the use of chemical fertilizers, improved sanitation, general health measures, and higher life expectancy.

As each earlier invention increased the amount of energy and survival advantage available to man, so it adjusted the ecological balance to favor the increase of his progeny. The latest growth change in human population since the onset of the industrial revolutions is, within all previous contexts, an extremely abnormal one; "It represents in fact, one of the greatest biological upheavals known in geological, as well as in human history."[2] In the longer range, of course, this expansion may be viewed as the natural evolutionary development of a unique species.

The first fifty years of this new phase, of adaptation and species extension through intensive industrialization, seemed to confirm the notion that man could indeed conquer nature, could free himself from the biological laws governing development of other species. But as the series of technological revolutions has multiplied in frequency and power amplification, this view has been somewhat tempered by the equivalent increase of knowledge about the overall effects on the planetary habitat.

Though it has been obvious for some time that we cannot simply extrapolate human development in terms of natural laws, and that Malthusian and other limits may not strictly apply, there are still many central questions of evolutionary adaptation through man's capacity to externalize his intellectual and physical means in symbolic and technological systems. He is, in this sense, more directly in control of his own future evolvement, but the extent of that control over the environ and over his own uncontrolled activities within the environ depends on his capacity to apply himself *consciously* to an adaptive process that has been largely unconscious.

Through his intelligence, man has enlarged his ecological niche to include the whole planet. His activities are no longer constrained to horizontal deployments around its surface, but extend increasingly into and beyond the atmosphere and beneath the oceans. These activities include the transformation of vast amounts of the material resources of the planet to his purposes.

> The mechanical revolution . . . brought into use strata of the earth previously beyond the reach of man. The subsurface was made to yield its wealth both of fossil fuels, the sources of inanimate energy itself, and of the metals required for the application and control of this new energy. Moreover, man pushed his frontiers upward as well. The air became a source of nitrogen; sunshine itself could be more fully used; radioactivity was discovered; and the energy of moving water came to be exploited in different ways and, hence, more fully. Generalizing, one might say that man pushed the exploitation of land vertically, both downward and upward. Land thus ceased to be identical with surface, with a thin layer of soil or surface minerals. It was no longer two dimensional; it spread out into the third dimension, to say nothing of the fourth dimension of the physicist.[3]

The scale of these activities and the expansion and proliferation of man-made systems now approach magnitudes in which they directly affect larger and larger areas, sectors, and relationships of the overall planetary system.

Man and the biosphere

The volume of air, water, and soil surrounding the earth, within which conditions are supportive of life, is variously termed the bio- or ecosphere, biofilm, or envelope. It extends vertically to a height of approximately 6 miles and downwards to the greatest known depths of the oceans, and to a few thousand feet below the earth's surface.

The life space is a unitary system of processes contained within these three layers of the atmosphere, the hydrosphere, and the geo- or lithosphere. In turn, these layers are conditioned by the energy radiations that provide motive power for the system. The major source of energy is from the sun, but there are also the kinetic and potential energies from the earth's gravitational system and the geothermal energy from the interior of the earth mass.

The atmospheric filtering of external radiation and the gravitational, pressure, and temperature constants provide a median environment for organic life. This environment is of a sufficiently steady state for long evolutionary change and of sufficient range to allow a great variety of species.

The planetary surface is relatively meager; about one-third of its 197 million square miles is dry land and the remainder is water. In human terms, we live at the bottom of an ocean of air, on a small island surrounded by an ocean of water. Within this life zone, most living forms are held close to the surface of the earth, but the evolutionary process has been specifically characterized by the enlargement of occupancy of the vertical and horizontal ranges of the biosphere. Our own most singular, and recent, exploit of life space extension has been to broach its limits by orbiting animals, plants, and men outside the earth's atmosphere.

Despite the close dimensions of the life zone and the relatively narrow tolerances endurable by living organisms, there are countless varieties of habitats within which forms of life pursue their cycles of individual growth and decay.

Man, of middle size in range and one of the least specialized of complex living forms, has almost evolved beyond the stage where he is constrained within any specific habitat or ecological niche parameters. These may be distinctly characterized for most other organisms by differences in medium, of earth, air, and water; in physiochemical factors of salinity, acidity, etc.; in temperature, pressure, and light availability. At one end of the scale we may distinguish such ecological habitats as climatic zones, ranging through the tropical, subtropical, temperate, subarctic, and arctic. At the other end we have organisms under several atmospheric pressures in the ocean depths, and those whose niche is on or within the tissues of another life form.

The fundamental relation between all organisms and their environ (as including other organisms) is the maintenance of life through various types of energy exchanges. The basic life materials are the chemical elements; thus, 99 percent of the human organism is composed of hydrogen, oxygen, carbon, nitrogen, calcium, and phosphorus, with various other trace elements in fractional amounts; water comprises 60 percent of its mass.

All such materials are, of course, energy – at varying levels of relatively temporal organization. We could therefore refer to all materials as energy whose mass and structural characteristics have a given stable configuration in the particular material state. Energy and materials are in constant and complexly regenerative flows between, and within, organisms and the environ.

The overall energy flux into and out of the biosphere and its larger containing earth system, from radiation received from the sun and that radiated outwardly from the earth, is roughly in balance. This allows us to consider the biosphere, theoretically, as a locally closed system within which no energy may be lost or gained overall. The energy flow within the biosphere, as a closed local system, should ultimately be reduced through its various exchange losses to an evenly dissipated end state of *entropy* or minimal energy flux.

This state of minimal order, of the final running down of the system, may be characterized partially by the process of organic decay. In this stage, the arrest of material growth and the slowing down of external and internal flows is finally resolved in the disintegration of the complex organic structure into its elementary constituents.

Entropy is also used, in terms of information, as a measure of uncertainty or disorder of knowledge. But to the extent that information increases order and predictability in the system and reverses the tendency toward running down, it is antientropic. As the agency or principle of complex ordering in the environ, its role has not yet been fully or clearly defined in relation to energy and material organization. It is significant, however, that while the amount of available energy and material elements in the ecosystem remains relatively constant, the amount of order increases. The bioevolutionary direction is toward increased complexity of order; information increases and accumulates.

> The information extracted from the environment by one organism does not in equal measure reduce the amount of information available to any other organism, nor does what is learned by one diminish the amount that can be learned by another. A genetic population in expanding its numbers increases, if anything – its per capita information supply, even if per capita supplies of materials and energy be reduced. . . . Evolution viewed as a "learning process" entails the incorporation of more information into population systems: 'In the long view there has been an increase in the complexity of genetic instructions [Medawar, 1961]' . . . Social organisms in sharing information increase the amount by increasing the distribution rather than inversely.[4]

Man's function in the ecosystem may then be viewed as

1   Entropic – in using energies to reduce complex material resources to simpler structures, i.e., where he acts as an unconscious biological agency as in food processing, reducing and extinguishing other organic populations, disordering towards malfunction of "natural" systems, in air, water, earth, pollution, etc.

2   Antientropic – where he uses energies more consciously to modify and transform his environ towards higher levels of complexity. Through the application of organized information/knowledge in his artificial systems he increasingly reprocesses, reorders and redistributes energy and materials in more, rather than less, complex forms.

The balance between man's entropic (disordering) propensities and his antientropic (ordering) propensities is, in this sense, a central point of our present discussions.[5] We can only surmise, in terms of our brief historical record, that this balance is already tipped, through evolutionary development, toward the antientropic processes as more favorable to the survival of the species.

The concept may also be extended beyond life on earth, toward the imminent engagement of man with extraterrestrial systems. Some of these, such as the moon, are of a different and apparently less complex order and of lower energy level. What may be the evolutionary effect of introducing antientropic bias into such entropically oriented systems? The question enlarges philosophically to the consideration of all life forms, including the nonhuman, as an antientropic process or principle. Our more immediately pressing consideration is, however, human life and society within the present confines of the biosphere.

The basic biological functions that we share with other organisms furnish only some of the parameters of our overall ecosystem requirements. Our further needs are complicated by the high degree of social development of the human species. Social patterns are more determinant of biological events than we generally concede.

We may schematize our ecosystem relations by labeling certain areas of the environ system and the human systems, at the same time bearing in mind that this is an extremely limited conceptual convenience. Such schematic models, in which divisions or "boxes" are set out in linearly connected fashion, can in no way approximate the dynamic complexity of our simplest relationships in which every aspect of every activity is interconnected.

Notes

1   R. B. Fuller, "Prospects for Humanity," *Saturday Review* (August 29, 1964).

2   *Energy Resources*. Washington, D.C.: Natl. Res. Council, Natl. Acad. Sci. Publ. No. 1000-D, Committee on Natural Resources, 1962.

3   Erich W. Zimmermann, *Introduction to World Resources*, Henry L. Hunker, ed. New York: Harper & Row, 1964.

4   O. T. Duncan, "Social Organization and the Ecosystem," in *Handbook of Modern Sociology*, R. L. Faris, ed. Skokie, Ill.: Rand McNally, 1964.

5   The hinge of this proposition rests, of course, with a specifically anthropocentric view of order.

Chapter 24

Krzysztof Wodiczko

DESIGNING FOR THE CITY OF STRANGERS [1999]

Source: Krzysztof Wodiczko (1999) 'Designing for the City of Strangers', in *Critical Vehicles: Writings, Projects, Interviews*, Cambridge, Mass.: MIT Press, pp. 4–15.

Krzysztof Wodiczko attained a degree in industrial design from the Warsaw Academy of Fine Art in the late 1960s. In the 1970s he emigrated from Poland, first to Canada and then to the USA. At the moment he runs the 'Interrogative Design Group' at the Massachusetts Institute of Technology. Today he is known primarily as an artist and much of his work speaks the language of contemporary avant-garde art. For instance, since the early 1980s he has been producing large-scale projections (of still and moving images) that are intended to intervene within the urban landscape (see Figure 24.1). Projected on to the side of buildings and monuments, the images (for instance, a giant padlock and chain on an empty building) are intended to constitute 'a symbol attack, a public psychoanalytic séance, unmasking and revealing the unconscious of the building, its body, the "medium" of power' (Wodiczko 1999: 47). Alongside the projections Wodiczko has been making a series of instruments (vehicles, communication devices, survival packs) intended for the use of homeless people and migrants.

His *Homeless Vehicle* (1988–9) is a good place to start when viewing Wodiczko's work as design practice (see Figure 24.2). Here his client group were homeless men and women, who participated in establishing the requirements for the vehicle and tested various versions of it. Yet while the vehicle had a function (to facilitate the role of homeless people in the city and to provide shelter for them), it also had a communicative aim: it was intended to make visible the invisible labour of the homeless (or 'evicts', Wodiczko's preferred term) in sustaining urban social relations. Thus the vehicle looked like a cross between a space-age rocket and a shopping trolley: it was designed to facilitate the collection of bottles and cans and to draw attention to itself, to fail to blend in.

The conjunction of utility and symbolic communication is at the centre of Wodiczko's design activity and becomes particularly vivid in his 'immigrant instruments'. Instruments like *Alien Staff* (1992–6) store information (video testimony, migration documents, photographs of loved ones and loved places) but they also demand attention (see Figure 24.3). In a world where design is often used to produce a mirage of social smoothness (all those refitted unemployment offices), *Alien Staff* speaks the catastrophic history of global migrations. *Alien Staff* facilitates communication, and it does so in the interests of the migrant: it 'must aid the stranger in making the transition to nonstrangeness while assisting the local in recognizing his or her own strangeness'.

Figure 24.1   Krzysztof Wodiczko, projection, Duke of York Column and steps, London, 1985 © Krzysztof Wodiczko, courtesy Galerie Lelong, New York.

As the text here testifies, part of Wodiczko's design brief is social reparation – to begin to heal the systemic tears in the social fabric. The rationale is compelling and seems more urgent by the day: if the 'public' (public monuments, public broadcasting) gives voice to the history and presence of the victors, then the memories and presence of the vanquished (those who are homeless, or placeless, or abused, or unwanted) remain locked in secret pockets of privacy. For design to help produce the conditions that would allow this private world to become public is *the* democratic activity *par excellence*.

Further reading: Deutsche 1996, 2002; Hebdige 1992, 1993; Highmore 2006; Hollier 1993; Kristeva 1991; Wodiczko 1999.

Figure 24.2 Krzysztof Wodiczko, *Homeless Vehicle*, 1988–9 (outside Trump Tower), aluminium and mixed media © Krzysztof Wodiczko, courtesy Galerie Lelong, New York.

The messiah interrupts history.

(Walter Benjamin, "Theses on the Philosophy of History", 1940)

City of the victors

ACCORDING TO WALTER BENJAMIN, the fact that things "go on" is a catastrophe. The city is a monumental stage for things to "go on" because it perpetuates both a spatial relationship between its inhabitants and its symbolic structures, and a psycho-social relationship among its dwellers. These two perpetuations must be perturbed to wake up the city and to save it from the bad dreams of the present, the nightmares of the past, and the catastrophes of the future. I would like to propose the possibility of a design practice that would interrupt these processes and could eventually help to heal the city's wounded psychosocial relations and its catastrophic reality.

Theorist Stéphane Mosès, in analyzing Benjamin's theological-political model of history, focuses on his concept of the *history of the victors*, which operates as a past "transmitted to us through a hermeneutical *tradition* that selects events, preserving some and rejecting others, at times determining their interpretation." It can easily afford to forget the catastrophes it has caused. I recognize this kind of history as the foundation or cement that stabilizes the continuity of the "legitimate" and "familiar" city. The history of the victors, the official presence of the official past, constitutes the *official city*. This official city is a lived tradition that celebrates, in everyday life, "the triumph of the strongest and the disappearance of the weakest."[1] Such a history (as represented in textbooks, national literature, films, and public monuments) cherishes a notion of progress that, according to Benjamin, is inevitably linked to a legacy of destruction.

Figure 24.3   Krzysztof Wodiczko, *Alien Staff*, 1992–6, mixed media, pictured in use in Stockholm ©
Krzysztof Wodiczko, courtesy Galerie Lelong, New York.

The history of a nation or city, like every synchronic narrative, collaborates with the *history of catastrophe* by celebrating the lineage of "our" progressive and victorious traditions. To avoid future catastrophes, daily disclosures of the often-hidden destructiveness of the present must be linked to critical recollections of past disasters. This sort of critical approach to history has been – and continues to be – an intuitive and interruptive survival practice of every immigrant.

"The inertia that perpetuates past injustices can only be broken by the eruption of something radically new; unpredictable," says Stéphane Mosès, building on Benjamin's analysis. The history of the victors must be confronted and interrupted by the *memory of the nameless* or the *tradition of the vanquished*. In staging such an interruption and bringing these traditions to light, the stranger – the vanquished of today – functions as a prophet or messenger. Each time the experience of a stranger is shared and understood, the city revives and returns to its conscious life as a democratic hope for us all. To heal one voiceless stranger, then, is to heal the entire city.

City of the vanquished

Tremors and aftershocks caused by the end of the Cold War are being felt across the planet. As the old and stable ideological front lines have vanished, a new war has begun, no longer cold and seemingly bloodless, but often hot, like fire, and openly bloody. Refugees are fleeing new religious wars, new chauvinisms, and new nationalisms. For many, the end of the Cold War has been the end of their world, their identity, their community, and the beginning of a new diaspora.

With the official account of the population of refugees soon to reach 40,000,000, the United Nations has called the last quarter-century the "Migration Era." The influx of immigrants to the United States has now reached the historic levels of the nineteenth-century immigration wave. By the year 2010, foreign-born residents and citizens will probably outnumber U.S.-born inhabitants in most American cities. By then, these cities will undoubtedly be the sites of the greatest challenges and hopes for democracy in the United States.

Historically, the city has always been a hope for the displaced. And today, as it was in the past, our cities are worth nothing and will be condemned to destruction if they cannot open themselves to strangers. Look back at Sodom and Gomorrah! Tens of millions of these strangers now traverse and transgress frontiers and borders that are simultaneously internal and external, geopolitical and psycho-social, ethical and spiritual, private and public. Identities and communities are disintegrating, multiplying, crossing, shifting, and reconfiguring, sparking fear and violence among those who feel invaded by others, who import speechless pain.

Immigrant utopia

As part of the second largest wave of immigration in U.S. history, these wanderers will be confronted by the multitude of divided and competing groups of both U.S.- and foreign-born residents. But unlike the immigrants of the first wave, these new refugees enter cities that are already fully built, with their architectural, ideological, and monumental theaters in place. It is up to these newcomers, then, to transform and unbuild the cities by inserting their presence, their performances, and their histories into the collective memories and democratic discourses of the city itself. The city is reconceived with each new immigrant, assuming that an open communication exists between the immigrant and all others. Too often, however, such openings exist only as wounds, a result of the wars that created the need for these large-scale migrations in the first place, or as a kind of psychosomatic symptom of the fundamentally asymmetrical nature of this passage, for immigrants do not have the rights enjoyed by citizens. But within each immigrant lives an entire city, often richer, more complex, and more hopeful than the public one – the city to come.

This Benjaminian utopia is, according to Stéphane Mosès, "a hope lived in the mode of the present." To survive, the immigrant must establish a utopia, a "no-place" that is located in the present time, not hidden behind the horizon of some idealized future. Why should the immigrant just add to the perpetuated misery of past immigrant experience? Why should this degrading experience, now taken for granted as part of the romantic patrimony, be endlessly imposed on every future immigrant, who must wear it like a pillory of American identity? No! The "no-place" should be a "No!-place." And once formulated in the immigrant's mind, it must be projected onto both the future and the past. The No!-place is an unacceptable place, the site of "my personal experience that I refuse to accept for today, for tomorrow, and forever, for myself, my children, for everyone, immigrants and nonimmigrants alike." "My utopia," says the immigrant, "proposes a vision of hope in which the society of tomorrow houses no place for the perpetuation of the kind of experience I am forced to live through today, the kind of misery that your immigrant parents and grandparents were forced to accept yesterday." The immigrant's No!-place is at once a vision, a criticism, and a resistance.

Cultivation of the tradition of the nameless has a self-defensive function as well: to survive, the stranger must guard against the fate of nomads, who, first deprived by the victors of their history (and even the right to have a history), were later forced to function as merely geographic subjects. As the French philosophers Gilles Deleuze and Félix Guattari teach us, "The defeat of the nomads was such, so complete, that history is one with the triumph of States."[2] Just as we have been told that nomads "invented nothing," so we have presumed that migrants and immigrants have nothing to contribute to public discourse. But the most questionable question, "Where are you from?," should never replace "In what way can your past and present experience contribute to everybody's well-being today and tomorrow?"

The infusion of the tradition of the vanquished (a critical-visionary history) into the history of the victors (a catastrophic-progress history) can be made by strangers thanks to their *political intuition of the present*. Such an intuition realizes the danger of repeating yesterday's injustices today and tomorrow. Every day a new history needs to be written, one that will retrieve the tradition of the vanquished. This new history, what Nietzsche would call a "critical history," is announced by the stranger and can help to sustain the agonistic democratic process. As philosopher Simon Critchley points out, "Democracy is the form of society committed to the political equality of all its citizens and the ethical inequality of myself faced with the Other. . . . Thus the rational order of the *polis* is justified by a philosophical language which criticizes the *polis* in the name of what it excludes or marginalizes, the pre-rational one-for-the-other of ethics."[3] In other words, democracy can be kept alive by an ongoing recognition, exposition, and legalization of the strangers' "illegitimate" experience, their "illegible" past, and their "illegal" present.

Transitional artifice

As psychoanalytic theorist Julia Kristeva writes, "Your speech has no past and will have no power over the future of the group: why should one listen to it? . . . One will listen to you only in absent-minded, amused fashion, and one will forget you in order to go on with serious matters. The foreigner's speech can bank only on its bare rhetorical strength, and the inherent desires he or she has invested in it." Unfortunately, this perception by the nonstranger also conforms to the symptomatic condition of the stranger: "Settled within himself, the foreigner has no self. Barely an empty confidence, valueless, which focuses his possibilities of being constantly other, according to others' wishes and to circumstances. I do what *they* want *me* to, but it is not 'me' – 'me' is elsewhere, 'me' belongs to no one, 'me' does not belong to 'me,' . . . does 'me' exist?"[4] As Kristeva's statement suggests, strangers need to gain confidence in the possibility of communicating their own experiences, and they need to be able to communicate this confidence as well. The stranger must learn to take his or her own experience seriously. To gain this confidence, however, the stranger must find a communicative form for the experience, then establish a playful distance from it.

Conversely, the nonstranger, or "local," must gain a playful distance from his or her own fear of the stranger to establish a healthy curiosity that will foster communication and closer contact. The presence of a stranger evokes in the nonstranger a well-hidden secret: the recognition of one's own strangeness. The stranger is unfamiliar and uncanny (*unheimlich* in German, or "unhomely"). The uncanny, Freud says, is everything that "ought to have remained hidden but has come to light." Kristeva claims that the ideal situation would be one in which the nonstranger recognized his or her own uncanny strangeness. As she says, "The foreigner is within me, hence we are all foreigners. If I am a foreigner, there are no foreigners." In search of an antixenophobic society, Kristeva notes Freud's stress on "those [esthetic] works in which the uncanny effect is abolished because of the very fact that the entire world of the narrative is fictitious. Such are fairy tales, in which the generalized artifice spares us any possible comparison between sign, imagination, and material reality. As a consequence, artifice neutralizes uncanniness and makes all returns of the repressed plausible, acceptable, and pleasurable."[5]

In sum, the state of being a stranger accumulates as an experience with no form, no language, no expression, and no right to be communicated, and thus becomes a dangerous psychic symptom. This stranger-ness is a strangely familiar, secret, and uncanny condition that we all share and that, when repressed in the ideological caves of our subjectivity, can sometimes explode in the face of an actual stranger. Between the speechless pain of the actual stranger and the sequestered fear of one's own strangeness lies the real frontier to be challenged. Can art operate as a revelatory, expressive, and interrogative passage through such a frontier? Can it be an inspiration, provocation, and opening act for a new form of communication in a nonxenophobic community? If the stranger is a prophet who interrupts history, today's artists and designers should help the prophet by designing special equipment for such an intervention.

The prophet's prosthesis

Such equipment would be the result of "interrogative design," a critical articulation of what is most questionable and unacceptable in the present: the stranger's pain in survival. The oldest and most common reference to this kind of articulation and design is the bandage. A bandage covers and treats a wound while at the same time exposing its presence. Its presence signifies both the experience of pain and the hope of recovery. Is it possible to develop this concept further? Could we invent a bandage that would communicate, interrogate, and articulate the circumstances and the experience of the injury? Could such a transformed bandage address the ills of the outside world as perceived by the wounded? To see the world as seen by the wound!

In the complexity of the contemporary urban context, this equipment becomes a device for communication and mediation – design as tactical media, its purpose being to treat not only the individual human suffering but also the external society that produced the wound. Could this device create new conditions that would soon render the need for it obsolete? Or, if needed, could it become a prosthesis, a (semi)permanent extension of the body (politic)? Such design requires thinking both clinically (therapeutically) and critically.

Over the centuries and millennia, the memory and tradition of the nameless developed certain *tactical* features against the *strategic* character of the history of the victors. Those features, according to Benjamin, have a profoundly "interactive" character based on "nonlinearity, radical negativity," performativity, and "arrest of time." The tactics of this tradition consist of storytelling, magic, miracle, humor, and entertainment (refer back to Freud). This is a "discontinuous tradition while continuity is that of the victor."[6] The tradition of the vanquished brings something new and unknown to the understanding of lived time, transposing subjective experience from the personal sphere to the historical.

Even in those societies that are most open, inviting, and attentive to the displaced, the psychological needs of immigrants are far less recognized than those of children, for instance. But like children, immigrants must develop their autonomous identities in the process of psychic development, independent of internal and external conditions or personal cultures. And they must do so in an experimental, creative, and playful way, in an atmosphere of internal and external trust. Yet, unlike children, they cannot expect the necessary protective space, normally provided by parents or society, for such experiment and play. On the one hand, then, immigrants are treated as hopeless and voiceless, incapable infants or defiant children. On the other hand, they are expected to be super-adults, self-motivated entrepreneurs, and fully independent individuals capable of facing a harsh new world. At the same time, the locals are treated as infants by the immigrants, who believe that the hostile or "naive" native residents do not understand the "sophistication" of the newcomers. The immigrants expect the locals to be super-adults and to extend themselves in special ways to understand foreign customs, ideas, and experiences. Both locals and aliens must refuse to be infantilized or expected to be super-adults.

This situation demands a new artifice that would serve both needs: inspiring playful distance and playful contact, as well as reinforcing the stranger's confidence in communicating the experience of alienation. To defuse xenophobic paranoias, one important function of this psycho-social artifice would be to neutralize the uncanniness evoked by the presence of a stranger. To do this, such an artifice should take the form of a special kind of equipment designed to function as a "fictitious narrative," one that nonetheless preserves and disseminates an emotional understanding of a painful and unacceptable reality.

On the other hand, if this psycho-social artifice is to be of any use to the stranger, it would have to function as, in D. W. Winnicott's terms, a "transitional object" or "transitional phenomenon," or, in extreme cases, as a transitional prosthesis. For the immigrant, such equipment would have to be perceived as neither internal nor external but belonging to a "[third zone] of experience in the potential space between the individual and the environment." This space "depends on experience which leads to trust. It can be looked upon as sacred to the individual in that it is here that the individual experiences creative living."[7]

The zones, spaces, and objects that immigrants invent are the territories of play, distance, irony, and humor: the uncanny in the locals' terrain, where the familiar and the unfamiliar wrestle with each other and where the lost land argues and jokes in a mother tongue with the promised land, speaking in the newly acquired language of a new critical history and a new vision of hope. The new kind of "transitional object" must be created here, where the zones of experience of the newcomer and the local can be encouraged, overlapped, and shared. But it is the immigrant who must introduce such an object first. The immigrant is the one who, in order to survive, must learn how to be both provocative and tactful.

Left alone with such newly designed equipment, the immigrant could create a space where he or she could accept, shape, even enjoy the complexity and originality of his or her own strange and often painful experiences. Bringing the instrument into the open would create the sacred and ethical space of the "third zone." This space exists not only between the stranger and the nonstranger but also between the inner and outer worlds of the stranger; between the stranger, the nonstranger, and the "third person" (who may or may not be a stranger, and who represents the point of view of "we," of the larger society as a whole); and, lastly, as in the case of the *Alien Staff*, between prerecorded speech and improvised live speech, contained and "broadcast" by the instrument and performed by the stranger.

In this way, the newly designed equipment could inspire a birth of a new community, even a temporary and momentary rebirth of democratic public space based on the agonistic speech acts and discourses that Hannah Arendt supported, enacted in a place that allows for the "unleashing of passions." Georges Bataille called such a place "sacred." This space will be constituted through the use of the Immigrant Instruments, which, in this way, will become "sacred objects." It will be constituted on the site of the newcomer, who is the stake of the society to come and the new mentality to be born.

The return of the said

To summarize, the interruption of the victors by the nameless can only happen through the design and implementation of a new psycho-cultural artifice – transitional object, which, on the one hand, will help the stranger to open up and come forward and, on the other hand, will encourage the nonstranger and other strangers to bring themselves closer to the stranger's experience and presence. This will inspire the new discourse in which the strangeness can be shared across all social boundaries.

In doing so, such new equipment will provide both the means and the field of play, where the speechless can creatively articulate their "saying," interrupting the flow of the "said." Armed with the new equipment, strangers will hopefully gain new rhetorical power to wrestle with the power of the "said." The interactive character of the encounter with the "said," the irony and humor of this unsolicited performance, will help to articulate, expose, and eventually disseminate the image of their unstable identity as well as the complex world of their multiplicity and their internal antagonisms, all overlapping in the process of becoming. Despite all of the power thus gained, the stranger, speaking from the bottom of the experience of the vanquished, will not resemble the victor in speech. As Emmanuel Levinas would say, the stranger, during the performance, will appear as the "said," but this time as the "justifiable said," since the traces of the original "saying" will remain the sole basis of his or her speech act.[8]

The stranger equipped with the immigrant instrument will be able to speak back to all of those strangers or nonstrangers who would like to cast the stranger in some preconceived mold of an individual or collective identity. The strangers and their doubles – the instruments – could disagree with each other or with anybody who wants to fuse the strangers into a particular culture or community. The use of the immigrant instruments, while encouraging trust, can displace any preconceptions of communion and commonality, protecting the stranger's right to exist as a unique singular human being and the right to announce or denounce his or her affiliations and associations.

The summary of the main points for the design of a new equipment for strangers:

Proposition 1: Strangers in their relation to the self and to the nonstranger (as well as to other strangers) need a thing-in-between, an equipment-artifice that will open up discussion and allow them to reveal and to share (communicate) their experiences, identities, visions, and unique strangenesses.

Proposition 2: Such equipment (communicative instrument) is an emergency need in today's migratory era, and the first user of the instrument must be the immigrant, followed by other foreigners, and then all of those native locals who are so profoundly estranged, infantilized, silenced, and excluded that they resemble the immigrant, even if they did not experience crossing the "proper" geopolitical borders.

Proposition 3: Such equipment, which I call the Immigrant Instrument, must offer healing powers to its users, overcoming the ever-present fear of one's own strangeness, as well as communicating the strangeness with playfulness, confidence, and power. For this purpose, the Instrument must operate as a psychological container (the confident companion) and as a social opening (displayed-presenter), the stranger's speaking double.

Proposition 4: The Immigrant Instrument must bring the interlocutor closer to the stranger. To achieve this goal, the Instrument must first take attention away from its user and bring the focus on itself as a "bizarre," "magical," "strange," or "curious" object, cliché, totem, attribute, technological gadget, or prosthetic device. In the second stage of its operation, the Instrument will expose, at a close distance, the stranger as speech-act virtuoso, who, armed with and empowered by the new media technology and ancient instrumental know-how, will be able to entertain and announce her or his critical and prophetic presence. Achieving such goals, the Instrument will increase the user's communicative abilities despite all psychic, linguistic, and cultural barriers in the context of the present-day xenophobia.

Proposition 5: The Immigrant Instrument must operate both as a transitional object (Winnicott) and as a communicative artifice (Kristeva).

Proposition 6: The Immigrant Instrument must function as an artifice, inspiring playful distance and playful contact. The foreigners must learn to take their own experience seriously; to see, however, that one's own often painful experience requires the ability to establish a playful distance from it. Conversely, to establish a communicative contact with the stranger, the nonstranger must gain equally playful distance from his or her fear of the stranger.

Proposition 7: The situation of today's immigrant (who is both a psychic and a social symptom) requires an instrument that would help its operator to become both the patient and the doctor. Self-healing must be combined with healing others, being healed while healing, making whole, and articulating and curing wounded psycho-social relations.

The Immigrant Instrument must aid the stranger in making the transition to nonstrangeness while assisting the local in recognizing his or her own strangeness. This will contribute, as Kristeva would like, to the formation of a communicative cross-stratum based on shared multiplicity of identities in an unstable process of becoming a community or, better, a community of becoming, the only commonality of which will be its communicated uncanny strangeness.

Notes

Fragments of this previously unpublished essay were delivered as parts of lectures for Harvard University, the Public Art Fund Lectures at the Cooper Union, New York, the Institute of Contemporary Arts, London, and the Institute of Contemporary Art, Boston.

1   Stéphane Mosès, "The Theological-Political Model of History," *History and Memory* 1 (Tel Aviv University, 1989), pp. 11, 13.

2   Gilles Deleuze and Félix Guattari, *Nomadology: The War Machine*, trans. Brian Massumi (New York: Semiotext(e), 1986), p. 73.

3   Simon Critchley, *The Ethics of Deconstruction: Derrida and Levinas* (Oxford: Blackwell, 1991), pp. 235, 239.

4   Julia Kristeva, *Strangers to Ourselves*, trans. Leon S. Roudiez (New York: Columbia University Press, 1991), pp. 20–21, 8.

5   Sigmund Freud, "The Uncanny," in *The Standard Edition of the Complete Psychological Works of Sigmund Freud* (London: Hogarth Press, 1955), vol. 17, p. 225; Kristeva, *Strangers to Ourselves*, pp. 192, 187.

6   See the discussion of Benjamin in Mosès, "The Theological-Political Model of History."

7   D. W. Winnicott, *Playing and Reality* (London: Tavistock, 1971), p. 103.

8   For an elaboration of the Levinasian concepts of "saying" and "the said," see the chapter "A Levinasian Politics of Ethical Difference," in Critchley, *The Ethics of Deconstruction*, pp. 229–236.

Chapter 25

Celeste Olalquiaga

THE CRYSTAL PALACE [1999]

Source: Celeste Olalquiaga (1999) *The Artificial Kingdom: A Treasury of the Kitsch Experience*, London: Bloomsbury, pp. 30–45.

Celeste Olalquiaga is a theorist and historian of kitsch. For her, kitsch is a critical element in our mass-produced world, the phenomenon that simultaneously mourns and celebrates our artificial world. Kitsch can be found ready-made in objects (the ubiquitous snow-globes that you find in any tourist shop) or it can be bequeathed on to the object (1950s atomic-style ashtrays, for instance, rediscovered in the present). In an earlier book Olalquiaga quotes the novelist Milan Kundera describing the feeling and affect of kitsch:

> Kitsch causes two tears to flow in quick succession. The first tear says: How nice to see children running on the grass! The second tear says: How nice to be moved, together with all mankind, by children running on the grass! It is the second tear that makes kitsch kitsch.
>
> (Kundera cited in Olalquiaga 1992: 36)

Thus kitsch is often seen as inauthentic culture trading in second-hand experience, shop-soiled sentiments and degraded artistic forms. What Olalquiaga does is not to simply refuse such an assessment, but to suggest that kitsch's cultural tone, its second-degree sentimentality, is an essential element of the designed culture of industrial modernity. To denounce kitsch is to fail to see its fundamental role in shaping culture.

For Olalquiaga, mass-produced designed objects arrive on the historical stage already marked as kitsch. They already carry the scent of nostalgia, the whiff of putrefaction. Nowhere is this more evident than in the use of natural motifs on industrial products: machinery draped in metal vines, for instance. Kitsch then is modernity's unending desire to preserve what it is killing, to crystallise its destructive force. Today modern supermarkets like to display sepia-toned photographs of shops from the 'good-old-days', and to pretend that their fish counters are really small street markets. These are the kitsch shrines to the very thing the supermarkets vindictively obliterate. Modern cars still carry the emblems and names of animals as morbid trophies that honour the industrialisation of road-kill.

In this extract Olalquiaga makes a bold claim: 'With its uninhibited emphasis on display, proliferation and artifice, and the global proportions of its reach as a trade fair, the Crystal Palace pretty much inaugurated the modern era as we know it.' By treating the Great Exhibition of 1851 as both the moment when industrial modernity was historically established, and as an outstanding example of kitsch, Olalquiaga fulfils the critical promise that Walter Benjamin offered when he wrote that 'World exhibitions are places of pilgrimage to the commodity fetish' (Benjamin 1999: 17). Benjamin's truncated formula, which captures the way that these showcases of global industrial design combined a melancholic religiosity with a feverish desire for profit, is fleshed out in Olalquiaga's work. In her hands the Crystal Palace becomes part glass sarcophagus, part iridescent department store.

Further reading: Auerbach 1999; Highmore 2003; Ngai 2005a; Olalquiaga 1992; Piggott 2004; Purbrick 2001.

Figure 25.1   The Crystal Palace (interior) from *Dickinson's Comprehensive Pictures of the Great Exhibition of 1851* (London, 1854).

We suppose that in a few months the glittering palace of iron and glass, the most unique and remarkable building in the world, will be as entirely a thing of the past as the ice-palace of the Empress of Russia that thawed in the summer sun.

Illustrated London News on the Crystal Palace, Saturday, October 11, 1851[1]

THE VAST COMMERCIAL expansion of glass during the nineteenth century greatly enhanced the modern pleasure of looking and collecting. In England, the glass market changed dramatically after the heavy taxes imposed on its importation from France were lifted in 1845, while in Italy, centuries-old glassmaking traditions underwent an important revival. Besides opening a whole new range of decoration and design, the availability and versatility of glass paved the way for a novel kind of preservation and visual display that promoted a highly voyeuristic optical sensibility, starting with the Parisian arcades.

The possibility of observing from a safe distance grants both a temporal remove (the case of natural history specimens and dioramas) and the disengaged but empowering anonymity that comes from being the subject of a voracious gaze whose object is confined and subordinated. This very distance changes the status of the object, which loses its commonness to become a thing worthy of such attention. So, while until now display had basically remained secondary to function – practical, religious or cognitive – with the advent of industrialization the lack of uniqueness of mass-produced objects was offset by the spectacularity of their presentation.

It is very fitting, then, that the first monumental-scale exhibit of industrial products took place in London's 1851 Crystal Palace. Following the arcades' paradigm – which would be emulated throughout the nineteenth century, accounting for covered passageways in London, fastuous galleries in Milan and Naples, and enormous commercial centers in Berlin and Moscow – the Crystal Palace was a gigantic structure of iron and glass dedicated to a new way of looking, that of the potential consumer. With its uninhibited emphasis on display, proliferation and artifice, and the global proportions of its reach as a trade fair, the Crystal Palace pretty much inaugurated the modern era as we know it.[2]

Formally the "Great Exhibition of the Works of Industry of All Nations," the Crystal Palace was built as a glittering homage: it was a place where people went to render honor, in the form of amazement and admiration, to the mass production that became Western culture's new form of royalty. Built in a record seven months and located in Hyde Park, the Crystal Palace covered eighteen acres – and six elm trees – with 956,165 square feet of panes of sheet glass. It was the first entirely mass-produced building, using new construction materials and a gridiron plan later to become the basis for constructing skyscrapers.

The first of the great world's fairs (there were fifty-eight international fairs between 1851 and World War I, eleven of which were considered major), the Crystal Palace received six million people, a daily attendance average of 42,831 – with reduced cost of admission on certain days – during the six months it remained open, from May through October 15, 1851. It was visited by everyone from Queen Victoria, who went with her children up to twice weekly in the first months and had her own retiring room in the premises, to those that had never before left their villages, such as eighty-five-year-old Dolly Pentreath, who walked almost three hundred miles to the Crystal Palace from her hometown of Penzance, carrying mackerel on her head to pay for lodging.[3]

"Neither crystal nor a palace, it was a bazaar," complained someone of the overwhelming display of over 100,000 articles from 14,000 exhibitors (half of which were British) that occupied eleven miles of stalls. Besides displaying the most recent products of Western industrial mechanization (a hydraulic press, marine and fire engines and locomotives, many of which were kept in motion with steam from boilers outside the palace), the exhibit, divided by sections, displayed an unprecedented accumulation that included raw materials and manufactured goods – textiles, jewelry and medical instruments – from around the world. The first international trade fair had something for everyone and a few things for no one, like the knife with 1,851 blades, a cross between a Christmas tree and a cactus; the "Silent Alarum Bed," which would throw the sleeper on the floor at a certain time; and the "talking telegraph," where a head in a box moved its mouth while code symbols appeared above it in flags. It also had a "Model Dwelling House" whose design was supervised by Prince Albert, the driving force behind the Great Exhibition, and a model of a floating church, both of which probably paled next to the model of the Liverpool docks, complete with sixteen hundred fully rigged ships.[4]

Perhaps no one expressed their feelings about this new era better than Victoria herself, a woman whose attachment to objects became so obsessive in her last years that she would not allow any of her innumerable possessions to be thrown away or even altered, and if something – a carpet, a curtain – fell into total disrepair, she would have it replicated to perfection. When even this was not enough, she had all of her belongings photographed from several angles, and the photos – along with their corresponding entries indicating not only the objects' main features but also their exact location in the rooms of her domains – placed in huge albums through which the elderly queen browsed at leisure. More than sixty years before, Victoria had been one of the first to compare the awe that she felt at the magnitude of the Great Exhibition to a religious experience: ". . . it was magical – so vast, so glorious, so touching," she wrote in her diary about the Crystal Palace's inauguration. "One felt filled with devotion, more so than by any service I have ever heard."[5]

An unprecedented opportunity for business competition and expansion, the Crystal Palace also became a meeting place for friends and lovers, an escape for middle-class women and a didactic outing for families, easily merging industrial affluence and leisure time. As such, it was the forebear of those microcosmic universes known as shopping malls and amusement parks; and, in fact, an amusement park of a very special kind the Crystal Palace became, once the Great Exhibition was over and its massive structure was dismantled, relocated and reassembled in 1854 on Sydenham Hill, a half-hour away from the heart of London. During its first thirty years the Sydenham Crystal Palace was visited by about two million people a year, a transit load for which special railway lines were built. The palace overflowed with special attractions that took place inside the building, in its immediate surrounding woods or in the boating-lake: balloon ascents, rose shows, cat and dog shows, trade fairs, art exhibitions, electrical, mining and photographic exhibitions, music festivals, and meetings of societies such as the National Temperance League and the Salvation Army.

A bizarre mix of all kinds of activities, the Sydenham Crystal Palace even housed schools of art, science, literature, music and engineering. Among its many spectacles the most popular and dramatic seem to have been the war shows: "Invasion," orchestrated by John M. East, drew about twenty-five thousand spectators for each performance, during which a life-size village, with its shops, church and school, was destroyed by enemy bombs, "the screams of trapped and dying children coming from the ruins," and later reconstructed for the next performance. A nineteenth-century Disneyland, the palace's last and biggest event was the construction in miniature of the British Empire for the coronation of King George V in 1911, complete with a railway on which visitors could tour, among other things, a South African diamond mine and an Indian tea plantation.[6]

Despite its popularity, the Crystal Palace went bankrupt that same year and was confiscated and later used as a naval depot during World War I. Rescued from total oblivion by a private fund set apart for this purpose before the war, for the next twenty-five years the palace sat silent, a shadow of its former splendor, on top of Sydenham Hill, coming alive only on Thursday evenings for fireworks. It is ironic that these never started any accidents, because, melting away as the *Times* had figuratively predicted eighty-five years before, on November 30, 1936, the Crystal Palace was swept by an unrelated fire that destroyed it in less than six hours, its darkened ruins later to be made into a national park.[7]

Perhaps the most outstanding criticism of the time leveled against the Great Exhibition centered on the eclectic character of its numerous works of art and the massive application of organic design to manufacture and industry. Foreign and national exhibits were accused of breaking with "pure" classical form, thus indulging in bad taste, reckless romanticism, narrativity and, worse than anything else, banality, eventually adding up to that most vilified of all artistic phenomena, a profanity so young that only around this time did it acquire a name: kitsch. And kitsch the Crystal Palace had galore, particularly the garden variety, like the bucolic sculpture of the Prince of Wales as a shepherd, or the use of crucifixes and rosaries for product display.[8]

Most offensively for its critics, the design presented at the 1851 exhibition sought to imitate nature, an overabundance of iron leaves, glass flowers and wooden antlers making of the Crystal Palace a sort of immense, transparent winter garden whose fauna and flora were wonderfully frozen. Making the novel world of industrial production more familiar by shaping it after plants and animals, this mixing of the old with the new ideologically "naturalized" machinery and manufacture by giving them the appearance of being products of nature rather than of human labor. In this combination of the organic and the mechanical, nineteenth-century design strived to create those "wish images" where the world appeared harmonious and effortless – in a word, utopian.[9]

Yet, at an exhibit whose explicit goals included the reunion of aesthetics and manufacture, it was not this utopian aspiration that was abhorred but the degree to which "the naturalist school of ornament" took it: unlike previous organic styles, the Victorian ornament was not a decorative element of the object, but became its central feature.[10] This "disastrous confusion of ornament and design" became the target of condemnation, not only for relegating the primary function of the object to a secondary position, but also – and perhaps more importantly for kitsch – because once function had been thrown to the winds, what followed was an unbounded proliferation that paved the way for another kind of displacement, that of the original by the copy: "Nothing can be worse than art at second-hand, more especially when the associations and feelings of the two sets of workers, the original and the imitators, are totally different."[11]

The Victorian love of "imitation and disguise" went even further, eventually blurring the limits between fantasy and reality in what may be considered either a botched attempt at realism or a fantastic vision of reality, according to one's point of view. This is the case with the use of natural history specimens, which although increasingly popular as collectibles since the Renaissance, became truly massive commodities in the nineteenth century. An integral part of the developing genre of trade known as world's fairs, this booming market was represented in the Crystal Palace by thousands of specimens, including the already extinct dodo bird and three or four hundred varieties of hummingbirds.

In most of these, taxidermy, as it had been developed since the sixteenth century, consisted in the precise rendition of the animal's physical appearance, a radical departure from the ancient embalming methods that had "sought to preserve the substance of the body rather than its form," often with totally unrecognizable results.[12] Full of respect for their dead and for all sacred species, neither the ancients nor the early natural history collectors would have ever dreamt up anything like the anthropomorphic exhibits at the Crystal Palace. Among the most outrageous were Hermann Ploucquet's extremely popular "comicalities" – fifteen hundred in total – where birds, weasels, cats, hares and other animals were posed to depict "comical, humorous and interesting scenes in animal life," like the group of ermines sitting at a table sipping tea from teacups while another member of their party plays the piano.[13]

By the late 1800s, stuffed animals and anthropomorphic displays gave way to the rage for "animal furniture," with the representations of animal parts replaced by the animal parts themselves: elephants' feet served as liquor stands, chairs stood on the four legs of rhinoceros or zebras, hat stands were made from antlers, tiger jaws held clocks and ostrich legs stopped doors. This fad was attributed to women's use of entire birds – instead of only feathers – on their hats in the 1860s, which was followed by the craze for tiger and bear claw jewelry, until the jungle effect invaded the entire home. "For some reason, innumerable monkeys were sold to light up billiard-rooms, the little animals swinging from a hoop with one hand and carrying the lamp in the other. After a time people other than those who had dead pet monkeys wanted to possess these unique lamps, so that defunct simians from the Zoo had to be eagerly bought up, and Mr. Jamrach, the famous wild beast importer, was vexed with orders for *dead* monkeys."[14]

Rather than its reaching for a utopian "natural" experience through technology, one could say the Crystal Palace's best-kept secret was its justified fear of losing a world that it loved all too well but was slowly sacrificing to scientific and industrial progress. With the organic standing metaphorically for use value and for production unmediated by technology (and therefore presumably having a more direct relationship to reality), the loss of the organic was perceived as the death of a dimension from which Western culture had derived a great deal of its meaning for centuries.

This became particularly discernible at the moment when the organic was dealt a mortal blow by modernization, with ornamental plants and animals quite literally representing a last-ditch effort to retain a sense of belonging to the natural order.[15] While the traditional concept of nature was still topically retained as a nominal assurance that things were not as radically different as they seemed, nature had already moved one degree away from its former status. Whereas it used to provide a model for understanding or organizing a certain sense of the world, now nature became an icon of itself, valid for representing the beauty of a supposedly orderly and predictible phenomenon which humans could refer to for ontological orientation.

The constant overlapping of the scientific approach to nature and organic ornamentation in the 1800s is perhaps the best indication of how ambiguous this new role of nature still was. The attack against the kind of organic ornamentation sponsored by the Great Exhibition was a clear reaction to a modernity that sought to fragment what had been perceived until then as an unproblematic whole – the role of nature in culture, no matter how distorted – while simultaneously attempting to retain part of this meaning under a new guise. Yet, instead of railing against the exhibition's overall objectification of nature (in the use of live plants as "a new and delightful sort of furniture ornament," for instance), the attack focused on only one aspect of this materialization, that which transformed a transcendental notion into industrial décor.[16]

In other words, rather than a critique against the new modes of production and consumption taking place at the Crystal Palace, what surfaces is the struggle between two concepts of nature, both of which claim exclusive ownership over the organic realm: the traditional one, where a theologized view of nature provided culture with symbolic meaning; and the modern one, which destroyed this view by reformulating nature according to rational, scientific paradigms and techniques, while simultaneously and contradictorily seeking to regain through this fragmented emblem what, by its own doings, was permanently gone.

Like the demise of that aura to which nature is inextricably bound as the bearer of a sense of authenticity, the downfall of the natural order triggered an immediate longing for and glorification of what was lost. Consequently, nature knows in the nineteenth century an unparalleled popularity, although always in a role subordinated to human whims: either fossilized in the emerging field of natural history or abstracted in the Romantic sensibility's quest for an immanent spirituality. In both cases, nature's modern role as the mirror of a human-centered cosmos is reproduced in its object status, with science and industry constantly perfecting ways to retain this evanescent realm.

Notes

1   "In the year 1740, the Empress Anne of Russia, caused a palace of ice to be erected upon the banks of Neva. This extraordinary edifice, was 52 feet in length, 16 in breadth, and 20 feet high, and constructed of large pieces of ice cut in the manner of free-stone. The walls were three feet thick. The several apartments were furnished with tables, chairs, beds, and all kinds of household furniture of ice. In front of the edifice, besides pyramids and statues, stood six cannon, carrying balls of six pounds' weight, and two mortars, entirely made of ice. As a trial from one of the former, an iron ball with only a quarter of a pound of powder was fired off, the ball of which went through a two-inch board, at sixty paces from the mouth of the piece, which remained completely uninjured by the explosion. The illumination in this palace, at night, was astonishingly grand." From "A Palace built of Ice," in Samuel G. Goodrich, *The Cabinet of Curiosities, or Wonders of the World Displayed: Forming a Repository of Whatever is Remarkable in the Regions of Nature and Art, Extraordinary Events, and Eccentric Biography* (New York: Piercy and Reed, 1840), vol. 1, p. 180.

2   Surprisingly, no one seems to mention the arcades as the obvious architectural precursors of the Crystal Palace. Most writers are content to cite the story of how it was designed by a royal gardener, Joseph Paxton, who, inspired by the structure of green-houses, rough-sketched it on a piece of paper, putting an end to the difficult quest for a winning design for the exhibition. For the history of the Crystal Palace, see Patrick Beaver, *The Crystal Palace, 1851–1936: A Portrait of Victorian Enterprise* (London: Hugh Evelyn, 1970).

3   On world's fairs, see Jane Shadel Spillman, *Glass from World's Fairs, 1851–1904* (Corning, NY: Corning Museum of Glass, 1986). On who attended the trade fairs, Toshio Kusamitsu, "Great Exhibitions Before 1851," in *History Workshop Journal*, no. 9 (Spring 1980): 70–78. Queen Victoria's routine is described in Beaver, *The Crystal Palace*, p. 64, and in the following excerpt from the exhibit's catalog: "Whatever may have been the weather, or however crowded the interior, Her Majesty has devoted, almost daily, until the close of the session of Parliament released her from attendance in London, several hours to visits to the Crystal Palace; inspecting each department in succession, and selecting from many of them such objects as gratified her taste, or were, for other reasons, considered to possess claims upon her attention." From *The Art Journal Illustrated Catalogue of the Industry of All Nations* (London: George Virtue, 1851), p. xxiii. The story of Dolly Pentreath, who even had a meeting with the queen, is told by Paul Hollister, Jr., in *The Encyclopedia of Glass Paperweights* (Santa Cruz, Calif.: Paperweight Press, 1970), p. 38.

4   Beaver, *The Crystal Palace*, pp. 47–56.

5   Ibid., p. 41. On Queen Victoria's object obsession, see Lytton Strachey, *Queen Victoria* (New York: Harcourt, Brace and Co., 1921), pp. 398–401. Victoria's collection, along with the numerous exhibits presented to the exhibition's organizers after it closed, eventually became a substantial part of London's Victoria and Albert Museum, and also gave rise to the Science Museum and Library, the Natural History Museum, the Geological Museum, the Imperial Institute, the Royal College of Science, the Royal School of Mines, the City and Guilds College, the Royal College of Art, the Royal College of Music, the Royal College of Organists and the College of Needlework.

6   Beaver, *The Crystal Palace*, p. 110. Charles Brock's fireworks displays were considered the most spectacular of all, with "every naval battle of any importance reproduced in fire on Sydenham Hill. The last one was the Battle of Jutland, which had to be seen to be believed. As huge battleships, outlined in fire, bombarded each other from opposite sides of the lake, the explosions of the shells were reflected in the water as they might have been at sea. Ships blew up and slowly sank. . . ." (ibid., p. 132).

7   For a childhood reminiscence of the palace's old age, see "The End," pp. 141–48 in Beaver, *The Crystal Palace*. The ruins of the Crystal Palace can be visited on Sundays, although little more than steps and broken statues remains. However, there are occasional walking tours and a great souvenir store run by the volunteers of The Crystal Palace Foundation. In 1853 New York City built its own Crystal Palace, a replica of the English one, in what is now Bryant Park. It also housed the World's Fair of the Industry of All Nations, and burned down in 1856.

8   Beaver, *The Crystal Palace*, pp. 57–59. The word "kitsch" is of German origin and began to be used in the mid-1800s in Munich to degrade certain forms of art. Its etymology includes *verkitschen*, to make cheap, and *kitschen*, to collect junk from the street. See Matei Calinescu, "Kitsch," in *Five Faces of Modernity* (Durham, N.C.: Duke University Press, 1987), pp. 225–62. For the essay that inspired the decades-old criticism against kitsch, see Hermann Broch, "Kitsch and Art-with-a-Message" (1933), reprinted in Gillo Dorfles, ed., *Kitsch: The World of Bad Taste* (New York: Bell Publishing, 1968), pp. 49–67; this is the uncredited source of Clement Greenberg's influential text "The Avant-Garde and Kitsch" (1939), in Dorfles, pp. 116–26. Broch later expanded his own essay into "Notes on the Problem of Kitsch" (1950), also in Dorfles, pp. 68–76. See also his *Hugo von Hoffmannstahl and His Time: The European Imagination, 1860–1920*, trans. and ed. Michael P. Steinberg (Chicago: Chicago University Press, 1984). Dorfles's anthology has been a cult classic on kitsch since the 1970s. The anti-kitsch position that it endorses (for which Broch's and Greenberg's early texts were fundamental) remains to be challenged. I attempt to do so in practice here, as well as in "Holy Kitschen," in my *Megalopolis: Contemporary Cultural Sensibilities* (Minneapolis: University of Minnesota Press, 1992). I also outline the history of the kitsch debate in a short essay entitled "The Dark Side of Modernity's Moon," in *Agenda*, no. 28 (Summer 1992): pp. 22–25.

9   On Benjamin and the utopian aspect of organic ornamentation, see Buck-Morss, "Mythic Nature: Wish Image," *The Dialectics of Seeing*, pp. 110–58.

10   John Gloag, *Victorian Taste: Some Social Aspects of Architecture and Industrial Design from 1820 to 1900* (Newton Abbot: David and Charles, 1979), pp. 130–58. Phrases quoted in this and the following paragraph are from this text.

11   Robert W. Edis, "Decoration and Furniture of Town Houses," a series of lectures delivered to the Society of Arts in 1880, as quoted in Gloag, *Victorian Taste*, p. 158.

12   "Taxidermy, and Ethnographical Models," in John Tallis, *Tallis's History and Description of the Crystal Palace, and the Exhibition of the World's Industry in 1851* (London and New York: John Tallis and Co., 1852), vol. 2, pp. 187–91.

13   I owe this reference, and my initial acquaintance with the Crystal Palace, to Miriam Gusevich's "Purity and Transgression: Reflections on the Architectural Avantgarde's Rejection of Kitsch" (Milwaukee: Center for Twentieth Century Studies, working paper no. 4, Fall 1986). Her argument for the ermines as kitsch is consistent with what I will later distinguish as nostalgic kitsch.

14   William G. Fitzgerald, "Animal Furniture," *Strand Magazine* 12 (Sept. 1896): 273–80.

15   As I have been suggesting, the distinction of the natural world as an object of inquiry or collection (as opposed to a symbol) started long before the nineteenth century, which is really the culmination of this process.

16   "The Vegetable World," in *Art Journal Illustrated Catalogue*, p. viii. This essay was omitted from the catalog's 1995 reprint by Gramercy Books.

Chapter 26

Tony Fry

FROM WAR TO WARRING [1999]

Source: Tony Fry (1999) 'From War to Warring', in *A New Design Philosophy: An Introduction to Defuturing*, Sydney: University of New South Wales Press, pp. 38–47.

Tony Fry is the founding director of the EcoDesign Foundation in Sydney, Australia. A product of the hot-house intellectual atmosphere of the Centre for Contemporary Cultural Studies in Birmingham in the late 1970s and early 1980s, Fry has developed an ecological approach to design that is of monumental proportions. His initial approach to the designed world is relatively familiar: it is the dialectical understanding that design is both a product of human agency, while also being itself a social agent. In Fry's words: 'designers design in a designed world, which arrives by design, that designs their actions and objects, or more simply: we design our world, while our world designs us' (Fry 1999: 6).

But it is in the light cast by the issue of sustainability and unsustainability that Fry's work comes alive. The question that Fry poses is insistent and consequential: 'How is it possible to gain that ability to act to sustain what needs to be sustained in conditions that devalue and negate that with sustaining capability for the sake of short term gains and immediate gratification?' (Fry 1999: viii) The answer to this question is the critical activity of 'defuturing' – which is a sort of design deconstruction aimed at revealing the unsustainability that is inscribed into the very fabric of our designed worlds. Defuturing is aimed at a full audit of unsustainability, which is seen as the essence of much of the way that the world is plotted, and it requires that we reconceive how we think about both history and the future. Defuturing is itself a temporal paradox; it understands that the past is in front of us and that the future is behind us. According to Fry:

> We need to remind ourselves that the future is never empty, never a blank space to be filled with the output of human activity. It is already colonised by what the past and present have sent to it. Without this comprehension, without an understanding of what is finite, what limits reign and what directions are already set in place, we have little knowledge of futures, either of those we need to destroy or those we need to create.
>
> (Fry 1999: 11–12)

The future is already written, history shows what is plotted. In this sense history becomes an urgent task for the future, for taking stock of how extensive unsustainability is.

To privilege war in relation to design, as Fry does in the text that follows, is to grasp the defutured in its ontological state: war is design at its most unsustainable. It is also design at its most innovative, and ironically its most 'productive'. From the perspective of television, contemporary wars (especially those with American involvement) often seem like marketplace showcases for the very latest in 'cutting-edge' design. The body-bags are the dreadful productivity.

Further reading: Bevan 2007; Colomina 2007; Fry 1983, 1989, 2003; Martin 2007.

MAN LIVES IN war. As Heraclitus put it: 'War is the father of all, and king of all. He renders some gods, others men, he makes some slaves, others free.'[1] Whoever we are, wherever we are from, we have all been touched by war: its historicity is, in variable proximity, equally ours. As we reach back into time, we find we are all unavoidably either the conquerors or the conquered, the colonisers or the colonised. War is always before us: as ideology, the threat of an other, the pressure of constrained populations, a contest of resources. The reasons for war are ever proclaimed to remain present, as are the reflexes towards force. The image of war constantly assaults us, and we call it news, drama, pleasure, play. We constantly function within its shadow. Even in the most peaceful of social environments – whether as fiction, fear, image, style, rhetoric – war still designs the emotional topography of men and women.

One and the other, beginning and ending, inside and outside, subject and object and that whole raft of binaries, not least war and peace, seem so 'natural' and so 'given'. Our language, its categories and our thinking belie the existence of the most intimate of couplings and the absolute perspectival problem of our position of observation and proximity to the 'observed'. The violence, disruptions, forces and extremes that are war, alter points of view and perspectives, which means that war always brings much more into feeling, hearing, touch and sight than just itself. War continually begs address beyond a 'violent historical event' or as a vectorial designing force that goes well beyond any possibility and means of bounding an event.

The links between military and civil research, the arms trade and national economies, the technological spin off from weapons development and military technologies are all taken as read. Our position is the claim that war is the defutured inscribed in us, our technology, and our world.

Machine 1: The Macedonian phalanx

The machine is an organisation of a system of interactive parts into a functional operational whole, and therefore requires an understanding of structure. The first machines were war engines – weapons – and weapons as we know them are prehistoric. The spear is at least 40,000 years old; the bow about 15,000.

Some of the most organised war machines were human. Refined from 500 years of development that stretched from the Assyrian technologies of war to the hoplite phalanx of Classical Greek warfare, the Macedonian phalanx, created in 360 BC, under Philip and Alexander, was both machine and machine part. It was formed from a square of 256 men, called a *syntagma*, that was arranged into a *taxis* of six syntagma. Each armoured man was armed with a four and a half metre long *sarissa* pike. Each syntagma was precision-drilled in side and arc movements. The enemy was not attacked by the phalanx, rather it was the anvil that the hammer, the cavalry, drove the enemy onto.

Besides acknowledging the environmental and ontologically designing condition of war we need to ask, following on from the discussion of technology above, what war has to do with functionalism and technology beyond the obvious relation between innovation and fighting machines. Why raise the question of war at all? First of all, as a practice predicated upon destruction, nothing is as unsustainable as war. Second, in an endeavour to grasp the nature of ontological designing, it will be argued that the question of war is unavoidable, for it is perhaps the most overt instance of such designing.

War is the starkest site of technology, but equally it is also the starkest expression of the human's constant return to the non-human. It is in war that we discover that the non-human both pre-dates and post-dates 'man'. Moreover, as indicated, war is the absolute other of sustainability, not only in terms of the destructive consequences of weapons, or war's ability to produce social and psychological devastation or its desensitisation of concern for environments (given or fabricated) but also in its total disregard for the consequences of the depletion and loss of potential human, material and immaterial resources. In this respect destruction always travels two ways – forward into the war zones and back into the ecologies from which the resources come, be they used or not. The concern registered here is not so much about design for war but rather design by war.

The power of war – as a disposition of human-constructed force over time – is beyond calculation. This is to say, and to say so in such a way as to invite plural interpretation, that the form that human life has taken cannot be separated from war as its very agency, technology and event. Neither the histories of the artefacts nor the narratives of war ever get anywhere near war's actual historicity or ontological designing. The claim being made is fundamental: war is the most extreme case of ontological designing.

Machine 2: The stirrup

Stirrups came into use in the third century AD by Chinese cavalry, and four centuries later in the West. They turned man and horse into a single machine unit. Combined with a saddle built up at either end to restrict longitudinal movement the stirrup enabled the rider armed with a lance, controlled with one arm, to function from a semi-rigid platform that had the ability to absorb a shock force while guiding the horse's reins with the free arm. The result was great mobility and an ability to transfer the force of the body weight and speed of a charging stallion to the point of a weapon with unprecedented violence.

Ontological designing (the designing of the designed as it acts in and on the world) at its most general, has been exposited as 'worlding' – the undirected world-making of the directional agency of the created world, including its designed forms and processes. At its most specific, ontological Design is the directional consequence of the 'thing-ing' (the on-going effects and environmental impacts) of some 'thing' designed. There is no condition more violent or dramatic in which things and worlds meet and clash than war. While every war is not a world war, every war is a war of worlds. War is being cast here as the name of an unsustainment between things and worlds that perpetuates the defutured well beyond any contained event. At the same time, war starkly discloses the ontological character of Design in the way it exposes its agency as directive of events, technologies, forms, relations, experience, knowledges, subjectivities, imaginations, psyches and memories, but with a very limited degree of directive or design control. War manifests the full mobilisation of instrumental reason in the service of designated causal outcomes, and the standing of all that is mobilised upon the unreason of unpredictable and untraceable consequences. The history of a war culminates in a moment of victory or defeat, whereas the historicity of war is its unnarrated continuum as it violently transformed and transforms conditions of being and beings.

Reframing as enframing

War, as an absolute preoccupation, is an unthinking. War is a closure of horizons, it is occupation by instrumental aim, an enframing powered by 'total mobilisation' in which everything (mind, body, matter, spirit, energy, love, ethnicity, gender and labour) is totalised. War, by image, design, technology and action, negates a developmental notion of human being, while the rhetoric of humanism conceals the loss.

War as a festival of excess and sacrifice always exceeds itself. One problem of thinking war is thinking its delimitation, finding an edge. Where is that line that divides war from that shadow of destruction out of which all life comes? We ever live on this line, as it both divides and connects creation and destruction. Here is the line to think the relation between war and the crisis that is the defutured. Crisis and the defutured are, however, no easier to delineate than war.

War, as it imposes itself on Earth, acts with total disregard, and in so doing exposes the frame of 'our' anthropocentrism like nothing else can. Its destruction arrives to continually reimpose our original moment of forcing our being into being. Certainly from the Western perspective, and echoing Hegel, war makes visible that 'force is everything': it brings everything into being and takes everything away. But more than this, war has also become that place that 'shows forth' the inseparable 'other than humanity' (itself a designation of ethnocentric force) within and between the human. Rather than it having a given and secured condition, 'being human' is a relative and mostly unstable state that humanist discourse mis-represents by universal and essentialist claims. Being human, in those cultures in which this mode of being is designated, always hangs in the balance. War tips things either way. Selves transcend their individualisa-tion and become a species being together with and for an other, they also degenerate to instinctive creatures without value or reference. In war it is possible to see more overtly than in any other circum-stance that unsustainability does not just centre on modes of actions of beings in their worlds but just as much upon the particular mode of the being of a being. In other words sustainability exposes the limits of the abstract division between self, ecology and environment.

War was always and remains deeply implicated in the extension of productivism. This is seen most starkly across the West's five-hundred-year (and more) employment of force and deployment of the technological tools and forms of war all to clear a space, install and expand the structuring of productivism in its global meta-infrastructural form – modernity. In the name of lawful appropriation, the removal of the obstacles to trade, acceleration of economic development and the need to impose 'enlightened' ideologies, force was employed as 'right and just'. Here is the inter-national competitive historicity of war as a means to force 'a' world into being, to draw colonised space as a map of worlded imposition and to break 'beings-together' away from the cultures of their own creation, and transform them into subjects and nations.[2]

Machine 3: Mechanical vision

The telescope was invented in the Netherlands at the start of the seventeenth century. Not many years after the semaphore was invented. By the late eighteenth century semaphore towers were in use with signal arms that could be arranged in the order of 200 configurations. These enabled complex messages to be sent and were viewable by telescope up to 10 kilometres apart. This meant a message could be sent about 400 kilometres in a day. No horse-mounted dispatch relay system could get near this distance. Machines with power to extend human vision have con-tinued to be developed from this moment. The strategic target finding eye, an eye that images or informs, is a key war machine. This is the machine that enables an aircraft laser weapon to shoot down an air to air missile travelling toward it at 3500 kilometres per hour, or a smart bomb to reach its target.

The violence of productivism was not simply a matter of its explicit manifestation but also the imposition of its regulatory order on the mind of an other.[3] Order and organised matter were emplaced as the order of 'man' and one God. The worlding of all other determinate powers and gods was to be materially and immaterially destroyed, usually by war.

The rise and arrival of Eurocentrism authored a particular anthropocentric human being who was to become a global sign and agent of the unsustainable. Being human, violence, unsustainability and warring are clearly always implicated in each other. If this point is recognised the agenda of environmentalism, design, aesthetics, ethics and politics radically changes.

The most confronting result of such a recognition is that we are ever locked into anthropocentrism and while not able to be both human and free, there is a great deal of difference between being interpellated by the anthropocentric drive and confronting it in such a way as to live, by decision and by design, in a disposition of accepted responsibility. (This is an ontology rather than a condition of enforced consciousness.)

The destructive impetus of war, especially when technologically assisted, converges in many ways with the unsustainable character of 'consumption' which is one of the general features of the system of dysfunctional exchange that is economic modernism. Both the economy of peace and the economy of war of modernity have treated resources as infinitely disposable. That war had the ability to consume/dispose so voraciously meant that the war and arms economy became an integral element of the modern economy. Making (for) war was one of the fastest ways to get rich. In this context, it is worth remembering the cybernetic principle that life systems not only can tolerate some destruction but depend upon it. When, however, destruction goes over the line, when it no longer fuels creation, then a terminal condition sets in.

War, as a functional system, destroys before a single shot is fired. Its agency has always been activated prior to the sighting of an enemy. Equally, its destruction continues well beyond the final silence of the battlefield. War has been extended ecstatically, the battle ground is substance, image, everywhere, electronic and smart.

While war is brutal, strident and overt, it can also insinuate its way into our lives in the most concealed manner. War can be both the most intolerable conditions and a tolerated backdrop. In extremes, it can be all consuming action or an unnoticed televisual image. Meanwhile, war also becomes woven into being in-human as the sensibility of 'the metaphysic of living by command' which produces inhumanism. There is that 'carrying on as normal' against the everyday presence of war in close proximity, which in the age of the televisual – which has made the theatre of war the world stage – it always is. Moreover, be it on the streets of Kabul, Jakarta, Sarajevo, Tel Aviv, or wherever it is on the day where the camera and conflict converged, we have all got used to seeing people going about their daily lives amid the activity of declared or undeclared urban warfare. This is part of the image of war we see, or directly encounter, almost daily.

War has imploded as grand causes have fragmented and 'the enemy' has proliferated. We lie in bed at night in the knowledge that somewhere urban warfare is always going on. In such settings, the lines between public and private police forces and the military are now very thin. Compound living, with razor wire, high fences, guard dogs, human activity detectors, video camera monitoring, armed guards and fortress mentalities, is now 'normality' for the wealthy and for corporate interests in many and diverse parts of the world. South Africa and Brazil boast some of the most extreme examples of this, as does Papua New Guinea. There is, of course, another trend for the wealthy to live in walled, electronically protected and patrolled spaces. Here is an architecture of emergency.

Machine 4: The tank road

The Reichsautobahnen was formed as a corporation in 1933 to construct the autobahn system which, as far as Hitler was concerned, was to be the best motorway system in the world. The layout, design, strength and construction of the system, which has been claimed as the most impressive of all the achievements of the Third Reich, was for military rather than civil needs. This motorway system copes with the weight and volume of today's traffic because it was built to transport tanks. Moreover, its layout was not based on linking major urban centres but on a grid to take troops to and up and down Eastern and Western borders. As a United States postscript: the post-war American highway program of linking individual states into an inter-state system was funded as a defence measure.

Re-turning

We have already noted that modern war stands on a structure of modernity, and that both modernity and war stand on the production of structure – productivism. There is always that erasure in the beginning which accompanies whatever is brought to presence.[4] At the same time, one is ever caught out by finding oneself back at the beginning. These philosophically inflected observations may seem far distant from the 'reality of war': they are not.

Machine 5: Pre-loaded logistics

As a result of its 'Mechanisation and Modernisation' plans of 1960, the United States Navy introduced containers and container ships. This push by the military, combined with the Vietnam War, powered the international shipping container revolution.

War produces breakdowns which defuture, but war is increasingly driven by techno-cybernetic systems that 'get the result', while at the very same moment installing dysfunction. Productivism increasingly meets its own dysfunctional product. Techno-cybernetics are, in fact, profoundly lacking in the self-sustaining qualities that define ecological cybernetic structures. Here is the return to destruction, and the finitude of life, in the failure of 'our mode of being here' to secure that (the 'here') upon which it, and other forms of life, depend. Power, violence, force, order, politics all get cited in some way or another as the structural components in the making and conduct of war. Yet these figures explain little in themselves, they all beg close interrogation. More than this, there is a structure of war that a phenomenology of war has the ability to uncover. This goes to the violence of design as forced direction, imposed knowledge and universal time.

The necrological call of war, as the experience of heightened authenticity, still resonates. War destroys community but it also creates a surrogate bond after its loss. Additionally, in an epoch of the deepening dysfunctionality of community, as yet another face of unsustainability, there are new and residual desires for other ways of being together that deliver a certain internal social cohesion within a group, but at the price of broader social damage. The gang can be the extreme social expression of this. While it is a manifestation of breakdown, it also transposes the conflict models of unity against the enemy and solidarity in war into the condition of dysfunction that is a response to, and thus accelerates the situation.

Reframing in the light of modern war

The form of war has, and continues to, change. There are certainly three trends that warrant identification.

Firstly the spatiality of war has become far more complex. While wars are still geographically delineated, and formally declared, they also proliferate as fragmented conflicts. We see this not least in parts of Africa, Asia and Eastern Europe, where the structure of a nation disintegrates and repressed social formations reassert themselves. Here is a breakdown of the designing of the map and its accompanying political matrix of colonialism. In these circumstances lines of demarcation are unclear, there is no clear single cause of conflict, but a series of agendas flowing from a 'return of the repressed'; there is no defined war zone; no distant semiological separation between the terrorist, the soldier and the criminal; no defined division between the military and the civilian (or even between soldiers and children); no unambiguously military targets; no legible event structure of battles but often totally unpredictable outbursts of violence; and no containment of conflict within event time (while a moment of origination may be identifiable there is no certainty as to when conflict is terminated, rather it just smoulders and flares up from time to time). In these circumstances military planning shifts from the disposition of large standing forces to the creation and use of rapid deployment forces and small irregular units working outside 'rules of engagement'. Such circumstances dramatically alter how a target is identified and engaged. The way unsustainability is manifested in these conditions is of course not the ground zone obliteration of warfare of mass destruction but rather a continual environmental degradation that follows from the dysfunction of infrastructure (the breakdown of water systems, power supplies, road systems and so on).

The second point is directly linked to the first. Modern war has in significant part been dematerialised. This means it is not contained in just one space of conflict. From Vietnam onward, war has been waged in the space of the televisual as well as on the ground. This takes us to designed and designing forms, such as the image of war where a 'theatre of war' is constituted as a television set upon which events unfold with the audiences becoming players in the action of staged events. There are many examples, like the set piece battles organised for video recording by the Mujahideen in Afghanistan, IRA bombings in Ireland, United States military press corps officially distributed film footage during the Gulf War, and Hamas auto-destructive human bombs in Israel. People die for the image: making it, trying to obtain it, as a result of an interpretation of it, and in wishing to live up to it. Equally, people are being made in the form of the image, they are born into it. The control of the image, its management, is now a major feature of the politics and conduct of war.

Image relations have now become absolutely integral to the technology of 'smart weapons'. The image takes the future away. War imaging now flows across conflict zones, time, space, subject, memory, desire and media. The war 'machine' is now far more than functional systems complexity in the immaterial space of televisual media. The images of reported conflict flow along with historical and fictional images to constitute the warscape of public perception in which the psychology of warring becomes naturalised. The image of war has simply become one more visual element of everyday life that folds into the normalisation of unsustainability by worlding it as 'reality'. The genres of news media divide the picturing of crisis between 'ecological disaster' and 'conflict crisis', yet such a division actually fuels crisis by its de-relationalisation. Picturing the news of separate crisis events, that themselves are often staged and almost always edited, in fact conceals the crisis – it creates a 'crisis of crisis'. The televisual experience confirms that the slippage between 'being at'; war and 'being in' war is no simple division. These experiences are not the same but they do implicate each other in action, memory and dream.

The third change is the imperative for forward planning of the use of rapid deployment forces arising out of the spectre of future 'eco-wars'. With increasing demands on earth's resources from unevenly distributed and rapidly growing populations, the availability of fresh water, oil, fertile soil and forests, are increasingly becoming strategic concerns. It is around the disjuncture of supply and demand of these staples of nations that many future conflicts are being anticipated. The notion of eco-wars has arrived, and water is now deemed an inflammatory liquid. The theology of productivity that stems from productivism, and the associated aspiration to a universal high standard of living, promoted by economic modernism, drive this situation. In its condition of silent expectation, the inhumanity of humanism awaits another of its disasters. The crisis of crisis ensures that with the arrival of every disaster, the accumulative crisis, that begs the naming of a state of emergency to prevent the emergency, never gets named. The dangers unconsidered by anthropocentrism and the limited temporal horizon of human beings ever press. On the latter point one can say that in the scale of movement of geophysical events, human-induced climate change is travelling at the speed of light whereas from the myopic human perspective there is all the time in the world! There is almost no sense of the historicity of crisis, not least because science deludes itself with facts while looking in the wrong place for the truth (it has not learnt the first lesson of the confrontation with anthropocentrism).

Notes

1   Fragment 53, *Heraclitus Fragments* (trans TM Robinson), University of Toronto Press, Toronto, 1987, p. 36. A modern return of this articulated spirit of war was the German anarchofascist writer Ernst Jünger who respoke Heraclitus in his evocation of war as 'the father of all things', as cited by Michael Zimmerman, *Heidegger's Confrontation with Modernity*, Indiana University Press, Bloomington, 1990, p. 51.

2   One can note as an aside, that all contemporary searches for national identity come down to a picking through the ruins of colonisation, devastation and occupation. Here is the condition of mutual non-recoverability. Neither the coloniser nor the colonised can recover this history, because, for the one, identity cannot come out of darkness and, for the other, it cannot arise from the unrecoverable. The only possibility of invention is the return of the same.

3   Within the narrative of Western thought, the moment when productivism began to bring almost all we know into presence (while unknowingly driving that which had to be fundamentally sustained into concealment) has been assigned to the pre-Socratic period of Greek culture. The crucial 'fact' here is not the truth, or otherwise, of this moment but rather the actuality of its occurrence. Most significantly, the consequence of this rupture was that in establishing the very foundations of Western (and thus modernist) thought, the essential grounds of sustaining being were concealed. The implication of the production of this concealment was that the very thing that now gets called unsustainability arrived not as a consequence of the effects of modernity but as part of its causality. Moreover, sustainability, from the very birth of reason, has been there as a question of thinking, of ethics as much as one of biology. Certainly it is possible to read the entire works of Aristotle as an expression, and at times an almost direct statement, of acknowledgement of this observation.

4   See Jacques Derrida, 'Violence and Metaphysics' in *Writing and Difference* (trans Alan Bass), University of Chicago Press, Chicago, 1978, pp. 79–153.

Chapter 27

Ashoke Chatterjee

DESIGN IN INDIA: THE EXPERIENCE OF TRANSITION [2005]

Source: Ashoke Chatterjee (2005) 'Design in India: The Experience of Transition', *Design Issues*, 21, 4, pp. 4–10.

In 1947 modern independent India was born. Amid violence, partition and a 'tryst with destiny', independent India came into existence on a platform of technological and scientific socialism. The belief in science and technology as a way of governing, reforming and trying to meet the needs of a vast and disparate population, meant that design had an important role in fashioning the new India. Combining a vision of 'the modern' with a revaluation of India's traditional craft activities (promoted by Gandhi), the new government under Jawaharlal Nehru invited various European and American designers to participate in forging the design culture of India. The architect Le Corbusier, for instance, helped design the city of Chandigarh, and the Los Angeles design team of Ray and Charles Eames was asked to produce recommendations for training Indian designers, engineers and craftspeople. The symbiotic relationships established in this moment are crucial for understanding postwar design culture: India stood out as the central example of how design might act for the benefit of humankind in reshaping social worlds in more egalitarian, more progressive ways.

In the text that follows Ashoke Chatterjee brings this story up to date, to show how the design culture of India (which is still indebted to the heritage of technological socialism) continues to face old and new national and global challenges. The Gandhian heritage of craft, self-reliance and sustainability is becoming increasingly relevant as rural poverty and ecological calamities constantly demand local as much as central solutions. The vast ambition of scientific and technological progressivism has to face the fact that after more than sixty years it has had only limited success in overcoming the massive poverty to be found in India. The intensification of market globalisation means India has to compete on a platform whose interests are geared towards transnational economic wealth rather than to the needs of the billion or more people who live in India.

Ashoke Chatterjee has had, and continues to have, a central role in the promotion of design and craft in India. He has been the director of India's prestigious National Institute of Design (NID) and has worked on a number of projects concerned with water management and environmental issues. For Chatterjee 'dignity, service and love' continue to be at the heart of contemporary design in India, and by maintaining that commitment India should stand as an example to others. India continues to be the country of radical unevenness: of intense technological sophistication and innovation, and drastic impoverishment of technical means; of significant wealth and extreme, catastrophic poverty.

It is in many ways a microcosm of global unevenness. India, then, is the site of planetary hope for design culture.

Further reading: Eames and Eames 1958; Mitter 1977; Prakash 2002; Spivak 2000.

C **G ROAD IS AHMEDABAD'S** pride: a new shopping boulevard that turns its back on the crowded bazaars of this medieval city. Steel and glass store fronts, coffee shops, Pizza Hut, the latest in home entertainment, sportswear, fashion and ethnic chic – international brand names from India and overseas, flashing in neon to attract Ahmedabad's affluent youth to a "happening place" that demonstrates the power of what is emerging as the largest consumer market in the world. It wasn't always this way. When I arrived in Ahmedabad in 1975, a "happening" meant sampling the street life of Manek Chowk, the heart of Ahmedabad's tradition as India's textile capital, around which revolved a rich pattern of community living and craft activity. It was in these lanes and marketplaces that Ahmedabad's craft and merchant guilds flourished for generations, giving the city a reputation that rivaled sixteenth century London. Seven bridges span the dry riverbed of the Sabarmati River, which separates Manek Chowk and old Ahmedabad from C G Road and the high-rise sprawl of the new city. The traffic hurling back and forth – handcarts and camel carts, and an occasional elephant, to compete with the city's passion for the newest in two-, three-, and four-wheeled speeders – is symbolic of India's passage to and from modernity, and its search for a confident identity that can link five-thousand years of history with a future in which change is the only certainty.

It is from this experience of transition that design in India takes its meaning. Mahatma Gandhi, arriving in India from South Africa almost a century ago, established his ashram retreat along the banks of the Sabarmati. His "experiments with truth" began in Ahmedabad, experiments intended to bring freedom to his subjugated people and to build a society that could "wipe every tear from every eye." Self-reliant systems of design and production were inherent in Gandhi's mission. They were directed at serving basic needs through a demonstration of social justice and a respect for nature's balance. Symbolic of this quest was Gandhi's campaign for the boycott of British textiles, and for the home production of handspun, handwoven "khadi," the livery of freedom which was to evolve into a handloom revolution that is in itself India's greatest achievement in contemporary design. A few kilometers down the riverside from Gandhi Ashram is the campus of the National Institute of Design. Established here some forty years ago, the NID was one of several specialist institutions of contemporary knowledge created by free India to ensure that its youth were at the frontiers of knowledge; harnessing it for the developmental needs of a giant democracy mired in postcolonial poverty. The NID was the first attempt by any developing country to use the design disciplines inherited from the Bauhaus as a tool for national regeneration. The catalyst for its creation was an extraordinary one. Barely a decade after Independence, India invited Charles and Ray Eames of Los Angeles to suggest how design could assist the growth of Indian industry. Government officials were expecting a feasibility report. What they got was an extraordinary statement of design as a value system, as an attitude that could discern the strengths and limitations of both tradition and modernity, and as a profession that could use the wisdom of such insights to make wise decisions about India's future:

> In the face of the inevitable destruction of many cultural values – in the face of the immediate need of the nation to feed and shelter itself – a desire for quality takes on a real meaning. It is not a self-conscious effort to develop an aesthetic – it is a relentless search for quality that must be maintained if this new Republic is to survive.[1]

Four decades later, if one is to search for the impact of design on contemporary India, C G Road may offer an easier vantage point than Manek Chowk. Graduates of the NID, and of the other design schools that followed it, are part of the international look and the product excellence showcased in the shopping malls of every Indian city. Indian brands that Indian designers have helped build compete successfully at home and overseas, from machine tools, automobiles, and watches, to an astonishing range of textiles, garments, entertainment and media products, and crafts redesigned to meet contemporary needs. All this represents a major transformation from yesteryear. In the early years of the NID's founding, India's market was carefully protected to encourage local production and discourage competition from imports – a policy that reflected the urge for self-reliance that had marked the freedom struggle under Gandhi's leadership. Indian planners were attempting to blend Gandhian and Marxist principles with the nation's multicultural ethic, and to do this through centralized planning. A competitive market would be tolerated, but not allowed to reign supreme. Entrepreneurship and the profit motive (which the Indian Diaspora had taken across the globe) were discounted at home as something vaguely disreputable. Industry, public as well as private, had difficulty in comprehending the importance of design in an environment where consumer choice was deliberately limited. Designers struggled with the contradictions of advocating excellence in a marketplace that did not appear to need it, and in social sectors which needed convincing evidence (which only a competitive marketplace could provide) that investment in design was worthwhile. When India's first design graduates emerged in the mid-1970s, the business community regarded design as a postponable luxury, or as an option to be applied after a product was developed rather than integrated into the development process.

Not surprisingly, the first career opportunities appeared wherever competition existed: in export industries, in working with traditional crafts threatened by mass production, and in the advertising industry. Traditional crafts, conservation of cultural heritage, exhibitions to communicate the Indian experience at home and abroad, service to small- and medium-sized enterprises looking for new markets, programs for health and literacy – these were the demonstrations that won for India (and for the NID) the first international recognition of design for development. In 1979, this recognition brought the United Nations, through the United Nations Industrial Development Organization (UNIDO) in Vienna, to the NID campus in Ahmedabad for the first-ever UN conference on design. It was an effort to share the Indian experience with the global community, and its outcome was the Ahmedabad Declaration on Industrial Design for Development. The Declaration articulated a global mission for design: that "designers in every part of the world must work to evolve a new value system which dissolves the disastrous divisions between the worlds of waste and want, preserves the identity of peoples and attends to the priority areas of need for the vast majority of humankind."

The conference suggested actions essential to the achievement of the Declaration, and these were endorsed by UNIDO. Several national and international institutions used the opportunity to reinforce the thinking that had begun to emerge through Europe's "green movement," pointing out that the "world of waste" was being rejected by the very societies that spawned consumerism. The 1979 Declaration should have been a watershed event for design in India, inspired as it was by the Indian experience. Yet the Declaration in India remained largely a statement of intent, and less one of achievement. It came at the opening of a decade that was to reject the socialist paradigm, and what many regarded as its Gandhian baggage. Instead, national policy turned toward global and domestic competitiveness, and to measures that could stress international market success as a new hallmark of self-reliance. Design began to move into the center of corporate strategies, and a profound semantic shift accompanied that movement.

Sometime in the 1980s, the term "designer" changed from a noun to an adjective; and the image of a good Indian life from Gandhian austerity to one of "Just do it." The new consumer culture accelerated as part of a young Prime Minister's decision to open India's door to globalization. Rajiv Gandhi took the first steps of dismantling protectionism. With that, design awareness accelerated at a speed that would have been impossible to even imagine at the time the Ahmedabad Declaration was signed. Designers who had been urging industry for years to acknowledge the centrality of their role now were being challenged to deliver design of a quality and at a speed entirely new to their experience.

India's own information technology (IT) revolution took off in the engineering campuses that had been created soon after Independence as India's technological frontiers. The computer began to impact every aspect of design training and service, opening vast new horizons of application. A gigantic media boom hit India, with a proliferation of products and channels that convincingly demonstrated design as the cutting edge for market survival. Soon, the fashion industry stormed in, challenging concepts of identity treasured by generations of Indians with its relentless promotion of an "international" (read European and North American) look, and an equally relentless demand for speed and quality. Media hype essential to a fashion culture quickly made it the most obvious expression of design in India, and design education soon was redefined in the public mind as a passport to glamour and wealth. Liberalization and globalization became the gospel of a new generation of international managers from India, leading an expanding middle class that was young and increasingly affluent. Their dreams of a "first-world" life-style soon would be fueled along the C G Roads of an India busily redefining itself in the language of global trade. Despite massive swings in the world economy, the market for design has expanded rapidly, and young professionals emerging from design schools are quickly absorbed by industry. Using design to build "Brand India" as a global presence is a job that Indian industry is doing well. Watching the shoppers rush by on C G Road, can one say that Indian design has arrived at last, and that the mission that began with the Eames's report is well on its way to fulfillment?

It often is said that whatever generalization applies to India, the opposite is equally true. Design is no exception: its success is in an organized marketplace that caters to a middle class as large as all of Europe, and to expanding prospects overseas. Its contribution will be essential to the role India now demands of being taken seriously as an economic power. Design capability is reflected in the improved competitiveness ratings accorded to India by the World Economic Forum's annual surveys, including its report for 2002/2003. The UNDP's human development reports tell another story. Here, India ranks among the lowest in the world. The reality is that the vast majority of India's one billion citizens live in rural settings and urban slums that remain well outside organized systems of commerce. For them, the quality of life remains abysmal, touched only at the farthest fringe by interventions from designers motivated by the early inspiration that defined a new Indian profession. For the visionaries who created the NID, the marketplace was an arena of interaction to be treated with great respect. It was here that quality had to be demonstrated, made practical, and given the power to change attitudes and behaviors. Thus market success was essential to demonstrate the value of design to the broader needs of a quality of life. Today, it often is seen as its only value.

The challenge is to innovate a client system that can harness design skills toward products and services that finally must deliver a freedom from want for all Indians. Such a system cannot reject market mechanisms. Instead, it must use them with the highest degree of managerial competence to build new sources of support for developmental priorities that can be sustained without total dependence on government programs. If this is to happen, Indian design must evolve strong partnerships and networks with institutions of civil society. Tomorrow, these institutions will be the prime clients of design for development.

In the years of centralized planning that followed India's Independence, government was the prime engine of social change in India. This is no longer the case, and recent years have seen a strong movement away from official controls and patronage to demands for decentralization, with decision-making and problem-solving at the local level. In the current period of transition that marks India's new fascination for market economics, government is withdrawing from the "commanding heights" it once occupied, leaving a social vacuum that private enterprise cannot be expected to fill. The case for design, carefully built over the years, had just begun to impact planners when major shifts in policy took place. Planners in New Delhi and the state capitals now are preoccupied with new priorities, and the case for design for development will have to be made elsewhere. The answer may be found in the newly empowered civil institutions. Building their understanding and support for design then can be used to restore real needs to the center of design education and training. If this is to be achieved, it is India's design schools that will need to assume the responsibility for forging the partnerships that can provide a client system responsive to issues of real need. This must be accepted as a marketing job; one that will require articulating the case for design with the highest level of professional skill. Support must come from "funders" – governments, international agencies, and industries – currently besieged with competing applications. Therefore, potential donors must be attracted by hard-headed proposals, carefully prepared with budgets, timelines, and benchmarks for monitoring progress. These are skills that the social sector often lacks, but without them no one will listen.

An immediate step might be to document key experiences in design for development from the past: documented to demonstrate the design process as a proven strategy for poverty alleviation. The case must be built to demonstrate economic and social impacts, cost benefits, extension and replication opportunities, the barriers and the opportunities for sustainability, as well as the possible cost to India of not involving designers in efforts for social change. Indian designers have demonstrated the potential of design for development. This now could be used for advocacy: the regeneration of crafts, the protection of fragile ecosystems and environments, the conservation of scarce materials, aids for the less able (India has the largest population of such persons in the world), communication and media efforts that have impacted campaigns for health and for human rights (particularly those of women and children), the generation of new opportunities for sustainable livelihoods, educational materials that help enliven the bleakness of India's classrooms, and the application of ergonomics to the reduction of drudgery, fatigue, and occupational ill-health in India's workplaces and homes. Social scientists, particularly economists, and professional managers need to be recruited to help make the case for design credible and water-tight.

Critical to the success of such an Indian effort will be to link it with global efforts toward sustainability. Perhaps the most important of these emerged from the Earth Summit at Rio in 1992 as Agenda 21, with its urgent demand for alternative patterns of consumption that are compatible with ecological sustainability. Despite all the disappointments of the past decade, the power of Agenda 21 has been demonstrated again at Johannesburg in 2002, and it remains the most important element in rethinking lifestyles and development patterns in India's industrialized North as well as developing South. Another key opportunity for integrating design has come through the United Nations Development Program (UNDP) in New York, and its new system of Human Development Reports. This system transforms the traditional understanding of living standards currently limited to measurements of gross national product and per capita income. Instead, the HDR approach defines development and progress in terms of a quality of life that can enlarge people's choices and their capacity to fulfill them. In 1998, the HDR investigated consumption from a human perspective – consumption *for* development – in what could be interpreted as a charter for design in the new millennium.

Other opportunities have emerged. These include movements for the empowerment of women and for consumer protection, the new respect for the knowledge and wisdom of indigenous traditions, the revival of crafts worldwide, the search for alternative patterns of income generation and employment to meet the needs of expanding populations, the growing respect for institutions and professions that have a capacity for interdisciplinary teamwork, and the search for values more enduring than brand names. All of these forces represent major opportunities for demonstrating the power of design. None of them was as strong or as clearly organized as they are today when the Ahmedabad Declaration on Industrial Design for Development was ratified in 1979. Each force suggests an opportunity to communicate the experience and contribution of designers around the world, brought together in a collective strength that can help take their efforts to scale. Charles and Ray Eames in their India Report spoke of design as an ultimate expression of "dignity, service and love." Contemporary design in India began with that message. Almost half a century later, India can help to ensure that this message remains as the non-negotiable heart of design as a twenty-first century profession in India and in every other part of the world.

Note

1   Charles and Ray Eames, *The India Report* (Ahmedabad: National Institute of Design, 1958).

PART SIX

DESIGN TIME

INTRODUCTION TO PART SIX

IS THERE A sense of time that is peculiar to the world of design? Is there a dominant tempo or rhythm to this artificial world? Perhaps the safest answer would be an immediate and resounding; 'No, of course not.' Design cultures include any number of different durations: the seasons of the fashion industry (spring/summer, autumn/winter) mockingly relate to the natural seasons, whereas the passing of generations of gaming consoles and mobile phones seems to take its pulse from the heart beat of the research and development laboratory. Similarly, any complex site of design (say a domestic room, a kitchen, for instance) is filled with any number of devices and utensils whose provenances would need to be gauged across millennia, centuries and years. Cooking a meal using the latest high tech sophistication also requires metal pans and wooden spoons. In a global context, at any one moment, there is a vast array of design temporalities being lived (terms like the 'developing world' and the 'developed (or over-developed) world' point to the uneven temporalities involved).

Yet it is precisely here that we do find a temporality that is peculiar to design, and one that has enormous consequences. The very fact that when people describe large landmasses as 'developing' or 'developed' they are thinking in the temporality of design (what is the communication infrastructure like in Botswana?) suggests that the global 'clock' is set to design-time. Of course it is precisely the fiction that there is an established temporality of progress (owned by the 'design leaders' in the West) that positions the non-West in the role of having constantly to play catch-up. No doubt the years to come will show that such rhythmic dominance was particularly stupid and will see Western cultures desperate to 'catch up' with sustainable forms of living that, in a few places in the world, are centuries old.

Design-time sways to the rhythm of capitalist production and consumption. Nowhere is this more evident than in the cycles of invention and obsolescence that circulate in design-time. Of course as writers like Evan Watkins point out, obsolescence isn't the obliteration of a design technology: it is the geographical re-situating of a design technology (into the hands of those with fewer financial resources). In this way the temporal dimension of design-time has spatial effects: this is the chronotope (the space-time) of design. It is hardly going to be news to many to say that this chronotope is wasteful, exploitative and ecologically damaging. It is also a chronotope that hides the more complex dimension of 'real' design-time (the plural times of design actuality, of contradictory effects and so on). Thus one of the challenges that the study of design culture faces is the fashioning of more ethical, more descriptive and more explanatory versions of time.

Chapter 28

Siegfried Giedion

ANONYMOUS HISTORY [1948]

Source: Siegfried Giedion (1948) *Mechanization Takes Command: A Contribution to Anonymous History*, New York: Norton, 1969, pp. 2–11.

The Swiss design theorist and historian Siegfried Giedion (1888–1968) spent his life investigating and promoting modernism in its vernacular and professional forms. Like other incisive critics of design (Siegfried Kracauer and Reyner Banham, for instance) Giedion had a practical and a philosophical knowledge: he had initially studied engineering and had gone on to take a doctorate in art history under the supervision of Heinrich Wölfflin. Alongside his writing Giedion was the founder and secretary of the Congrès Internationaux d'Architecture Moderne (CIAM) from 1928 until its dissolution in 1959. CIAM was the central forum for the promotion of modernist architecture and urban planning across the globe.

In his 1948 book, *Mechanization Takes Command*, Giedion traces the lineage of machines and machine forms, like the assembly line, which he finds first, not in the production of automobiles, but in the industrialised slaughtering of animals in the 1870s. *Mechanization Takes Command* takes its objects from the workplace (urban and rural) and the home (food preparation, washing and furniture). This follows on from an earlier, more experimental work, *Building in France, Building in Iron, Building in Ferro-Concrete* (1928), where Giedion provides his first explanation of the purpose and power of 'anonymous history'. His argument is beguilingly simple: given that the most highly regarded buildings of industrial modernity work to veil their relationship to industry ('the nineteenth century cloaked each new invention with historicizing masks', 'each was senselessly buried beneath stone stage sets'), then the historian of industrial modernity can't afford to look at that century's most prized possessions. They must look elsewhere. For Giedion in *Building in France* it meant looking at constructions built without the involvement of celebrated architects: the constructions of a vernacular (or 'collective') modernism were to be found in more anonymous buildings – in bridges, factories, shops, industrial sheds and so on. In *Mechanization Takes Command* he extends this to include nearly every device that was in circulation by the middle of the twentieth century.

Giedion's historical understanding of design objects informed his evaluation of contemporary design. For him the form of our object-world articulated the deep social structure of the past. Thus the promotion of modernist design was always, for Giedion, a social programme:

> Today we need a house that corresponds in its entire structure to our bodily feeling as it
> is influenced and liberated through sport, gymnastics, and a sensuous way of life: light,

transparent, movable. Consequentially, this open house also signifies a reflection of the contemporary mental condition: there are no longer separate affairs, all domains interpenetrate.

(Giedion 1929, cited in Heynen 1999: 36)

Further reading: Georgiadis 1993; Giedion 1928/1995, 1941/1980; Heynen 1999.

HISTORY IS A magical mirror. Who peers into it sees his own image in the shape of events and developments. It is never stilled. It is ever in movement, like the generation observing it. Its totality cannot be embraced: History bares itself only in facets, which fluctuate with the vantage point of the observer.

Facts may occasionally be bridled within a date or a name, but not their more complex significance. The meaning of history arises in the uncovering of relationships. That is why the writing of history has less to do with facts as such than with their relations. These relations will vary with the shifting point of view, for, like constellations of stars, they are ceaselessly in change. Every true historical image is based on relationship, appearing in the historian's choice from among the fullness of events, a choice that varies with the century and often with the decade, just as paintings differ in subject, technique, and psychic content. Now great historical panoramas are painted, now fragments of everyday things suffice to carry the feeling of an epoch.

The historian deals with a perishable material, men. He cannot calculate the course of future events like the astronomer. But in common with the astronomer, he may see new constellations and hitherto invisible worlds appearing over the horizon. And like the astronomer, he must be an ever-watchful spectator.

His role is to put in order in its historical setting what we experience piecemeal from day to day, so that in place of sporadic experience, the continuity of events becomes visible. An age that has lost its consciousness of the things that shape its life will know neither where it stands nor, even less, at what it aims. A civilization that has lost its memory and stumbles from day to day, from happening to happening, lives more irresponsibly than the cattle, who at least have their instincts to fall back upon.

History, regarded as insight into the moving process of life, draws closer to biological phenomena. We shall speak little, here, of general lines and great events, and then only when necessary to connect occurrences with the bedrock in which they are rooted.

We shall inquire in the first line into the tools that have molded our present-day living. We would know how this mode of life came about, and something of the process of its growth.

We shall deal here with humble things, things not usually granted earnest consideration, or at least not valued for their historical import. But no more in history than in painting is it the impressiveness of the subject that matters. The sun is mirrored even in a coffee spoon.

In their aggregate, the humble objects of which we shall speak have shaken our mode of living to its very roots. Modest things of daily life, they accumulate into forces acting upon whoever moves within the orbit of our civilization.

The slow shaping of daily life is of equal importance to the explosions of history; for, in the anonymous life, the particles accumulate into an explosive force. Tools and objects are outgrowths of fundamental attitudes to the world. These attitudes set the course followed by thought and action. Every problem, every picture, every invention, is founded on a specific attitude, without which it would never have come into being. The performer is led by outward impulses – money, fame, power – but behind him, unbeknown, is the orientation of the period, is its bent toward this particular problem, that particular form.

For the historian there are no banal things. Like the scientist, the historian does not take anything for granted. He has to see objects not as they appear to the daily user, but as the inventor saw them when they first took shape. He needs the unworn eyes of contemporaries, to whom they appeared marvelous or frightening. At the same time, he has to establish their constellations before and after, and thus establish their meaning.

History writing is ever tied to the fragment. The known facts are often scattered broadcast, like stars across the firmament. It should not be assumed that they form a coherent body in the historical night. Consciously, then, we represent them as fragments, and do not hesitate, when necessary, to spring from one period to another. Pictures and words are but auxiliaries; the decisive step must be taken by the reader. In his mind the fragments of meaning here displayed should become alive in new and manifold relations.

Before we entered upon the present work we tried, at Yale University in the winter of 1941, to suggest in broad outline what brought us to anonymous history. At that time we could not foresee how far the inquiry was to lead. For this very reason a few passages as then spoken may not be out of place:

Any inquiry today into the rise of our modern way of life must remain incomplete. There is no lack of works tracing the broad political, economic, or sociological trends of our time. Specialized researches into the various fields are also available. But few bridges have been thrown between them.

If we seek a more general insight into the rise of our way of life – of our comfort, of our attitudes – we are stopped at every turn by gaps and unanswered questions.

We know furthermore that isolated studies are inadequate to embrace the complex structure of the nineteenth century. More than the bare history of an industry, an invention, an organization, we have to observe what was occurring in various other fields at the same time. Then we see that without conscious forethought phenomena simultaneously arise, bearing striking similarities to one another. They need only be displayed side by side to call into consciousness the tendencies and sometimes the meaning of their period.

Iron filings, these small insignificant particles, by the interference of a magnet become form and design, revealing existing lines of force. So, too, the details of anonymous history can be made to reveal the guiding trends of a period.

Our task is clearly outlined: to inquire how our contemporary life, with its mixture of constituent and chaotic elements, came about. The difficulty lies in sifting and separating those facts that may be called constituent and that are the true pointers of their age. Once this has been done the material does the rest.

Anonymous history is directly connected with the general, guiding ideas of an epoch. But at the same time it must be traced back to the particulars from which it arises.

Anonymous history is many sided, and its different departments flow into one another. Only with difficulty can they be separated. The ideal in anonymous history would be to show simultaneously the various facets as they exist side by side, together with the process of their interpenetration. Nature does this in the eye of the insect – a lens of multiple facets – fusing its distinct images of the outer world into an integrated picture. The individual does not have such power. We must be grateful if this objective is fulfilled only in the fragment.

Procedure

In *Space, Time and Architecture* we attempted to show how our period came to consciousness of itself in a single field, architecture.

Now to broaden the scope, we shall observe the coming about of mechanization, that almost unescapable influence over our way of life, our attitudes, our instincts.

We shall deal with mechanization from the human standpoint. Its results and its implications cannot be simply stated. The prerequisite is that we should understand its tools, even if our interest here is not a technical one. It is not enough for a physician to know that a body is attacked by a disease. Even if he is not a bacteriologist, he must push his research into usually invisible realms, he must have a modest knowledge of bacteriology, he must know when the organism was attacked and how the tuberculosis spread. Likewise, the historian cannot dispense with the microscope. He cannot relent in tracing the theme to its origins. He has to show when an idea first appears; how quickly or slowly it spreads or disappears. He cannot confine himself to mechanization alone any more than the doctor can to bacteria. He must take psychic factors into reckoning, for often they exert a decisive influence. In our case art represents the psychic factor. It will serve as the surest aid to an understanding of certain phenomena.

We begin with the concept of Movement, which underlies all mechanization. There follows the Hand, which is to be supplanted; and Mechanization as a Phenomenon.

Mechanization of the complicated craft

The elimination of the complicated handicraft marks the beginning of high mechanization. This transition takes place in America during the second half of the nineteenth century. We shall meet with it in the callings of the farmer, the baker, the butcher, the joiner, and the housewife. But only in one instance shall we follow it closely: in the masterful transformation of the door lock from handicraft to mechanized production.

The means of mechanization

The symptom of full mechanization is the assembly line, wherein the entire factory is consolidated into a synchronous organism. From its first appearance in the eighteenth century down to its later and decisive elaboration between the two World Wars, the assembly line is an American institution. What we shall have to say about it is but roughly carved out. So far as we know, no historic account yet covers this most significant factor in America's productive capacity. For this reason, but especially because they closely touch upon human problems, the assembly line and scientific management will be given somewhat closer treatment.

Mechanization encounters the organic

What happens when mechanization encounters organic substance? Here we face the great constants running through human development: soil, growth, bread, meat. The questions involved are but narrow sectors of a far broader complex: man's relation today to those organic forces that act upon and within him. The catastrophes that threaten to destroy civilization and existence are but outward signs that our organism has lost its balance. Their causes lie deeply buried in the great anonymous movements of the epoch. Our contact with the organic forces within us and outside of us has been interrupted – a paralyzed, torn, chaotic condition. This contact is increasingly menaced as the tie with basic human values becomes frayed. Here, if anywhere, overturn has become inevitable.

   We shall therefore open with the question: What happens when mechanization meets an organic substance? And shall close by inquiring into the attitude of our culture toward our own organism.

Mechanization of agriculture

After remaining stationary for a thousand years, the structure of the farmer is revolutionized. At first in literary and tentative ways, in the eighteenth century; experimentally in the first half of the nineteenth century; sweepingly in the second half. England forms the hub of the movement during the eighteenth century, the American Middle West during the latter half of the nineteenth. Here begins what is perhaps a new chapter in the history of man: a changed relation to the soil and the uprooting of the farmer.

Of the instruments of mechanization we shall touch only the reaper, which by its replacement of the hand holds the most important place among the tools of mechanized agriculture.

Bread

What happens when mechanization comes up against an organic substance, bread, which, like the door lock or the farmer, belongs among the symbols of humanity? How did mechanization alter the structure of bread and the taste of the consumer? When did this mechanization set in? How are popular taste and production related to one another?

Meat

What are mechanization's limits in dealing with so complex an organism as the animal? And how does the elimination of a complicated craft – such as the butcher's – proceed?

Still of unmeasured significance is mechanization's intervention in the procreation of plants and of animals.

Mechanization encounters human surroundings

What happens to the human setting in the presence of mechanization?

Dangerous tendencies declare themselves before the advent of mechanization (on which the whole blame is thrown) and independently of it. There is no doubt that nineteenth-century mechanization facilitated these trends. But they appear distinctly in the interior before the impact of mechanization is felt.

The changing conception of comfort: medieval comfort

We shall look to the late medieval period for a secure starting point. Here lie the roots of our existence and of our continuous development. Since typological researches in this field are unfortunately lacking, the Middle Ages will be included and dealt with from this point of view. What interests us in the first line here is the type of comfort developed in different periods. How did the Middle Ages understand comfort? How does the medieval conception differ from our contemporary view? Where do connecting links exist?

To take a short path, we shall follow the relation between man and space. How does man order his intimate setting in the fifteenth century, the eighteenth, the nineteenth the twentieth? How, in other words, has his feeling for space changed?

A parallel question is that of *human posture* in the various periods, and of posture's projection into seating.

Comfort in the eighteenth century

The creation of modern sitting comfort is to be sought in the Rococo. The Rococo's great power of observation in shaping furniture organically so as to favor relaxation of the body forms a counterpart to that period's exploration of the plant and animal world.

Late eighteenth-century England is primarily concerned with the technical virtuosity of the cabinet-maker, and affords, within the most refined type of handicraft, a foretaste of the mechanized furniture of the nineteenth century.

The nineteenth century

The beginnings of ruling taste

More than in the Rococo, in which Louis XV's role was not a very active one, a particular type of man becomes decisive in the Empire: Napoleon. Here phenomena appear, such as the devaluation of symbols, which have been laid at the door of mechanization alone.

The mechanization of adornment

The misuse of mechanization to imitate handicraft production and the use of substitute materials comes to the fore in England between 1820 and 1850. The blurring of the instincts is clearly recognized by English Reformers around 1850. Through criticism and encouragement, attempts are made to influence industry directly.

The reign of the upholsterer

From the upholsterer's hand comes that cushion furniture of the latter half of the century which seems to have lost all structure. These are transitory products of a surprising longevity. To avoid vague judgments, we have thought it useful to consider them typologically.

What types are found? In what way are they connected with mechanization? How is their form related to the introduction of spiral springs? When do they first come into use?

The Surrealists have given us keys to the psychic unrest that haunted mechanized adornment, cushion furniture, and the whole interior.

The constituent furniture of the nineteenth century

Over against the ruling taste stands the unexplored complex of 'patent-furniture.' In this case, mechanization is harnessed to the opening of new fields. Here, where unobserved, the creative instinct of the nineteenth century reveals itself, fulfilling needs formerly without solution. This furniture that answers to the posture of the nineteenth century is the work of the engineer. It is based on movability and adjustability to the body. In America, between 1850 and the late 'eighties there grew a facility never known in Europe for solving *motion problems* of this kind, which America lost back to the influence of ruling taste after 1893.

The constituent furniture of the twentieth century

The initiative now passes into European hands. The new furniture created in this period is bound up with the spatial conceptions of the new architecture. It is a furniture of *types*, not of individual pieces. It is the work, with few exceptions, of the architects who at the same time became the leaders of contemporary building.

Mechanization of the household

The mechanizing of the housewife's work is not unlike the mechanizing of the other complex handicrafts. The alleviation of domestic drudgery proceeds along like paths: first, through mechanization of the work process; and again by its organization. Both are best observed in America, in the early 'sixties, and – at their peak – in the period between the two World Wars.

Questions that require an answer are, among others:

Is household rationalization connected with the status of woman in America? Is it rooted in the Quaker or the Puritan outlook?

The organization of the kitchen had its starting point in the new architectural movement in Europe around 1927. It came about in the general reshaping of the house.

We have placed the mechanization of the hearth at the head of the various mechanisms. An ever-growing concentration and automatization of the heat source is observed – from the coal range to electric cooking. This trend seems to be still in progress.

We shall survey the various aids to mechanical comfort in the household, their individual appearance and general acceptance. Central among them are the mechanized cleaning appliances: for washing, for ironing, for dishwashing, for removing dust, etc. The influence of feeling upon the aspect of the appliances cannot be overlooked: streamline style.

Only when the mechanical appliances had already been worked out and were becoming popularized did the interest of American industry turn to the integration of the appliances within the work process. Thus emerging in the mid-'thirties, the streamline kitchen was raised, with its devices, into the idol of the house.

It was in the time of full mechanization that the domestic servant question, recognized around 1860 as irreconcilable with democracy, became an immediate problem: the servantless household. Connected with the servant problem was the attempt to reduce the ever-rising cost of mechanical utilities by a rationally planned mechanical core of the house.

Mechanization of the bath

The history of its technical equipment affords no standard by which to evaluate the modern bath. Closer insight is immediately gained in registering the uncertainty and wavering throughout the century from the moment a choice between types became necessary.

Just as it left no style untouched, the nineteenth century left none of the historical types untried. But scant progress was made, outside of reformistic propaganda or the development of luxury bathrooms. For the masses of the population, only the cheapest mode of bathing was seriously debated.

The chaos around 1900 appears in the failure of the expert to recommend a single satisfactory bathtub. But even this would have offered no historically acceptable standard, and the question remains: is bathing a simple ablution, or is it part of a broader concept, regeneration of the human organism? Looking backward, we find that in past cultures the bath was embodied in types affording total regeneration. Though shortened to the utmost, a typology of Western regeneration will have to be drawn up. Ancient, Islamic, Late Gothic, Russian regeneration seem to reflect a common archetype, its path traceable to the interior of Asia.

All these types aim not merely at outward ablution, but at a total vivification of the body by differentiated means, which vary with the culture. Our civilization from the waning Middle Ages on has believed that it can do without a systematic type of regeneration to help the organism recoup the damage which each civilization in its own way entails.

Mechanization did no more than give a glittering façade to the most primitive type of bath.

Toward a typological approach

A treatment of problems suited to our day will constantly bear interrelations in mind. This leads to a typological approach. The history of styles follows its theme along a horizontal direction; the history of types along a vertical one. Both are necessary if things are to be seen in historical space.

The specialistic approach that grew in strength through the nineteenth century brought stylistic history to the fore. Typological thinking rarely finds a place there, and mainly when unavoidable, as is the case in the encyclopedias of furniture. The French contributions around 1880, in which a vein of universality still runs, are the more satisfactory in this respect. The large *Oxford English Dictionary* too is sometimes a friend in need.

We are interested in following the growth of phenomena, or if one will, in reading their line of fate, over wide spans of time. Vertical sections make it possible to trace the organic changes of a type.

How far a type need be followed back into its history varies with the case. There are no rules or recipes. It is not the historian who guides, but the material. Some of the developments will call for far-reaching retrospect, others only for rapid backward glances. What is essential is the panoramic and simultaneous view. This may lead to discontinuous treatment. For only through simultaneous perception of various periods and of various fields within a period can there be insight into the inner growth.

Conceiving of history as constellations, the historian can claim one more freedom. He assumes the right to observe at close range certain phenomena, certain fragments of meaning, while omitting others from his field of attention. This may lead to unwonted proportions, as in contemporary painting when a hand is made to spread over the picture while the body remains a hint or a fragment. This freedom in handling proportion is no less necessary when one seeks to represent the meaning of historical complexes.

Dates

The historian's objectivity may be voiced in a treatment faithful to the nature of the material as well as to its constellations in time.

Dates are the historian's yardstick. They enable him to measure off historical space. In themselves or when pinned to isolated facts, they are as meaningless as the numbers on a ticket. But conceived in interrelation, that is vertically and horizontally connected within the network of historical objects, they delimit constellations. In such cases dates take on meaning.

Dates marking when and where phenomena first appear or have become commonplace in various spheres form complexes that give objective insight into growth.

Chapter 29

Evan Watkins

SOCIAL POSITION AND THE ART OF
AUTOMOBILE MAINTENANCE [1993]

Source: Evan Watkins (1993) 'Social Position and the Art of Automobile Maintenance', in *Throw-aways: Work Culture and Consumer Education*, Stanford: Stanford University Press, pp. 89–96.

In 1961 the philosopher of everyday life Henri Lefebvre wrote: 'In "consumer society" . . . the manufacturers of consumer goods do all they can to manufacture consumers. To a large extent they succeed' (Lefebvre 1961/2002: 10). Evan Watkins' book *Throwaways: Work Culture and Consumer Education* can be read as one of the most sustained accounts of how this is achieved. The argument on which the book is premised follows Lefebvre's initial proposition that consumer culture manufactures consumers. For Watkins this means taking the pedagogic function of commodities and consumer culture seriously. Commodities and the literature surrounding them train us: they furnish us with new desires, new expectations, new skills, while simultaneously getting us to jettison previous abilities and satisfactions. Take, for example, the fridge and the consumer culture of chilled, supermarket-packaged food. In fridge-oriented food cultures many goods that used to live in cup-boards have migrated to the fridge, including vegetables. Buying packaged vegetables, storing them in fridges and believing in their quality encourages some activities while discouraging others. Consumer culture is educating chilled-food users to believe in the pedagogy of the packaging: follow the nutrition guidelines, and, most emphatically, believe the expiration date. To hand over authority to the expiration date would, in the end, mean discarding older skills that are reliant on visual and olfactory senses to tell you when something is 'off'.

Watkins argues that what consumer culture has to teach us is the lesson of 'up-to-date-ness'. The rhythm of this pedagogy promotes a constant turnover of commodities and the practices that they afford: obsolescence is not only a central phenomenon of this rhythm, it also becomes a form of social production. Thus while things become outmoded, so too do the populations for whom they still have value. As Michelle Henning glosses it: 'Marginalized and exploited populations that are charac-terized as obsolescent are surrounded by obsolescent material culture, and out of necessity, they engage in obsolescent cultural practices' (Henning 2007: 54). To maintain a car that is twenty years old is to maintain a car that is at least sixteen years 'out of date' (according to the rhythm of obsolescence), and to signal your own outmoded-ness in contemporary culture.

The historical transformation that structures Watkins' account is the shift from production-led culture to consumption-led culture. The corresponding pedagogy requires a shift from what Watkins calls a 'natural' coding (the ideological belief that the dominant order is the natural order of things) to a 'techno-ideological' coding that takes its authority from technological innovation. The class culture that is produced is shaped by the uneven distribution of contemporary technology and the circulation of obsolescent things:

> As so-called third world countries, as well as part-time workers, a great many racial and ethnic 'minorities,' and poor people generally in the United States know all too well, obsolete technologies don't disappear as they become obsolete. Obsolescence means the possibility of *appearance*; it is a precondition for the availability of technologies to these groups.
>
> (Watkins 1993: 26)

It may turn out that in the attempt to build a sustainable future, ecological politics will find common cause with a social politics based around something as out-of-date – something as 'obsolescent' – as class consciousness.

Further reading: Gendron 1986; Henning 2007; Wollen and Kerr 2002.

OUT OF CONTEXT, such terms as "care" and "maintenance" don't typically suggest masculine activities, and as a result when deployed concerning car work they have been linked with more immediately recognizable masculine ideologies of automotive performance and individualistic, even "frontiersman"-style, appeals to do-it-yourself stuff. But what interests me here particularly is how the effects of changing automotive technologies are plotted to define both care and maintenance.

With very recent-model cars, in contrast to seventies and even early eighties models, relatively little can be done without enormously expensive diagnostic equipment and very specialized tools to perform adjustments. For example, one common tune-up job often done at home would involve setting the gap between the breaker points in the distributor, and that would mean the use of a simple instrument called a feeler gauge, which consists of a number of different-thickness blades inserted between the open points to determine the gap. For some time, however, meeting manufacturer specifications exactly has required not only a feeler gauge but also an instrument called a dwell meter, which can measure electronically the number of degrees the distributor cam rotates while the breaker points are closed. No longer prohibitively expensive, dwell meters are widely available and easy to use. They perform the same function, after all, as a feeler gauge. But still newer electronic ignition systems, in contrast, do away with distributor breaker points altogether. Such systems are more efficient, require less maintenance – and are virtually impossible to do anything about at home when, inevitably, they do break down. And that is the key point. It's not that a home mechanic couldn't learn a different and complicated technology; that's happened often enough. It's that there's little to do at all without far more comprehensive and *expensive* equipment than a dwell meter.

In relation to such changes, several things have happened in the literature of automotive work. Much of the space in car magazines that in the past would have been taken up with outlining procedures to get the most out of timing and distributor fine-tuning, as well as carburetor adjustment and refitting exhaust systems, is now given over to "detailing," an almost obsessive involvement in fit and finish rather than performance. Probably the fastest growing discourse about cars, however, involves both books and articles in a wide range of magazines targeted for what their titles "boldly" recognize: auto work for "dummies," for "the compleat idiot," for someone who wants a "greaseless adventure" – and, of course, for women. Along with maintenance in these terms, and consistent with other forms of consumer self-help literature, there is a continual emphasis on self-protection – how not to get ripped off by garage mechanics, used-car dealers, when purchasing a new car, and so on. The shift, in other words, is of both gender and class. The men to whom this marketing is addressed are targeted as middle- and upper-middle-class men used to purchasing someone else's labor to do the work. Detailed instructions for oil changes, for example, seem necessary only for men who've barely glanced at a car's engine before.

For a number of reasons, I think it worth considering this new form of car-maintenance discourse in terms of a more generally pervasive discourse of nostalgia. Most obviously, the appeal – like that of *American Graffiti* and other more recent examples – seems inextricably linked to the re-creation of a moment in the technological past. As a result, the appeal is not just "you can do it," but "you can do it, *too*," where the force of that "too" has nothing to do with people now working as auto mechanics on late-model cars, but with individuals "just like yourself" who some time "in the past" used to spend a great deal of time tinkering with the family car at home. Second, it's a discourse far more overt than other forms of nostalgia about its ostensibly cross-gender implications. Women are invited to abandon their feminized prohibitions against "getting dirty," to learn to love it, and to amaze any prehistoric males in sight with their knowledge. Men are invited correspondingly to be sensitive, caring, and careful workers with their hands, not Camel-smoking punks gearing up for the drag strip. Third, the frontier ideologies of do-it-yourself are at once preserved and updated with a kind of urban guerrilla mythology directed against evil forces lurking everywhere in the jungle (e.g., *Mugged by Mr. Badwrench*). This alignment is then correlated with a notion of similar technological continuity: cars still work in basically the same ways as in the past, only with some new refinements you need to master. Finally, and most crucially, there is – albeit often muted in the midst of all this upbeat advice – a thematic of loss no less pervasive than in any nostalgia production. All the wealth of detailed information can hardly disguise the fact that with newer cars there is very little that can be done at home; there's no obvious labor referent for the information. Donna Sclar, for example, in *Auto Repair for Dummies*, talks at great length about the pleasures of working on carburetors and the gratifying results that follow from the smallest adjustment, and this in a book aimed at owners of newer cars that almost uniformly do not have carburetors, but rather fuel-injection systems requiring a diagnostic computer and expensively specialized tools to perform adjustments. Much of the information then has to do not with your work, but with what to tell your mechanic to look for as a problem: the identification of strange noises, and so on.

Alongside this upscale marketing of car maintenance, however, there exists another kind of discourse, directed at what must be recognized, I think, as the repair of *older* cars; not in that long-familiar sense of restoring "classic" European Jaguars or Mercedeses or Austin Healeys, and so on, but simply fixing up ten- to twenty-five-year-old Fords, Chevys, Plymouths, and cheap-end available VWs, Datsuns, and Toyotas, just to keep them running. Shop manuals, *Chilton* reissues, and specialized manufacturer's instructions (such as those put out by Holley carburetors, for example) are the primary carriers of this discourse. You'll find here no instructions about how to locate the oil filter by color and shape, and the like. A *Chilton* manual's typical procedures for rebuilding an entire engine often take up little more space than instructions for oil changes in upscale discourse. Safety warnings, in contrast, will loom large (they are often the only pages in color) and, unlike the work procedures, may seem insultingly obvious to buyers familiar with upscale discourse.

Such different discourses "mean" in different ways. It's possible without much exaggeration to refine a sense of the nostalgia of an upscale discourse of maintenance into a recognition of pastiche in something like Jameson's sense. Stylistically, the form is a collection of what often seem idiosyncratic accretions – from a whole range of current self-help, fitness and diet, and still vaguely "countercultural" texts such as the descendants of Pirsig's *Zen and the Art of Motorcycle Maintenance* – linked with a curiously empty but nevertheless evocative appeal to artisanal labor and communities of work. All the above then function to obliterate anything like a "real" past or a real history of labor skills, leaving only an empty "look" of the past. Alternatively, that style might be read through Baudrillard's simulation as selling the notion of home labor, home activity itself, as part of what Baudrillard calls a "hyperlogic" of consumption, having reached an extreme point of replacing any signified of production with (literally) the consumption of consumption, as if *that* were productive labor (as indeed it would be in the "obscene" world of "mass" consumption Baudrillard describes). Either way, upscale discourse becomes one familiar version of the postmodern, a perilously unmoored chain of floating signifiers whose combinatory structures yield momentary flashes of what looks like significance, but whose meaning finally strings through an endlessly self-referential circuit of consumption.

While perhaps then epistemologically "empty," such upscale discourse is nevertheless educational, most immediately about how to read what I've been calling repair discourse. This latter will inevitably seem in contrast a more stable, "representational" language, dependent on an assumed security of reference. The detail of instructions in upscale discourse tells you that should you happen to run across instead such things as a *Chilton* manual's abrupt command to "remove the intake manifold," then you're in the presence of the survival of an *older* set of assumptions about discursive signification itself. The instruction, in other words, has to do not only with how to go about changing an oil filter but also with a model of cultural change that would explain why it is that the discourse of *Chilton* manuals and the like now appears remote, opaque, and uninformative. It's a survival from a now obsolete technological past, which will make no particular sense to you facing a new car's engine in the present. The message is a crucial one, for like consumer self-help literature generally, an upscale discourse of car maintenance is not intended to intimidate you with what you don't know or can't do. Thus there's nothing particularly abstract or "academic" about how such a lesson in reading should be part of upscale discourse. It is powerfully functional, alleviating potential anxieties about the performance of maintenance work by turning what could otherwise be felt as a debilitating recognition of lack of resources into an enabling understanding of changing technologies. That is, the discursive "emptiness" of reference supplies an exercise in grasping the conditions of change, and implies that the "performance" at issue here has relatively little to do with work on cars.

In upscale discourse, cultural change, as involving the differences in practices of discursive signification, is not only plotted in direct relation to technological change but also in relation to the social positionalities of those engaged in the work of car maintenance. Such discourse implies that *Chilton* manuals and the like had at one time a generally available field of discursive reference because they addressed technologies generally available to the home mechanic to work with. The nostalgia evoked in upscale discourse's fascination with automobile technologies that existed in the past – carburetors, for example – can be extended easily enough to home mechanics themselves, who in their "natural" surroundings in the past can appear as heroized examples of individual labor skills and resources. But car work isn't simply a thing of the past; while you may never have occasion to remove the intake manifold, somebody may have to. The terms of performance upscale discourse addresses have to do with how you deal with that "somebody." This, then, is where the educational message of discursive technological obsolescence turns into an interventional force in the configurations of social position.

The "somebody" you deal with in the present is not the nostalgically recreated picture of individual labor skills, but what happens to that heroic figure when it "survives" into a very different present. Just as the discourse of a *Chilton* manual will in the present seem uninformative and potentially intimidating, likewise the "survival" to whom that discourse might still make a great deal of sense will seem "awkward" at best, vicious at worst. What the home mechanic "survives" into is the service worker, who is likely to try to "mug" you with price ripoffs for repairs that are "shoddily" done in any case; the occupant of "low-income" neighborhoods, who offends your esthetic sensibilities with trashy yards, car parts, and blocked-up cars all over the place; the "insensitive," who ignores ecological imperatives with polluting exhausts and freeway detritus. The home mechanic survives as a figure who stands as a forbiddingly *masculine* sign of a no longer useful gender economy.

Yet for anyone who *must* engage in it now, car repair work is not so very different from a wide range of traditionally sanctioned women's work. Like women's work, it is repair labor, and is labor intensive, requiring low-tech and often improvisational skills with the relatively cheap materials and tools at hand. It's often performed during time snatched from other and more conspicuously determined concerns. It's almost invisible socially, except perhaps as an "eyesore" when it fails – producing then stalled cars along freeways, or cars blocked up in yards in "poor" neighborhoods and trailer parks. It's unproductive labor, both in a traditional Marxian sense and in the newer meaning of labor that contributes little to a consumer economy. Most important, it's often essential to family and household, when working conditions force people to cope with multiple low-paying jobs in widely scattered locations. My analogy between the necessity of car repair in these terms and the familiar conditions of "women's work" is hardly an exact parallel. Nevertheless, similarities in the qualities, skills, utility, and circumstances of the work do exist, and the recognition of similarities is obscured by the ideological determinations of gender and class positions powerfully reinforced by the ostensibly cross-gender implications of upscale discourse.

When in that discourse women are invited to do their own car work, to cross gender territories, the crossing is imaged as a taking up of new freedom, a refusal of the limitations of a feminized "lifestyle." It should be clear, however, that whatever mobilities this gender crossing might promise to women remain class-specific. While working-class women are certainly no strangers to "getting dirty" or to wearing old and shapeless clothing to do work of all kinds around the house, the shame of exposure in such a state is no mere relic of an older lifestyle, to be happily abandoned for a new, positive attitude toward work, dirt, and old clothing. For working-class women at least, the discourse of upscale maintenance doesn't function as "liberating," but as a vicious reminder of all the conditions of their lives that won't change no matter how much they improve their "attitude."

The male target audience for upscale discourse, in contrast, is invited to learn the patience and care with hand labor that women already purportedly possess, and at the same time to join a long tradition of masculine activity. But in terms of repair labor the class barriers of this gender mobility are almost absolute, for what certain men are invited to engage in as a freely chosen acquisition of new skills and forms of self-satisfaction is for others a grimly imposed logic of necessity. The very possibility of crossing gender territories, in either case, is plotted as strictly as the visibly marked territories to be crossed. You can cross gender territories as a class privilege, as something that comes with upward mobility, which marks your "progress" beyond the hopelessly outdated "traditions" still preserved in the surviving pockets of working-class life.

To the extent that upscale discourse sells an image of performing as a home mechanic, it's no mistake to see that image as an empty one in terms of the semiotic structure of the discourse, and to locate it, as Baudrillard would suggest, within the field of consumer practices rather than the field of work. What I've been arguing is that its conditions of meaning still function as part of an educational process. This car-maintenance discourse is first of all a lesson in how to read, where the immediate reference is not car work but another discourse, that of repair, whose process of signification belongs to "the past." Thus upscale discourse becomes a theoretical model of cultural change, a way of making sense of such changes in signification across the appearance of new, sophisticated automotive technologies. This model is very familiar at that, as, like most theories of the postmodern, it offers signifying practices as the best clue to the dynamics of change and the best available means to "read" the complex of technological innovations that alter the categories and norms of everyday behavior.

As consumer self-help literature, the model of change is then made to address potential anxieties about engaging in the work of car repair, insofar as it restructures perceptions of social position through its narrative of survivals. Those who engage in the actual work of repair at home are positioned not as groups of the population condemned to that work by current conditions, but as survivals from the past. That is, someone employed at Minit-Lube, changing the oil on Accords and Beamers, keeping up perhaps two late-seventies cars for use of self and family members at similar service-sector jobs, and thumbing through whatever literature may be available to guide that repair work, is not seen in terms of a current social organization requiring more and more people to live and work in such conditions. Rather, that person is positioned as a survival, a once-common figure of home labor now lost in a world where low-tech repair work is only an odd, marginalized pocket in the midst of coefficients of drag and multipoint fuel-injection systems. The "proper" heir to the confident, masculine, self-reliant home mechanic of the past is not really such survivals, but precisely the performing agency of the reader of upscale discourse in the present, empowered with the mobility to move across fixed categories of gender division and with the class lifestyle of the upwardly mobile. Upscale discourse sells an image of performing as a home mechanic, but while the performance has almost nothing to do with working on cars, it's not *just* an empty image. It's part of an educational process of instruction and of social stratification. As a model of cultural change, the educational narrative may have been linked to very different political values than in other forms of postmodern theorizing, where typically it is the "survivals" instead who are focused upon as victims of a relentless march of capitalist "colonizing" now cannibalistically feeding on even its own immediate past in the rush of change. Yet despite the differences in politics, the narrative structures remain remarkably congruent. In whatever political version, there's no room to recognize a sense in which "such people" are not really survivals at all.

Chapter 30

Michel Serres (with Bruno Latour)

THE PAST IS NO LONGER OUT-OF-DATE
[1995]

Source: Michel Serres (with Bruno Latour) (1995) 'The Past is No Longer Out-of-date', in *Conversations on Science, Culture, and Time*, translated by Roxanne Lapidus, Ann Arbor: University of Michigan Press, pp. 48–62.

Michel Serres has pursued the path of the polymath with the sort of unswerving dedication usually only found in arch specialists. More unnervingly his knowledge crosses the firmest of all disciplinary boundaries: that between the sciences (physical and abstract) and the humanities and social sciences. Educated in advanced maths, physics, the classics and philosophy, Serres writes about science, about ecology, about education, about the senses, in a manner that really does defy categorisation. His erudition is evident on every page, as too is his total impatience with received ideas about science: 'What a sign of the times, when, to cruelly criticize a book, one says that it is only poetry' (Serres 1995: 44)!

One of Michel Serres' most insightful ideas is also uncannily simple: it is the idea that the past hasn't finished with us. The past doesn't pass; it isn't something that can be kicked away like a ladder, when you've climbed to the next level. Instead the past accrues as sedimentation and as revivals. The consequences of this position for thinking about truth and for thinking about history are enormous. For instance, it makes the question of up-to-date-ness decidedly more awkward. This is an example that Serres alludes to in the text that follows:

> Consider a late-model car. It is a disparate aggregate of scientific and technical solutions dating from different periods. One can date it component by component: this part was invented at the turn of the century, another, ten years ago, and Carnot's cycle is almost two hundred years old. Not to mention that the wheel dates back to neolithic times. The ensemble is only contemporary by assemblage, by its design, its finish, sometimes only by the slickness of the advertising surrounding it.
>
> (Serres 1995: 45)

If the present moment contains such a variety of durations within a single assembly, then clearly a notion of time that is laid down like a track where the next thing supersedes the previous one simply won't do. For Serres, time percolates; it brews up odd connections across times and places. Sometimes a recent development throws the past into relief in a way that will make the work of the ancients seem like the most cutting-edge thought possible.

Throughout Serres' writing a host of critical insights are produced. Yet it is also work that is very much antagonistic to the values of contemporary Anglophone scholarship: there would be few people in academia who would want to promote the value of 'intuition'; nor many that would agree that 'reason is statistically distributed everywhere; no one can claim exclusive rights to it' (Serres 1995: 99). Serres' work is an extraordinary testimony to the possibilities opened up when science and literature come together. Yet he also warns about the possibility that, when such coming together is really achieved, it might simply fail to interest either party. Such a fate would be our profound loss, and would tell us more about the vested interests in the disciplines than about the difficulty of cross-disciplinary work.

Further reading: Assad 1999; Brown 2002; Connor 2005; Serres 1980/2007, 1988, 1997.

BL   You're going too fast. This problem of time is the greatest source of incomprehension, in my opinion. What makes other people's "past" empty, frozen, nontemporal, is the supposition that the past is out-of-date.

MS An excellent way of putting it. In former times this was called a rupture – there is a chasm between Lucretius' atoms and those of Perrin, between mythic antiquity and contemporary science, which makes the past bygone and the present authentic. This thesis has always seemed to me quasi-religious: it supposes that between long-lost times and the new era there is some advent, some birth of a new time.

BL   Are you saying that the rationalist idea of epistemological ruptures is itself an archaic idea?

MS Let me say a word on the idea of progress. We conceive of time as an irreversible line, whether interrupted or continuous, of acquisitions and inventions. We go from generalizations to discoveries, leaving behind us a trail of errors finally corrected – like a cloud of ink from a squid. "Whew! We've finally arrived at the truth." It can never be demonstrated whether this idea of time is true or false.

But, irresistibly, I cannot help thinking that this idea is the equivalent of those ancient diagrams we laugh at today, which place the Earth at the center of everything, or our galaxy at the middle of the universe, to satisfy our narcissim. Just as in space we situate ourselves at the center, at the navel of the things in the universe, so for time, through progress, we never cease to be at the summit, on the cutting edge, at the state-of-the-art of development. It follows that we are always right, for the simple, banal, and naive reason that we are living in the present moment. The curve traced by the idea of progress thus seems to me to sketch or project into time the vanity and fatuousness expressed spatially by that central position. Instead of inhabiting the heart or the middle of the world, we are sojourning at the summit, the height, the best of truth.

This diagram allows us permanently (yes, *permanently*, since the present is always the last word on time and truth; "permanently" – that's a good paradox for a theory of historical evolution) to be not only right but to be righter than was ever possible before. Now I believe that one should always be wary of any person or theory that is always right: he's not plausible; it's not probable.

BL   For me, for an ordinary reader, what makes your demonstration unbelievable – improbable – is that you can't treat Lucretius as a contemporary, because his science is obviously obsolete. And it's the scientists, the epistemologists, who constantly argue that there is no scientific thought before themselves.

MS Scientists often think like Descartes: "No one has thought before me." This Descartes-effect produces good publicity, very effective and convincing: "No one ever thought such-and-such until I said it." This boast contradicts the *Philosophia perennis* and is totally absurd.

BL   It's this kind of philosophy that makes the past totally distant. It's obvious to us moderns that, as we advance in time, each successive stage outstrips the preceding one.

MS But that's not *time*.

BL That's what you need to explain to me — why this passage of time is not time.

MS That's not time, only a simple line. It's not even a line, but a trajectory of the race for first place — in school, in the Olympic Games, for the Nobel Prize. This isn't time, but a simple competition — once again, war. Why replace temporality, duration, with a quarrel? *The first to arrive, the winner of the battle, obtains as his prize the right to reinvent history to his own advantage.* Once again dialectics — which is nothing more than the logic of appearances.

More profoundly, time alone can make co-possible two contradictory things. As an example, I am young and old. Only my life, its time or its duration, can make these two propositions coherent between themselves. Hegel's error was in reversing this logical evidence and in claiming that contradiction produces time, whereas only the opposite is true: time makes contradiction possible. This error is the source of all the absurdities recounted since then on war, "the mother of history."

No, war is mother only to death, first of all, and then perpetually to war. It gives birth only to nothingness and, identically, to itself. So, destruction repeats itself, which is the reason for the eternal return of debate. History fairly regularly vindicates those who don't believe in such Hegelian schemas.

The hypothesis that before a given generation there was no science denies all temporality, all history. On the other hand, tradition often gives us ideas still filled with vitality.

BL Excuse me, but where do you get this idea from?

MS Can I return to my training? I earned a degree in classical studies, in Latin and Greek, and I was also trained in science, earning two degrees in mathematics. Through my entire life I have never abandoned this double route. I still read Plutarch and the great physicists, at the same time, as a refusal of the separation between science and literature, of this divorce that informs the temporality of so-called contemporary thought.

BL This same separation? The separation between literature and science?

MS Yes. The Age of Enlightenment was very instrumental in categorizing as irrational any reason not formed by science. Now, I maintain that there is as much reason in the works of Montaigne or Verlaine as there is in physics or biochemistry and, reciprocally, that often there is as much unreason scattered through the sciences as there is in certain dreams. Reason is statistically distributed everywhere; no one can claim exclusive rights to it.

This division thus is echoed in the image, in the imaginary picture that one makes of time. Instead of condemning or excluding, one consigns a certain thing to antiquity, to archaism. One no longer says "false" but, rather, "out-of-date," or "obsolete." In earlier times people dreamed; now we think. Once people sang poetry; today we experiment efficiently. History is thus the projection of this very real exclusion into an imaginary, even imperialistic time. The temporal rupture is the equivalent of a dogmatic explusion.

On the one hand, there's the gradual disappearance of great authors — those whose ancient culture refers to the archaic age of poetry, which no one needs. On the other hand, scientists, as the only "contemporaries," speak the truth about the world or the brain, math or physics. Since you know the United States well, you know with what delight it consigns Europe to Pompeii or the era of the great cathedrals. It's an excellent way of saying, "Today, we are advancing while you are in charge of the museums." History lends a certain impression of reality to self-promotion.

Scientists at the beginning of this century didn't yet feel this divorce. Jean Perrin, in *Les Atomes*, cites Lucretius from the beginning and even performs anew experiments and observations inspired by the Latin text. In his study you'll find an annotated copy of Lucretius. Another example: at the beginning of his *Celestial Mechanics* Laplace passes in review all the mechanists who preceded him, starting with the ancient Greeks.

BL Now you're introducing another confusion. In the case of Laplace or Perrin it's a recapitulation, demonstrating the growth of reason. All scientists can sketch out a brief history in which they place themselves at the pinnacle of reason, after centuries of groping.

MS That's right — you're correct — and I am saying the same thing.

BL If I understand correctly, your own way of showing the past has nothing to do with the growth of reason?

MS No.

BL What is the articulation between the distinction, on the one hand, of the sciences from the humanities and, on the other, of the out-of-date or long-lost past from the uniquely rational present?

MS That took place in the eighteenth century, which sought to remove all rationality from anything that was not science: it's science's bid to take over the totality of reason. Those areas suddenly bereft of reason include religion, of course, literature and the humanities, as well as history and the past: they are all consigned to the irrational. And the nineteenth century of Sturm und Drang will confirm this momentous decision by confining all literary movements to myths and dreams. In this regard, the history of science, epistemology, scientists, and even the man in the street went along with this idea, which is the source of the usual historical diagram: reason later, unreason before. What can we call this, except prejudice?

The converse prejudice is no more enlightening, though — claiming that we have totally forgotten an initial intuition received and developed only by certain pre-Socratics, among the ancient Greeks. This intuition emanates, of course, from the greatest denigrators of science and technology. So, we have a nice symmetry, like the two lions we were speaking of earlier!

If the redoubtable problem of historical time could be resolved so simply, we would know about it.

BL But you, you claim that, as the saying goes, those who ignore history are condemned to repeat — on the contrary — out-of-date arguments and philosophical movements.

MS Yes.

BL So, you want to escape from both of these?

MS To ignore the past is often to run the risk of repeating it. How many times have we read a book intoxicated with recent invention, whose author boasts of having finally escaped from certain ideas and ways of feeling and perceiving, which he innocently repeats without realizing it! We could name ten examples.

Neither judgment nor absence of judgment

BL Having said this, there is a problem. Your argument completely contradicts the most fundamental thesis of Bachelard's and Canguilhem's philosophy of the official sciences, embraced in France, at least, by all scientists. The distinction Canguilhem makes between history and epistemology is clear. History collects facts, even if they are false. Epistemology has the task of judging, of outlawing the false and only keeping the true. Your definition of the passage of time no longer has any rapport with the dogma of French epistemology.

MS Let's remain fair: Canguilhem wrote an excellent article on Auguste Comte, in which he praises him for not deprecating things from an earlier era — from the age of superstition.

Since I had abandoned epistemology, I also dropped any judgmental perspective. Criticism is never fertile, and evaluation of the sciences is not even possible, since they fluctuate so rapidly. Although it is valued in academia, criticism is easy, temporary, fugitive, quickly out of style. If yesterday's truth is tomorrow's error, then in the sciences it likewise happens that the error condemned today will sooner or later find itself in the treasure house of great discoveries.

Furthermore, it is stimulating to restore to material judged irrational the respect owed to straight reason, even if it means redefining the latter. For example, finding an authentic science in Lucretius, in authors, poets, novelists, or theologians – thousands of whom used to call themselves rational.

BL So, we should abandon both the belief that they are out-of-date and the possibility of judging them on the basis of the current state of science?

MS The so-called current state of science. Who can affirm that this is really contemporary, except the inventors, who are present and active in the forefront of discovery? This question and the immense difficulty in answering it make what Sartre called "commitment" very problematical. Who is truly of our era, can you tell me?

BL But to say this is to abandon the idea that, by being ignorant of certain arguments, we will repeat even older ones.

MS True.

BL But to do that is completely to realign eras.

MS In the end we'd almost have to speak of uneducating. As soon as you bring together on an island all those who are right and who assume the right to judge everything and you abandon everything else, by ignoring this *everything else*, you run the risk of repeating it. To forget exposes one to repeating.

BL So, your own principle of movement . . .

MS . . . is to struggle against forgetting. As a result, your reproach to me about ignoring history is reversed; in other words, who really speaks about history?

BL Yes, but now we run into another difficulty: your history is not Bachelardian, in the sense that it is not the sanctioned history.

MS No, since I suspend all judgment. Have you noticed that the term *sanctioned* comes both from the law and from religion, to reaffirm *sanctified*?

BL But, furthermore, your history is not historicist, in the sense that you don't want to go and recover history as it was for the people of the period. That doesn't interest you either. You want neither the sanctioned history of the epistemologists nor the dated, historicist, documentary history of the historians. Is it because you want this bygone history to live again now?

MS Yes. To take up again the example of Lucretius, contemporary physics at least allows us to reread him, but in an oblique manner, and finally to discover some actuality that is still active. What do we mean by oblique here? That if you translate atom by atom, you will not get very far. You must look somewhat alongside, or more globally, at the system of turbulence. In the last century William Thomson still was assimilating atoms to vortices in fluids, so the tradition I am reviving dates from two thousand years ago and has been forgotten for scarcely a hundred years. It doesn't necessarily come to us from remote antiquity. Sometimes things that seem to have been forgotten for a long time are actually conserved quite close to us. Which is the reason for the time lapse I'm talking about.

Even the best disciples of Descartes have forgotten their master on this point: he is much more the forerunner of contemporary physics than Newton, who only yesterday was held by our predecessors to be more modern. Yes, vortices are pulling ahead of universal attraction, far from being reduced to a fiction of physics, as Leibniz said. The heavens of the galaxies, of meteorologists, even the space of particles are more and more Cartesian – sown by whirlwinds and turbulences.

BL Yes, but to say that this is a time that is still active – this is not a historian's position either. In none of your books do you attempt to "reconstitute the cultural environment of Lucretius," to "seek out the texts he might have read," and thereby utilize history to transport us from our era to that of the Romans.

MS No.

BL What always interests you is the reverse movement. To take Lucretius, to leap over the philosophers who discount him by saying he's obsolete, and to bring him to the hypotheses that are current in physics.

MS That's right. What's more, this is a way – a strategy, a ruse – to answer another question: that of loss. Everything has its price. As science advances, we rarely evaluate the substantial cultural losses that correspond to the gains. Literature becomes evanescent through a loss of substance, while, on the other hand, there is a considerable gain in scientific intelligence – in both content and institutions.

This is behind my temptation to write a defense and an illustration of the humanities – in the face of, in opposition to, and for the benefit of scientists themselves. To say to them: "Lucretius thinks more profoundly and even more rationally than many of today's scientists. A novelist like Zola invented thermodynamic operators well before the science of thermodynamics; he introduced them without even realizing it. Read this or that poem by Verlaine." I want to show a certain *reason* in its emerging state and illustrate it for the benefit of academic reason.

BL Yes, but with a double difficulty. You reuse authors and texts considered by the epistemologists to be proscribed and out-of-date.

MS "When you hear that Beethoven is out-of-date, listen to the music of those who make such claims," said Schumann with a smile. "Usually, they are nothing but composers of flat romances."

BL But at the same time, you aren't preserving texts on the same grounds as the humanities usually do – those of historicism.

MS Sometimes, not often.

BL You never say, "Let us respect them at least for their difference, for their eccentricity, as an interesting witness to bygone days." For you it's never a question of exoticism . . .

MS You're right.

BL . . . their past and their difference do not cancel out their effect of reality, of rationality. You don't respect their difference in the way that a historian or an ethnologist would. You place them on the same footing as the most modern theses.

MS Yes.

BL At the obvious risk . . .

MS . . . of not being heard by either the Latin scholar who has no use for hydrodynamics or the scientist who laughs at the *clinamen*. This defines the solitude of those who seek: it's not too serious; what matters is what's correct. Who is not isolated, when he is seeking?

BL This is the problem we must address.

MS In fact, professional risk does exist. You have to accept paying its price – knowing that, on the one hand, humanists no longer recognize their customary Lucretius and that, on the other, scientists are totally uninterested in this story.

Except that this is starting to change. The theoreticians of turbulence are starting to say, "Yes, in fact, there is already in Lucretius this kind of thing." Except that each important discovery suddenly reveals an intelligent past behind a recent obstruction. With each new advance there is new amnesia! Each invention reveals both the real and the historical.

BL We'll come back to this point later. So, time experienced as present allows you to circumvent both those who claim that time is out-of-date and who are in fact immobile and those who say, "The only way to respect temporality is through the work of historians." This would define your enterprise.

MS It's almost a resurrection of dead texts. But since the university, through a maximal bifurcation, produces scientists, on the one hand, and purely literary scholars, on the other, messages destined for both parties are not well received.

BL Before we talk about that I want to make sure that I've rightly understood what you were saying — that the particular approach to time that interests you is the other side of the coin from the separation of the humanities and the sciences. This separation obliges the humanities to be historicist, to be content with the remains of the past, and to maximize their difference. The sciences are Bachelardian in their spontaneous philosophy — that is, they completely cancel out their past, in a sense from hour to hour, from year to year.

MS Yes.

BL So it's the same two-pronged problem: to settle the problem of time and to settle the problem of the sciences.

A different theory of time

MS It's a matter of interdisciplinarity.

BL But doesn't this suppose another temporality, a nonmodern way of considering the passage of time?

MS This is truly the fundamental question. Whether it's the scientific hypothesis, on the one hand, which we have called the hypothesis of excellence, or, on the other hand, that of historicism, the two suppose that time develops in a linear fashion — that is, that there really is an enormous distance, more than a score of centuries, between Lucretius and today's physics. Whether this time is cumulative, continuous, or interrupted, it always remains linear.

BL Because of succession. Or successions of revolutions, as described by the epistemologists or even Foucault.

MS There you are. But time is in reality somewhat more complicated than that. You no doubt are familiar with chaos theory, which says that disorder occurring in nature can be explained, or reordered, by means of fractal attractors.

BL Yes. According to this, chance is nonetheless determined, and disorder is produced by an underlying order.

MS Exactly. But in this, order as such is harder to perceive, and customary determinism has a slightly different appearance. Time does not always flow according to a line (my first intuition of this is in my book on Leibniz [284–6]) nor according to a plan but, rather, according to an extraordinarily complex mixture, as though it reflected stopping points, ruptures, deep wells, chimneys of thunderous acceleration, rendings, gaps — all sown at random, at least in a visible disorder. Thus, the development of history truly resembles what chaos theory describes. Once you understand this, it's not hard to accept the fact that time doesn't always develop according to a line and thus things that are very close can exist in culture, but the line makes them appear very distant from one another. Or, on the other hand, that there are things that seem very close that, in fact, are very distant from one another. Lucretius and modern theory of fluids are considered as two places separated by an immense distance, whereas I see them as in the same neighborhood.

In order to explain these two perceptions we must, in fact, clarify the theory of time. The classical theory is that of the line, continuous or interrupted, while mine would be more chaotic. Time flows in an extraordinarily complex, unexpected, complicated way . . .

BL So, it is not you who travel through time but, rather, the elements that become close in this chaotic time?

MS Certainly. Time is paradoxical; it folds or twists; it is as various as the dance of flames in a brazier — here interrupted, there vertical, mobile, and unexpected.

The French language in its wisdom uses the same word for weather and time, *le temps*. At a profound level they are the same thing. Meteorological weather, predictable and unpredictable, will no doubt some day be explainable by complicated notions of fluctuations, strange attractors. . . . Someday we will perhaps understand that historical time is even more complicated.

BL In any case, it doesn't "pass."

MS Yes, it passes, and also it doesn't pass. We must bring the word *pass* closer to *passoir* – "sieve." Time doesn't flow; it percolates. This means precisely that it passes and doesn't pass. I'm very fond of the theory of percolation, which tells us things that are evident, concrete, decisive, and new about space and time.

In Latin the verb *colare*, the origin of the French verb *couler*, "to flow," means precisely "to filter." In a filter one flux passes through, while another does not.

BL But it doesn't pass in the form of a fluid. It's not a fluid.

MS Who knows?

BL It is perhaps turbulent, but not linear . . .

MS "*Sous le pont Mirabeau coule la Seine . . .*" [Beneath the Mirabeau Bridge flows the Seine . . .] – thus flows classical linear time. But Apollinaire, who had never ever navigated, at least on fresh water, hadn't studied the Seine enough. He hadn't noticed the counter-currents or the turbulences. Yes, time flows like the Seine, if one observes it well. All the water that passes beneath the Mirabeau Bridge will not necessarily flow out into the English Channel; many little trickles turn back toward Charenton or upstream.

BL They don't flow like parallel trickles.

MS It's not always laminar. The usual theory supposes time to be always and everywhere laminar. With geometrically rigid and measurable distances – at least constant. Someday it will be said that that is eternity! It is neither true nor possible. No, time flows in a turbulent and chaotic manner; it percolates. All of our difficulties with the theory of history come from the fact that we think of time in this inadequate and naive way.

BL All the theologians agree with you.

MS Really? Maybe that's why I so greatly admire Péguy's work.

BL His Clio? *[Clio: Dialogue between History and the Pagan Soul.]*

MS Yes, *Clio*. In it one sees, from the evidence, a time that is completely turbulent.

From this you understand how Lucretius can be as close to us as our neighbor and, conversely, how contemporary things can become very distant.

BL You have a topologically bizarre space as your reference for understanding time.

MS There is in Lucretius a global theory of turbulence, which can make that time really understandable. His physics seems to me truly very advanced. Along with the contemporary sciences, it holds out the hope of a chaotic theory of time.

BL Everyone has heard you say this, and no one believes you.

MS Nonetheless, fairly simple mathematics can also easily bring one to such an idea. A certain theory of numbers reorders their sequence in such a way that near neighbors become very distant, while, inversely, distant numbers come closer. It's fun, instructive, and has a strong influence on intuition. Once you've entered into this kind of thinking you realize how much all of what we've said about time up till now abusively simplifies things.

More intuitively, this time can be schematized by a kind of crumpling, a multiple, foldable diversity. If you think about it for two minutes, this intuition is clearer than one that imposes a constant distance between moving objects, and it explains more. Everyone is amazed that after 1935 the Nazis, in the most scientifically and culturally advanced country, adopted the most archaic behavior. But we are always simultaneously making gestures that are archaic, modern, and futuristic. Earlier I took the example of a car, which can be dated from several eras; every historical era is likewise multitemporal, simultaneously drawing from the obsolete, the contemporary, and the futuristic. An object, a circumstance, is thus polychronic, multitemporal, and reveals a time that is gathered together, with multiple pleats.

BL You are explaining here a sentence I was going to ask you to explain from your book Le Tiers-Instruit, *which speaks of precisely these non-metrical diversities: "I have always used a process of abstraction like this, which could be called topological, and whose principle consists of describing non-metrical diversities — in this case, the network."*

MS Yes. If you take a handkerchief and spread it out in order to iron it, you can see in it certain fixed distances and proximities. If you sketch a circle in one area, you can mark out nearby points and measure far-off distances. Then take the same handkerchief and crumple it, by putting it in your pocket. Two distant points suddenly are close, even superimposed. If, further, you tear it in certain places, two points that were close can become very distant. This science of nearness and rifts is called topology, while the science of stable and well-defined distances is called metrical geometry.

Classical time is related to geometry, having nothing to do with space, as Bergson pointed out all too briefly, but with metrics. On the contrary, take your inspiration from topology, and perhaps you will discover the rigidity of those proximities and distances you consider arbitrary. And their sim*pli*city, in the literal sense of the word *pli* [fold]: it's simply the difference between topology (the handkerchief is folded, crumpled, shredded) and geometry (the same fabric is ironed out flat).

As we experience time — as much in our inner senses as externally in nature, as much as *le temps* of history as *le temps* of weather — it resembles this crumpled version much more than the flat, overly simplified one.

Admittedly, we need the latter for measurements, but why extrapolate from it a general theory of time? *People usually confuse time and the measurement of time,* which is a metrical reading on a straight line.

BL So mathematics, which is your model, is not metrical?

MS It can easily become so. Sketch on the handkerchief some perpendicular networks, like Cartesian coordinates, and you will define the distances. But, if you fold it, the distance from Madrid to Paris could suddenly be wiped out, while, on the other hand, the distance from Vincennes to Colombes could become infinite.

No, time does not flow as people think it does. The time we spontaneously use imitates the succession of natural integers.

BL So, it's never a case of your inventing the proximities, in your opinion? Whereas for a modernist, time passes, falls behind him, is obsolete.

MS Archaisms can always be found among us, while Lucretius, in some instances, is right on top of things, as they say.

Let me tell you a true story. Have you ever heard how some brothers, in their seventies, were grouped around their father for a funeral vigil, weeping for a dead man aged thirty or less? He had been a mountain guide and, following an accident, had disappeared into a crevasse in the high mountains. He reappeared more than a half-century later, deposited in the valley by the glacier, perfectly conserved, youthful, from the depths of the cold. His children, having grown old, prepare to bury a body that is still young. That's the source of this alpine scene, which is precisely an anachronism, and is admittedly rare here, but often observed — between a writer and his critics. Art, beauty, and profound thought preserve youth even better than a glacier!

Admire how, on the problem of time, an unpretentious true story agrees with recent science, to produce good philosophy.

BL   It's precisely this biographical and philosophical bizarreness that sets you apart from modernists and makes you so difficult to read.

MS   We are archaic in three-fourths of our actions. Few people and even fewer thoughts are completely congruent with the date of their times. Recall what we were saying earlier about the present.

BL   Yes, but it's not enough to say it that way. A modernist could say it also. But for him it would mean that the archaic is repressed, dangerous, that it could leap out at us. Whereas for you it is a positive affirmation.

MS   Why the specter of this pointless repression? Antiquity is there, most often, without needing any air pump (a truly obsolete instrument) to drive it back.

BL   For you archaicism is not a holdover of which we still need to rid ourselves more completely. That would be the position of Bachelard, for example.

MS   Maybe. Everything depends on the way you understand the passage of time.

Chapter 31

N. Katherine Hayles

THE MATERIALITY OF INFORMATICS: AUDIOTAPE AND ITS CULTURAL NICHE [1999]

Source: N. Katherine Hayles (1999) 'The Materiality of Informatics: Audiotape and its Cultural Niche', in *How We Became Posthuman: Virtual Bodies in Cybernetics, Literature, and Informatics*, Chicago: University of Chicago Press, pp. 207–21.

N. Katherine Hayles is Professor of English and Media Arts at University of California, Los Angeles. After an initial career as a research chemist Hayles switched disciplines to study literature and has since become a leading theorist of the 'posthuman' condition. Posthumanism designates not a decisive physical actuality, but a set of technological shifts, material phenomena, and related concerns about these shifts and phenomena, that suggest that older ideas of the 'human' as an ideological 'subject' are in jeopardy. For some theorists the posthuman points in the direction of virtuality, as human life migrates to digital existences, on webs and networks. For Hayles the posthuman is simultaneously ultrahuman – posthumans are creaturely beings in contact with a world of machines (and the human as animal is one of the best ways of initially dismantling an ideology of the human) – and a virtual avatar existing across various media.

In this extract from her book *How We Became Posthuman* Hayles is looking at how information storage and retrieval alter a conception of human life. Taking the example of the tape-recorder – now a technology on the edge of obsolescence – Hayles looks at the way the materiality of information recodes human forms. Her guide is the one-time 'beat' writer and general avant-garde literary experimenter William Burroughs. Importantly Hayles treats Burroughs as a theorist of the posthuman who simultaneously reflects on the posthuman while also performing 'it'. Burroughs then is a speculative theorist who uses fiction to map the terrain of the possible, the probable and the performative. Hayles doesn't interpret Burroughs so much as join him in conversation.

While some of the speculative theoretical work that emerged in the wake of the information revolution seems to be overly seduced by its gee-whiz-ness of computer culture and to lose touch with the materiality of information (the physical tools that are coding, storing and retrieving data, as well as the human bodies that are operating these tools, becoming bored staring at screens, developing repetitive strain injury by using computer mice and so on), Hayles' speculative work is always materially (and historically) grounded. Her definition of the term 'informatics', for example, usefully ranges across the micro- and macro-levels of posthuman life:

> By 'informatics', I mean the material, technological, economic, and social structures
> that make the information age possible. Informatics includes the following: the late
> capitalist mode of flexible accumulation; the hardware and software that have merged

telecommunications with computer technology; the patterns of living that emerge from and depend on access to large data banks and instantaneous transmission of messages; and the physical habits – of posture, eye focus, hand motions, and neural connections – that are reconfiguring the human body in conjunction with information technologies.

(Hayles 1999: 313)

Since the advent of 'ubiquitous computing' (the presence of computers, and computer-like operating systems, in a massive variety of devices, from cars to fridges) the condition of the post-human is becoming increasingly linked to the ideal consumer of design culture.

Further reading: Badmington 2000; Borgmann 2001; Hayles 2002; Turkle 1997.

IN HIS GROUNDBREAKING work *Reading Voices: Literature and the Phonotext*, Garrett Stewart asks not how we read, or why we read, but where we read.[1] He decides we read in the body, particularly in the vocal apparatus that produces subvocalization during silent reading. This subvocalization is essential, he argues, to the production of literary language. Language becomes literary for Stewart when it cannot be adequately replaced by other words, when that particular language is essential to achieving its effects. Literary language works by surrounding its utterances with a shimmer of virtual sounds, homophonic variants that suggest alternative readings to the words actually printed on the page. Subvocalization actualizes these possibilities in the body and makes them available for interpretation. Several interesting consequences flow from this argument. First, the bodily enactment of suppressed sound plays a central role in the reading process. Second, reading is akin to the interior monologue that we all engage in, except that it supplies us with another story, usually a more interesting one than that provided by the stream of subvocalized sound coming out of our own consciousness. Third, the production of subvocalized sound may be as important to subjectivity as it is to literary language.[2]

We are now in a position to think about what tape-recording means for certain literary texts. Audiotape opens the possibility that the voice can be taken out of the body and placed into a machine. If the production of subvocalized sound is essential to reading literary texts, what happens to the stories we tell ourselves if this sound is no longer situated in the body's subvocalizations but is in the machine? Often histories of technology and literature treat technology as a theme or subject to be represented within the world of the text. I want to take a different approach, focusing on the technical qualities of audiotape that changed the relation of voice and body, a change [William] Burroughs associates in *Ticket* [*That Exploded*] with the production of a new kind of subjectivity. In the mutating and metamorphosing bodies of *Ticket*, we can see a harbinger of the posthuman body. These mutations are intimately bound up with internal monologues that, in Burroughs's view, parasitically inhabit the body. But I am getting ahead of my story. First we need to trace the development of the audio technology that he uses to effect this startling view of discourse as a bodily infestation.

Born in the early 1900s and coming of age after World War II, audiotape may already be reaching old age, fading from the marketplace as it is replaced by compact disks, computer hypermedia, and the like. The period when audiotape played an important role in U.S. and European consumer culture may well be limited to the four decades of 1950–90. Writing his cybernetic trilogy – *The Ticket That Exploded, The Soft Machine*, and *Nova Express* – in the late 1950s and 1960s, William Burroughs was close enough to the beginnings of audiotape to regard it as a technology of revolutionary power. Long after writing dissociated presence from inscription, voice continued to imply a subject who was present in the moment and in the flesh. Audiotape was of course not the first technology to challenge this assumption, and the cultural work it did can best be understood in the context of related audio technologies, particularly telephone, radio, and phonograph.

Telephone and radio broke the link between presence and voice by making it possible to transport voice over distance.[3] Before audiotape and phonograph, however, telephone and radio happened in the present. Speaker and listener, although physically separated, had to share the same moment in time. Telephone and radio thus continued to participate in the phenomenology of presence through the simultaneity that they produced and that produced them. In this sense they were more like each other than either was like the phonograph. By contrast, the phonograph functioned primarily as a technology of inscription, reproducing sound through a rigid disk that allowed neither the interactive spontaneity of telephone nor the ephemerality of radio.

The niche that audiotape filled was configured through the interlocking qualities of the audio technologies that preceded it, in a process Friedrich Kittler has aptly called "medial ecology".[4] Like the phonograph, audiotape was a technology of inscription, but with the crucial difference that it permitted erasure and rewriting. As early as 1888, Oberlin Smith, at one time president of the American Society of Mechanical Engineers, proposed that sound could be recorded by magnetizing iron particles that adhered to a carrier.[5] He was too busy to implement his idea, however, and the ball passed to Valdemar Poulsen, a young Danish engineer who accidentally discovered that patterns traced on the side of a magnetized tuning fork became visible when the fork was dipped in iron powder. When the fork was demagnetized, the patterns were erased. He saw in the imprinting and erasure of these patterns the possibility of a recording device for sound, using iron wire as the carrier. Its immediate commercial use, he imagined, would lie in providing tangible records of telephone conversations. He called the device a "Telegraphone," which he understood to signify "writing the voice at a distance." At the 1900 Paris Exposition, he won the Grand Prix for his invention.[6] Despite extensive publicity, however, he was not able to raise the necessary capital in Europe for its development. By 1903 the patents had passed to the American Telegraphone Company (ATC), which raised a huge amount of money ($5,000,000) by selling stock. Five years later the owners of ATC had still not built a single machine. Their main business, in fact, turned out to be raising money for the machines rather than actually producing the machines. When they did finally turn out a few operational devices in 1911, using the famous model Phoebe Snow to advertise them as dictation machines, the sound quality was so bad that the Dupont Company, after installing them in a central dictation system, ended up suing. The questionable status of the machines was exacerbated during World War I, when the Telefunken Company of America was accused of using them to encode and transmit secret messages to Germany. From the beginning, audiotape was marked with the imprint of international capitalism and politics as surely as it was with the imprint of voices.

By 1932, steel tape had become the carrier of choice in high-end machines, and the British Broadcasting Corporation (BBC) became actively interested in the development of steel tape, using it to carry the Christmas address of King George V in that year. Film tape, created by coating paper or plastic tape with iron oxide and feeding it through a ring-shaped head, appeared on the scene by 1935.[7] The great advantage of film tape was that it could be easily spliced, but originally it had such poor sound quality that it could not compete with steel tape. The problem of establishing good correspondence between sound frequency and the pattern on film tape (that is, controlling hysteresis) was partly solved by the introduction of high-frequency bias in 1938.[8] By 1941 the sound quality of film tape had so improved that it was competitive with steel tape in studio work. On the consumer market, machines with wire were still common. It was not until after World War II that systematic research was carried out to find the optimum coating material for film tape, and only in 1948 was the first American patent issued for a magnetic recording machine using film tape and a ring head. The use of film tape then expanded rapidly, and within a decade it had rendered steel tape obsolete, with film tape being used in the consumer market as well as the professional studios.

By the late 1950s, then, magnetic tape had acquired the qualities that, within the existing cultural formation, gave it the force of paradox. It was a mode of voice inscription at once permanent and mutable, repeating past moments exactly yet also permitting present interventions that radically altered its form and meaning. These interventions could, moreover, be done at home by anyone who had the appropriate equipment. Whereas the phonograph produced objects that could be consumed only in their manufactured form, magnetic tape allowed the consumer to be a producer as well. The switches activating the powerful and paradoxical technoconceptual actors of repetition and mutation, presence and absence, were in the hands of the masses, at least the masses who could afford the equipment.

The paradoxical qualities that magnetic tape was perceived to have in the late 1950s were forcefully expressed by Roy Walker, involved in making tape-recordings for the BBC during this period. "Anyone who has made a BBC recording and been in on the editing session may emerge feeling that he can no longer call himself his own. Cuts and transpositions can be and are made. Halves of sentences spoken at different times can be amalgamated to let a speaker hear himself say the opposite of what he knows he said. Hearing oneself say something and continue with something else said half an hour earlier can be peculiarly disconcerting. You might have the feeling that if you went quickly out of the studio you might catch yourself coming in."[9] His language locates the disconcerting effect both in the time delay ("sentences spoken at different times can be amalgamated") and in the disjunction between voice and presence ("he can no longer call himself his own"). When these qualities of audiotape were enacted within literary productions, a complex interplay was set up between representational codes and the specificities of the technology. When voice was displaced onto tape, the body metonymically participated in the transformations that voice underwent in this medium. For certain texts after 1950, the body became a tape-recorder.

When Burroughs wrote *The Ticket That Exploded*, he took seriously the possibilities for the metonymic equation between tape-recorder and body.[10] He reasoned that if the body can become a tape-recorder, the voice can be understood not as a naturalized union of voice and presence but as a mechanical production with the frightening ability to appropriate the body's vocal apparatus and use it for ends alien to the self. "The word is now a virus" (*TTE*, p. 49), the narrator says in a phrase indebted to the Buddhist-inspired idea that one's sense of selfhood is maintained through an internal monologue, which is nothing other than the story the self tells to assure itself that it exists.[11] Woven into this monologue are the fictions that society wants its members to believe; the monologue enacts self-discipline as well as self-creation. Burroughs proposes to stop the interior monologue by making it external and mechanical, recording it on tape and subjecting the recording to various manipulations. "Communication must become total and conscious before we can stop it," the narrator asserts (*TTE*, p. 51). Yet splicing tape is far from innocuous. Once someone's vocalizations and body sounds are spliced into someone else's, the effects can feed back into the bodies, setting off a riot of mutations. The tape-recorder acts both as a metaphor for these mutations and as the instrumentality that brings them about. The taped body can separate at the vertical "divide line," grotesquely becoming half one person and half another, as if it were tape spliced lengthwise. In a disturbingly literal sense, the tape-recorder becomes a two-edged sword, cutting through bodies as well as through the programs that control and discipline them.

In *The Ticket That Exploded*, the body is a site for contestation and resistance on many levels, as metaphor, as physical reality, as linguistic construct, and last but hardly least, as tape-recorder. The tape-recorder is central to understanding Burroughs's vision of how the politics of co-optation work. Entwined into human flesh are "pre-recordings" that function as parasites ready to take over the organism. These "pre-recordings" may be thought of as social conditioning, for example an "American upper middle-class upbringing with maximum sexual frustration and humiliations imposed by Middle-Western matriarchs" (*TTE*, p. 139), which not coincidentally matches Burroughs's own experience. A strong sense of sexual nausea pervades the text, and sexuality is another manifestation of pre-recording. Parodically rewriting the fable in Plato's *Symposium* about the spherical beings who were cut in half to make humans, the narrator asserts: "All human sex is this unsanitary arrangement whereby two entities attempt to occupy the same three-dimensional coordinate points giving rise to the sordid latrine brawls. . . . It will be readily understandable that a program of systematic frustration was necessary in order to sell this crock of sewage as Immortality, and Garden of Delights, and *love*" (*TTE*, p. 52).

The idea of two entities trying to occupy the same space is further reinforced by the vertical "divide line" crossing the body, the physically marked line in bone, muscle, and skin where the neural canal of the month-old fetus closes to create the beginnings of the torso.[12] The early point at which the "divide line" is imprinted on human flesh suggests how deeply implicated into the organism are the pre-recordings that socialize it into community norms. In one scene the narrator sees his body "on the operating table split down the middle," while a "doctor with forceps was extracting crab parasites from his brain and spine – and squeezing green fish parasites from the separated flesh." "My God what a mess," the doctor exclaims. "The difficulty is with two halves – other parasites will invade sooner or later. . . . Sew him up nurse" (*TTE*, p. 85). As the doctor intimates, the body is always already fallen. Divided within itself rather than an organic unity, it is subject to occupation and expropriation by a variety of parasitic forms, both cultural and physical.

Chief among these parasitic forms is "the word." It is a truism in contemporary theory that discursive formations can have material effects in the physical world. Without having read Foucault and Derrida, Burroughs came to similar conclusions a decade earlier, imagining "the word" as the body's "Other Half." The narrator stated: "Word is an organism. The presence of the 'Other Half' a separate organism attached to your nervous system on an air line of words can now be demonstrated experimentally." The experiments to which the narrator alludes were performed by, among others, John Cunningham Lilly, who in the late 1950s and 1960s used isolation tanks to test the malleability of human perception.[13] The experiments required subjects to enter a dark tank and to float, cut off from all sensory input, in water kept at body temperature. The narrator mentions that a common "hallucination" of subjects in sense withdrawal was "the feeling of another body sprawled through the subject's body at an angle" (*TTE*, p. 49). "Yes quite an angle," the narrator ironically remarks, identifying the sensation as the subject's perception of his "other half," the word virus that invades the organism until it seems as intrinsic to the body as flesh and bone.

For the narrator, the proof of this parasitic invasion and infection is the interior monologue we all experience. "Modern man has lost the option of silence," he asserts. "Try to achieve even ten seconds of inner silence. You will encounter a resisting organism that *forces you to talk*. That organism is the word" (*TTE*, pp. 49–50). Burroughs's project is to offer the reader as many ways as he can imagine to stop the monologue, to rewrite or erase the "pre-recordings," and to extricate the subject from the parasitic invasion of the "Other Half." Tape-recorders are central to this project; "it's all done with tape recorders," the narrator comments (*TTE*, p. 162). One strategy is to "externalize dialogue" by getting "it out of your head and into the machines" (*TTE*, p. 163). He suggests that the reader record the last argument the reader had with a boyfriend or girlfriend, putting the reader's side of the argument on one recorder and the friend's side on the other. Then the two recorders can argue with each other, leaving the human partici-pants free to stop replaying the conversation in their heads and get on with their lives. The narrator also suggests recording random sounds on a third machine – snippets from a news broadcast, say – and mixing them in too. The intrusion of the random element is significant; it aims to break the reader not only out of personal obsessions but also out of the surrounding, culturally constructed envelope of sounds and words. "Wittgenstein said: 'No proposition can contain itself as an argument,'" the narrator remarks, interpreting this as follows: "The only thing *not* prerecorded in a prerecorded universe is the prerecording itself which is to say *any* recording that contains a random factor" (*TTE*, p. 166).

The intrusion of randomness is important in another way as well, for Burroughs is acutely aware of the danger that he might, through his words, spread the viral infection he is trying to combat. It is important, therefore, that disruptive techniques be instantiated within the text's own language. These techniques range from his famous use of the "cut-up," where he physically cuts up previously written narratives and arbitrarily splices them together, to more subtle methods such as shifting between different linguistic registers without transition or explanation.[14] Perhaps the single most important device is the insistent pressure to take metaphors literally – or put another way, to erase the distinction between words and things. Language is not merely like a virus; it *is* a virus, replicating through the host to become visible as green fish in the flesh and crab parasites tearing at the base of the spine and brain. In Burroughs, the material effects of language do not need to be mediated through physical discipline to re-form the body, for example through the prescribed postures and gestures used to teach penmanship in the eighteenth and nineteenth centuries. With a writer's license, he makes language erupt directly into the body. The body itself, moreover, is treated as if it physically were a recorder, regulated by the principles that govern magnetic tape in its reproduction, erasure, and reconfiguration. Here, within the represented world of the text, techniques of inscription merge with incorporated practices in a cyborg configuration of explosive potential. The double edge of this potential is not difficult to understand, for the reifying and infective power of words can be defused only through other words, which can always turn against their master and become infectious in turn. Making the word flesh is both how the virus infects and how the vaccine disinfects. In either case, the flesh will not continue unchanged.

The pressure toward literalization can be seen in the narrative sections that use the conventions of science fiction to figure the invasion of the word as a physical operation (early on the narrator announces, "I am reading a science fiction book called *The Ticket That Exploded*" [*TTE*, p. 5]). On this track, Earth has been invaded by the alien Nova mob, so-called because their strategy is to drive the planet to extreme chaos or "nova." The mob includes such creatures as heavy-metal addicts from Uranus, sex addicts from Venus, and other parasitic organisms that can occupy human flesh. "Nova criminals are not three-dimensional organisms – (though they are quite definite organisms as we shall see) – but they need three-dimensional human agents to operate" (*TTE*, p. 57). A single parasitic alien can take over hundreds of humans, stringing together its hosts to form rows of "coordinate points," analogous to lines of print or to phonemes subordinated through grammar and syntax. The reputed leader of the mob is an appropriately bimorphic creature called variously "Mr. Bradly Mr. Martin," "Mr. and Mrs. D," or simply "the Ugly spirit." In this instantiation of the "Other Half," the word itself is split down the middle.

A counterinvasion has been staged by the Nova police, whose weapons include radio static, "camera guns" that destabilize images by vibrating them at supersonic speeds, and of course tape-recorders. Recruiting "Mr. Lee" (this pseudonym used often by Burroughs was his mother's maiden name), the district supervisor tells Mr. Lee that he will receive his instructions "from books, street signs, films, in some cases from agents who purport to be and may actually be members of the organization. There is no certainty. Those who need certainty are of no interest to this department. This is in point of fact a *non-organization* the aim of which is to immunize our agents against fear despair and death. We intend to break the birth-death cycle" (*TTE*, p. 10). One of the criminals the department seeks is Johnny Yen, whose name suggests sexual desire. "Death *is* orgasm *is* rebirth *is* death in orgasm *is* their unsanitary Venusian gimmick *is* the whole birth death cycle of action," the narrator explains. He proceeds, apparently exasperated, to make his point even more obvious. "You got it? – Now do you understand who Johnny Yen is? – The Boy-Girl Other Half strip tease God of sexual frustration – Errand boy from the death trauma" (*TTE*, p. 53).

On this track, the action can be read as a physical contest between the Nova mob and the Nova police, as when a police operative from Minraud blows a mob crab guard into smithereens. But if the word is a parasite with material effects, the distinction between metaphor and actuality, representation and reality, is moot. Thus another strategy of resistance is the "Rewrite Room," the space from which comes the exposé of Johnny Yen cited above. Johnny Yen is not blown away but rather is rewritten to become a rather enchanting green fish boy, an amphibious life-form (a benign bimorphic creature) living in the canals and mating with Ali the street boy in a nonhuman life cycle that destabilizes the human sense of what constitutes the body, life, and death. The crisis of mutation, the recognition that pattern is always already penetrated by randomness, is here associated with a form of embodiment that moves through a froth of noise as easily as a fish through water.

For human subjects, however, this destabilization is bound to be threatening rather than simply liberating, for the narrative attempts to put into play all the boundaries that define human subjectivity. Body boundaries are often literally disintegrated, for example by the Sex Skin, an organism that surrounds its victims with a second skin that gives its victims intense sexual pleasure while dissolving and ingesting them. Positioned against the clear threat of this kind of sexual delirium are tape-recorders, potentially liberating but also not without danger. Recording one's body sounds and splicing them into someone else's can free one from the illusion that body sounds cannot exist apart from the interior monologue. But just as

Burroughs's words can become parasitic if not self-disrupted, so these sounds have the potential to constitute a parasitic monologue in turn. According to the narrator, the splicing produces a strong erotic reaction. If it is expressed in actual sexual contact "it acts as an aphrodisiac . . . nothing more. . . . But when a susceptible subject is spliced in with someone *who is not there* then it acts as a destructive virus," ironically becoming the phenomenon it was meant to counteract (*TTE*, p. 20).

As well as disrupting words audibly present, Burroughs wants to create – or expose – new ones from the substrata of the medium itself. He describes experiments based on "inching tape," manually rubbing the tape back and forth across the head at varying speeds. "Such exercises bring you a liberation from old association locks . . . you will hear words that were not in the original recording new words made by the machine different people will scan out different words of course but some of the words are quite clearly there." The technique gives new meaning to Marshall McLuhan's aphorism "The medium is the message," for it is "as if the words themselves had been interrogated and forced to reveal their hidden meanings it is interesting to record these words literally made by the machine itself" (*TTE*, p. 206). Here Burroughs envisions incorporating practices that can produce inscriptions without the mediation of consciousness.

He actually performed the tape-recorder experiments he describes from the late 1950s through the late 1970s. He inched tape to create, as he heard it, new words; he recorded radio broadcasts and spliced the tape to achieve an aural "cut-up"; and he held the microphone to the base of his throat and tried to record his own subvocal speech. As if anticipating Christian fundamentalists who hear Satanic messages hidden in records and tapes (people whose sensibilities he would no doubt enjoy outraging), he also read from his books, including *The Nova Express* and *The Ticket That Exploded*, and spliced the readings in with music played backward. The recordings have been preserved, and some of this archival material has been collected in a phonograph album entitled "Nothing Here Now but the Recordings."[15] Late one night I traveled to the music library at the University of California at San Diego to listen to the album. Even though the experience of sitting in the nearly deserted high-tech facility, insulated from exterior sound, was eerily conducive to hearing the words that Burroughs claims are there, some of the passages are clearly of historic interest only. In particular, the section that records subvocal speech is virtually unintelligible as patterned sound. Perhaps paradoxically, I found the recording less forceful as a demonstration of Burroughs's theories than his writing. For me, the aurality of his prose elicits a greater response than the machine productions it describes and instantiates.

The power of that writing is evident in the "writing machine" section of *The Ticket That Exploded*. The narrator describes an "Exhibition," which includes "a room with metal walls magnetic mobiles under flickering blue light and smell of ozone" (*TTE*, p. 62). The room is situated, of course, inside a tape-recorder. Normally, narrative fiction leaps over the technologies (printing press, paper, ink) that produce it and represents the external world as if this act of representation did not require a material basis for its production. Burroughs turns this convention inside out, locating the "external" world *inside* the techno-logical artifact. The move constructs a completely different relation between fiction and the material means of its production, constituting the technology as the ground out of which the narrative action evolves. This technique hints that the technology is not merely a medium to represent thoughts that already exist but is itself capable of dynamic interactions *producing* the thoughts it describes. At issue, then, is the technology not only as a theme but as an articulation capable of producing new kinds of subjectivities.

The tape-recording qualities important in the Exhibition are the twin and somewhat contradictory powers of inscription and mutation. Unlike marks on paper, this writing can easily be erased and rewritten in other forms. As spectators clink through turnstiles of the Exhibition, "great sheets of magnetized print held color and disintegrated in cold mineral silence as word dust falls from demagnetized patterns" (*TTE*, p. 62). The description points to the attraction the recorder has for Burroughs. Sound, unlike print, dies away unless it is constantly renewed. Its ephemerality calls forth a double response that finds material expression in the technology. On the one hand, magnetic tape allows sound to be preserved over time; in this respect it counters the ephemerality of sound by transforming it into inscription. On the other hand, inscriptions can be easily erased and reconfigured; in this sense, it reproduces the impermanence of sound. Burroughs was drawn to both aspects of the technology. The inscription of sound in a durable medium suited his belief that the word is material, whereas the malleability of sound meant that interventions were possible, interventions that could radically change or eradicate the record.

At the Exhibition, language is inscribed through "word dust" that falls from the walls as pervasively as smog particles from the Los Angeles sky. Anticipating videotape, Burroughs imagines that "picture dust" also falls from the walls. "Photomontage fragments backed with iron stuck to patterns and fell in swirls mixing with color dust to form new patterns, shimmering, falling, magnetized, demagnetized to the flicker of blue cylinders pulsing neon tubes and globes" (*TTE*, pp. 62–63). When the Nova police counterinvade the planet, "falling" phrases repeatedly appear, as if they were news bulletins read over and over on the radio: "Word falling – Photo falling – Time falling – Break through in Grey Room"; "Shift linguals – Cut word lines – Vibrate tourists – Free Doorways – Pinball led streets – Word falling – Photo falling – Break through in Grey Room – Towers, open fire" (*TTE*, p. 104); "cut all tape"; "Break through in Grey Room – 'Love' is falling – Sex word is falling – Break photograph – Shift body halves" (*TTE*, p. 105). The "Grey Room" evidently refers to the mob's communication and control center, perhaps the "board room" where, the narrator tells us, multinationals plot to take over outer and inner space.

In opposition to the linear centralized control of the "Grey Room" is the chaotic recursivity of the Exhibition. Here there is no clear line between those who act and those who are acted upon. The traffic flow through the room is structured like a recursive loop. As the spectators pass, they are recorded "by a battery of tape-recorders recording and playing back moving on conveyor belts and tracks and cable cars spilling the talk and metal music fountains and speech as the recorders moved from one exhibit to another." The narrator remarks parenthetically, "Since the recorders and movies of the exhibition are in constant operation it will be readily seen that any spectator appears on the screen sooner or later if not today then yesterday or tomorrow" (*TTE*, p. 64). Thus spectators move along within the room, hearing and watching recordings of themselves as the recordings are played back from machines that are also moving along a conveyor belt. Their reactions as they hear and watch are also recorded in turn by other machines, creating an infinite regress in which body and tape, recording and voice, image and sight, endlessly reproduce each other. Within this world, it makes a weird kind of sense for bodies to mutate as easily as spliced tape, for the distinction between reality and representation has been largely deconstructed. "Characters walk in and out of screen flickering different films on and off" (*TTE*, p. 64); bodies split in half lengthwise; screens show two films simultaneously, half of one on one side, half of the other on the other side; a writing machine "shifts one half one text and half the other through a page frame on conveyor belts" (*TTE*, p. 65). Inscriptions, bodies, sounds, and images all follow the same dynamics and the same logic of splices running lengthwise to create mutated posthuman forms that both express and strive to escape from the conditioning that makes them into split beings.

In a wonderfully oxymoronic phrase, Burroughs calls the place where culture produces its replicating sound and image tracks the "reality studio." "Clearly no portentous exciting events are about to transpire," the narrator says, implicitly mocking the melodrama of his own space-alien track. "You will readily understand why people will go to any lengths to get in the film to cover themselves with any old film scrap . . . anything to avoid the hopeless dead-end horror of being just who and where you all are: dying animals on a doomed planet." Connecting capitalist financing with cultural productions (as if remembering the American Telegraphone Company), he continues: "The film stock issued now isn't worth the celluloid its [*sic*] printed on. There is nothing to back it up. The film bank is empty. To conceal the bankruptcy of the reality studio it is essential that no one should be in position to set up another reality set. . . . Work for the reality studio or else. Or else you will find out how it feels to be *outside the film*" (*TTE*, p. 151).

As the text draws to a close, the narrator directs the reader's attention to the possibility that the reality studio may indeed be closing down and that the reader will therefore shortly be outside the film, off the recording. A similar message is given in a different medium, when at the end of the penultimate section, the print of the text is disrupted by several lines of cursive script, English alternating with Arabic. Each line runs through a permutation of "To say good by silence," with the lines gradually becoming more random and indecipherable as they proceed down the page (*TTE*, p. 203). Perhaps Burroughs is trying to prepare the reader for the panic that sets in when the interior monologue is disrupted and, for the first time in one's life, one hears silence instead of language. For whatever reason, he takes extraordinary care to achieve a feeling of closure unusual in his works from this period. Compared with *Naked Lunch*, the ending here is formally elaborate and thematically conclusive.

Echoing *The Tempest*, the text as it winds down splices in dialogue from Shakespeare's play with visions of contemporary technologies. "i foretold you were all spirits watching TV program – Terminal electric voices end – These our actors cut in – A few seconds later you are melted into air – Rub out promised by our ever-living poet – Mr. Bradly Mr. Martin, five times our summons – no shelter in setting forth" (*TTE*, p. 174). The splices invite the reader to tease out resonances between the two works. Whereas insect imagery predominates in *Naked Lunch*, in *Ticket* the usual form of nonhuman life is aquatic or amphibian, recalling Caliban's characterization as a "fishy monster." Prospero conjures spirits from the air, and yet his magic has a terrible materiality; he can, we are told, raise bodies from the dead. Most of all he is a supreme technician, blending illusion with reality so skillfully that his art can effect changes in the real world. Burroughs aims for nothing less, using language to disrupt the viral power of the word, creating recordings to stop the playbacks that imprison our future in the sounds of our past. If the tape-recorder is, as Paul Bowles called it, "God's little toy," *The Ticket That Exploded* is the tape that reveals this god-machine's life-transforming possibilities (Bowles quoted in *TTE*, p. 166).

"What we see is dictated by what we hear," the narrator of *Ticket* asserts (*TTE*, p. 168). There is considerable anecdotal evidence to support his claim. Whereas sight is always focused, sharp, and delineated, sound envelopes the body, as if it were an atmosphere to be experienced rather than an object to be dissected. Perhaps that is why researchers in virtual reality have found that sound is much more effective than sight in imparting emotional tonalities to their simulated worlds.[16] Their experiences suggest that voice is associated with presence not only because it comes from within the body but also because it conveys new information about the subject, information that goes deeper than analytical thought or conscious intention. Manipulating sound through tape-recorders thus becomes a way of producing a new kind of subjectivity that strikes at the deepest levels of awareness. If we were to trace the trajectory suggested here to the end of the period when audiotape held sway, it would lead to texts such as C. J. Cherryh's *Cyteen* trilogy, where the body has become a corporate product molded by "taking tape," that is, listening to conditioning tapes that lay the foundation for the subject's "psychset." Burroughs anticipates Cherryh's implication that the voice issuing from the tape-recorder sounds finally not so much postmodern as it does posthuman.

Where hope exists in *Ticket*, it appears as posthuman mutations like the fish boy, whose fluidity perhaps figures a type of subjectivity attuned to the froth of noise rather than the stability of a false self, living an embodied life beyond human consciousness as we know it. But this is mere conjecture, for any representation of the internal life of the fish boy could be done only in words, which would infect and destroy exactly the transformation they were attempting to describe. For Burroughs, the emphasis remains on subversion and disruption rather than creative rearticulation. Even subversion risks being co-opted and taken over by the viral word; it can succeed only by continuing to disrupt everything, including its own prior writing.

In this chapter, I have been concerned with Burroughs's fictions not only as harbingers of the posthuman but, more immediately, as sites where body/embodiment and inscription/incorporation are in constant and dynamic interplay with one another. As we have seen, in the Exhibition, inscriptions fall from the walls to become corporeal "word dust"; incorporations are transformed into inscriptions through video- and audio-recording devices; bodies understood as normative and essentialized entities are rewritten to become particularized experiences of embodiment; and embodied experience is transformed, through the inscriptions of the tape-recording, back into essentialized manifestations of "the word." The recursivities that entangle inscription with incorporation, the body with embodiment, invite us to see these polarities not as static concepts but as mutating surfaces that transform into one another, much like the

Möbius strip that Grosz imagines for her "volatile bodies." Starting from a model emphasizing polarities, then, we have moved toward a vision of interactions both pleasurable and dangerous, creatively dynamic and explosively transformative.

It is no accident that recursive loops and reflexive strategies figure importantly in these transformations, for Burroughs shared with Humberto Maturana and Philip K. Dick an appreciation for how potently reflexivity can destabilize objectivist assumptions. Whereas Maturana located reflexivity in biological processes and Dick placed it in psychological dynamics, Burroughs located it in a cybernetic fusion of language and technology. Mutating into and out of the tape-recorder, the viral word reconfigures the tape-recorder as a cybernetic technology capable of radically transforming bodies and subjectivities. As for the "external" world, where clear divisions separate observer from system, human from technological artifact, Maturana, Dick, and Burroughs agreed (although for different reasons) that there is no there there. Whatever the limitations of their works, they shared a realization that the observer cannot stand apart from the systems being observed. In exploring how to integrate observer and world into a unified field of interaction, they also realized that liberal humanism could not continue to hold sway. Just as the tide of posthumanism that Norbert Wiener had struggled to contain could not be held back, neither could the technological advances in informatics, advances that would soon displace second-wave issues with third-wave concerns.

Notes

1   Garrett Stewart, *Reading Voices: Literature and the Phonotext* (Berkeley: University of California Press, 1990).

2   Eric Havelock argues that modern subjectivity, with its sense of stable ego and enduring identity, was a historical invention that correlated with the transition from orality to writing: see *Preface to Plato* (Cambridge: Harvard University Press, 1963).

3   The literature on these technologies is extensive. For a useful brief discussion, see Douglas Kahn and Gregory Whitehead, eds., *Wireless Imagination: Sound, Radio, and the Avant-Garde* (Cambridge: MIT Press, 1992), especially Douglas Kahn's chapter "Introduction: Histories of Sound Once Removed," pp. 1–30.

4   See Friedrich A. Kittler, *Discourse Networks, 1800–1900*, translated by Michael Metteer (Stanford: Stanford University Press, 1990). Also relevant is Friedrich A. Kittler, "Gramophone, Film, Typewriter," translated by Dorothea von Mücke, *October* 41 (1987): 101–18, in which Kittler wrote: "The technical differentiation of optics, acoustics, and writing around 1880, as it exploded Gutenberg's storage monopoly, made the fabrication of so-called man possible. His essence runs through apparatuses" (p. 115). Nothing could be more applicable to Burroughs's view of tape-recording.

5   The pioneering papers in the development of magnetic tape-recording are collected in Marvin Camras, *Magnetic Tape Recording* (New York: Van Nostrand Reinhold Company, 1985). His brief introductions to the sections provide a valuable (if sketchy) history, which I have drawn on here.

6   For the patent description of the Telegraphone, see V. Poulsen, "Method of Recording and Reproducing Sounds or Signals," in Camras, *Magnetic Tape Recording*, pp. 11–17. The model exhibited in Paris differed somewhat from the patent description.

7   A description of the film and ring head is given in H. Lubeck, "Magnetic Sound Recording with Films and Ring Heads," in Camras, *Magnetic Tape Recording*, pp. 79–111.

8   A useful review of this work is J. C. Mallinson, "Tutorial Review of Magnetic Recording," in Camras, *Magnetic Tape Recording*, pp. 229–43.

9   Roy Walker, "Love, Chess, and Death," in Samuel Beckett, *Krapp's Last Tape: A Theater Notebook*, edited by James Knowlson (London: Brutus Books, 1980), p. 49.

10   William S. Burroughs, *The Ticket That Exploded* (New York: Grove Press, 1967) (hereafter cited in the text as *TTE*).

11   This idea of an interior monologue shoring up a false sense of self is also important in Francisco J. Varela, Evan Thompson, and Eleanor Rosch, *The Embodied Mind: Cognitive Science and Human Experience* (Cambridge: MIT Press, 1991). For an extensive discussion of how tape-recorders can be used to disrupt the word virus, see William Burroughs, *Electronic Revolution* (Bonn: Expanded Media Editions, 1970), pp. 1–62.

12   Cary Nelson has an excellent discussion of the body in relation to space in Burroughs's work, including *The Ticket That Exploded* and its companion novels: "The End of the Body: Radical Space in Burroughs", in *William S. Burroughs at the Front: Critical Reception, 1959–1989*, edited by Jennie Kerl and Robin Lydenberg (Carbondale: Southern Illinois University Press, 1991), pp. 119–32.

13   John Cunningham Lilly gives an account of these experiments in his autobiographical account *The Center of the Cyclone: An Autobiography of Inner Space* (New York: Julian Press, 1972). In a characteristically literalizing passage, Burroughs suggested that isolation tanks could literally dissolve body boundaries: "So after fifteen minutes in the tank these Marines scream they are losing outlines and have to be removed – I say put two marines in the tank and see who comes out – Science – Pure science – So put a marine and his girl friend in the tank and see who or what emerges –" (*TTE*, p. 83).

14   The cut-up method is described in many places by Burroughs and others; see, for example, Daniel Odier, *The Job: Interviews with William S. Burroughs* (New York: Grove Press, 1969), p. 14, and William S. Burroughs, "The Cut-Up Method of Brion Gysin," *Re/Search* #4/5 (San Francisco: Re/Search Publications, 1982), pp. 35–8. Robin Lydenberg lucidly discusses the political and theoretical implications of the practice in *Word Cultures: Radical Theory and Practice in William S. Burroughs' Fiction* (Urbana: University of Illinois Press, 1987). Laszlo K. Gefin contextualizes the practice in the avant-garde techniques of collage in "Collage Theory, Reception, and the Cut-Ups of William Burroughs," *Perspectives on Contemporary Literature: Literature and the Other Arts* 13 (1987): 91–100. Anne Friedberg, "Cut-Ups: A Synema of the Text," in Skerl and Lydenberg, *William S. Burroughs*, pp. 169–73, traces the cut-up method through the dadaists.

15   Robin Lydenberg has a good discussion of Burroughs's experiments with tape-recordings, including this album, in "Sound Identity Fading Out: William Burroughs' Tape Experiments," in Kahn and Whitehead, *Wireless Imagination*, pp. 409–33.

16   Brenda Laurel and Sandy Stone, private communication.

Chapter 32

Peter Hitchcock

CHRONOTOPE OF THE SHOE (TWO) [2003]

Source: Peter Hitchcock (2003) 'Chronotope of the Shoe (Two)', in *Imaginary States: Studies in Cultural Transnationalism (Transnational Cultural Studies)*, Urbana: Illinois University Press, pp. 118–52.

This final piece of writing (Peter Hitchcock's 'Chronotope of the Shoe (Two)') returns us to the topic of the first one in this collection: the commodity and its secret. In contemporary culture, casual athletic shoes (trainers or sneakers) have become a distinctive commodity that also, to a large degree, seems to epitomise commodification itself. As Hitchcock shows, the various companies that make sneakers (Nike, Reebok, Adidas, Puma, Lacoste and so on) outsource the production of shoes to workers in 'developing' countries like South Korea, Taiwan and Malaysia where labour can be bought for very little money. The shoes are then sold in 'over-developed' countries for a great deal of money. This disparity is hidden in the shoe and by the shoe, which is transformed (through design and promotion) into a magical product that is highly desirable, fashionable and, for some, collectable. The sneaker is produced in thousands of different styles, and these styles are attached to various logos and brand names that anchor them. The sneaker, then, also demonstrates the way that the 'distinctiveness, difference and newness' of a particular commodity (which is often all you are really paying for) is only a minor derivation of the surface design while the functional structure remains constant.

For his inquiry into the sneaker commodity Hitchcock uses the concept of the 'chronotope'. He takes the term from the Russian literary theorist Mikhail Bakhtin. Bakhtin's translators explain the chronotope as: 'A unit of analysis for studying texts according to the ratio and nature of temporal and spatial categories represented. . . . The chronotope is an optic for reading texts as x-rays of the forces at work in the culture system from which they spring' (Emerson and Holquist in Bakhtin 1981: 425–6). For Bakhtin 'the chronotope makes narrative events concrete, makes them take on flesh, causes blood to flow in their veins' (Bakhtin 1981: 250). Thus it is the most social aspect of a literary text, and the one that is played out across its form and content. If a narrative is made up of a series of events, then the chronotope of literature is the orchestration of time and space (for instance, in the picaresque novel, the road movie and so on) that allows events to be 'shown forth' in a particular way.

While Bakhtin concentrates on literature, the concept of the chronotope shouldn't be limited to narrative forms. In Bakhtin's hands the chronotope opens up literature to the historical geography of the real world. For Hitchcock the chronotope is the critical antidote to the fetish of the commodity. The attention to the chronotope of the shoe is a way of insisting that what is hidden by the commodity (the real history of the production, the geographical unevenness of its circulation) is inscribed in the shoe in physical form. The chronotope is what allows Hitchcock to follow 'the trace of a Jakarta woman shoe worker in a rubber sole and, as we will see, a working-class African American male dead in the streets of Chicago with his shoes removed'.

Further reading: Abbas and Erni 2005; Bakhtin 1981; Goldman and Papson 1999.

[. . .]

KARL MARX ONCE suggested that a commodity "is a very strange thing, abounding in metaphysical subtleties and theological niceties."[1] A social history of the shoe would show as much, for there is no commodity in modern history with a greater capacity to confound thingness and spirit, use value and exchange, desire and displacement, and production with consumption.[2] The commodity stands in for Being where Being itself threatens the logic of the commodity form. The shoes (pairs, hence the "two" of my title) deconstruct the binaries that bind while yet confirming the convenience of their duality (the commodity status of shoes makes their use and their function as objects of desire both separable or collapsible within a marketing machine). Rather than elaborate the social history implied above, I want to examine in more detail the contemporary chronotope that links culture and capital in the aura of the shoe. In the manner of Gilles Deleuze and Félix Guattari, one could state that the aura of the shoe spreads, rhizomelike, across the globe as an (almost) metaphysical index of desire in capital (indeed, to be "over the shoes" is an expression of desire). But while this allows an understanding of the theological and theoretical inside/outside of the shoe it does not coordinate the affective points of responsibility that historically have left the trace of a Jakarta woman shoe worker in a rubber sole and, as we will see, a working-class African American male dead in the streets of Chicago with his shoes removed.

To chart this chronotope I will elaborate the *pointure* (as Derrida describes it) or pricking of the shoe in theory, and the rise of a particular commodity, the athletic shoe. The aim throughout will be to map the "metaphysical subtleties and theological niceties" of commodity culture as it currently confers aphanisis on the workers of the world (even when, or precisely because, the workers are positioned between the earth and the people who use them[3]). I have three claims that are central to commodity critique: first, a materialist understanding of transnational capitalist commodification is not simply a problem of totality, but one of imagination;[4] second (but a point that is, in essence, inextricable from the first), time/space compression in transnational commodity culture offers an abstruse simultaneity that necessitates a reevaluation of the fetish and fetishism;[5] third, commodity desire is no more inevitable than responsibility – both desire and responsibility are produced within regimes of truth that are irreconcilable – their contradictions are themselves an index of the world system.

The chronotope of the shoe invokes a Bakhtinian framework of affective responsibility – a means to fathom the logic of the commodity.[6] In Bakhtin's interpretation, the chronotope was multivalent, a complex constituent feature of his developing "historical poetics" that could link recurring literary devices across cultural history.[7] Yet this immediately marks Bakhtin's chronotope as a contradictory concept. If, as Bakhtin argues, literary chronotopes develop from and respond to specific extraliterary contexts, then how can these chronotopes be manifest transhistorically? Michael Holquist suggests that we distinguish between chronotope as a device or category of narrative and the principle of chronotopicity itself. The latter refers to time/space relations that structure the always already mediated condition of art and life.[8] As Bakhtin notes, "Out of the actual chronotopes of our world (which serve as the source of representation) emerge the reflected and *created* chronotopes of the world represented in the work."[9] While chronotopicity is not a stable bridge between art and life, it nevertheless draws attention to the mediatory functions of time and space in their interrelation. Beside its transhistorical inclinations, however, there are other obvious weaknesses in Bakhtin's articulation of the concept. For instance, the concrete forms of everday life that Bakhtin summons draw attention to the situatedness of *his* critique from which one must ask what it would mean to specify "the actual chronotopes of our world." Would one not be forced, by the very terms of Bakhtin's exegesis, to particularize quite radically what is "ours" in that phrase? And what are the processes by which "our" world gets generalized so that in a chronotopic economy "our" world might stand in for others? Again, one must distinguish quite carefully the "worldliness" that Bakhtin advocates, despite and because of its correlations with the transnationalism of the commodity form. My point is this: If, as Katerina Clark and Michael Holquist contend, the chronotope is "a concept for engaging reality,"[10] then we would do well to examine the chronotopes of that world and not just their artistic or literary correlatives *in isolation* that are the hallmarks, for better or worse, of the "world" about which Bakhtin wrote in "Forms of Time."

When we are in life we are not in art and vice versa, as Bakhtin muses. But of course, chronotope, like dialogism and exotopy, is a Bakhtinian bridging concept that links these autonomous yet interdependent worlds: "However forcefully the real and represented world resist fusion . . . they are nevertheless indissolubly tied up with each other and find themselves in continual mutual interaction; uninterrupted exchange goes on between them, similar to the uninterrupted exchange of matter between living organisms and the environment that surrounds them."[11] Bakhtin is recalling the thought of Alexander Ukhtomsky from whom he first heard and used the word *chronotope* in 1925. There is little use in substituting directly these comments on uninterrupted exchange with the production of value in exchange represented by the commodity form. Can they be coordinated or tied up within cultural critique, however, without losing the specificity of either? And, if the aura of the shoe, the athletic shoe in particular, is enabled by what Fredric Jameson calls the cultural logic of late capitalism[12] – indeed, is symptomatic of its transnationalism – can these terms be interrelated without inexorably reproducing the inclusionary fantasy of worldliness that most transnational corporations (TNCs) tout as the very integer of their success?

Here, the chronotope is a story of a shoe and the worker to which it refers. The invocation of the shoe, however, does not build a world picture of culture and capital at the present time (for representation itself will remain the problem and not the provider) yet it can implicate cultural critique in the fate of the increasingly absent or disappearing worker whose labor "disappears" in the commodity form but now also vanishes in the commodification of theory itself. The strategy I recommend is not only to inscribe the shoe within a metonymic chain of affective being, but also to elaborate the shoe within a code of affective answerability. The shifting registers of the symbolic of the shoe are less about the capabilities of the cultural researcher than about the abject culpability of the Same. The aim is not the production of guilt (however some may revel in the discourse of victimhood); rather, I seek the production of a counterlogic, one which challenges the tidy knowledge that the trail of the shoe might leave. Cultural critique cannot (following Gayatri Spivak's powerfully argued notion)[13] make the subaltern (Indonesian shoe worker) speak, but it can attend to a geopolitical imagination that challenges the production of that "existence" on a world scale.

The shoe is magical, both within the history of the commodity and the psychological compulsions of modern "man." The shoe is *the* emblem of the fetishism that links the commodity to desire. And the most magical shoe of all is currently the athletic shoe because it is simultaneously a symbol of cultural capital, physical prowess, self-esteem, economic and psychic overinvestment, and crass economic exploitation; in fact, it epitomizes late capitalist flexible accumulation *and* continuing masculinist regimes of desire and disavowal.[14] Although Donald Katz has a different argument in mind, he stated the case quite nicely in 1994: "The name-brand athletic shoe might seem an unlikely seminal artifact of these last years of the twentieth century, but that is clearly what the shoes have become."[15] One brand in particular demonstrates the aura of the shoe for Katz, and that is Nike – named after the Greek goddess of victory, and a company that marks the triumphalism of transnational corporate élan.[16] This "seminal artifact" conjures the chronotope that is our chief concern and runs from the culture of consumption to the international division of labor and the critical methods that must be answerable to both.

What is the magic of capital for late capitalism? In 1962 Phil Knight "faked out" a Japanese athletic shoe company and became their distributor in the United States under the name Blue Ribbon Sports. Ten years later Jeff Johnson, an employee of Blue Ribbon Sports, sat bolt upright in his bed one morning and blurted the word, "Nike." Phil Knight was looking for a new moniker for the company and its sports shoes. Within thirty years the name of the winged goddess of victory became synonymous with the success of American transnationalism in recreational footwear, enough, for instance, to produce nearly $10 billion of annual sales and profits of $800 million in 1997 alone (a year in which Nike sold more than three hundred pairs of shoes a minute).[17] But Nike has also faced severe problems in its form of globalization. With the economic downturn in Asia in 1997–98, changes in fashion demand, classic overproduction caused by its contract futures, financial and social instability in its main production hubs like Indonesia, and burgeoning opposition in Asia and in Nike's "homeland" to transnational sweatshop practices, Nike saw its profits drop by 35 percent in the first quarter of 1998; indeed, in the second quarter of that year it reported a net loss of $67.6 million – a disaster quickly followed by layoffs and public-relations campaigns. It has since recovered, but it is clearly subject to intense competition/opposition at home and abroad. Despite these shifting fortunes and the emergence of a formidable antiglobalist and anti-World Trade Organization network, the story of Nike has become a legend in American capitalist history, a lesson in tremendous company growth and a benchmark for savvy marketing tactics. To underline the latter, one should note that Nike is not really in the business of making shoes: What it does is market shoes. The shoes themselves are made through contracting and subcontracting in twelve- to eighteen-month production cycles outside its major market, the United States. Currently, Nike uses more than 700 factories worldwide that employ more than 500,000 people (110,000 in Indonesia).[18] It is the metaphysical subtleties of the shoe that Nike has harnessed with a godlike touch that few have matched. Yet who is vanquished in Nike's "victory," and what other rendezvous of victory is possible in the nexus of culture and capital?

The chronotope of the shoe immediately invites questions of desire (the projection of the fetish and its disavowal) that are more than a subtheme: They describe both the limits of a geopolitical cultural trans-nationalism and the geopolitical in general at this historical juncture. Thus, the worker "exists" at the nexus of economic integration, spatial differentiation, cultural globalization, *and* masculinist disavowal. While the notion of existence as aphanisis follows Marx's analysis of the commodity to a certain degree, it also links the fate of the worker in contemporary forms of engendered power. The financialization and transnationali-zation of the globe is partial (despite the triumphalism that its proponents proclaim) but significant enough to throw into relief the patriarchal and capitalist ideologies that inform its mode of accumulation. These must insistently be made answerable to the being of the worker, however decentered that self has become. The task is not to make visible that which has been transmogrified beyond recognition (for that visibility is also often at man's behest): The point is to understand the contemporary processes (psychic, social, economic, political) by which workers must be rendered a convenient abstraction – the shoe for the flesh.[19]

Nike makes shoes in Indonesia.[20] Indonesia is a country that needs no "national allegory" to understand its integration into global capitalist and cultural relations. (Here I agree with Aijaz Ahmad's cogent critique that Jameson's characterization of the "Third World" text is an exercise in "positivist reductionism."[21]) Indonesia's contemporary ties to the world system begin in 1965, first with a military coup, then with the overthrow of Sukarno and his populist regime, and the subsequent crushing of the Communist Party (PKI) by the Western-backed forces of Suharto.[22] Suharto's "New Order" meant several things: a political system that continually steamrollered any and all forms of opposition to its "beneficence" (what was left of the PKI was outlawed in 1966, and periodic social unrest, like the riots of 1984 were quickly "remedied"); a foreign policy that has not been beyond a little old-style colonialism to maintain hegemony in the Indonesian archipelago (the process of incorporating East Timor cost several hundred thousand lives, but in the aftermath of Suharto's "withdrawal" from the political scene and an East Timorese independence move-ment sanctioned first by Suharto's "interim" successor, B. J. Habibie, then Wahid, and most recently Megawati Sukarnoputri, that bloody annexation is being remedied to some degree[23]); an enforcement of constitutional rule that often meant a narrow interpretation of the *Pancasila* (the Five Principles originally devised by Sukarno as a basis for the modern Indonesian state[24]); and an opening to foreign investment that undoubtedly raised living standards in many sections of the population but did not fundamentally address the root causes of systemic inequalities that attract transnational corporations in the first place. Development in Indonesia has meant this and more.

The periodic World Bank country reports on Indonesia make for dry and clinical reading.[25] The studies appear to have been prodded by the typical traumatic stress associated with massive foreign investment and the exploitation of Indonesia's natural resources (including large oil reserves, a factor that has clearly spurred growth but, because of the geopolitical significance of oil prices, has often meant internationally produced austerity programs – and strategic silence on state-sponsored atrocities). The piles of statistics on poverty rates in Indonesia are a measure of the World Bank's own hesitation about investment strategies.[26] Not surprisingly, poverty rates are highest in the agricultural sector. Families are generally bigger, wages lower, and living conditions substandard compared to their urban counterparts, especially those in Jakarta. In several reports the concern is about the social and political consequences of fostering a large and generally poor underemployed population (Indonesia's population is now the world's fourth-largest). And, of course, the economics of development strategy are closely tied to this. The Suharto regime, mindful of any IMF or World Bank attempts to influence the internal politics of the state, generally followed the advice of these reports and the examples of other Asian "miracle" economies like Taiwan, Malaysia, and South Korea by drawing surplus labor into other segments of production. But industrialization has raised not only real wages but the specters of class division on the one hand, and environmental disaster on the other (the latter has included the deliberate setting of massive forest fires but also an explosion of urban blight). Both now threaten to drive transnationals away, but in the early years of the New Order these considerations were distant, to say the least.

Indeed, it is tempting to say that Indonesia garners importance not because it makes shoes, but because it was made for shoes, which is of course merely to underline that transnational capitalism is not that interested in what Indonesia might otherwise "represent."[27] The political, social, and economic circumstances of Indonesia after 1965 increasingly made it ripe for exactly the mode of light industry, low-tech, labor-intensive "development" symbolized by shoe production. Yet this capitalist desire is simultaneously a masculinist desire, both a product of the search for higher profit margins in the process from production to consumption *and* a symptom of global fetishistic disavowal. The shoe stands in both for the desire that compels it and the actual conditions that inform it. This means not only the feminization of the developing world through the rubric of transnational market "penetration" (such language is not marginal but part of the very texture of the socioeconomic relations that accompany it); it also means that the internationalization of markets has attempted to efface the psychic inscriptions on the commodity form by exporting the nonrepresentation of the worker to the farthest corners of the globe (farthest, that is, from the object of the commodity's production – the consumer).

What starts out, then, as a conventional narrative about the onward march of late capitalist "development" in the Newly Industrialized Countries (NICs) in the thrall of TNCs becomes a web of complex synergy that the commodity presents as its natural apotheosis. To be sure, the roots of this process of commodification of relations on a world scale can be found in Marx's reading of industrialization, but there it was seen as the rallying point of a unifying labor movement conscious of the world that left it underfoot; now, however, it is the mark of amnesia and aphanisis – the great complexity of commerce that precedes the arrival of the commodity is repressed (disavowed). The commodity appears in its advertisement, and not in the hands of the shoemaker or rubber molder twelve thousand miles away. Naturally, a capitalist is taciturn about using the immiseration and inequality built into the production of the commodity as a way to sell it: That is one of the meanings of capitalism. But it is only now, in the transformed time/space relations of global capital, that criticism of this process seems beyond the powers of the cognitive. Even radical approaches to knowledge like cultural studies inadvertently buttress this point of view by concentrating on the subversive meanings of the consumer – what the consumer does with the commodity. The worker is either an old shoe or has disappeared, except as an ironic integer of her or his continuing absence from the realm of social, economic, and political power.

Again, a different sense of time/space critique does not solve that absence, as if a chronotopic imagination alone might disarticulate the logical consistency of superexploitation. Yet the internationalization of cultural critique, with all its dangers, may be a necessary evil if one is to understand culture's implication in the order of things and thingness at this time. The story of Indonesia in the twentieth century was one of colonization, occupation, revolution, independence, counterrevolution, development, integration, and so forth. That it was also the disjecta membra, the refracting shards of Western capital and culture, is not a coincidence, however specific that narrative must be. That continues to be the real foundation of the chronotope of the shoe.

No shorthand version of Indonesian politics and economics will provide an adequate understanding of the tremendous changes wrought on society by the New Order's version of modern statehood.[28] The transmigration program of relocating large numbers of people to outlying islands in order to ease the burdens of population explosion in Java would itself serve as a case study of the disjunctions of Indonesian development (during and after colonization). And, of course, given the rapacious sway of transnational capital, some comparison with the business practices of the Dutch East India Company in the preceding centuries would also shed light on the differences in the extraction of surplus value from labor today.[29] From the above, three characteristics, however, have particular relevance to Indonesia's recent integration into the global economy: an excess of labor suitable for labor-intensive low-wage light-industrial production; little or no organized labor infrastructure; and an authoritarian regime that routinely disregarded the nominally democratic nature of Indonesian statehood epitomized in the five principles in order to smooth the flow of capital in and out of the country.

In terms of the Asian economic miracle since the end of World War II, this adds Indonesia to a metonymic chain that has included Taiwan, Malaysia, and South Korea. As transnationals move around Asia (and that obviously includes Asian transnationals, particularly those of Japan), competition for cost effectiveness has intensified. Interestingly, as the Asian markets seek out cheaper production costs, many of the companies who were subcontracted to boost production in places like Taiwan and South Korea are now subsubcontracting in other emerging economies. This is certainly true of Indonesia, and it appears to be the case in China, which is rapidly becoming the metonym to supplant all others in this process. Focusing on Indonesian shoe production is not meant to stand in unproblematically for developments of this kind elsewhere in the region, but rather it emphasizes what elements disrupt an otherwise tidy metonymy. In the end, it is not simply desire for cheaper labor in accordance with the appropriate prerequisites that produces these changes but also the logic of desire itself – that which does not favor mere cause and effect, but abstruse simultaneity.

The chronotope of the shoe can be schematized as a psychic compulsion linked simultaneously to gender hierarchization and commodity fetishism, a narrative that comprises the actual production of a shoe within regimes of capital, and a tale of the embodied labor of a shoe worker here interpellated in the Indonesian economy. The shoe is a particularly useful way to understand the chronotope of culture and capital because it accentuates the process of desire intrinsic to the logic of global circuits of production and consumption. The importance of the shoe relates simultaneously to its status as a commodity and to its function as fetish. In Freud's famous formulation, fetishism is a masculine prerogative – a reflex to the "horror of castration"[30] produced by the boy's belief in the woman (the mother) having a penis. The boy does not repress the contradictory evidence of this projection so much as disavow it (*Verleugnung*), a process that more properly describes the function of a fetish as an external reality. Why the shoe emerges as a fetishistic substitute for the "absent female phallus" is only hinted at in Freud's explanation: He avers that the young boy fixates on the shoe or the foot at the very moment of disavowal as the boy glimpses the woman's genitals from below. In the absence of the phallus the boy fantasizes its presence: The shoe, particularly the woman's shoe, becomes the metonym for something that it is not; namely, the belief that the Being of female is male.

More of a sketch than an essay, Freud's thoughts on fetishism have produced a plethora of interpretation. Indeed, recent discussion would seem to underline still further the importance and the controversy of this piece.[31] The psychic significance of Freud's formulation is accentuated by its ambivalent relation to its cognates in political economy, anthropology, and literary theory in which its critical function alternates between touchstone and gravestone. Marx preempts the Freudian turn to a certain extent by associating fetishism with the general aura of the object as a commodity. Behind what he refers to as the "hieroglyph" of the product lies value, which Marx explores as the social character of labor, precisely what the money-form's relationship to the commodity must erase or deny. In Freud's theory, the object arises as a presence for something that was never there; for Marx, the commodity stands in for a real absence, the social labor that produced it. In *Feminizing the Fetish*, Emily Apter explores a "curious compatibility" between these readings, a space where the commodity's "secret" and the "strangeness" of consciousness form (and here she quotes from Michel Leiris) an "affective ambivalence, that tender sphinx we nourish, more or less secretly, at out core."[32] Apter persuasively theorizes ambivalence as a "third term," as the space where fetish, fetishism, and theories of fetishism ("the fetishism of fetishism") seem to mutually deconstruct – and is thus a place where "feminizing" becomes both necessary and ineluctable, as long as one limits its function to literary narrative (the textual examples that Apter provides). Whatever the ambivalence of Marx's own tropes on fetishism,[33] the "metaphysical subtleties" of the commodity do not stand in the same relation as Freud's fetishist to the fetish. Not quite.

Within commodity fetishism the social relations in exchange between commodities stand in for the social relations of those human beings who have labored to produce them. The illusory aspect of commodity fetishism is that the value of the commodity appears inherent to it, whereas its value is not natural, but social. This is a *real relation*, not simply a representational fallacy. One can easily accept Jean Baudrillard's exegesis of simulacra on this point,[34] but not the overhasty displacement of the economic onto the signifying chain for the very same reason. Thus, commodities can simulate one another without reference to an actual original (which never existed, hence the link to psychic fetishism), but labor value does not exist as an imaginary referent to the commodity even if it is presented as such. In addition, in the rush to find equivalence between Freudian "affect" and commodity effect it is easy to overlook that commodity fetishism is specific to the relations among things (that is, their exchange value), but fetishizing the shoe or foot is a displaced relation of subject and object, not two shoes' *danse macabre*.

If one links together the processes involved in the production and consumption of athletic shoes, several familiar patterns begin to emerge. To think these simultaneously within the chronotope is itself, as I have suggested, something close to fantasy (something hallucinogenic in Derrida's parlance), but is never-theless the first circle of affective responsibility. Within production there is primarily a woman worker. She is hired because she is cheap and because she is dexterous (she has to be able to work inside and outside the shoe with great speed).[35] She is also assumed to be noncombative in terms of labor rights and, while unmarried, "free" to work long hours. With increasing unemployment on the land, the woman worker is lured from the village to the emerging urban centers in Indonesia. Nike moves to Indonesia from the middle of the 1980s at the same time that this labor force is itself emerging in the Indonesian economy. Light industry of this kind continues to be crucial for the Indonesian government in picking up the slack in industrial development caused by the reining in of its oil business in the international market. As noted, the World Bank played a large role in this "retooling," and some $350 million of foreign aid poured into Indonesia over three years in the late 1980s for light industry development, including shoe factories (DK 185). In 1988 Indonesian athletic shoe exports stood at $4 million, but by 1993 this had risen to $1.5 billion. For Nike, the switch to production in Indonesia becomes more attractive at this time both because of almost nonexistent government oversight in their form of business and because labor costs in South Korea and Taiwan in particular were beginning to eat into profit margins. Since Indonesia was seen to lack a sufficient managerial class, Nike encouraged the importation of managers from other parts of its Asian operations – a move that often caused friction with the Indonesian workforce (including strikes and the destruction of facilities). In 1991, for instance, the *Far Eastern Economic Review* reported a woman line worker for Nike in Indonesia protesting that "They [the Korean managers] yell at us when we don't make production quotas and if we talk back they cut our wages" (DK 172).[36] While working conditions for women workers have improved, athletic shoe production is still a harmful and exploitative business. The solvents used to glue the soles of these shoes are highly toxic and, even when the extractor fans are working well, the women constantly breathe fumes. Interestingly, the cofounder of Nike, Bill Bowerman, often made shoe prototypes using similar glue solvents and was eventually crippled by them. He developed neuropathy, a degenerative nerve condition often experienced by shoe and hatmakers. Nike opens and closes factories with such speed in its search for cheap labor that its workers are probably spared most of the long-term effects of glue sniffing. But the neuropathy remains in transnational exploitation itself.

To be sure, Nike's labor practices in Asia are unremarkable for late capitalist transnationalism.[37] Subcontractors scour emerging economies for the usual characteristics mentioned above and sufficient infrastructure to get raw materials in and the finished product out within the requisite business cycles. Some of Nike's shoe lines require more skill than others. (Air Jordans, for instance, were still made in South Korea at the Tae Gurang Industrial Company's factory called "T2" long after most of the other production lines had been shifted to Indonesia and China.) In the main, however, the price of the shoe is connected fundamentally to its image much more than the cost of the skill required to make it. Where the artwork, Van Gogh's shoe paintings for instance, might evoke the product-being of a whole community, the image of the athletic shoe provides a status in excess of the performance provided by the shoe's design. Nevertheless, the truth in *pointure* shares much of the epistemological form of the truth in advertising where shoes are concerned. To maintain the responsibility at issue one must continually reconnect these elements of the shoe's aura; that is, the sheer weight of marketing mystique with the object of superexploitation in the developing world, the woman worker.

The condition of women workers in Indonesia is overdetermined by several interlocking factors that facilitate the Nike "miracle." Among those mentioned so far, the nature of the government is vital. Despite the violent resistance to the newly restrictive Pancasila from the moment it was drafted into law in 1984 (which resulted in the Tanjung Priok massacre of protestors by the New Order in September of that year), in general the fate of women in the workforce is guided by the Pancasila's democratic absolutism. Women must know their place as wives and mothers but, when interpellated by the dictates of light industrial need, they must further submit to paternalism in the workplace.[38] Although this does not completely negate the possibility of industrial action (as mentioned, there have been significant strikes against Nike in Indonesia) it minimizes the risk by making protest appear against the foundations of continuing Indonesian nationhood. This limit on worker solidarity is not the monopoly of Indonesia; it is, rather, the unimaginable of contemporary regimes of time/space in capital. The limit always appears to emerge elsewhere.

One of these highly regulated women workers in Indonesia in the 1990s was Sadisah. In 1992 Jeffrey Ballinger, a labor activist who has done much to raise serious questions about Nike's Asian business practices, displayed one of her pay slips in *Harper's Magazine* to make visible, in an obvious way, the cost of Nike's business in the Asian market.[39] In April of that year Sadisah's wage was 14 cents per hour for a total of $1.03 for a 7.5-hour day – significantly less than the government's figure for "minimum physical need." Sadisah, like the other 114 workers on her Nike line, was forced by material need to work long hours of overtime. Ballinger reports that an International Labor Organization survey found that 88 percent of women workers in Indonesia on Sadisah's wage were malnourished. Sadisah herself has come from a peasant community to make Nike's shoes and now can afford to rent a shack without electricity or running water. The cost of her labor to make one pair of Nike athletic shoes is about 12 cents. In the American market these shoes will sell for $80 to $150 a pair.

When Derrida writes of surplus value in his shoe essay he does not consider the maker, not even for a sentence, in the production of surplus value. To raise this specter (of Marx, and more besides) is not simply a question of restitution – to somehow claim or appropriate these shoes for their rightful owner, the shoemaker. Sadisah, on the contrary, remains with the shoe, in its stitching and gluing, just as the shoe stays with her, in her poverty and in her body (the effects of both the vapors, and long-term exposure to the purple lights that have often been used to illuminate the glue employed in the soling process). She exists in the shoe in a way that the capitalist cannot. Where the shoes in Van Gogh's painting leave a trace of the subject as owner, as user, the shoe itself is always already the embodied labor of its maker (yet without the laborer's body). Air Max, Nike's most successful running shoe, illustrates the presence of this Being quite succinctly. The sole is see-through, like Cinderella's shoes, but here it is so that the consumer can see and show that "air is real," as one commentator puts it,[40] that you are indeed walking on compressed air. (It is no coincidence that Air Max is Nike's most fetishized shoe: The 1995 model, for instance, remains a collector's item.) There is the Being of Sadisah, there, where she is entirely absent, see-through, invisible. Her labor is to be walked upon because she is there, in her absence. Note, this is not a realistic representation of embodied labor, which must, necessarily, remain abstract. The Being of Sadisah is an abstraction; whereas "air is real" is an imaginary resolution of this real contradiction (to borrow from Althusser on ideology). But, occasionally, the shoe worker reminds the owner as consumer of her absent presence, for her pricking can chafe the foot, or the sole can burst, leaving the owner disconsolate but aware, briefly, that the air-to-be-seen was a product-being out of sight: the shoes had been made.[41]

In April 1992, Sadisah earned $37 net for her month's labor. Ballinger, an AFLCIO researcher, notes an alarming disparity between this figure and that of the earnings of Michael Jordan at that time. Jordan, the linchpin of Air Jordan marketing, received $20 million from Nike in 1992 for endorsing the shoe that bears his name. Ballinger calculates that it would take 44,492 years for Sadisah to earn this amount based on Nike's payments to her. The disparity lies in the power of the image, in the mystique of "branding," in the unfettered circulation of commodity culture. Yet opposition to the nefarious aspects of such circulation is not uncommon and, as it turns out, Nike has been one of the most prominent targets of transnational labor and consumer resistance. Ballinger's article represented something of a watershed in media awareness of the plight of women workers like Sadisah. Ballinger himself formed a group in 1994, Press for Change, that published a Nike Newsletter to expand public awareness in the United States of the real price of a pair of Nikes.[42] The campaign against Nike intensified both because of labor action in the workplace and a concomitant media activism where Nike least expected it. Jose Ramos Horta, an East Timorese Nobel Peace Prize winner in 1996, encouraged and emboldened American labor and human-rights organizations to get involved in protesting rights abuses in Indonesia (not just in East Timor, but on islands like Java, where Nike's interests were extensive). Global Exchange took up the challenge and, with Press for Change, brought a Nike worker to the United States in 1996 on a consciousness-raising tour. While presence does not simply reverse the logic of aphanisis I have invoked, it remains a forceful answer to the conveniently missing worker in transnational corporate discourse. Cicih Sukaesih had been fired by a Nike subcontractor in Indonesia in 1992 for organizing workers like Sadisah to press for at least Indonesia's minimum wage (about $1.30 a day at that time). In *Reclaiming America*, Randy Shaw recounts the highlights of Sukaesih's American tour. Sukaesih arrived in Washington, D.C., during a fashion industry forum (in which she was not allowed to participate).[43] She had her photograph taken with Kathie Lee Gifford, perhaps America's most famous "reformed" sweatshopper, and also visited a Footlocker store to try on the Nike shoes she made but could not afford to wear. In New York, Sukaesih joined a protest outside a Nike Town (one of the company's superstores) and in Chicago requested a meeting with Michael Jordan, who, predictably, was unavailable. Sukaesih even made a visit to Nike's corporate headquarters in Beaverton, Oregon (another example, according to Phil Knight, of labor activists' "terrorist tactics"). Nobody from management would meet with her or Medea Benjamin of Global Exchange, a PR snafu that only served to intensify media coverage of the tour. Despite a well-oiled image machine, Nike was faced with the same quandary as the philosophers: the question of Being changes dramatically once the shoemaker is acknowledged.[44]

This acknowledgment goes beyond the pious liberal reflex to wear a supportive badge and shoes with a different product label. Newer anti-sweatshop organizations and more established NGOs have built a sustainable human/worker-rights network, despite corporate attempts to buy out such entities in order to shore up their transnational image (Nike, for instance, has promised almost $8 million over a five-year period to one such organization, Global Alliance). In general, the athletic shoe industry is dominated by the empty gesture of voluntary compliance or codes of conduct that lack enforcement procedures. Workers are less isolated, however, than they were a decade ago, and consumer awareness may yet produce the affective responsibility at issue here in a global imaginary. Indeed, the prospects of a more transnational dialogism have been considerably enhanced not just by having a shoe worker testify in consumer markets, but by having NGOs and individuals work on the ground precisely in those areas disavowed in the past. In late August 2000, for instance, Jim Keady, an American former soccer pro, worked in a Nike shoe factory in the suburbs of Jakarta in order to publicize Nike's continuing reliance on paltry wages. The $1.20 he received each day for his labor was not enough to keep him nourished and he fell ill from the ordeal. Responding to Keady's personal campaign, Nike said he had "trivialized and demeaned the lives of Indonesians who work in factories. . . . Given his privileged, Western perspective, Mr. Keady does not understand . . . the value and importance of a job . . . in Indonesia."[45]

Mindful that even Keady's firsthand experience does not do justice to the complexities of corporate culture, let us focus briefly on Beaverton itself, the epicenter of Nike's "global imagery" and a "corporate Xanadu," as Katz calls it. "Nike World Campus" is a key node in the geopolitical imaginary of the chronotope. Of Nike's more than six thousand American workers, most are based in Beaverton. It is an extraordinary think tank devoted to the magic of the commodity form, to the marketing of image. For instance, in the mid-1980s Nike was big but had not yet become a transnational "player" like McDonald's or Coca-Cola. Then, in 1984, the company signed Michael Jordan to its roster and there began a marketing partnership that would give Jordan name recognition beyond belief and Nike global brand power. Consider the "Jordan Flight" television commercial developed at Beaverton in 1985. As Jordan glides toward the basketball rim the soundtrack emphasizes the roar of jet engines. The image is slowed down to enhance the fact that Jordan is in flight; indeed, he stays in the air for ten seconds. This human impossibility is precisely the point: Jordan has become the equivalent of the goddess whose name graces the ad. He can fly. Just before his retirement in 1993 (he has since made a comeback, retired again, and made another comeback), Jordan noted, "What Phil [Knight] and Nike have done is turn me into a dream." Here there is a bizarre correlation with the immiseration of Sadisah and Sukaesih somewhere offscreen in the shoe factory, as if the hyperreality of Jordan's flight is inseparable from the phantom in Air that the worker represents in Nike's sole. It is only in Beaverton, where Adam Smith's old invisible hand is still at work, that these complementary components must be kept apart, unlaced and unglued.

The Nike World Campus at Beaverton is a world removed from the factories in Indonesia. Responding to Katz's questions, Nike employees said the Campus was "like being in a playground" and that it was "a factory for fun" (DK 49). The workforce is young (but not as young as the women workers in Asia) and often display a highly motivated sports mentality.[46] The corporate identity of Nike is predominantly white and male even if the sportspeople who endorse its products are not. (Buildings are named after Nike success stories like Alberto Salazar, Bo Jackson, and Joan Benoit Samuelson.) While this is unremarkable for American capitalism it cannot be separated from the implications of Nike's global sway. The interior walls of each building are drenched with sports paraphernalia and associated imagery (Katz compares them to frat houses). This, however, goes beyond the trappings of jock culture: It is part of the very fabric of corporate life that makes up Nike's "matrix" structure. To read book-length studies of Nike like *Swoosh* and *Just Do It* is to understand that transnational corporatism itself depends on a working logic that is thoroughly masculinist. The activities at Nike management retreats (called "Buttfaces"), corporate parties ("Nike Nites"), and the annual Nike "Beer Relays" are perhaps the most obvious symptoms of the Beaverton mindset. But the dominance of testosterone in Nike activities has still more glaring "high" points: for instance, in December 1979, when the company went public (and Phil Knight became wealthy to the tune of $178 million) no women employees were offered stock in the company (even Carole Fields, onetime controller for Nike and nicknamed "Dragon Lady," got nothing from the stock options). Similarly, even after the decision to move into the emerging and lucrative market for women's aerobic shoes in 1987 (and only after Reebok had profited handsomely from this line), it was several years before women were invited to "the boys' club in Beaverton" (as Katz calls it) to take a more active role in this marketing process (incidentally, this was a financial success, and by 1992 Nike was the leader in the aerobics niche[47]). In the playground, however, the fun is mostly male and insistently so.

The matrix structure at Beaverton must acknowledge the material force of the Asian women workers even as the images it creates are the material reality that denies this link beyond the World Campus. While "exposing the technology" might allow one to "see the air," it also belies the stark contradiction and dependence between two material forces of production, the physicality in the fetishism if you will. Both aspects are integral to the time/space coordinates of the shoe. They are, in Bakhtin's terms, "the knots of narrative that are continually tied and untied" in an apparently empty continuum. Inside the World Campus, the designers, consciously or not, wrestle with the implications of this ineluctable link. Although they all have a "license to dream,"[48] the designers must work with the contractors and subcontractors to render their imagination profitable.[49] The cost of the material components is one consideration, and Nike has, over the years, developed a highly integrated system for bringing together materials made in different parts of the globe. The production of air pockets or sacs, the air that can be seen, is not trusted to the Asian market: the heart of Nike's "technology" is produced in the United States by a company called "Tetra," then shipped to Asia for assembly in the shoe itself. Lightweight leather substitutes like Durabuck are made by a Japanese affiliate. (Nike came up with Durabuck while its lab technicians were working on Michael Keaton's Batboots for *Batman*.) And the designers must also take note of regional variations in color tastes around the globe even though preferences among youth culture often change at rates that are out of sync with the production process. Of course, Nike advocates a high degree of homogenization (a mainstay of economies of scale), something facilitated by the power of the brand, but augments its "branding" with what it calls a "psychographic" view of the marketplace. When Nike designers are indulging in "free association," they are also targeting particular psychic profiles. This is one of the ways that masculinism (and other logics of Being) gets built into the shoe.

Cultural critics find the hard-edged rationalism of marketing anathema to cultural understanding, and yet it seems to me we seriously misapprehend the cultural logic of capital by suppressing the realities of corporate culture while celebrating somewhat traditional symptoms of art in the marketplace. What the Nike psychographic approach attempts is a breakdown of market segmentation in any one production cycle. This is represented as a triangle whose apex is dominated by Nike's leading profile target: the sixteen- to twenty-six-year-old "hardbody" male "sports driver." The fetishistic impulses of this group sets the standards for the rest (including the women's segments). These young males (again, the primary market is in the United States, but global sales continue to expand) will shell out the $80–$170 for "top of the line" models (even this last word is in step with the overall logic). This segment is designated "Max," although it is not reserved solely for the Air Max line. The next segment is called "Perf" (performance) and targets athletes and aspiring athletes who might actually gain from the design technologies in the shoe. Beneath this is the "Core" segment, which is also called the middle or "kill" zone where Nike makes most of its sales. The Core identify with Perf and Max yet usually lack both the body and the psychological investment to make as much use of Nike's high-profile shoes. Eighty percent of Nike's shoes are not used for their intended purpose. (Nike always contests this figure, but gradually and grudgingly "fashion" has pushed aside "athletic" in the symbolic of the shoe that Nike presents.) At the base of the Nike psychographic triangle is the "Entry" segment, those people who must be weaned onto Nikes by an incessant combination of peer-driven, price-driven, and advertising-driven campaigns. While brand loyalty is difficult in the ephemeral life of an athletic shoe (Max, for instance, may choose another line precisely because Core and Entry are choosing theirs), the psychographic approach is also beholden to the paradox of commodity fetishism in general: The consumer must be made to sustain his or her private fantasy even though he or she covets an object or image that is traded publicly. The savvy theorist has an answer to this dilemma, but then so too do Nike's marketing gurus, like Jim Riswold, who says of the psychography: "it never appeared to me as part of some grand strategy. I mean, it's not nineteenth century philosophy" (DK 151). Quite. Commodity desire gets a lot more help than Marx (or Freud for that matter) could envisage. The magic of the fetish requires the magic of money. In 1997, for example, Nike spent $975 million on promotion.

Most of Nike's shoe lines play to and reinforce conventional definitions of masculinity. Just as the Greeks used Nike to symbolize victory in war (at one point they clipped her wings to keep "victory" in

Athens), so Nike laces the sports profile with the language of aggression. Featured shoe models have included Air Assault, Air Barrage, Air Force, Air Magnum Force, Air Raid, and even Air Stab. Other companies in the business have marketed shoes like "Run'N'Gun," "Predator," "Marauder," "Shooter," and "Slasher." (It is noticeable that with the increased focus on every aspect of sneaker production the politics of naming has retreated to the relatively safe havens of cliché, abstraction or technobabble – Air Pegasus, Air Current RW, or Air Accel Low.) The association of sport and violence is not surprising, but it has other repercussions along the chain of affective responsibility than the epistemic violence that produces the superexploitation of Asian women workers. Before considering that in more detail, let us consider the design process of a typical Nike shoe.

For instance, the Air Carnivore was first dreamed up by Bill Worthington in 1992 and remains in many ways an archetypal lesson in Nike's creative logic. The path from idea to actual shoe is a laborious one: out of curiosity Nike employees once sketched out the process of a shoe's development, and the resulting map, cognitive or otherwise, was sixty feet long. Even then, the designer is weighed down by doubt. Worthington muses, "The question now was whether the consumer would be able to appreciate the technology inside the shoe, or to understand its true personality" (DK 159). This is something of my own approach in stressing the chronotope of the shoe. Worthington, however, stops short in his assessment of Air Carnivore's time/space coordinates: "People will tell each other about the Carnivore. They'll say, 'Here's a shoe that represents the aggression of sports'" (DK 159). The aggression takes on another meaning in Pusan, South Korea, where the Carnivores were made. The Carnivores would be one of factory T3's last production runs in 1993 as Nike moved still more production to Indonesia, China, and Vietnam. The name of the shoe is a fitting metaphor for Nike's labor practices: by the end of 1993, 3,500 T3 workers, mostly women, had been laid off. The graffiti on the factory walls included the demand: "We want to be compensated for working our brains out!" (DK 165) They were not.

Meanwhile back in Beaverton, a price structure was worked out for the shoe. Before they were fired (or disavowed in my schema), the T3 workers were paid about $4.50 for every pair of Carnivores made. (This labor cost was considered too high alongside the margins available from workers like Sadisah and Sukaesih elsewhere in Asia.) Nike paid the subcontractor about $29.50 for each pair of Carnivores (60 percent of the price went to product materials). "Landing" the shoe in the consumer market would take another $7.40 (including duties). After taxes and another $15 for running the operation at Nike World Campus, the company would have a $5.50 profit built into the shoe. The retailer would pay about $70 for the Carnivore, the consumer up to $60 more than that depending upon demand and promotions (if the line becomes coveted, the price can soar – a little retail hoarding can exacerbate this effect, as it did with the infamous Air Max '95 whose margins expanded by up to 40 percent). While the women in Pusan look for employment in the emerging service industries, Nike will chase "nations farther down the developmental ladder" (DK 168) – places where a $130 pair of sneakers can still be made, not worn.[50]

The Air Carnivore looks like it could eat jobs and dollars as fast as it creates them. It is predominantly green (when first pitched at an annual sporting goods show in Atlanta the Nike salesperson barked "Vegetarians beware") and appears to abjure the natural contours of a foot. The bulkiness of the shoe is an illusion, since the synthetic materials used render it quite light. The sole is purple and black, and deeply striated into "pods" of supporting rubber. The upper of the shoe is deformed by several straps of Velcro which, like the advertising images, hold the shoe together around the foot. These straps are part of an "anti-inversion" collar which is both heavily indebted to technobabble and to a desire to prevent the ankle from turning should this cross-trainer actually be used for cross-training. The top of the shoe is dominated by a third Velcro strap which sticks, rather than stitches, the subject in the shoe (to complicate the metaphor so heavily analyzed by Derrida and the series of allusions I have made thus far). The inside of the shoe sports a Neoprene sock. This "Dynamic Fit Sleeve" allows the foot to move and breath inside a shoe whose outside suggests completely the opposite – anti-inversion indeed. We are far removed from Van Gogh's peasant shoes here, but other peasants are not completely erased: in the belly of the Air Carnivore a tiny label testifies "Made in South Korea."

The belly of a shoe? Worthington, the designer, is unequivocal: "This shoe is like an animal. It's like a living, breathing thing instead of an inanimate consumer product" (DK 127). Just as the Greeks anthropomorphized a symbol of military success, so our young designer gives life to the fetish of his desire. And what inspired this fearful symmetry? Worthington, like other Nike designers, is a self-professed "culture pirate" and, unlike most others at the World Campus, the designers often draw their imagery from outside the world of sports. The Air Carnivore owed its animal nature as much to the films *Jurassic Park* and the *Alien* series as it did to man's "natural" aggression (when Katz interviewed Worthington, the latter's office featured stills from *Alien*). Worthington also drew up a cartoon character to "image" the shoe's effect on its owner. An average kid, "Bert Starkweather," becomes "Bolt Stingwater" (Luke Skywalker?) in his Carnivores and proceeds to "win drag races on foot and step on people's faces" (DK 128). Could it be that this creativity never leaves the shoe, but becomes part of its affective image, its commodity aura, its product-being?

Obviously, the suggestion is not that merely by buying into the image one becomes the character that the designer projects but, nevertheless, if the main point of such consumption is not in fact the practical utilization of sporting technology for sport, then how the shoe is made and marketed stands in for (and contradicts) a corporate claim that is otherwise "ethically neutral." In contemporary capitalism, the violence of representation is also, and always already, the violence of production and consumption. To separate off the moment and malevolence of Image from the Being in production and consumption is to collude with precisely those avatars of this epoch who claim that image is everything and representation is, in itself, the sole arbiter of debates about the mode of production in and outside culture. The chronotope of the shoe suggests that the time and space of athletic shoe production across the globe curve toward simultaneity but in fact maintain context-specific criteria that appear to render them incommensurable. The inside/outside of commodity production, like the inside/outside of the shoe itself, is indeed inseparable, but how easy has it become to reduce the sign of worker presence/absence in production to a label tucked away from view? Two examples may elaborate the cycle of violence that is endemic to the production and circulation of commodities at the moment when fetishism must disavow its responsibility to the real, and indeed, to Reality.

Nike is taking greater control over its production and distribution operations in Asia as a result of the bad press it has received about the labor practices it fosters. (The Code of Conduct it trumpets still sidesteps the question of independent verification, but there is no doubt that Nike has been forced to reveal more detail about its day-to-day operations in Asia – it has even printed the addresses of some of the factories where it subcontracts.) Yet responsibility is a very relative state of mind in Nike's corporate ideology, since when accused of crass exploitation of its Asian workers Nike's spokespeople continue to maintain a dogged moral neutrality. This line of argument proposes that either problems occur because of the nature of the market or that Nike can hardly be held responsible for the internal socioeconomic (and political) conditions of the countries where it bases its production operations. The record, as I have already implied, underlines that Nike, like many TNCs, actively seeks and supports conditions of this kind. In addition, a program Nike describes as "Futures" exacerbates poor labor relations because, by securing future orders from retailers six to eight months in advance, the tendency is to speed up production quotas in Asia and reduce flexibility in the hours of work on the line. Other spinoff practices within this mode of production include the nightly confinement of young women workers to the dormitories within the factory grounds.[51] The apex of these violations is, of course, the wage itself, and here violence begets violence. In Serang, near Jakarta, in 1992 Nike workers went on strike and demanded a 15 percent pay increase. While this may sound excessive to some, in fact it amounts to only 24 cents a day at 1992 exchange rates. When the local subcontractor, a South Korean, refused to bargain, the women workers smashed windows at the factory and overturned furniture. Rather than jeopardize the production cycle, the owner caved in.[52] But, as the Korean workers in Pusan testify, workers take a risk with such activity: Nike can "just do it" elsewhere. In the five years leading up to this strike the company had closed twenty of its Asian factories and opened another thirty-five. And anyway, the TNC can say that any industrial action is the result of the contractors' malfeasance, not the company that pulls their strings.

But if the violence of production has material effects on workers like Sadisah, then there is a concomitant violence in the culture of consumption that accompanies it. Nike's psychographic approach to the market has had another valence in the symbolic of the shoe: for American inner-city youth racked by unemployment and the lure of drug culture, the athletic shoe offers *status*. Again, the athletic shoe company will claim that the imaging of a particular desire is not an endorsement of its consequences, which are, in the first place, overdetermined by a host of other causal factors. But when Nike's cofounder William Bowerman proclaims that one should "play by the rules, but be ferocious" the difficulty is believing that the second emotion can be contained by the civic duty of the first. Nike themselves have not "played by the rules" to the extent that (according to *Swoosh*) they have used bribery in the past, kited checks, "dumped" inventory, and avoided custom duties.[53] And, if Nike's labor practices are anything to go by, the rule in athletic shoe production is that there are no rules, at least none that need strict compliance. One reason the slogan "Just do it!" is so enticing is surely that it imagines a world bereft of rules, a world in which "being ferocious" is some Darwinian compulsion. Do we really believe that the slogan "Just do it by the rules" would have the same effect in the competitive frenzy that is the athletic shoe market? And even if the desire to win in athletic competition can be characterized as "ferocious," is that the same desire communicated in such Nike models as "Air Stab" and "Air Carnivore"? The goddess of victory is smiling.

In 1989 Michael Eugene Thomas was strangled to death by his friend David Martin for his $115 pair of Air Jordans. The same year Johnny Bates was shot to death for his Air Jordans, and Raheem Wells was murdered for his Nikes. In Chicago in 1990 there were, on average, fifteen violent crimes committed per month over athletic shoes (up to fifty a month if one includes warm-up jackets and other sports-related garments).[54] Jordan and Spike Lee have been singled out in the past for their Nike advertising campaigns of the late 1980s in which "Just do it!" became a street knowledge that dovetails with the "ferocious" reality of urban crime. In their defense, Nike played the race card by suggesting that it was typical of race bias in the media that African Americans were being blamed for contributing to the violence already heaped at the doorstep of low-income African American communities. To the extent that white celebrities are not routinely singled out for their contributions to cultures of violence (dozens of Hollywood names immediately come to mind), Nike's point is well taken, but the company's race relations contain their own history of bias. As we have seen, while Michael Jordan made $20 million a year for footwear endorsements, Nike's predominantly white American marketing managers pitted Asian workers against one another (Korean versus Indonesian, Indonesian versus Chinese) in a game of wages tag in which the only defining qualities of racial esteem are the profit margins that accrue to their location. In the United States, Operation PUSH, the Chicago-based civil-rights group, mounted a campaign against Nike because of its poor record in minority hiring in the United States and because of its failure to provide support in the communities where a disproportionate amount of Nike products are sold (disproportionate in terms of income to sales, not total sales). PUSH also discovered that, at the time, Nike had no African American executives and did not use a single African American-run company to promote its products. Nike was cashing in on the image of African American athletes while cashing out on any responsibility to African American communities in general.[55] Naturally, Nike's public-relations department has worked on these issues. (TNCs usually have philanthropic programs – which in some cases provide tax breaks – to ward off the accusation that they are in the business of economic exploitation.) Nevertheless, the larger issue remains whether a transnational corporation should be held accountable for the forms of identification with its "global power brand."

The fetish is a lure. Nike spends millions of dollars each year to cultivate an "emotional tie" (as Phil Knight describes it) to the athletic shoe but disavows this connection at the point where its psychography facilitates an irrational logic of possession. Yet this is intrinsic to the commodity form and does not resolve itself in fine-tuning an image attached (with Velcro) to it. To murder someone for their Nike shoes is irrational in the extreme but is symptomatic of, among other socioeconomic factors, the culture of possession in general. Van Gogh's shoes may well have symbolized the eclipse of valorized peasant communities (certainly this is Heidegger's belief), but the fetishistic overinvestment in the athletic shoe is no less significant: it conjures the madness and malevolence of a particular form of globalism that is itself deracinating peasant communities in different parts of the world *simultaneously and in the same affective space*. In the chronotope of the shoe, pricking stitches Sadisah to Thomas: the maps must be redrawn continually to account for this time/space continuum.

Commodity fetishism is not the same as the psychological compulsion sketched by Freud, but the centrifugal aura of the athletic shoe within contemporary transnational capitalism shows how one may be dialogically implicated with the other. Branding accentuates this overlap in the psychic and economic coordinates of the newest World Order – a relationship that is crucial to athletic shoe culture. Violence, epistemic and real, is not an accidental by-product of the matrix of contemporary commodity production but is vital to it, while the "costs" of production and consumption are necessarily rendered invisible or inconsequential. For Nike, the desire to expand sales far outweighs the use-value of their athletic shoes. In 1993, 77 percent of American young men said they wanted a pair of Nikes (even if they could not afford to buy them); some knew more than a dozen of the models available that year; others even knew the stock numbers. In the "teenager to young adult male" bracket, Americans owned more than ten pairs of sporting footwear *each*. In 1997, 350 million pairs of athletic shoes were sold in the American market alone (although increases in sales have slowed and, in some markets, have actually shrunk).

Michael Haines has a Nike obsession. When interviewed by Katz he had already collected almost forty pairs. Interestingly, his "fetish" (as his mother calls it) began in the early 1980s when he first spotted the see-through air sole of the Air Max. His desire, piqued by the appearance of absence, became at one point almost uncontrollable – he was forced to hide new pairs around the house and, when that aroused suspicion, he persuaded his father to buy them instead. Most of the shoes have never been worn and are revered almost solely for their associative effects. To read what Haines has to say about his shoes is to face the superaddressee of commodity production: "They have to face backward on the shelf because they're so much more . . . beautiful from behind"; "if I could have a new pair every day"; "I still love to come home during school breaks and come up here to open the doors" [of the cupboard that houses his collection]; "I love them. I love thinking about opening the box for the first time. I love taking them out. Just talking about them gets me . . . I don't know" (DK 262–63). The sexual dynamic of Haines's attachment may be exaggerated and frankly bizarre, but few CEOs in the athletic shoe business would be upset by a desire directly connected to a company's advertising machine. How much commodity desire is enough desire? Can this be calibrated, or is the love of these shoes incalculable such that the violence of the sweatshop and the street is an inadvertent by-product for which responsibility is an empty concept? Nike does not merely satisfy a need for athletic footwear, it deliberately creates a need far in excess of what is necessary (this, of course, is one of the meanings of capitalism). Yet conventional wisdom would have it that Haines hurts no one by coveting his shoes. In truth, his personal fixation has been purchased and in that exchange his desire is globally localized (to borrow once more from contemporary TNC lore) just as Sukaesih and Sadisah's labor has been interpellated in an international network of capital exchange. The names and the products may change, but as long as the logic of these connections remains predominantly unimagined, then the commodity fetish will continue to be naturalized: the ontology of the commodity, the Being of the shoe, will present itself as a normative Being of culture. And what seems like an adjunct to cultural discourse is in fact what silently defines it.

Sadisah does not speak to us in these pages, and neither does Sukaesih (even through reported speech).[56] The shoes don't speak either (although, on this point, the Nike designers are close to the philosophy of art proposed by Heidegger, Jameson, and Derrida[57]). Even by acknowledging Sukaesih's presence in the United States and foregrounding the immense, and generally successful, campaigns to defamiliarize the governing tenets of global sneaker production, this record does not undo the cognitive fix in "Just Do It!" The athletic shoe will pass out of TNC production exploitation not because people will stop running but because the "victory" invoked is not about running.[58] Indeed, the chronotope of the shoe is only about the essence of the shoe at all to the extent that such a commodity is a narrative about the international division of labor. Similarly, Indonesia is not miraculously mapped (even as it is integrated into global circuits of commodity production and exchange) by the affective points of time and space that I have sketched above (and no handy reference to shadow theater will wrest it from that chiaroscuro). Shoe production does not give us the magic key to the intense vicissitudes of Indonesian history since independence. All I argue here is that the athletic shoe industry has inscribed itself in a particular form of nation building that is nevertheless uninterested in the Subject that such a process confers. To imagine the links in the aura of the shoe is what must be risked if criticism is to be responsibly positioned in global analysis. For the commodity, the chronotope becomes something of a heuristic device, "the place where the knots of narrative are tied and untied," but a place that is always displaced by the logic of desire in the marketplace and by the desire for a logic that is not stitched by authoritarian regimes of truth. The imagination required is less surefooted not only because the product-being of the contemporary commodity is dispersed fantastically, but because there is no language adequate to the global representation of the worker. While Nike has global imagery, there is yet no global imaginary that can transform the developmental ladder that the TNC typically exploits. So even when activists counter corporate tokenism by organizing independent labor watchdogs like the Workers Rights Consortium, there remains a tremendously powerful ideological machine that says such efforts are blind to the good that economic exploitation brings. Nicholas Kristof and Sheryl WuDunn, for instance, blithely contend that sweatshops are the economic linchpin of Asian modernization. ("They're dirty and dangerous. They're also the major reason Asia is back on track.")[59] In the nineteenth century, a similar paucity of global imagination allowed the British to believe that the opium trade was performing the same miracle. If antisweatshop organizations head off the descent into cynicism, smugness, and glibness, the structural logic of commodity production and consumption weighs heavily on counterhegemonic discourse. Indeed, merely by detailing the deaths that result from a psychic overinvestment in the commodity, one does not break the production of desire that informs it. What then, is the point of chronotopic critique?

I have borrowed chronotope from Bakhtin as he borrowed it from Ukhtomsky (and, indeed, Einstein), "as a metaphor (almost, but not entirely)"[60] to draw together seemingly disparate elements of the world system attached (artists, workers, philosophers, inner-city youth, and cultural critics alike) by affective responsibility. We have no alibi for this responsibility (the boycott of selected consumer items is ultimately beside the point) because, as Bakhtin reminds us, we cannot claim to be anywhere else but where we are in Being. Cultural criticism must do much more than express concern for the wasted humanity of capitalist production (a somewhat sentimental, humanist answerability) by making the deracinated Being of the commodity form imaginable. But this responsibility is also about meaning, which Bakhtin suggests can only become part of our social experience when it takes on "the form of a sign." The shoe is not perhaps the "hieroglyph" that Bakhtin had in mind and that is partly why his formulation has been refigured in my argument by the "hieroglyph" that Marx identified. Just as our philosophers overlook the maker, so Bakhtin's hypostatization of the novel placed formal limits on the range of social experience imaginable. That the novel can conjure the world of commodity culture is undeniable; the test of a geopolitical imaginary is whether it can imagine how the commodity can conjure in the opposite direction. This is not ultimately about the cognitive abilities of the cultural critic (or his or her humanist inclinations) but, more importantly, about forms of collective reciprocity disrupting the aura of the commodity that anxiously purports to embrace a world economy with its own cultural transnationalism. This kind of answerability does not exclude individualist efforts like Keady's to dramatize the human costs of globalizing capitalist consumer desire, since he evokes a responsibility that can catalyze collectivity across borders. To imagine the world otherwise continues to be the challenge, not by individual volition, however, but by alternative forms of socialization. Only then will the shoe be on the other foot.

Notes

1   Karl Marx, *Capital*, vol. 1, trans. Ben Fowkes (New York: Penguin, 1976), 163.
2   The main reason for this is primarily the shoe's contradictory status within and between commodity fetishism

and its psychosocial cognates. This is a huge and separate debate in its own right, and one that dances among the lines that follow. For a wideranging and suggestive collection in this regard, see Emily Apter and William Pietz, eds., *Fetishism as Cultural Discourse* (Ithaca, N.Y.: Cornell University Press, 1993). Appropriately, the cover of this book features a pair of shoes bound tightly together – it's an illustration by Mary Kelly entitled "Supplication."

3   Here I allude to Jacques Derrida's reading of Martin Heidegger in "Restitutions of the Truth in Pointing [*pointure*]," in *The Truth in Painting*, trans. Geoffrey Bennington and Ian McCleod (Chicago: University of Chicago Press, 1987). In general, I use Lacan's interpretation of Jones on aphanisis to underline the difference between the meaning that is ascribed to the commodity and the "disappearance" of the labor that marks its very possibility. The "fading" of the worker as subject is a function of her relationship to the commodity form under capitalism.

4   The geopolitical imagination eschews the totalizing impulse of the dialectic at the same time as it resists the aestheticizing tendencies of the dialogic. If this imagination is indeed "representable," the commodity under transnational capitalism is its most prescient instance.

5   Part of this reevaluation is manifest in the work of William Pietz, particularly in a series of articles entitled "The Problem of the Fetish" published in *Res: A Journal of Aesthetics and Anthropology* 9 (Spring 1985): 12–13, 13 (Spring 1987): 23–45, and 16 (Autumn 1988): 105–23, and in his essay "Fetishism and Materialism" in *Fetishism As Cultural Discourse*, ed. William Pietz and Emily Apter (Ithaca, N.Y.: Cornell University Press, 1993), 119–51. I must say, however, that Pietz's general rejection of what he characterizes as "semiological" readings of Marx on fetishism seriously underestimates the significance of the imagination and the imaginary in commodity desire. The affective responsibility I explore is predicated on a materialist approach to semiosis.

6   This, of course, is not how Bakhtin uses *responsibility*, which, in his early essays at least, is a means to foreground an ethical responsibility in aesthetics that is often antagonistic to the neo-Kantian Marburg school from which Bakhtin nevertheless drew sustenance. For Bakhtin's sense of responsibility ("answerability"), see his *Art and Answerability*, trans. Vadim Liapunov, ed. Michael Holquist and Vadim Liapunov (Austin: University of Texas Press, 1990). What I will attempt to do with both Bakhtinian answerability and chronotope is reinscribe them within an economy of difference that does not resolve itself in an aesthetic "ought." The globalization of commodity culture answers traditional notions of authoring with the magic of the fetish: It "speaks" to them. But it also marks out new territories of practical engagement for the academic, for whom responsibility cannot remain an "academic" inquiry. For this sense of responsibility, see, for instance, Gayatri Chakravorty Spivak, "Responsibility," *boundary* 2 (Fall 1994): 19–64.

7   See Mikhail Bakhtin, "Forms of Time and of the Chronotope in the Novel: Notes towards a Historical Poetics," in *The Dialogic Imagination*, trans. Caryl Emerson and Michael Holquist, ed. Michael Holquist (Austin: University of Texas Press, 1981), 84–258. The chronotope has engendered intense disputes among Bakhtinians. My effort here is to accentuate its spatial possibilities in the critique of the commodity form.

8   See Michael Holquist, *Dialogism: Bakhtin and His World* (London: Routledge, 1990), 108–25.

9   Bakhtin, "Forms of Time," 253.

10   Katerina Clark and Michael Holquist, *Mikhail Bakhtin* (Cambridge, Mass.: Harvard University Press, 1984), 278.

11   Bakhtin, "Forms of Time," 280.

12   Fredric Jameson, *Postmodernism; or, The Cultural Logic of Late Capitalism* (Durham, N.C.: Duke University Press, 1991).

13   Gayatri Chakravorty Spivak, "Can the Subaltern Speak?" in *Marxism and the Interpretation of Culture*, ed. Cary Nelson and Lawrence Grossberg (Urbana: University of Illinois Press, 1988), 271–313.

14   The culture of sport is very big business in the United States: even in the early 1990s it already represented a market of more than $60 billion.

15   Donald Katz, *Just Do It: The Nike Spirit in the Corporate World* (New York: Random House, 1994), 9. Subsequent references to this work will be included in the main text as DK plus page number.

16   In addition to the book by Katz, Nike has been eulogized and criticized in J. B. Strasser and Laurie Becklund, *Swoosh: The Unauthorized Story of Nike and the Men Who Played There* (New York: Harper, 1993). The "swoosh" is Nike's trademark – vaguely reminiscent of the goddess's wing but more evocative of a secret diacritic. Such is the brand recognition of Nike that it can market all manner of shoes and clothing merely by adding the "swoosh."

17   These figures are reported in Andrew Hsiao, "Standing Up to the Swoosh," *Village Voice*, 10 October 2000, 41–43.

18   See Hsiao, "Standing Up to the Swoosh."

19   This, therefore, is not a humanist response to the inhumanity of the commodity for the worker. In *Capital*, vol. 1, Marx is quite explicit about the twofold character of embodied labor in the commodity and its connection to the socialization of consciousness. The issue of embodied labor must be kept separate from that of the worker as commodity, or as an exploitable cost of production.

20   Nike also makes/has made athletic shoes in South Korea, Taiwan, Vietnam, Bangladesh, and China. These countries may be interchangeable for transnational capital but they are not for this argument.

21   See Aijaz Ahmad, *In Theory* (London: Verso, 1992), 97. A further problem, as Ahmad well knows, is that even if one focuses one's critique in relation to a national paradigm, the necessary expertise calls into question the globalism of the critique itself, and not just the blithe country hopping of the TNC. The answerability of theory is bound by a cognitive shortfall, one that prescribes and denatures even the most ardent openness to global others.

22   The U.S. Central Intelligence Agency's role in this is still hotly debated (it was clearly involved in the civil war of the 1950s), as are the consequences for American foreign policy in the aftermath of the genocide that swept Indonesia at that time (the estimates of murdered PKI members, sympathizers, and anti-Suharto supporters of all persuasions range from 250,000 to one million). By 1967 Sukarno's power was effectively nullified and opposition to Suharto had either "disappeared" or was languishing in prison (in the late 1960s Indonesia could boast more than 100,000 political prisoners). A critical account of the coup is provided in Benedict R. O'G. Anderson and R. T. McVey, *A Preliminary Analysis of the October 1, 1965, Coup in Indonesia* (Ithaca, N.Y.: Cornell University Press, 1971). A useful, if general, reading of the period can be found in Robert Cribb and Colin Brown, *Modern Indonesia* (London: Longman, 1995).

23   We are still too close to the events of 1998–99 in East Timor to gauge the success of East Timorese independence. At that time, the Indonesian military and its sponsored thugs, usually termed "militia," officially withdrew from East Timor and a UN peace-keeping contingent led by Australia took up positions in Dili, the capital, and elsewhere. Little, if any, mention was made of Western, particularly American, machinations in the invasion of 1975 (or, for instance, the military and economic support provided by Australia to Suharto's regime afterward). Indeed, the international community has trodden gingerly over the issue of Indonesian violence in the region in order to maintain its sinuous ties to Indonesia's far more important geopolitical economy. Again, this schema of desire and disavowal (with its attendant diplomatic amnesia) is deeply embedded in the logic of globalization. For a polemical critique of the Indonesian invasion of East Timor, see Matthew Jardine, *East Timor: Genocide in Paradise* (Tucson, Ariz.: Odonian Press, 1995).

24   To borrow from Benedict Anderson's famous formulation, the Pancasila are about as good an example of how communities get "imagined" as one could find (the principles are belief in God, national unity, humanitarianism, people's sovereignty, and social justice and prosperity). Sukarno kept them sufficiently vague to smooth over the obvious divisions that racked the Indonesian archipelago in the aftermath of colonization. If the geopolitical imagination merely replays the deficiencies of the imagined community epitomized in the Pancasila, then it must fail as an adequate critical apparatus.

25   See, for instance, D. Cherchichovsky and O. E. Meesook, *Poverty in Indonesia: A Profile* (Washington, D.C.: World Bank, 1984); and C. Iluch, *Indonesia: Wages and Employment* (Washington, D.C.: World Bank, 1985).

26   Consider the World Bank monograph *Indonesia: Strategy for a Sustained Reduction in Poverty* (Washington, D.C.: World Bank, 1990). The World Bank reports that in 1987 30 million Indonesians lived in poverty (17 percent of the population at that time). Indonesia had one of the lowest per capita incomes, lowest life expectancy, and lowest number of doctors per capita in the world (1 doctor for 9,460 people). The World Bank recommends that, because of the limited feasibility of expanding Indonesia's rice farming, the country embark on a course of light industrial, labor-intensive manufacturing. Several years (and millions of Nike shoes) later, the World Bank reports (in *Indonesia: Environment and Development* [Washington, D.C.: World Bank, 1994]), that the problem is overindustrialization from the expansion and inclusion of the workforce in manufacturing (by the end of the decade, this represented 45 percent of Indonesia's GDP). The World Bank asks where Indonesia is going to get the foreign capital to sustain such an industrial workforce and wonders at the same time whether the severe pollution (particularly on Java) is a catastrophe waiting to happen. Income, life expectancy, and the number of doctors have all improved, but these reports reveal that the World Bank, foreign governments, and foreign

corporations have all played a part in exacerbating underlying systemic problems in Indonesia. The effects of greater pollution, for instance, and indeed of industrialization in general, may well lower life expectancy in the years to come. While there is little rigidity to developmental models in Asia, the experience of urban centers like Jakarta and Taibei might give the World Bank some pause about the prospects of Beijing or Shanghai.

27   Unless the selling of a representation itself is at stake. While there is no space here to detail the intricacies of "cultural diplomacy," it is clear that the Indonesian government has attempted in the past to sell an image of the nation that provides a cultural compensation for its otherwise authoritarian operations – and that foreign governments and corporations are entirely complicit with this process (since to overlook a massacre or two might garner economic preferences). See, for instance, Clifford Geertz's trenchant assessment of the "Festival of Indonesia" in the United States in 1991 in "The Year of Living Culturally," *New Republic*, 21 October 1991, 30–36; and Brian Wallis, "Selling Nations," *Art in America* 79 (September 1991): 85–91.

28   One of the best English-language studies is provided by Benedict R. O'G. Anderson, *Language and Power: Exploring Political Cultures in Indonesia* (Ithaca, N.Y.: Cornell University Press, 1990). See also J. D. Legge, *Indonesia* (Sydney: Prentice Hall of Australia, 1980); and Leslie Palmier, ed., *Understanding Indonesia* (Aldershot, England: Gower, 1985).

29   For instance, the infamous *Cultuurstelsel*, or Forced Cultivation System (which basically paid for the Netherlands' debts, costs of war, and public works programs *in Holland* from 1830 to 1869), is an object lesson in colonial excess *and* modes of labor exploitation in Indonesia.

30   Sigmund Freud, "Fetishism," trans. Joan Riviere, in vol. 21 of *The Standard Edition of the Complete Psychological Works of Sigmund Freud* (London: Hogarth, 1961), 154.

31   Most of the innovative work in this area does not just take issue with the normative function that Freud provides for this "minor perversion" but unpicks the model of masculinity it seems to imply. This includes feminist appropriations and renegotiations that, while not necessarily complementary, have "feminized the fetish" in significant ways. See, for instance, Donald Kuspit, "The Modern Fetish," *Artforum*, October 1988, 132–40, in which he argues that some contemporary women artists fetishistically mimic the phallic mother in order to attach the power of birth to the creation of their objects. Researching the *aliénistes* (as the nineteenth-century French psychiatrists often called themselves), Jann Matlock reinterprets the phenomenon of women as clothing fetishists in "Delirious Disguises, Perverse Masquerades, and the Ghostly Female Fetishist," *Grand Street* (Summer 1995): 157–71. In a highly original reading of fetishism's economic and psychic interrelations, Linda Williams explores how ambivalent phallocentrism can structure even the conventional masculinist narratives of hardcore pornography in "Fetishism and the Visual Pleasure of Hard Core: Marx, Freud, and the 'Money Shot,'" *Quarterly Review of Film and Video* 11, no. 2 (1989): 23–42.

32   Emily Apter, *Feminizing the Fetish* (Ithaca, N.Y.: Cornell University Press, 1991), 2.

33   And these are many, especially as they slide into and contradict Marx's metaphors for ideology. For a provocative reading of the function of metaphor for Marx's concepts, see W. J. T. Mitchell, *Iconography: Image, Text, Ideology* (Chicago: University of Chicago Press, 1986). While not subscribing to a Marxist position, Mitchell is careful to distinguish the tactical, historical deployment of metaphors in Marx's arguments. What can and cannot be seen in the commodity fetish remains vital to the present polemic but as an indication of a continuing dissymmetry between visualization and imagination.

34   Jean Baudrillard, *Simulations*, trans. Paul Foss, Paul Patton, and Philip Beitchman (New York: Semiotext[e], 1983).

35   Indeed, the proletarianization of Asian women emphasizes either dexterity or eyesight and often both. For a keen analysis of the treatment of women workers under transnational capitalism, see Annette Fuentes and Barbara Ehrenreich, *Women in the Global Factory* (Boston: South End Press, 1983).

36   The disciplinary zeal of the managers is reinforced by the ideological underpinnings of the Pancasila, which encourage dutiful submission and *ibuism*, the belief that a woman should primarily act as a mother without demanding power or prestige in return. Clearly, women workers have resisted every element of this desire, despite the threat of wage cuts or dismissal.

37   Yet the higher Nike's profile, the more vocal the resistance against such business practices has become. For capitalist investors, however, Nike is an exemplary organization. In 1993 *Money* magazine included Nike in a list of six American companies who offered investors returns of up to 47 percent per annum. See Ellen Stark, "Making Money on America's Top Money," *Money*, June 1993, 114–17.

38   The conservative reinterpretation of the Pancasila as a document that supports patriarchy is detailed in Cribb

and Brown, *Modern Indonesia*. For an important essay on the enlistment of young peasant women into the Indonesian industrial workforce, see Diane L. Wolf, "Linking Women's Labor with the Global Economy: Factory Workers and Their Families in Rural Java," in *Women Workers and Global Restructuring*, ed. Kathryn Ward (Ithaca, N.Y.: Cornell University Press, 1990), 25–47. In *Factory Daughters* (Berkeley: University of California Press, 1992) Wolf has written one of the most extensive and detailed analyses of the effect of globalization on Javanese women workers. For some pertinent discussion of the cultural representations of the effects of the Pancasila for women, see Tineke Hellwig, *In the Shadow of Change: Images of Women in Indonesian Literature* (Berkeley: University of California Press, 1994).

39   See Jeffrey Ballinger, "The New Free Trade Heel," *Harper's Magazine*, August 1992, 46–47. In 1993 Ballinger appeared in a special edition of "Street Stories" on CBS that focused on Nike's operations in Indonesia. Ironically, the main factory featured was about the cleanest shoe manufacturing plant on the planet. Nevertheless, the program reported that a strike at another Indonesian plant had resulted in twenty-two workers being "suspended," and it did document the practice of confining the women workers to the plant dormitories. Katz (*Just Do It*) provides plenty of details on this and other evidence of Nike's misdeeds in Asia, but his critique remains a long way from condemnation.

40   Quoted in Strasser and Becklund, *Swoosh*, 501.

41   It also reminds the business community of Nike's economic vulnerability. Michael Janofsky, for instance, recalls the misfortune of Quincy Watt, the American runner, whose Nike shoes came apart during a race at the world track and field championships in Stuttgart in August 1993. Watt, an Olympic champion, finished fourth. Janofsky uses this as an occasion to discuss a quarter in which Nike's earnings dropped. He suggests that "Just Do It" be amended to "Just Glue It." See Michael Janofsky, "Market Place," *New York Times*, 24 September 1993, D6.

42   Much of Ballinger's activism on Nike in Indonesia is recorded in Jeff Ballinger and Claes Olsson, eds., *Behind the Swoosh: The Struggle of Indonesians Making Nike Shoes* (Uppsala: Global Publications Foundation, 1997).

43   Shaw's book provides a fairly detailed chapter on the human- and labor-rights campaigns directed at Nike in the 1990s as part of a general argument on new forms of activism in the United States. See Randy Shaw, *Reclaiming America: Nike, Clean Air, and the New National Activism* (Berkeley: University of California Press, 1999).

44   This is a subtext that runs through the collection *No Sweat*, ed. Andrew Ross (New York: Verso, 1997). The campaign against sweatshop practices in the United States has achieved numerous victories, but, as Ross points out, eradicating the worst excesses of the fashion industry does not remove the tyranny of substandard wages as a whole in clothing and shoe production. And, given the sharp mobility of contemporary transnational corporations, continued vigilance must be maintained to ensure that subcontracting does not simply reproduce sweatshop conditions in a new location. The latter is a major reason for a company to go global in the first place.

45   See Hsiao, "Standing Up to the Swoosh," 43.

46   For more on the cultlike campus at Beaverton, see James Servin, "Camp Nike: It's Not a Job, It's a Lifestyle," *Harper's Bazaar*, June 1994, 46–48. In another odd twist in economic history, a psychology professor suggests that the model for the Nike World Campus was the athletic sports camps provided in Eastern Europe under Communism!

47   See Kate Bednarski, "Convincing Male Managers to Target Women Customers," *Working Woman*, June 1993, 23–24, 28. Not surprisingly, the language of this article is generally in step with capitalist consciousness. There is no recognition, for instance, that Nike had been "targeting" women workers for quite some time. In effect, the women managers disavow the women workers just like their male counterparts, although that is not the same as saying that a woman's identification with the shoe is simply the equivalent of male fetishism; it is to acknowledge, however, that male fetishism is hegemonic. For an article that reconnects the woman as producer to woman as consumer, see Cynthia Enloe, "The Globetrotting Sneaker," *Ms.*, March–April 1995, 10–15. For more on this form of global critique, see Cynthia Enloe, *The Morning After: Sexual Politics at the End of the Cold War* (Berkeley: University of California Press, 1993).

48   Katz (*Just Do It*, 130) describes a process of invention at Nike World Campus that is indistinguishable from artistic reverie and is nurtured "in a general ambience of youthful, free-associative creativity that is invariably tempered by some flavor of sophisticated wit."

49   On this point, labor is the deciding factor: "No matter how inspired a new technical design, style statement, or marketing campaign, the entire industry's productive processes were still based on how fast the women in Pusan, South Korea, and Indonesia could glue together by hand up to twenty-five pieces of a single shoe" (ibid., 174).

50   Vietnam and Bangladesh are more recent additions to this game.

51   The factory dormitories are widespread, but this has been a particular feature of Nike's Chinese operations. The retort has been that this is for "security reasons" and has nothing to do with the fear that the workers might become romantically involved, want to start families, or even choose another line of work.

52   See Mark Clifford, "Spring in Their Step," *Far Eastern Economic Review*, 5 November 1992, 56–57. The title refers to Nike's practice of hopping from one Asian country to the next in search of cheap labor.

53   None of this is particularly surprising for a capitalist organization. Nike's annual reports detail several other practices that may or may not abide by the rules of risk management for capital. The company uses both derivatives and hedging as financial instruments, both of which are subject to greater extremes of volatility than are most accounting practices. Interestingly, in fiscal 1997, Nike issued about $300 million of debt securities, the proceeds from which were swapped into Dutch guilders, ostensibly to smooth the financing of European operations. Since the company also hedges using currency contracts, it might be interesting to trace the life of these guilders. Obviously, that the Dutch were the primary colonial force in Indonesia is an irony easily missed by Nike's accountants.

54   For more on the culture of killing for sportswear, see Rick Telander, "Senseless," *Sports Illustrated*, 14 May 1990, 36–49. See also Katz, *Just Do It*, 268–70. On Tuesday, 19 December 1995, in New York a man went berserk in a shoe store after being told that the Nike hightops he had ordered had not yet arrived. He pulled out a 9mm pistol and shot dead five people. The man had been previously diagnosed with schizophrenia. While Nike cannot be blamed for individual acts of madness like this, a culture of active responsibility does not resolve itself in the mere fact of diagnosis.

55   See, for instance, Wiley M. Woodward, "It's More Than Just the Shoes," *Black Enterprise*, November 1990, 17.

56   My point here is simply that such speech does not constitute the truth of the commodity, not that testimony is irrelevant.

57   Heidegger, "Origin of the Work of Art," 161, claims the Van Gogh painting "spoke" the Being of the thing, the product-being in the shoes. Jameson's comment that Warhol's "Diamond-Dust Shoes" "doesn't really speak to us at all" implies that Van Gogh's effort does (Jameson, *Postmodernism*, p. 8). And Derrida's entire investigation is about how the truth "speaks" in painting. Derrida suggests that Heidegger makes the peasant shoes "speak" — once they are painted, "these shoes talk" (Jacques Derrida, *The Truth in Painting*, translated by Geoffrey Bennington and Ian McCleod [Chicago: University of Chicago Press, 1987], p. 323). My point is that these figures of speech are written into the product-being of commodity fetishism.

58   Indeed, the rise in popularity of rugged "outdoor" shoes and boots has already redrawn the athletic shoe market. Nike, of course, has switched production accordingly and expanded its focus on apparel. It also experimented with another slogan, "I can," which carries enough existential baggage to rewrite this chronotope again.

59   Nicholas D. Kristof and Sheryl WuDunn, "Two Cheers for Sweatshops," *New York Times Magazine*, 24 September 2000, 70–71.

60   Bakhtin, "Forms of Time," 84.

Bibliography

Abbas, Ackbar and John Nguyet Erni, eds (2005) *Internationalizing Cultural Studies: An Anthology*, Oxford: Blackwell.

Acland, Charles R., ed. (2007) *Residual Media*, Minneapolis: University of Minnesota Press.

Agrest, Diana, Patricia Conway and Leslie Kanes Weisman, eds (1996) *The Sex of Architecture*, New York: Harry N. Abrams.

Ahmed, Sara (2006) *Queer Phenomenology: Orientations, Objects, Others*, Durham, NC and London: Duke University Press.

Altieri, Charles (2003) *The Particulars of Rapture: An Aesthetics of the Affects*, Ithaca: Cornell University Press.

Ames, Kenneth L. (1984) 'Meaning in Artifacts: Hall Furnishings in Victorian America', in *Material Culture Studies in America*, ed. Thomas J. Schlereth, Nashville: American Association for State and Local History, pp. 206–21.

Anderson, Stanford (1987) 'The Fiction of Function', *Assemblage*, 2, pp. 18–31.

Appadurai, Arjun, ed. (1986) *The Social Life of Things: Commodities in Cultural Perspective*, Cambridge: Cambridge University Press.

—— (2006) 'The Thing Itself', *Public Culture*, 18, 1, pp. 15–21.

Arvatov, Boris (1925) 'Everyday Life and the Culture of the Thing (Towards a Formulation of the Question)', translated by Christina Kiaer, *October*, 81, 1997, pp. 119–28.

Asendorf, Christoph (1993) *Batteries of Life: On the History of Things and their Perception in Modernity*, translated by Don Reneau, Berkeley, Los Angeles and London: University of California Press.

Assad, Maria L. (1999) *Reading with Michel Serres: An Encounter with Time*, Albany: SUNY Press.

Atkins, Jacqueline M. (2005) *Wearing Propaganda: Textiles on the Home Front in Japan, Britain and the United States*, New Haven: Yale University Press.

Attali, Jacques (1977) *Noise: Political Economy of Music*, translated by Brian Massumi, Minneapolis: University of Minnesota Press.

Attfield, Judy (1994) 'The Tufted Carpet in Britain: Its Rise from the Bottom of the Pile, 1952–1970', *Journal of Design History*, 7, 3, pp. 205–16.

—— (1999) 'Bringing Modernity Home: Open Plan in the British Domestic Interior', in *At Home: An Anthropology of Domestic Space*, ed. Irene Cieraad, Syracuse: Syracuse University Press, pp. 73–82.

—— (2000) *Wild Things: The Material Culture of Everyday Life*, Oxford and New York: Berg.

—— (2002) 'Moving Home: Changing Attitudes to Residence and Identity', *Journal of Architecture*, 7, pp. 249–62.

Attfield, Judy and Pat Kirkham, eds (1995) *A View from the Interior: Women and Design*, London: The Women's Press.

Auerbach, Jeffrey A. (1999) *The Great Exhibition of 1851: A Nation on Display*, New Haven and London: Yale University Press.

Augé, Marc (1986/2002) *In the Metro*, translated by Tom Conley, Minneapolis: University of Minnesota Press.

—— (1992/1995) *Non-Places: Introduction to an Anthropology of Supermodernity*, translated by John Howe, London: Verso.

Auslander, Leora (1996) *Taste and Power: Furnishing Modern France*, Berkeley: University of California Press.

Aynsley, Jeremy (2004) *Pioneers of Modern Graphic Design: A Complete History*, 2nd edn, London: Mitchell Beazley.

Bachelard, Gaston (1958) *The Poetics of Space*, translated by Maria Jolas, Boston: Beacon Press.

Bacon, Edmund N. (1976) *Design of Cities*, Harmondsworth: Penguin.

Badmington, Neil (2000) *Posthumanism*, Readers in Cultural Criticism, Basingstoke: Palgrave.

Baker, Nicholson (1989) *The Mezzanine*, Cambridge: Granta.

Bakhtin, Mikhail (1981) *The Dialogic Imagination: Four Essays*, translated by Caryl Emerson and Michael Holquist, Austin: University of Texas Press.

Banham, Reyner (1960/2002) *Theory and Design in the First Machine Age*, London: Architectural Press.

—— (1969) *The Architecture of the Well-Tempered Environment*, London: Architectural Press.

—— (1973) *Los Angeles: The Architecture of Four Ecologies*, Harmondsworth: Penguin.

—— (1981) *Design by Choice*, ed. Penny Sparke, London: Academy Editions.

Barthes, Roland (1957/1973) *Mythologies*, translated by Annette Lavers, London: Granada.

—— (1967/1990) *The Fashion System*, translated by Matthew Ward and Richard Howard, Berkeley, Los Angeles and London: University of California Press.

Baudelaire, Charles (1964) *The Painter of Modern Life and Other Essays*, translated by Jonathan Mayne, New York: Da Capo and Phaidon.

Baudrillard, Jean (1968/1996) *The System of Objects*, translated by James Benedict, London: Verso.

Bauman, Zygmunt (2004) *Wasted Lives: Modernity and its Outcasts*, Cambridge: Polity Press.

Bayley, Stephen (1986) *Twentieth-Century Style and Design*, London: Thames and Hudson.

Beard, Alice (2002) ' "Put in Just for Pictures": Fashion Editorial and the Composite Image in *Nova* 1965–1975', *Fashion Theory*, 6, 1, pp. 1–20.

Bell, Genevieve (2006) '*Satu Keluarga, Satu Komputer* (One Home, One Computer): Cultural Accounts of ICTs in South and Southeast Asia', *Design Issues*, 22, 2, pp. 35–55.

Benjamin, Walter (1928) 'Toys and Play: Marginal Notes on a Monumental Work', in *Selected Writings, Volume 2: 1927–1934*, Cambridge, Mass. and London: Harvard University Press, 1999, pp. 117–21.

—— (1999) *The Arcades Project*, translated by Howard Eiland and Kevin McLaughlin, Cambridge, Mass. and London: Harvard University Press.

Betts, Paul (2004) *The Authority of Everyday Objects: A Cultural History of West German Industrial Design*, Berkeley, Los Angeles and London: University of California Press.

Bevan, Robert (2007) *The Destruction of Memory: Architecture at War*, London: Reaktion.

Blake, Peter (1976) *The Master Builders: Le Corbusier, Mies van der Rohe, Frank Lloyd Wright*, New York: W.W. Norton.

Blunt, Alison (2005) *Domicile and Diaspora: Anglo-Indian Women and the Spatial Politics of Home*, Cambridge: Blackwell.

Bonsiepe, Gui (1991) 'Designing the Future – Perspectives on Industrial and Graphic Design in Latin America', *Design Issues*, 7, 2, pp. 17–24.

Borgmann, Albert (2001) *Holding on to Reality: The Nature of Information at the Turn of the Millennium,* Chicago: University of Chicago Press.

Bourdieu, Pierre (1972/1990) *Outline of a Theory of Practice,* translated by Richard Nice, Cambridge: Cambridge University Press.

—— (1979/1989) *Distinction: A Social Critique of the Judgement of Taste,* translated by Richard Nice, London and New York: Routledge.

Bourke, Joanna (1996) 'The Great Male Renunciation: Men's Dress Reform in Inter-war Britain', *Journal of Design History,* 9, 1, pp. 23–33.

Bowlby, Rachel (2000) *Carried Away: The Invention of Modern Shopping,* London: Faber and Faber.

Boym, Svetlana (1994) *Common Places: Mythologies of Everyday Life in Russia,* Cambridge, Mass.: Harvard University Press.

—— (2001) *The Future of Nostalgia,* New York: Basic Books.

Bresnahan, Keith (2003) 'Housing Complexes: Neurasthenic Subjects and the Bourgeois Interior', *Space and Culture,* 6, 2, pp. 169–77.

Breward, Christopher (2004) *Fashioning London: Clothing and the Modern Metropolis,* Oxford: Berg.

Brown, Bill (1996) *The Material Unconscious: American Amusement, Stephen Crane, and Economies of Play,* Cambridge, Mass.: Harvard University Press.

—— (2003) *A Sense of Things: The Object Matter of American Literature,* Chicago: University of Chicago Press.

—— ed. (2004) *Things,* Chicago: University of Chicago Press.

Brown, Steven D. (2002) 'Michel Serres: Science, Translation and the Logic of the Parasite', *Theory, Culture & Society,* 19, 1, pp. 1–27.

Buck, David N. (2000) *Responding to Chaos: Tradition, Technology, Society and Order in Japanese Design,* London: Spon Press.

Bull, Michael (2000) *Sounding out the City: Personal Stereos and the Management of Everyday Life,* Oxford and New York: Berg.

Burgin, Victor (1996) *In/Different Spaces: Place and Memory in Visual Culture,* Berkeley: University of California Press.

Buse, Peter, Ken Hirschkop, Scott McCracken and Bertrand Taithe (2005) *Benjamin's* Arcades: *An unGuided Tour,* Manchester: Manchester University Press.

Bush, Christopher (2007) 'The Ethnicity of Things in America's Lacquered Age', *Representations,* 99, pp. 74–98.

Caillois, Roger (1958/2001) *Man, Play and Games,* translated by Meyer Barash, Urbana and Chicago: University of Illinois Press.

Caplan, Ralph (2005) *By Design: Why There Are No Locks on the Bathroom Doors in the Hotel Louis XIV and Other Object Lessons,* Oxford and New York: Berg.

Castle, Terry (1988) 'Phantasmagoria: Spectral Technology and the Metaphorics of Modern Reverie', *Critical Inquiry,* 15, pp. 26–61.

Catterall, Claire, ed. (1999) *Food: Design and Culture,* London: Laurence King.

Çelik, Zeynep (1996) 'Gendered Spaces in Colonial Algiers', in *The Sex of Architecture,* ed. Diana Agrest, Patricia Conway and Leslie Kanes Weisman, New York: Harry N. Abrams, pp. 127–40.

—— (1997) *Urban Forms and Colonial Confrontations: Algiers under French Rule,* Berkeley, Los Angeles and London: University of California Press.

—— (1999) 'Colonial/Postcolonial Intersections: *Lieux de mémoire* in Algiers', *Third Text,* 49, pp. 63–72.

—— (2000) 'Colonialism, Orientalism and the Canon', in Iain Borden and Jane Rendell, *InterSections: Architectural Histories and Critical Theories,* London: Routledge, pp. 161–9.

—— (2004) 'Framing the Colony: Houses of Algeria Photographed', *Art History,* 27, 4, pp. 616–26.

Chambers, Ross (1994) 'Meditation and the Escalator Principle (on Nicholson Baker's *The Mezzanine)',* *Modern Fiction Studies,* 40, 4, pp. 765–806.

Chatterjee, Ashoke (2005) 'Design in India: The Experience of Transition', *Design Issues,* 21, 4, pp. 4–10.

Chauncey, George (1994) *Gay New York: Gender, Urban Culture, and the Making of the Gay Male World, 1890–1940,* New York: Basic Books.

—— (1996) '"Privacy Could Only Be Had in Public": Gay Uses of the Streets', in *Stud: Architectures of Masculinity*, ed. Joel Sanders, New York: Princeton Architectural Press, pp. 224–60.

Child, Jack (2005) 'The Politics and Semiotics of the Smallest Icons of Popular Culture: Latin American Postage Stamps', *Latin American Research Review*, 40, 1, pp. 108–37.

Cieraad, Irene, ed. (1999) *At Home: An Anthropology of Domestic Space*, Syracuse: Syracuse University Press.

—— (2002) '"Out of my Kitchen!" Architecture, Gender and Domestic Efficiency', *Journal of Architecture*, 7, pp. 263–79.

—— (2004) 'Milk Bottles and Model Homes: Strategies of the Dutch Association for Correct Living (1946–1968)', *Journal of Architecture*, 9, pp. 431–43.

Clancy, Deirdre (1996) *Costume since 1945: Couture, Street Style and Anti-Fashion*, London: Herbert Press.

Clifford, James (1988) *The Predicament of Culture: Twentieth-Century Ethnography, Literature, and Art*, Cambridge, Mass.: Harvard University Press.

Coleman, Debra, Elizabeth Danze and Carol Henderson, eds (1996) *Architecture and Feminism*, New York: Princeton Architectural Press.

Collingham, Lizzie (2005) *Curry: A Biography*, London: Chatto and Windus.

Colomina, Beatriz, ed. (1992) *Sexuality and Space*, Princeton: Princeton Papers on Architecture.

—— (1996) *Privacy and Publicity: Modern Architecture as Mass Media*, Cambridge, Mass.: MIT Press.

—— (2007) *Domesticity at War*, Cambridge, Mass.: MIT Press.

Conekin, Becky E. (2003) *'The Autobiography of a Nation': The 1951 Festival of Britain*, Manchester and New York: Manchester University Press.

Conekin, Becky E., Frank Mort and Chris Waters, eds (1999) *Moments of Modernity: Reconstructing Britain 1945–1964*, London: River Oram.

Connor, Steven (1997) 'The Modern Auditory I', in *Rewriting the Self: Histories from the Renaissance to the Present*, ed. Ray Porter, London and New York: Routledge, pp. 203–23.

—— (2005) 'Michel Serres' Five Senses', in *Empire of the Senses: The Sensual Culture Reader*, ed. David Howes, Oxford and New York: Berg, pp. 318–34.

Conway, Hazel, ed. (1992) *Design History: A Student's Handbook*, London and New York: Routledge.

Cooke, Lynne and Peter Wollen, eds (1998) *Culture Beyond Appearances*, New York: New Press.

Cosgrove, Stuart (1984) 'The Zoot-Suit and Style Warfare', *History Workshop Journal*, 18, pp. 77–91.

Cottom, Daniel (1988) 'On the Dignity of Tables', *Critical Inquiry*, 14, 4, pp. 765–83.

Cowan, Ruth Schwartz (1989) *More Work for Mother: The Ironies of Household Technology from the Open Hearth to the Microwave*, London: Free Association Books.

Craik, Jennifer (1993) *The Face of Fashion*, London: Routledge.

Cranz, Galen (2000) *The Chair: Rethinking Culture, Body and Design*, New York: W. W. Norton.

Crary, Jonathan (1984) 'Eclipse of the Spectacle', in *Art after Modernism: Rethinking Representation*, ed. Brian Wallis, Boston: Godine, pp 283–94.

—— (1989) 'Spectacle, Attention, Counter-Memory', *October*, 50, Autumn, pp. 96–107.

—— (1990) *Techniques of the Observer: On Vision and Modernity in the Nineteenth Century*, Cambridge, Mass.: MIT Press.

—— (1999) *Suspensions of Perception: Attention, Spectacle, and Modern Culture*, Cambridge, Mass.: MIT Press.

—— (2002) 'Géricault, the Panorama, and Sites of Reality in the Early Nineteenth Century', *Grey Room*, 9, pp. 5–25.

Csikszentmihalyi, Mihaly (1991) 'Design and Order in Everyday Life', *Design Issues*, 8, 1, pp. 26–34.

—— (1997) *Finding Flow: The Psychology of Engagement with Everyday Life*, New York: Basic Books.

Daniels, Inge M. (1999) 'Japanese Material Culture and Consumerism: A Review of Recent Work', *Journal of Material Culture*, 4, 2, pp. 231–40.

Dant, Tim (2004) 'The Driver-car', *Theory, Culture & Society*, 21, 4/5, pp. 61–79.

Davies, Margery W. (1982) *Woman's Place is at the Typewriter: Office Work and Office Workers 1870–1930*, Philadelphia: Temple University Press.

Debord, Guy (1967) *Society of the Spectacle*, translated by Donald Nicholson-Smith, New York: Zone Books, 1994.

Deutsche, Rosalyn (1996) *Evictions: Art and Spatial Politics*, Cambridge, Mass.: MIT Press.

—— (2002) 'Sharing Strangeness: Krzysztof Wodiczko's *Ægis* and the Question of Hospitality', *Grey Room*, 6, pp. 26–43.

Dickerman, Leah, ed. (1996) *Building the Collective: Soviet Graphic Design, 1917–1937*, New York: Princeton Architectural Press.

Donald, James (1999) *Imagining the Modern City*, London: Athlone Press.

Douglas, Mary (1979) *Purity and Danger: An Analysis of Concepts of Pollution and Taboo*, London: Routledge and Kegan Paul.

Doy, Gen (2002) *Drapery: Classicism and Barbarism in Visual Culture*, London: I. B. Tauris.

Drobnick, Jim, ed. (2006) *The Smell Culture Reader*, Oxford: Berg.

Dunlap, David W. (1997) 'Architecture in an Age of Disability', *New York Times*, 1 June, sec. 9.1.

Eames, Charles and Ray Eames (1958) 'The Eames Report', *Design Issues*, 7, 2, 1991, pp. 63–75.

Eastlake, Charles (1878/1986) *Hints on Household Taste*, 4th edn, New York: Dover.

Eleb-Vidal, Monique and Anne Debarre-Blanchard (1989) *Architectures de la vie privée: Maisons et mentalités XVIIe–XIXe siècles*, Brussels: Archives d'Architecture Moderne.

—— (1995) *L'invention de l'habitation moderne: Paris 1880–1914: Architectures de la vie privée, suite*, Paris: Éditions Hazan et Archives d'Architecture Moderne.

English, Bonnie (2007) *A Cultural History of Fashion in the Twentieth Century: From the Catwalk to the Sidewalk*, Oxford: Berg.

Entwistle, Joanne (2000) *The Fashioned Body: Fashion, Dress and Modern Social Theory*, Cambridge: Polity Press.

Ernyey, Gyula (1988) 'Developmental Problems and Possibilities in Times of Change', *Design Issues*, 5, 1, pp. 82–6.

Evans, Jessica (1986) 'The Imagined Referent: Photographic Constructions of Handicap and the Imperfect Body within the Institutions of Charity', *Block*, 12, pp. 71–82.

Fathers, James (2003) 'Peripheral Vision: An Interview with Gui Bonsiepe Charting a Lifetime of Commitment to Design Empowerment', *Design Issues*, 19, 4, pp. 44–56.

Feher, Michel, ed. (1997) *Fragments for a History of the Human Body (Parts One to Three)*, New York: Zone Books.

Fischer, Claude S. (1994) *America Calling: A Social History of the Telephone to 1940*, Berkeley: University of California Press.

Fisher, Philip (2002) *The Vehement Passions*, Princeton: Princeton University Press.

Floré, Fredie (2004) 'Lessons in Modern Living: Home Design Exhibitions in Belgium 1945–1958', *Journal of Architecture*, 9, pp. 445–62.

Flusser, Vilém (1983) *Towards a Philosophy of Photography*, London: Reaktion Books, 2000.

—— (1999) *The Shape of Things: A Philosophy of Design*, London: Reaktion Books.

—— (2002) *Writings*, translated by Erik Eisel, ed. Andreas Ströhl, Minneapolis: University of Minnesota Press.

—— (2004) *The Freedom of the Migrant: Objections to Nationalism*, translated by Kenneth Kronenberg, Urbana: University of Illinois Press.

Forty, Adrian (1986) *Objects of Desire: Design and Society since 1750*, London and New York: Thames and Hudson.

—— (1989) 'Of Cars, Clothes and Carpets: Design Metaphors in Architectural Thought: The First Banham Memorial Lecture', *Journal of Design History*, 2, 1, pp. 1–14.

Foster, Hal (2002a) 'The ABCs of Contemporary Design', *October*, 100, pp. 191–9.

—— (2002b) *Design and Crime (and Other Diatribes)*, London: Verso.

Foucault, Michel (1963/1976) *The Birth of the Clinic*, translated by A. M. Sheridan, London: Tavistock.

—— (1975/1982) *Discipline and Punish: The Birth of the Prison*, translated by Alan Sheridan, Harmondsworth: Penguin.

—— (1996) *Foucault Live: Collected Interviews, 1961–1984*, ed. Sylvère Lotringer, New York: Semiotext(e).

—— (1976/1984) *The History of Sexuality. Volume One: An Introduction*, translated by Robert Hurley, Harmondsworth: Penguin.

—— (1977) 'Language to Infinity', in *Language, Counter-Memory, Practice: Selected Essays and Interviews*, translated by Donald F. Bouchard, New York: Cornell University Press, pp. 53–67.

—— (1980) *Power/Knowledge: Selected Interviews and Other Writings, 1972–1977*, translated by Colin Gordon, New York: Pantheon Books.

Fournier, Marcel (2006) *Marcel Mauss: A Biography*, translated by Jane Marie Todd, Princeton: Princeton University Press.

Frampton, Kenneth (1985) *Modern Architecture: A Critical History*, London: Thames and Hudson.

—— (2001) *Le Corbusier*, London: Thames and Hudson.

Francastle, Pierre (1956/2000) *Art and Technology in the Nineteenth and Twentieth Centuries*, translated by Randall Cherry, New York: Zone Books.

Fredrickson, Laurel (1999) 'Vision and Material Practice: Vladimir Tatlin and the Design of Everyday Objects', *Design Issues*, 15, 1, pp. 49–74.

Freeman, June (2004) *The Making of the Modern Kitchen: A Cultural History*, Oxford: Berg.

Freud, Sigmund (1901/1975) *The Psychopathology of Everyday Life*, translated by Alan Tyson, Harmondsworth: Penguin.

—— (1926/1979) 'Inhibitions, Symptoms and Anxiety', *On Psychopathology*, Harmondsworth: Penguin.

Freund, Peter (2001) 'Bodies, Disability and Spaces: The Social Model and Disabling Spatial Organisations', *Disability & Society*, 16, 5, pp. 689–706.

Fry, Tony (1983) 'Cultural Politics, Design and Representation', *Block*, 9, pp. 40–9.

—— (1989) 'A Geography of Power: Design History and Marginality', *Design Issues*, 6, 1, pp. 15–30.

—— (1999) *A New Design Philosophy: An Introduction to Defuturing*, Sydney: University of New South Wales Press.

—— (2003) 'The "Futurings" of Hong Kong', *Design Issues*, 19, 3, pp. 71–82.

Fuller, Matthew (2005) *Media Ecologies: Materialist Energies in Art and Technoculture*, Cambridge, Mass.: MIT Press.

Fuller, R. Buckminster (1981) *Critical Path*, New York: St Martin's Press.

Fuss, Diana (1992) 'Fashion and the Homospectatorial Look', *Critical Inquiry*, 18, 4, pp. 713–37.

—— (2004) *The Sense of an Interior: Four Writers and the Rooms that Shaped Them*, New York and London: Routledge.

Galison, Peter (1990) 'Aufbau/Bauhaus: Logical Positivism and Architectural Modernism', *Critical Inquiry*, 16, 4, pp. 709–52.

Gallo, Rubén (2005) *Mexican Modernity: The Avant-Garde and the Technological Revolution*, Cambridge, Mass. and London: MIT Press.

Gardiner, Michael E. (2000) *Critiques of Everyday Life*, London and New York: Routledge.

Gartman, David (1994) *Auto Opium: A Social History of American Automobile Design*, London and New York, Routledge.

Gendron, Bernard (1986) 'Theodor Adorno Meets the Cadillacs', in *Studies in Entertainment: Critical Approaches to Mass Culture*, ed. Tania Modleski, Bloomington and Indianapolis: Indiana University Press, pp. 18–36.

Georgiadis, Sokratis (1993) *Siegfried Giedion: An Intellectual Biography*, translated by Colin Hall, Edinburgh: Edinburgh University Press.

Giedion, Siegfried (1928/1995) *Building in France, Building in Iron, Building in Ferro-Concrete*, translated by J. Duncan Berry, Santa Monica: The Getty Center for the History of Art and the Humanities.

—— (1941/1969) *Space, Time and Architecture: The Growth of a New Tradition*, 5th edn, Cambridge, Mass.: Harvard University Press.

—— (1948/1969) *Mechanization Takes Command: A Contribution to Anonymous History*, New York: Norton.

—— (1954) *Walter Gropius: Work and Teamwork*, London: Architectural Press.

Gigante, Denise (2005) *Taste: A Literary History*, New Haven: Yale University Press.

Gilroy, Paul (1992) 'Wearing Your Art on Your Sleeve: Notes towards a Diaspora History of Black Ephemera', *Ten: 8*, 2, 3, pp. 129–37.

Gitelman, Lisa and Geoffrey B. Pingree, eds (2003) *New Media 1740–1915*, Cambridge, Mass.: MIT Press.

Goffman, Erving (1967) *Interaction Ritual: Essays on Face-to-Face Behaviour*, Chicago: Aldine.

Goggin, Gerard (2006) *Cell Phone Culture*, London and New York: Routledge.

Goldman, Robert and Stephen Papson (1999) *Nike Culture: The Sign of the Swoosh*, London: Sage

Goodall, Phil (1983) 'Design and Gender', *Block*, 9, pp. 50–61.

Gorman, Carma, ed. (2003) *The Industrial Design Reader*, New York: Allworth Press.

Grau, Oliver (2003) *Virtual Art: From Illusion to Immersion*, Cambridge, Mass. and London: MIT Press.

Gray, Camilla (1962/1986) *The Russian Experiment in Art, 1863–1922*, London: Thames and Hudson.

Green, Nancy L. (1997) *Ready-to-Wear and Ready-to-Work: A Century of Industry and Immigrants in Paris and New York*, Durham, NC and London: Duke University Press.

Greenhalgh, Peter, ed. (1990) *Modernism in Design*, London: Reaktion Books.

Gronberg, Tag (1998) *Designs on Modernity: Exhibiting the City in 1920s Paris*, Manchester: Manchester University Press.

Guffey, Elizabeth E. (2006) *Retro: The Culture of Revival*, London: Reaktion Books.

Guillén, Mauro F. (2006) *The Taylorized Beauty of the Mechanical: Scientific Management and the Rise of Modernist Architecture*, Princeton: Princeton University Press.

Gullestad, Marianne (1992) *The Art of Social Relations: Essays on Culture, Social Action and Everyday Life in Modern Norway*, Oslo: Scandinavian University Press.

Gumbrecht, Hans Ulrich and K. Ludwig Pfeiffer, eds (1994) *Materialities of Communication*, translated by William Whobrey, Stanford: Stanford University Press.

Hadlaw, Janin (2003) 'The London Underground Map: Imagining Modern Times and Space', *Design Issues*, 19, 1, pp. 25–35.

Hall, Edward T. (1966) *The Hidden Dimension: Man's Uses of Space in Public and Private*, New York: Doubleday.

Hall, Stuart (1992) 'What is this "Black" in Black Popular Culture?' in *Black Popular Culture*, ed. Michele Wallace, Los Angeles: Bay Press, pp. 21–33.

Halle, David (1993) *Inside Culture: Art and Class in the American Home*, Chicago: Chicago University Press.

Hamon, Philippe (1992) *Expositions: Literature and Architecture in Nineteenth-Century France*, translated by Katia Sainson-Frank and Lisa Maguire, Berkeley, Los Angeles and Oxford: University of California Press.

Hand, Martin and Elizabeth Shove (2004) 'Orchestrating Concepts: Kitchen Dynamics and Regime Change in *Good Housekeeping* and *Ideal Home* 1922–2002', *Home Cultures*, 1, 3, pp. 235–56.

Haraway, Donna J. (1991) *Simians, Cyborgs, and Women: The Reinvention of Nature*, London: Free Association Press.

Harootunian, Harry (2000) *History's Disquiet: Modernity, Cultural Practice, and the Question of Everyday Life*, New York: Columbia University Press.

Harris, Daniel (2000) *Cute, Quaint, Hungry and Romantic: The Aesthetics of Consumerism*, New York: Da Capo Press.

Harrison, Martin (1992) *Appearances: Fashion Photography since 1945*, London: Jonathan Cape.

Haruhiko, Fujita (2001) 'Notomi Kaijiro: An Industrial Art Pioneer and the First Design Educator of Modern Japan', *Design Issues*, 17, 2, pp. 17–31.

Hawkins, Gay (2006) *The Ethics of Waste: How We Relate to Rubbish*, Sydney: University of New South Wales Press.

Hay, Gerhard, ed. (1975) *Literatur und Rundfunk 1923–1933*, Hildesheim.

Hayden, Dolores (1981) *The Grand Domestic Revolution: A History of Feminist Designs for American Homes, Neighborhoods, and Cities*, Cambridge, Mass.: MIT Press.

—— (1984/2002) *Redesigning the American Dream: Gender, Housing, and Family Life*, New York: W. W. Norton.

Hayles, N. Katherine (1999) *How We Became Posthuman: Virtual Bodies in Cybernetics, Literature, and Informatics*, Chicago: University of Chicago Press.

—— (2002) *Writing Machines*, Cambridge, Mass.: MIT Press.

Hays, Michael K. (1992) *Modernism and the Posthumanist Subject: The Architecture of Hannes Meyer and Ludwig Hilberseime*, Cambridge, Mass. and London: MIT Press.

Hebdige, Dick (1979) *Subculture: The Meaning of Style*, London and New York: Methuen.

—— (1987) 'The Impossible Object: Towards a Sociology of the Sublime', *New Formations*, 1, pp. 47–76.

—— (1988) *Hiding in the Light: On Images and Things*, London and New York: Routledge.

—— (1992) 'The Machine is *Unheimlich*: Wodiczko's Homeless Vehicle Project', *Public Address: Krzysztof Wodiczko*, Minneapolis: Walker Art Centre, pp. 54–67.

—— (1993) 'Redeeming Witness: In the Tracks of the Homeless Vehicle Project', *Cultural Studies*, 7, 2, pp. 173–223.

Helfand, Jessica (2001) *Screen: Essays on Graphic Design, New Media, and Visual Culture*, Princeton: Princeton Architectural Press.

Henkin, David M. (1998) *City Reading: Written Words and Public Spaces in Antebellum New York*, New York: Columbia University Press.

Henning, Michelle (2007) 'New Lamps for Old: Photography, Obsolescence, and Social Change', in *Residual Media*, ed. Charles R. Acland, Minneapolis: University of Minnesota Press, pp. 48–65.

Heskett, John (2002) *Toothpicks and Logos: Design in Everyday Life*, Oxford: Oxford University Press.

Heynen, Hilde (1999) *Architecture and Modernity: A Critique*, Cambridge, Mass. and London: MIT Press.

Highmore, Ben (2003) 'Machinic Magic: IBM at the 1964–1965 New York World's Fair', *new formations*, 51, pp. 128–48.

—— (2004) 'Homework: Routine, Social Aesthetics, and the Ambiguity of Everyday Life', *Cultural Studies*, 18, 2–3, pp. 306–27.

—— (2005) *Cityscapes: Cultural Readings in the Material and Symbolic City*, Basingstoke and New York: Palgrave Macmillan.

—— (2006) *Michel de Certeau: Analysing Culture*, London and New York: Continuum.

—— (2007) 'Walls without Museums: Anonymous History, Collective Authorship, and the Document', *Visual Culture in Britain*, 8, 2, pp. 1–20.

Hill, Jonathan, ed. (1998) *Occupying Architecture: Between the Architect and the User*, London and New York: Routledge.

Hine, Thomas (1987) *Populuxe*, London: Bloomsbury.

Hitchcock, Peter (2003) *Imaginary States: Studies in Cultural Transnationalism (Transnational Cultural Studies)*, Urbana: Illinois University Press.

Hollier, Denis (1993) 'While the City Sleeps: Mene, Mene, Tekel, Upharsin', *October*, 64, pp. 3–15.

Hollis, Richard (2001) *Graphic Design: A Concise History*, London: Thames and Hudson.

—— (2006) *Swiss Graphic Design: The Origins and Growth of an International Style, 1920–1965*, London: Laurence King.

Humble, Nicola (2005) *Culinary Pleasures: Cookbooks and the Transformation of British Food*, London: Faber.

Imrie, Rob (1996) *Disability and the City: International Perspectives*, London: Paul Chapman.

Iverson, Margaret (1993) *Alois Riegl: Art History and Theory*, Cambridge, Mass.: MIT Press.

Iwabuchi, Koichi (1998) 'Marketing "Japan": Japanese Cultural Presence under a Global Gaze', *Japanese Studies*, 18, 2, pp. 66–75.

—— (2002) *Recentering Globalization: Popular Culture and Japanese Transnationalism*, Durham, NC: Duke University Press.

Jackson, Anna (1992) 'Imagining Japan: The Victorian Perception and Acquisition of Japanese Culture', *Journal of Design History*, 5, 4, pp. 245–56.

Jackson, Lesley (2001) *Robin and Lucienne Day: Pioneers of Contemporary Design*, London: Mitchell Beazley.

Jackson, Stevi and Shaun Moores, eds (1995) *The Politics of Domestic Consumption: Critical Readings*, London: Harvester Wheatsheaf.

Jaffé, H. L. C. (1986) *De Stijl: The Dutch Contribution to Modern Art*, Cambridge, Mass. and London: Belknap Press, Harvard University Press.

Jameson, Fredric (1998) *The Cultural Turn: Selected Writings on the Postmodern, 1983–1998*, London: Verso.

Jameson, Fredric and Masao Miyoshi, eds (1998) *The Cultures of Globalization*, Durham, NC: Duke University Press.

Johnson, James H. (1995) *Listening in Paris: A Cultural History*, Berkeley: University of California Press.

Julier, Guy (2000) *The Culture of Design*, London: Sage.

—— (2006) 'From Visual Culture to Design Culture', *Design Issues*, 22, 1, pp. 64–76.

Jütte, Robert (2005) *A History of the Senses: From Antiquity to Cyberspace*, translated by James Lynn, Cambridge: Polity Press.

Keyvanian, Carla (2000) 'Manfredo Tafuri: From the Critique of Ideology to Microhistories', *Design Issues*, 16, 1, pp. 3–15.

Kiaer, Christina (2005) *Imagine No Possessions: The Socialist Objects of Russian Constructivism*, Cambridge, Mass. and London: MIT Press.

Kiaer, Christina and Eric Naiman, eds (2006) *Everyday Life in Early Soviet Russia: Taking the Revolution Inside*, Bloomington and Indianapolis: Indiana University Press.

Killen, Andreas (2006) *Berlin Electropolis: Shock, Nerves, and German Modernity*, Berkeley: University of California Press.

Kinross, Robin (1988) 'Herbert Read's *Art and Industry*: A History', *Journal of Design History*, 1, 1, pp. 35–50.

Kirkham, Pat (1995) *Charles and Ray Eames: Designers of the Twentieth Century*, Cambridge, Mass. and London, MIT Press,

Kittler, Friedrich A. (2001) 'Computer Graphics: A Semi-Technical Introduction', *Grey Room*, 2, pp. 30–45.

—— (1986/1999) *Gramophone, Film, Typewriter*, translated by Geoffrey Winthrop-Young and Michael Wutz, Stanford: Stanford University Press.

Knipfel, Jim (1999) *Slack Jew: A Memoir*, New York: Berkeley Books.

Knox, Paul L. (1987) 'The Social Production of the Built Environment: Architects, Architecture, and the Post-Modern City', *Progress in Human Geography*, 11, 3, pp. 354–78.

Komardjaja, Inge (2001) 'New Cultural Geographies of Disability: Asian Values and the Accessibility Ideal', *Social and Cultural Geography*, 2, 1, pp. 77–86.

Kracauer, Siegfried (1995) *The Mass Ornament: Weimar Essays*, translated by Thomas Y. Levin, Cambridge, Mass.: Harvard University Press.

Kramarae, Cheris, ed. (1988) *Technology and Women's Voices: Keeping in Touch*, London: Routledge and Kegan Paul.

Kristeva, Julia (1991) *Strangers to Ourselves*, translated by Leon S. Roudiez, New York: Columbia University Press.

Kuisel, Richard (1993) *Seducing the French: The Dilemma of Americanization*, Berkeley, Los Angeles and London: University of California Press.

Kwinter, Sanford (2001) *Architectures of Time: Toward a Theory of the Event in Modernist Culture*, Cambridge, Mass. and London: MIT Press.

Lagae, Johan (2004) 'Modern Living in the Congo: The 1958 Colonial Housing Exhibit and Postwar Domestic Practices in the Belgian Congo', *Journal of Architecture*, 9, pp. 477–94.

Latour, Bruno (1996) *Aramis, or the Love of Technology*, translated by Catherine Porter, Cambridge, Mass.: Harvard University Press.

Lavin, Maud (2001) *Clean New World: Culture, Politics, and Graphic Design*, Cambridge, Mass.: MIT Press.

Lavin, Sylvia (2004) *Form Follows Libido: Architecture and Richard Neutra in a Psychoanalytic Culture*, Cambridge, Mass. and London: MIT Press.

Lavrentiev, Alexander N. and Yuri V. Nasarov (1995) *Russian Design: Tradition and Experiment, 1920–1990*, translated by Flora Fischer, London: Academy Editions.

Leach, Neil, ed. (1999) *Architecture and Revolution: Contemporary Perspectives on Central and Eastern Europe*, London and New York: Routledge.

Lefebvre, Henri (1958/1991) *Critique of Everyday Life: Volume 1*, translated by John Moore, London: Verso.

—— (1961/2002) *Critique of Everyday Life: Volume Two, Foundations for a Sociology of the Everyday*, translated by John Moore, London and New York: Verso.

—— (1968/1984) *Everyday Life in the Modern World*, translated by Sacha Rabinovitch, New Brunswick: Transaction Publishers.

Lehmann, Ulrich (2000) *Tigersprung: Fashion in Modernity*, Cambridge, Mass. and London: MIT Press.

Leiris, Michel (1938) 'The Sacred in Everyday Life', in *The College of Sociology 1937–39*, ed. Denis Hollier, Minneapolis: University of Minnesota Press, 1988, pp. 24–31.

—— (1948) *Scratches: Rules of the Game Volume 1*, translated by Lydia Davis, Baltimore and London: The Johns Hopkins University Press, 1997.

Leslie, Esther (1998) 'Walter Benjamin: Traces of Craft', *Journal of Design History*, 11, 1, pp. 5–13.

Lingis, Alphonso (1994) *Foreign Bodies*, New York and London: Routledge.

Lipovetsky, Gilles (1994) *The Empire of Fashion: Dressing Modern Democracy*, translated by Catherine Porter, Princeton: University of Princeton.

Loos, Adolf (1987) *Spoken into the Void: Collected Essays 1897–1900*, translated by Jane O. Newman and John H. Smith, Cambridge, Mass. and London: MIT Press.

Loxley, Simon (2006) *Type: The Secret History of Letters*, London: I. B. Tauris.

Lupton, Deborah (1996) *Food, the Body and the Self*, London, Thousand Oaks and New Delhi: Sage.

Lupton, Ellen (1986) 'Reading Isotype', *Design Issues*, 3, 2, pp. 47–58.

—— (1993) *Mechanical Brides: Women and Machines: From Home to Office*, Princeton: Princeton Architectural Press.

—— (1996) *Mixing Messages: Graphic Design in Contemporary American Culture*, Princeton: Princeton Architectural Press.

—— (2002) *Skin: Surface, Substance and Design*, Princeton: Princeton Architectural Press.

Lupton, Ellen and J. Abbott Miller (1992) *The Bathroom, the Kitchen, and the Aesthetics of Waste (A Process of Elimination)*, New York: Kiosk.

—— (1999) *Design, Writing, Research: Writing on Graphic Design*, London: Phaidon.

McCarthy, Anna (2001) *Ambient Television: Visual Culture and Public Space*, Durham, NC and London: Duke University Press.

McDonough, Tom (2007) *'The Beautiful Language of My Century': Reinventing the Language of Contestation in Postwar France, 1945–1968*, Cambridge, Mass.: MIT Press.

McDowell, Colin (1997) *Forties Fashion and the New Look*, London: Bloomsbury.

McHale, John (1969) *The Future of the Future*, New York: George Braziller.

McHale, John and Magda Cordell McHale (1978) *Basic Human Needs: A Framework for Action*, New Brunswick: Transaction Books.

Maciuika, John V. (2000) 'Adolf Loos and the Aphoristic Style: Rhetorical Practice in Early Twentieth-Century Design Criticism', *Design Issues*, 16, 2, pp. 75–86.

McLuhan, Marshall and Quentin Fiore (1967/1996) *The Medium is the Massage: An Inventory of Effects*, Corte Madera: Gingko Press.

Madge, Pauline (1993) 'Design, Ecology, Technology: A Historiographical Review', *Journal of Design History*, 6, 3, pp. 149–66.

—— (1997) 'Ecological Design: A New Critique', *Design Issues*, 13, 2, pp. 44–54.

Maguire, Patrick J. and Jonathan M. Woodham, eds (1997) *Design and Cultural Politics in Postwar Britain: The Britain Can Make It Exhibition of 1946*, London and Washington: Leicester University Press.

Maharaj, Sarat (1991) 'Arachne's Genre: Towards Inter-Cultural Studies in Textiles', *Journal of Design History*, 4, 2, pp. 75–96.

Mally, Lynn (1992) *Culture of the Future: The Proletkult Movement in Revolutionary Russia*, Berkeley: University of California Press.

Marchand, Roland (1995) 'The Designers go to the Fair, II: Norman Bel Geddes, The General Motors "Futurama", and the Visit to the Factory Transformed', in *Design History: An Anthology*, ed. Dennis P. Doordan, Cambridge, Mass. and London: MIT Press, pp. 103–21.

Marcus, Sharon (1999) *Apartment Stories: City and Home in Nineteenth-Century Paris and London*, Berkeley: University of California Press.

Margolin, Victor, ed. (1990) *Design Discourse: History, Theory, Criticism*, Chicago: University of Chicago Press.

—— (1998) *The Struggle for Utopia: Rodchenko, Lissitzky, Moholy-Nagy, 1917–46*, Chicago: University of Chicago Press.

—— (2002) *The Politics of the Artificial: Essays on Design and Design Studies*, Chicago: University of Chicago Press.

Marling, Karal Ann (1994) *As Seen on TV: The Visual Culture of Everyday Life in the 1950s*, Cambridge, Mass.: Harvard University Press.

Martin, Randy (2007) *An Empire of Indifference: American War and the Financial Logic of Risk Management*, Durham, NC and London: Duke University Press.

Marvin, Carolyn (1988) *When Old Technologies were New: Thinking about Electrical Communication in the Late Nineteenth Century*, New York and Oxford: Oxford University Press.

Marx, Karl (1844/1977) *Economic and Philosophical Manuscripts of 1844*, London: Lawrence and Wishart.

—— (1867/1976) *Capital: A Critique of Political Economy – Volume One*, translated by Ben Fowkes, Harmondsworth: Penguin.

Massey, Anne (1995) *The Independent Group: Modernism and Mass Culture in Britain 1945–59*, Manchester: Manchester University Press.

Massumi, Brian (2002) *Parables of the Virtual: Movement, Affect, Sensation*, Durham, NC and London: Duke University Press.

Mauss, Marcel (1923/1990) *The Gift: The Form and Reason for Exchange in Archaic Societies*, translated by W. D. Halls, London: Routledge.

—— (1934) 'Techniques of the Body', translated by Ben Brewster, *Economy and Society*, 2, 1 (1973), pp. 70–88.

—— (2006) *Techniques, Technology and Civilisation*, ed. Nathan Schlanger, New York and Oxford: Durkheim Press and Berghahn Books.

Mazon, Mauricio (1988) *Zoot-suit Riots: The Psychology of Symbolic Annihilation*, Austin: University of Texas Press.

Meikle, Jeffrey L. (2001) *Twentieth Century Limited: Industrial Design in America, 1925–1939*, Philadelphia: Temple University Press.

Michael, Mike (2006) *Technoscience and Everyday Life: The Complex Simplicities of the Mundane*, Maidenhead: Open University Press.

Michael, Vincent (2002) 'Reyner Banham: Signs and Designs in the Time without Style', *Design Issues*, 18, 2, pp. 65–77.

Mirzoeff, Nicholas (2004) *Watching Babylon: The War in Iraq and Global Visual Culture*, London: Routledge.

Mitchell, Timothy (2002) *Rule of Experts: Egypt, Techno-Politics, Modernity*, Berkeley, Los Angeles and London: University of California Press.

Mitter, Partha (1977) *Much Maligned Monsters: A History of European Reactions to Indian Art*, Chicago: Chicago University Press.

Mizuta, Kazuo (1993) *The Structures of Everyday Life in Japan in the Last Decade of the Twentieth Century*, Lewiston, NY: Edwin Mellen Press.

Molotch, Harvey (2003) *Where Stuff Comes From: How Toasters, Toilets, Cars, Computers and Many Other Things Came to Be as They Are*, London and New York: Routledge.

Montague, Ken (1994) 'The Aesthetics of Hygiene: Aesthetic Dress, Modernity, and the Body as Sign', *Journal of Design History*, 7, 2, pp. 91–112.

Moon, Michael (1998) *A Small Boy and Others: Imitation and Initiation in American Culture from Henry James to Andy Warhol*, Durham, NC: Duke University Press.

Moon, Michael, Eve Kosofsky Sedgwick, Benjamin Gianni and Scott Weir (1994) 'Queers in (Single-Family) Space', *Assemblage*, 24, pp. 30–7.

Morley, David (2003) 'What's "Home" Got to Do with It?: Contradictory Dynamics in the Domestication of Technology and the Dislocation of Domesticity', *European Journal of Cultural Studies*, 6, 4, pp. 435–58.

Morris, Meaghan (1998) *Too Soon, Too Late: History in Popular Culture*, Bloomington and Indianapolis: Indiana University Press.

Morse, Margaret (1998) *Virtualities: Television, Media Art, and Cyberculture*, Bloomington: Indiana University Press.

Mort, Frank (1996) *Cultures of Consumption: Commerce, Masculinities and Social Space in Late Twentieth Century Britain*, London: Routledge.

Mukerji, Chandra and Michael Schudson, eds (1991) *Rethinking Popular Culture: Contemporary Perspectives in Cultural Studies*, Berkeley: University of California Press.

Mumford, Lewis (1938/1983) *The Culture of Cities*, New York: Harcourt, Brace, and World.

Naylor, Gillian (1971) *The Art and Crafts Movement: A Study of its Sources, Ideals and Influence on Design Theory*, London: Studio Vista.

Ndalianis, Angela (2005) *Neo-Baroque Aesthetics and Contemporary Entertainment*, Cambridge, Mass.: MIT Press.

Nesbit, Molly (2000) *Their Common Sense*, London: Black Dog.

Nesbitt, Kate, ed. (1996) *Theorizing a New Agenda for Architecture: An Anthology of Architectural Theory 1965–1995*, Princeton: Princeton Architectural Press.

Ngai, Sianne (2005a) 'The Cuteness of the Avant-Garde', *Critical Inquiry*, 31, pp. 811–47.

—— (2005b) *Ugly Feelings*, Cambridge, Mass.: Harvard University Press.

Nye, David E. (2006) *Technology Matters: Questions to Live With*, Cambridge, Mass.: MIT Press.

Ockman, Joan, ed. (1993) *Architecture Culture 1943–1968: A Documentary Anthology*, New York: Rizzoli.

Olalquiaga, Celeste (1992) *Megalopolis: Contemporary Cultural Sensibilities*, Minneapolis: University of Minnesota Press.

—— (1999) *The Artificial Kingdom: A Treasury of the Kitsch Experience*, London: Bloomsbury.

Oliver, Paul (1994) *Dunroamin: The Suburban Semi and its Enemies*, London: Pimlico.

Overy, Paul (1991) *De Stijl*, London: Thames and Hudson.

Panofsky, Erwin (1927/1997) *Perspective as Symbolic Form*, translated by Christopher S. Wood, New York: Zone Books.

—— (1995) *Three Essays on Style*, ed. Irving Lavin, Cambridge, Mass.: MIT Press.

Pantzar, Mika (1997) 'Domestication of Everyday Life Technology: Dynamic Views on the Social Histories of Artifacts', *Design Issues*, 13, 3, pp. 52–65.

Papanek, Victor (1985) *Design for the Real World: Human Ecology and Social Change*, London and New York: Thames and Hudson.

Paul-Lévy, Françoise and Marion Segaud (1983) *Anthropologie de l'espace*, Paris: Éditions du Centre Georges Pompidou, CCI.

Pawley, Martin (1990) *Theory and Design in the Second Machine Age*, Oxford: Basil Blackwell.

Perec, Georges (1978/1987) *Life: A User's Manual*, translated by David Bellos, London: Collins Harvill.

—— (1997) *Species of Spaces and Other Pieces*, translated by John Sturrock, Harmondsworth: Penguin.

Periton, Diana (2004) 'The "Coupe Anatomique": Sections through the Nineteenth Century Parisian Apartment Block', *Journal of Architecture*, 9, pp. 289–304.

Petroski, Henry (1990) *The Pencil: A History of Design and Circumstance*, London: Faber.

—— (1999) *Remaking the World: Adventures in Engineering*, New York: Vintage Books.

—— (2006) *Success through Failure: The Paradox of Design*, Princeton: Princeton University Press.

Pevsner, Nikolaus (1936/1991) *Pioneers of Modern Design: From William Morris to Walter Gropius*, Harmondsworth: Penguin.

Piggott, J. R. (2004) *Palace of the People: The Crystal Palace at Sydenham 1854–1936*, London: Hurst.

Pink, Sarah (2004) *Home Truths: Gender, Domestic Objects and Everyday Life*, Oxford and New York: Berg.

Plant, Sadie (1992) *The Most Radical Gesture: The Situationist International in a Postmodern Age*, London and New York: Routledge.

Podro, Michael (1982) *The Critical Historians of Art*, New Haven and London: Yale University Press.

Pool, Ithiel de Sola, ed. (1977) *The Social Impact of the Telephone*, Cambridge, Mass.: MIT Press.

Poster, Mark (2001) *What's the Matter with the Internet?* Minneapolis: University of Minnesota Press.

Prakash, Vikramaditya (2002) *Chandigarh's Le Corbusier: The Struggle for Modernity in Postcolonial India*, Seattle and London: University of Washington Press.

Pred, Allan (1995) *Recognizing European Modernities: A Montage of the Present*, London and New York: Routledge.

Probyn, Elspeth (2005) *Blush: Faces of Shame*, Minneapolis: University of Minnesota Press.

Purbrick, Louise (1993) 'The Dream Machine: Charles Babbage and his Imaginary Computers', *Journal of Design History*, 6, 1, pp. 9–23.

—— ed. (2001) *The Great Exhibition of 1851: New Interdisciplinary Essays*, Manchester: Manchester University Press.

—— (2007) *The Wedding Present: Domestic Life beyond Consumption*, Aldershot: Ashgate.

Putnam, Tim (1988) 'The Theory of Machine Design in the Second Industrial Age', *Journal of Design History*, 1, 1, pp. 25–34.

—— (2004) 'The Modern Home and the Evolution of the House', *Journal of Architecture*, 9, pp. 419–29.

Putnam, Tim and Charles Newton, eds (1990) *Household Choices*, London: Futures Publications.

Pynchon, Thomas (1973/2000) *Gravity's Rainbow*, New York: Vintage.

Rabine, Leslie W. (2002) *The Global Circulation of African Fashion*, Oxford: Berg.

Rabinow, Paul (1989) *French Modern: Norms and Forms of the Social Environment*, Chicago: University of Chicago Press.

Rafael, Vicente L. (2003) 'The Cell Phone and the Crowd: Messianic Politics in the Contemporary Philippines', *Public Culture*, 15, 3, pp. 399–425.

Rakow, Lana (1992) *Gender on the Line: Women, the Telephone, and Community Life*, Urbana: University of Illinois Press.

Rancière, Jacques (2004) *The Politics of Aesthetics: The Distribution of the Sensible*, translated by Gabriel Rockhill, London and New York: Continuum.

—— (2007) *The Future of the Image*, translated by Gregory Elliott, London: Verso.

Rapoport, Amos (1969) *House Form and Culture*, London: Prentice-Hall.

Rappaport, Erika Diane (2000) *Shopping for Pleasure: Women in the Making of London's West End*, Princeton: Princeton University Press.

Reed, Christopher (2006) 'Design for (Queer) Living: Sexual Identity, Performance, and Décor in British *Vogue*, 1922–1926', *GLQ*, 12, 3, pp. 377–403.

Retort (2005) *Afflicted Powers: Capital and Spectacle in a New Age of War*, London: Verso.

Rice, Charles (2004) 'Rethinking Histories of the Interior', *Journal of Architecture*, 9, pp. 275–87

Richards, Thomas (1990) *The Commodity Culture of Victorian England: Advertising and Spectacle 1851–1914*, Stanford: Stanford University Press.

Robbins, Bruce (2007) 'The Smell of Infrastructure: Notes toward an Archive', *boundary 2*, 34, 1, pp. 25–33.

Robbins, David, ed. (1990) *The Independent Group: Postwar Britain and the Aesthetics of Plenty*, Cambridge, Mass. and London: MIT Press.

Ronell, Avital (1991) *The Telephone Book: Technology, Schizophrenia, Electric Speech*, Lincoln, Nebr.: Bison Books.

Rosselin, Céline (1999) 'The Ins and Outs of the Hall: A Parisian Example', in *At Home: An Anthropology of Domestic Space*, ed. Irene Cieraad, Syracuse: Syracuse University Press, pp. 53–9.

Roth, Nancy (2004) 'Flusser, At Last', *Oxford Art Journal*, 27, 3, pp. 433–5.

Rothschild, Joan, ed. (1999) *Design and Feminism: Revisioning Spaces, Places and Everyday Things*, New Jersey: Rutgers University Press.

Rowe, Peter G. (1993) *Modernity and Housing*, Cambridge, Mass.: MIT Press.

Rudofsky, Bernard (1964/2003) *Architecture without Architects: A Short Introduction to Non-Pedigreed Architecture*, Albuquerque: University of New Mexico Press.

Rybczynski, Witold (1986) *Home: A Short History of an Idea*, London: Penguin.

Sanders, Joel ed. (1996) *Stud: Architectures of Masculinity*, New York: Princeton Architectural Press.

Sartre, Jean-Paul (1938/2004) *Nausea*, translated by Robert Baldick, Harmondsworth: Penguin.

Scannell, Paddy (1996) *Radio, Television and Modern Life*, Oxford: Blackwell.

Schivelbusch, Wolfgang (1977) *The Railway Journey: The Industrialization of Time and Space in the 19th Century*, New York: Berg.

—— (1988) *Disenchanted Night: The Industrialization of Light in the Nineteenth Century*, translated by Angela Davies, Berkeley, Los Angeles and London: University of California Press.

—— (1993) *Tastes of Paradise: A Social History of Spices, Stimulants, and Intoxicants*, translated by David Jacobson, New York: Vintage Books.

Scholder, Amy (2003) *Replay: Game Design and Game Culture*, New York: Peter Lang.

Schwartz, Frederic J. (1996) *The Werkbund: Design Theory and Mass Culture before the First World War*, New Haven and London: Yale University Press.

—— (1999) 'Cathedrals and Shoes: Concepts of Style in Wölfflin and Adorno', *New German Critique*, 76, pp. 3–48.

—— (2005) *Blind Spots: Critical Theory and the History of Art in Twentieth-Century Germany*, New Haven: Yale University Press.

Schwartz, Vanessa R. (1998) *Spectacular Realities: Early Mass Culture in Fin-de-Siècle Paris*, Berkeley, Los Angeles and London: University of California Press.

Seago, Alex and Anthony Dunne (1999) 'New Methodologies in Art and Design Research: The Object as Discourse', *Design Issues*, 15, 2, pp. 11–17.

Sedgwick, Eve Kosofsky (2003) *Touching Feeling: Affect, Pedagogy, Performativity*, Durham, NC: Duke University Press.

Sennett, Richard (1986) *The Fall of Public Man*, London and Boston: Faber and Faber.

—— (1990) *The Conscience of the Eye: The Design and Social Life of Cities*, London: Faber.

Serres, Michel (1980/2007) *Parasite*, translated by Lawrence R. Schehr, Minneapolis: University of Minnesota Press.

—— (1988) 'Turner translates Carnot', in *Calligram: Essays in New Art History from France*, ed. Norman Bryson, Cambridge: Cambridge University Press, pp. 154–65.

—— (1997) 'Science and the Humanities: The Case of Turner', *SubStance*, 83, pp. 6–21.

Serres, Michel (with Bruno Latour) (1995) *Conversations on Science, Culture, and Time*, translated by Roxanne Lapidus, Ann Arbor: University of Michigan Press.

Short, Frances (2006) *Kitchen Secrets: The Meaning of Cooking in Everyday Life*, Oxford: Berg.

Shove, Elizabeth (2003) *Comfort, Cleanliness and Convenience: The Social Organization of Normality*, Oxford: Berg.

Shove, Elizabeth and Dale Southerton (2000) 'Defrosting the Freezer: From Novelty to Convenience', *Journal of Material Culture*, 5, 3, pp. 301–19.

Siebers, Tobin (1998) *The Subject and Other Subjects*, Ann Arbor: University of Michigan Press.

—— (2003) 'What can Disability Studies Learn from the Culture Wars?' *Cultural Critique*, 55, pp. 200–14.

—— (2006) 'Disability Aesthetics', *Journal for Cultural and Religious Theory*, 7, 2, pp. 63–73.

Silverman, Debora L. (1989) *Art Nouveau in Fin-de-Siècle France: Politics, Psychology, and Style*, Berkeley: University of California Press.

Simmons, Philip E. (1992) 'Toward the Postmodern Historical Imagination: Mass Culture in Walker Percy's "The Moviegoer" and Nicholson Baker's "The Mezzanine"', *Contemporary Literature*, 33, 4, pp. 601–24.

Smith, Terry (1993) *Making the Modern: Industry, Art, and Design in America*, Chicago: University of Chicago Press.

Sparke, Penny (1986) *An Introduction to Design and Culture in the Twentieth Century*, London: Unwin Hyman.

—— (1988) *Italian Design 1870 to the Present*, London: Thames and Hudson.

—— (1995) *As Long as it's Pink: The Sexual Politics of Taste*, London: HarperCollins.

—— (2004) 'Studying the Modern Home', *Journal of Architecture*, 9, pp. 413–17.

Spigel, Lynn (1992) 'Installing the Television Set: Popular Discourses on Television and Domestic Space, 1948–1955', in *Private Screenings: Television and the Female Consumer*, ed. Lynn Spigel and Denise Mann, Minneapolis: University of Minnesota Press, pp. 3–38.

Spitz, René (2002) *Hfg Ulm: The Political History of the Ulm School of Design, 1953–1968*, Stuttgart: Editions Axel Menges.

Spivak, Gayatri Chakravorty (2000) '~~Megacity~~', *Grey Room*, 1, pp. 8–25.

Standage, Tom (1998) *The Victorian Internet: The Remarkable Story of the Telegraph and the Nineteenth Century's Online Pioneers*, London: Weidenfeld and Nicolson.

Stein, Gertrude (1980) *The Yale Gertrude Stein*, selected by Richard Kostelantez, New Haven and London: Yale University Press.

Sterling, Bruce (2005) *Shaping Things*, Cambridge, Mass.: MIT Press.

Sterne, Jonathan (2003) *The Audible Past: Cultural Origins of Sound Reproduction*, Durham, NC: Duke University Press.

Stewart, Susan (1993) *On Longing: Narratives of the Miniature, the Gigantic, the Souvenir, the Collection*, Durham, NC and London: Duke University Press.

Stoler, Ann Laura (1995) *Race and the Education of Desire: Foucault's* History of Sexuality *and the Colonial Order of Things*, Durham, NC and London: Duke University Press.

Stoller, Paul (1997) *Sensuous Scholarship*, Philadelphia: University of Pennsylvania Press.

Sullivan, Louis (1918/1979) *Kindergarten Chats and Other Writings*, New York: Dover.

Sutton, David E. (2001) *Remembrance of Repasts: An Anthropology of Food and Memory*, Oxford and New York: Berg.

Tafuri, Manfredo (1973/1992) *Architecture and Utopia: Design and Capitalist Development*, translated by Barbara Luigia La Penta, Cambridge, Mass. and London: MIT Press.

—— (1980/1990) *The Sphere and the Labyrinth: Avant-Gardes and Architecture from Piranesi to the 1970s*, translated by Pellegrino d'Acierno and Robert Connolly, Cambridge, Mass. and London: MIT Press.

Taylor, Lou (2002) *The Study of Dress History*, Manchester: Manchester University Press.

Teasley, Sarah (2003) 'Furnishing the Modern Metropolitan: Moriya Nobuo's Designs for Domestic Interiors, 1922–1927', *Design Issues*, 19, 4, pp. 57–71.

Teymur, Necdet (1996) 'The Materiality of Design', in *The BLOCK Reader in Visual Culture*, ed. John Bird, Barry Curtis, Melinda Mash et al., London and New York: Routledge, pp. 148–66.

Thomas, Nicholas (1991) *Entangled Objects: Exchange, Material Culture, and Colonialism in the Pacific*, Cambridge, Mass. and London: Harvard University Press.

Thompson, Emily (2004) *The Soundscapes of Modernity: Architectural Acoustics and the Culture of Listening in America, 1900–1933*, Cambridge, Mass. and London: MIT Press.

Thompson, Michael (1979) *Rubbish Theory: The Creation and Destruction of Value*, New York: Oxford University Press.

Thorburn, David and Henry Jenkins, eds (2004) *Rethinking Media Change: The Aesthetics of Transition*, Cambridge, Mass. and London: MIT Press.

Tiffany, Daniel (2000) *Toy Medium: Materialism and the Modern Lyric*, Berkeley: University of California Press.

Tobin, Joseph J., ed. (1992) *Re-Made in Japan: Everyday Life and Consumer Taste in a Changing Society*, New Haven: Yale University Press.

Troy, Nancy J. (1983) *The De Stijl Environment*, Cambridge, Mass. and London: MIT Press.

Tupitsyn, Margarita (1999) *El Lissitzky: Beyond the Abstract Cabinet*, New Haven: Yale University Press.

Turkle, Sherry (1997) *Life on the Screen: Identity in the Age of the Internet*, New York: Simon and Schuster.

Turner, Victor (1969) *The Ritual Process: Structure and Anti-structure*, Chicago: Aldine Publishing Company.

Van Gennep, Arnold (1909/1981) *Les rites de passage*, Paris: Éditions Picard.

Verschaffel, Bart (2002) 'The Meanings of Domesticity', *Journal of Architecture*, 7, pp. 287–96.

Vidler, Anthony (2000) *Warped Space: Art, Architecture, and Anxiety in Modern Culture*, Cambridge, Mass. and London: MIT Press.

Vincentelli, Moira (1989) 'Reflections on a Kabyle Pot: Algerian Women and the Decorative Tradition', *Journal of Design History*, 2, 2–3, pp. 123–38.

Walker, John A. (1989) *Design History and the History of Design*, London: Pluto.

Wallace, Michele, ed. (1992) *Black Popular Culture*, Los Angeles: Bay Press.

Walsh, Claire (1995) 'Shop Design and the Display of Goods in Eighteenth-Century London', *Journal of Design History*, 8, 3, pp. 157–76.

Ward, Janet (2001) *Weimar Surfaces: Urban Visual Culture in 1920s Germany*, Berkeley, Los Angeles, and London: University of California Press.

Warin, Megan and Simone Dennis (2005) 'Threads of Memory: Reproducing the Cypress Tree through Sensual Consumption', *Journal of Intercultural Studies*, 26, 1–2, pp. 159–70.

Watkins, Evan (1993) *Throwaways: Work Culture and Consumer Education*, Stanford: Stanford University Press.

Watson, Thomas J. Jr. (1990) *Father, Son & Co.: My Life at IBM and Beyond*, New York: Bantam Books.

Wheeler, Wendy (2006) *The Whole Creature: Complexity, Biosemiotics and the Evolution of Culture*, London: Lawrence and Wishart.

Whiteley, Nigel (1987) *Pop Design: Modernism to Mod*, London: Design Council.

—— (2002) *Reyner Banham: Historian of the Immediate Future*, Cambridge, Mass. and London: MIT Press.

Whitford, Frank (1984) *Bauhaus*, London: Thames and Hudson.

Wigley, Mark (1995) *White Walls, Designer Dresses: The Fashioning of Modern Architecture*, Cambridge, Mass. and London: MIT Press.

—— (2001) 'Network Fever', *Grey Room*, 4, pp. 82–122.

Willett, John (1978) *The New Sobriety: Art and Politics in the Weimar Period 1917–33*, London: Thames and Hudson.

Williams, Rosalind (1982) *Dream Worlds: Mass Consumption in Late Nineteenth-Century France*, Berkeley, Los Angeles and Oxford: University of California Press.

Wills, Gary (1989) 'Message in the Deodorant Bottle: Inventing Time', *Critical Inquiry*, 14, pp. 497–509.

Wilson, Elizabeth (2000) *Bohemians: The Glamorous Outcasts*, London: I. B. Tauris.

Windsor, Alan (1981) *Peter Behrens: Architect and Designer 1868–1940*, London: The Architectural Press.

Winnicott, D. W. (1985) *Playing and Reality*, Harmondsworth: Penguin.

Wodiczko, Krzysztof (1999) *Critical Vehicles: Writings, Projects, Interviews*, Cambridge, Mass.: MIT Press.

Wollen, Peter and Joe Kerr, eds (2002) *Autopia: Cars and Culture*, London: Reaktion Books.

Woodfield, Richard, ed. (2001) *Art History as Cultural History: Warburg's Projects*, Amsterdam: G + B Arts.

Woodham, Jonathan (2004) 'Design and Everyday Life at the *Britain Can Make It* Exhibition 1946: "Stripes, Spots, White Wood and Homespun versus Chintzy Armchairs and Iron Bedsteads with Brass Knobs"', *Journal of Architecture*, 9, pp. 463–76.

Worpole, Ken (2000) *Here Comes the Sun: Architecture and Public Space in Twentieth-Century European Culture*, London: Reaktion Books.

Wright, Gwendolyn (1991) *The Politics of Design in French Colonial Urbanism*, Chicago and London: University of Chicago Press.

Yeh, Wen-hsin, ed. (2000) *Becoming Chinese: Passages to Modernity and Beyond*, Berkeley: University of California Press.

Zielinski, Siegfried (1998) *Audiovisions: Cinema and Television as Entr'actes in History*, Amsterdam: Amsterdam University Press.

—— (2006) *Deep Time of the Media: Toward an Archaeology of Hearing and Seeing by Technical Means*, translated by Gloria Custance, Cambridge, Mass. and London: MIT Press.

Zimmerman, Claire (2004) 'Photographic Modern Architecture: Inside "the New Deep"', *Journal of Architecture*, 9, pp. 331–54.

Žižek, Slavoj (1989) *The Sublime Object of Ideology*, London: Verso.

Index